MW01504002

NIMROD

The World's First AntiChrist

CJ Wilson

Copyright © 2024 by Make It Plain Publishing LLC.

All rights reserved. No part of this book may be used or reproduced in any form whatsoever without written permission except in the case of brief quotations in critical articles or reviews.

Printed in the United States of America.

Cover design by Cara Wilson

Biblical Timeline

From Noah to Christ

Noah (3898 - 2950 BC)
Died at age 950 [Gen. 9:28]
*Had 3 Sons: Shem, Ham, Japheth [Gen. 9:18-19]
Global Flood/Deluge (3298 BC)

<u>Nimrod</u> (son of Cush, the son of Ham, the son of Noah)

Abraham (2166 - 1991 BC)
Died at age 175 [Gen. 25:7]

Isaac (2066 - 1886 BC)
Died at age 180 [Gen. 35:28]

Jacob (2006 - 1859 BC)
Died at age 147 [Gen. 47:28]

Birth of Christ (0 AD)

MLK on Power

Power properly understood is nothing but the ability to achieve purpose. One of the great problems of history is that the concepts of love and power have usually been contrasted as opposites, polar opposites, so that love is identified with the resignation of power, and power with a denial of love. What is needed is a realization that power without love is reckless and abusive, and love without power is sentimental and anemic. Power at its best is love implementing the demands of justice, and justice at its best is power correcting everything that stands against love.

Martin Luther King Jr.

Nimrod: The World's First AntiChrist

Contents

Nimrod: The World's First AntiChrist

Matthew 24:5

For many shall come in my name, saying, I am Christ: and shall deceive many.

Jesus

Noah and Sons

Genesis 6: 5-7

And GOD saw that the wickedness of man *was* great in the earth, and *that* every imagination of the thoughts of his heart *was* only evil continually. 6 And it repented the LORD that he had made man on the earth, and it grieved him at his heart. 7 And the LORD said, I will destroy man whom I have created from the face of the earth; both man, and beast, and the creeping thing, and the fowls of the air; for it repenteth me that I have made them.

Imagine how God feels.

Take a second, breathe, and put what you are doing on pause. Block out everything, every noise, every sound, every voice, and try to sharpen your focus. Take a second and imagine how God feels. We don't do this enough. Now go back, read the verses above again, and try to look at humanity from the perspective of God, looking at HIS own creation, disobey HIM. After everything HE had done, HIS creation chose to go away from HIM. So much so that God himself repented that HE made mankind. That's incredible, and not in a good way. HE made man, HE made angels, HE made all. Men had daughters, angels came down and corrupted the seed of man thus creating children that became giants, which were called the nephillim. Despite that, HE gave mankind so much power and dominion, only to be slapped in the face with disobedience and dysfunction. It was not that humanity didn't know better, they chose worse. They chose to do evil. They had been taught evil doctrine by Semjaza and the second set of fallen angels who the scriptures above are referring to. The result of this unholy mixing of DNA made giants, which in turn led the whole world away from the LORD. Again, the world was in a chaotic state. This type of global climate moved God to want to destroy mankind because of its sins against him. In fact, humanity's sin was so great that it even had infiltrated the animals of earth through evil practices (bestiality, idolatry, etc.). For these acts, God had seen enough. It was time to make a change. That change would come via the Great Flood.

In HIS infinite wisdom, God chose a man named Noah, the 8th descendant from Adam, who was just and perfect in his generation to continue the human race. To be clear, this doesn't mean he was perfect and without sin, only Jesus did that, but it means that he was a man who practiced good in the eyes of God and sought holiness before God. Why is knowing that Noah was the 8th man from Adam important? In biblical numerology, the number 8 means new beginnings. The birth, purpose, and life of Noah meant a new beginning for humanity, all humanity. Noah began building the Ark as a single man at 480 years old. He married a woman named Naamah, the daughter of the great man Enoch (Jasher 5:16). By her, he had 3 sons, Shem, Ham, and Japheth.

Genesis 6:10

And Noah begat three sons, Shem, Ham, and Japheth.

For the next 102 years, this family unit did the work in preparation for the launch of the Ark. When his 3 sons came of age, Noah went to Eliakim son of Methuselah, to ask for his daughters to marry his sons.

Jasher 5:35

Then Noah took the three daughters of Eliakim, son of Methuselah, for wives for his sons, as the Lord had commanded Noah.

Noah's family went from one man to 8 people, all committed to do the service of the LORD.

The Flood, which we all have heard about, occurs due to mankind's disobedience to God. All flesh was destroyed that wasn't inside Noah's Ark. For 364 days, this family maintained the Ark and its residents. Finally, after God sent a wind to stop the rain and the land began to appear, the Ark rested on the Mountain of Ararat, which is in modern-day Turkey.

Genesis 8: 1-5

And God remembered Noah, and every living thing, and all the cattle that was
with him in the ark: and God made a wind to pass over the earth, and the waters
asswaged; 2 The fountains also of the deep and the windows of heaven were
stopped, and the rain from heaven was restrained; 3 And the waters returned from
off the earth continually: and after the end of the hundred and fifty days the
waters were abated. 4 And the ark rested in the seventh month, on the seventeenth
day of the month, upon the mountains of Ararat. 5 And the waters decreased
continually until the tenth month: in the tenth month, on the first day of the
month, were the tops of the mountains seen.

Mt Ararat

© National Geographic

After God allowed Noah and his sons to go forth out of the Ark, Noah built an altar to give thanks to God for his grace and mercy. The smell of the sacrifice to the LORD touched the heart of God in pleasure. God used the Flood to cleanse the Earth of sin, the same way a person uses water to clean a dirty shirt. The sacrifice by Noah was an example to us all of how simple deeds and consideration of God moves HIS heart, even when HE is angry, and justifiably so.

Genesis 8:21

And the LORD smelled a sweet savour; and the LORD said in his heart, I will not again curse the ground any more for man's sake; for the imagination of man's heart *is* evil from his youth; neither will I again smite any more every thing living, as I have done.

God cemented his covenant with Earth and humanity by giving us the rainbow in the sky as a reminder that HE will never again destroy the world by water. To this point in history, this has held true. There are over 200 flood stories worldwide in different cultures that tell of a world restarting flood. Whether it be different character names, outcomes, plots, twists, etc., the story is the same. The rainbow stands as a receipt of this act.

It is here that the story of Noah and his sons take off. It is here where humanity, as we know it, takes off.

Genesis 9: 18-20

And the sons of Noah, that went forth of the ark, were Shem, and Ham, and Japheth: and Ham *is* the father of Canaan. 19 These
are the three sons of Noah: and of them was the whole earth overspread. 20 And Noah began *to be* an husbandman, and he
planted a vineyard:

Reader, please note from above what the word husbandman means: farmer. After the Great Flood, Noah became a farmer of grapes. The grapes he grew still grow wild to this day around the base of Mt. Ararat. The oldest winery known to mankind is there. People ask why, of all things, did Noah become a grape farmer to make wine? Allow me to ask you a question: if you became privy to the information he knew, a hundred plus years in advance, and then you saw the world wiped out, literally, hearing the screams and horror of the dying people and animals outside the Ark, the tossing and turning of the waves, animals screaming in fear on the inside of the Ark, scared family members as well who are trusting him even though they don't know if the Ark will hold up, etc. How would you cope once you are allowed to leave knowing that the only people left alive were you and your 7 family members? Oh, and add to the equation that you were locked in a floating zoo for a full lunar year as well. Yeah, you'd probably knock Noah out of the way trying to build a winery to drown out your sorrows.

To be clear, I am not advocating getting drunk or anything like that, but only Noah knew what he knew and experienced what he experienced. Having a vineyard is not wrong. Several biblical characters owned a vineyard to make wine. Look deeper. No other man could understand the pain he went through. No other man in human history has his testimony. Only God knew that pain, which is why Noah was allowed to live 350 years after the Flood as a reward of his obedience.

It is out of his drunken state, however, that we pick up speed on getting to know how the world was repopulated. The immediate Biblical event surrounding the exit from the Ark allows the story to speed up.

Genesis 9: 20-24

And Noah began *to be* an husbandman, and he planted a vineyard: 21 And he drank of the wine, and was drunken; and he was uncovered within his tent. 22 And Ham, the father of Canaan, saw the nakedness of his father, and told his two brethren without. 23 And Shem and Japheth took a garment, and laid *it* upon both their shoulders, and went backward, and covered the nakedness of their father; and their faces *were* backward, and they saw not their father's nakedness. 24 And Noah awoke from his wine, and knew what his younger son had done unto him.

Wow. Ham, the younger son of Noah, saw his father naked in his tent, drunk. The fact that he saw his father unclothed was one thing, but the manner in which he looked upon him without covering him was another. In ancient cultures, any child seeing the nakedness of their parent becomes a shame to the entire family. Ham in this situation is no different. Even if it was an accident, he could have covered his father so he wasn't exposed to others. This is why Shem and Japheth came along, walking backwards, to cover their father. For this purpose, when Noah awoke and found out what happened, he cursed his own grandson, who hadn't been born yet.

For centuries, many have wondered why Noah cursed his grandson Canaan instead of his own son, the offender, Ham. This choice has caused much division and debate among the races and religions as to the why and reason of Noah. Also, the question is asked about the purpose of God allowing Noah to do so. The answer was given in the restart of mankind, where God would call home for the chosen, and where HE would eventually come to call the world back unto himself. Curse and gift, perspective is key.

Ham: Establishing Africa

Genesis 10:6

And the sons of Ham; Cush, and Mizraim, and Phut, and Canaan.

After the Flood waters went down, Ham went his way south with his family from Mt. Ararat. In the process of his journey toward a warmer climate, his sons Cush, Mizraim, Phut, and Canaan began to have children as well. In fact, Ham's family grew more and faster than that of his brothers.

Jasher 7:9

Japheth 460 men

And the sons of Tiras were Benib, Gera, Lupirion and Gilak; these are the sons of Japheth according to their families, and their numbers in those days were about four hundred and sixty men.

Jasher 7:18

Shem 300 men

These are the sons of Shem, according to their families; and their numbers in those days were about three hundred men.

Jasher 7:14

Ham 730 men

These are the sons of Ham, according to their families, and their numbers in those days were about seven hundred and thirty men.

As time progressed forward while the Hamites traveled south, several of Ham's grandsons and great grandsons began to break away from the family and establish themselves among their cousins, the sons of Shem and Ham in what is now called the Near or Middle East. Two of Ham's sons, Mizraim and Phut, continued to travel south. They noticed the beautiful greenery of modern Syria and the powerful mouth of the Euphrates and Tigris River. They moved on and decided to continue further South. They saw the only river in the world that flows North, the Nile River, and decided to settle closely. Mizraim settled along the Nile River while his brother Phut and his sons traveled a little further along the coastline of the Mediterranean Sea. These two men and their families became the first Biblical settlers of what later was named by the Romans as Africa. To be clear, Africa's original name was not Africa. The continent itself was called Alkebulan, meaning "mother of mankind" or better known as the "Garden of Eden". The initial piece of land, however, was and still is in the northeastern corner of the continent. Coming from Mt. Ararat, they settled into the Nile Delta. They called it Kemet, which means 'Black Land', due to its dark and rich soil that runs along the Nile River.

Name	Meaning	Settled
Mizraim	Double, Distress	Egypt
Phut	Gift	Libya

Their brother, Canaan, the one cursed by his grandfather Noah for his father's sin, decided to settle the area not too far from his father and grandfather. That area during Old Testament times became known as Canaan, later the Promised Land. Even though he was cursed, from a curse came a blessing. The curse of Canaan was that he was going to be a servant to his brothers. One who sets and serves. The land he settled became the servant to the world because it became the land promised to Abraham, a Semite (Shem), through which every nation was and continues to be served. It was renamed Israel and Palestine later, but more importantly, it became the place where our Lord Jesus the Christ was born, ministered, died, was resurrected, and ascended back to his throne in Heaven from. HE is that promise, and the land initially settled by Canaan was where that promised was manifested. God and his infinite wisdom is unmatched.

Name	Meaning	Settled
Canaan		Servant

Israel/Syria/Jordan, Near East = Promised Land

Ham, the father of the group, traveled and eventually settled among his grandchildren and great grandchildren in what is known as modern day Uganda. If you travel to Uganda or use the Ugandan Travel Guide, they will tell you of the original people called the Nilo or Hamites. Uganda is south of modern-day Sudan, west of Kenya, east of the Congo, and southwest of Ethiopia. Ham is the father of Africa although his children take the credit for the many widely successful civilizations and empires that sprang from him. In essence, Ham settled the central part of Africa and his offspring spread over the continent from there. Africa's father is rooted at its heart.

Cush, the oldest son of Ham, took a different route. He went east, following the Euphrates and Tigris Rivers into a beautifully lush and green place. It is there, in the land between the rivers, did he begin to establish himself. The land he settled became known as Mesopotamia or 'The Fertile Crescent' or 'The Land Between The Two Rivers'. Do these names sound familiar? It should. In middle and high school, world history classes begin with the teachings of the early civilizations of earth and the 1st recorded civilization was named Sumer. Perhaps you remember the term 'The Cradle of Civilization'. That is ancient Sumer. Well, guess what? Sumer means 'the black-headed people'. Guess what Cush means?

Name	Meaning	Settled
Cush	Black Face	Ethiopia (Nubia)

Black face. Ancient Sumer was settled and civilized by Cush, the son of Ham. How do we know that? The first city built after the flood was named Kish, named after its builder, Cush.

M.I.P.

The Cradle of Civilization was built by black-faced people.

Cush, at this point, had 5 sons (Gen. 10:7). Those sons eventually journeyed southwest to settle by their uncles while their father traveled into this lush land between the rivers. This is very important to know before we move to the next chapter. The knowledge, information, and secrets of their father Cush would change the world in more ways than you have ever known. Cush had a secret, a big, little, secret. Be patient with us, we will explain to you how.

Cuneiform Tablet
© Khan Academy

While establishing the world's first civilization, the Sumerians began their own writing system. It became known as the world's first writing system. That system became known as cuneiform. It is a wedge-shaped form of writing that was imprinted into soft clay. They created word signs into clay which later became known as pictographs. This style of writing was copied by many great civilizations to follow including the Akkadians, Babylonians, Hittites, and Assyrians. All are mentioned in the Bible.

Before we move on, I want you to know the contributions of the Sumerians so you will understand the significance of this people. Without them and their developments, the world would not have many things or at least they would be delayed in discovery. The Sumerian civilization introduced both a writing and number system, sun-dried bricks, wheeled carts, and perhaps more importantly, irrigation for farming. These people were absolute geniuses. Without their early technological advances, we would not have the information to be able to sustain life on the planet on such a wide scale basis. Every nation learned from their standard of life first, then improved on the model they set in order to advance beyond the destruction of the Flood. We all have learned from the Sumerians whether you like it or not, whether we know it or not.
After establishing the city of Kish and jump starting the Sumerian civilization, Cush had other plans to move southwest behind his children and grandchildren. His sons settled the southwestern corner of modern-day Saudi Arabia and East Africa.

Ancient Kish
© Al-Monitor

Sons of Cush

Name	Meaning	Settled
Seba	Drunkard	Eritrea
Havilah	Trembling	Djibouti
Sabtah	Encirclement	Yemen
Raamah	Thunder	Southwest Saudi Arabia
Sabtecha	Striking	unknown

While everything we read here about Cush is very interesting and somewhat inspiring, especially his establishing the Sumerian civilization and king dynasty at Kish, take a second to remember an important point of reference regarding his contribution to the world. Remember what I mentioned regarding a secret he was carrying? Cush, a great builder and brilliant mind, although an old man at this point in his life, was carrying a dirty yet POWERFUL secret. Let's give him his flowers now because what you are about to read concerning him will make you want to throw a boulder at him later.

Clothing Made By God Hand's

Genesis 3:21

Unto Adam also and to his wife did the LORD God make coats of skins, and clothed them.

Wow. I know, for many people, this is the first time you may have read this. For others, this will be the first time you have paid attention to this verse other than reading it on the way to the end of the chapter in Genesis. Please take a second and really examine what you just read. Adam and Eve, father and mother of ALL creation, had clothing made of skins, made by the HANDS OF GOD himself! That can be a book and movie all unto itself. Regardless, this is such a powerful verse. If nothing else, it shows the connection, grace, and mercy of God, considering the betrayal HE just went through that we all are still fighting. HE made clothing, with the same hands that made man, HE made clothing to cover the man, even though covering wasn't made for man. The master coverer, covering, but I digress.

For those who are interested in fashion, the arts, sowing, and knitting, take a look at this closely. The gift that you have comes from the LORD. HE is the grand designer. All artistic abilities come from HIM. For those who don't understand, please adhere to the perspective that the arts are a wisdom, yes, a creative process that we all don't possess. It's actually a spirit that comes from God that you can use as a tool to create things that's beyond the normal understanding of humanity or not. Sounds crazy? Read:

Exodus 28: 3-4

And thou shalt speak unto all that are wise hearted, whom I have filled with the spirit of wisdom, that they may make Aaron's garments to consecrate him, that he may minister unto me in the priest's office. 4 And these are the garments which they shall make; a breastplate, and an ephod, and a robe, and a broidered coat, a mitre, and a girdle: and they shall make holy garments for Aaron thy brother, and his sons, that he may minister unto me in the priest's office.

Notice how the scripture in verse 3 state that God fills people with the 'spirit of wisdom' to make garments? The holiest garments that was made in Jewish history was made for Aaron, the first priest of Israel. This is the power of fashion, art, knitting, and sowing. It's special. I personally don't have that gift or wisdom, but I respect those that do. Read the following for further validation of how special God thinks of designers and creators.

Exodus 35:35

Them hath he filled with wisdom of heart, to work all manner of work, of the engraver, and of the cunning workman, and of the embroiderer, in blue, and in purple, in scarlet, and in fine linen, and of the weaver, even of them that do any work, and of those that devise cunning work.

God honors designers, and so do I. With all due respect and humility, thank you!

With that said, let's refocus on what the original designer put together in the garden. After man fell from immortality, via sin, and was cursed to exit Eden, God decided to cover his children even though they disobeyed him. When Adam first ate of the fruit of the tree of knowledge, he and his wife made a decision to cover themselves because they realized they were naked.

Genesis 3:7

And the eyes of them both were opened, and they knew that they were naked; and they sewed fig leaves together, and made themselves aprons.

But God.

Even in HIS disappointment, God still decided to cover HIS loved ones. Let me repeat this for everyone, especially men with families and young men who will become heads of families: God decided to cover HIS loved ones even after their disappointment and choosing to go away from HIM. Before HE sent Adam and Eve out of the Garden, HE personally designed clothing for them so they can be covered in the world. HE knew that without proper covering, their bodies would deteriorate in the elements outside of the Garden. This is how leadership works. Even in disappointment, lead. Even in disappearance, cover.

Genesis 3:21

Unto Adam also and to his wife did the LORD God make coats of skins, and clothed them.

So, now that we read this, a HUGE elephant-sized question is standing in the middle of the room.

Where or what ever happened to Adam's Clothing?

Well, strap up. Here comes the ride...

Jasher 7:25

For after the death of Adam and his wife, the garments were given to Enoch, the son of Jared, and when Enoch was taken up to God, he gave them to Methuselah, his son.

And...

Jasher 7:26

And at the death of Methuselah, Noah took them and brought them to the ark, and they were with him until he went out of the ark.

And...

Jasher 7:27

And in their going out, Ham stole those garments fro Noah his father, and he took them and hid them from his brothers.

Then…

Jasher 7:28

And when Ham begat his first born Cush, he gave him the garments in secret, and they were with Cush many days.

BOOM!

Well, if you didn't know, now you know. Now you know what Cush's secret was! Now you know why Cush went a different way in discovering the New World. The wisdom from the hands of the creator himself was stolen by Ham and given to his son Cush, who hid them from his brothers just as his father had done. As we go forth in the book, you will learn how much power and wisdom was in these clothes that was made with heavenly hands. The power to create the universe made these clothes. The power to alter the universe was in these clothes. There is power in presentation.

Truth is stranger than fiction.

A Mighty One in the Earth

After establishing Kish, Cush was ready to move south. He had done some good, but at the same time and as you have read, Cush had done some bad, especially in the eyes of the LORD. As he progressed in age and set his sights on leaving Sumer, he had a decision to make about the garments made from the hands of God himself that his father Ham had stolen from Noah. The decision he made would change human history forever.

Jasher 7:29

And Cush also concealed them from his sons and brothers, and when Cush had begotten Nimrod, he gave him those garments through his love for him, and Nimrod grew up, and when he was twenty years old he put on those garments

Yes, you read that right. Cush, because of his love of his young son in his old age, he gave the sacred clothes of Adam and Eve to his youngest son, Nimrod. This is a perfect example of how dysfunction is passed down through the ages through lessons and or DNA. A father gives a stolen product to his son knowing that what he had stolen was perhaps the most powerful item on Earth. Dysfunction.

The clothing was special. Cush knew the power of those garments. His father Ham knew that the hands of God had fashioned these clothes and whoever possess them can take on godly aided power. I know, this sounds like a movie or sci-fi tale, but it is not. Where do you think they get these superhuman stories from? For example, let's look at the Ark of the Covenant and the power it possessed as described in scripture.

Powers of the Ark of the Covenant:

- The Jordan River stopped flowing as the Ark crosses (Josh. 3: 14-17)
- Thousands die at the site of the Ark (1 Sam. 6)
- Outbreak of tumors and disease among the Philistines (1 Sam. 5: 6-12)
- Caused the walls of Jericho to fall (Josh. 6: 6-20)
- Death to anyone who touched it against the will of God (2 Sam. 6: 6-8)

Moses was instructed by God to build the Ark (Ex. 31: 1-7). The craftsmen that helped Moses build it was Bezalel and Oholiab (Ex. 37:1). With that said, the Ark was built by men under the blessings and wisdom of God giving these people Godly intelligence to build this sacred chest. The clothing of Adam and Eve weren't made by human hands. They were made by the hands of God himself. Think about that for a second. Imagine the power of that in comparison to the power of the Ark of the Covenant. One was built by human hands and it had unworldly power. Imagine the literal clothes made from the hands of God! Humbling. Some people have a lucky shirt, shoes, pants, socks, etc. Some people have family heirlooms that are emotionally charging or empowering when they see or feel them. So, image what you would feel with these garments?

Cush, knowing how powerful these garments were, gave them to the son of his old age. This same type of admiration was also shown later by Jacob (Israel) when he made a coat of many colors for Joseph, the son of his old age.

Genesis 37:3

Now Israel loved Joseph more than all his children, because he was the son of his old age: and he made him a coat of many colours.

Nimrod, the 5th son of Cush (Gen. 10:7), grew up in Sumer watching his father Cush build and create culture. These two attributes, building and creating, will be mainstays in Nimrod's life as you will see in the book. At this point in his life, Nimrod was the baby boy, beloved of his father. At the age of 20, his father gave him the sacred garments. Before the gift was given, he was just the son whom his father loved. After the gift, everything changed. The world changed. He changed. History changed. With a gift, he became the Mighty One in the Earth.

Genesis 10:8

And Cush begat Nimrod: he began to be a mighty one in the earth.

Nimrod went from being another one in the Earth to the mighty one in the Earth. Being a mighty one in the Earth is one thing, but being called a mighty one in the Earth by God is a whole different thing. Reader, please note: there is no other biblical character given this title. No one! From Adam to Revelation, no one. Only Nimrod.

Only Nimrod.

Remember that.

The Hunter

Genesis 10:9

He was a mighty hunter before the LORD: wherefore it is said, Even as Nimrod the mighty hunter before the LORD.

What a compliment! Wow. What a compliment indeed. Nimrod had to be an outstanding young man at hunting for God himself to say that Nimrod was a mighty hunter before HIM. This is an amazing salutation to given to a man, especially in the Word of God. Notice how scripture says 'the' mighty hunter before the LORD and not 'a' mighty hunter before the LORD. This shows the exceptional ability of Nimrod that separates him throughout the age of the writing history of the Bible. He's one of one.

Why is this important? Well, consider this: for the first time in human history, mankind was given the ability to eat meat. Prior to the flood, they only ate the meat of vegetables or fruit, which means the edible parts. When God made Adam, HE made man to eat from the Earth. Man was given every green thing to eat (Gen. 1:29). This is important to examine when questioning how the people from the early biblical days lived so long. Their open secret was that they lived in a more oxygen rich environment and they ate green herbs from the Earth. Hunting was not a thing. Wildlife was allowed to grow and multiply. It wasn't until after the Flood that man was given the opportunity to eat meat from animals.

Genesis 9: 1-3

And God blessed Noah and his sons, and said unto them, Be fruitful, and multiply, and replenish the earth. 2 And the fear of you and the dread of you shall be upon every beast of the earth, and upon every fowl of the air, upon all that moveth upon the earth, and upon all the fishes of the sea; into your hand are they delivered. 3 Every moving thing that liveth shall be meat for you; even as the green herb have I given you all things.

With this being said, please understand how dynamic and different Nimrod was at hunting. For him to be considered a mighty hunter before the LORD, he was a hunter of epic proportion. Prior to the flood, mankind were herbivores. After the flood, carnivores. To eat both meat and vegetables makes you an omnivore. Nimrod could have been an omnivore, but there wasn't a carnivore on the planet, human or otherwise, that could hunt like Nimrod. He was the king of the New World jungle. So, a question begs to be asked: how did he become so skilled at hunting?

Jasher 7:30

And Nimrod became strong when he put on the garments, and God gave him might and strength, and he was a mighty hunter in the earth, yea, he was a mighty hunter in the field, and he hunted the animals and he built altars, and he offered upon them the animals before the Lord.

There's the answer. The garments he put on gave him might and strength that came directly from the LORD GOD himself. This is very important to know and understand. Nimrod was empowered by God to become such a mighty hunter. Even though his grandfather had stolen the garments and his father concealed them from his brothers, God blessed Nimrod. Why?

Nimrod honored God with the blessing of his hunting as mentioned in the verse above. As a young man of 20 years old, he gave honor to God for giving him this might and strength. That's very important to understand about Nimrod's story. In his origin, he was a man that followed the God of his fathers, especially Noah, his grandfather.

Reader, please pay close attention to the following concept as it will help explain Nimrod's original character traits. He started out living in the ways of Abel, the son of Adam, who would give God his first and best. This was very pleasing to the LORD. Nimrod knew God and disciplined himself in a way that was admirable and respectful. In return, God blessed him.

Genesis 4:4

And Abel, he also brought of the firstlings of his flock and of the fat thereof. And the LORD had respect unto Abel and to his offering:

This is how Nimrod became the hunter of all hunters: humility breeds power into prowess.

Fame and Family Fights

Jasher 7: 31-32

And Nimrod strengthened himself, and he rose up from amongst his brethren, and he fought the battles of his brethren against all their enemies round about. 32. And the Lord delivered all the enemies of his brethren in his hands, and God prospered him from time to time in his battles, and he reigned upon earth.

The reputation of Nimrod became widespread. He was the beloved son of his father Cush and everyone knew it. His older brothers knew of his unique abilities and even they were respectful of their younger brother and his gifts. Keep in mind, Nimrod was the youngest of 5 brothers, the baby boy. Whereas in most biblical families the oldest son gets the most respect and reputation along with the responsibility of upholding the family. Nimrod is the exception. His reputation gave him the ability to align himself with others because they recognized his ability to establish dominance through hunting and the favor of God. He used his reputation as a great hunter like a marketing plan to strengthen himself amongst his brothers first, then the rest of the world. He fought his brothers' battles and won, earning him respect to the point that he became a ruler. God prospered him.

Nimrod was successful, very successful, especially for his age. To be clear, the youngest of a family unit being a ruler with or over his older brothers is taboo at this point in human history. Families with multiple sons did not send the youngest son into battle or dangerous situations. Why? Because, if the older sons die, the youngest son would be the keeper and namesake of the family to stay alive. An example of this concept is seen with Jacob (Israel) deciding not to send Benjamin, his youngest son, to Egypt during the famine while all the older brothers were sent to buy grain. Jacob understood the risk of sending his sons into a dangerous situation that they possibly wouldn't return from for the sake of their overall family. He had already lost Joseph at that point, so losing Benjamin, the youngest, was not up for discussion. Also, to draw a parallel, Benjamin as the child of Jacob's older age, just like Nimrod to Cush. The youngest must be protected so the family can be preserved. Nimrod broke that mold.

Genesis 42:2

But Benjamin, Joseph's brother, Jacob sent not with his brethren; for he said, Lest peradventure mischief befall him.

Allow for me to reiterate that Nimrod was successful because of God, even when he did things on his own. Go back and read verse 32 of Jasher 7 again. Take notice of how it said from 'time to time' God would deliver him. That means that Nimrod would win some battles on his own, other times God would deliver victory to him. Either way, Nimrod's fame grew so much that he became his own entity in the Earth to the point that he became a ruler amongst his own family. That's BIG, considering he was the youngest son. His reputation became a brand or hashtag for greatness in the biblical days.

Jasher 7:33

Therefore it became current in those days, when a man ushered forth those that he had trained up for battle, he would say to them, Like God did to Nimrod, who was a mighty hunter in the earth, and who succeeded in the battles that prevailed against his brethren, that he delivered them from the hands of their enemies, so may God strengthen us and deliver us this day.

This is incredible! Like God did to Nimrod, who was a mighty hunter in the earth, who succeeded in the battles fighting for his brothers, that he delivered them from the hands of their enemies, so may God strengthen us and deliver us this day. This was the original 'Mamba Mentality', the great warrior creed, the declaration of readiness for war. Nimrod had no parallel in hunting animals or men. He stood alone and the world population at that time stood and spoke in recognition of his prowess.

Notice again, God is involved, even in the reputation of Nimrod. Men would pray that God strengthen and deliver them as HE did Nimrod. To be clear, idolizing someone who is successful is an age-old human condition. Nimrod forced humanity to consider God, even in their training for war. He made it abundantly clear with the altars he built after his victories that God was supreme. The LORD was his source of strength and power and the whole world knew it. For twenty years, Nimrod ruled and followed this path as his father and brothers continued to build and expand themselves in ancient Sumer. But there's something about fame that gets into the human heart and changes a person, even a righteous or God loving human, if you are not careful to ward it off.

Jasher 7: 34-45

And when Nimrod was forty years old, at that time there was a war between his brethren and the children of Japheth, so that they were in the power of their enemies. 35. And Nimrod went forth at that time, and he assembled all the sons of Cush and their families, about four hundred and sixty men, and he hired also from some of his friends and acquaintances about eighty men, and be gave them their hire, and he went with them to battle, and when he was on the road, Nimrod strengthened the hearts of the people that went with him.

Fame. His cousins, the sons of Japheth, which settled in areas close to the Euphrates and Tigris Rivers, came to have war with one another. Notice how the sons of Japheth didn't war with Nimrod? They took issue with his brothers. Why? Fame. Everyone knew Nimrod was great. He was like a young Mike Tyson. Everyone knew who he was. His older brothers however, that's a different story. His brothers were at war, again, and they needed their little brother to help them fight against their cousins. In fact, they were already in the hands of their enemies, as verse 34 states. It is clear in scripture that the sons of Japheth were a serious threat to Cush' sons, including Nimrod. The WHOLE family of men showed up to fight. Nimrod even hired some of friends to help him fight his cousins. Even with that, the sons of Cush didn't feel secure. Nimrod, sensing the low morale of his family in regards to the possible outcome of the war and annihilation of his whole family, stopped the men on the side of the road. This is where fame can help a cause, if used correctly. Reputation can inspire confidence.

Jasher 7:36

And he said to them, Do not fear, neither be alarmed, for all our enemies will be delivered into our hands, and you may do with them as you please.

These few words changed the game. Just a few words from the mighty one in the Earth changed the morale. Just like that, low morale became high confidence. That's leadership. That's charisma. Guess what happened next?

Jasher 7:37

And all the men that went were about five hundred, and they fought against their enemies, and they destroyed them, and subdued them, and Nimrod placed standing officers over them in their respective places.

Just like that, Nimrod was now the mightiest warrior in the Earth. He just beat the sons of Japheth. Only the sons of Shem remained in abundance in the Earth because Cush was a son of Ham, one of the 3 sons of Noah. Please take in mind, there weren't millions or billions of people on Earth at this point. There were thousands of people, multiplying as God charged them to. So, a victory of this magnitude was beyond huge, it was global. To give this perspective, please read carefully...

Nimrod won the 1st **Real** World War

I know, you have probably never heard of this. The victor of the "1st" World War as we know it were the Allied Powers (France, Italy, Russia, the British Empire and the US). What ironic about the "Allies" were that there as 5 nations, just like the 5 sons of Cush. The youngest son, Nimrod, got the credit for the victory. The US, also the youngest of the victor nations, was the last nation to enter the war, received a lot of the credit for winning WW1 as well. The sons of Cush had already been at war with the sons of Japheth, then Nimrod came along and finished the job. The world was at war for 3 years (1914-1917) before the US entered in 1917. It ended in 1918. Interesting how things tend to repeat themselves in history, but I digress.

Jasher 7:38

And he took some of their children as security, and they were all servants to Nimrod and to his brethren, and Nimrod and all the people that were with him turned homeward.

Nimrod took the children of the Japhethites and made them servants, not slaves. This is important to understand the difference. Servants were treated as people. Slaves were treated as a debt or property. Nimrod used these children as collateral to ensure that the Japhethites don't return for war again or their children would be killed. Also, they were taken to be taught the ways of Nimrod. A cultural exchange. How do we know this? This practice was copied throughout history when one nation conquered another, popularized by the Babylonians with the Hebrews during the Babylonian Captivity. King Nebuchanezzar II, a man who fashioned himself after Nimrod and even took on the title of Nimrod as all Babylonian kings did (King of the World), took the Hebrew princes into his royal house to indoctrinate and culturally change their thought process. The prophet Daniel, Shadrach, Meshach, and Abednego were captive princes in the royal house of Babylon.

Daniel 1: 3-7

And the king spake unto Ashpenaz the master of his eunuchs, that he should bring certain of the children of Israel, and of the king's seed, and of the princes; 4 Children in whom was no blemish, but well favoured, and skilful in all wisdom, and cunning in knowledge, and understanding science, and such as had ability in them to stand in the king's palace, and whom they might teach the learning and the tongue of the Chaldeans. 5 And the king appointed them a daily provision of the king's meat, and of the wine which he drank: so nourishing them three years, that at the end thereof they might stand before the king. 6 Now among these were of the children of Judah, Daniel, Hananiah, Mishael, and Azariah: 7 Unto whom the prince of the eunuchs gave names: for he gave unto Daniel the name of Belteshazzar; and to Hananiah, of Shadrach; and to Mishael, of Meshach; and to Azariah, of Abednego.

Fame and Family. This was Nimrod's big moment. His Family was the reason he stayed at war. His Fame was the reason his enemies didn't want war. His Frame was the reason his Family wanted him to fight. His Fame is the reason he took the children of the Japhethites as servants to be taught as Family. His God was the reason he had Fame, Frame, and Family.

Jasher 7: 39-40

And when Nimrod had joyfully returned from battle, after having conquered his enemies, all his brethren, together with those who knew him before, assembled to make him king over them, and they placed the regal crown upon his head. 40. And he set over his subjects and people, princes, judges, and rulers, as is the custom amongst kings.

Nimrod emerged from the war with his cousins as the man of men in the Earth. He had grown from the youngest son and pride of his father Cush, to the mighty hunter before the LORD, to a mighty warrior, to the ruler in his family, to king. For 20 years he was everything mentioned great except king. But once he was given his crown at the age of 40, Fame and Family changed. He was no longer little brother or the mighty hunter. He was King, King Nimrod.

Terah

Genesis 11: 24-26

And Nahor lived nine and twenty years, and begat Terah: 25 And Nahor lived after he begat Terah an hundred and nineteen years, and begat sons and daughters. 26 And Terah lived seventy years, and begat Abram, Nahor, and Haran.

Much of what we know of Terah is written in the genealogy of Abraham as his father, but that's it. We aren't really taught about him and what he actually did in the world. All we really know is that he was the father of Abram, later renamed Abraham by God, and that he died in land far away from the land of his fathers. But that changes today. We will learn who and how impactful of a man Terah was on the shaping of the world beyond just being Abraham's dad. Brace yourself. This is a complicating character.

Jasher 7:41

And he placed Terah the son of Nahor the prince of his host, and he dignified him and elevated him above all his princes.

The same Terah that is mentioned in Genesis 11 is the same Terah that was put in charge of Nimrod's forces. Terah was a cousin of Nimrod. He was a descendant of Shem, the 8th son from Noah. This is the first scriptural recorded act for Nimrod as King. He chose to elevate Terah to being the prince of princes. Everyone was to see and respect him, second only to Nimrod himself. The same type of designation is used in the story of Joseph and Pharaoh after Joseph interpreted Pharaoh's dreams that all his so-called seers could not.

Genesis 41: 39-40

And Pharaoh said unto Joseph, Forasmuch as God hath shewed thee all this, *there is* none so discreet and wise as thou *art*: 40 Thou shalt be over my house, and according unto thy word shall all my people be ruled: only in the throne will I be greater than thou.

Terah was positioned for greatness. Who wouldn't want to be crowned as prince of princes with only one person having more say than you? Nimrod was the man, the King, the mighty one in the earth. Everyone respected and feared him. That same guy chose Terah as his prince of princes! What an honor! Beautiful right? Well, this designation will explain a lot about the story of both Nimrod and Abraham. Just keep in mind, as we offer a bit of advice to all, beginning with myself...

All promotions aren't elevations. Some are excavations, deep digs into your life that could be chaos creators.

Someone should have told Terah.

Becoming A god

Jeremiah 17:9

The heart is deceitful above all things, and desperately wicked: who can know it?

Fame. It has a way of changing a man's heart. It has a way of warring on your thoughts, feelings, and emotions. It has a way of changing your daily routines. Things you used to do, you change. Things you used to say, you don't. Places you used to go, you stop going. Fame can cause a change of heart. If not to you personally, it definitely will cause a change in the people around you. Fame, it's the most addictive drug on Earth. It always has been, always will be. Fame, if not careful, can take the most dedicated of humanity and turn them into a vanity minded person. Fame, it can get into the heart and change how you see the world. More importantly, Fame can get into the heart and change how you see God. But as you see in Jeremiah 17:9, the heart is deceitful. This means that the place from which your feelings flow is vulnerable, like an open wound. It was made perfect, but became infected, because of Adam's sin. Fame is a like bacteria that can get in the blood and spread throughout the body, metaphorically. When it gets to the heart, it appears as a remedy, but it is really an agent of chaos, if not handled correctly. Fame can be deceiving, which once in the heart can cause you to be self-absorbed and high minded, making the heart deceitful above all things, making it and or you desperately wicked to maintain that Fame. In the end, a person can become someone you don't recognize because of a change of heart. Who can know it, the heart? This is why you must guard your heart against things that are deceiving. From the heart flows the you that God will see and judge. From the heart, like a river, flows the real you of life. Guard it carefully, or it will have you on guard.

Proverbs 4:23

Keep thy heart with all diligence; for out of it are the issues of life.

Now, let's redirect our attention back to the man of the hour, Nimrod, the famous king. His reputation is known to all mankind on Earth. He is the man. He is revered. He is respected. He is loved. He is ruler. He is undisputed. But as we have just learned about the heart and how God views it, especially when Fame is injected into it, something changed in Nimrod. The man who started out following in the ways of Noah, behaving and giving thanks to the LORD like Abel, the one who put on the clothing of God to gain supernatural abilities and built altars to the LORD to showcase his deference to the Master of the Universe, was now different. Something in his heart changed. When the eyes and admiration came, his foundation shifted.

Jasher 7:42

And whilst he was reigning according to his heart's desire, after having conquered all his enemies around, he advised with his counselors to build a city for his palace, and they did so.

Subtly, not all at once, Nimrod's heart changed. He is now ruler of the known world at this time and he did as he pleased. As he pleased. Subtle. This is a very dangerous thing. This is where tyranny was born. This is where absolution was hatched. This is where dictator was formed. When a ruler makes rules to the desire of their own heart, then the only one looking to be satisfied is self, the heart, not the needs of the people for whom you rule. This is where new idolatry was born. This is where God ceases to be sovereign in one's eyes. More scarily, this is where making thine-self a god was created in the Earth. Nimrod the god is born, in his heart, ruling according to his heart's desire. His desire, his heart.

While feeling like he can do all according to his satisfaction, he desired to have a palace built to his liking. This palace would need to be fit for a king. He planned with his advisors to build this palace for him, not them. What were they going to say, no? You cannot forget, these are the same men that made him their king (Jasher 7: 39-40), they can't say no. So, what did they do? They built accordingly.

Jasher 7:43

And they found a large valley opposite to the east, and they built him a large and extensive city, and Nimrod called the name of the city that he built Shinar, for the Lord had vehemently shaken his enemies and destroyed them.

The large valley they found opposite to the east was near the Tigris River. That area is called the Fertile Crescent, Mesopotamia, modern-day Iraq. It's the same area his father Cush had settled, but west of the city of Kish. The city he founded was closer to the modern-day Persian Gulf. The bible agrees:

Genesis 11: 1-2

And the whole earth was of one language, and of one speech. 2 And it came to pass, as they journeyed from the east, that they found a plain in the land of Shinar; and they dwelt there.

While all of this seems business as usual from a historical perspective, something very subtle is happening before your eyes that you may have missed. I want you to notice something in your reading. In Jasher 7:42, Nimrod conspires to build a palace. In verse 43, it says that the city was built and named Shinar. Sounds good, but there is a problem: there is no city, as in terms of a gathering place with parameters and walls, named Shinar in the records! In the history of ancient Mesopotamia, there is no city named Shinar. With that said, it begs the question: are the holy scriptures inaccurate? No. Well, what's the issue?

Ancient Hebrew scholars interpret the name Shinar to be two different things. The first interpretation is Sumer. As mentioned before, this is the same geographical area of modern-day Iraq and the ancient civilization that Cush settled when building Kish with his sons. But that's an area, not a city. Instead, there is a city, a great city, a city that is spoken of in the Bible from Genesis to Revelation. The city is named Babylon. This city is also called Shinar, representing not just an actual city, but an area. It encompasses both titles. In the beginning, however, it wasn't named Babylon, it was named Shinar, meaning 'That What is Young'. It was a new city, young in the Earth. But it grew into something that regenerates itself into various different cultures, including our own (Western Civilization), making it old yet always being young. Nimrod ruled it all. It would grow to be called another name, which we will get into later.

Jasher 7: 44-45

And Nimrod dwelt in Shinar, and he reigned securely, and he fought with his enemies and he subdued them, and he prospered in all his battles, and his kingdom became very great. 45.And all nations and tongues heard of his fame, and they gathered themselves to him, and they bowed down to the earth, and they brought him offerings, and he became their lord and king, and they all dwelt with him in the city at Shinar, and Nimrod reigned in the earth over all the sons of Noah, and they were all under his power and counsel.

This is how Nimrod became a god, in his own heart and the heart of men. He conquered all those who opposed him. He won all his battles. His kingdom grew from a few settlements to the whole of the known world at that time. Notice in verse 45 where it says 'ALL nations and tongues heard of his fame'? That means everyone knew him, everyone. There was not one group of people who didn't hear of this man. Again, this is not to say there are billions of people on the planet at this point, but it is to say that there was a 100% ratio of all people knowing who this one man was. Imagine the power of that. It's the small pool, biggest fish example in real life. No man was more Famed than him, including his father and uncles who were written of biblically that were still alive at that time.

Nimrod's next move was to gather all people of the Earth to him. Stop for a second and think about this. He had ALL the people of Earth regather to come to him. Think of how powerful that is. There is only one who should have the power to do so: God. Think of it. All people, coming together, for one man. For what? As it said immediately afterwards, to have them bow down and bring him offerings. Yes, you read that right. Nimrod called these people from where they were in the Earth, to abandon their homes and lives, to bow down and give him offerings for being their lord and king. The world had to live in Shinar, his area, his city, with him as their ruler.

Remember how Nimrod came on the scene as an humble young man, wearing the garments of Adam and Eve made by the hands of God, a mighty hunter before the LORD, building altars and give offerings to say thank you to God for his abundance of blessings? He was good in the eyes of the LORD. Well, now Nimrod is requiring the same be done for himself by the people, all people. How did this happen? His heart changed. In his heart, iniquity was found. There is ONLY one other being in the universe that this happened to that was created to worship God, as he did, for a time, until iniquity was found in him, in his heart. Guess who that one being was? Lucifer.

Ezekiel 28:15

Thou wast perfect in thy ways from the day that thou wast created, till iniquity was found in thee. 16 By the multitude of thy merchandise they have filled the midst of thee with violence, and thou hast sinned: therefore I will cast thee as profane out of the mountain of God: and I will destroy thee, O covering cherub, from the midst of the stones of fire. 17 Thine heart was lifted up because of thy beauty, thou hast corrupted thy wisdom by reason of thy brightness: I will cast thee to the ground, I will lay thee before kings, that they may behold thee.

This is how Nimrod became a god amongst men. He stopped following the LORD and started following Lucifer. He exchanged the selfless to become selfish. He went from being wise to being wicked. Reader, be careful out there, it's a slippery slope, all of which starts in the heart. Lucifer was the 1st, unfortunately, he won't be the last. Nimrod was 1st.

Jasher 7:46

And all the earth was of one tongue and words of union, but Nimrod did not go in the ways of the Lord, and he was more wicked than all the men that were before him, from the days of the flood until those days.

Mardon

Jasher 7:47

And he made gods of wood and stone, and he bowed down to them, and he rebelled against the Lord, and taught all his subjects and the people of the earth his wicked ways; and Mardon his son was more wicked than his father.

Wow. This is idolatry at its finest. Not only did Nimrod accept worship from the people of the earth, but he built gods of wood and stone for the people to worship. He himself bowed down and worshipped them. He errored but more egregiously, he led the world to do the same against the LORD. This practice of idolatry got its birth place with Nimrod. He is the father of idolatry. What do I mean by idolatry?

The term idolatry means the worship of a physical object as a god, an immoderate attachment or devotion to something. Whether it be a person, place, or thing, if it becomes #1 in your life above God, you are practicing idolatry. You are following in the footsteps of Nimrod. He is your father. Not your literal father, obviously, but your life path father. Anything that gets the attention and admiration of your first attention, thought, devotion, commitment, discipline, love, and sacrifice, is idolatry. Check your life inventory and see if there are areas of idolatry.

Do you see how powerful this is? Can you see how idolatry is all around us? Can you see how it's an old issue yet it's young enough to change with the current, which is the very definition of Shinar? God despises idolatry. Look at these verses and see what the Bible says about it.

- Jonah 2:8
- Psalms 16:4
- Isaiah 44: 9-11

God himself said…

- Exodus 20: 3-6
- Leviticus 19:4
- Isaiah 45:20

There are various different forms of idolatry.

- Colossians 3:5

M.I.P.

Anything that gets in the place of God is idolatry.

What makes the issue with Nimrod's behavior worse is that he taught his family to do the same. His son, Mardon, was a student to his teacher, his father. What's crazy is that scripture said that Mardon was more wicked than his father. How can that be so?

Nimrod knew God, the real God, the one true God. He knew him personally. He knew what he was doing was wrong because he had experience with God. The one true God is the one who protected him in his youth, empowered the clothing he wore that made him invincible, gave him his kingdom, and allowed him to have a family. Nimrod knew the power and realness of God. They knew one another, personally. However, Mardon did not know God. Mardon only knew what his father had taught him: evil. He could take steps to displease God in ways that Nimrod knew not to do. That's the fragility of parenting. Our experiences are not that of our children. We MUST keep that in mind. No matter how we grew up and lived life, those experiences will never be understood by our children no matter what, even if they practice the same things as us. This is the case with Nimrod and Mardon.

Jasher 7:48

And every one that heard of the acts of Mardon the son of Nimrod would say, concerning him, From the wicked goeth forth wickedness; therefore it became a proverb in the whole earth, saying, From the wicked goeth forth wickedness, and it was current in the words of men from that time to this.

Mardon was his father's son. He was wicked, so much so that he too became famous, like his father. As son to the god of men and king of the Earth, Mardon had his pick of whatever he deemed his desire. From his heart flowed wickedness, which became his reputation. Mardon became the poster child for evil. Imagine that.

Before we move forward in the book, let's break down who Mardon really was, who he came to be, and how he is still present in this world. We'll break it down.

Nimrod built the city of Shinar, also known as Babylon. Nimrod became polytheistic, a worshipper of many gods. When you research the origin of the city of Babylon, you will see many inscriptions and archaeological findings of many different gods. It's quite amazing to see how committed and devoted to these stone carvings and images the people were. Many of the artifacts are still in good shape with the colorings still visible. Again, the people followed Nimrod and his belief structure to the gods.

Regardless of where you start in your research, they all will lead back to the chief god of Babylon. His symbols are everywhere. He is considered the patron or king of the gods of Babylon. It was made clear for us to discover not only who but how powerful this being was revered to be. It is really amazing, but guess what the patron God of Babylon name is? Marduk.

(Marduk's symbol animal, the mušḫuššu or "snake-dragon" at the Detroit Institute of Arts. This is a glazed brick relief from the city of Babylon itself, dating to the Neo-Babylonian period.)

Marduk's symbol was a snake-dragon. A serpent. We all know about the serpent in the garden and how Satan used it to deceive Eve and then Adam. The serpent was a creation of God, good in the eyes of God, but was used because of its God-given ability to be more cunning and craftier than any other animal the LORD had created (Gen. 3:1). Just the same as Satan used the serpent to do evil, he can use men to do evil. This was the idea of using the image of the snake. Let's M.I.P. this image down so you can understand why Marduk's symbol was specifically chosen.

As for the dragon part of the image, dragons too were and still are real. I know, you probably want to close this book and head for the hills after me saying this, but allow me to show you in the Bible where dragons are real and how the changing of a name plus propaganda tactics caused people to view dragons as make believe. Again, this book is for educational purposes.

Biblical History:

- Deuteronomy 32:33
- Job 30:29
- Psalms 44:19
- Psalms 148:7
- Isaiah 27:1
- Micah 1:8

World History:

Prior to 1841, dragons were called just that, dragons. In 1842, Sir Richard Owen, an English scientist, coined the term dinosaur to replace the word dragon. This is the same man that founded the Natural History Museum of London in 1881. His ability to change a word made him go from being a nobody in the world of science to being equally as renown as Charles Darwin, the survival of the fittest guy. In fact, they were rivals. There's more I can include here about Sir Richard Owen, but I digress. Research the name Sir Richard Owen yourself and see if we are wrong.

The root or etymology of the word dinosaur is split. Its' split greek spelling is *deinos*, meaning terrible. The other side of the word spelling is *sauros*, meaning lizard. Combined, you have deinos-sauros, meaning terrible lizard. When translated into Latin you get dinosaurus, or dinosaur. This word was taken and implemented into dictionaries throughout the British Empire, which was taught to the masses worldwide. How do you think it became widely used and taught in schools all over the world? So yes, dragons have always been and will always be. Mankind changed and accepted the name which throws you off the trail of the truth of God and his word. This is not a fairy tale, this is real life.

Now, more information on Marduk.

As king of the gods of Shinar or Babylon, Nimrod designed specific responsibilities to the god. According to Dr. Joshua Marks, writer for worldhistory.org and co-founder of Ancient History Encyclopedia, Marduk is key to understanding Babylonian history.

"Marduk was the patron god of Babylon, the Babylonian king of the gods, who presided over justice, compassion, healing, regeneration, magic, and fairness, although he is also sometimes referenced as a storm god and agricultural deity. His temple, the famous ziggurat described by Herodotus, is considered the model for the biblical Tower of Babel. The Greeks associated him with Zeus and the Romans with Jupiter. He is depicted as a human in royal robes, carrying a snake-dragon and a spade."

What's also important to understand about Marduk is that he has another nickname that describes him. He's referred to as Bel. The alternate spelling of Bel is Ba'al, Lord of thunderstorms, Lord of the flies. Do not be confused by all of these different names. Different people or tribes have different names for the same person in different languages. They all describe one being, Marduk. He was the god of the people, protector of the city, the chief wicked one.

There is an interesting book written by Takayoshi Oshima named *Babylonian Prayers to Marduk*, which is a compilation of archaeological documents that were put together for anyone to read about the mass devotion in the ancient world to Marduk. The people even went so far in their letters to one another to open with a greeting of '...May god Marduk keep you in good health!' (Pg. 268, *Babylonian Prayers to Marduk*). Again, this was and continues to be serious business. To the people, Marduk was the spiritual power of Babylon, a force of nature that gave them a sense of calm and present hope. This is the chief god that Nimrod set up as an idolator for the people to worship, nor the LORD God of Heaven.

In the end, the reason we need to know about Marduk or Bel or the more biblically known name of Ba'al is because they are so-called spiritual entities that Mardon would have followed. Not only Mardon, but the known world at the time. Mardon was the physical Marduk. Again, keep in mind, the whole known world was living in this area since Nimrod called them to Shinar. They all worshipped Nimrod, Marduk, and the gods he made. Do not be deceived. This was all intentional, including indoctrinating his son Mardon. Why? To send a message to God:

The concept was to establish a ONE WORLD GOVERNMENT with Nimrod as the head.

Marduk would be the chief god.

Mardon would be the next in line behind Nimrod.

New World Order.

But God.

You can keep your snake in the grass.

My God always has a ram in the bush.

Birth of Abraham

Jasher 7: 49-51

And Terah the son of Nahor, prince of Nimrod's host, was in those days very great in the sight of the king and his subjects, and the king and princes loved him, and they elevated him very high. 50. And Terah took a wife and her name was Amthelo the daughter of Cornebo; and the wife of Terah conceived and bare him a son in those days. 51. Terah was seventy years old when he begat him, and Terah called the name of his son that was born to him Abram, because the king had raised him in those days, and dignified him above all his princes that were with him.

Shalom. God is Great! Look at what the LORD has done. In the midst of the rise of Nimrod and his abundantly wicked son Mardon, the wisdom of God was already at play. Nimrod had a son, Mardon, to which he had a choice: to teach him good or evil. Nimrod chose the latter. He could have taught him about the same God that gave him his Fame and ability to be victorious in battle to which he became King of the World at that time. He could have taught him that the clothing he wore, designed by the hands of God himself, was the real power behind the throne. He could have taught him to follow the ways of Noah, Enoch, and Methuselah, but he didn't. Instead, he decided to teach him evil, to not walk as a man of the sovereign God, the only God. He chose the same path of Lucifer, the bringer of light or enlightenment.

Evil is blinding, even when it is planning, masquerading as an angel of light or enlightenment. As Nimrod grew in fame, so did his plans to secure himself by elevating the most trusted people around him. The man who everyone loved that accepted the ways of Nimrod was Terah, who had already received a promotion as 2nd in command when Nimrod received kingship. But during this time of empire expansion, he gave Terah more powers to rule. While all of this sounds good for Terah, God was displeased in the works of Nimrod. From within the 2nd elevation of Terah would come the wisdom of God to restore the world back to himself, away from the idolatrous world king. Just as God gave the people of Earth 120 years to get themselves together and change their lives with Noah, he gave Nimrod a chance to get himself together as well. He could see the heart of the man and the evilness of his son Mardon. The LORD himself had a plan, and the wheels were sent into motion.

While the world was carrying on business as usual and Nimrod at the center of it, Terah took a wife, Amthelo, who gave birth to a son when Terah was 70 years old. This is amazing, for two different reasons.

First, the number 70 means judgment in biblical numerology. It was the age of 70 that God decided to send judgment into the world through the 2nd highest official in Nimrod's kingdom. Think of it. Terah had his pick of the women of the world, young and old. To the wicked Nimrod and Mardon, image who and what they had at their disposal. Terah, being a man that the king and all the princes loved, what woman couldn't he have? With that said, he had no children nor wife, for 70 years. To be married and to begin having children at 70 years old is a blessing within itself. But the child, the son that was born, was a son born in purpose. God had seen enough. It was time to issue out judgement and the birth of this son was going to bring Nimrod and the world to a reckoning.

Second, Terah named his son Abram, meaning exalted father. Did you get that? He was a child, already being named an exalted father. Wow! Terah could see something that had not happened yet. As he was being exalted and made a first-time father himself, he gave his son the name which means exalted father. Wow! Again, these are the wheels and wisdom of LORD at play, in the middle of sinful and idolatrous behavior. Through the genealogy of Shem, in service to the house of Ham, was Abram born.

Genesis 11: 10-26

These are the generations of Shem: Shem was an hundred years old, and begat Arphaxad two years after the flood: 11 And Shem lived after he begat Arphaxad five hundred years, and begat sons and daughters.12 And Arphaxad lived five and thirty years, and begat Salah: 13 And Arphaxad lived after he begat Salah four hundred and three years, and begat sons and daughters.14 And Salah lived thirty years, and begat Eber: 15 And Salah lived after he begat Eber four hundred and three years, and begat sons and daughters.16 And Eber lived four and thirty years, and begat Peleg: 17 And Eber lived after he begat Peleg four hundred and thirty years, and begat sons and daughters.18 And Peleg lived thirty years, and begat Reu: 19 And Peleg lived after he begat Reu two hundred and nine years, and begat sons and daughters.20 And Reu lived two and thirty years, and begat Serug: 21 And Reu lived after he begat Serug two hundred and seven years, and begat sons and daughters. 22 And Serug lived thirty years, and begat Nahor: 23 And Serug lived after he begat Nahor two hundred years, and begat sons and daughters. 24 And Nahor lived nine and twenty years, and begat Terah: 25 And Nahor lived after he begat Terah an hundred and nineteen years, and begat sons and daughters.26 **And Terah lived seventy years, and begat Abram**, Nahor, and Haran.

The events surrounding the birth of Abraham would turn the wheels of judgment even more. In Shinar magic and astrology was all a part of daily life. Worshipping Marduk and the various different gods were all a part of the norm. Studying the stars, information taught to humanity via the fallen angels called the watchers, were well practiced in the kingdom of Nimrod. It is through this practice, on the celebratory night of the birth of Abram, did God decide to send a message.

Jasher 8:1

And it was in the night that Abram was born, that all the servants of Terah, and all the wise men of Nimrod, an conjurors came and ate and drank in the house of Terah, and they rejoiced with him on that night.

While everyone was partying and drinking...

Jasher 8:2

And when all the wise men and conjurors went out from the house of Terah, they lifted up their eyes toward heaven that night to look at the stars, and they saw, and behold one very large star came from the east and ran in the heavens, and he swallowed up the four stars from the four sides of the heavens.

God was working, moving the stars, for a coming star....

Jasher 8:3

And all the wise men of the king and his conjurors were astonished at the sight, and the sages understood this matter, and they knew its import.

The studiers of the stars knew something special was happening...

Jasher 8:4

And they said to each other, This only betokens the child that has been born to Terah this night, who will grow up and be fruitful, and multiply, and possess all the earth, he and his children for ever, and he and his seed will slay great kings, and inherit their lands.

The men saw the Fame of this son…

Jasher 8:5

And the wise men and conjurors went home that night, and in the morning all these wise men and conjurors rose up early, and assembled in an appointed house.

After the party, a meeting was needed in the morning…

Jasher 8:6

And they spoke and said to each other, Behold the sight that we saw last night is hidden from the king, it has not been made known to him.

The king did not know what the real KING had said in the heavens…

Jasher 8:7

And should this thing get known to the king in the latter days, he will say to us, Why have you concealed this matter from me, and then we shall all suffer death; therefore, now let us go and tell the king the sight which we saw, and the interpretation thereof, and we shall then remain clear.

Their words translated really means "Let's tell the king to save our own lives."

Jasher 8: 8-13

And they did so, and they all went to the king and bowed down to him to the ground, and they said, May the king live, may the king live. 9. We heard that a son was born to Terah the son of Nahor, the prince of thy host, and we yesternight came to his house, and we ate and drank and rejoiced with him that night. 10. And when thy servants went out from the house of Terah, to go to our respective homes to abide there for the night, we lifted up our eyes to heaven, and we saw a great star coming from the east, and the same star ran with great speed, and swallowed up four great stars, from the four sides of the heavens. 11. And thy servants were astonished at the sight which we saw, and were greatly terrified, and we made our judgment upon the sight, and knew by **our wisdom** the proper interpretation thereof, that this thing applies to the child that is born to Terah, who will grow up and multiply greatly, and become powerful, and kill all the kings of the earth, and inherit all their lands, he and his seed forever.12. And now our lord and king, behold we have truly acquainted thee with what we have seen concerning this child. 13. **If it seemeth good to the king to give his father value for this child, we will slay him before he shall grow up and increase in the land, and his evil increase against us, that we and our children perish through his evil**.

This is how evil works and thrives in the world today. If you don't know, if you suspect, if you wonder, etc. This is a blueprint of how devious the minds of men are. The so-called wise men of the world, well off and socially positioned to succeed in life, those with extraordinary gifts and minds, group up and plot things that would be shameful if the eyes of the people knew THE TRUTH. They are privy to information that the rest of the world do not have. They make decisions that seem to benefit the masses when in reality, it's to benefit themselves. Please look at the verses above and dissect them carefully. They saw what they saw and decided to do damage control. They thought about their place in life, how they would be affected. At no point did you read where they considered the people. At no point did you read that they congratulated Terah and gave thanks for the sign in the heavens. At no point did you read that they humbled themselves to what they saw. No. These were men who were supposed to be mature and representatives of the people as governmental figures who saw an astonishing thing. They saw stars moving in the sky to mark the birth of this child. This child was special and they knew it. Instead of dealing in immediate truth, they decided to meet to find a way to live in an ongoing lie. The plan to kill a child of a friend in order to a keep a king in power was how the meeting adjourned. They decided to kill a man's seed, his child, his namesake, his family line, his blessing, so they can rule. They declared war on a man who they called their friend. They declared war on a man they just partied with. They declared war on a man they just celebrated his promotion. They declared war on a man with a promise from heaven. More importantly.....they declared war on the plan of God.

This is the very definition of politics: war without fighting.

Little did Nimrod know, the plan for the saving of humanity was happening right under his nose.

With the birth of Abram, God was sending a message on 3 levels.

1. Above the heads of men in the stars, he had made a declaration of judgment.

Psalms 50:6

And the heavens shall declare his righteousness: for God is judge himself. Selah.

2. Among men, in the earth, he will bring judgment.

Psalms 9:8

And he shall judge the world in righteousness, he shall minister judgment to the people in uprightness.

3. In the hearts of men shall he judge.

1 Samuel 16:7

But the LORD said unto Samuel, Look not on his countenance, or on the height of his stature; because I have refused him: for *the LORD seeth* not as man seeth; for man looketh on the outward appearance, but the LORD looketh on the heart.

What a crazy way and world to be born into, for a purpose this newborn did not know. With that said, Welcome to the world Abram!

Thanks Terah.

Envy

James 3:16

For where envying and strife *is*, there *is* confusion and every evil work.

Jesus' half-brother James said this. The man who grew up in the house with Jesus the Christ, said these words under the inspiration of the LORD himself. Who would know what this looks like better than the brother of the man the world became envious of. James 3:16 is a very important scripture in the whole wisdom of the Bible. Reread the verse before going forward and check your own inventory in your life. Analyze if you are experiencing this emotion, is it happening to you from someone else, have you or are you indulging in envious schemes, or do you know someone who is practicing envy. When you look closely, look what else has the capability to come out of envy: every evil work. Not some evil work, but every evil work. Needless to say, this is not good.

Envy is where this section begins.

Jasher 8: 13-14

If it seemeth good to the king to give his father value for this child, we will slay him before he shall grow up and increase in the land, and his evil increase against us, that we and our children perish through his evil. 14. And the king heard their words and they seemed good in his sight, and he sent and called for Terah, and Terah came before the king.

After hearing the words of the "wise men" that saw the heavens move with the birth of Abram, Nimrod had a choice to make. Consider his options: 1) he could disregard the information and keep going about his business, 2) he could have the wise men killed for saying such a thing about a fully devoted man to the cause as Terah had shown himself to be, or 3) take their advice and have the child killed. Two of the choices were evil, which means that Nimrod had a 67% chance of choosing wrong. Guess which one Nimrod chose? Door #3. He chose evil, with no hesitation. What's really crazy is that after promoting a man he trusts like no other and allowing him to celebrate his marriage and the birth of a son, Nimrod was easily ready to take life from the same man he celebrated. I guess Terah wasn't really his friend. Fame was his friend. This child's Fame was already rivaling his own in the minds of the wise men. There was no room for two people at the top, only one. This is why evil sounded good in the eyes of Nimrod.

Who do you know is envious of a two-day old child???
Evil. I digress.

Terah is then summoned to the king. While in his presence, pay close attention to the conversation between so-called friends.

Jasher 8: 15-16

And the king said to Terah, I have been told that a son was yesternight born to thee, and after this manner was observed in the heavens at his birth. 16. And now therefore give me the child, that we may slay him before his evil springs up against us, and I will give thee for his value, thy house full of silver and gold.

Look at the evil. Look at the scheme. Look at the deception. Look at the so-called friendship.

Nimrod acknowledged the abnormal star pattern connected to the child. That's good, but just like the serpent in the garden with Eve, he only told partial truth to cause a deeper destruction. Nimrod was direct, and disrespectful in my opinion, to ask Terah for his son's life, especially the son of his old age to murder for the sake of his own peace of mind. Nimrod disrespected Terah even further by telling him that he will reward the death of his son with a home full of gold and silver. In modern-day terms, it's like getting a multimillion dollar check from someone to watch your newborn child be killed. No amount of money can replace the thought, memory, and moment with a child, especially in older age. But again, as said in Jasher 7:42, Nimrod ruled in any way his heart desired. Me over We at its nastiest.

Now was the time for Terah's response.

Jasher 8: 17-21

And Terah answered the king and said to him: My Lord and king, I have heard thy words, and thy servant shall do all that his king desireth. 18. But my lord and king, I will tell thee what happened to me yesternight, that I may see what advice the king will give his servant, and then I will answer the king upon what he has just spoken; and the king said, Speak. 19. And Terah said to the king, Ayon, son of Mored, came to me yesternight, saying, 20. Give unto me the great and beautiful horse that the king gave thee, and I will give thee silver and gold, and straw and provender for its value; and I said to him, Wait till I see the king concerning thy words, and behold whatever the king saith, that will I do. 21. And now my lord and king, behold I have made this thing known to thee, and the advice which my king will give unto his servant, that will I follow.

Terah appears to be trying to filibuster, which means he's using a lot of words to delay the actual issue at hand. Sounds like an American politician, but I digress. He's looking for the right thing to say, as any person would, without offending the king, while saying a bunch of words that mean nothing in the grand scheme of things. Nimrod wasn't buying it.

Jasher 8: 22-24

And the king heard the words of Terah, and his anger was kindled and he considered him in the light of a fool. 23. And the king answered Terah, and he said to him, Art thou so silly, ignorant, or deficient in understanding, to do this thing, to give thy beautiful horse for silver and gold or even for straw and provender? 24. Art thou so short of silver and gold, that thou shouldst do this thing, because thou canst not obtain straw and provender to feed thy horse? and what is silver and gold to thee, or straw and provender, that thou shouldst give away that fine horse which I gave thee, like which there is none to be had on the whole earth?

Again, Nimrod wasn't buying it. But what he didn't know is that Terah was using what happened the night before as an example of how they both should look at the situation at hand. By giving his response above, Nimrod tied himself to a judgement that he didn't see coming from his own mouth.

Jasher 8: 25-26

And the king left off speaking, and Terah answered the king, saying, Like unto this has the king spoken to his servant; 26. I beseech thee, my lord and king, what is this which thou didst say unto me, saying, Give thy son that we may slay him, and I will give thee silver and gold for his value; what shall I do with silver and gold after the death of my son? who shall inherit me? surely then at my death, the silver and gold will return to my king who gave it.

Nimrod's whole foot was in his mouth.

There was nothing he could say.

Jasher 8:27

And when the king heard the words of Terah, and the parable which he brought concerning the king, it grieved him greatly and he was vexed at this thing, and his anger burned within him.

Nimrod now has a nasty anger cocktail swirling. He has envy mixed with jealousy and deceit. Instead of pouring his scheme down the drain, his pride and ego kicks in, thus adding anger to the drink.

Jasher 8: 28-29

And Terah saw that the anger of the king was kindled against him, and he answered the king, saying, All that I have is in the king's power; whatever the king desireth to do to his servant, that let him do, yea, even my son, he is in the king's power, without value in exchange, he and his two brothers that are older than he. 29. And the king said to Terah, No, but I will purchase thy younger son for a price.

The cocktail spins. Nimrod maintains his position, appealing to the financial gain in exchange for a human life. Recognize closely what is happening. You see it everyday in today's society. A person with money and power that feels like they can get what they want, when they want, defuse any issue, sacrifice others for self-gain, or just simply pay to make a situation go away. Don't get me wrong, it takes finances to keep things operational, especially when relating to the maintenance of people, organizations, and or business. But this is heartless. Sounds crazy right? Not so much. It's normal in our society. How so? People give up their children everyday in exchange for a check from the government. Some people have children for other people just to make money. There are whole organizations who profit from the death of infants, promoting abortions in exchange for money. This is the mindset of Nimrod, today. People and Government, take note.

Jasher 8: 30-31

And Terah answered the king, saying, I beseech thee my lord and king to let thy servant speak a word before thee, and let the king hear the word of his servant, and Terah said, Let my king give me three days' time till I consider this matter within myself, and consult with my family concerning the words of my king; and he pressed the king greatly to agree to this. 31. And the king hearkened to Terah, and he did so and he gave him three days' time, and Terah went out from the king's presence, and he came home to his family and spoke to them all the words of the king; and the people were greatly afraid.

3 days. 3 whole days. That's it. For the life of your son and family's name on the Earth through that son, just 3 days to think about an agreed upon death. 3 days. Not the amount of years of service he gave to Nimrod. Not the total number of battles he waged and won with Nimrod. Not the amount of time devoted to a man and his cause above his own. Not the commitment and devotion to changing your spiritual life because of Nimrod. Not humbling yourself to be elevated by the world king. Not even from the same clan, Terah was a Semite whereas Nimrod was a Hamite. Not being happy for a man that just had a son at 70 years old. None of those things counted when envy came into the picture. None of them. For all his work. For his service. For all his time. 3 days. To add insult to injury, Terah had to beg or beseech the king for that. 3 days.

The scripture says that the people were greatly afraid. You know why? Because they saw and felt in person the power of Nimrod. Consider Terah's family thought process at that moment. How much do you really matter in the eyes of the king? How much do we really have to give to show our commitment to the cause? Who does he really care about? He has a son, doesn't he understand? Where is the empathy or sympathy? How can anyone do this to a man that everyone loves and has done you no harm?

How just is that? What causes this type of response and action, especially between "friends"? Envy. Read the definition of envy and you will see why it is a strong drink, a cocktail, a deceiver to the senses.

Envy = painful or resentful awareness of an advantage enjoyed by another joined with a desire to possess the same advantage

Please take heed to the words of James, the half-brother of Jesus. Do not become like Nimrod, having the whole world at your fingertips and it not be enough. Cherish what you have, give thanks for what you don't. Perhaps the LORD of the Universe is doing you a favor, protecting you from yourself, or a coming destruction. It's a choice. Understanding the timing of things is a God thing. Wanting more time is a man thing.

Someone else' success or fortune is not your own, and vice versa. Besides, success is a mask. It comes with a price that everyone is not willing to pay. Let someone else's joy live while you kill the hate. Give God credit in all things and avoid trying to take away someone else' light because you may be in the shadows. Understand that the son, excuse me, the sun, can make a shadow the bright spot, depending on the angle of the object. Perspective is key. By ignoring James' advice, you are building the breeding ground for every kind of evil to be available, EVERY kind of evil. When Jealousy and Envy reside in your heart, it's not the information you receive that defile you. It's how you respond to the information and what comes from you that defiles you. Nimrod took information and decided in his heart to do as he pleased, allowing jealousy, envy, and pride to abound.

Don't be like Nimrod, numbskull. Be like Christ.

Mark 7: 14-16

And when he had called all the people *unto him*, he said unto them, Hearken unto me every one *of you*, and understand: 15
There is nothing from without a man, that entering into him can defile him: but the things which come out of him, those are they that defile the man. 16 If any man have ears to hear, let him hear.

The Sacrifice

Romans 11:33

O the depth of the riches both of the wisdom and knowledge of God! how unsearchable *are* his judgments, and his ways past finding out!

God has a way to get done what HE needs to get done. It's called HIS will. HE has a way to reverse actions without reversing time. HE allows things to happen so a greater good can be done. I must admit, I don't understand it at times. I really don't. There are things that God will do or allow that makes me look at HIS decisions and not like it. For example, I have lost loved ones, children, that I have no clue why they died. The memory hurts to think of. For my family also that lost loved ones, the same. Again, I don't understand God's reasoning in some things, I don't. I disagree at times, I do. I don't understand why HE allows evil people to prosper. I don't understand why the rich get richer and the poor get poorer on such a wide scale. I don't understand how little unseen bacteria and viruses can take down a visible giant. I don't understand world hunger, it literally makes zero sense to me. But there is something that I cling to that gives me comfort in the midst of the pain, disagreement, and confusion.

Romans 8: 38-39

For I am persuaded, that neither death, nor life, nor angels, nor principalities, nor powers, nor things present, nor things to come, 39 Nor height, nor depth, nor any other creature, shall be able to separate us from the love of God, which is in Christ Jesus our Lord.

With that said, let's get into a tough reading.

Jasher 8: 32-33

And it was in the third day that the king sent to Terah, saying, Send me thy son for a price as I spoke to thee; and shouldst thou not do this, I will send and slay all thou hast in thy house, so that thou shalt not even have a dog remaining. 33. And Terah hastened, (as the thing was urgent from the king), and he took a child from one of his servants, which his handmaid had born to him that day, and Terah brought the child to the king and received value for him.

3 days had past. Evil is relentless. Not only did Nimrod push the envelope on paying for the child, but now he is ready to kill his so-called friend and all in his family household, including the dog. That's cold. That's wrong. That's evil.

In his fear, Terah exchanged the child of his servant that was born that day with Abram, and took the child to Nimrod. Yes, I can't explain it. I don't understand it. Some things are just beyond me. What happens next is even worse.

Jasher 8:34

And the Lord was with Terah in this matter, that Nimrod might not cause Abram's death, and the king took the child from Terah and with all his might dashed his head to the ground, for he thought it had been Abram; and this was concealed from him from that day, and it was forgotten by the king, as it was the will of Providence not to suffer Abram's death.

When the scripture says the LORD was with Terah in the matter, it shows that God had compassion to be with him in the moment. As tough of a decision this was, God was with Terah. Sometimes we don't understand how. Sometimes we don't understand why. But we do have to keep in mind that HE is with us. Whenever things such as this happen, God allows it for a greater good to come out of it. We can't always see it, and again, I don't always understand or agree, but God doesn't need understanding or agreement to be God. HE alone is God.

Nimrod smashed the head of the child that he thought would bring him to an end. He did it right in front of the man that he believed was the father. Imagine the pain of that moment. The chaos of that moment. The pain of the real parent, the servant of Terah. The loss of the family of the servant that gave up their child so Abram can live. The evil of this moment combined with the switching of the child is equally bad. Am I calling God wrong? No. I'm simply saying I don't understand the mind of God on matters such as this. HIS ways are beyond both my and our understanding. Even though the parents and child weren't named, we do offer our condolences to the family and spirit of both parents and child that remain nameless in this situation. Even though Nimrod didn't have a heart, we do. Peace to their resting spirit.

As the scripture says, it was the will of God's providence that Abram not be killed. So, what is providence? Divine guidance or care. It was the divine guidance of God that this happened. This was only the beginning.

Jasher 8: 34-35

And Terah took Abram his son secretly, together with his mother and nurse, and he concealed them in a cave, and he brought them their provisions monthly. 36. And the Lord was with Abram in the cave and he grew up, and Abram was in the cave ten years, and the king and his princes, soothsayers and sages, thought that the king had killed Abram.

Terah was broken. Imagine the impact of these events, experiencing the fear of losing your family, having a member of your household family killed to protect another, witnessing a child's head bashed into the ground, by a man who had claimed and proclaimed you to be his right-hand man. Unbearable. Terah had not only lost a child in his house via his servant, but he had to hide his wife and nurse along with Abram so Nimrod wouldn't double back and have his whole family killed had he found out the child of the stars was still alive.

Let's observe what the 2nd most powerful man on Earth had to endure. 1) He lost the comfort of his wife in his home. 2) He didn't have a chance to raise his own son. 3) The things he was celebrated for and the woman who gave him the son for whom he was celebrating was now sent away for her own protection. 4) For months, he had to send the provisions needed to make sure his family was taken care of in secret. 5) Meanwhile, Nimrod had forgotten the issue. That's how evil and blinded his mind was. Terah had to sneak supplies to his family, living in a cave. Think about that for a second. Consider how disturbed Terah had to be. This is the 2nd most powerful man in Nimrod's kingdom, and he was living in a personal prison of power. This is the trick of power for those who seek it or want to be close to real power. It's the things you don't see that keep certain people in power. While Shiner is being built into the cradle of civilization, cities and towns all under the thumb of Nimrod, Terah was living in absolute terror. A rich man with global influence had his whole family living in a cave, unprotected, while he was living in a palace, protected. Anything could have happened to his wife, nurse, and Abram while they lived in that cave. They were in the wilderness, alone, two women and a child, no protection. As a husband and a father, this had to hurt. It strikes at your core. He essentially lost his family just the same as his child servant who had been killed and then forgotten by Nimrod. With one decision, in 3 days, Terah's whole life had changed.

This section is called 'The Sacrifice' in recognition of the unnamed servant who sacrificed his life for the story of Abram to go forth. This unnamed child from an unnamed household servant is very humbling. When you look at the story as we have, as gruesome as it is, you still miss an important factor: the child that was killed was born on the same day it died! Let's reread the verse and notice this very important detail...

Jasher 8: 32-33

And it was in the third day that the king sent to Terah, saying, Send me thy son for a price as I spoke to thee; and shouldst thou not do this, I will send and slay all thou hast in thy house, so that thou shalt not even have a dog remaining. 33. And Terah hastened, (as the thing was urgent from the king), and he took a child from one of his servants, which his handmaid had born to him that day, and Terah brought the child to the king and received value for him.

This was a newborn child. A child of new life. A child that had just seen the light of day, the breath of air, a short touch of love, gone. We don't know the child's name, but every culture and continent on this planet has been affected by the sacrifice of the unknown child. This family's loss was everyone's gain, in some capacity or another. Through Abram, the whole world would be blessed. Now watch this....God, in his infinite wisdom, allows us to expand from the unknown into knowing him through teachers who understand the sacrifice of the unknown. The apostle Paul, when visiting Athens, visits the tomb of the unknown god on Mar's Hill, the debating place for all the Greek philosophers. From here, he teaches the European continent's greatest thinkers of the 'Unknown God'.

Acts 17: 22-23

Then Paul stood in the midst of Mars' hill, and said, Ye men of Athens, I perceive that in all things ye are too superstitious. 23
For as I passed by, and beheld your devotions, I found an altar with this inscription, TO THE UNKNOWN GOD. Whom
therefore ye ignorantly worship, him declare I unto you.

Meanwhile, God was working his plan. Abram was growing and growing strong. For 10 years he lived and grew as a cave dweller. But God was with him. That's more than enough for anyone. Nimrod and all his counsel thought Abram was dead. But God. He makes the unknown, known. He makes the known, unknown. Therefore, we salute the sacrifice of the unknown child and its family. We are eternally grateful to know that the unknown God made it known about your sacrifice. We love you!

Psalms 73:26

My flesh and my heart faileth: ***but* God** *is* the strength of my heart, and my portion for ever.

Origin of the 1st Hebrew

Genesis 11:27

Now these *are* the generations of Terah: Terah begat Abram, Nahor, and Haran; and Haran begat Lot.

While Abram was growing up in a cave in Mesopotamia with his mother and nurse, his two older brothers Nahor and Haran were of age and were starting their own families. The offspring of this family unit will be major players throughout human history.

Jasher 9: 1-3

And Haran, the son of Terah, Abram's oldest brother, took a wife in those days. 2. Haran was thirty-nine years old when he took her; and the wife of Haran conceived and bare a son, and he called his name Lot. 3. And she conceived again and bare a daughter, and she called her name Milca; and she again conceived and bare a daughter, and she called her name Sarai. 4. Haran was forty-two years old when he begat Sarai, which was in the tenth year of the life of Abram; and in those days Abram and his mother and nurse went out from the cave, as the king and his subjects had forgotten the affair of Abram.

As you can see, Haran was 32 years older than Abram. He is the oldest son of Terah. He had a son, Lot, when he was 39 then he had two daughters, Milca (Milcah) and Sarai, with Sarai being born when he was 42. Sarai was born when Abram was 10 years old. They were born and lived in Ur, the city of the Chaldees, a prosperous city in the kingdom of Nimrod.

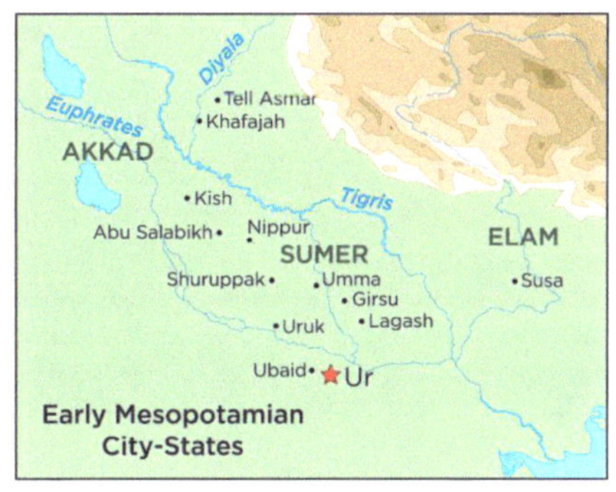

Early Mesopotamian City-States

After spending 10 years in a cave, living to avoid Nimrod and his government, it was time for young Abram to leave. His mother and nurse had done a great job of hiding and protecting him while his father Terah provided the provisions they needed to survive. After 10 years, Nimrod and company believed him to be dead and the issue forgotten.

But God.

Jasher 9:5

And when Abram came out from the cave, he went to Noah and his son Shem, and he remained with them to learn the instruction of the Lord and his ways, and no man knew where Abram was, and Abram served Noah and Shem his son for a long time.

Amen! As mentioned earlier in the book. God's plan was set in motion. The wheels were turning. It was time. While Nimrod made the whole world worship as he worshipped, polytheistic, God had a plan for the young Abram. He was sent to live with the only monotheists on the planet at the time who worshipped one God, the only God, the men who the world still respected, including Nimrod. Abram was sent to the father of the Semite family, Shem, and his father, the great Noah, who was still alive in the Earth. Noah lived 350 years after the flood, so he would still have been alive during this time (Gen. 9:28).

There is an important parenting lesson here for all to learn about the development of a son. When Abram came of age, his family sent him to be with the patriarchs of his family to learn the ways of God and life, the root of all manhood. They sent a young boy to old men to learn what he needed to know to become a man. Being that his father was not available, these women knew that a boy needed a man to teach a boy how to become a man. This is an important lesson in understanding manhood from both the male and female perspective. At some point in the life of a young male, he needs an older man to show him the pathway of manhood. Whether he gains that experience when he's younger or older, a man needs a man for manhood development. The process and transition into manhood from boyhood is the job of a man, not a woman. This is not disrespectful to a woman. It's actually a compliment. We need one another to continue the human race. The decision Terah and his wife made was to secure Abram's growth spiritually, mentally, and physically. This is a process designed by God, not man. Regardless of the reason why a man isn't in the life of their son, good or bad, finding a Godly or good man in the family is key to the development of the child. It doesn't take anything away from you as a parent. All it does is add value and capital to the life of your son. For example, you can send your son to get this training during the summer when school is out. It also gives you a break when you need it (wink, wink). Abram was raised under these conditions.

Jasher 9:6

And Abram was in Noah's house thirty-nine years, and Abram knew the Lord from three years old, and he went in the ways of the Lord until the day of his death, as Noah and his son Shem had taught him; and all the sons of the earth in those days greatly transgressed against the Lord, and they rebelled against him and they served other gods, and they forgot the Lord who had created them in the earth; and the inhabitants of the earth made unto themselves, at that time, every man his god; gods of wood and stone which could neither speak, hear, nor deliver, and the sons of men served them and they became their gods.

For 39 years, Abram was being tutored by Noah and Shem. Wow! Imagine the lessons learned there. To be present to hear the conversations, the directions, the stories, the experiences, the testimonies. Wow. To God be the glory! From childhood to adulthood, from 10 to 49, Abram learned from Noah and Shem how to serve God Almighty. Just as Nimrod was raised by Cush teaching him the ways of God so much so that he started out giving God credit for his successes, Abram was given sound teaching to know God from his youth. His mother introduced God to him at 3 years old for seven years, he then learned from Noah and Shem from 10 to 49. Abram knew THE God in the midst of a world of many so-called gods. He knew the ONE, the same ONE Nimrod knew.

Nimrod, on the other hand, progressed to go opposite of the LORD. He taught men rebellion, which is likened to witchcraft (1 Sam. 15:23). He forgot God, just as he forgot the child who's head he smashed into pieces thinking it was Abram. He taught mankind to have an independent god unto themselves with Marduk being the chief god. Nimrod was teaching the world to rebel against the LORD in the same ways the people did prior to the Great Flood.

Jasher 9. 7-10

And the king and all his servants, and Terah with all his household were then the first of those that served gods of wood and stone. 8. And Terah had twelve gods of large size, made of wood and stone, after the twelve months of the year, and he served each one monthly, and every month Terah would bring his meat offering and drink offering to his gods; thus did Terah all the days. 9. And all that generation were wicked in the sight of the Lord, and they thus made every man his god, but they forsook the Lord who had created them. 10. And there was not a man found in those days in the whole earth, who knew the Lord (for they served each man his own God) except Noah and his household, and all those who were under his counsel knew the Lord in those days.

Even though Terah made the right decision to send his son to Noah and Shem, who did right in the eyes of the LORD, he did not do right in his devotion to God for himself. He indulged in idol worship with the rest of the world, choosing survival of self in this world over revival of self in the world to come. Always be mindful, bad company corrupts good character.

1 Corinthians 15:33

Be not deceived: evil communications corrupt good manners.

The following verses will explain the reason why Abram became Abraham later in the Bible, earning him the nickname of the father of faith. As you read, please understand the process of his decision. Every person who struggles in whether to believe in God or not can start here and try this process. Decide for yourself, in the most primitive way you can, whether God be true or not. You can find out the answer to the question in nature. Let's read:

Jasher 9: 11-15

And Abram the son of Terah was waxing great in those days in the house of Noah, and no man knew it, and the Lord was with him. 12. And the Lord gave Abram an understanding heart, and he knew all the works of that generation were vain, and that all their gods were vain and were of no avail. 13. And Abram saw the sun shining upon the earth, and Abram said unto himself Surely now this sun that shines upon the earth is God, and him will I serve. 14. And Abram served the sun in that day and he prayed to him, and when evening came the sun set as usual, and Abram said within himself, Surely this cannot be God? 15. And Abram still continued to speak within himself, Who is he who made the heavens and the earth? who created upon earth? where is he?

Abram set out on a course to find out God on his own. He decided to test who or what God is for himself, separate and apart from the teachings of Noah and Shem. He looked to the sun, and began to pray to it. Sun worship was common in Nimrod's Shinar. This was Abram's first step in finding truth for himself.

Sun Worship in Ancient Mesopotamia

According to researcher Dr. Ruth Horry:

Šamaš (Sumerian Utu) is the god of the sun. He brings light and warmth to the land, allowing plants and crops to grow. At sunrise Šamaš was known to emerge from his underground sleeping chamber and take a daily path across the skies. As the sun fills the entire sky with light, Šamaš oversaw everything that occurred during the daytime. He thus became the god of truth, judgements and justice. Šamaš also played a role in treaties, oaths and business transactions, as he could see through deceit and duplicity. As a defender of justice, the sun god also had a warrior aspect. Šamaš played a similarly

Samas, Sumerian sun god Utu
© British Museum

important role in the realm of the dead as he did in the living world. The spirits of the dead were thought to enter the netherworld via a passage on the horizon in the extreme western part of the world. In some traditions, this passage was the same entrance that led to Šamaš's underground dwelling, and to which he returned at sunset each evening.

Abram noticed that the sun had a short time to rule, during the day. He concluded this cannot be God. Why? Because he or it (the sun), is limited. The sun cannot be God if it is limited to the day. So, Abram did a test to see if perhaps the sun went to a different place.

Jasher 9:16

And night darkened over him, and he lifted up his eyes toward the west, north, south, and east, and he saw that the sun had vanished from the earth, and the day became dark.

The sun was nowhere to be found. He looked in all four directions, no sun. Abram now knows that the sun is not God. It had now become dark outside, so he decides to look up.

Jasher 9: 17-18

And Abram saw the stars and moon before him, and he said, Surely this is the God who created the whole earth as well as man, and behold these his servants are gods around him: and Abram served the moon and prayed to it all that night. 18. And in the morning when it was light and the sun shone upon the earth as usual, Abram saw all the things that the Lord God had made upon earth.

Uh oh. Here comes both conflict and controversy. Abram began to worship the moon as God as he thought the stars were its servants in the night sky. He worshipped them all night. The moon god was known as Nanna or Sin.

Moon Worship in Ancient Mesopatamia:

According to Dr. Joshua Mark:

Nanna (also known as Nannar, Nanna-Suen, Sin, Asimbabbar, Namrasit, Inbu) is the Mesopotamian god of the moon and wisdom. He is one of the oldest gods in the Mesopotamian pantheon and is first mentioned at the very dawn of writing in the region c. 3500 BCE. His cult center was the great temple at Ur, and he is frequently mentioned in hymns and inscriptions from the Ur III Period (2047-1750 BCE) as the chief god of the pantheon with the epithet Enzu, lord of wisdom. His importance is evident in the number of inscriptions which refer to or praise him and the stories in which he features.

Nanna or Sin
© New World Encyclopedia

Important Note: Nanna/Sin was the patron god of the city Ur of the Chaldees

Nanna or Sin also carries another name today. There is a monotheistic belief structure that has the same sign as the symbol of worship for the ancient Sumerians (We'll get into that later).

Spoiler alert....Nanna was the "Crescent Moon" god.

Scholar Stephen Bertman adds:

The Mesopotamians thus conceived of day, illuminated by the sun, as emanating from the darkness of night and the lesser light of the moon. As the time of lovemaking, the night and the moon were linked to the goddess of the erotic. As a source of light, the moon was also viewed as humanity's protector against acts of criminality undertaken under the cover of darkness even as the illuminating and all-seeing sun was looked upon as a guardian of justice (122).

When the morning came, Abram noticed something: the moon went away just as the sun did. Neither ruled with absolution. Both went away. Abram was looking for the God of the Universe that never went away. He was looking for Jehovah Adon Kol Ha-arets, The LORD of All the Earth. In the morning, after seeing all these things, Abram concluded the moon and stars, like the sun, was not God.

Jasher 9:19

And Abram said unto himself Surely these are not gods that made the earth and all mankind, but these are the servants of God, and Abram remained in the house of Noah and there knew the Lord and his ways' and he served the Lord all the days of his life, and all that generation forgot the Lord, and served other gods of wood and stone, and rebelled all their days.

By going through the process of ruling out sun and moon worship, Abram eliminated the most prominent gods of the ancient world. Sun and moon worship are worldwide cultural norms for early civilization worship. People worshipped them, and to this day many others do as well, not realizing Abram tested this for us so we don't have to do the same. Using logic and reason, he realized both the sun and moon had to have a creator that governs them since they rise and fall each day. They didn't have the power to remain nor were they responsive to worship. Therefore, he concluded that they cannot be God. The real God must be greater than the sun and the moon, because they are limited in their power and domain. He concluded they are servants of God, not God. Moses, years later and the writer of the book of Genesis, would concur (Gen. 1: 14-19) with Abram. Abram educated us from the perspective of the ancient Sumerians, future Akkadians and world renown Babylonians who were masters in astronomy and astrology. Moses would educate us from the perspective of ancient Egyptian science, being that he was both priest and prince, knowing the secrets of Egyptian religion. Abram and Moses both testify that celestial worship is vanity.

Deuteronomy 4: 19-20

And lest thou lift up thine eyes unto heaven, and when thou seest the sun, and the moon, and the stars, even all the host of heaven, shouldest be driven to worship them, and serve them, which the LORD thy God hath divided unto all nations under the whole heaven. 20But the LORD hath taken you, and brought you forth out of the iron furnace, even out of Egypt, to be unto him a people of inheritance, as ye are this day.

This personal trial was enough for Abram to decide to live for God and be opposite of the world. The process of finding out God on your own is a testimony unto itself. Why? Because God desires relationship with us, personally. HE loves it. HE loves us. What Abram did was honorable and serves as an example for us in how we learn and grow to know HIM. He tried God for himself, which is key in relational development with the LORD. He saw what the world was doing and decided to stand on the other side of its belief structure. He chose God, the LORD, for himself. His decision was the creation of a whole new thought process, belief structure, and people. Even though he hadn't taken a wife yet or had children, the birth of a nation was happening in the process of the making of the man. His name meant exalted father. Abram was establishing his belief and relationship with God for himself. This act of standing on the other side against the world and choosing God came to be given a name:

Hebrew = to stand on the other side.

You have now witnessed the making and shaping of the first Hebrew.

Abram would not earn the title of Hebrew publicly until later in his story. But as for now, he has internally made the decision to stand away from the world and believe in the ONE true God, unlike Nimrod. This is how salvation works for the believer to this day. The change must occur to you then within. God desires truth in the innermost part. Just as Abram became Hebrew from within, with the changing of his mind and the renewing of his heart, so are we in salvation. Whether we be Jew or Gentile, we must become a Hebrew at heart, one who stands with God against the belief structure of a Nimrod built world system. Amen.

Romans 12:2

And be not conformed to this world: but be ye transformed by the renewing of your mind, that ye may prove what is that good, and acceptable, and perfect, will of God.

The Tower

Genesis 11:1

And the whole earth was of one language, and of one speech.

One World Language, One World Government, One World Leader, Nimrod. If you take nothing else from this particular section, you must understand the first sentence. This is essentially it, the destination. Everything else is the detail of this sentence, and the details are incredible. Genesis gives us the entree, the book of Jasher gives us the details to describe the same event. Let's proceed.

Genesis 11:2

And it came to pass, as they journeyed from the east, that they found a plain in the land of Shinar; and they dwelt there.

Question: who are the "they" that the Bible is referring to?

The book of Jasher says...

Jasher 9: 20-22

And king Nimrod reigned securely, and all the earth was under his control, and all the earth was of one tongue and words of union. 21. And all the princes of Nimrod and his great men took counsel together; Phut, Mitzraim, Cush and Canaan with their families, and they said to each other, Come let us build ourselves a city and in it a strong tower, and its top reaching heaven, and we will make ourselves famed, so that we may reign upon the whole world, in order that the evil of our enemies may cease from us, that we may reign mightily over them, and that we may not become scattered over the earth on account of their wars. 22. And they all went before the king, and they told the king these words, and the king agreed with them in this affair, and he did so.

Answer: Phut, Mitzraim, Cush, Canaan, and their families (the world population) are the "they" Genesis 11:2 is referring to.

Keep in mind, the world had been recalled by Nimrod to one place, the valley of Shinar, to live with him in ancient Sumer to be taught the ways of their king. As it says in Genesis, they all spoke the same language so there was no confusion. They lived in the same area, they traveled together, everything was done as one.

The princes of Nimrod were his uncles, the sons of Ham. They all counseled their nephew even though he was the king of the world. They came together to scheme to build a tower so they themselves can be elevated above everyone in the world. This is very important to know in the big scheme of things. They wanted to rule over the world as Nimrod did, just in a different way. Sure, Nimrod was the king, but they knew if they could be elevated in some capacity, they too would receive praise and power, similar to Nimrod. Reader, please keep in mind, it was not the initial plan of Nimrod to build this tower. It was his family, those seeking their claim to fame, their own power pull. That's very important to note as we move along.

The sons of Ham conspired to build a tower to heaven. Read verse 21 again. The desire was for them to be elevated and famous, like Nimrod. There's that word again, Fame. I told you before, it's the most addictive drug known to mankind. They wanted to build this tower to heaven. My apologies for the repetitive language, but you must really think about that for a second. What would possess a man to want to build a tower to heaven? Well, we have our answer. Evil that merges both the physical and metaphysical world. The only way they could do this is if they got permission to do so from their nephew and king, Nimrod, who was interconnected with the most evil of evils in the world, the Fallen One. Nimrod had to consider the prospect of this possibly happening. By doing so, history changed. Mr. Wicked himself did what you read he did and no, this is not a Jared's commercial, but he said yes! From that point on, they were about the business of getting this done.

As Genesis 11:2 says, they traveled west (from the east) to look for a place to build this tower. They didn't take a few people to see it. They took everyone, every man they could find, to help with the Tower.

Jasher 9:23

And all the families assembled consisting of about six hundred thousand men, and they went to seek an extensive piece of ground to build the city and the tower, and they sought in the whole earth and they found none like one valley at the east of the land of Shinar, about two days' walk, and they journeyed there and they dwelt there.

600,000 men for this one cause was an open rebellion. To be clear, unifying for one cause, one reason, even in disobedience, is amazing. They sent people out to search the known world and no place was like the location they found that was just a 2-day walk from Shinar. They found a valley that fit their scheme. This was not only intentional but a showcase of engineering genius. Why? When building a tall building, you must dig deep into the ground for stability so the building can have a solid foundation that won't allow the building to tilt over. A valley is picture perfect to build such a structure since the ground is already de-elevated, giving them an opportunity to build a tower which appears to be coming from within the Earth to the heavens. They didn't want the natural elevation of God's work to get the credit, such as a hill or mountain. They wanted the credit and glory. All engineers and architects learn this in school, that all skyscrapers must have a deep base before you can build up. It's like a tall tree: no matter how tall or wide or length of limbs the tree has, it's only as strong as the root, which is deep in the Earth. This is architectural design 101. With the valley only being a 2-days' walk from Shinar, the supply train wouldn't be interrupted to build the tower and a city around it.

Genesis 11: 3-4

And they said one to another, Go to, let us make brick, and burn them throughly. And they had brick for stone, and slime had they for morter. 4 And they said, Go to, let us build us a city and a tower, whose top may reach unto heaven; and let us make us a name, lest we be scattered abroad upon the face of the whole earth.

The plan to build the tower began with making brick for stone and using slime for mortar. This tower was going to take tons of bricks and slime to complete this task. But why bricks and slime?

Bricks represented the idea of something being permanent.

Slime will rise to the surface when moved, yet it is a sticky substance, like glue. when heated, it hardens, like a rock.

M.I.P.

They wanted to build a tower that was permanent and sustainable as a rock without rocks

Why did they build it without rocks? Rocks were God-made, brick are not. Again, they wanted the credit. Besides, they and Nimrod knew who the ROCK was, Jehovah Sal'l, The LORD, my Rock!

Psalms 18:2

The LORD *is* my rock, and my fortress, and my deliverer; my God, my strength, in whom I will trust; my buckler, and the horn of my salvation, *and* my high tower.

Before we go forward, allow us to make something clear about what you are reading. Do not be deceived. The Tower you are reading about here is the original skyscraper building! Yes, you read that right. Take a second and think about the following questions, critically.

Why does every major city on the planet have skyscrapers and a skyline? Why do the skyscrapers reach into the sky? Why are they needed and why is it common to have skyscrapers?

Well, keep reading. We've partially answered these questions already.

As the uncles of Nimrod said, they wanted to be exalted, elevated, to rule over the people. Think of the books you read, the movies you see, the plot of those using and building these monuments. There's a common theme: self-promotion, self-rule, self-elevation.

Challenge: go watch the movie *Skyscraper* (2018) with Dewayne 'The Rock' Johnson. Great movie, a lot of action, I loved it! However, listen carefully to the words that are being used to describe the origin of these monuments to men. Test what you read here, biblically and historically, then apply it to your everyday life and what you see with your own eyes. Truth is stranger than fiction.

Let's proceed to answer the other questions with scripture.

Jasher 9:24

And the building of the tower was unto them a transgression and a sin, and they began to build it, and whilst they were building against the Lord God of heaven, they imagined in their hearts to war against him and to ascend into heaven.

There it is! Now we're getting to the good stuff! It wasn't just that they wanted to build a tower to heaven and leave it alone when they were done. They wanted to build a tower to heaven to go to war against God! That's a different type of arrogance! They imagined in their hearts to do this, the very place that God sees, the heart. They wanted it to be apparent to the LORD when HE sees them that there is no misinterpretation of intent, they wanted to displace the LORD off HIS throne, in HIS domain, like a modern-day coup d'état. Wow!

Jasher 9:25

And all these people and all the families divided themselves in three parts; the first said We will ascend into heaven and fight against him; the second said, We will ascend to heaven and place our own gods there and serve them; and the third part said, We will ascend to heaven and smite him with bows and spears; and God knew all their works and all their evil thoughts, and he saw the city and the tower which they were building.

Let's align the groups so you can get a clear picture of what you just read:

Group One

Go up into heaven, fight against God

Group Two

Go up into heaven, put their own gods in place, and serve them there

Group Three

Go up into heaven, kill God with weapons (bows and spears)

Group One's intention was to simply to ascend into heaven and fight God. This makes 0 sense but you can see the arrogance of the heart of man. They actually believed that they could 1) go into heaven, 2) fight God, and 3) defeat the invisible All-Powerful Spirit that gave them life. Their desire was for power and authority.

Group Two's intention was to rise up above God and to place their own gods in HIS position, thus creating a pantheon (group of gods). By placing their own gods in HIS place, which is idolatry, they (humans) would be the gods, being that the gods they were placing in the place of God were created by their own hands. They could create the perception the world would see and eventually believe. This group's desire was to control perception through deception. The key word is control.

Group Three's intention was to kill God, plain and simple. How were they going to do it? With arrows and spears. They believed they could go to war with God in heaven, and kill HIM with weapons of wood, stone, and possibly iron. The same way the "invincible" mighty hunter of Earth Nimrod expanded his kingdom to the known world without rival, it was time to take on God, the same one that gave Nimrod his powers to begin with. They believed they could make God, a spirit, bleed. Not only did they believe they could make HIM bleed, but they believed they could make HIM die, the Spirit that gives life, the Father of All Spirits. This group's desire was to monopolize Godship.

*** The motive of Nimrod in building the tower was to WAR against God***

Ladies and gentlemen, this is not a test, but a testimony for mankind to read and understand that God is real. The same man, Nimrod, who gained his fame and power from God, is now ready to lead a war on the LORD of the Universe himself. This is not a fairy tale. This is scripture, unadulterated, for you to see how wicked and evil a person can become. Starting out in church is good, but some of the vilest men in history began their journey in church or in an environment where God was understood to be sovereign and real. Please make note of this statement. For example, Adolf Hitler grew up in church, actually he wanted to be a priest early in life. That didn't turn out well. Later in the book, we will return to this section and give you details to collaborate my claim. This is NOT to say don't go to church. Allow me to be clear. What I am saying is that even the devil will go to church, he came from heaven itself, so you can't be surprised when you see such evil going on within a person that perhaps started in the church but turns against God. The heart of a man can change. Again, the title of this book is called *Nimrod: The World's 1st AntiChrist*, meaning there have been many more that came after him with a final one on the way, but I digress.

Let's address these haters of God, group by group, before the LORD steps in. There are some people who would like to take the stand to address the 3 groups before HE does.

Biblical Characters Question the Minds of Men...and Nimrod

Rulers **Job** and **Solomon**, can you please address Group 1

Group 1 - How can you build into heaven to fight against God when not even the heavens can contain HIM? Do you know how high HE is? How deep HE is? How wide HE is? Can you size God up?

Job says...

He's Deeper than HELL, Higher than HEAVEN, Longer than the SEA, Wider than the EARTH

Job 11: 7-9

Canst thou by searching find out God? canst thou find out the Almighty unto perfection? 8 It is as **high as heaven**; what canst thou do? **deeper than hell**; what canst thou know? 9 The measure thereof is **longer than the earth**, and **broader than the sea**.

(Keep in mind, mankind at this point thought these elements mentioned in Job were limitless)

Solomon says…

The heaven you are trying to go into cannot contain him. So, how are you going to do it?

1 Kings 8:27

But will God indeed dwell on the earth? behold, **the heaven and heaven of heavens cannot contain thee**; how much less this house that I have builded?

Worship Leaders **Nehemiah** and **Moses** requests the microphone to testify to Group 2

Group 2 - You want to build into heaven to replace God so you can worship your own gods, that you made, correct? If you made them of stone and wood, wouldn't that make you their gods? Better yet, where did the wood and stone come from?

Nehemiah says…

Nehemiah 9:6

Thou, even thou, art LORD alone; thou hast made heaven, the heaven of heavens, with all their host, the earth, and **all things that are therein**, the seas, and all that is therein, and thou preservest them all; and the host of heaven worshippeth thee.

Moses testified on behalf of something the LORD said…

Exodus 20: 2-6

I am the LORD thy God, which have brought thee out of the land of Egypt, out of the house of bondage. 3 **Thou shalt have no other gods before me**. 4 **Thou shalt not make unto thee any graven image, or any likeness of any thing that is in heaven above, or that is in the earth beneath, or that is in the water under the earth**: 5 Thou shalt not bow down thyself to them, nor serve them : for I the LORD thy God am a jealous God, visiting the iniquity of the fathers upon the children unto the third and fourth generation of **them that hate me**; 6 And shewing mercy unto thousands of **them that love me**, and **keep my commandments**.

Prophets **Isaiah** and **John** volunteer to address Group 3

Group 3 - Didn't somebody already try to ascend above the mountain of God to replace him in heaven? Wasn't there already war in heaven? How did that turn out?

Isaiah says…

Lucifer's Desire led to Lucifer's Fall. He was where you are trying to go, Heaven. He tried this takeover nonsense already. He failed…to the Earth, where you are building from.

Isaiah 14:12

How art thou fallen from heaven, O Lucifer, son of the morning! **how art thou cut down to the ground**, which didst weaken the nations! 13 **For thou hast said in thine heart**, **I will ascend into heaven, I will exalt my throne above the stars of God: I will sit also upon the mount of the congregation**, in the sides of the north: 14 **I will ascend above the heights of the clouds; I will be like the most High**.

John says...

There was War in Heaven already. Satan tried it, and failed. He had an army with him that were angels, and failed. You have an army with you, men, and you expect to succeed?

Revelation 12: 7-9

And **there was war in heaven**: Michael and his angels fought against the dragon; and the dragon fought and his angels, 8 **And prevailed not**; **neither was their place found any more in heaven**. 9 And **the great dragon was cast out**, **that old serpent, called the Devil**, and **Satan**, which deceiveth the whole world: **he was cast out into the earth**, and **his angels were cast out with him**.

Shhhh! Be quiet and listen up! The LORD is about to testify....

To Groups 1, 2, and 3

Isaiah 44: 6-11

Thus saith the LORD the King of Israel, and his redeemer the LORD of hosts; I am the first, and I am the last; and **beside me there is no God**. 7 And who, as I, shall call, and shall declare it, and set it in order for me, since I appointed the ancient people? and the things that are coming, and shall come, let them shew unto them. 8 Fear ye not, neither be afraid: have not I told thee from that time, and have declared it? **ye are even my witnesses. Is there a God beside me? yea, there is no God; I know not any.** 9 They that make a graven image are all of them vanity; and their delectable things shall not profit; and they are their own witnesses; they see not, nor know; that they may be ashamed. 10 **Who hath formed a god, or molten a graven image that is profitable for nothing**? 11 Behold, all his fellows shall be ashamed: and the workmen, they are of men: let them all be gathered together, let them stand up; yet they shall fear, and they shall be ashamed together.

(Mic drop)

Well, well. Let's go back to the tower. Nothing else to see here.

Jasher 9:27

And when they were building they built themselves a great city and a very high and strong tower; and on account of its height the mortar and bricks did not reach the builders in their ascent to it, until those who went up had completed a full year, and after that, they reached to the builders and gave them the mortar and the bricks; thus was it done daily.

© Burj Khalifa

Not only did they build a tower, but they built a city around the tower. It was a sight to behold. The structure of the tower was so large and enormous that it would take a full year for a man to go from the base of the tower to the top. Image that. Even with all the skyscrapers of today, NONE of them are the size of the original tower. No skyscraper today is big enough that if a man was to start walking today it would take a year to go to the top. With elevators, obviously you could reach the top in a minute or two. Walking up or down the staircase would take a long time, but not a year. For example, the Burj Khalifa in Dubai is the tallest building in the world. It is 2,717 feet high. A Frenchman, Alain Robert, climbed the stairs of the building from the bottom to the top. It took him 6 hours, 13 minutes, and 55 seconds to achieve this Guinness world record. While this is an amazing feat, and congrats to Mr. Robert, but the Burj Khalifa is not the Tower of Nimrod. We're talking a whole different animal, a whole different building. The builders of this wondrous abomination was so committed to the task, that life itself didn't matter if it was lost by the workers. The only thing that mattered was getting this evil done, even if it took a year to walk from the bottom to the top.

Jasher 9:28

And behold these ascended and others descended the whole day; and if a brick should fall from their hands and get broken, they would all weep over it, and if a man fell and died, none of them would look at him.

They didn't care. These men were committed to evil and didn't care about the consequences thereof. This is what evil can do. As mentioned before, evil doesn't care about anything or anyone as it is blinding to those who indulge thereof. Just as Nimrod didn't care after he smashed the head of a newborn child to pieces to secure his future as king, neither did the workers of the Tower care when someone died. This project was so vast and large that if a brick fell from above and killed someone, they wouldn't even stop to mourn the death of the person who was killed. Think of how demented you would have to be to do such a thing. They didn't stop or pause to check on the person. They wouldn't even look at the person. They wouldn't cry when a man died but they would cry if a brick fell to the ground and broke. That's how valueless human life had become in this plan to overtake God. That's evil, that's cold, that's Nimrod.

While all of this was going on, God was taking note of what they were doing. He knew what was going on and more importantly, he knew their thoughts (Jash. 9:26). So, one day, our God decided to make a visit.

Genesis 11:5

And the LORD came down to see the city and the tower, which the children of men builded.

This is so beautiful. The LORD our God is El Rai, the God who Sees. He came down to see this building that his haters were building. Imagine that. The same God they hated, came down to see them. This is such a teachable moment that I have to pause my writing for a breaking news moment. Give me one second, we'll be back in a flash!

Breaking News: Haters of God acknowledge that he does exists! Haters of God acknowledge that he does exists!

This is SO IMPORTANT when understanding true evil and those who dispute God. You cannot dispute something or someone who doesn't exist. No matter how you slice it, you cannot dispute something that doesn't exist. If it doesn't exist, why dispute it? If you dispute something that doesn't exists, doesn't that mean it's something psychologically wrong with you? It's just a question. Something to think about, right?

Back from the Breaking News Break...

While the LORD was looking at the tower and all of the evil associated with it, something happened. The men that were building it were in a place that they could try to execute their plans. Remember the 3 groups? Guess what happened next?

Jasher 9:29

And the Lord knew their thoughts, and it came to pass when they were building they cast the arrows toward the heavens, and all the arrows fell upon them filled with blood, and when they saw them they said to each other, Surely we have slain all those that are in heaven.

Yes, you read that right. These men began to fire arrows into the sky towards the heavens. We cannot make this up. These men cast their weapons into the sky to really try to kill God and the heavenly host. When they saw the arrows return to the Earth with blood on them, they were filled with joy! Why? They honestly believed that they had did something special. They honestly believed that they had did what no one else had done. They believed that they had done what Satan/Lucifer could not do. Think of the madness of this moment. These men believed that they were the ones to do something so special and magical that not even the devil himself could do to God. The arrows had blood on them!

But God.

Jasher 9: 30-31

For this was from the Lord in order to cause them to err, and in order; to destroy them from off the face of the ground. 31. And they built the tower and the city, and they did this thing daily until many days and years were elapsed.

Look at the wisdom of God. Hallelujah! Hallelujah! Hallelujah! The LORD, in his infinite wisdom, allowed this to happen for a long time. He didn't want them to think this was a momentary victory. He allowed this illusion to occur for his glory. Observe the wisdom of our God:

2 Thessalonians 2: 11-12

And for this cause God shall send them strong delusion, that they should believe a lie: 12 That they all might be damned who believed not the truth, but had pleasure in unrighteousness.

God allowed them to believe such foolishness so HE could gather them together to execute judgement. HE allowed it for years, every day, so HE could send a global message of who HE is and what HE is capable of doing. HE allowed the people to think initially that they had killed all the host of Heaven. Instead of leaving their delusion alone and abandoning the project, they decided to continue to shoot their arrows and spears into the heavens, with each weapon returning with blood on it. Imagine the arrogance and blatant blasphemy of these men, thinking that they were not only killing those in heaven, but that they were killing the creator. Why would God allow this to happen? So others will not follow this thought process which will eventually result in destruction. How does this relate to modern time? Go research Space Force and its weapons in the sky. God didn't agree with it then, HE certainly doesn't agree with it now. HE had a plan then, HE has a plan now.

Genesis 11: 6-7

And the LORD said, Behold, the people *is* one, and they have all one language; and this they begin to do: and now nothing will be restrained from them, which they have imagined to do. 7 **Go to**, **let us** go down, and there confound their language, that they may not understand one another's speech.

Before we go forward in the book, let's address the 'Go to, let us' part of what God said in verse 7. Who is God talking to? This is very important so we will *Make It Plain* for you.

Genesis 1:26

And God said, **Let us** make man in our image, after our likeness: and let them have dominion over the fish of the sea, and over the fowl of the air, and over the cattle, and over all the earth, and over every creeping thing that creepeth upon the earth.

In Genesis 1:26, the 'let us' words that God used was HIM speaking to HIMself during creation. HIS WORD spoke creation into existence. HE is a Spirit, which is Holy, the Holy Spirit. Because HE is HIS WORD, as the Father of All, HE created man in HIS image, in HIS likeness. HE created man to have mind, body, and spirit, as one person. HE operates as God the Father (creator, mind), God the Son (servant, came in the flesh/body), and God the Holy Spirit (life source, spirit). Just like we consult within ourselves, so did God. HE has no one to counsel HIM. Why? Because HE is God.

Isaiah 40:13-14

Who hath directed the Spirit of the LORD, or being his counseller hath taught him? 14 With whom took he counsel, and who instructed him, and taught him in the path of judgment, and taught him knowledge, and shewed to him the way of understanding?

In Genesis 11:6-7, the 'Go to, let us' being used that God spoke was HIM speaking to a group outside of HIMself. HE was speaking to a group of angels whose role in existence is to please God.

Jasher 9:32

And God said to the seventy angels who stood foremost before him, to those who were near to him, saying, Come let us descend and confuse their tongues, that one man shall not understand the language of his neighbor, and they did so unto them.

So, now you see the difference. God sent HIS angels down to confound the languages of the people so that they couldn't understand one another. Remember, Nimrod called the whole world to him using one language. There was no confusion or need to learn a different way to speak. There was one language, one government, one leader....until God said enough.

Imagine the LORD of the Universe, along with 70 of the most powerful angels God created who stands in front of HIM, descend to the Earth. Can you imagine what that would have looked like? All of the arrows and spears shot into the heavens. All of the provoking that was done against HIM. All of the arrogance, and ignorance. All of the taunting, blasphemy, and disdain toward the creator. Nimrod wanted HIS attention, well, he got it. Instead of coming down in dramatic fashion, God came down in stealth. Why stealth? Whereas Nimrod used open and loud arrogance, God used wisdom, unassuming and quiet. It would send the loudest message, one that has stretched throughout the test of time.

God and HIS host of angels descended while the people were working, doing their normal things. While they were busy, something happened. One man working spoke to the next man and didn't understand him. One by one, no one could understand one another. From the bottom to the top of the Tower, confusion. Confusion creates chaos. Chaos creates change. The world that Nimrod and his advisors had created had just been flipped, just like that. For the first time, the people couldn't understand one another, which proves that even your haters that join up against you can be broken by a misunderstanding or lack of communication. If they can't understand one another, how can they get a job done?

In the midst of the confusion, the LORD had an assignment for the 70 angels. Remember the 3 groups who had their blasphemous plans to rearrange heaven? God had plans for them. It was time to execute judgement. How fitting of a word for the occasion. What's even more fitting is the number 70 and its meaning. Remember, Terah was 70 years old when he had Abram. God sent down 70 angels to execute his judgment on the builders of the tower. The number 70 means judgment...interesting.

Jasher 9: 33-34

And from that day following, they forgot each man his neighbor's tongue, and they could not understand to speak in one tongue, and when the builder took from the hands of his neighbor lime or stone which he did not order, the builder would cast it away and throw it upon his neighbor, that he would die. 34. And they did so many days, and they killed many of them in this manner.

Confusion brought frustration, frustration brought anger, anger brought chaos, and chaos brings destruction. This is the delusion that God sent down to confuse the so-called 'wise' men of the Earth. These men turned on one another and forgot their original plan to build the Tower. These same men believed the lie of the bloody arrows. They worked increasingly hard to accomplish their goals to displace and kill God. In the end, all it brought them was tower-on-tower crime.

As for the 3 groups, the LORD itemized their punishments. Observe:

Jasher 9: 35

And the Lord smote the three divisions that were there, and he punished them according to their works and designs; those who said, We will ascend to heaven and serve our gods, became like apes and elephants; and those who said, We will smite the heaven with arrows, the Lord killed them, one man through the hand of his neighbor; and the third division of those who said, We will ascend to heaven and fight against him, the Lord scattered them throughout the earth.

M.I.P.

Group 2: they became like apes and elephants, men who lived like beasts

Group 3: the LORD himself killed them by turning them against one another

Group 1: they were scattered throughout the Earth

Boom! Judgment. God sent a message. HE executed HIS judgment in a different order to make sure the world would carry this lesson with them for every nation to know. Each group brought this upon themselves following the leadership of Nimrod and his counselors. Group 3 was killed off immediately. The other two groups HE handled a little bit differently.

Group 2 became like apes and elephants, men who lived like beasts of the field. They were meant to live in groups or herds, migrate and group think, then die. While both apes and elephants are animals we see in zoos and are more of the easily tamable animals, they are beasts of the field, not humans. God likened this group and their minds to such animals. Don't be surprised by this. God did this in scripture to other men who took on the title and mind of Nimrod. HE did this to show them that they are not and will never be God, ever. HE showed them and others that HE is God and God alone. Let's look at some examples to show how God is not to be played with.

King Nebuchanezzar II

(King of Babylon, took on the name/title/crown of Nimrod, aspired to become World King)

Daniel 4: 28-33

All this came upon the king Nebuchadnezzar. 29 At the end of twelve months he walked in the palace of the kingdom of Babylon. 30 The king spake, and said, Is not this great Babylon, that I have built for the house of the kingdom by the might of my power, and for the honour of my majesty? 31 While the word was in the king's mouth, there fell a voice from heaven, saying, O king Nebuchadnezzar, to thee it is spoken; The kingdom is departed from thee. 32 And they shall drive thee from men, and thy dwelling shall be with the beasts of the field: they shall make thee to eat grass as oxen, and seven times shall pass over thee, until thou know that the most High ruleth in the kingdom of men, and giveth it to whomsoever he will. 33 The same hour was the thing fulfilled upon Nebuchadnezzar: and he was driven from men, and did eat grass as oxen, and his body was wet with the dew of heaven, till his hairs were grown like eagles' feathers, and his nails like birds' claws.

Paul Spoke to Men Who Were 'like' Beasts at Ephesus

1 Corinthians 15:32

If after the manner of men I have fought with beasts at Ephesus, what advantageth it me, if the dead rise not? let us eat and drink; for to morrow we die.

Peter Describes Ungodly Men, Blasphemous Seducers

2 Peter 2:12

But these, as natural brute beasts, made to be taken and destroyed, speak evil of the things that they understand not; and shall utterly perish in their own corruption;

This is the penalty for Group 2 thinkers. They are the group thinkers or those who hide in groups. They go along to get along. They are self-willed but group think so they fall in with whatever madness the culture or current is taking them. They don't have their own minds and thoughts, as Peter called them cursed children (2 Pet. 2:14). This group still lives in the Earth. Be mindful of the in-crowd and culture led thoughts. You may be joining a group that practices how to displease God. The remnant from the Tower.

As for Group 1, HIS judgement was simple and more harsh, in my opinion.

Genesis 11:8

So the LORD scattered them abroad from thence upon the face of all the earth: and they left off to build the city.

God decided to let this group live so they can send the message of the Tower to all nations. Had God destroyed all people at the Tower, no one would be left to tell the tale of what happens to those that defy God. The original name of the Tower was the Tower of Shinar. After God and the 70 angels descended to Earth to cause the confusion and confounding of the languages, it became known by another name:

Genesis 11:9

Therefore is the name of it called Babel; because the LORD did there confound the language of all the earth: and from thence did the LORD scatter them abroad upon the face of all the earth.

M.I.P.

The Tower of Babel is called the Tower of Confusion

Why Babel? Because Babel means confusion.

So, what happened to the Tower once the people were scattered?

Jasher 9: 36-39

And those who were left amongst them, when they knew and understood the evil which was coming upon them, they forsook the building, and they also became scattered upon the face of the whole earth. 37. And they ceased building the city and the tower; therefore he called that place Babel, for there the Lord confounded the Language of the whole earth; behold it was at the east of the land of Shinar. 38. And as to the tower which the sons of men built, the earth opened its mouth and swallowed up one third part thereof, and a fire also descended from heaven and burned another third, and the other third is left to this day, and it is of that part which was aloft, and its circumference is three days' walk. 39. And many of the sons of men died in that tower, a people without number.

Amen. Just as God executed judgement on the 3 Groups, HE also executed judgment on the building itself because of the evil transgressions of the men who built it. 1/3 of the Tower was swallowed by the Earth itself. Another 1/3 was burned up with fire from heaven. The final 1/3 was left as a reminder to the rest of mankind not to repeat or reinvent. God was not playing around. There isn't an accurate count of how many people died in the construction or deconstruction of the Tower. Only God knows how that.

So, this begs another question before we close this section: where is the 1/3 that remains? Is it still visible for the world to see? Translation, where was the Tower of Babel?

Answer: I thought you'd never ask!

The Tower of Babel was built as a 2-day walk from the city of Nimrod called Shinar, which was later named Babylon. It ended up being a 3-day walk (Jash. 9:38) with the size of the Tower and the city built around it, called Eridu. A person in good shape or physically fit, as these people were (daily diet/walking), walking a mile every 10-12 minutes was normal. That equates to about 6 miles an hour. If someone walked from 8am to 8pm, for 12 hours straight, they could walk 72 miles in a day. 2 days = 144 miles. 3 days = 216 miles. Well guess what the distance is from the archaeological ruins of Babylon to Eridu? About 215 miles. The Tower of Babel was at Eridu. Boom!

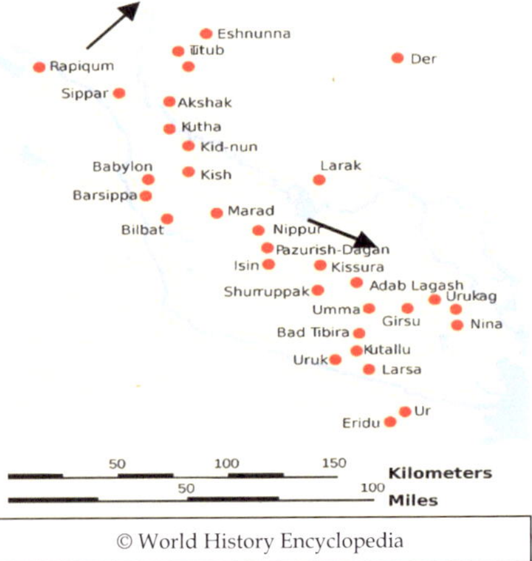

© World History Encyclopedia

In Jasher 8:43, the city that Nimrod built after his wars in the North with the Japhethites was large and extensive. It was where his palace was built. If you notice in the scripture, it said the city was opposite the east, meaning west or in the west. The city that is west of his original stomping grounds is Kish, the city his father Cush founded after the flood. Look at the map and see for yourself. In the land of Shinar, in the area of Babylon, Nimrod called the world to be gathered. There were smaller towns and cities that were being built, but they were centered around Nimrod and his desires. Ur, in the south land of Shinar was being built around the same time. It was here that Terah made his home. Remember, Nimrod was expanding his territory as the world population began to grow. The birth of Abram occurred in Ur of the Chaldees, not too far from Eridu. The ancient city of Ur is a special place in the history of the world. From Ur, you could see the Tower of Babel, which means Terah could see the Tower from his home. That's how tall and big the Tower of Babel was!

As the scriptures told us, Nimrod was in the same city of Ur when Abram was born. This is very important to understand. Terah and the people of Ur would have seen the Tower being built on a daily basis. While Nimrod continued to rule and build up his kingdom, he taught the world evil even faster than the Tower itself. There are countless artifacts in the cities of Mesopotamia from this time period that reflect idol worship on a mass scale. The following is a list of the gods and their attributes that Nimrod taught the people:

Anu/An - father of the gods, caused the flood

Adad - god of weather

Assur - god of war

Ianna - fertility goddess

Enki/Ea - god of water, told Noah to build the Ark

Marduk - chief god, god of justice, told his father Anu to kill 'noisy' mankind in the flood

Ishtar - goddess of war

Nanna/Sin - moon good

Nebo - god of knowledge

Nergal - god of the underworld (death)

Ninurta - god of farming

Shamash - sun god

Reader, please take note: there are 12 gods, each worshipped in a different month of the year, just as the book of Jasher said Terah did (Jash. 9:8). Also, notice how Nimrod took the truth of God and changed the story of the flood. Notice how he gave the real responsibilities of God, by himself, to different gods, made of stone, wood, and Nimrod's imagination. These are the pantheon of gods that Nimrod created in Jasher 7:47.

Before we move forward, let's address the common language of humanity and how the people of Shinar were educated. It all began with Noah and his sons. The oral language was Semitic, the language of Shem. The system of writing they used was the cuneiform system that Cush helped them develop. They created the school system that we have today worldwide, which they called Edubba. The history of the Sumerians and their educational system is one of the first lessons your children learn in world history classes in middle and or high school. Check their books and see if it for yourself. I have taught World History for 5 years in public schools in Texas and have seen several different history books from all kinds of publications. They all teach the same thing. They all teach about the cradle of civilization being in Sumer and the people there were super intelligent and developing the modern school system with cuneiform as an example of that. All the technology and human civilization advancements made by these people were due to the intelligence and high science of the sons of Noah. To be clear, the Sumerians were a highly advanced society, which is why they could build a tower to heaven, something no other civilization has been able to do since. The Sumerians were world builders, the same world we live in now. It was built and ruled by Nimrod.When Cush and his brothers went to Nimrod to tell them of the tower they wanted to build, they found it. They searched everywhere but no place was like the place they found at Eridu, which is in a valley. In Genesis 11:2, the Bible says they journeyed or traveled from the east, which means that Eridu was west of where they were. Again, this brings us full circle back to the city of Shinar (later named Babylon). Eridu was southwest of the city of Ur but there is an important factor to understand about the way people traveled in ancient times. They journeyed parallel to rivers so they can have access to water and food. From the city of Shinar/Babylon in the north, Eridu would appear to be west even though it is southeast. Why? Because the Euphrates River flows south and bends east towards the Persian Gulf which would mean the city and tower of Eridu/Babel was west of the Euphrates. This aligns geography and scripture to match.

In relation to Abram, the valley of Eridu was just a few hours walk from the city of Ur where Terah's home was. If Nimrod needed his #2 guy in charge, that would be a quick summoning on foot or horseback. Biblical history and world history tell the world's story if you know how to read it. So, you see, the Bible is right again.

Before we conclude the Tower section, we need to explain the difference between the words Babel and Babylon. This has been taught for many years to be the same. I've heard and seen all kinds of messages, sermons, and videos about them both being the same place. Whereas the intent was good, the information was incorrect. This is why we as researchers want to clear this up. The term Babel means 'confusion' (Gen.11:9), which was located at Eridu in the southwestern corner of Shinar. The term Babylon means 'gate of the gods'. Babylon is in the north, Babel in the south. Two different cities, two different meanings, two different purposes for its founding. Babel was founded as a tower to be a temple to the god Enki against God. Shinar/Babylon was built as a palace to welcome Nimrod into his kingdom, thus the term gate of the gods. It is here that Nimrod introduced the world to idolatry or belief in different gods, strange gods. At Babel, Nimrod's leadership led to the confusion of the languages, thus the phrase the Tower of Confusion. Although both places were a beacon of evil in the world, they were two different cities with two different agendas. Both would be signature cities in world history.

In conclusion, here's what Nimrod and his followers didn't know when desiring to build the Tower of Babel: flesh and blood cannot go to nor inherit the kingdom of God. They called it heaven. Had they known that, they would have known that arrows and spears were useless against God. HE is a spirit, and spirit cannot be killed or bloodied, especially with weapons made of wood, iron, and stone. Remember, we had Job, Solomon, Nehemiah, Moses, Isaiah, and John speak to these groups about who the LORD is and what HE is capable of. But they didn't listen. The Tower was built for man to elevate his way into godship, which is not what God designed, which is why HE destroyed the Tower. Had HE killed everyone who did this, it would have been another global flood type of catastrophe, where only a few people would have survived. Instead HE allowed a group to live to tell this story as a warning not to repeat. HE left another group alive to serve as living examples of men likened to beast because of their blasphemous behavior and the consequences of those that follow the same path. Since that time, mankind has tried to find different ways to rebuild different types of Towers, called skyscrapers, to redo what Nimrod and his crew did. All have been unsuccessful. Sure, they are majestic and awe-inspiring to behold, but they are not pro-God buildings. They are monuments to men. The reason why they all have been unsuccessful is because they miss the point that Nimrod missed: God's space is not human. The corruption of humanity cannot go and be in the presence of incorruption, which is God. Even Enoch, who never died, but was translated (changed from human to spirit), could not enter God's presence in heaven, as a human. No Tower has that power.

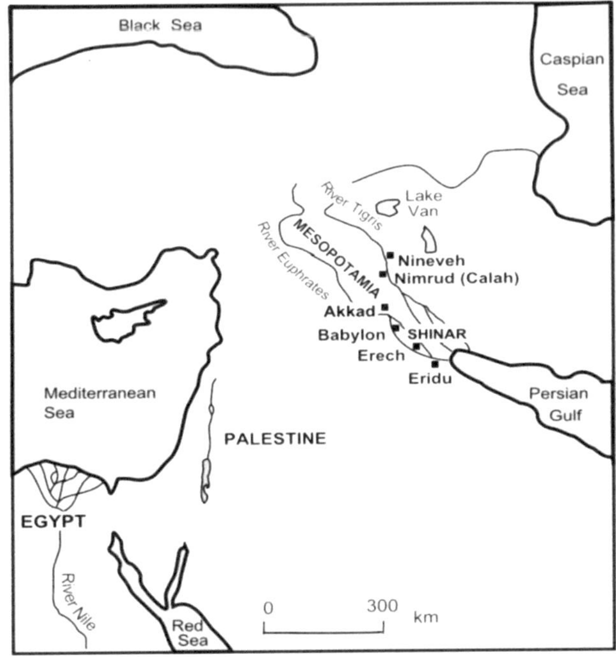

1 Corinthians 15:50

Now this I say, brethren, that flesh and blood cannot inherit the kingdom of God; neither doth corruption inherit incorruption.

Birth of the Races

Genesis 10:32

These are the families of the sons of Noah, after their generations, in their nations: and by these were the nations divided in the earth after the flood.

This section has been a hot topic of discussion for MANY years. There has been all kinds of debates, studies, archaeological findings, suggestions, etc., about the origin of the races. To be honest, they are pretty intriguing to read in relation to the different perspectives' scholars draw from their research. There's a lot of information out there to analyze. Regardless of the perspective, the only one that really counts in the grand scheme of things, is God's. Here's what is really interesting to think about when it comes to this take: imagine spending years of your life chasing perspectives of people who are ever changing, which we all are allowed and free to do, but when it all ends at death, you meet the ONE who allowed you to make that choice that saw it ALL from the beginning, who has no motive to lie or deceive. Do you think the ONE, Elohim Chayim (the Living God), Elohenu Olam (the Everlasting God) will care to consider an opinion or perspective of humans when HE has the final say on ALL matters? Humans have a lifetime to choose perspectives, which is limited. God is eternal, which is unlimited. Choosing HIS way is the final say. Choosing HIS WORD is the way.

When we look at the question of the races as we know it, they all begin with Noah and his Sons. This is very instrumental in understanding the story of *Nimrod: The World's First Anti-Christ*. So, instead of belaboring the time, let's lay out how the birth of the races began.

The term "race" as defined by Merriam-Webster's dictionary means any one of the groups that humans are often divided into based on physical traits regarded as common among people of shared ancestry. The key to the definition of race are written in the last two words: shared ancestry. There is a shared ancestry of the human race, which means there is a common designer: God.

It was God who chose Noah and his family to survive the Flood. Through his family do we get the nations of the world that we have today. Yes, Noah's 3 sons are the originators of all the races. Shem, Ham, and Japheth. The DNA of those three men are found in every human being on the planet and the physical traits we have in or on our bodies validate it, and we will provide the information and science for that. Everything God planned for the post-Flood world was intentional. It all had a designed purpose. In fact, we will even show you who was the first child born in the New World and what his purpose was. God is a purposeful being, HIS existence is intentional, so is HIS will. We are a part of HIS will.

According to Henry M. Morris, writer for *Science and the Bible,* who published an article on scibi.org, every human being has DNA that is traced back to three men with the same genetic number, who in turn have the same genetic code number that they share in common that comes from one man. I know, a historian trying to speak scientific is confusing within itself, my apologies, so let's *Make It Plain...*

M.I.P.

Every man has a genetic # number

There are only 3 different genetic #s that are common when analyzing DNA, regardless of race or global location or nation (we speaking about the human, not the nationality)
Those 3 different #s, when analyzed, share one common #
The one common # is the ancestor or father of the three different genetic #s found in every man on Earth

Whew! Clarity is key. With that said, let us give you the science to validate this claim and then we will show you how the Bible validates science before there was DNA science to trace truth. Brace yourself, it's about to get deep....

Is it Shem, Ham, or Japheth? At Genesis and Genetics, we have examined Y-chromosome genomes searching for Noah and his three sons. They were easy to find. According to our analysis, if you have the rs17306671 Y-chromosome mutation nucleotide A, you are from Shem. The rs9786139 Y-chromosome mutation nucleotide A means you are from Ham. And if you have the rs3900 Y-chromosome mutation nucleotide G, you are from Japheth. Of course, if you are a woman, you don't have a Y-chromosome; so, you will have to get your father's or brother's DNA.

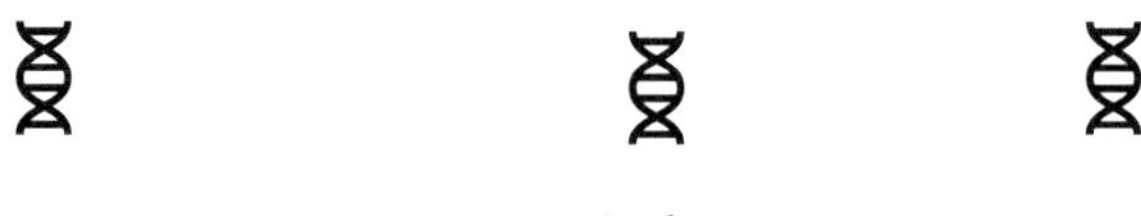

And...

The following presents the easy-to-follow logic and analysis which anyone can repeat.
We started by looking for all Y-chromosome mutations/markers with a frequency of more than 5 percent. This was easy by taking existing phylogenetic trees and looking for which markers had a frequency of more than 5 % of the population.
Next, we took one single human Y-chromosome genome (HG02461 a man from Gambia, Africa). We found that he had a marker at L15, re9786139. This marker is in approximately 38 percent of the world's male population. So, we knew our African from Gambia came from our ancient ancestor with the L15 marker.
Then we continued to look at individual human genomes from other places in Africa, Japan, China, Europe, South America, and North America. We found that all our subjects were related to one of just three major groups. Specifically, these groups were L15/ rs9786139, M9/ rs3900, and M429/ rs17306671. The implication is that our original male ancestor had three sons. Consequently, all male humans were born from these three sons.

Outstanding. Plain and somewhat simple. Yes, every human male on the planet can be traced back to one man and his three sons, who share his DNA code within their own code. It is truly amazing to sit down and read this scientific approach with mathematical evidence to verify what the scriptures have said for thousands of years. It's incredible. I encourage you to go and read the entire article. Perspective.

But wait, there's more.

There has been a debate among scientists for many years about whether or not there are 3 to 5 races of human beings on the planet. Let's analyze both groups and see how the Word of God solves the scientific debate.

For the scientists who say that there are 3 races:
Negroid (African)
Caucasian (European)
Mongoloid (Asian)

For the scientists who say that there are 5 races:
African
Asian
European
*Oceanian
*Native American

First, let's take a look at the group who believes that there are 5 races of people. There is an argument that comes with the last two groups, the Oceanian and Native Americans, being either included or excluded because of the migration factors on the human body due to climate change and survival. Regardless, they are the same, human. These two groups share the belief that the African, Asian, and European race are valid. They disagree about the Oceanian and Native American groups, which divides the room. While they argue, scripture makes this argument so easy to answer.

Genesis 10:32

These are the families of the sons of Noah, after their generations, in their nations: and by these were the nations divided in the earth after the flood.

Simple. Easy. Straight forward. From Noah, his DNA, his family, comes ALL the nations of the world. Obviously, he is a descendant from Adam, the first man, but the Flood refocused humanity back to Noah and his sons continuing the human race. Noah and his wife were pure in blood, directly connected and untainted by the fallen angels and Nephilim. This is the other reason for the Flood, to refocus the purity of humanity. I know, that seems very simplified, so let's give more details.

1. We have learned that Ham settled Africa. That's the Negroid grouping.
2. We have learned that Japheth settled Europe. That's the Caucasian grouping.
3. We have learned that Shem settled the Near East, Asia. That's the Mongoloid grouping.

Well, what about the Oceania and Native American races? Where are they biblically? Let's work.

Genesis 10:25

And unto Eber were born two sons: the name of one was Peleg; for in his days was the earth divided; and his brother's name was Joktan.

Dr. John D. Morris of the *Institute of Creation Research* addressed this question for us:

"The traditional interpretation relates Peleg's day to the division of language/family groups at the Tower of Babel. Comparing the lineage of Shem, which includes Peleg, to the lineage of Ham, which includes Nimrod, leader of the rebellion at Babel, we find it likely that Peleg was born soon after the dispersion (assuming the genealogies are complete). Thus it would have been reasonable for his father Eber to name a son in commemoration of this miraculous event. One "separator" did occur sometime after the dispersion. The Ice Age, which followed the Flood, would have caused sea level to be an estimated 600 feet lower than today, since such a great volume of water was trapped as ice on the continents. Such a lowering of today's seas would reconnect the continents once again. The connected continents would have aided in both animal and human migration following both the Flood and the dispersion, as commanded by God (Genesis 8:17; 11:4,8,9). Then the ending of the Ice Age and the melting of the ice sheets would cause sea level to rise, covering the land bridges and "dividing" the continents after migration had occurred."

Wow! How thank you Dr. Morris for the information and research. The resetting of the bodies of water allowed travel to occur over the planet. This movement from the Tower because of the changing of the languages led people to venture all over the world we know today. This is where you get the Oceania and Native American groups. Change of climate, change of pigmentation, change of physiological traits, change of cultures.

ALL still come from Shem, Ham, and Japheth.

To be clear, what we consider race and the importance thereof is NOT important to God. Race was used as a divider by mankind to separate people, according to man's standards. God used language to separate people. But again, race is not important to God like it is to us, especially in the Western world. This was NOT a biblical issue. In fact, races weren't used in the terminology of biblical authors. Tribes and who your father was is the separator in scripture, which is not the same as race. Your ability to gain respect, riches, and honor was based on those two things: tribal and patriarchal allegiances. There were family members with different skin complexions and or body structures, like Jacob and Esau, but they were twin brothers. Jacob (Israel) was smooth skinned, Esau was hairy and course. Jacob had darker skin than Esau, who was considered to be red skinned.

Genesis 25:25

And the first came out red, all over like an hairy garment; and they called his name Esau.

Race and how it divides people today is evil. It was later in the "evil-ution" of man did skin color begin to matter relative to the value and worth of a life. When empires began to form in the western world (Europe, West African Slave Trading, North and South American exploitation, Marco Polo's Chinese Expeditions, etc.), so did using race as a separator and denigrator of humanity. It's not an old issue, as in regards to the age of the world, yet evil nonetheless.

In the western world, black skin has been deemed a negative for hundreds of years. It couldn't be further from the truth, but for conversation sake, if you know anything about US history at all, obviously race matters. As the author of *Biblical Black History*, I can tell you that I wish I didn't have to write that book. I really do. Why? Because it didn't matter to the actual characters of the book and most importantly to God. There is no black, white, red, green, yellow, purple, pink, whatever "color" you choose, in heaven. Our God is bigger than that. He sees the heart of a man, which is literal and figurative, which is all the same. Every man's heart is pinkish/red, like all the other organs God designed. Every man has sinned in his heart, regardless of your skin color, social status, economic class, health condition, etc. The heart is what God sees and what God judges, period.

1 Samuel 16:7

But the LORD said unto Samuel, Look not on his countenance, or on the height of his stature; because I have refused him: for the LORD seeth not as man seeth; for man looketh on the outward appearance, but the LORD looketh on the heart.

This verse alone should have solved the race issue, especially here in America, if people want to know what God really thinks about skin color, beauty, money, intent, etc. HE sees YOU through you. This is further proof into why God is God, HE doesn't think like men do, thank God.

I wrote *Biblical Black History* to lay out the historical and biblical data in simple, concise language to prove that most of the biblical characters were African or Asian, which would be considered black in the western world. If my words make you uncomfortable, good. The truth is stranger than fiction. There are millions of people, as history has proven, that have been conditioned to think race first, especially in America, mostly teaching that the white race was first. It should be the human race first, but I digress. My work was to start the process of reconditioning people to the Truth of God's Word over the word of a conqueror or colonizer. Both master and slave must bow to God in intelligence or bow to sin in ignorance. Both intelligence and ignorance start with an I, which means that the choice is up to YOU and I.

There are few European characters in the Bible, even though the Greek language was used in the New Testament in places, thanks to Alexander the Great, a European. Daniel, a Hebrew prophet, was a "black" man by western standards. If you want the proof, go get *Biblical Black History* and read it or just research the ancient Hebrews and how they were identical in appearance to their Canaanite cousins, who are historically known as dark-skinned people. There are many archaeological studies that show the proof. A good book to read to find those truths was written by journalist Gert Muller named *The Ancient Black Hebrews: The Forensic Proof Simply Explained*. Regardless, in Daniel chapter 7, the prophet prophesied about a beast to come, a leopard, that would rise up and rule. It would have wings like a bird on its back, meaning it would move swift in its victories, which if you study Alexander the Great's battle history, he was the youngest world ruler in history with the vastness of the imperial land he controlled. It's ridiculous how much land he conquered and what's more stunning is that he spread the Greek language via conquest from Greece to Asia. Daniel was Hebrew, a dark-skinned man, prophesying about a coming Greek, a white man, who was going to change world history. The Greek people at that point in history lived in city states, nothing special. If you notice in Daniel 7, the description of the coming ruler was an animal, not a skin color. The content of the character of this empire and its ruler was the emphasis, not his race. Most of the biblical characters were highly melanized people, or in western world terminology, black. The people in those times cared about the tribe, not the skin. The only concern they had relating to your skin was if you had leprosy or not. That's it.

In the end, we must understand the why of the races. God took 3 brothers from the same father to showcase his own wisdom and intelligence. The unbeliever has no excuse. It doesn't matter how you look, it matters how you act. They looked different, but have the same father. They had different ambitions, same father. They settled different continents, same father. Shem and Ham, darker skinned. Japheth means fair, which speaks to his lighter skin. Japheth settled Europe, Ham settled Africa, Shem settled Asia. Simple. That is the intelligence of God.

The key to understanding the races, which rarely ever gets talked about, is the mother of the races. Eve is the mother of humanity as a whole, but it is Noah's wife who's the mother of the three races. Her name was Namaah. All three of her sons were different looking children, born in a different time, built to multiply in the Earth. These three sons had the same mother, same father. She was the wife of Noah, witness to the destruction of mankind, yet she remained faithful and a servant. Noah gets a lot of credit for being righteous as scripture says, so you must understand how important his wife is in that statement and along that journey. She and her sons helped Noah build the Ark. This should let you know a lot about Namaah and how exceptional she had to be as a person, woman, wife, and mother.

To be clear, there is only one race of people on the planet that has scientifically been proven to be able to birth distinctly different pigmentation from same the womb: the highly melanized woman. In the western world, a "black" woman. In mostly every school world history textbook, our children have been taught that the birthplace of humanity began in Africa. The oldest bones found on Earth have been discovered there. The garden of Eden, if you trace the four rivers that flow from it, all point to the Near East/Africa region. A highly melanized or by western standards, black woman, can have a so-called black child, red child, yellow child, or when there is a mutation or lack of melanin released into the pigmentation development in the womb, an albino child (which would appear Caucasian). All of these children can have the same parents, but the multi-plex of variations of skin color in the DNA of the highly melanized woman are incredible and undenied. So yes, Namaah, wife of Noah and mother to Shem, Ham, and Japheth, had to be a highly melanized woman as well. Not that it matters in the grand scheme of life to the spiritually mature, but again, we must recognize that a great injustice has been done to condition people to separate one another because of their race. Many have grown to hate themselves or others because of this great barrier. You wouldn't have great leaders such as Gandhi, MLK, Cesar Chavez, etc., fighting for human and civil rights if whole nations of people weren't conditioned to be hateful, spiteful, ignorant, and deceptive. That has to change.

Regardless of the look of a man, no matter where they live in the Earth, they are still under the watchful eye of God that sees into every place (Prov. 15:3). Shem, Ham, and Japheth had one father, Noah, and one Father, God. For this reason, we have no excuse in understanding who our Father is regardless of how our brother looks. Your DNA comes from your father. DNA itself was created by God, THE Father. This is the wisdom of God.

God took Shem and made him the leader of the group through whom the world spoke his language when exiting the ark (Semitic language, Hebrew). He gave Ham the privilege of settling the continent that would eventually produce the most people and resources known to mankind, even to this day (Africa). He gave Japheth the ability to intermingle and intermix within the territories of his brethren to become an exchanger of skills and talents that he would take credit for, whether it be right or wrong (Europe). It's biblical.

Genesis 9:27

God shall enlarge Japheth, and he shall dwell in the tents of Shem; and Canaan shall be his servant.

Each son of Noah has had descendants of theirs become rulers of big portions of the then known world. Thutmose III, Alexander the Great, Xerses I, Nebuchadnezzar II, Genghis Khan, Shaka Zulu, Charlemagne, Julius Caesar, Octavian Augustus, and many others all shared the world ruler crown. All were chasing one idea: one world united under one ruler. While all tried, ALL failed. Only one has reached that pinnacle. Only one. That one is the one to whom this book is named, Nimrod. That one is the blueprint for the coming world ruler that will unite the nations into One World Order. He that is to come is exactly like he that has already been. History has a tendency to repeat itself.

In conclusion, we now understand that the races come from Noah, through Namaah, to Shem, Ham, and Japheth. These three sons and their wives gave us nations, each having similarities but just as different as night and day. The genetic codes of these brothers are just as strong today as it was thousands of years ago in each and every human on this planet. The real race we should be concerned with is where we will spend eternity. God separated mankind at the Tower with languages, not skin color, or their DNA. He demonstrated to the world that without proper communication, even brothers can separate. Men should race to join one another in their worship of the Creator instead of fleeing to their corners and cultures to worship creation. The language separation at the Tower gave mankind the opportunity to send praise to the LORD of Host in every different language given, with the 70 angels serving as witnesses. But the pride and evil of mankind wouldn't allow them to do so. Nevertheless, mankind and Satan himself could not deny the LORD his just due praise. Reader, please take note because the following is so important:

Over the course of time, every language that was introduced to the world at the Tower will declare the glory of the LORD. Not only that, they will be offered his grace via the Gospel to reunite creation with Creator. This is why the Gospel must be preached throughout the world BEFORE Christ returns or descends. Remember, God and the 70 angels descended on the Tower to destroy and disperse. He will return to save and judge. His desire is not that we build a Tower, but to be a watchman as on a tower. This is the true will of God.

Ezekiel 3:17

Son of man, I have made thee a watchman unto the house of Israel: therefore hear the word at my mouth, and give them warning from me.

This is why Nimrod is so important in world history. He is the one for whom we must keep watch. He represents the man who promotes the agenda of Satan, which is anti-human. This is why the coming AntiChrist is the 2.0 version of Nimrod. This is why the Gospel must be preached throughout the world, in every tongue, in every language. This is the real race, not skin color or culture. But the race against evil, against judgement, against Hell-fire. Believers must endure. Why? Because it is a race. Jesus said it best...

Matthew 24: 13-14

But he that shall endure unto the end, the same shall be saved. 14 And this gospel of the kingdom shall be preached in all the world for a witness unto all nations; and then shall the end come.

City Builder

Genesis 10:10

And the beginning of his kingdom was Babel, and Erech, and Accad, and Calneh, in the land of Shinar.

The Tower of Babel was destroyed. Languages have changed. Many people have deserted Shinar. Nimrod is still king. The world is starting over again but in a different way. God restarted the world the first time by sending the Flood. He restarted it again by confusing the languages to scatter the people out over the world since Nimrod called them all to him in the valley of Shinar at Eridu. 1/3 of the Tower is remaining, as God left it. There were still people left that spoke the same language of Nimrod. His kingdom was intact even though many of the people and princes were gone. It was now time for Nimrod to re-establish dominance in the world. How did he do it the first time? Through war and building. How would he do it this time?

Jasher 11: 1-2

And Nimrod son of Cush was still in the land of Shinar, and he reigned over it and dwelt there, and he built cities in the land of Shinar. 2. And these are the names of the four cities which he built, and he called their names after the occurrences that happened to them in the building of the tower.

Nimrod lost the war with God. There was no way around it. He knew that the people who survived and saw the Tower's destruction saw his defeat as well. The Tower was dedicated to the Sumerian freshwater god named Enki and was a display of Nimrod's power to do as he pleased. The defeat at the Tower could have crippled him and his ego. Whereas some would see this as an embarrassment and change their outlook on life, Nimrod saw this as an opportunity to expand his kingdom. The princes that were once servants of his that spoke different languages were still going to fear him if he showed his ability to be strong. In the ancient world, one of the best ways to show power and strength was the ability to build. Nimrod knew he was vulnerable at this point but the best way to mask his weakness was to build fortresses and cities to strengthen himself against those that thought now was the time to usurp him. He may not have been a match for the God of heaven with the sky-scraping Tower, but building walled cities would give him leverage over men who may see this as an opportunity to take the throne. It was time to re-establish himself. War and build. That's the blueprint.

Jasher 11:3

And he called the first Babel, saying, Because the Lord there confounded the language of the whole earth; and the name of the second he called Erech, because from there God dispersed them.

The Tower of Eridu dedicated to the god Enki was destroyed. Nimrod had a city built around it. Instead of allowing the name of the city to continue to be Eridu, he renamed the city Babel, meaning confusion. From that day the Tower was called the Tower of Babel. Nimrod called it and the city itself that name because of what the LORD had done.

Babel = confusion

City of Erech or Uruk
© The Archaeologist

The second city he built was called Erech, or Uruk, meaning long. Do not be mistaken about the name of the city. It is intentional and purposeful. Nimrod built this city from an egotistical point of view. Do not be deceived. If you have learned nothing else about the world king, the driving force behind his power is pride. The city Erech sounds like the word we use today, erect, which means to stand tall or long. It's a term usually associated with male genitalia. Where do you think it comes from? Nimrod. This city was built to be symbolic of self-pride and disdain for God. Why do we take such an approach? Let's look at some of the details of the ancient city and how it was built.

Erech was the largest city in the world when Nimrod had finished building it. The city layout was shaped like a circle with high and thick brick walls. In the center were two temples or as the Sumerians called them, Ziggurats. Both ziggurats were higher than the other buildings surrounding it in the city. One was built to Anu the Sumerian sky god, which had a white top. The other was made to Ishtar the goddess of war and fertility, who's alternate name is Eanna. The base of the temple made to Ishtar still remains. Nimrod wanted the LORD to see this image from above. Even though he didn't believe in God anymore to follow him, he knew God existed. Again, its design was intentional. For a man to build a city and then name it Erech or Uruk in the shape of genitalia is no accident. One of the ziggurats having a white top in a city name Erech is a coincidence? Sounds crazy and possibly an isolated incident, right? No. Many modern-day structures that reach into the sky look different from above as opposed to eye level viewing. Playing on people's ignorance is the easiest way to get rich, powerful, and famous in this world. It's an old concept.

Most historians and archaeologists consider Erech to be the first city in the world. We know otherwise, but their findings validate scripture, that it existed and we know who built it. The city of Erech was known for religion and science study. Yes, you read that right. Before schools, colleges, and universities, people were studying the things we now live by. Education is not new. It began in temples and homes and spread throughout the world. The Sumerians called them Edubbas. These people were looking for different ways to figure out the universe and more importantly, how did the LORD of heaven do what HE did and why. Nimrod wanted the people to continue in their ways of distorting the truth of God while creating a narrative of himself and others being god by tracing HIS footsteps and claiming HIS glory. Today, that's called science. Pottery and thousands of artifacts were found on this site including a library.

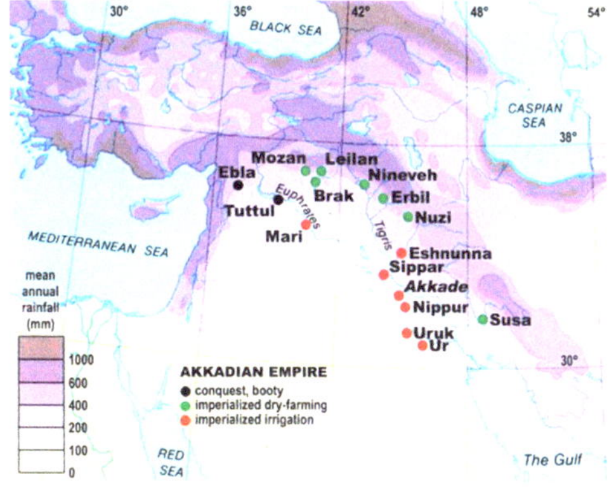

Jasher 11: 4-5

And the third he called Eched, saying there was a great battle at that place; and the fourth he called Calnah, because his princes and mighty men were consumed there, and they vexed the Lord, they rebelled and transgressed against him. 5. And when Nimrod had built these cities in the land of Shinar, he placed in them the remainder of his people, his princes and his mighty men that were left in his kingdom.

Sargon I
© National Geographic

The third city founded by Nimrod was Eched or Accad (Akkad). Some translations spell it as Agade. It takes this name because a great battle took place in this region, to the north of Shinar, which established Nimrod in the north. The city itself has not yet been found by archaeologists but we do know that the kingdom of Accad existed and thrived under Sargon I, who later unified Mesopotamia under one ruler, just as Nimrod did. The Akkadians took on the name after Nimrod placed the people in the city as verse 5 says. The people of Sumer that stayed under the leadership of Nimrod that lived in the area now had secure walls to defend themselves against possible threats. Accad is believed to be built in between the Tigris and Euphrates as a fortress and reminder of a previous victory. Remember, people in the ancient world traveled near water routes and rivers so they can have access to water and food. Building a city at the site where both rivers curve themselves toward one another is very smart and strategic. The Accadians or Akkadians were known for being very warlike and agriculturally wealthy. As time would progress, this city-state would grow to mimic the size and power of the kingdom of Nimrod.

The fourth city built by Nimrod was named Calneh or kalneh. The alternate name for the city is named after the builder itself, Nimrud. The name means fortress of Anu in Sumerian with a dual meaning as mentioned in Jasher 11:4 as the city where the great men of Nimrod were defeated in war with God. The city itself was built along the Tigris River in the northeast corner of Nimrod's kingdom. Calneh was a city renowned for its elaborate palaces and temples. Calneh was built similar to the other cities Nimrod built but it was much further north. This fortress was a beautiful city that was built to send a message to all peoples in the north that were thinking of invading the heart of Shinar. The city carries his namesake as a reminder to all people along the Tigris River in the north that Nimrod was king and he has the power to influence. Please keep in mind, there were no forklifts, cranes, and major modern machinery to get this built. But as you can see in the image above, Nimrod was an excellent builder and architect. His building projects have stood for thousands of years. The city itself was still available for people to see until April of 2015 when the terrorist group ISIS destroyed the ruins of the city on live television for the world to see. Their reasoning was because there were numerous images of ancient gods and civilization that were built and designed by Nimrod. The images were polytheistic, which was taken as an offense to Islamic group. The irony is that UNESCO, the United Nations Educational Scientific and Cultural Organization, declared Nimrud's destruction as a war crime. So again, the city that was built to showcase rebellion and power by having elaborate palaces and ziggurats was destroyed by a group that lives in rebellion seeking power.

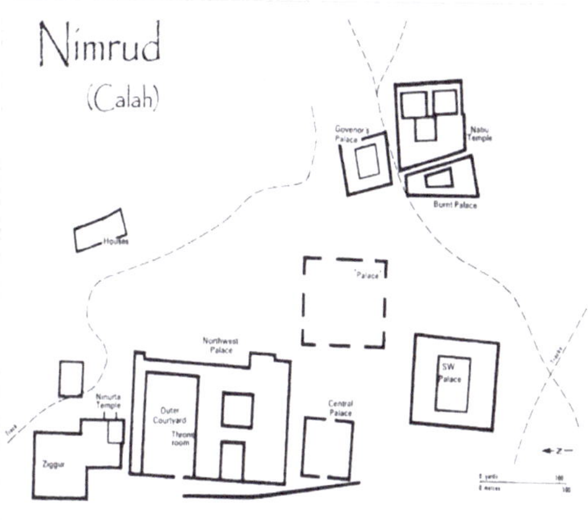

Calneh/Nimrud
© History Today

In the end, we understand the mindset of the city builder that Nimrod became. The idea of building these cities was to strategically position himself against others that may want to harm him. There were many settlements built along the Tigris and Euphrates rivers that eventually grew into towns then cities, but none were as major as the four cities of Nimrod. Just as the people believed there were four corners to the Earth, so did Nimrod built four cities to fortify his defenses so he could see his possible enemies coming from afar. To the West of Babel, a desert. To the South, the Persian Gulf. To the East, unexplored land that was being discovered by the Madai (Medes/Indians) and Sinites (Chinese). To the North, the sons of Shem and Japheth. He knew that as long as he protected himself to the North, he would reign securely for enough time that he could re-strengthen his forces and return to war. By building ziggurats to the gods, he could still control the minds of the people to obey him by creating idols made by his hands and his servants. War was coming and Nimrod knew it. But how? His kingdom was split and many kings had been established in the new world that spoke different languages that were trading with his princes in Shinar. They knew he was weakened and just like any wounded animal around other hungry animals, they smelt blood and opportunity. This was all designed and allowed by God because of the birth of a child many years in advance that said Nimrod's kingdom would fall. The time of the prophecy to unravel itself was fast approaching, and Nimrod felt it coming.

Long live the king.

Jasher 11:5

And when Nimrod had built these cities in the land of Shinar, he placed in them the remainder of his people, his princes and his mighty men that were left in his kingdom.

The *god* Killer

Genesis 11:27

Now these are the generations of :: Terah begat Abram, Nahor, and Haran; and Haran begat Lot.

Abram, Abram, Abram. The man who has the reputation as being the father of the Faith and the first Hebrew, is a man with a deeper history than you know. We will walk through some of his feats as an example of how God allows the sun to shine through in the midst of darkness. We will also show how God, in the future, will allow good people who seek HIM to come back to the LORD when the Antichrist comes on the scene after Christ returns. The blueprint for how to deal with the Antichrist and those in the world today can be found in the following section beginning with verse 27 of Genesis 11. It starts with family, as all education does.

Jasher 11: 13-15

And in the fiftieth year of the life of Abram son of Terah, Abram came forth from the house of Noah, and went to his father's house. 14. And Abram knew the Lord, and he went in his ways and instructions, and the Lord his God was with him. 15. And Terah his father was in those days, still captain of the host of king Nimrod, and he still followed strange gods.

Parents, please pay attention. Pay close attention. Your life and lifestyle are being analyzed and studied by your children. Whether or not you think they see what you do is not up to you. God allows them, us, you, to see things that a parent doesn't think they see. Even if you send them away or you as the parent go away, a child has the DNA of their parent. They will find the world whether you teach them or not. The same God that gave them to you and forms them in the womb of their mother is the same God that will call them to HIM, whether you are in agreement or not. This parental concept is the perfect parallel to the story of Terah and his sons. Abram was the youngest of 3 sons, the child of his father's old age. When he was 10 years old, he was sent to live with Noah and Shem at Mt. Ararat. When he was 49, he decided to find out for himself who the LORD was. After concluding that the sun, the moon, and the stars were not God, he decided that the same LORD that Noah and Shem worshipped and taught him was the One. Now, at the age of 50, Abram sets off back down the Fertile Crescent to the city of Ur of the Chaldees (Chaldeans) to rejoin his family. He was coming back with an agenda and a heart that followed the LORD. Even though he knew his father was the 2nd in command over Nimrod's empire and he was hidden from the king's wrath as a child, he had no idea that his father was an idol worshipper who followed the ways of Nimrod with manmade gods. Remember, Abram grew up in a cave in the wilderness away from his father.

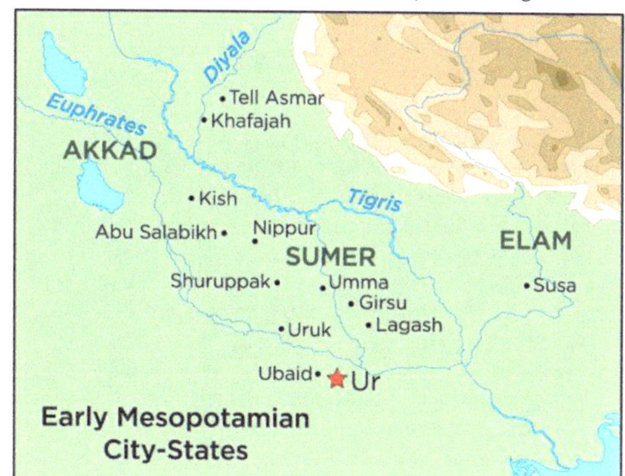

The clash between father and son is about to begin.

Jasher 11: 16-17

And Abram came to his father's house and saw twelve gods standing there in their temples, and the anger of Abram was kindled when he saw these images in his father's house. 17. And Abram said, As the Lord liveth these images shall not remain in my father's house; so shall the Lord who created me do unto me if in three days' time I do not break them all.

Foolishness angers the righteous. I will say it again. Foolishness angers the righteous. After traveling from modern-day Turkey to Iraq on foot, you would think perhaps Abram would have a different disposition when arriving at his father's house. Instead, his eyes were opened immediately to the lifestyle of Terah. Upon entering his father's home, he saw 12 gods in their temples or shrines, all manmade. Terah, an idol worshipper, had built shrines in his home to the gods Nimrod had made for him and the world. This angered Abram. Instead of enjoying his return to the house he never lived in to rejoin his family, he was on edge. He decided to make a vow unto himself that within 3 days, if he hadn't broken all the idols, he would want to be broken by God himself for not completing the task. A serious conversation with dad was on deck.

Jasher 11: 18-22

And Abram went from them, and his anger burned within him. And Abram hastened and went from the chamber to his father's outer court, and he found his father sitting in the court, and all his servants with him, and Abram came and sat before him. 19. And Abram asked his father, saying, Father, tell me where is God who created heaven and earth, and all the sons of men upon earth, and who created thee and me. And Terah answered his son Abram and said, Behold those who created us are all with us in the house. 20. And Abram said to his father, My lord, shew them to me I pray thee; and Terah brought Abram into the chamber of the inner court, and Abram saw, and behold the whole room was full of gods of wood and stone, twelve great images and others less than they without number. 21. And Terah said to his son, Behold these are they which made all thou seest upon earth, and which created me and thee, and all mankind. 22. And Terah bowed down to his gods, and he then went away from them, and Abram, his son, went away with him.

Abram was hot! Children, especially sons, listen carefully. Instead of going to his father with disrespect, he went to his father calm, in respect, but having logic in his approach. He could have chosen the easy path of frustration, anger, disrespect, and rage, but he didn't. Abram was more concerned with getting the situation right over getting his feelings heard and expressed. This is a very important example to diagnose when addressing deep issues with parents.

Ancient Sumerian Home

Terah, as a rich man, lived in a big house. Most Sumerian homes were either 2 or 3 story homes. There was a garden in the center of the home, which is where the family spent most of their time together. The inner parts of the house were cool and people mostly slept on the roof of their homes in the summer. The outer court was a place for showcasing the wealth of the home, which would be on display for anyone passing by. The inner court would be a large well-kept area that was built for welcoming, worshipping, and entertainment. The outer court, a passage way. To walk into the inner court of the house and see gods set up would be normal in ancient Sumer, especially during Nimrod's reign.

Abram approached his father with foundational questions about creation and who was responsible for life itself. His father pointed to wood and stone carved idols, in his house. As Abram looked upon them, his father bowed and worshipped these items in his home, in the center of his home, symbolic of these gods being the center of his life. After praying to them in front of his son, they both left the courtyard and went to another place in the home. This is important to know because Abram has now seen his father commit spiritual fornication right in front of him. Also, what's worthy of noting is that Abram didn't dispute or fight with his father in the moment. There is a way to disagree with a parent without becoming disrespectful. Let's read more.

Jasher 11: 23-27

And when Abram had gone from them he went to his mother and sat before her, and he said to his mother, Behold, my father has shown me those who made heaven and earth, and all the sons of men. 24. Now, therefore, hasten and fetch a kid from the flock, and make of it savory meat, that I may bring it to my father's gods as an offering for them to eat; perhaps I may thereby become acceptable to them. 25. And his mother did so, and she fetched a kid, and made savory meat thereof, and brought it to Abram, and Abram took the savory meat from his mother and brought it before his father's gods, and he drew nigh to them that they might eat; and Terah his father, did not know of it. 26. And Abram saw on the day when he was sitting amongst them, that they had no voice, no hearing, no motion, and not one of them could stretch forth his hand to eat. 27. And Abram mocked them, and said, Surely the savory meat that I prepared has not pleased them, or perhaps it was too little for them, and for that reason they would not eat; therefore tomorrow I will prepare fresh savory meat, better and more plentiful than this, in order that I may see the result.

The same woman that raised Noah in a cave is the same woman that provided the opportunity for grace and reconciliation. Notice how she didn't ask questions or pry into the business of her son and husband. The kid, which means a baby goat, was the sacrifice used to bring revelation. Abram used the meat to test the wood and stone to see if they could fend for themselves. They couldn't. Abram, as other prophets after him, made fun of the idols that couldn't do anything. All of this was done without his father knowing it. Why? Sometimes the dysfunction of our parents need to be tested first before approaching them and causing disruption.

Jasher 11: 28-33

And it was on the next day that Abram directed his mother concerning the savory meat, and his mother rose and fetched three fine kids from the flock, and she made of them some excellent savory meat, such as her son was fond of, and she gave it to her son Abram; and Terah his father did not know of it. 29. And Abram took the savory meat from his mother, and brought it before his father's gods into the chamber; and he came nigh unto them that they might eat, and he placed it before them, and Abram sat before them all day, thinking perhaps they might eat. 30. And Abram viewed them, and behold they had neither voice nor hearing, nor did one of them stretch forth his hand to the meat to eat. 31. And in the evening of that day in that house Abram was clothed with the spirit of God. 32. And he called out and said, Wo unto my father and this wicked generation, whose hearts are all inclined to vanity, who serve these idols of wood and stone which can neither eat, smell, hear nor speak, who have mouths without speech, eyes without sight, ears without hearing, hands without feeling, and legs which cannot move; like them are those that made them and that trust in them.

The spirit of God is amazing! Sometimes, when we are operating in peace and purpose, the greatest opportunities for God to show up, happens, even in a dispute. As you read above, Abram repeated the process of offering to the gods of his father but to no avail. He had had enough and he patiently became angry. In his patience, the spirit of God came upon him to speak to the issues of the world by seeing the evil in his own father's house. Again, read carefully. In Abram's patience, the spirit of God came upon him to speak to the issues of the world by seeing the evil in his father's house! Sometimes, parents, the greatest reflection of the world and where you stand on issues are on full display in your house. A divided heart will lead to a divided house. When the spirit of the LORD speaks, it doesn't differentiate between who you like or dislike, family or foe. It speaks, as it did through Abram, about the wickedness of the world and its displeasure in the eyes of the LORD. Terah was not exempt.

Jasher 11: 34-37

And when Abram saw all these things his anger was kindled against his father, and he hastened and took a hatchet in his hand, and came unto the chamber of the gods, and he broke all his father's gods. 34. And when he had done breaking the images, he placed the hatchet in the hand of the great god which was there before them, and he went out; and Terah his father came home, for he had heard at the door the sound of the striking of the hatchet; so Terah came into the house to know what this was about. 35. And Terah, having heard the noise of the hatchet in the room of images, ran to the room to the images, and he met Abram going out. 36. And Terah entered the room and found all the idols fallen down and broken, and the hatchet in the hand of the largest, which was not broken, and the savory meat which Abram his son had made was still before them. 37. And when Terah saw this his anger was greatly kindled, and he hastened and went from the room to Abram.

Abram was done. The spirit of the LORD was upon him. God detests idols. HE is a jealous God. Why? Because HE deserves all the worship, glory, praise, credit, attention, etc. that we can give HIM. HE created all, not some manmade idol that needed man hands to have shape. Abram destroyed all the idols except one. Why? Leaving one and placing the weapon in the hands of the biggest idol will lead his father to think that the head god killed the other gods in displeasure. The trap was set. If they believed the head god did it, then there would be no need to worship any other god but the head god. Or, if the head god didn't do it and Abram did, why couldn't they protect themselves from a human? The logic of offering a sacrifice to the gods to test the dysfunction of his father was genius. Abram knew what Moses came to learn and teach the children of Israel many years later: Our God is a jealous god. One of the easiest ways to set HIM off or anger HIM is to worship other gods.

Deuteronomy 6: 13-15

Thou shalt fear the LORD thy God, and serve him, and shalt swear by his name. 14Ye shall not go after other gods, of the gods of
the people which are round about you; 15(For the LORD thy God is a jealous God among you) lest the anger of the LORD thy God
be kindled against thee, and destroy thee from off the face of the earth.

Dad was in his feelings. Terah is upset, angry, and ready to challenge his son for the destruction of his idols. Let's rephrase it. A parent is upset, angry, and ready to challenge their child when their dysfunction is called out. Abram actually tried his father's ways to see if there was a worth in worshipping idols. When he saw it was useless, he allowed the spirit of God to come upon him to destroy his father's obsession. It's amazing to see how emotional we can get to keep our foolishness going in the face of our children and when they call us on it, we flip out. Perhaps, the innocence or spirit of God is in them, trying to call us back to HIM, through them? Perhaps.

Jasher 11: 38-42

And he found Abram his son still sitting in the house; and he said to him, What is this work thou hast done to my gods? 39. And
Abram answered Terah his father and he said, Not so my lord, for I brought savory meat before them, and when I came nigh to
them with the meat that they might eat, they all at once stretched forth their hands to eat before the great one had put forth his
hand to eat. 40. And the large one saw their works that they did before him, and his anger was violently kindled against them, and
he went and took the hatchet that was in the house and came to them and broke them all, and behold the hatchet is yet in his hand
as thou seest. 41. And Terah's anger was kindled against his son Abram, when he spoke this; and Terah said to Abram his son in
his anger, What is this tale that thou hast told? Thou speakest lies to me. 42. Is there in these gods spirit, soul or power to do all
thou hast told me? Are they not wood and stone, and have I not myself made them, and canst thou speak such lies, saying that the
large god that was with them smote them? It is thou that didst place the hatchet in his hands, and then sayest he smote them all.

Terah wanted to defend his gods. Think about this for a second. A man, creation, was trying to defend his gods, the alleged creators. Abram told his father how he tried his ways and offered the gods a meal. They responded to the displeasure of the head god, and he chopped them into pieces. Terah knew Abram was lying. How? Because he knew the gods he worshipped couldn't do anything. He knew it. He admitted it. It's amazing to see how far someone will go to deceive themselves.

Jasher 11: 43-49

And Abram answered his father and said to him, And how canst thou then serve these idols in whom there is no power to do any thing? Can those idols in which thou trustest deliver thee? can they hear thy prayers when thou callest upon them? can they deliver thee from the hands of thy enemies, or will they fight thy battles for thee against thy enemies, that thou shouldst serve wood and stone which can neither speak nor hear? 44. And now surely it is not good for thee nor for the sons of men that are connected with thee, to do these things; are you so silly, so foolish or so short of understanding that you will serve wood and stone, and do after this manner? 45. And forget the Lord God who made heaven and earth, and who created you in the earth, and thereby bring a great evil upon your souls in this matter by serving stone and wood? 46. Did not our fathers in days of old sin in this matter, and the Lord God of the universe brought the waters of the flood upon them and destroyed the whole earth? 47. And how can you continue to do this and serve gods of wood and stone, who cannot hear, or speak, or deliver you from oppression, thereby bringing down the anger of the God of the universe upon you? 48. Now therefore my father refrain from this, and bring not evil upon thy soul and the souls of thy household. 49. And Abram hastened and sprang from before his father, and took the hatchet from his father's largest idol, with which Abram broke it and ran away.

Boom! Now that a father has admitted dysfunction, we can address the truth and be transparent in it. That's what Abram did, in the spirit of God, the spirit of Truth, in a way that was rational to the mind of his father. Abram, before he could address the world, he first addressed his father. He reminded his father of the God of Noah and Shem, his fathers. He reminded him of the same God Nimrod once worshiped but turned away from. Terah didn't ask who this God was because he knew better. Terah knew this God, yet he went against HIM. He made his own gods, like we do today, but I digress. Abram challenged his father to the truth of life. After doing so, he fled, dagger in hand. Remember, when Abram was born, his father sent him away to protect his life. Now, Abram was fleeing his father to save his own life. The house of Terah was not a place for Abram, in infancy and adulthood. There's a message in that: dysfunction in family is optional, even when you don't have a choice. Abram was building his resume to impact the world, right from his father's home. He now has a new reputation:

The god killer!

The Fire Walker

Genesis 11:28

And Haran died before his father Terah in the land of his nativity, in Ur of the Chaldees.

Terah is angry, very angry! More so than that, he is fearful. His son Abram has done something that was against the law of Nimrod. Dismantling the gods was an act that no one could get away with, especially the 2nd in command to Nimrod. Treason! Anger and fear consumed the same father that had a child killed so his child could live. The child that was allowed to live is the same child that had just caused this anger and fear. So much so that he is willing to risk death to himself to side with Nimrod to administer justice to his own son. Terah, in his feelings and dysfunction, had forgotten the prophecy surrounding his own son. But not God.

Jasher 11: 50-52

And Terah, seeing all that Abram had done, hastened to go from his house, and he went to the king and he came before Nimrod and stood before him, and he bowed down to the king; and the king said, What dost thou want? 51. And he said, I beseech thee my lord, to hear me--Now fifty years back a child was born to me, and thus has he done to my gods and thus has he spoken; and now therefore, my lord and king, send for him that he may come before thee, and judge him according to the law, that we may be delivered from his evil. 52. And the king sent three men of his servants, and they went and brought Abram before the king. And Nimrod and all his princes and servants were that day sitting before him, and Terah sat also before them.

Defending dysfunction. This is what Terah had resorted to. He lied to Nimrod 50 years ago and allowed for him to kill a child to protect his own. He now calls the acts of Abram evil because he smashed the gods of Nimrod, the gods he made with his own hands, the gods of his dysfunction and disrespect. This is pride operating at its finest. This man basically went and told on his own son because he felt disrespected in his own house. It's ridiculous. What's really crazy is that the king had forgotten what he had done. He had forgotten that this same complaint of his son was rooted in a lie that was 50 years old. This serves as another example of what's done in the dark will eventually come to the light. Even if that light is dark.

Nimrod's focus, however, was not in the lie, but what lies behind the lie: prophecy. Now that Terah is there, in his presence, ready to undo what he had done, destroying Nimrod's fear of losing his kingdom was #1 on his to-do list. Abram was found and summoned to the king in front of his fearful father.

Jasher 11:53

And the king said to Abram, What is this that thou hast done to thy father and to his gods? And Abram answered the king in the words that he spoke to his father, and he said, The large god that was with them in the house did to them what thou hast heard.

Uh oh. The time has come. Finally, the two men whose story cannot be told without acknowledging the other have finally met. God had allowed so much to happen so this moment would be perfect so the world can bear witness to HIS power. Prepare yourself for the sparks to fly!

Jasher 11: 54-60

And the king said to Abram, Had they power to speak and eat and do as thou hast said? And Abram answered the king, saying, And if there be no power in them why dost thou serve them and cause the sons of men to err through thy follies? 55. Dost thou imagine that they can deliver thee or do anything small or great, that thou shouldst serve them? And why wilt thou not sense the God of the whole universe, who created thee and in whose power it is to kill and keep alive? 56. 0 foolish, simple, and ignorant king, woe unto thee forever. 57. I thought thou wouldst teach thy servants the upright way, but thou hast not done this, but hast filled the whole earth with thy sins and the sins of thy people who have followed thy ways. 58. Dost thou not know, or hast thou not heard, that this evil which thou doest, our ancestors sinned therein in days of old, and the eternal God brought the waters of the flood upon them and destroyed them all, and also destroyed the whole earth on their account? And wilt thou and thy people rise up now and do like unto this work, in order to bring down the anger of the Lord God of the universe, and to bring evil upon thee and the whole earth? 59. Now therefore put away this evil deed which thou doest, and serve the God of the universe, as thy soul is in his hands, and then it will be well with thee. 60. And if thy wicked heart will not hearken to my words to cause thee to forsake thy evil ways, and to serve the eternal God, then wilt thou die in shame in the latter days, thou, thy people and all who are connected with thee, hearing thy words or walking in thy evil ways.

FEAR! None. Zero.

This is the Abram that you didn't know. This is the courage that you read about from the prophets. This is the bravery reflected in the apostles. This is the directness of those that know their God. This is the uncompromising nature of those that gave their lives in the Roman Coliseums for their LORD. This is what a true man or woman of God will do in the face of real so-called power and evil. This is what you and I should look like when defending our faith. It is not a soft spoken, let's hold hands, I just want to be friends type of Faith. In the face of life and death, similar to Stephen in the book of Acts, your faith cannot be compromising. Stand on business! Our father's business!

Abram was not into negotiating truth. Man, I love this! It is so inspirational. Abram challenged Nimrod to truth, the thing that he is supposed to represent, but even the great Nimrod knew his gods were nothing. He challenged Nimrod to remember the God who created him, that Nimrod knew, but chose not to teach to the world. He reminded him of the evil that the people before the flood had done to provoke God to wrath and he was following the same ways. Abram called him wicked, foolish, simple, and ignorant. Finally, he told him how he will die in his latter days and those who believe like him. Yes, you read that right. Abram told the ruler of the known world at the time the truth of God in a direct, straight to the point, I'm not trying to appease or hurt your feelings, type of way. This is the God we serve. HE will give you what to say and the truth to stand on, just as HE did Abram.

Jasher 11:61

And when Abram had ceased speaking before the king and princes, Abram lifted up his eyes to the heavens, and he said, The Lord seeth all the wicked, and he will judge them.

When you understand evil, you understand that it's not about the person, but the power behind the person that must be addressed. Evil lives and hides in groups, afraid to stand on its own. Why else do you think the fallen one had to deceive other angels to fall with him? Why didn't he go his way on his own? Think of it. Why does the evil of this world always look to be validated by others who think the way it does? I digress, it's just a question.

Ephesians 6:12

For we wrestle not against flesh and blood, but against principalities, against powers, against the rulers of the darkness of this world, against spiritual wickedness in high places.

Now that Abram has spoken his peace, it was time for Nimrod to show his piece.

Jasher 12: 1-5

And when the king heard the words of Abram he ordered him to be put into prison; and Abram was ten days in prison. 2. And at the end of those days the king ordered that all the kings, princes and governors of different provinces and the sages should come before him, and they sat before him, and Abram was still in the house of confinement. 3. And the king said to the princes and sages, Have you heard what Abram, the son of Terah, has done to his father? Thus has he done to him, and I ordered him to be brought before me, and thus has he spoken; his heart did not misgive him, neither did he stir in my presence, and behold now he is confined in the prison. 4. And therefore decide what judgment is due to this man who reviled the king; who spoke and did all the things that you heard. 5. And they all answered the king saying, The man who revileth the king should be hanged upon a tree; but having done all the things that he said, and having despised our gods, he must therefore be burned to death, for this is the law in this matter.

I told you. Evil hides in groups. There is a lack of accountability in groups. Look at what you read again. Nimrod called all his pundits, his vassals, the leaders of the nations of the world, to his presence to get their opinion on such a matter. There was already a law against what Abram did, but it's clear that Nimrod couldn't remember the law because he had been hit over the head with truth. What's even crazier here is that everyone came, again, and everyone knew Terah. The way he described Abram's lack of fear and boldness in speech was a threat to not only Nimrod's power, but their power as well (verse 3). That is very important to understand. Power must have fear to maintain power. It's an ingredient that gives evil such a good flavor to the wicked. Nimrod knew this and it's why he gave the details of the meeting with Abram to his followers. He, Nimrod, by himself, could not make the decision. He needed the group.

The group of leaders chose two things to do to destroy the idea of what Abram had done. They knew how to kill the man, but it was the idea that they really wanted to kill. Using the law that Nimrod had made would be the foundation to do their will to the man or any man that followed Abram's thought process. By speaking with no fear before the king, he must be hung, on a tree (think about Jesus, crucified on a cross, made of a tree, who spoke to the rulers of his day in the same manner). But they wanted more. For disposing of their gods, Abram must be burned, purged from their society, unwanted. Fire is the ultimate consumer, so why not send a message to mankind that anyone who despises the gods of their hands should be burned to death, unworthy of a burial, a Hell of their own creation.

Jasher 12:6

If it pleaseth the king to do this, let him order his servants to kindle a fire both night and day in thy brick furnace, and then we will cast this man into it. And the king did so, and he commanded his servants that they should prepare a fire for three days and three nights in the king's furnace, that is in Casdim; and the king ordered them to take Abram from prison and bring him out to be burned.

For 3 days and 3 nights, a furnace was created in Casdim. The alternate spelling of Casdim is Kasdim, meaning Ur-Kasdim. This is the same city, Ur of the Chaldees, that Abram was born in. In his own city, in the city of his father, in his hometown, was he to be burned to death. What a welcome party.

Jasher 12: 7-9

And all the king's servants, princes, lords, governors, and judges, and all the inhabitants of the land, about nine hundred thousand men, stood opposite the furnace to see Abram. 8. And all the women and little ones crowded upon the roofs and towers to see what was doing with Abram, and they all stood together at a distance; and there was not a man left that did not come on that day to behold the scene. 9. And when Abram was come, the conjurors of the king and the sages saw Abram, and they cried out to the king, saying, Our sovereign lord, surely this is the man whom we know to have been the child at whose birth the great star swallowed the four stars, which we declared to the king now fifty years since.

Almost a million men to one. The world was on one side, and Abram was alone on the other. The women and children of the world was brought together to witness this event. Scripture goes so far to even tell you that they stood on the rooftops, which is where most people in the ancient world slept in the summer to keep cool. They stood on towers, because the main tower at Babel had been destroyed, to see. Every man on the planet came to see this. I'll repeat, EVERY man on the planet came to see this. Nimrod had the world's eyes and attention to showcase his power and justice as his desire to put Abram on a display to send a message. The haters of Abram even remembered that this is the child they saw born and his prophecy was written in the heavens 50 years prior to this. Every kingdom was present to see the destruction of the man who killed the gods, the gods of his father. In an indirect way, strategically, Nimrod was also sending a message to his blind witnesses that with the death of Abram, his kingdom would be secured. Now, the same men who saw the star in the sky and understood the prophecy 50 years prior about the end of Nimrod's reign, knew this moment was pivotal. The kings that were subordinates to Nimrod did not. But again, real evil never really tells the full story.

While all of this was happening, Terah was watching. Sure, he finally got justice for what Abram had done, but in his fear, he didn't realize who he was really dealing with. Evil doesn't really forget things, it hides them until the right time to do more evil. Observe...

Jasher 12: 10-11

And behold now his father has also transgressed thy commands, and mocked thee by bringing thee another child, which thou didst kill. 11. And when the king heard their words, he was exceedingly wroth, and he ordered Terah to be brought before him.

They didn't forget. Nimrod may have forgot, but his sages and "wise" men did not. They reminded the king of Terah's lie. Not only should the man Abram be killed but his father who deceived the king should be brought to justice as well. This is the danger of hiding in groups. The group is never really for you, but the group. Dysfunction has consequences. Terah is about to learn the hard way.

Jasher 12: 12-15

And the king said, Hast thou heard what the conjurors have spoken? Now tell me truly, how didst thou; and if thou shalt speak truth thou shalt be acquitted. 13. And seeing that the king's anger was so much kindled, Terah said to the king, My lord and king, thou hast heard the truth, and what the sages have spoken is right. And the king said, How couldst thou do this thing, to transgress my orders and to give me a child that thou didst not beget, and to take value for him? 14. And Terah answered the king, Because my tender feelings were excited for my son, at that time, and I took a son of my handmaid, and I brought him to the king. 15. And the king said Who advised thee to this? Tell me, do not hide aught from me, and then thou shalt not die. 16. And Terah was greatly terrified in the king's presence, and he said to the king, It was Haran my eldest son who advised me to this; and Haran was in those days that Abram was born, two and thirty years old.

See what fear can do. Fear can make you tell the truth to hide a lie to tell another lie to hide as the truth. This man, Terah, is something else. In order to preserve his own life from the group, he decided to say his oldest son was his advisor on lying to the king. This was ridiculous. This man, #2 in the kingdom, more esteemed by Nimrod than all the other kings that operated under his rule, was afraid to die on his own. He lied, again, in the presence of the king to cover his own butt. He initially used the emotional card in verse 14 to see if that would stop Nimrod. It didn't. Instead, he gave up his oldest son, his first namesake, to die in his stead. Shameful.

Jasher 12: 16-17

But Haran did not advise his father to anything, for Terah said this to the king in order to deliver his soul from the king, for he feared greatly; and the king said to Terah, Haran thy son who advised thee to this shall die through fire with Abram; for the sentence of death is upon him for having rebelled against the king's desire in doing this thing. 18. And Haran at that time felt inclined to follow the ways of Abram, but he kept it within himself.

For the record, Haran, the oldest son of Terah, did not advise his father to kill his youngest brother. Haran was sentenced to death for a crime he did not commit. His father knew it and was willing to allow not only one of his sons to die but two, the oldest and the youngest. This, again, is what fear can do. Haran, the oldest, in his time he spent noticing the demeanor and boldness in which his younger brother operated, secretly admired Abram. He could see his younger brother was a man of conviction, choice, and logic. He didn't care about his age, just his ability. You never know whose watching you when you are focused on the LORD. Haran was tuned in to his brother. The key here is that he kept it to himself. Although admirable, this is not ideal. There is a message here but I will save it until later.

Jasher 12: 18-23

And when Terah had spoken this to the king concerning Haran his son, the king ordered Haran to be seized with Abram. 21. And they brought them both, Abram and Haran his brother, to cast them into the fire; and all the inhabitants of the land and the king's servants and princes and all the women and little ones were there, standing that day over them. 22. And the king's servants took Abram and his brother, and they stripped them of all their clothes excepting their lower garments which were upon them. 23. And they bound their hands and feet with linen cords, and the servants of the king lifted them up and cast them both into the furnace.

Well, Abram was there. With the whole world watching, literally, it was time for the fire. He and his brother Haran, who was completely innocent by the way, were gathered together to be purged of this world. One was bound for telling the truth, the other for a lie being told on him, by their father. They were stripped of their clothes except their under garment (underwear), humiliated before the world. Tied up, held up, and thrown into the fire. This was supposed to be it. This was supposed to be the end of a life journey for Abram. This was supposed to be the end of the line for good men in the earth. The Satanic influence in detecting good in people had found its way to Abram and Haran. Abram had given himself to the LORD completely. Haran desired to do so but did it internally, not showing himself to be completely committed. They were both thrown into the fire, two sons of the same fire.

As they were both held up then cast down into the furnace, the belief of solidifying his kingdom for good was a second away, literally. Nimrod was a second away from becoming lord of the earth. He may not be lord of heaven as he tried with the Tower of Babel, but with Abram's death, he would become lord of the earth, being that there was no man willing to follow the God he knew other than Noah and Shem in the north at Mt. Ararat, and as old men, they were not fighters but mountain men who lived in caves. The time was now, a second away from immortality.

But God.

Jasher 12: 24-25

And the Lord loved Abram and he had compassion over him, and the Lord came down and delivered Abram from the fire and he was not burned. 25. But all the cords with which they bound him were burned, while Abram remained and walked about in the fire.

Esh Oklah! Esh Oklah! Esh Oklah!

What does Esh Oklah mean? Moses will tell you...

Deuteronomy 4:24

For the LORD thy God is a consuming fire, even a jealous God.

The LORD God IS a consuming fire. HE is not a fire, but a consuming fire. The fire is not God. The fire is not to be worshipped, as some cultures do. HE is the very element that makes fire, fire. HE can take a bush, set it on fire, and the bush not be burned up. HE is the same God that sent his spirit, the holy spirit, to descend on humanity at Pentecost, that the spirit passed one to another as a fire. HE is the same God that walked in the fire with Shadrach, Meshach, and Abednego. HE is the same God that when HIS spirit rests on you it's like fire shut up in your bones as the prophet Jeremiah says. HE is God, and HE is the One that can do all things. HE is the same God that said HIS ministers are a flame of fire.

The LORD allowed the cords to be burned to showcase that the fire is real and powerful, but not more than HE. God loved Abram for his willingness to follow HIM against all odds. The numbers were literally a million to one, and he still chose God. He didn't relent, compromise, or operate in fear. He knew God and accepted HIM as such. That moved the LORD, the creator of all, to operate on his behalf. The flame from this fiery furnace was so great that all the people of the world could look in and see anything and everything in the fire, including Abram and his brother Haran. One could assume many looked on in sheer horror, especially the children, as they watched these two men be thrown into the fire, not understanding they were witnessing an execution. On the contrary, one could also assume there were others there excited to see such an event.

When Abram and his brother were brought to the furnace, they were cast or thrown into the fire, which is horrific when you think about it. Two brothers, both the son of Terah, Nimrod's right-hand man. Abram was there because of what he believed. Haran was there because his father lied on him. After being thrown in, something amazing happened. The world was made witness to something extraordinary. Whereas one brother was walking in the flame, the other was consumed.

Jasher 12:26

And Haran died when they had cast him into the fire, and he was burned to ashes, for his heart was not perfect with the Lord; and those men who cast him into the fire, the flame of the fire spread over them, and they were burned, and twelve men of them died.

Haran was burned to death. The LORD did not give him the same favor HE had given to Abram. Why? Because Haran didn't fully commit to the ways of God. He inwardly wanted to follow the LORD but he didn't outwardly give him his allegiance. This is a very important lesson. There are MANY people today that talk that "I'm saved, I believe in God, I'm a believer talk" but really, they are halfhearted followers of the one true God. Haran had a chance and choice, but chose admiration over acclimation. He symbolizes those that choose how a believer is seen over actually being a believer. Being thrown into the fire is symbolic of being thrown into judgement. Because he wasn't an actual believer, he was burned, which is exactly what scripture says about the non-believer, regardless of whether they lived a good life, was pro-God and or was a morally good person. God desires us to choose him or not. The purpose of being thrown into the fire is so we can be purged of the non-essential elements. God wants us to be pure in him, like gold.

1 Peter 1:7

That the trial of your faith, being much more precious than of gold that perisheth, though it be tried with fire, might be found unto praise and honour and glory at the appearing of Jesus Christ:

And…

Proverbs 17:3

The fining pot is for silver, and the furnace for gold: but the LORD trieth the hearts.

Consider the example of Abram and Haran. One was all in, one was almost in. When the LORD calls, when HE gives you a chance, you must accept HIM. It is a choice. Haran had a chance to accept HIM, inwardly and outwardly, to join with his brother in the fullness of God, but he didn't. This is not to judge Haran, that's God's job. However, this is a message that was taught throughout the ages, including by Jesus himself, that no man can serve two masters (Matt. 6:24). You cannot be almost with God, no different than any healthy relationship you desire to have or be in. You cannot inwardly desire HIM but outwardly agree with the world. In the compassion for humanity, I hate it for Haran, but this is a lesson for the world to recognize and adjust accordingly. The same applies to the 12 men that were following orders who died from the heat of the furnace. Think of how hot this furnace had to be! This should give you an idea of the intensity of the hatred of Nimrod for Abram and things that represent God and good in this world. This same fire that was so hot that it killed Haran and the 12 soldiers will be the same fire that the coming Anti-Christ will have to destroy the saints and all things that are good, including those that are morally good people but non-believers, like Haran.

The fire that burns in men is more than figurative speaking, but a spiritual one as well. The spirit that animates the body we live in is likened to a flame on a candle. As we live, it burns, bright. When we die, it is extinguished. Esh Oklah, which means 'the LORD is a consuming fire', gives us an understanding of the value that God himself places in fire. It is meant to consume, to purify, to warm, to seal, to punish, to purge, to be a light. For example, God made HIS ministers a flame of fire (Heb. 1:7), which can be seen with the spiritual eye in the spiritual world by spiritual beings. The human eye can't see this. This is why our belief in HIM is like fire shut up in our bones because we burn for HIM. Abram was the first one to exemplify this type of faith in the world after the flood. Therefore, if you are HIS fire, you can live in HIS fire, furthermore, you can walk in the fire.

Jasher 12:27

And Abram walked in the midst of the fire three days and three nights, and all the servants of the king saw him walking in the fire, and they came and told the king, saying, Behold we have seen Abram walking about in the midst of the fire, and even the lower garments which are upon him are not burned, but the cord with which he was bound is burned.

Look at what the LORD has done! The fire is not god. God is God, in the fire. HE gave Abram the ability to walk in the fire. Not only did he walk in the fire, he did it for 3 days and 3 nights! This is the God that we serve. Even though Haran was burned to death in the fire, Abram was untouched while being covered by the LORD. Imagine seeing a man, walking in a furnace, for 3 days! The LORD put Abram and HIS power to give and take life on full display for the world to see. No one noticed this more than Nimrod's princes. After watching Abram walk in the flame for 3 days, they had seen enough. It was time to tell Nimrod.

Jasher 12:28

And when the king heard their words his heart fainted and he would not believe them; so he sent other faithful princes to see this matter, and they went and saw it and told it to the king; and the king rose to go and see it, and he saw Abram walking to and fro in the midst of the fire, and he saw Haran's body burned, and the king wondered greatly.

Only God can make evil second guess itself. Reread verse 28 again. The princes of Nimrod, which were his own family members, told him that Abram was alive and walking in the fire. They could see him. Everyone could see him! If it was a person or two saying someone was walking in the fire, they could be dismissed and or attached to a god or goddess. But everyone saw Abram. The trusted servants of Nimrod saw him. They reported back to say the same thing as the previous princes. It was time for Nimrod to go take a look for himself.

He couldn't believe it! No one could believe it. With all the power and influence Nimrod had, this power he was looking at was too much. He knew it wasn't a fluke or trick because he could see the charred body of Haran in the fire. He saw what everyone else saw, man walking in the furnace. The scripture said he wondered greatly, which means he was trying to figure out what he was really looking at. This is what the power of God can do to the proud. There was only one thing to do to get an answer...

Jasher 12: 29-31

And the king ordered Abram to be taken out from the fire; and his servants approached to take him out and they could not, for the fire was round about and the flame ascending toward them from the furnace. 30. And the king's servants fled from it, and the king rebuked them, saying, Make haste and bring Abram out of the fire that you shall not die. 31. And the servants of the king again approached to bring Abram out, and the flames came upon them and burned their faces so that eight of them died.

When God is involved, no man can intervene. When God does what HE does, it doesn't matter what a man does. Nimrod's servants, the same people who created the furnace, could not come close to the same fire they made. 8 more men died, a total of 20, following orders. What does that mean? Following evil comes with a price, your life. Following God comes with a price as well, your life. What's the difference? One takes life, one gives it.

After noticing the effects of approaching this vast fire, Nimrod humbled himself. The same God he looked away from that gave him everything that he had was showcasing to him HIS power and might. Man is no match for God, and Nimrod knew that. It took this live example that the world saw firsthand to send the message: the God of heaven is the real and ONLY God. HE is power, not man. Nimrod clearly hadn't learned his lesson from the Tower. Even in the wickedness of his heart, Nimrod knew who he was dealing with and it was time to stop the madness. From a political standpoint, the longer Abram walked in the fire, the weaker his position as king and ruler of the world would become. He had to get Abram out of that fire.

Jasher 12:32

And when the king saw that his servants could not approach the fire lest they should be burned, the king called to Abram, O servant of the God who is in heaven, go forth from amidst the fire and come hither before me; and Abram hearkened to the voice of the king, and he went forth from the fire and came and stood before the king.

No mas! Nimrod couldn't take it anymore. He openly admitted to the fact that the God who is in heaven is the real God and Abram was HIS servant. This is so beautiful on so many levels. Pride comes before destruction and Nimrod's pride was causing his own destruction. No man could approach this fire, the same fire men created, but a man of God could not only approach it but he could walk in it for 3 days and 3 nights without being burned. The great Nimrod himself couldn't do what he saw, and he knew it. In a position of submission to the moment, he gave in. This is a message to evil and those who think your pride will last in the face of the Great One: you will submit. Either you will submit now or later, but either way, like the world's most powerful man, you will eventually submit and admit who God really is.

Now that Abram has been called, something very important is about to happen that is critical for the purpose of this work. Pay close attention to the following verses and how Abram, Nimrod, and the world responds to the power of God.

Jasher 12: 33-37

And when Abram came out the king and all his servants saw Abram coming before the king, with his lowergarments upon him, for they were not burned, but the cord with which he was bound was burned. 34. And the king said to Abram, How is it that thou wast not burned in the fire? 35. And Abram said to the king, The God of heaven and earth in whom I trust and who has all in his power, he delivered me from the fire into which thou didst cast me. 36. And Haran the brother of Abram was burned to ashes, and they sought for his body, and they found it consumed. 37. And Haran was eighty-two years old when he died in the fire of Casdim. And the king, princes, and inhabitants of the land, seeing that Abram was delivered from the fire, they came and bowed down to Abram.

There is no answer for God, period. Nimrod called HIM the God of heaven, which is true. Abram called HIM the God of heaven and earth. Notice the subtle difference. Nimrod calling HIM the God of heaven, although true, leaves out the God of Earth, which is the title Nimrod reserved for himself. Abram, hearing what Nimrod said, understood what those titles meant. To clarify and give the proper honor to God that is due to HIM, Abram told the king himself who God was. This is why it's important to know the God in whom you serve. The devil may be in the details, but so is the wisdom of God that the devil will try to use against you.

Abram told Nimrod and the world who saved him and how he trusted in HIM. There were no tricks involved and finding Haran's burned body was the proof. This is why the opening verse to this section in Genesis 11 speaks to Haran dying "before" his father Terah in Ur of Chaldees. Now you know how and why. God is so great! Also, to show how fragile people's belief structure really is when they are not connected to the real God, they resorted back to a form of idolatry and bowed down to Abram.
Reader, please understand the power of this moment, when Abram was faced by the servants and princes of Nimrod. Abram had the same opportunity to accept their worship that Nimrod had when he was younger. Nimrod, using the garments of Adam and Eve made by the hand of God, accepted their worship and became the king of the world. Abram, on the other hand, only had his undergarments on, which the fire couldn't burn. The same undergarments weren't made from God' hands, but manmade garments, like we have today. Regardless, the power of God protected him from the fire, which kills every man, including Abram's brother Haran. Abram had a chance to become the new Nimrod, accept worship, become a god, become the new Nimrod. All he had to do was stand there and accept the praise of the people who bowed to him. That's it. The leaders of nations and all the people were bowing to Abram. If he accepted this moment, like Nimrod did when he became king, he would be the world ruler and the omen that was spoken of him at his birth would be validated. Abram declined. He took the moment to give God the glory and honor HE deserves, in the presence of Nimrod. This was a real power move through humility.

Jasher 12:38

And Abram said to them, Do not bow down to me, but bow down to the God of the world who made you, and serve him, and go in his ways for it is he who delivered me from out of this fire, and it is he who created the souls and spirits of all men, and formed man in his mother's womb, and brought him forth into the world, and it is he who will deliver those who trust in him from all pain.

To God be the glory! Abram gave it up. He gave it up. Instead of accepting the glory, he gave the credit to God in the face of his enemies. He taught the world leaders a lesson and gave them the blueprint of how to get back to God. No part of his words or demeanor was about himself, but God. He was intentional in his deflection of praise while the world watched. This is so amazing to see. Whereas Nimrod accepted the adulation and created a whole reputation based on the gifts of God in the clothing made for Adam and Eve, Abram had his clothing burned off only to see God do an even greater work. Again, this is the God that we serve.

Jasher 12: 39-43

And this thing seemed very wonderful in the eyes of the king and princes, that Abram was saved from the fire and that Haran was burned; and the king gave Abram many presents and he gave him his two head servants from the king's house; the name of one was Oni and the name of the other was Eliezer. 40. And all the kings, princes and servants gave Abram many gifts of silver and gold and pearl, and the king and his princes sent him away, and he went in peace. 41. And Abram went forth from the king in peace, and many of the king's servants followed him, and about three hundred men joined him. 42. And Abram returned on that day and went to his father's house, he and the men that followed him, and Abram served the Lord his God all the days of his life, and he walked in his ways and followed his law. 43. And from that day forward Abram inclined the hearts of the sons of men to serve the Lord.

This is how Abram gained his wealth. It wasn't because he was a merchant or his father Terah or some other story (there are many out there). Scripture tells you how he became wealthy. God has a way of allowing people that are evil to support a good cause. Take note. They may not agree with you, they may dislike your position, they may wholeheartedly see things from a different perspective than you. But when you do what the LORD says, HE has a way to make those same people store up goods for themselves only to have it given to you for a greater work to be done that their evil could not do.
Kings of other nations now knew of Abram. From that point on to today, this name means something to world leaders. That name, Abram, means 'alone, he has everything.' Alone, he has a God that is all powerful. There is a country saying that I heard old men say when I was a boy that applies here: some people deserve a whole lot of leave alone! That was Abram. By himself, with the LORD of heaven looking over his shoulder, no man wanted to be the enemy of such a man. They gave him gifts and some of the men of different nations begin to follow him and his ways. He went from being one man to 300 followers, just like that. That's what God will do when you serve HIS will.

What God did at the Tower of Babel first proved that Nimrod was not the ruler of heaven. Now, he was being proven to not be the ruler of earth. Kings came and bowed to his nemesis Abram, in his presence, in the city of Ur (chasdim). This had to be a tough pill to swallow for Nimrod. How does a person recover from such when your arch enemy becomes a hero in your own home?

As for Abram, before the furnace, he was known to his father as the god killer. He now has another nickname to be added to his resume: *the fire walker*. Let's Make It Plain...

One man wore clothes, became a king, taught men to serve many gods, kingdom is shrinking.

One man wore fire, became a servant, taught men to serve one God, kingdom is growing.

Luke 3: 16-17

John answered, saying unto them all, I indeed baptize you with water; but one mightier than I cometh, the latchet of whose shoes I am not worthy to unloose: he shall baptize you with the Holy Ghost and with fire: 17 Whose fan is in his hand, and he will throughly purge his floor, and will gather the wheat into his garner; but the chaff he will burn with fire unquenchable.

The Holy Spirit is the same spirit that overtook Abram when he earned the nickname god killer at his father's house. The fire through which Christ baptizes us is the same fire that is in HIS ministers. The fire of the furnace Abram walked in does not compare to the fire shut up in our bones. By default, that makes every TRUE believer in the makeup of Abram. It's just that our furnace is different. When we stand on HIS word, we stand on HIS fire. That, by default, makes us all fire walkers.

Thank you Father God. Thank you father Abram.

Jeremiah 23:29

Is not my word like as a fire? saith the LORD; and like a hammer that breaketh the rock in pieces?

Sarai

Genesis 11: 29-30

And Abram and Nahor took them wives: the name of Abram's wife was Sarai; and the name of Nahor's wife, Milcah, the daughter of Haran, the father of Milcah, and the father of Iscah. 30 But Sarai was barren; she had no child.

Look at God! It is not good for a man to be alone, so God designed woman for man. HE didn't design man for man, or woman for woman, but woman for man. This is not my opinion or thought in motion seeking an audience to be validated. The body of woman was designed to receive connection with a man as the man was created to give connection. This is the divine wisdom of God, easily explained in HIS WORD. The scripture is my foundation with God being its source. Don't believe me? I don't have to use Genesis to prove this, I have a more direct message.

1 Corinthians 11: 8-9

For the man is not of the woman; but the woman of the man. 9 Neither was the man created for the woman; but the woman for the man.

God has a plan. It may not work like we want when we want, the way we want, but HE is God and HIS ways are not our ways. HIS thoughts are not our thoughts. HE designed a woman to be the fit for a man. Women are unique in their nature. Why? Because God took them from man while being uniquely gifted by the hands of God to be what we are not in nature. As a man, we are the opposite of them. For the duration of time a man is dating or looking for the one, he mimics Adam, the first man. He is asleep. Everyone that comes and goes in his life is like a character in the dream of a play. You truly don't wake and live until that One comes. This is why God put Adam to sleep while HE fashioned woman. When HE was finished designing her, with no time put on how long Adam slept, God was busy putting 'she' together.

When God finished, HE woke Adam up and stood there alongside woman, ready for Adam to connect with her. This is the wisdom of God and the first marriage. Yes, marriage is not a man thing, it's a God thing. The idea of a man giving a woman away and or walking her down the isle is a rendition of the original marriage in which God the Father gave away HIS daughter, woman, to man. Even for atheist and satanists, it's a practice instituted by God. Man is asleep until SHE is ready. Science has even proven that girls physically, mentally, emotionally, and hormonally, mature faster than boys do. Yet they come from a man. See how God gives us balance? It's a beautiful thing when you get it.

With that said, in walks Sarai.

Jasher 12:44

And at that time Nahor and Abram took unto themselves wives, the daughters of their brother Haran; the wife of Nahor was Milca and the name of Abram's wife was Sarai. And Sarai, wife of Abram, was barren; she had no offspring in those days.

Nahor is the older brother of Abram, the middle son of Terah. After walking in the fire and being admonished by the world, God allowed for Abram to have an Adam-like moment, to wake up. When he did, HE presented Abram with Sarai his niece, the daughter of his dead brother Haran, as his wife. Please keep in mind the time and societal norms in the world. This was a common practice for population purposes for close family members to marry one another. God allowed this for a time then HE forbad it once the earth was spread out and discovered after the Tower fell. Sarai being chosen for Abram was a cultural norm. In a more intimate way, Abram shared the last moments of Sarai's father life, Haran, in the furnace. Their connection was forged in fire, a trauma bond of epic proportions.

The term Sarai means princess in Hebrew. This woman is a woman of women. Her story is epic. Her father was burned alive in a fire because her grandfather lied. Her father, Haran, had three children. One son and two daughters. His first child was named Lot, who we will discuss later. His second child was a girl, Milcah, which name means queen. She would later become the biblical grandmother of Rebecca, the future wife of Isaac, the mother of Esau and Jacob, who was later to be named Israel by God. Sarai was her little sister. She was 40 years old when she married Abram, her uncle. So, it's needless to say but these women are two important figures in world history. Without them, there is no Israel as we knew and know it.

Sarai was a woman that was fashioned to see and live a great life as the youngest daughter of Haran. He was the oldest son of the #2 in command in the world. You can imagine the gifts and lifestyle she received as the granddaughter to Terah. Understanding this type of lifestyle is major in looking at Sarai's story and seeing it unfold. Think of it: her sister Milcah name means queen and her name means princess. It speaks for itself. It also gives you an indicator that Haran was a real modern-day girl dad to name his daughters queen and princess. Their names allow us to know the expectations of their treatment for any man that would become suitors. Needless to say, both of their uncles, Nahor and Abram took them as wives.

Ruins of Ancient City of Haran

Haran was a man of good standing in the eyes of Nimrod. How do we know this? Because he had his own land in the north of the land of Shinar or Mesopotamia. Whereas Terah lived in Ur, in south Mesopotamia, Haran settled land in the northern section of Nimrod's kingdom and even had a city built bearing his name. The city itself was built near a tributary that flows into the Euphrates River. His children would have been well kept and admired amongst the people of Shinar.

Sarai was in a unique place in life. Her father afforded her and her siblings a good life. She would have had things that most people of the ancient world did not have access to. Children, however, she did not have. But that was set to change. By marrying Abram, who also had no children, she was about to walk into a life with a man whom is known universally and eternally as the father of nations. Her father was a partial believer in God. Her husband was a full believer in God. This was the foundation of their relationship.

As a new wife, Sarai walked into a relationship without children and couldn't have children after they were married. Scripture says she was barren. For women then and now, this is a hard thing to embrace. With everything Sarai had seen and gone through, nothing would prepare her for what was to come in her life. She was designed for greatness. A testimony among testimonies of what God can do. Without her, there is no promise fulfilled by God. We spend a lot of time speaking about Abram her husband, and rightfully so, but without her and her contribution to the will of God as a princess, the future Father of Faith wouldn't be. Just as he is the father of nations, she is the mother, who was barren. To Sarai, who's name too would be changed alongside her husband, we bow and salute you, princess mother!

Isaiah 51:2

Look unto Abraham your father, and unto Sarah that bare you: for I called him alone, and blessed him, and increased him.

Leaving **Ur**

Genesis 11: 31-32

And Terah took Abram his son, and Lot the son of Haran his son's son, and Sarai his daughter in law, his son Abram's wife; and they went forth with them from Ur of the Chaldees, to go into the land of Canaan; and they came unto Haran, and dwelt there.

Abram is now a married man. Nimrod is still king of Shinar. The kings of the world were back in their kingdoms. All was calm, but it was time for the plan of God to go forth. Abram, the world-famous fire walker and man of God, was living in a land where evil still reigned. Despite the fact that Abram proved to Nimrod and the world that God is God, and beside HIM there is no other, the delusion of power and the foothold of evil still prevailed in the minds and nature of man. Abram knew this. Even though Nimrod gave Abram riches, Abram knew that living in Ur was not his final resting place, it was his launching pad. Culturally, men lived near their families to keep their families intact as they would act as workers and servants to one another. This is what the word son and daughter mean. Take note:

Son means to continue the house, which means servant
Daughter means my (a possessive word [ex. My daughter Ashley = my Ashley])

Abram knew that the evil of Nimrod would not coexist with the greatness of the good of God. The idea of starting a family in Ur would be a problem that Abram did not want Sarai to bare even though Sarai was barren. The Sumerian pantheon of gods and goddesses were still dominant in Shinar. Proof of this was as simple as walking outside and seeing what we now call the Great Ziggurat of Ur. It was a temple built to the Sumerian moon god Nanna, also called Sin. This temple, called a ziggurat, was the highest building on the landscape for anyone to see for miles around. It would have been a beautifully built masterpiece of clay bricks, made similar to the recently destroyed Tower of Babel, but on a much smaller scale. The ziggurat was the center of life in Ur. Its ruins still exists to this day.

Great Ziggurat of Ur
© Khan Academy

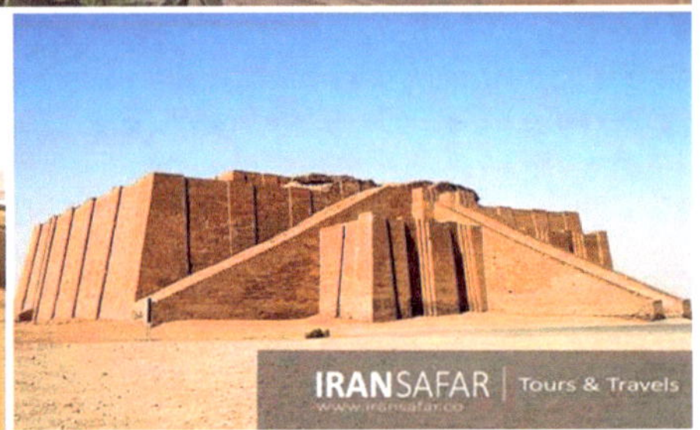

Ziggurat of Ur (What Abram and Sarai would have seen everyday)
© IRANSAFAR

Meanwhile, in Babel (Eridu)...

Jasher 12: 45-46

And at the expiration of two years from Abram's going out of the fire, that is in the fifty second year of his life, behold king Nimrod sat in Babel upon the throne, and the king fell asleep and dreamed that he was standing with his troops and hosts in a valley opposite the king's furnace. 46. And he lifted up his eyes and saw a man in the likeness of Abram coming forth from the furnace, and that he came and stood before the king with his drawn sword, and then sprang to the king with his sword, when the king fled from the man, for he was afraid; and while he was running, the man threw an egg upon the king's head, and the egg became a great river.

Question: Nimrod dreamed of seeing Abram with a drawn sword. What was the sword?

Hebrews 4:12

For the word of God is quick, and powerful, and sharper than any twoedged sword, piercing even to the dividing asunder of soul and spirit, and of the joints and marrow, and is a discerner of the thoughts and intents of the heart.

Answer: The sword is Truth.

Jasher 12: 47-49

And the king dreamed that all his troops sank in that river and died, and the king took flight with three men who were before him and he escaped. 48. And the king looked at these men and they were clothed in princely dresses as the garments of kings, and had the appearance and majesty of kings. 49. And while they were running, the river again turned to an egg before the king, and there came forth from the egg a young bird which came before the king, and flew at his head and plucked out the king's eye.

Wow! Instead of asking a question here, I think it is better to lay this out because there is a lot going on. An egg, a river, 3 men, a young bird and an plucked-out eye of the king. We will decode the items for you as the spirit of the living God allows. But first, let's see how Nimrod responded.

Jasher 12: 50-52

And the king was grieved at the sight, and he awoke out of his sleep and his spirit was agitated; and he felt a great terror. 51. And in the morning the king rose from his couch in fear, and he ordered all the wise men and magicians to come before him, when the king related his dream to them. 52. And a wise servant of the king, whose name was Anuki, answered the king, saying, This is nothing else but the evil of Abram and his seed which will spring up against my Lord and king in the latter days.

The fearless king now has fear. We can dive into the irony and hypocrisy of that, but there's another item that requires our attention. Nimrod called all of his so-called wise men to him to help interpret his dream. After hearing it, only one of his counselors, Anuki, had a perspective. Who is this random person that just so happen to be mentioned in scripture? Why is he important in the presence of Nimrod, the ruler of Shinar? Who was Anuki?

Anuki means wisdom. In ancient Sumeria, his name is derived from the pantheon of gods that Nimrod created. An alternative spelling of his name is the Anunna or Anunnaki, which in Hebrew is bene-haelohim. In scriptural text, *the fallen angels*. Yes, you are reading this correctly. They were regarded as the determiner or judges of the fates of humanity. Anuki was a representative of the gods and goddesses who are the centerpiece of Sumerian and Akkadian history, which is why Anuki was in the presence of Nimrod. His report of Abram is an accurate take on how the story of the Anunnaki and Sumerian Kings List rival that of the scriptures. Truth is stranger than fiction. Anuki had more to say...

Jasher 12: 53-56

And behold the day will come when Abram and his seed and the children of his household will war with my king, and they will smite all the king's hosts and his troops. 54. And as to what thou hast said concerning three men which thou didst see like unto thyself, and which did escape, this means that only thou wilt escape with three kings from the kings of the earth who will be with thee in battle. 55. And that which thou sawest of the river which turned to an egg as at first, and the young bird plucking out thine eye, this means nothing else but the seed of Abram which will slay the king in latter days. 56. This is my king's dream, and this is its interpretation, and the dream is true, and the interpretation which thy servant has given thee is right.

Wow. Another omen of the end of the reign of Nimrod via Abram. This time, directly to his face, from the representative of the fallen angels themselves, Anuki. Even evil knows that God is the ONE. Wow.

Jasher 12: 57-58

Now therefore my king, surely thou knowest that it is now fifty-two years since thy sages saw this at the birth of Abram, and if my king will suffer Abram to live in the earth it will be to the injury of my lord and king, for all the days that Abram liveth neither thou nor thy kingdom will be established, for this was known formerly at his birth; and why will not my king slay him, that his evil may be kept from thee in latter days? 58. And Nimrod hearkened to the voice of Anuki, and he sent some of his servants in secret to go and seize Abram, and bring him before the king to suffer death.

How soon, how soon do people forget. The same man that walked in the fire is back on the king's radar to kill? Again? Two years removed from the event that the whole world saw and now we're back to square one: killing Abram. If the fire couldn't kill Abram, what made Nimrod think that the hands of humans can? How soon did they forget that even the men that threw Abram into the fire was killed. The men who were sent to bring Abram out of the fire was killed. Why now would Nimrod send more men to get the same man, thinking or expecting a different result? This, by definition, is insanity, which is doing the same thing over and over again yet expecting a different result. However, the fear of a good man has no expiration date.

Abram was minding his own business establishing himself in the land while the king was dreaming of him. That's what you call living in someone's head, rent free. The king of the world had everything at his disposal, things, people, access, etc. Anything he wanted was at his fingertips, except Abram. The threat of a good man was too much for Nimrod and his minions to handle, which is a blueprint for evil.

By taking the advice of Anuki, killing Abram is the only way to stop the prophecy from coming true and Abram's seed from killing the king. Keep in mind, Abram didn't have children at that time and his wife was barren. So, here's a message within a message: your enemies believe in your future even if you don't. With that said, all haters are the same. They see things that sometimes you can't. That's why it's important to have haters: they are the reminders in your present of your future greatness. Abram's hater was actually having dreams about him.

Jasher 12: 59-60

And Eliezer, Abram's servant whom the king had given him, was at that time in the presence of the king, and he heard what Anuki had advised the king, and what the king had said to cause Abram's death. 60. And Eliezer said to Abram, Hasten, rise up and save thy soul, that thou mayest not die through the hands of the king, for thus did he see in a dream concerning thee, and thus did Anuki interpret it, and thus also did Anuki advise the king concerning thee.

In the midst of your haters, your planners and plotters of your downfall, God will get a message through to you of what's coming. Haters forget in the middle of their plots that there is a God that hears all and sees all, knows all, feels all, and no place is hidden from him. This is no exception. Anuki's interpretation of Nimrod's dream was overheard by a man who was assigned to Abram. Eliezer heard some vital information that was a part of a much larger plan of God. His warning to Abram set off a chain of reactions that are all biblically backed information. It's so amazing! Now watch God work...

Jasher 12: 61-62

And Abram hearkened to the voice of Eliezer, and Abram hastened and ran for safety to the house of Noah and his son Shem, and he concealed himself there and found a place of safety; and the king's servants came to Abram's house to seek him, but they could not find him, and they searched through out the country and he was not to be found, and they went and searched in every direction and he was not to be met with. 62. And when the king's servants could not find Abram they returned to the king, but the king's anger against Abram was stilled, as they did not find him, and the king drove from his mind this matter concerning Abram.

Abram listened to Eliezer and left the city of Ur in southern Shinar. He headed to the north to Mt. Ararat to seek safety again with Noah and Shem. This shows how there is a difference between the eyes of God and the eyes of evil. The eyes of evil couldn't see Abram. The eyes of the LORD directed Abram's escape. When the men couldn't find him, they returned to Nimrod to give the report. Again, look at how our God works...

Jasher 12:63

And Abram was concealed in Noah's house for one month, until the king had forgotten this matter, but Abram was still afraid of the king; and Terah came to see Abram his son secretly in the house of Noah, and Terah was very great in the eyes of the king.

Wow! This is incredible. After everything that had happened, Terah came to check on his son. After all the lies, worshipping false gods, getting angry with Abram, the death of his oldest son, the fear of Nimrod, the constant search for Abram, the die at any moment culture, the betrayal of the Sumerian sages who once celebrated him, etc., Terah was still a father. He could have easily turned his back on his son and never saw him again. He could have decided to join the search party to find Abram to have him killed so he could get back in good favor with the king and others. He could have just forgotten Abram and lived his life out with a whole different energy, but he didn't. Terah was a father, from the lineage of Shem, who was still living. Terah left his home in Ur, and found his son in the house of Noah in modern-day Turkey. He looked in a place that a father would, that soldiers wouldn't. Why is this important?

It's never too late, mom or dad, after whatever mistake(s) you may have made in the life of a child, you can ALWAYS look for them to set the record straight. Why? As Terah found out, at the end of the day, with humility and love, you are still a parent. Regardless of what a child thinks of you, adult or not, they still come from you. As long as you have breath in your body, you have a chance. Take it. Terah did.

Jasher 12: 64-69

And Abram said to his father, Dost thou not know that the king thinketh to slay me, and to annihilate my name from the earth by the advice of his wicked counsellors? 65. Now whom hast thou here and what hast thou in this land? Arise, let us go together to the land of Canaan, that we may be delivered from his hand, lest thou perish also through him in the latter days. 66. Dost thou not know or hast thou not heard, that it is not through love that Nimrod giveth thee all this honor, but it is only for his benefit that he bestoweth all this good upon thee? 67. And if he do unto thee greater good than this, surely these are only vanities of the world, for wealth and riches cannot avail in the day of wrath and anger. 68. Now therefore hearken to my voice, and let us arise and go to the land of Canaan, out of the reach of injury from Nimrod; and serve thou the Lord who created thee in the earth and it will be well with thee; and cast away all the vain things which thou pursuest. 69. And Abram ceased to speak, when Noah and his son Shem answered Terah, saying, True is the word which Abram hath said unto thee.

Humbled. This is how you humble yourself, parents, to get your children back. It's not just about going after them, but when you find them, be willing to listen to the perspective they give. Put your pride to the side and just listen. Your perspective may be valid and at some point, they need to be expressed. But this is a perfect example of how to humble yourself and just be available to hear and feel the pain of the perspective of your child. Abram gave Terah what we call a real talk session, man to man, son to father. Notice how Abram spoke with confidence and directness. He didn't bite his tongue, disrespect, show distain for, or anything negative towards his father. He could have chosen violence, but he didn't. He honored the house of Noah by speaking truth to his father Terah. He even challenged his father to leave the foolishness of this world behind and journey along with him to the land of Canaan, the land named after the same son that was cursed by Noah. Oh, and he said it in Noah's house! That's how bold Abram was. Shem, the founding father of the Semite people was sitting there observing the whole conversation and he agreed with Abram. Think about that for a second. The man who created the whole group of people that you descend from, hundreds of years old, sitting there and agreeing with your son and his perspective. To commend Terah, he said nothing, listened, and honored Shem by hearing Noah. This is how to correct a family issue such as this. It also shows the importance of having an elder available to hear a matter out for the embetterment of the family. It's so beautiful how the simple words of Shem's agreement with Abram caused the following...

Jasher 12:70

And Terah hearkened to the voice of his son Abram, and Terah did all that Abram said, for this was from the Lord, that the king should not cause Abram's death.

He listened. Dad, mom, he listened. If you are having an issue with a parent, please take this section and have a family reading session to lay the foundation for the conversation. If you are having an issue with connecting with a child, please take this section and humble yourself to this story. It's scripture based and it gives all the credit and glory to God for the opportunity to bring a family together as it should be. Abram didn't grow up in the house with Terah. Terah didn't really know his son. Abram disapproved of his father's lifestyle. Terah didn't approve of how Abram went about his business as well. Terah lied to protect his son as a newborn then lied to have his oldest son killed along with Abram to protect his own life. Abram destroyed property in his father's house that he didn't grow up in on his welcome back arrival in Ur. Whatever the case, Terah humbled himself and listened. He could've told his side, but he didn't. He didn't send Abram's mother to smooth the conversation over or anything like that. He went, by himself, AS A MAN, to take whatever came with the conversation: good, bad, or otherwise. This is a great example of redemption. How?

By Terah listening, the whole story of Abram takes off after this happens as you will read in the next section. Without Terah humbling himself, the story would have been different. By listening to the voice of his son, the whole world changed. To add another element to this amazing story and plan of family reconciliation, this was all done at Mt. Ararat, in Noah's house, in the land of Haran, the son that was killed in the fire of Ur.

In the land of his son that was lost, a son was found.

Again, look at how our God works on our behalf...if you let HIM.

Thanks, Terah.

Jasher 13:1

And Terah took his son Abram and his grandson Lot, the son of Haran, and Sarai his daughter-in-law, the wife of his son Abram, and all the souls of his household and went with them from Ur Casdim to go to the land of Canaan. And when they came as far as the land of Haran they remained there, for it was exceedingly good land for pasture, and of sufficient extent for those who accompanied them.

Death of Noah

Genesis 12:1
Now the LORD had said unto Abram, Get thee out of thy country, and from thy kindred, and from thy father's house, unto a land that I will shew thee:

Abram and his family, including his father Terah and nephew Lot, left Noah's home and settled in the land of his dead brother Haran in the north. To be clear, when the scripture says that they left Ur, it means that they did not return to Ur after Abram left to go hide in the house of Noah. While in Haran, the LORD spoke to Abram and told him to leave the land of his kindred to go to the land he will show him. That land was named Canaan, which was to the southeast of Haran. Abram obeyed and left Haran for Canaan.

Everyone didn't go to Canaan with Abram. His father Haran, brother Nahor, and nephew Lot remained in the land of their deceased brother. Meanwhile, the LORD called home the man that made the world a home to humanity again.

Ark remains at Mt. Ararat in Turkey
© NY Post

Jasher 13:9
At that time, at the end of three years of Abram's dwelling in the land of Canaan, in that year Noah died, which was the fifty-eighth year of the life of Abram; and all the days that Noah lived were nine hundred and fifty years and he died.

At the age of 58, Abram witnessed the death of the great Noah. The man who lived in accordance to the way of the LORD and teacher of HIS ways to Abram himself, Noah the obedient, died. He was 950 years old. Bravo and respect to his name, spirit, and contribution to the world. Because of his obedience and willingness to work, the world that we know and live in was preserved and allowed because of his decision to stick with God vs. the world and their gods. He was crucial in the development of Abram and his Godly worldview. Without Noah, the old world would have been forgotten as a teaching tool against idolatry. With Noah, the new world would not have an opportunity to know the real LORD of heaven. Thank you, father Noah, you were more than the builder of the ark. You gave us an opportunity to know God. That's an ark within itself. By your obedience, we learned that the ark was a precursor to Christ. Thank you, Amen!

Calling Abram

Isaiah 43:1

But now thus saith the LORD that created thee, O Jacob, and he that formed thee, O Israel, Fear not: for I have redeemed thee, I have called *thee* by thy name; thou *art* mine.

As Abram and Sarai lived in Canaan, Abram began to teach the Canaanites the ways of the LORD. Keep in mind, the sons of Canaan knew of the LORD via their grandfather, Noah, but they followed the ways of Nimrod their cousin. They worshiped many different gods, as they painted them on the walls of the caves they lived in and the cities they built. It is in this new land that Abram would plant the initial seeds of faith that would prove to be a global game changer.

Genesis 12: 7-8

And the LORD appeared unto Abram, and said, Unto thy seed will I give this land: and there builded he an altar unto the LORD, who appeared unto him. 8 And he removed from thence unto a mountain on the east of Bethel, and pitched his tent, having Bethel on the west, and Hai on the east: and there he builded an altar unto the LORD, and called upon the name of the LORD.

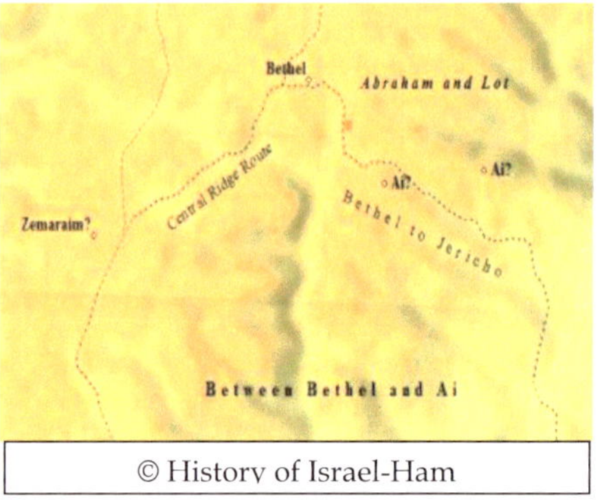

© History of Israel-Ham

Abram followed the ways of the LORD. He went when God said go. He listened, which is the key, he listened. God always prefer obedience over sacrifice. This is why God took Abram to the land between Bethel and Ai. It was here, in isolation, that God allowed Abram to make an altar to serve HIM. This encounter with the real God, the God of Noah and Shem, made Abram the man he would become. This is also a lesson for us all. When we are called to be separate from the world, don't look at it as punishment, but rather an opportunity to worship the LORD as Abram did. It was in this remote place, in the middle of nowhere, did God make a promise to Abram to give him the land to build his family on. In return, Abram built an altar, symbolizing the sacrifice of all after being promised the blessings of all, a family. A man who had no children of his own was promised land that would become the Promised Land. God making this promise to Abram was the fulfillment of the curse Noah placed on Canaan (Gen. 9: 20-29). See how God can turn a bad thing into a great thing? All you have to do is listen.

God has a unique way of doing things, especially when it comes to calling HIS chosen. Despite the fall of man, God chose the bloodline through which HE would dwell amongst us. When the whole of mankind became contaminated and almost destroyed by the Nephilim and Giants, it was through Noah and the Flood that God reestablished HIS will and way. By the names of men through the lineage of Adam to Noah, God showed what HIS plan was. Take a good look and see what the LORD was doing through the meaning of names...

Adam = Man

Seth = Appointed
Enosh = Mortal
Kenan = Sorrow, but
Mahalael = The Blessed God
Jared = Shall Come Down
Enoch = Teaching
Methuselah = His Death Shall Bring
Lamech = the Despairing
Noah = Comfort, Rest

M.I.P.
Man Appointed Mortal Sorrow, but The Blessed God Shall Come Down Teaching. His Death Shall Bring the Despairing Comfort, Rest

= Jesus the Christ

Methuselah is the key to the calling. He is the oldest living human to ever live, dying when he was 969 years old. He was also Noah' grandfather. Methuselah was a minister of God in the Earth when all of mankind turned against God. He lived during the age of the giants, which means this man had seen some things that we can only imagine. All of the people who followed God during that time died. Why? The LORD, in his mercy, took the Godly people away from the evil in the Earth to spare them from the Nephilim. Methuselah was the only one left, whose job was to preach the word and prophesy to the rest of humanity to repent.

Jasher 5: 5-10
And all who followed the Lord died in those days, before they saw the evil which God declared to do upon earth. 6 And after the lapse of many years, in the four hundred and eightieth year of the life of Noah, when all those men, who followed the Lord had died away from amongst the sons of men, and only Methuselah was then left, God said unto Noah and Methuselah, saying, 7 Speak ye, and proclaim to the sons of men, saying, Thus saith the Lord, return from your evil ways and forsake your works, and the Lord will repent of the evil that he declared to do to you, so that it shall not come to pass. 8 For thus saith the Lord, Behold I give you a period of one hundred and twenty years; if you will turn to me and forsake your evil ways, then will I also turn away from the evil which I told you, and it shall not exist, saith the Lord. 9 And Noah and Methuselah spoke all the words of the Lord to the sons of men, day after day, constantly speaking to them. 10 But the sons of men would not hearken to them, nor incline their ears to their words, and they were stiffnecked.

Methuselah preached until he died, seven days before the flood occurred. After the death of Methuselah, only Noah was left as righteous in the Earth. Then the flood happened. After the flood ended, Noah and family came out of the Ark at Mt. Ararat. This is where Noah stayed as his sons spread out into the new world. It is through Shem, the son of Noah, we get Abram. Through Abram, we eventually get the Christ, Jesus, who the lineage of Adam to Noah speaks about. It was the death of Methuselah that caused the flood to come about, which is why his name means '*his death shall bring*.' Just as Methuselah was called to preach, Noah was called to lead and live, and now, Abram was called to set a new course of obedience in the Earth for mankind. This is why God had to take Abram to an isolated place to reveal to him HIS plan to fulfill HIS promise and showcase HIS power. It was all a plan, which began before the world was created.

That's why when God calls, you have no choice but to listen to HIM.

2 Timothy 1:9
Who hath saved us, and called us with an holy calling, not according to our works, but according to his own purpose and grace, which was given us in Christ Jesus before the world began,

Meanwhile…

In Egypt

© National Geographic Education

© Univ. of Chicago

© British Museum

Origin of Pharaoh

Reader, this section will be an explosive one to read. Why? Because it will counter what has been taught for hundreds of years from historical scholars about Egyptian history. As a lover of history itself, especially Egyptian history, understanding the origins of the Egyptian way of life is always fun to read and learn about. You read about the many different gods, their perspective of how they created the world and the things in it, and how they decided to center the world along the Nile River. You read about the different dynasties, their rise and fall, so far and so on. Again, it's fascinating information! When you read the stories and majestic hieroglyphics, one can become engulfed in the beauty of a people who left behind so many artifacts of their existence, past, power, and believed future, which is incredible.

The story of their existence is highlighted in the position of the rulers of Egypt and the power they held to uphold the civilization and its place in the world. These rulers, who are the most remembered of Egyptian history outside of the staggering pyramids and belief structure, always seem to be iconic whether their reign is long or short-lived. Many of them, like Thutmoses III and Ramses, are some of the most studied historical figures worldwide for their attributes to society and governmental political structure. In history, these rulers began as kings then became what we know as pharaohs, which is where we will shift our focus for this particular section. This is where we jump in and begin the process of understanding why and how the term pharaoh came about, who was the first, and how the office of pharaoh in Egypt connect all future rulers to Nimrod. Also, you will see how the position of the ruler of Egypt is important in the big picture of history, both for Christ and the Anti-Christ. Buckle up.

We have previously learned that the man who settled Egypt (post-flood), from which comes the name Egypt, is Mizraim, the son of Ham, the son of Noah. Mizraim means distress, which is both the Aramaic and Hebrew name for Egypt. It has been called many different names throughout history, like Kemet (meaning the 'black land'), but the biblical name of the country in the most north-eastern corner of Africa is called Egypt.

Egypt, an African Country
© BBC

Before we move forward, we must give you some information then 'Make It Plain' for you to understand how science, history, and scripture coincide with one another to give you a clear picture of what you are reading about the origin of Egyptian civilization. I know, in most scholarly arenas, these three don't normally agree. But we are looking through the lenses of Truth to see something special, as a teachable moment, where all three mix.

According to Jimmy Dunn, writer of The Origin of Egyptian Civilization for TourEgypt.net,

"The Egyptologists of the early 20th century concluded that the classic ancient Egyptian civilization had been brought to the Nile Valley by a "dynastic race" of invaders. They believed that the invaders were both culturally and politically superior to the native Prehistoric Egyptians, and that they swiftly established themselves as rulers of the country. At the time, the dubious science of cranial metrology, that is, using skull measurements to attempt to determine racial characteristics, was fashionable. It was also used in support of this "superior race" theory in Egypt."

Science and history both agree that a "superior" race ruled early Egypt. This so-called superior race was Mizraim and his sons, as the Bible calls them the sons of Ham (meaning Ham's bloodline). They were considered superior because of their knowledge and advancement in civilization.

What's important to understand is that there were a small group of people already living in the area of Egypt, not calling themselves Egyptians. The incoming sons of Mizraim are the reason the inhabitants of this area of Africa were called Egyptians. This should not be puzzling due to the fact that Mizraim and his sons learned from their father Cush, the creator of the Mesopotamian/Sumerian civilization in modern-day Iraq. The origin of a new post-flood societal structure was learned then passed down to these men. The language they spoke was a different dialect than those surrounding them because of the confusion of the languages at the Tower of Babel. Their knowledge of how to build, organize, teach, and preserve civilization all come from the kingdom of Shinar's ruler, the Tower of Babel's builder, Mizraim's nephew, Nimrod.

Genesis 11:9

Therefore is the name of it called Babel; because the LORD did there confound the language of all the earth: and from thence did the LORD scatter them abroad upon the face of all the earth.

Why is this important to know? Because men of history who become rulers of nations learn and adopt these principles and information then use them to take, maintain, and or enhance their agenda of ruling the world. They repeat history because they know that people don't read or pay attention to history. As a history teacher, I learned that kids turn off learning history for a few reasons, mainly because they claim that it's boring. They have no idea that none of the other subjects in education matter without history remembering them or keeping record of the importance of that subject relative to the present or future. This is why history matters to the top minds on the planet, they know it's the secret sauce. What may be new to you is old news to world leaders. For example, Adolf Hitler used this knowledge and phraseology to create a concept of a 'superior' or 'master' race to exterminate millions of Jewish people. He taught the German people that they were descendants of a once superior race and their time to ascend to rulership had finally come to pass. They were taught that they were the greater seed of man, higher knowledge-minded, most advanced, spiritually greater, civilization creators and destroyers. This is what he instilled, amongst many other concepts, all of which come from studying Nimrod and Egyptian history. This is also a reason why Hitler invaded Egypt during World War 2. So yes, reading this information is very important to know.

Jimmy Dunn also states..

"These superior, invading people were believed to have come from a land to the east of Egypt, reflecting the widespread view that the Orient was a primary source of early culture. The royal art of Egypt during the 1st Dynasty was thought to be similar to that found in Mesopotamia, and so many believed that the earliest kings of Egypt came from present day Iraq."

Mesopotamia/Sumer/Shinar is "East" of Egypt
© WordPress Ancient Mesopotamians

Again, history and science agrees with scripture in our findings that these 'invaders' that settled Egypt and created a political rulership came from "east of Egypt". If you look at the map of the middle east, Mesopotamia or modern-day Iraq is East of Egypt.

The Fertile Crescent civilization of the Sumerians is historically known as the 1st civilization in the world. The people that spread out from the Tower of Babel's fall allowed for small groups of people to go to different regions of the world, like Egypt, to establish themselves. A larger group of people coming in to establish themselves as rulers and politically structured would be viewed as invaders or different. So yes, history, science, and scripture agree. Boom!

Narmer Tablet
© Khan Academy

The first king of Egypt is believed in legend and history to be called Narmer, the catfish king. He is described as a leader that subjugated the smaller groups of people living in Upper and Lower Egypt. You can find the record of his takeover and ascent to power on the Narmer Tablet. He's called the catfish king for two reasons, which are very important to understanding the narrative of how the pharaoh position came to be in world history.
Catfish are scavengers. They feed on small, dying, or dead fish. They know how to rise to becoming the biggest fish in a small pond rather quickly, which is why catfish are in abundance in the wild. This was the identity of Narmer's rise to power. He fed on the smaller groups of inhabitants in Egypt, taking over rather quickly, using the spoils of war to become the king.

Narmer, however, was not his real name. Like several other figures in history, taking on another name is normal, especially if you are a ruler. Catfishing people or appearing to be someone then actually looking or being opposite of what you project, in this world today, is also called catfishing. That was Narmer, the catfish king. He was known as Narmer, but in reality, he was Mizraim, the man whom Egypt is named after. As history has shown us and the Narmer tablet exemplifies, he came from the east as a conqueror then became a ruler and builder of a nation. He established civilization as the father of a historically rich culture.

Establishing Egypt along the Nile River was not the work of a single man. It took many years and many hands to establish the Egypt that history remembers. Mizraim had help establishing his domain and we know who helped him. Just as he learned from Cush and Nimrod, his brother and nephew, establishing a kingdom is easier done when having family that are trustworthy around you to help build your infrastructure. Mizraim, a father of 7 sons, allowed them to settle alongside him to create borders of small tribes to carve out their land. The objective was for the groups to protect one another as one, regardless of political rise and fall, thus protecting the land of their father, as one people. They would come to settle different regions around their father's land, but they would always be interconnected with Egypt being the land of their father.

1 Chronicles 1: 11-12

And Mizraim begat Ludim, and Anamim, and Lehabim, and Naphtuhim, 12 And Pathrusim, and Casluhim, (of whom came the Philistines,) and Caphthorim.

As you see, 7 sons, unique in name and purpose. Now, let's take a look at who they were, what their name means, what tribe or nation did they become, and what's noteworthy about them.

Biblical Name	Meaning	Ancient Group	Noteworthy
Ludim	nativity	Lydians,	Mercenaries for Egypt (Jer. 46:9)
*Anamim	responding waters (tribal)	unknown,	intermixed

Lehabim	flames, swords	(tribal) intermixed with the Libyans
Naphtuhim	*engravers (Egyptians)*	*known as the true Egyptians*
Pathrusim	mouthful of dough (Pathrosites)	lived in Upper Egypt (south)
Casluhim	fortified (Philistines)	warlike, coastal people
Caphthorim	a crown (Cretans)	coastal people, settled Crete

Now, let's take a look at where these sons settled, geographically, to give a better understanding of how these brothers helped to solidify Egypt as a nation.

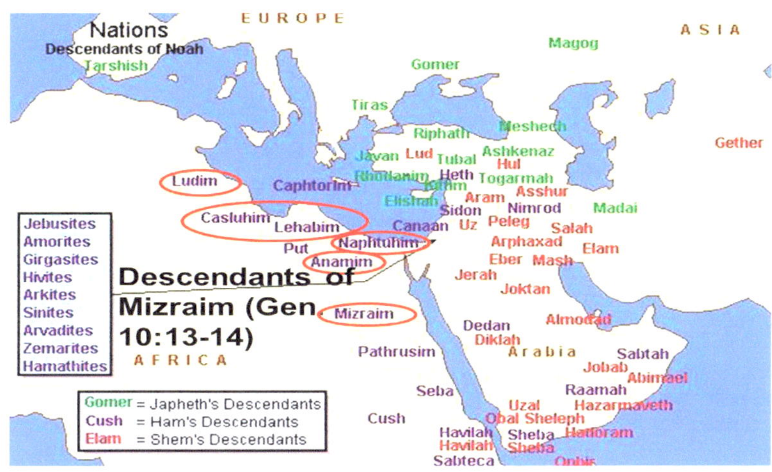

After the rule of Narmer (Mizraim) or Menes, the establishment of the Egyptian way of life took off. In the Egyptian book of kings, this time period is considered the 1st dynasty. Narmer ruled then gave his kingdom over to one of his sons, Anamim, who intermixed with his brothers. The Anamim settled in the plush Nile Delta in the north next to the beautiful Mediterranean Sea.

Upon accepting the land of Egypt as his to rule, Anamim decided to follow his father in changing or adding a name to his own. This process of name changes in Egypt will come to be called a nebty name, which gives a ruler 5 royal names. Anamim would officially change his name to Anom.

Jasher 7:11

And the sons of Mitzraim were Lud, Anom and Pathros, Chasloth and Chaphtor.

Genesis 10: 13-14

And Mizraim begat Ludim, and Anamim, and Lehabim, and Naphtuhim, 14And Pathrusim, and Casluhim, (out of whom came Philistim,) and Caphtorim.

1 Chronicles 1: 11-12

And Mizraim begat Ludim, and Anamim, and Lehabim, and Naphtuhim, 12 And Pathrusim, and Casluhim, (of whom came the Philistines,) and Caphthorim.

M.I.P.

Anamim = Anom

Amen, let us continue.

As Anom began to rule, he too established his kingdom and the belief structures of his father. The belief in Egyptian religious customs, better known as the Egyptian Pantheon of gods, continued. Narmer continued polygamy in Egypt the same way he learned it in Mesopotamia, except he changed the names and other minut details of worship which is what separates Babylonian deities from the Egyptian gods. We will get into that later. Anom became known for his many religious activities and reforms within Kemet to enhance the power and presence of the 'gods' in the people's common day-to-day life. This is huge when considering how the position of Pharaoh came to be more of a religious title over the political title of king. In history, you won't find him as Anom, but by one of his other names, one of which is Hor-Aha. In Greek, he is called Athotis. He will later become deified as a god because of his religious and scientific work. He led a few building projects but working in secret or obscurity became his signature. His rule as king of Egypt is remembered as a time of religious enhancement. As the son of Narmer (Mizraim), he had his tomb built adjacent to his father's, which is in the necropolis of the kings of the 1st Dynasty at Abydos.

King Hor-Aha Inscription
© Ancient Egypt Online

Tomb of King Hor-Aha at Abydos
© Tour Egypt

Anamim = Anom = Hor-Aha = Athotis

It is here where we can dive into the origin of pharaoh. Prior to this time, the rulers of Egypt were called kings, ruling in a governmental and political sense of the word. The priest ruled in the temples and places of worship. The priest had their place and the king held his. They were not co-joined. Narmer (Mizraim) is the 1st king to unite both the Upper and Lower lands of Egypt into one, his sons and the smaller groups that he conquered. His son Anamim or Anom continued his father's work, just in a different way, by unifying the north and south through religious works. Narmer could be called the 1st pharaoh, as many scholars have over the years, but he was not officially seen in that light according to scripture which shows a distinct difference in tag and title. It is here where we discover a hidden in plain sight secret that will make your biblical reading of scripture easy to diagnose regarding Egypt.

Jasher 14:1

In those days there was in the land of Shinar a wise man who had understanding in all wisdom, and of a beautiful appearance, but he was poor and indigent; his name was Rikayon and he was hard set to support himself.

Rikayon was a Sumerian man, from the land of Shinar, which means he was a man living in the kingdom of Nimrod. The descriptions of him was that he was a wise man who understood the concept of wisdom in all things plus he was an attractive man to look at. This is VERY important to know for our final destination within this section and the overall scope of Nimrod's influence. If Rikayon' attributes were on a dating site, he would receive all kinds of attention and direct messages for his positives. The problem someone would encounter with him once they actually get to know him would be the negatives, which are just as impactful and glaring. Just as many people choose to overlook the negatives and attach themselves to the positives throughout history, but this section, I hope, serves as a warning to those who do so or are in danger of devastation. Pleases look at the whole picture of a person first before making a life decision. We'll explain.

Jasher 14:1 says Rikayon' was poor and indigent, which means to feel or show anger because of something unjust or unworthy. It means he was poor, financially, and lived in an angry spirit because he felt as though life had been unjust towards him. Sure, he was wise and had the capabilities to be compensated for his gift if placed in the right position, but his place in the world at the time, in Nimrod's kingdom, was to be a poor but wise man. To be clear, there is nothing wrong with being a man of common living yet wise in the eyes of God and those you matter to. But, to some people, like Rikayon, that wasn't enough. His inability to support himself or pay for a comfortable life was too much for him to handle. This is a psychological breeding ground for change in a person's life. Either a person will change for the better or change for the worse. Most life stories of people going from rags to riches begin at this place in one's mind. On the contrary, so does self-implosion and deep depression. It's a thin line.

Jasher 14:2

And he resolved to go to Egypt, to Oswiris the son of Anom king of Egypt, to show the king his wisdom; for perhaps he might find grace in his sight, to raise him up and give him maintenance; and Rikayon did so.

As we see, another king has now come to power in Egypt. Anom at this point had given his kingdom to Oswiris, his son, to be king over Egypt. Oswiris, as his father before him, is historically called by a different name. That name is Djer.

M.I.P.

Oswiris = Djer

King Djer Inscription

© Tour Egypt

Oswiris, historically, was known for his militaric mind and introduction of human sacrifice in religious festivals. He was the first recorded ruler to record his battles outside of Egypt (inscription at Wadi Halfa). One of the most important things to know about Oswiris, outside of his thirst for human sacrifice, was that he created a textbook about anatomy that was found and used by the Greeks, who used Egyptian science to create their schools. He was deeply associated with the study of the dead, the underworld, and all things relating to the human body. Yes, this was a clever, smart, powerful human being, but he had a dark side, a very dark side. Osiris, the god of the underworld, who's symbolized in Egyptian religion to represent death, resurrection, and agricultural fertility, tomb was discovered in 1898 by a poor French archaeologist Emile Amelineau. His discovery of the 'Tomb of Osiris' was later to be found out to be the actual tomb of Djer, which the book of Jasher calls Oswiris. Reader, do you think that Oswiris and Osiris, both lovers of the dead, both teachers of how the underworld works, both rulers of Egypt, both lovers of human anatomy, both worshipped in Egypt, are two different people? Do you find it a coincidence that both share the same tomb? Let's continue.

As we see in Jasher 14:2, it was during Oswiris' reign that Rikayon decided to leave the land of Nimrod in Shinar and venture to Egypt to possibly improve his life. He decided to use his wisdom for a price and power, which was valued among the sons of Mizraim who were carving out their own space in the world. This led Rikayon to leave Shinar and go southwest into Egypt.

Jasher 14: 3-4

And when Rikayon came to Egypt he asked the inhabitants of Egypt concerning the king, and the inhabitants of Egypt told him the custom of the king of Egypt, for it was then the custom of the king of Egypt that he went from his royal palace and was seen abroad only one day in the year, and after that the king would return to his palace to remain there. 4. And on the day when the king went forth he passed judgment in the land, and every one having a suit came before the king that day to obtain his request. And when Rikayon heard of the custom in Egypt and that he could not come into the presence of the king, he grieved greatly and was very sorrowful.

Upon arriving in Egypt, Rikayon inquired about the king from the Kemetic people themselves. This was very important for his strategy on how to improve his life situation after his move to the black land. When he found out that the king only showed himself to the people once a year, his feelings were hurt and his plan deeply disrupted. He needed exposure for the chance at opportunity. Without it, his plan meant nothing. But why?

Oswiris followed in the customs of his father, Anom or Hor-Aha, who was known for being an obscure or hidden king. Remember the dark side of Oswiris, how he dealt in darkness and human sacrifice practices. He was not a man of the people to be seen and heard openly. This was a culture shock for Rikayon who was used to the culture of Nimrod, who was visible before men in Shinar. Nimrod was known to the world as a king but before that, a mighty hunter before the LORD in the Earth. Also keep in mind that Nimrod invited the whole world to the Tower of Babel to see him and his great work, which took years to complete. So yes, only seeing the king 1 time a year, in passing, was a huge culture shock for Rikayon or any outsider who was not used to the Egyptian way of life. With the king being out of reach, so was his chance of leaving poverty.

Jasher 14: 6-9

And in the evening Rikayon went out and found a house in ruins, formerly a bake house in Egypt, and he abode there all night in bitterness of soul and pinched with hunger, and sleep was removed from his eyes. 7. And Rikayon considered within himself what he should do in the town until the king made his appearance, and how he might maintain himself there. 8. And he rose in the morning and walked about, and met in his way those who sold vegetables and various sorts of seed with which they supplied the inhabitants. 9. And Rikayon wished to do the same in order to get a maintenance in the city, but he was unacquainted with the custom of the people, and he was like a blind man among them.

When you don't know, you don't know. This part of the story sounds like the age-old stories of actors and actresses who ventured to Hollywood, thinking they would become the world's next star. They get there, see how different of a culture it is than where they come from, then face a decision: do I assimilate or vacate. This is the very decision the wise, good looking, yet angry man Rikayon faced. He chose to assimilate. Instead of quitting, he decided to figure out a way to survive through the year until the time of the king's passing. He saw how the marketers bought and sold one to another, making a way for themselves. He figured he could do it, but because he wasn't Egyptian and didn't know all the customs of the land, he felt as a blind man among them. He needed to find a way to connect with the people so he could sustain himself until the opportunity presented itself. This would require patience, work, and more importantly, a new plan of action.

Jasher 14: 10-13

And he went and obtained vegetables to sell them for his support, and the rabble assembled about him and ridiculed him, and took his vegetables from him and left him nothing. 11. And he rose up from there in bitterness of soul, and went sighing to the bake house in which he had remained all the night before, and he slept there the second night. 12. And on that night again he reasoned within himself how he could save himself from starvation, and he devised a scheme how to act.

Wow. Rikayon tried the right way. He tried. He tried to sale vegetables to make a living, but because he didn't know the customs of the land and people, he was an unwanted competitor in the market. The people who saw what he was doing came and took his vegetables and way of making a living away from him. He wasn't one of them. Rikayon had to go back to the vacant baker's shop with no food, no way of making a living, no plan. It was in his hunger, his anger, his despair, his rejection, his bitterness, and his frustration, a new plan was devised. This is dangerous territory for any person to be in. Making a plan from this state of mind usually yields a dangerous result and this situation is no different. In fact, the world will forever be changed from a decision made in a vacant bakery in Egypt on a day that is not remembered in history.

Jasher 14: 14-15

And he rose up in the morning and acted ingeniously, and went and hired thirty strong men of the rabble, carrying their war instruments in their hands, and he led them to the top of the Egyptian sepulchre, and he placed them there. 14. And he commanded them, saying, Thus saith the king, Strengthen yourselves and be valiant men, and let no man be buried here until two hundred pieces of silver be given, and then he may be buried; and those men did according to the order of Rikayon to the people of Egypt the whole of that year. 15. And in eight months time Rikayon and his men gathered great riches of silver and gold, and Rikayon took a great quantity of horses and other animals, and he hired more men, and he gave them horses and they remained with him.

The power of a good lie can make you rich if you are willing to empower those around you for your personal gain. This is exactly what Rikayon did. He used his wisdom to twist a situation to his benefit. Nowadays, it's called simply called business. Verse 14 says he 'acted ingenuiously', which means to have or show an unusual aptitude for discovering, inventing, or contriving. He created a plan to use the name of the king, Oswiris, to limit people from burying their own in this Egyptian graveyard or tomb. This is very clever, although contrived with a lie. He hired 30 men, although he had no money, to stop the people from being able to bury their dead in peace, which is a top priority in Egyptian culture. This is very insightful, very shrewd. Again, keep in mind the connection between Oswiris and Osiris with the dead.

Osiris

In Egyptian culture, if you don't know anything else, you understand that the burying of the dead and how you honor them is top of their list in respecting culture. Although the pyramids at that time weren't built as they are today, if you were living in the known world at that time you would know about the importance of burying the dead for families in Egypt. If you knew anything about the king, Oswiris, you would know of his love or thirst for the dark side of life which is death and all the sinister practices involved. Again, Oswiris was well versed in human sacrifice as a custom. Picking up on these facts then using it to your benefit to create revenue was very deceitful but lucrative for Rikayon. He went from earning silver and gold to livestock. With his newly acquired wealth, he empowered his workers with domesticated horses which was seen as an object of power amongst the common people. All of his riches gained came from lying on the king.

Jasher 14: 16-20

And when the year came round, at the time the king went forth into the town, all the inhabitants of Egypt assembled together to speak to him concerning the work of Rikayon and his men. 17. And the king went forth on the appointed day, and all the Egyptians came before him and cried unto him, saying, 18. May the king live forever. What is this thing thou doest in the town to thy servants, not to suffer a dead body to be buried until so much silver and gold be given? Was there ever the like unto this done in the whole earth, from the days of former kings yea even from the days of Adam, unto this day, that the dead should not be buried only for a set price? 19. We know it to be the custom of kings to take a yearly tax from the living, but thou dost not only do this, but from the dead also thou exactest a tax day by day. 20. Now, O king, we can no more bear this, for the whole city is ruined on this account, and dost thou not know it?

The time had come for the king to pass by and get a report of this town within his kingdom. The feedback given to him was not good. They let him know that the people have become impoverished due to a tax of the dead, which was not a custom of the Egyptian kings that came before him nor the kings they've heard of in other kingdoms. This wasn't even a custom of the pre-flood nations going all the way back to Adam, the father of all men. Yes, the Egyptians were aware of Adam, the first man.

This new tax was devastating the economy of this town and they could not sustain life with the heavy responsibility placed on them by the government mixing into a religious affair, which is the key point of this whole event. The people were alleging there was a governmental decree, via the king, that interfered with a religious event, which was not the responsibility of the king as he was not the final voice on religious affairs. That duty belonged to the high priest and his priests. Take note, this is an example of the recognition of the separation between church and state, thousands of years before the Europeans even thought to do so.

Jasher 14: 21-23

And when the king heard all that they had spoken he was very wroth, and his anger burned within him at this affair, for he had known nothing of it. 22. And the king said, Who and where is he that dares to do this wicked thing in my land without my command? Surely you will tell me. 23. And they told him all the works of Rikayon and his men, and the king's anger was aroused, and he ordered Rikayon and his men to be brought before him.

The king was hot! He was upset and angry! Rightfully so. His name, which meant power to the people, was being misused. This was a major violation in Egyptian society. Using the king's name for personal gain was a strike against the government itself, which is treason. The idea of doing such a thing meant death, immediately. This is why Oswiris, when hearing about this act, was wroth in anger because he knew what this meant and the optics thereof. He asked and the people told him who Rikayon was, what he did, and how he had gained riches. To add insult to injury, Rikayon did so in just 8 months' time. This angered the king and he sent for Rikayon. Normally, this would instill fear in someone, especially in ancient Egypt, but this was all a part of the plan Rikayon devised in his anger and rejection....in a vacant bakery.

Jasher 14:24

And Rikayon took about a thousand children, sons and daughters, and clothed them in silk and embroidery, and he set them upon horses and sent them to the king by means of his men, and he also took a great quantity of silver and gold and precious stones, and a strong and beautiful horse, as a present for the king, with which he came before the king and bowed down to the earth before him; and the king, his servants and all the inhabitants of Egypt wondered at the work of Rikayon, and they saw his riches and the present that he had brought to the king.

Flattery. Good old-fashioned flattery with a touch of deception. The king was in a trap and didn't realize it. This town, which had become poor and angry, was given a display of riches that both fooled them and cooled their anger, simultaneously. Take note of the deception: Rikayon used their children, about 1000 of them, and clothed them in beautiful silks and other fabrics, sat them on horses which represented power, and sent them one by one to the king, putting on a whole display of a perception of how Egyptians should or could look with the right person in charge. He included precious stones and a beautiful horse as a gift, special for the king himself. When it was his turn to present himself to the king, he came and bowed as a sign of the utmost respect to the man that he had plotted to see for almost a year. This great showcase of wealth and the idea of what a little town of people could be as a representative of the nation won over the minds of the same people that were angry with Rikayon. By telling an ugly lie, he used the beautiful things of the world to win over the same people who wanted to kill him by using their children as bargaining chips for his opportunity to never be broke again. Remember, this plan was created in anger and frustration in an abandoned baker's building in a small town of Egypt by a man who was poor and angry but wise and good looking. He was now in front of the king and he had his full attention. Mission accomplished.

Jasher 14: 25-26

And it greatly pleased the king and he wondered at it; and when Rikayon sat before him the king asked him concerning all his works, and Rikayon spoke all his words wisely before the king, his servants and all the inhabitants of Egypt. 26. And when the king heard the words of Rikayon and his wisdom, Rikayon found grace in his sight, and he met with grace and kindness from all the servants of the king and from all the inhabitants of Egypt, on account of his wisdom and excellent speeches, and from that time they loved him exceedingly.

The lie payed off. The king loved the message and the idea of what Rikayon offered him. The explanation of his process sealed the deal for the king, showcasing Rikayon' wisdom. He used a lie to get in the door of the hearts of people, to get an interview with the king, smoothed over his possible position in the presence of all the king's men, and just like that, he was in. Sounds a lot like our present-day capitalistic business structure. Wall Street tactics. Do whatever you need to do, at the expense of people, ethics, and morality, just to get rich or in the presence of riches. Capitalize for yourself at all costs for self-gain. Nevermind you use children to smooth over you transition. Nevermind you planned this with anger, frustration, and bitterness. Nevermind you became rich on other people's death and burial procedures. Nevermind any of that. The only thing that matters is winning at all costs and being placed in a better position than you were. Yes, reader, I hope you are starting to see why this book needed to be written, this section needed to be explained, and the perspective of how treacherous business in this world has a horrible root in world history. There is nothing new underneath the sun. What you and I see today has been going on for thousands of years.

Now strap your seatbelt on tight, the following verses are going to validate this section and introduce you to a term you have seen and used in school since you were a child. You have seen movies and images all your life of a certain person in a position of power called a certain name thinking that it is associated with power. Read carefully...

Jasher 14:27

And the king answered and said to Rikayon, Thy name shall no more be called Rikayon but **Pharaoh shall be thy name, since thou didst exact a tax from the dead**; and he called his name **Pharaoh**.

Boom! Here it is. The term Pharaoh was created for Rikayon. King Oswiris created the name Pharaoh because Rikayon found a way to tax the dead and their families, which is a separate economy unto itself. For that name, he is called Pharaoh. Wow! This is amazing!

The term pharaoh in the modern Merriam-Webster dictionary means a ruler of ancient Egypt. The position became known as both the governmental and religious leader of the people. In fact, Pharaoh became defined as the 'Lord of the Two Lands' and 'High Priest of Every Temple', meaning he was responsible for the entirety of Egypt (Upper and Lower) plus he had the final say on all religious worship in the kingdom. By the time the Greeks came to know what the Pharaoh was, they defined the name to mean the 'Great House' or pero, indicating he is the living and moving royal residence or palace of Egypt. The term Pharaoh would later be adopted by the ruler of Egypt within himself, not as a separate entity. The idea and office of pharaoh had just begun, created by Oswiris and worn by Rikayon.

Before we proceed, we must stop for a second and address a key question that may be going through your mind considering Rikayon: was the 1st Pharaoh of Egypt Egyptian or not? Good question, here's the answer. King Oswiris was Egyptian. The term Pharaoh is Egyptian. But, Rikayon was from the land of Shinar, which was in the kingdom of Nimrod. Rikayon would have been considered a Sumerian or Cushite, a black man. Obviously, the Egyptians, which are African, were and still are what westerners call black people. The office of Pharaoh is Egyptian and is associated or defined as being Egyptian, but the first person to hold that office was not. They were kindred peoples, but not the same tribal group. Both were from the sons of Ham, which means sunburnt, but from different sons of Ham's bloodline. Rikayon was not Egyptian, but he became the 1st Pharaoh, an Egyptian office of supreme power in Egypt.

Jasher 14: 28-29

And the king and his subjects loved Rikayon for his wisdom, and they
consulted with all the inhabitants of Egypt to make him prefect under the king.
29. And all the inhabitants of Egypt and its wise men did so, and it was made a
law in Egypt.

Notice the Serpent over the 3rd Eye
© Britannica

The cleverness of Rikayon, like a serpent, was working. He was accepted and revered by the Egyptians, who were lovers of all religions and wisdom. Laws were passed to validate his position so no one could question the man. Rikayon went from being poor and good looking to being rich, untouchable, and good looking in the eyes of the people of Egypt. All of this happened because of his serpent-like behavior. Coincidentally, this same type of behavior was worn on the head by every Pharaoh, right in front of the Pineal Gland or as the world calls it, the 3rd eye. The serpent wraps his body around the head of the Pharaoh, representing the cunningness or "wisdom" of the Pharaoh. The craftiness of the serpent is more impactful than all the other animals that God created on this planet. Sounds familiar?

Genesis 3:1

Now the serpent was more subtil than any beast of the field which the LORD God had made. And he said unto the woman, Yea, hath God said, Ye shall not eat of every tree of the garden?

For the record, the term subtil means cunning, crafty, elusive. This is what the serpent represents. It sits in front of the 3rd eye, better known as the all-seeing eye, which is taught to be the mind's eye or the place in the brain where humans get their spiritual connections, perceptions, and or awareness. It's taught to be the gateway into a higher intelligence of self. In anatomy, as you learned Oswiris and his father Anom were lovers of, the pineal gland (3rd eye) is in the center in of the brain and is vital to the whole of the body. Zawn Villines wrote in an article for *Medical News Today*, which was medically reviewed by Dr. E. Luo,...

"The pineal gland is key to the body's internal clock because it regulates the body's circadian rhythms. Circadian rhythms are the daily rhythms of the body, including signals that make someone feel tired, sleep, wake up, and feel alert around the same time each day. The pineal gland , which is a hormone that helps regulate circadian rhythms. Melatonin is produced according to the amount of light a person is exposed to. The pineal gland releases greater amounts of melatonin when it is dark, which points to melatonin's role in sleep. Many supplement manufacturers offer melatonin as a "natural" sleep aid."

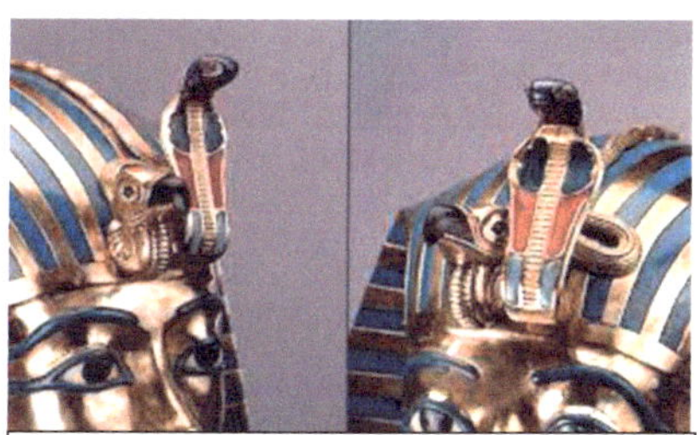

The Uraeus
© Egyptian History

In different cultures, the 3rd eye is described to have many different religious uses, which was first instituted by the Egyptians, namely Pharaoh. In ancient Indian cultures, it is described as the anja or 6th chakra, meaning a center of higher consciousness. The same is believed in Tao or Daoism in Japan. Hindus place a dot there and call it the tilaka, which is an expression of the supreme god Shiva. Buddhists consider it the place from which enlightenment comes 1st. Regardless, they all stem from the Egyptian belief as the source of empowerment and recognition of this body part as a connection to a higher self or spiritual world. Again, the Pharaoh would wear a serpent around the head, in front of the 3rd eye, to represent his cunningness and ability to control, see, and be the higher consciousness on Earth as the 'Lord of the Two Lands of Egypt', which they believed to be the center of the world. This all started with Rikayon, the wise and good-looking, angry liar who became the first Pharaoh. The serpent on the headdress is called the uraeus.

But wait, there's more.

Jasher 14:30

And they made Rikayon Pharaoh prefect under Oswiris king of Egypt, and Rikayon Pharaoh governed over Egypt, daily administering justice to the whole city, but Oswiris the king would judge the people of the land one day in the year, when he went out to make his appearance.

Prefect means a chief officer or magistrate within a government. In ancient Egypt, this office meant he was an untouchable person that only the king himself had more power than. Although this was a very dangerous position to place Rikayon in, the people loved him. They overlooked how he moved into his position of power via deceit. They accepted his shrewd deeds based on how good he could talk, how good he looked, and how he assimilated into the Egyptian belief structure by learning the ways of the dead. They overlooked his beautiful lie. By making him Pharaoh, he was given the permission to govern Egypt daily while the king could go into obscurity and only judge the people as a whole one day a year. By his positioning, he had become the ruler of Egypt, the ultimate judge over their day-to-day lives. Wow. All birthed from a beautiful lie, rooted in anger and frustration.

This, as you can probably see coming, was the end of the reign of Oswiris. Rikayon was crafty, cunning, and in his position as prefect of Egypt, he was in a position to do as he pleased. He could have stopped here and played his part within the kingdom, but ambition was in his heart from his start all the way back in Shinar with Nimrod. Again, his deeper, darker plan, made in anger, was playing itself out. Watch how the mind of a serpent works now that it sees a crack in the door to possible power.

Jasher 14:31

And Rikayon Pharaoh cunningly usurped the government of Egypt, and he exacted a tax from all the inhabitants of Egypt.

You cannot make this up. You see it for yourself. From ragged to ruler, anger to absolute, poor to power. This is how the cunning ability of the serpent to smoothly wrap itself around the mind of a person, using God given wisdom to create devastation and anti-God type behavior to gain power. A serpent will wrap itself around its prey and squeeze the life out of it so it can devour the carcass, whole. This story is no different. Rikayon took power from the king and taxed everyone in Egypt, not just the people in the town or the families of the dead, but everyone. At this point he was now the ruler over the government and the religious affairs of Egypt, which by modern definition describes the office of Pharaoh. The serpent was now ruler in Egypt.

Jasher 14: 32-33

And all the inhabitants of Egypt greatly loved Rikayon Pharaoh, and they made a decree to call every king that should reign over them and their seed in Egypt, Pharaoh. 33. Therefore all the kings that reigned in Egypt from that time forward were called Pharaoh unto this day.

One man, in the kingdom of Nimrod, went to his Egyptian neighbors, and had a position created for him that changed the world: Pharaoh. It's mischievous how he gained his power, but what's worse is that the people loved it. Do not consider this strange. God himself said..

Jeremiah 5: 30-31

A wonderful and horrible thing is committed in the land; 31 The prophets prophesy falsely, and the priests bear rule by their means; and my people love to have it so: and what will ye do in the end thereof?

God himself said that the people love liars. That people love to have it so. They love to be lied to. They love to have someone over them that are supposed to be doing right, lie to them and mislead them. They love to have priests, which are representative of preachers, prophets, etc., lie as their leaders. Look at the world today, is that not true? Look at the ancient world, was that not true? Look at the story of Rikayon, is this not true? Verses 32 and 33 in Jasher 14 clearly states that all the people in Egypt loved Rikayon. They loved him and accepted his behavior, even though he was a liar and usurper of authority. They made a decree, which lasted all the way to Cleopatra VII, the last true Pharaoh of Egypt. She too wore the serpent around her head, in front of the all-seeing eye, which has come to be known as the eye of Horus. Some scholars say Caesarion, the son of Julius Caesar and Cleopatra VII was the last Pharaoh of Egypt, but he was assassinated at an early age of 17 and ruled under the thumb of Rome, which is not really the office of a true Pharaoh. Regardless, they all wore the term, tag, title, and responsibility of being ruler of the people of Egypt. The office did expand as more Pharaohs had more responsibilities and religious obligations, but the very office of Pharaoh is rooted in deception, cunningness, ambition, and power.

Pharaoh Cleopatra VII
© Live Science

The title Pharaoh is mentioned 94 times in Genesis and 115 times in Exodus. Whereas the writers of the Bible never tell you the name of the Pharaoh, the emphasis is on the office and responsibilities of Pharaoh. This is very intentional. In my book *Biblical Black History: The Exodus*, we give you the name of the Exodus Pharaohs, beginning with Ahmose I to the actual exodus from Egypt Pharaoh being none other than Thutmoses III. As you can see here, we do our research and decode the Egyptian kings list and align it with biblical scripture to find who hasn't been named. As we have discovered, Rikayon, a Sumerian from the land of Shinar, which is the kingdom of Nimrod, was the first named Pharaoh. It is clear that the office of Pharaoh is important to not only the Hebrews for it to be recorded in the Bible, but more importantly, to God himself. Why? Because the Pharaoh grew to identify themselves as god on Earth. They were self-declared gods who ruled the government as a whole, the religious head of all temples, and the living image of a god/human in the minds of the people. Surrounding nations grew to mimic the structure of the Egyptians in some capacity and that influence begins with the Pharaoh.

Pharaoh represented the antithesis of the Abrahamic monotheistic worldview. Whereas Pharaoh was worshipped as a god, the Egyptians eventually grew to have over 2000 gods. There was a different god for almost every aspect of Egyptian life. Abram and his soon to be nation believed in one God, Yahweh. The later Exodus story of Moses vs. Pharaoh, freedom vs. slavery, real vs. fake, was an example of how Yahweh used the office of Pharaoh to showcase his own power to the world for ages to come. In Egypt, the Pharaoh and the gods, namely Ra (sun god) and Horus (the one-eyed falcon god), were the most impactful and respected gods. God himself gave recognition to the fact that people believed these gods to be real. HE chose what HE thought to be the best way to draw his people back to HIM, believe in HIS supreme power, break the spirit of the anti-God ruler, change the Egyptian people' worldview, and finalize the reality of HIM being God alone in the universe for all to know. How? HE decided to speak directly to the idea of the Egyptian gods and Pharaoh not being on HIS level. After the Exodus, there are more run-ins with Egyptian culture, wars, belief structures, and more.

Eye of Horus
© Britannica

The impact of the religious structure of Egypt impacted the whole world, even to this day. The so-called 'all-seeing eye of Horus' is famous throughout the world. Even on the American one-dollar bill, we can see this Egyptian image, an anti-God symbol. This image, which is called the wedjat or udjat eye in the Egyptian culture, is the eye of Horus that was plucked out by his "uncle" Set, god of the desert, his rival. Horus, the falcon head god, was a sky god. His right eye represents the sun, his left eye, the moon. This eye was used in funeral ceremonies, festivals, and healing practices. All of which were used in anti-God activities. Again, Pharaoh was the leader of this ritual as the head of all temples and religious practices in Egypt. Pharaoh was an idol to his people, accepting worship as a god. Pharaoh was an idolator, as he worshipped other gods, even as a self-proclaimed god himself. Pharaoh was an idol maker, as he endorsed the creation of idols to be worshipped by the people throughout the land of Egypt. He took on the name of Horus, the one-eyed, as all Pharaohs had to take on a Horus name as one of the 5 royal names of a Pharaoh. They all embodied the so-called power of the all-seeing eye of Horus. They assumed the position of all-seeing, all-knowing, a position and power belonging to God himself. This is blasphemy! The Pharaoh was the leader of idol worship in Egypt.

Psalms 135: 15-18

The idols of the heathen are silver and gold, the work of men's hands. 16 They have mouths, but they speak not; eyes have they, but they see not; 17 They have ears, but they hear not; neither is there any breath in their mouths. 18 They that make them are like unto them: so is every one that trusteth in them.

In the end, God had a prophecy and lamentation for the office of the Pharaoh of Egypt. Sure, we know about the Exodus story and how God interacted with Pharaoh Thutmoses III. We know about the plagues of Egypt and the drowning of their army, which archaeologists have found on the sea floor of the Red Sea. There are also traces about Egypt and the impact of their harsh behavior towards the Hebrews for the duration of the Bible. But one prophecy, which is very important in world history, was given by God to the prophet Ezekiel against Pharaoh. Again, God doesn't specify which ruler in particular, but the office or position of Pharaoh and whoever holds that responsibility in the aftermath of Rikayon's appointment. Most people have never read this prophecy, so please read it carefully.

Ezekiel 29: 1-7

In the tenth year, in the tenth month, in the twelfth day of the month, the word of the LORD came unto me, saying, 2 Son of man, set thy face against Pharaoh king of Egypt, and prophesy against him, and against all Egypt: 3 Speak, and say, Thus saith the Lord GOD; Behold, I am against thee, Pharaoh king of Egypt, the great dragon that lieth in the midst of his rivers, which hath said, My river is mine own, and I have made it for myself. 4 But I will put hooks in thy jaws, and I will cause the fish of thy rivers to stick unto thy scales, and I will bring thee up out of the midst of thy rivers, and all the fish of thy rivers shall stick unto thy scales. 5 And I will leave thee thrown into the wilderness, thee and all the fish of thy rivers: thou shalt fall upon the open fields; thou shalt not be brought together, nor gathered: I have given thee for meat to the beasts of the field and to the fowls of the heaven. 6 And all the inhabitants of Egypt shall know that I am the LORD, because they have been a staff of reed to the house of Israel. 7 When they took hold of thee by thy hand, thou didst break, and rend all their shoulder: and when they leaned upon thee, thou brakest, and madest all their loins to be at a stand.

Sobek, Crocodile (dragon) god of Nile

Wow. God is making it clear, especially in verse 3, that HE is against the Pharaoh of Egypt, who grew to consider himself the great dragon or crocodile in the midst of 'the river', which is the Nile River. The so-called dragon of the Nile is a man-made god called Sobek. God takes the position of a master fisherman who hunts this crocodile by causing all the fish to plug the scales of this crocodile as HE removes it from the river to be placed in the wilderness or desert, where crocodiles and fish cannot survive. The desert beast and birds will feast on the flesh of the dead king and his fish. This is an allegory of how the Pharaoh position will be removed from usage, those who aid the office of Pharaoh will be stripped away and thrown out with the Pharaoh, and different nations will come from the wilderness or world to will feast on the remains of this office. God will use the dismantling of this position to show the people of Egypt that God is the LORD, not Pharaoh. The Egyptian way of life and belief structure represented evil and slavery to the Hebrews. For such behavior, God will destroy this position.

With that said, did the prophecy of Ezekiel 29 ever come true? Did God really do what he said?

Well, if you read the rest of the chapter, God says that HE was going to make Egypt a 'lowly' kingdom and that for 40 years it would be a desolate wasteland. I know, if you think about it, Egypt was a world superpower during biblical times, decked in fine beauty and wondrous pyramids, temples, and occultic rituals on display for the world to see. For God to say that HE was going to make it a wasteland, it would have to take a long time to do, right? No, not at all. If God said it, God meant it, and HE doesn't need time as we do to make things fit.

The prophecy of Ezekiel 29 was given in biblical chronology around the year 572BC. Two years later, in 570BC, king Nebuchadnezzar of Babylon attacked Egypt in his quest for world domination. It was his 37th year as king. The Pharaoh of Egypt at the time was named Hophra. It was under his leadership as Pharaoh that God began to execute judgement on Pharaoh and Egypt as written in Ezekiel 29.

Jeremiah 44:30

Thus saith the LORD; Behold, I will give Pharaoh hophra king of Egypt into the hand of his enemies, and into the hand of them that seek his life; as I gave Zedekiah king of Judah into the hand of Nebuchadrezzar king of Babylon, his enemy, and that sought his life.

Babylonian Chronicle
© British Museum of History

Nebuchadnezzar left an inscription, called the Babylonian Chronicle, which you can find in the British Museum of History which details his attack on Egypt after he defeated the Arabs to the east. Thereafter, Egypt was a vassal state to the Babylonian rulers. Nebuchadnezzar would institute Amasis II as the vassal king of Egypt to rule for the duration of time of the Egyptian decline. The Persians would then overthrow the Babylonians and continue Egypt's servitude to a foreign nation, including Amasis II as governor. He would die 4 years after the 40-year prophecy was fulfilled in the year 526BC. Egypt continued its vassal-hood well into the years of Alexander the Great, the Ptolemy Empire years, Rome, and thereafter. All weak states. Following the Babylonian invasion, Egypt would never be a superpower in world history ever again. There were vassal kings and so-called Pharaohs of Egypt that came thereafter, but none were actual sovereign rulers of Egypt as the Pharaohs of old. The prophecy God given to Ezekiel and Jeremiah were fulfilled. Egypt was and continues to be a 'lowly' nation.

To make a long story short, Pharaoh is a position of self-elevation and one who accepts worship as a god, being both leader of church and state in Egypt. The Pharaoh was supposed to be a good looking, wise, and all-supreme being, as Rikayon believed himself to be. It ended up being a position that was broken, angry, and poor, the other attributes of Rikayon that was overlooked in his grand scheming and rise to power. Where he began, in the kingdom of Nimrod, would later be the place from which the office of Pharaoh would be destroyed, by a king from the land of Nimrod, Nebuchadnezzar II, the king of Babylon. Ironically, the name Babylon is derived from the word Babel, the Tower of Confusion, built by none other than the king of the world himself, Nimrod. See how it all falls down?

Leviticus 19:4

Turn ye not unto idols, nor make to yourselves molten gods: I am the LORD your God.

M.I.P.

Pharaoh is an idolator, idol, and idol maker, all of which is anti-God or antiChrist.

Isaiah 2: 11-12

The lofty looks of man shall be humbled, and the haughtiness of men shall be bowed down, and the LORD alone shall be exalted in that day.

Meanwhile….

In Canaan

3,200-Year-Old Canaanite Temple
© Daily Mail

Canaanite goddess
© Metropolitan Museum of Art

Canaanites
© Armstrong Institute of Biblical Archaeology

Abram and Egypt

Genesis 12:10

And there was a famine in the land: and Abram went down into Egypt to sojourn there; for the famine was grievous in the land.

Desperate times call for desperate measures. Abram, who was living in the wilderness between Bethel and Hai, was facing the same circumstances as everyone else living in the known world at that time. Scripture says that there was a famine, which means a lack of food, where he was living. As the owner of a large amount of livestock and the head of a household of several people, he needed to lead his house to a place where they can have food to survive. He decided to go down into Egypt to find it for everyone he was responsible for.

Brook of Egypt/Mizraim
© Open Bible Info

Jasher 15: 2-3

And Abram and all belonging to him rose and went down to Egypt on account of the famine, and when they were at the brook Mitzraim they remained there some time to rest from the fatigue of the road. 3. And Abram and Sarai were walking at the border of the brook Mitzraim, and Abram beheld his wife Sarai that she was very beautiful.

The brook of Mitzraim (Mizraim) or the brook of Egypt was the last stopping station before entering Egypt. It is what geologists call a natural border. This little tributary off the Mediterranean Sea was the natural marker for travelers to know that they were either leaving Egypt or entering it. While at this place to rest from their travel and water up for the rest of their journey, Abram had a chance to really look upon his wife, Sarai. He noticed how beautiful she was. To some, this may seem odd or strange, but as a husband myself, sometimes you get caught up in the daily hustle and bustle of life and forget to take a second and really see the beauty of the woman God has given you. It doesn't mean that you don't appreciate her or anything like that. It just means that when you put life on pause for a second and really look at her, you see the artwork of God that is noteworthy in her and it can cause a man to analyze life differently based on the beauty of woman. Taking this moment to see her in this fashion is likened to how Adam awoke from his sleep and saw woman (Eve) standing in front of him as his companion. Lord have mercy...I digress.

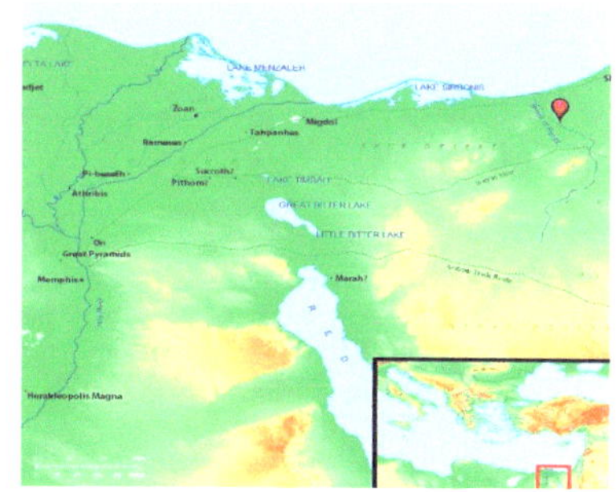

Genesis 12: 11-13

And it came to pass, when he was come near to enter into Egypt, that he said unto Sarai his wife, Behold now, I know that thou art a fair woman to look upon: 12 Therefore it shall come to pass, when the Egyptians shall see thee, that they shall say, This is his wife: and they will kill me, but they will save thee alive. 13 Say, I pray thee, thou art my sister: that it may be well with me for thy sake; and my soul shall live because of thee.

Yes, ladies, the you that we see can make a man start thinking like this. Abram, a good and wise man, really saw the amazingness of his wife Sarai and began to think of the possible evil of mankind and the change of culture they were about to walk into. On one hand, Abram is thinking about his own survival, a human's 1st instinct. On the other hand, he's thinking shrewdly, devising a scheme to live because of the reputation of the culture of the Egyptians and how ungodly they were. One would ask how could Abram know this about the Egyptians? For one, he was a wilderness traveler, so hearing about the customs of Egypt would not be foreign to him. Secondly, he knew from his days in Shinar that beautiful women were prizes to men of power, which killing another man to take his wife was not an uncommon practice for pagans. Even king David, much later in world and biblical history, had one of his soldiers (Uriah) killed so he could marry Bathsheba to become his own wife. How impactful was that in history? Bathsheba gave birth to a son named Solomon that became the next king of Israel and one of the wisest men to ever live. Again, a common yet evil practice.

Let's continue.

The hidden thing about Abram's outlook on entering Egypt and devising a plan to survive was that he didn't keep the information to himself. He told his entire household about this idea of survival.

Jasher 15: 6-7

And Abram commanded the same to all those that came with him to Egypt on account of the famine; also his nephew Lot he commanded, saying, If the Egyptians ask thee concerning Sarai say she is the sister of Abram. 7. And yet with all these orders Abram did not put confidence in them, but he took Sarai and placed her in a chest and concealed it amongst their vessels, for Abram was greatly concerned about Sarai on account of the wickedness of the Egyptians.

Imagine the culture of Egypt being so pagan that a man and his household has to stoop to all this just to get some food to survive and keep his family intact. Think about it. Can you image the next time you go to the grocery store, market place, or restaurant to buy food, you have to hide you wife or loved ones in the trunk of your car so the people operating the place don't kill you? How wild would that be? But again, desperate times call for desperate measures, and Lord knows how desperate a person can be if they are hungry.

Jasher 15: 8-13

And Abram and all belonging to him rose up from the brook Mitzraim and came to Egypt; and they had scarcely entered the gates of the city when the guards stood up to them saying, Give tithe to the king from what you have, and then you may come into the town; and Abram and those that were with him did so. 9. And Abram with the people that were with him came to Egypt, and when they came they brought the chest in which Sarai was concealed and the Egyptians saw the chest. 10. And the king's servants approached Abram, saying, What hast thou here in this chest which we have not seen? Now open thou the chest and give tithe to the king of all that it contains. 11. And Abram said, This chest I will not open, but all you demand upon it I will give. And Pharaoh's officers answered Abram, saying, It is a chest of precious stones, give us the tenth thereof. 12. Abram said, All that you desire I will give, but you must not open the chest. 13. And the king's officers pressed Abram, and they reached the chest and opened it with force, and they saw, and behold a beautiful woman was in the chest.

Something very unique just happened right in front of you. Notice how the king's guards pressed Abram about a tenth? Does this sound familiar? It should. We will discuss this later.

Before we move forward, please note who the Pharaoh is here. The king and Pharaoh is described as the same person. Why? Because at this point, the position of king and Pharaoh had been combined. Who was the person who did this at this point in Egyptian and scriptural history? Rikayon. He is the Pharaoh that we are reading about and the culture of which we are speaking. Please keep this in mind as we read on.

Abram's plan to conceal his greatest treasure, Sarai, was snuffed out pretty fast. How? He hid Sarai in a chest. The guards viewed the chest as a place where you hide precious jewels. This is a parallel to a wisdom of God. Inside the chest is where God hid the heart. Abram hid his wife in his chest, not thinking they would look to the place where one keeps the treasures of your heart, the precious stones, or your loved one, your precious stone. See how it all works?

Genesis 12: 14-15

And it came to pass, that, when Abram was come into Egypt, the Egyptians beheld the woman that she was very fair. 15 The princes also of Pharaoh saw her, and commended her before Pharaoh: and the woman was taken into Pharaoh's house.

The cat was out of the bag, for lack of a better phrase. The beauty of Sarai was seen by all. The lustful yet beauty appreciative eyes of the Egyptian people and princes was on full display. The very thing Abram feared was now at hand.

Jasher 15: 14-16

And when the officers of the king beheld Sarai they were struck with admiration at her beauty, and all the princes and servants of Pharaoh assembled to see Sarai, for she was very beautiful. And the king's officers ran and told Pharaoh all that they had seen, and they praised Sarai to the king; and Pharaoh ordered her to be brought, and the woman came before the king. 15. And Pharaoh beheld Sarai and she pleased him exceedingly, and he was struck with her beauty, and the king rejoiced greatly on her account, and made presents to those who brought him the tidings concerning her. 16. And the woman was then brought to Pharaoh's house, and Abram grieved on account of his wife, and he prayed to the Lord to deliver her from the hands of Pharaoh.

This is incredible, and not necessarily in a good way. The guards ran to Pharaoh to tell him of Sarai's beauty. Grown men, running to go tell another grown man that a married woman is so beautiful, so fine, that they wanted to bring her before him. It's offensive when you think of it. These men, as Jasher 15:15 says, were rewarded for doing so. Imagine the deceit and evil of this act. This is what you call covetousness, which is something God hates but Pharaoh loves.

Genesis 20:17

Thou shalt not covet thy neighbour's house, thou shalt not covet thy neighbour's wife, nor his manservant, nor his maidservant, nor his ox, nor his ass, nor any thing that is thy neighbour's.

Why do think God addresses covetousness in the 10 Commandments? He hates it.

While Pharaoh was blown away at Sarai's beauty, Abram was praying. His fear of losing her and his life was actively going through his mind. When he saw her taken away and put in Pharaoh's house, he knew what was going to happen next. He would lose his wife, then he would lose his life. At this point, in a foreign land, with evil customs established by Pharaoh, the only thing he could do is pray.

Reader, it is in moments like this that God allows your humanity to rise to the occasion to see who are you willing to trust: your nature or HIS. HE has already made promises to Abram about his future. HE has already called him out of Shinar and Nimrod to a new place to establish him and his name forever. Yet, HE allows Abram to fall into the hands of an evil ruler while having his whole household, including his wife, be taken with the eminent threat of death as the predictable outcome. In that moment, God seeks to see how committed to HIS Word you are. Abram could sit and accept his fate and forget his God. Or, he could pray to his God to deliver him. It's a culture issue.

Meanwhile, while Abram was grieving and praying, his wife Sarai was praying as well. This is very important to understand, ladies, as a woman of God and supporter of your husband. The same man that looks upon your beauty and follows God as your leader, at some point, will need you to help lead the group based on the situation you are in. The culture within your household will be put on display when chaos comes knocking on your door. Will you panic and give in? Will you look to blame and shame? Will you go down the path of least resistance? Or, will you take on the role of leadership by going to the supreme leader, God, and remind HIM of HIS promise to your husband? The same way your husband follows God, will you? Will you be praying and holding God to HIS Word, which HE loves? Or will you allow your emotions to win the day? Options, that's all, just options.

So, which option did Sarai choose?

Jasher 15: 17-19

And Sarai also prayed at that time and said, O Lord God thou didst tell my Lord Abram to go from his land and from his father's house to the land of Canaan, and thou didst promise to do well with him if he would perform thy commands; now behold we have done that which thou didst command us, and we left our land and our families, and we went to a strange land and to a people whom we have not known before. 18. And we came to this land to avoid the famine, and this evil accident has befallen me; now therefore, O Lord God, deliver us and save us from the hand of this oppressor, and do well with me for the sake of thy mercy. 19. And the Lord hearkened to the voice of Sarai, and the Lord sent an angel to deliver Sarai from the power of Pharaoh.

This, ladies and gentlemen, is the God we serve. HE heard her. Not him, but her. For those who think scripture is men oriented or dominated, please pay close attention to what you just read here. God has order and structure, as any good organization does. We can have our disagreements about it, but in the end, God's order is supreme because HE is the creator and designer of it all. We sometimes get caught up in mixing man's error with God's excellence. A man can claim God and do wrong. That is not to be mixed with the actual Word of God and how HIS design is perfect. These verses are the perfect example of how and why.

Sarai prayed and reminded God of HIS words to her husband. She bought in to the culture of their home. This is so beautiful. The hidden treasure of her husband was the culture of their home, not just the beauty of her figure. Both were Sarai. God hearkened or listened to her. Again, HE listened to her. There would be no Abraham as we know it without Sarai. We don't say this to contradict scripture, but had God not heard Sarai's prayer, Abram would face death, with no child to bring forth Israel, through which Jesus Christ would come. This was it. Had she not prayed. Had she not prayed. Had she not bought into the culture of what her husband introduced to her. Again, had she not prayed. This shows the balance of God in accepting both man and woman and how HE hears both. HE heard her so much so that he sent an angel to save her. The scripture did not say the angel was sent to save Abram, but to save Sarai. That's the power of a praying woman who is bought into the culture of her husband who is a man of God. I'm just saying, HE will send an angel on your behalf. Wow, just wow.

Let's see what the angel did...

Jasher 15: 20-22

And the king came and sat before Sarai and behold an angel of the Lord was standing over them, and he appeared to Sarai and said to her, Do not fear, for the Lord has heard thy prayer. 21. And the king approached Sarai and said to her, What is that man to thee who brought thee hither? and she said, He is my brother. 22. And the king said, It is incumbent upon us to make him great, to elevate him and to do unto him all the good which thou shalt command us; and at that time the king sent to Abram silver and gold and precious stones in abundance, together with cattle, men servants and maid servants; and the king ordered Abram to be brought, and he sat in the court of the king's house, and the king greatly exalted Abram on that night.

Look at God. Wow. The angel stood over them, symbolic of God looking over the situation. This is so beautiful. In the midst of chaos, the angel of the LORD gives words of peace and finality to a prayer that Sarai gave to the LORD God of Heaven. Do not fear, the LORD has heard you. Wow! This is amazing. A woman, in the presence of Pharaoh, with so much on the line, sees the angel and hears the words of God. Wow! It is the angel' presence that alters the response of Pharaoh, the so-called all-seeing demi-god who couldn't see the angel above his head nor hear the words of the angel's voice. This is our God at work.

The presence of the angel allows Pharaoh to elevate instead of eliminate Abram. Even though Sarai kept up the deception Abram told her, in saying they were siblings, God would see them through. Reader, do not mistake this as God condoning a deception, which would incite that God is okay with lying, which would be wrong and blasphemous. That is not what scripture nor myself is saying. What I am saying is that God allowed this to happen for the bigger picture of things because he has a looming judgement on Pharaoh and Egypt many times over because of the evil customs of the Pharaoh and the Egyptians. There is a punishment coming, so don't jump the gun and think that God will not punish the deception, liar, and the those who are okay with lying. This is just a step in the process of showcasing the supreme wisdom of God as a judge in live time, serving the greater good for generations to come. Let's proceed.

Genesis 12:16

And he entreated Abram well for her sake: and he had sheep, and oxen, and he asses, and menservants, and maidservants, and she asses, and camels.

Instead of death, Abram was given riches. He was given more livestock, menservants and maidservants, which are women. What the Egyptians meant for evil, God meant for good. This same phraseology would be used by Joseph, ironically in Egypt, when facing certain death but instead being elevated to 2nd in command in Egypt. Had Sarai been made queen of Egypt, she would have position of 2nd in command. See how God previews a thing before it becomes actualized? Joseph was one of the 12 sons of Israel, which would later be called the 12 tribes of Israel. Israel's original name was Jacob. Jacob's father was named Isaac. Isaac's father was named Abraham, which this story knows him as Abram. Isaac's mother name was Sarah, which this story knows her as Sarai. See how it works? There would be no Joseph or Israel in Egypt had it been no Abram and Sarai in Egypt. Amen.

Now that we see that Abram was enhanced, enriched, and restored, the punishment for the sins was at hand. Let's first see God address the covetousness of the Egyptians.

Jasher 15: 24-26

And when the king came near to Sarai, the angel smote him to the ground, and acted thus to him the whole night, and the king was terrified. 25. And the angel on that night smote heavily all the servants of the king, and his whole household, on account of Sarai, and there was a great lamentation that night amongst the people of Pharaoh's house. 26. And Pharaoh, seeing the evil that befell him, said, Surely on account of this woman has this thing happened to me, and he removed himself at some distance from her and spoke pleasing words to her.

Justice. You conspire and take with a lust in your heart, God has a way to deal with that. Pharaoh decided to reach out and touch the wife of the anointed Abram, and a plague comes into Egypt. Yes, you read this right. BEFORE the Exodus plagues of Egypt via Moses and Aaron, Abram and Sarai were responsible for sending plagues on Egypt via the angel of the LORD. This, ladies and gentlemen, is the justice given to the Egyptians for seeing, taking, and touching what belonged to God. This, ladies and gentlemen, is the justice that God has set for those that touch his anointed nowadays as well. God himself makes it clear in the book of Psalms that HE has a record of administering justice as the supreme judge of the world. By this name, God is named Jehovah Shafat, which means 'Jehovah is our Judge.'

Psalms 105: 7-16

He is the LORD our God: his judgments are in all the earth. 8 He hath remembered his covenant for ever, the word which he commanded to a thousand generations. 9 Which covenant he made with Abraham, and his oath unto Isaac; 10 And confirmed the same unto Jacob for a law, and to Israel for an everlasting covenant: 11 Saying, Unto thee will I give the land of Canaan, the lot of your inheritance: 12 When they were but a few men in number; yea, very few, and strangers in it. 13 When they went from one nation to another, from one kingdom to another people; 14 He suffered no man to do them wrong: yea, he reproved kings for their sakes; 15 Saying, Touch not mine anointed, and do my prophets no harm. 16 Moreover he called for a famine upon the land: he brake the whole staff of bread.

This is the God that we serve. HE doesn't stutter or misalign his words. We do. HE made this abundantly clear for all to see. HIS anointed are untouchable. They may be imperfect, wrong in a situation, etc., you still cannot touch them or do them any harm. These are God's words and HE means every syllable of it. Pharaoh tried to touch Sarai, and a plague broke out. Again, justice for covetousness. Don't play with the people of God. Even the so-called god of Egypt Pharaoh himself had to keep some distance from Sarai. He even humbled himself to speak pleasant words to her. That's what will happen when God steps in. The so-called elite and elect will humble themselves to you, because of HIM. Again, that's the God WE serve!

Genesis 12: 17-20

And the LORD plagued Pharaoh and his house with great plagues because of Sarai Abram's wife. 18 And Pharaoh called Abram, and said, What is this that thou hast done unto me? why didst thou not tell me that she was thy wife? 19 Why saidst thou, She is my sister? so I might have taken her to me to wife: now therefore behold thy wife, take her, and go thy way. 20 And Pharaoh commanded his men concerning him: and they sent him away, and his wife, and all that he had.

Well ladies, and gentlemen, there you have it. Pharaoh had seen enough. He called Abram to him and called it a day. Yes, Sarai was beautiful and all, but there was nothing but sickness going on in his household since they got to Egypt. Sarai had said they were siblings just as Abram had told her. Once Pharaoh found out the truth, he asked them to leave. Truthfully, he paid them to leave, which is a common practice for people with financial leverage to pay for "problems" to go away.

Jasher 15:30

Now therefore here is thy wife, take her and go from our land lest we all die on her account. And Pharaoh took more cattle, men servants and maid servants, and silver and gold, to give to Abram, and he returned unto him Sarai his wife.

Abram went to Egypt to find food. Instead, he found riches. He deceived Pharaoh about his relationship with his wife to save their lives. Their punishment was the terror of facing death and having to come back to the same man they lied to and confess their lie. People got sick because of their lie. Lies are sickening.

The Egyptians were punished with plague because of their covetousness. In the end, the Egyptians were restored and so was Abram. This would be the 1st meeting between the Egyptians and Abram the Hebrew, but certainly not the last. It is from this relationship we get the Exodus. It is from this relationship we get the 3 monotheistic belief structures on earth. More importantly, it is from this relationship we get the Christ.

Matthew 2: 14-15

When he arose, he took the young child and his mother by night, and departed into Egypt: 15 And was there until the death of Herod: that it might be fulfilled which was spoken of the Lord by the prophet, saying, Out of Egypt have I called my son.

From a lie, placed in a chest, eventually came The TRUTH, whom we are to place in our chest.

Amraphel

Genesis 14:1

And it came to pass in the days of Amraphel king of Shinar, Arioch king of Ellasar, Chedorlaomer king of Elam, and Tidal king of nations;

The verse above is very important, especially the name Amraphel, the king of Shinar. The naming of kings and their kingdoms will give indications of who and where in history we can pinpoint certain events. At this particular junction in biblical history, we are navigating the life of Abram. While that may serve as the headline, this verse and the next nine verses all describe a war that was going on in the known world.

Of all the kings mentioned in Genesis 14: 1-9, Amraphel is mentioned first? Why? As a student of history and biblical history, it tells a whole different story, kind of like a clue to study and investigate. There are several questions to be asked that highlight these men and their importance in the Bible but we must take a closer look at Amraphel. The key questions regarding him are as follows:

1. Who is Amraphel, king of Shinar?
2. What does his name mean?
3. Where is Shinar?
4. Who are these other kings and what is their relation to Amraphel?

Again, pay close attention to the names, their kingdoms, and the meaning of those names.

To begin, the king of Shinar has already been identified earlier in the book. Remember reading this...

Jasher 11: 1-2

And Nimrod son of Cush was still in the land of Shinar, and he reigned over it and dwelt there, and he built cities in the land of Shinar. 2. And these are the names of the four cities which he built, and he called their names after the occurrences that happened to them in the building of the tower.

Yes, you read that right. Nimrod was the ruler of Shinar. Even Merriam-Webster defines Nimrod as a descendant of Ham, a mighty hunter, and the king of Shinar. When we understand the definitions and parallel the time period, that would by default mean that Nimrod was known by another name. Shinar did not have 2 kings, just one. Yes, you got it right, Amraphel, the king of Shinar, is Nimrod! Don't be surprised by this as kings throughout history have had several names or what cultures call 'throne' names. For example, in ancient Egypt, Pharaohs would have 5 names (nebty)! They would take on the name Horus, Two Ladies, Golden Horus, King of Upper and Lower Egypt, and the son of Ra. The first 4 names would be given when the man became pharaoh, the last name when they are born.

To answer question #1 and #2 directly, Nimrod was Amraphel. The name Nimrod means great hunter, which is how he was identified by God in his origin, which was his purpose by the LORD himself. The name Amraphel means 'one that darkens counsel', which became Nimrod's elder role as the oldest king in the Earth. Let's M.I.P.

M.I.P.

One that darkens counsel = someone who gives evil advice or evil ideas

Why is this definition important? Because it shows how far into evil Nimrod had gone. He and his son had become so synonymous with evil that he became known by another name that represented the depth of his fall. He was associated with evil to the point that even the advice and thoughts coming from him represented evil in the minds of men. He became identified in name by his actions in thought. Think about that for a second. That's how evil of a man he had become.

To answer question #3, we, alongside biblical and secular historians, have identified Shinar as ancient Babylon, the Fertile Crescent, or modern-day Iraq.
Now that we have answered the first 3 questions, finding out who the other kings are and their nations are important in answering question #4 and understanding the role of Amraphel in verse 1 of Genesis 14.

Arioch, king of Ellasar
Chedorlaomer, king of Elam
Tidal, king of nations

Arioch means lion-like/to pluck. Several translations of this name mean 'lion like man'. This would indicate that Arioch was a man of great statute, power, and or influence. Ellasar was a city state on the eastern bank of the Euphrates River. It is called the ancient city of Larsa or the modern tourist site named Senqara. What's important to note about Ellasar is that it is also called Eri-Aku in the Sumerian language, a named closely associated with sun worship. Eri-Aku is written about in Sumerian cuneiform, who later became a vassal king of King Hammurabi, the lawgiver, another name for Nimrod. I digress.

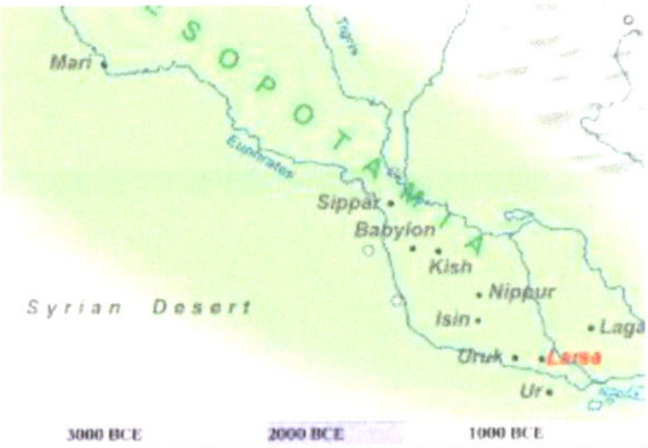

Ancient City of Ellasar is Larsa
© Sumerian Hub

Chedorlaomer has an incomplete meaning, beginning with chedor which means servant of - (kudur). The Elamites worshipped Lagamaru or Lagamal, meaning no mercy. This would mean Chedorlaomer name in title could mean 'servant of he who gives no mercy'. Being that the Elamites ruled modern-day western Iran centered at Susa and Khuzestan, the Elamite kingdom would have been next door to the kingdom of Amraphel (Nimrod).

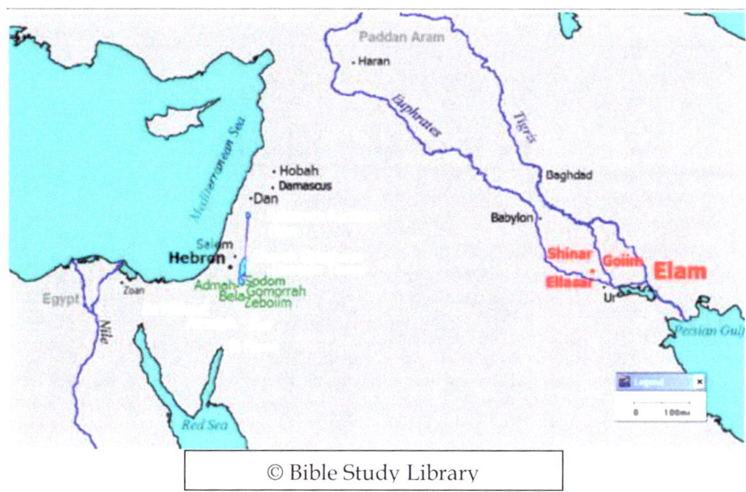

© Bible Study Library

The 3rd king is Tidal, which means high praise or splendor. The term nations associated with his kingdom comes from the Hebrew word Goiim or Goyyim, meaning nations. The Akkadian meaning of Goiim is the 'King of the Four Corners of the Earth'. Tidal would have been the ruler of many city-states in the middle eastern region east of the Tigris River but north of Elam and Shinar. These cities and nations popped up after the collapse of the Tower of Babel as men began to spread out over the world as the waters receded.

As you can see, these 3 kings all ruled the area around the fallen Tower of Babel, which was in Shinar, the realm ruled by Nimrod. The once all engulfing kingdom of Nimrod that governed the whole world was now broken into smaller kingdoms and or city-states that other men ruled. All of these kings and kingdoms were spinoffs of Amraphel (Nimrod) and his paganism. They are all connected in evil towards the LORD, which is why and how they came to war with the Canaanite nations to the west of them, where Abram resided.

I hope that you now have a better idea of how name changes can throw you off the trail of certain people if you don't know how those changes could merely be descriptions of said person. Nimrod, as we found, went by the name Amraphel as his story continued to expand in the world. He would come to be known by other names historically, which we will get into later in the work, like Hammurabi the Lawgiver. Every high school student in history class in the U.S. has to learn about Hammurabi's Codes and how he ruled with an iron fist. Students have no idea that Hammurabi is quite often translated and given to be an alternative name of Amraphel, who just so happens to be Nimrod. Again, use etymology and you will see how the meaning of the word describes the why, whereas history describes the who:

Nimrod = the mighty/great hunter
Amraphel = one who darkens counsel
Hammurabi = the lawgiver

M.I.P.
Same guy, the biblical Nimrod

War of the Kings

Genesis 14: 2-9

That these made war with Bera king of Sodom, and with Birsha king of Gomorrah, Shinab king of Admah, and Shemeber king of Zeboiim, and the king of Bela, which is Zoar. 3 All these were joined together in the vale of Siddim, which is the salt sea. 4 Twelve years they served Chedorlaomer, and in the thirteenth year they rebelled. 5 And in the fourteenth year came Chedorlaomer, and the kings that were with him, and smote the Rephaims in Ashteroth Karnaim, and the Zuzims in Ham, and the Emims in Shaveh Kiriathaim, 6 And the Horites in their mount Seir, unto Elparan, which is by the wilderness. 7 And they returned, and came to Enmishpat, which is Kadesh, and smote all the country of the Amalekites, and also the Amorites, that dwelt in Hazezontamar. 8 And there went out the king of Sodom, and the king of Gomorrah, and the king of Admah, and the king of Zeboiim, and the king of Bela (the same is Zoar;) and they joined battle with them in the vale of Siddim; 9 With Chedorlaomer the king of Elam, and with Tidal king of nations, and Amraphel king of Shinar, and Arioch king of Ellasar; four kings with five.

I know, this looks like a lot, but have no worries trying to understand it. We'll *make it plain* for you. The 4 kings of the east, which includes Nimrod (Amraphel), declared war on the kings or city-states of the west, the Canaanite nations. These Canaanite nations were a confederation or alliance. They are historically known as the Sodom and Gomorrah Alliance of Kings. These Canaanite nations payed tribute or royalties to Chedorlaomer for 12 years. In the 13th year, they decided not to pay, making their actions a rebellion to the Elamite king. Year 14, Chedorlaomer went to the west with a vengeance.

What's important to note about this war is that the once ruler of the world was now a vassal king himself. What does vassal mean? A person under the protection of a feudal lord to whom he has vowed homage and fealty. A person who is in a subordinate position or servant. Yes, kings and whole nations become vassals to others for various different reasons. In this case, Nimrod, the great hunter and once ruler of the world was a vassal king, who had to pay homage to Chedorlaomer, king of Elam. The fall of the Tower of Babel caused a tidal wave of change in the earth that impacted everyone, including the once thought of invincible Nimrod. Humble pie will change your appetite and sometimes where you sit when you eat, ask Nimrod.

Jasher 16:1

At that time Chedorlaomer king of Elam sent to all the neighboring kings, to Nimrod, king of Shinar who was then under his power, and to Tidal, king of Goyim, and to Arioch, king of Elasar, with whom he made a covenant, saying, Come up to me and assist me, that we may smite all the towns of Sodom and its inhabitants, for they have rebelled against me these thirteen years.

Nimrod was now considered one of the eastern or Elamite kings. They went out to fight against the 5 great kings of Sodom and Gomorrah. Even though Nimrod was now a vassal king, he was still regarded as the great hunter because of the skins of Adam and Eve made from the hands of God that made him lethal in hunting and killing. The meaning given to him as the mighty hunter before the LORD is not a good thing. It means he was a killer, a hunter of people. This is relative because of the other nations he and the alliance under Chedorlaomer would destroy along the way. With that said, we cannot look over the names of some of the other nations of people that are mentioned in Genesis 14: 2-9, not because of who they were, but what they were.

Noah's flood killed all of the giants. However, after the flood, there were spirits that remained that became what we know as demons. Where did the demons come from? Men and women under the influence of these fallen angels had children, which became giants (Enoch 6). The flood killed them. These spirits could not return to God, the father of All spirits, because their actual fathers were the visiting angels, who had been bound in everlasting chains under darkness, waiting for judgment (Jude 6-7). These same spirits remained, still able to influence, still able to distort, still able to alter the human genome, still able to cause chaos in the Earth, only because man was now open to this type of blasphemy. Now, it was man that was open to these of relationships and knowledge to alter the human genome. Now, there are a whole group or family of giants that had established themselves in Canaan, a perversion of humanity. Don't consider this to be odd. Remember, Noah cursed Canaan because of his father Ham's perversion. See how God works? Now let's look at the nations that the kings of the east killed before they came to the kings of the Sodom and Gomorrah alliance.

Name	Meaning	Giants?
Rephaims -	terrible ones	Yes
Zuzims -	those that move	Yes
Emims -	terrors/dreaded ones	Yes
Horites -	caveman/cave dweller	Yes
Amalekites -	to know and rebel	Yes
Amorites -	to say/utter	Yes

Canaan, Land of the Giants
© The History of Ancient Israel

While these kings fought one another, the 4 kings of the east defeated the 6 kings of early Canaan. This land was full of giants, and what makes it even more interesting, is that they were connected to the bloodlines of Shem, Ham, and Japheth. For example, the Zuzims, according to Genesis 14:5, were in the land of Ham, which if you look at the biblical maps of the time, it's talking about Canaan stretching down into what we know as Africa. Canaan, the son that was cursed by Noah, is historically known as dark skinned people. The Zuzims, a nomadic group of giants, moved around in the land but homeland was in Canaan, as the map shows.
The last two kingdoms mentioned were the Amalekites and Amorites. These two groups were not kingdoms yet even though they were mentioned in Genesis 14. Why then are they mentioned here? Because Moses, the author of Genesis and the first 5 books of the Bible, are describing the correlation of these people in advance and the region in which they dwelled to the people living during his time. For example, the Amalekites were the sons of Eliphaz (Esau's oldest son) and his concubine Timna, who was a Horite, the giant race mentioned above. Amalek wasn't born at this time, but much later (Gen. 36:12). The Horites were alive at this time and had intermingled with humans in this area, much like the giants of the pre-flood world. Timna, the eventual concubine of Esau, was from this bloodline of giants. Esau, the twin brother of Jacob (Israel) and great grandson of Abram (Abraham), mixed the bloodlines by having a child with a woman who had giantism in her DNA. This is why the Amalekites were adversaries of the Israelites and are well recorded in history as a giant race, both before and after the birth of Amalek. This is also the area and people Amalek settled amongst after he was born. Being that Amalek's mother was a concubine, he didn't share in the birth rights as his siblings who were born from the wives of Esau. Therefore, Amalek settled among the people of his mother, not his father, which was his birthright. As for the Amorites, they were the sons of Canaan, the son of Ham, the son of Noah (Gen. 10: 15-16). They became known as the warriors of the mountains or highland mountaineers. They were giants as well. The prophet Amos, in his book, claimed that they were as tall as the cedar trees (Amos 2:9).

As the kings of the east defeated the nations of giants that lived in Canaan, they finally came to the kings of the west, the rulers of Sodom and Gomorrah. You must understand how the kings of the west felt after hearing about the winning ways of their opposition from the east. They were not only defeating nations along the way, but they were defeating giants and families of giants. It was now the moment of truth as Chedorlaomer and Nimrod were ready to crush the rebellion.

Slime Pits of Siddiim
© iBible

As expected, the western kings were no match for the eastern kings. Chedorlaomer had the upper hand. Why? Because he had Amraphel, Nimrod the mighty hunter, on his side. As they continued their fighting, the kings of Sodom and Gomorrah themselves were scattered and chased into the valley of Siddim, which was full of slime pits. Others fled to the mountains to escape certain death. The kings that made it through the slime pits made it to the gates of Sodom to hide but the 3 kings of the east ransacked Sodom and Gomorrah.

Genesis 14: 10-11

And the vale of Siddim was full of slimepits; and the kings of Sodom and Gomorrah fled, and fell there; and they that remained fled to the mountain. 11 And they took all the goods of Sodom and Gomorrah, and all their victuals, and went their way.

Chedorlaomer wanted to send a message. Granted, he wanted to be paid for his lordship over the kings of the east and west. However, he wanted to send a message to all others that insubordination and disrespect will not be tolerated. He not only killed giants and destroyed the 5 kings of the west, but he looted and took all the goods from Sodom and Gomorrah to showcase his power. It's understandable, especially from a historical and political point of view, but in the midst of sending this message, someone was present living in the area that subscribed to a higher power than Chedolaomer.

There was a certain man living in Sodom that was under the divine eye of God. That man, who didn't know his story would take center stage in teaching the world how God's grace abounds and how HIS hedge of protection cannot be penetrated by any other power in the universe. That man was Lot, the nephew of Abram.

Genesis 14:12

And they took Lot, Abram's brother's son, who dwelt in Sodom, and his goods, and departed.

For all those reading, take note. God has a special protection promise for those that are "HIS".

Isaiah 41: 10-13

Fear thou not; for I am with thee: be not dismayed; for I am thy God: I will strengthen thee; yea, I will help thee; yea, I will uphold thee with the right hand of my righteousness. 11 Behold, all they that were incensed against thee shall be ashamed and confounded: they shall be as nothing; and they that strive with thee shall perish. 12 Thou shalt seek them, and shalt not find them, even them that contended with thee: they that war against thee shall be as nothing, and as a thing of nought. 13 For I the LORD thy God will hold thy right hand, saying unto thee, Fear not; I will help thee.

Lot, as we learned, chose to go live near Sodom and Gomorrah because the grass looked greener for his livestock. His split with his uncle Abram over land and flocks which led him to a place that he thought would be better. This is a lesson for all of us: God is the greener grass which will never whither and or be conquered. The land that Lot chose was green, but only temporarily. When the 4 kings came to sack Sodom and Gomorrah, Lot was taken with the spoils of war. Normally, in a situation like this, the men are killed and the women made sex slaves or servants. In this case, Lot was taken along with his wealth and family.

This should have been the end of Lot's story, but God. HE always has eyes watching and working HIS will, which means if you are connected to HIM, HE's watching and working for you. In this particular case, the LORD had eyes in the field during battle watching so the story can be told of how HIS promise to protect can never be broken, even if said promise is to someone else not present at the time. God's umbrella of protection covers not only the one HE promises it to but to those around them that remain under that umbrella.

Jasher 16:6

And they plundered all the cities of Sodom and Gomorrah, and they also took Lot, Abram's brother's son, and his property, and they seized all the goods of the cities of Sodom, and they went away; and Unic, Abram's servant, who was in the battle, saw this, and told Abram all that the kings had done to the cities of Sodom, and that Lot was taken captive by them.

Thank God for Unic. A fighter, a witness, a servant. This man, who history books never speak about, will be noted here for being a hero. His first-hand account of what happened and him choosing to go back to tell his master, Abram, that his nephew had been taken by the 4 kings that included Nimrod is a game changer. Of all the people he saw taken while Sodom and Gomorrah was being razed, he just so happen to see Lot and everything he had taken. By going back to Abram to tell of what he had seen, the LORD used a man that history books forget to bridge the gap between the man through whom the Christ would come and the world's 1st Anti-Christ. Again, thanks Unic, you are greatly appreciated.

When Abram heard the news, all you know what broke loose:

Genesis 14: 13-16

And there came one that had escaped, and told Abram the Hebrew; for he dwelt in the plain of Mamre the Amorite, brother of Eshcol, and brother of Aner: and these were confederate with Abram. 14 And when Abram heard that his brother was taken captive, he armed his trained servants, born in his own house, three hundred and eighteen, and pursued them unto Dan. 15 And he divided himself against them, he and his servants, by night, and smote them, and pursued them unto Hobah, which is on the left hand of Damascus. 16 And he brought back all the goods, and also brought again his brother Lot, and his goods, and the women also, and the people.

Well, there it is. Unic, which name has a dual meaning in association to a noun that means a thing which is the only one of its kind. The other meaning is associated with the title eunuch, which means a bedroom guard, whose job was to protect the living areas of women. Regardless, Unic is very unique in his positioning within the story of Nimrod as he's the witness who told Abram about the taking of Lot into custody of Chedorlaomer and Nimrod.

When Abram heard the news, he immediately gathered all his men, 318, and chased down the army of the 4 kings. Upon finding them, he divided his men into smaller groups as they attacked by night in the darkness. Keep in mind, Abram's 318 men spread out was facing an army of over 800,000 men (Jasher 16:2). Sounds crazy, right?! Size doesn't matter when it comes to the LORD of Heaven and Earth. His hand and power is the only size that matter.

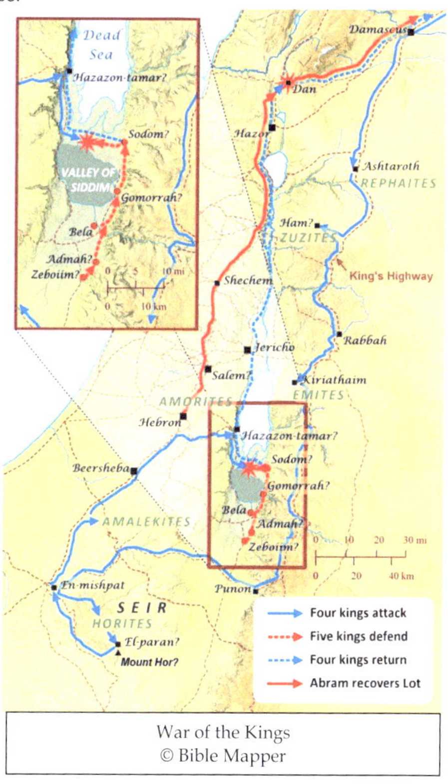

War of the Kings
© Bible Mapper

Attacking by night was not the custom for warfare at that time, so needless to say, this concentrated plan by Abram was meant to cause chaos and confusion while he penetrated the camp to find Lot and his family. Chasing an army through slime pits in the darkness was a very crazy move but one in which Abram trusted to be successful.

Genesis 14: 15-16

And he divided himself against them, he and his servants, by night, and smote them, and pursued them unto Hobah, which is on the left hand of Damascus. 16 And he brought back all the goods, and also brought again his brother Lot, and his goods, and the women also, and the people.

Abram won, gathered all that was taken, including Lot and his family, and returned the rest to the people. All 800,000 men were scattered into the wilderness. Gone. Only the 4 kings, including Nimrod, were left. The great army of the Elamite kings were destroyed. This is another loss to the reputation of Nimrod while Abram, the servant of God, wins again. This war and its result is another precursor to the coming war between Christ and the antichrist, followers of God and followers of the god of this world. We don't need the odds or superior numbers in our favor to win. We just need God. That's all.

Romans 8:31

What shall we then say to these things? If God be for us, who can be against us?

Melchizedek and Tithing

Genesis 14: 17-18

And the king of Sodom went out to meet him after his return from the slaughter of Chedorlaomer, and of the kings that were with him, at the valley of Shaveh, which is the king's dale. 18 And Melchizedek king of Salem brought forth bread and wine: and he was the priest of the most high God.

Amen. When the victory was won, when Nimrod and the 3 Elamite kings under Chedorlaomer had been dismantled and sent back home, Abram met with the king of Sodom. While attending this meeting, another king showed up whose seat of power was not too far away in the city of Salem. The name of this king and his attributes has been a mystery to many scholars, elders, pastors, and historians for generations. The city, Salem, is one of the most prized possessions on this planet although the name we know it to be now is not Salem. More importantly, the king bringing bread and wine to this meeting and the standard he laid for the rest of the world to follow created the idea of tithing to the LORD, which is used in every major religion on earth. There's a secret here that's hidden in plain sight that will reveal who HE is. Let's put on the glasses of Truth and use discernment to see the greatness of God.

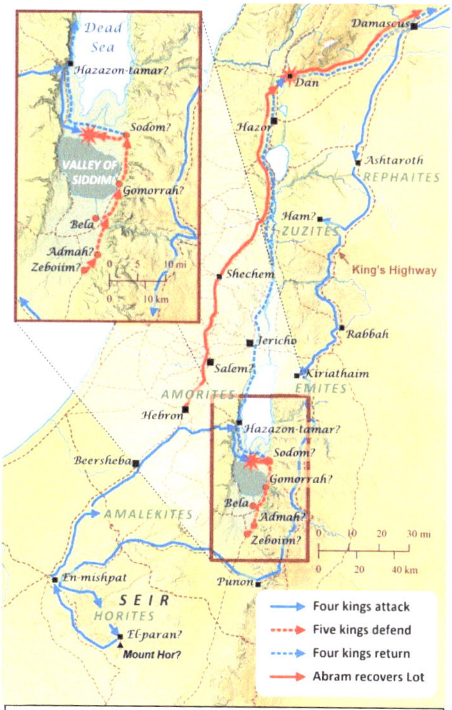

War of the Kings
© Bible Mapper

As the scripture says, the name of the king of Salem that approached Abram was Melchizedek. He's a very important figure in human history whose name is descriptive of the coming Christ, thousands of years in advance. The name Melchizedek in Hebrew means 'King of Righteousness'. In the ancient Canaanite language, it means 'my king is (the god) of Righteousness'. This is very important in translation because it reveals who Melchizedek really is.

M.I.P.

The king is (the god) of Righteousness = The king of Righteousness = God

The God of Righteousness made himself known to the Jebusites as El Elyon, which means Most High God. Please keep in mind that God is a revealer. Do not consider this strange for God to unveil HIMself to people by using a different name or appearance. For example, HE told Moses that by the name Jehovah HE was NOT known to Abraham (Abram), Isaac, and Jacob (Exodus 6:3). God chose the title Melchizedek to symbolize order in the Earth, via righteousness, in the position of a king and priest to align HIS future people, city, and land before they realized they were chosen.

The order of Melchizedek is heavenly, eternal. The later priesthood of Aaron through Melchizedek was earthly, temporary. HE ruled at Salem, later to be named Jeru-salem or Jerusalem, the holy city of God. The position of king means ruler. The position of priest means aligner and leader of the belief structure of the person and or people, who is authorized to perform sacred rites as a mediator between humanity and the divine. God even charges us to be of the order of Melchizedek, a practicer of righteousness (Psalms 110:4). Why? Because the spirit of God is Righteousness, which existed BEFORE the flesh of Jesus the Christ was made, which is why Jesus himself said that before Abraham (Abram) was, I Am (John 8:58), which meant before Abraham (Abram) was even born, HE existed. The spirit WITHIN Christ was God, because God is a spirit (John 4:24), which leads to the concept of God being the king of righteousness. God in Christ is Righteousness. The verification of this was written by the Apostle John in Revelation 19:11 as God revealed HIMself as a rider on a white horse.

Revelation 19:11

And I saw heaven opened, and behold a white horse; and he that sat upon him was called Faithful and True, and in righteousness he doth judge and make war.

There is only one who can administer true righteousness and justice: the LORD God himself. How he chooses to send forth this message into the earth for man to see and follow is his choice and right as God. This is why Melchizedek was chosen for such a time to be an example of an eternal connection to God that far exceeded the physical reflection. God is righteousness because God is the ultimate right.

So, what's the difference between Melchizedek and Christ? Melchizedek represented righteousness and rulership in the Earth from a position of power. Christ represents righteousness and rulership in the Earth from a position of servitude. Melchizedek ruled Salem for a time. Christ rules the world forever.

Hebrews 7: 15-16

And it is yet far more evident: for that after the similitude of Melchisedec there ariseth another priest, 16 Who is made, not after the law of a carnal commandment, but after the power of an endless life.

Melchizedek's role brought about the idea of the law aligning man to God (via Moses), physically. Christ' role brings about the fulfillment of the law which aligns man to God (via Jesus), spiritually. Melchizedek instituted the tithe to mankind as a sacrifice to God. Christ is the tithe on the behalf of mankind, serving as the final sacrifice. Melchizedek's appearance to Abram made it possible for the Order of Righteousness to be passed through the bloodline of Abram to his future offspring and priestly tribe, the Levites, which is Earthly. Christ' appearance with Abram made it possible for the lifestyle of righteousness to be accepted in the hearts of men for All to become Holy priests unto God himself forever, through faith, which is spiritual. God is the Greatest!

Question: How did Abram (Abraham) see Christ when he died thousands of years in advance before Jesus' birth?

Answer: I thought you would never ask...

John 8: 56-58

Your father Abraham rejoiced to see my day: and he saw it, and was glad. 57 Then said the Jews unto him, Thou art not yet fifty years old, and hast thou seen Abraham? 58 Jesus said unto them, Verily, verily, I say unto you, Before Abraham was, I am.

Amen.

Armana Letters
© Dept. of Archaeology
Univ. of Cambridge

The ancient settlement of Salem was founded by Shem, the son of Noah. Shem, who lived to be 600 years old (Gen. 11: 10-11), was still alive during this time when Abram met Melchizedek. Salem was inhabited by the Canaanite group called the Jebusites, who became idol worshippers after the time of Shem and Melchizedek, even to the time of King David. However, during the time of Shem, they were worshippers of God. The city itself sits between 2 hills, Mt. Olives and Mt. Zion. According to the Armana Letters, the Akkadian people recorded the name of the city as U-ra-salim, meaning "peace", which is what the name Salem means. The city would later become known as Jeru-salem (Jerusalem), meaning the city of peace, the capital of Israel and beloved city of God. From Salem did Melchizedek rule.

Genesis 14:19-20

And he blessed him, and said, Blessed be Abram of the most high God, possessor of heaven and earth: 20 And blessed be the most high God, which hath delivered thine enemies into thy hand. And he gave him tithes of all.

Melchizedek came and blessed Abram. That was the mission. He fully recognized the heart of Abram, the work it took to win, and the power it took for the victory. In that blessing, he also introduced the term tithe, in which Abram gave a 10th of his spoils. Please read the following verses of the section carefully to get an understanding of what Abram was giving. It will make tithing relative in today's world, which is key in understanding what tithing should mean.

Genesis 14: 21-24

And the king of Sodom said unto Abram, Give me the persons, and take the goods to thyself. 22 And Abram said to the king of Sodom, I have lift up mine hand unto the LORD, the most high God, the possessor of heaven and earth, 23 That I will not take from a thread even to a shoelatchet, and that I will not take any thing that is thine, lest thou shouldest say, I have made Abram rich: 24 Save only that which the young men have eaten, and the portion of the men which went with me, Aner, Eshcol, and Mamre; let them take their portion.

Abram did not take anything that wasn't his from the battle against Nimrod and the kings of the east. Therefore, he didn't offer tithes on what wasn't his to give. This is very important to note. What belonged to the king of Sodom, Abram returned. He made a personal declaration, before God, to not take anything for himself from the king of Sodom. Why? So the king of Sodom couldn't say that he made Abram rich. Note the symbolism. Sodom would come to be known as one of the two cities of sin, later to be destroyed by the hand of God HIMself. This city and its ruler could not claim to make Abram rich over the God that Abram served, whose universally wealthy and the very concept of wealth is himself (Psalms 112:3). If Abram accepted wealth offerings from the king of Sodom, it would appear that the city of sin made Abram rich, which would be a contradiction to the promise of God, thus giving rise to belief structures allowing criminal institutions to fund or bankroll God's house. That wouldn't be godly or holy at all. Instead, Abram saved the people and goods of Sodom and in good countenance, he gave them the opportunity to start again, hopefully seeing the power of God to forgive and start over in good faith. If anyone was going to make Abram rich, he was resolved to commit to believing his increase would come from the LORD God himself. He only asked that the 318 men who were victorious with him be given their portion from the victory, but he himself, only the food they had eaten was sufficient for him to keep. This also shows how and what Abram tithed. It wasn't money, as you read in verse 24. He gave based on his increase, which just so happen to be the food, which was a spoil of the increase.

Tithing within itself has become a cringe effect word in churches worldwide. For some, it's a celebration of giving back to the LORD through the church to uphold and enhance the kingdom of God. To others, it's a depressing act of taking or giving to an organization that has been known to steal and cheat the very people who gave the spoils for increase. Regardless, it's a term that gets everyone' attention when spoken. Whereas we can write a whole book on tithing alone, which we may at a different time, we prefer to concise this information for you in the simplest form. Understanding the origin and essence of tithing with Abram will make the concept easier to comprehend in our modern-day life. Abram tithed a 10th of his increase, which was food. His followers tithed from their spoils, which included goods. The spirit of the tithe is to give a 10th of YOUR increase, not the expectations of whatever organization you are a part of. Even God told the prophet Malachi what HE expects in tithing:

Malachi 3:10

Bring ye all the tithes into the storehouse, that there may be meat in mine house, and prove me now herewith, saith the LORD of hosts, if I will not open you the windows of heaven, and pour you out a blessing, that there shall not be room enough to receive it.

Simple. Notice how God said to bring all the tithes in the storehouse, which means the church storage functions (pantry, bank accounts, storage facilities, etc.), so that there may be 'MEAT' in HIS house. So that there may be MEAT in HIA house. The MEAT HE is speaking to is the essential essence of sustaining life, which is food. The MEAT can also mean money, but it wasn't deliberately saying money as it has been preached throughout the world. It, meaning tithing, is NOT exclusive to money. For example, if you find a starving person within the community and give them cash instead of food, the cash won't fill their belly until they use that money to buy food. It's likened to a person that's sick. If you give them money instead of medicine, all the money in the world can't get them healthy again. Sure, the money can be used in the aftermath to do something to possibly remedy the situation, but money within itself doesn't fix the human condition. The MEAT addresses the intentional and non-intentional meaning of increase which is integral to understanding the spirit of God's tithe. The spirit of the tithe is to give the 10th of your increase, your essential things, which must be given to the LORD who gave you ALL that you have. If it's time, money, food, land, etc., it belongs to the LORD. Whatever your 'fruit' is, a 10th of that belongs to the LORD. It's that simple. It's not exclusive to one or another, especially money.

For those who have a question about tithing money, here's your answer:

Deuteronomy 14: 23-25

And thou shalt eat before the LORD thy God, in the place which he shall choose to place his name there, the tithe of thy corn, of thy wine, and of thine oil, and the firstlings of thy herds and of thy flocks; that thou mayest learn to fear the LORD thy God always. 24 And if the way be too long for thee, so that thou art not able to carry it; or if the place be too far from thee, which the LORD thy God shall choose to set his name there, when the LORD thy God hath blessed thee: 25 Then shalt thou turn it into money, and bind up the money in thine hand, and shalt go unto the place which the LORD thy God shall choose:

Context is key. In verse 23, there are descriptions of tithing to the LORD based on the increases in crops and livestock, essentials to human civilization. In verse 24, there's an explanation for those who live distant from the place God chose for you to tithe, which means God should choose where you tithe not the church you go to, there is a difference. Verse 25 gives the how, via money, to take to the place God chose for you to tithe. The understanding of verse 25 for tithing is not to push for money 1st, but as a replacement or go instead, depending on your life situation. Some families put themselves in poor life quality situations trying to tithe money instead of paying for food for themselves and their families, respectively. There are people who will never leave the poor threshold because they want to be obedient to God. To be clear, there is nothing wrong with the desire to be obedient to the LORD, which we all should want and do, daily. That is righteous. However, how they tithe is keeping them from prospering as scripture says. I know this is going to bother some people who live and die by the words of their pastor, who's living high in life while the people he tends to are living low in misery. Let me be clear: God never intended for mankind to tithe themselves into poverty or not be able to come out of it due to HIS plan. That's not HIS design. HIS blueprint is to teach a discipline of thankfulness and accountability for the upkeep of HIS kingdom by giving a 10th back to HE who gave you all. Your 10th may be someone else' 90% or means to survival. By administering your 10th to the place of HIS choosing, there is a freedom to give what is owed, which leads to understanding how to give an offering, which creates a cheerful giver, which the LORD loves (2 Cor. 9:7). It is not wise to give what you don't have in money then suffer to not have enough money to buy food and essentials, which can lead to all kinds of confusion and or violations of God, all because we do not understand scripture. The wiser thing to do is to buy your food then tithe a 10th of the food increase. That is giving God a 10th of your first fruits, as Abel did (Gen. 4:4), as God desires. Think about it for a second: how can you give God a 10th of the first fruits when you are giving the seeds away from which you produced the fruit? How can fruit reproduce without seeds? It can't. Keep the seeds, produce more fruit, tithe your first fruits which are your best fruit and the LORD will honor your tithe. This is what is being described in the spirit of the tithe. Again, context is key.

Proverbs 3: 9-10

Honour the LORD with thy substance, and with the firstfruits of all thine increase: 10 So shall thy barns be filled with plenty, and thy presses shall burst out with new wine.

As we go forward, let's take a closer look at Melchizedek and Abram' (Abraham) relationship. It is very important for you and I to know the background of this relationship as it will give us an example of how our daily walk with God plus the alignment of our faith, knowledge, and works versus the evil one can brighten our lamp to bring others to Christ. We can use it as a marker or sign to find righteousness in this world as opposed to leaving ourselves or people in the dark for the anti-Christ to mislead. Again, Abram's seed vs. Nimrod's seed. Whenever the name Melchizedek comes up and or the Order of Melchizedek, the question of whether or not he is God always get asked. We've already broken this down above, but we will give you a more concise yet comprehensive breakdown to answer that question more clearly and directly.

Hebrews 7: 1-3

For this Melchisedec, king of Salem, priest of the most high God, who met Abraham returning from the slaughter of the kings, and blessed him; 2 To whom also Abraham gave a tenth part of all; first being by interpretation King of righteousness, and after that also King of Salem, which is, King of peace; 3 Without father, without mother, without descent, having neither beginning of days, nor end of life; but made like unto the Son of God; abideth a priest continually.

Wow. Let's look at this very closely. We will break this down by the verse to *Make It Plain* (M.I.P.) who Melchizedek is in detail according to God's Word.

Verse 1 - Melchizedek is a king and priest of the most-high God (El Elyon in Hebrew). He left Salem to meet Abram after the battle was over.

Verse 2 - You must recognize that there is ONLY 1 King of Righteousness. There is ONLY 1 King of Salem or Peace. We see that Abram gave a tenth (1/10) of his increase to this King, giving recognition to this HIM as special and or unique. This offering to the King of Righteousness is the introduction of tithing to Abram (Abraham) and those that follow him or his way of faith. The word tithe is introduced, biblically, here.

Verse 3 - Notice how the scripture says 'without father, without mother, without descent, having neither beginning of days, nor end of life. Who else can have these characteristics? What human being can have these qualities? Let's break down what these descriptions mean.

1. Without father = always was
2. Without mother = wasn't born
3. Without descent = no relatives
4. No beginning of days = no birthday or birth date
5. No end of life = cannot die, eternal
6. Made like the Son of God = was made/appeared in flesh like Christ or Adam
7. Abideth a priest continually = eternally a priest, forever

Only 1 being in the history of the universe has these qualities:

God.

Let's take a scriptural look into understanding how, why, and where we can validate that God ALONE has these 7 attributes. But first, we must describe the nature of God via scripture, which can sum up all 7 superlatives in one.

John 4:24

God is a Spirit: and they that worship him must worship him in spirit and in truth.

The mere fact that God is a spirit, which means HE is not a man but a divine being, separates HIS nature from mankind. Being that HE is a spirit, HE has the ability to do things that the human cannot. Well, what kind of spirit is HE?

Leviticus 19: 1-2

And the LORD spake unto Moses, saying, 2 Speak unto all the congregation of the children of Israel, and say unto them, Ye shall be holy: for I the LORD your God am holy.

Holy. This is where and how you can define God as a spirit: Holy. HE is a Holy Spirit, which means that HE is THE HOLY SPIRIT.

Question: If HE is a Holy Spirit or THE HOLY SPIRIT, does that mean that there are other spirits?

Answer: Yes.

Question: Well, if there are other spirits, who's the creator or father of spirits? Wouldn't that spirit be the most powerful or rival spirit?

Answer: Yes, and I thought you would never ask..

Hebrews 12:9

Furthermore we have had fathers of our flesh which corrected us, and we gave them reverence: shall we not much rather be in subjection unto the Father of spirits, and live?

Boom! God is the Father of Spirits. HE is the most powerful of all spirits. HIS spirit is holy, thus making HIM THE HOLY SPIRIT. This is why HE as a spirit, which can take on any shape or form, as the most powerful of all spirits, can sum up all 7 descriptors of Melchizedek. The very nature of God is all-consuming and all-powerful. Nothing exists or have been created without HIM. HE is God.

Jeremiah 32: 17-18

Ah Lord GOD! behold, thou hast made the heaven and the earth by thy great power and stretched out arm, and there is nothing too hard for thee: 18 Thou shewest lovingkindness unto thousands, and recompensest the iniquity of the fathers into the bosom of their children after them: the Great, the Mighty God, the LORD of hosts, is his name,

Whereas this is enough information for some, we have the detailed scriptures below that align the descriptors of Melchizedek in Genesis with the testimonies about God throughout scripture.

Descriptors of Melchizedek (Hebrews 7: 1-3)

1. Without father = always was
2. Without mother = wasn't born
3. Without descent = no relatives
4. No beginning of days – no birthday
5. No end of life = cannot die
6. Made like the Son of God = was made/appeared in flesh like Christ or Adam
7. Abideth a priest continually = eternally a priest, forever

– –

Isaiah 43:10 (1. Without father 2. Without mother 3. Without descent)

Ye are my witnesses, saith the LORD, and my servant whom I have chosen: that ye may know and believe me, and understand that I am he: before me there was no God formed, neither shall there be after me.

1 Timothy 1:17 (4. No beginning of days 5. No end of life)

Now unto the King eternal, immortal, invisible, the only wise God, be honour and glory for ever and ever. Amen.

John 1:14 (6. Made like the Son of God)

And the Word was made flesh, and dwelt among us, (and we beheld his glory, the glory as of the only begotten of the Father,) full of grace and truth.

Hebrews 4: 14-16 (7. Abideth a priest continually)

Seeing then that we have a great high priest, that is passed into the heavens, Jesus the Son of God, let us hold fast our profession. 15 For we have not an high priest which cannot be touched with the feeling of our infirmities; but was in all points tempted like as we are, yet without sin. 16 Let us therefore come boldly unto the throne of grace, that we may obtain mercy, and find grace to help in time of need.

And

John 10:30

I and my Father are one.

Bonus Attributes of God which further validate Melchizedek as a form of God:

Isaiah 40: 13-14 (he has no elder, teacher, or leader)

Who hath directed the Spirit of the LORD, or being his counseller hath taught him? 14 With whom took he counsel, and who instructed him, and taught him in the path of judgment, and taught him knowledge, and shewed to him the way of understanding?

Isaiah 41:4 (God himself was 1st and will be last)

Who hath wrought and done it, calling the generations from the beginning? I the LORD, the first, and with the last; I am he.

Isaiah 45: 18-19 (Just as God spoke the heavens and earth into existence, he did the same with Righteousness)

For thus saith the LORD that created the heavens; God himself that formed the earth and made it; he hath established it, he created it not in vain, he formed it to be inhabited: I am the LORD; and there is none else. 19 I have not spoken in secret, in a dark place of the earth: I said not unto the seed of Jacob, Seek ye me in vain: I the LORD speak righteousness, I declare things that are right.

Isaiah 45: 22-25 (God is the Author of Righteousness and Justice)

Look unto me, and be ye saved, all the ends of the earth: for I am God, and there is none else. 23 I have sworn by myself, the word is gone out of my mouth in righteousness, and shall not return, That unto me every knee shall bow, every tongue shall swear. 24 Surely, shall one say, in the LORD have I righteousness and strength: even to him shall men come; and all that are incensed against him shall be ashamed. 25 In the LORD shall all the seed of Israel be justified, and shall glory.

King of Righteousness? HE is Righteousness.
Psalms 145:17

The LORD is righteous in all his ways, and holy in all his works.

King of Peace? HE is Peace.
2 Thessalonians 3:16

Now the Lord of peace himself give you peace always by all means. The Lord be with you all.

King of Jerusalem? HE is.
2 Chronicles 6:6

But I have chosen Jerusalem, that my name might be there; and have chosen David to be over my people Israel.

So again, there is only 1 with all these qualities, history, power, and abilities:

God.

There is another connection to Melchizedek being God that is quite often hidden in plain sight.
Read Genesis 14:18 again.

Genesis 14:18

And Melchizedek king of Salem brought forth bread and wine: and he was the priest of the most high God.

Bread and wine. Bread and wine. Does this phraseology sound familiar? There are 2 examples we will show you that showcases the wisdom of God spread throughout time to reveal HIMself and HIS amazing footprint.

1. First, Joseph, while in prison, will help you by interpreting the dreams of two men, a butler and baker, who were servants of the Pharaoh of Egypt...

Genesis 40: 12-13 (the butler, held Pharaoh's wine)

And Joseph said unto him, This is the interpretation of it: The three branches are three days: 13 Yet within three days shall Pharaoh lift up thine head, and restore thee unto thy place: and thou shalt deliver Pharaoh's cup into his hand, after the former manner when thou wast his butler.

Genesis 40: 18-19 (the baker, cooked Pharaoh's bread)

And Joseph answered and said, This is the interpretation thereof: The three baskets are three days: 19 Yet within three days shall Pharaoh lift up thy head from off thee, and shall hang thee on a tree; and the birds shall eat thy flesh from off thee.

M.I.P.

The wine represents restoration, as the butler was restored.
The bread represents sacrifice, as the baker was killed.

2. Jesus, at the last supper, fed the disciples...

Luke 22: 15-20

And he said unto them, With desire I have desired to eat this passover with you before I suffer: 16 For I say unto you, I will not any more eat thereof, until it be fulfilled in the kingdom of God. 17 And he took the cup, and gave thanks, and said, Take this, and divide it among yourselves: 18 For I say unto you, I will not drink of the fruit of the vine, until the kingdom of God shall come. 19 And he took bread, and gave thanks, and brake it, and gave unto them, saying, This is my body which is given for you: this do in remembrance of me. 20 Likewise also the cup after supper, saying, This cup is the new testament in my blood, which is shed for you.

The bread and wine is a symbol of Christ. Yes, thousands of years in advance. Melchizedek could have greeted Abram with all kinds of gifts, but he didn't. He chose to bring bread and wine to Abram to symbolize who he really was and the key ingredient to the promise he had already made to Abram regarding his future. The one who was the come, God in Christ, was to redeem mankind back to HIMself as a sacrifice. The bread symbolizes HIS body. The wine to symbolize HIS blood. With Jesus' body being the sacrifice, HIS blood being the cleansing agent, and HIS resurrection being our saving grace.

M.I.P.

The blood of Christ represents restoration, as the butler was in Joseph's story.
The bread of Christ represents sacrifice, as the baker was in Joseph's story.

See how God works? HE is consistent throughout the ages.

John 6: 32-35

Then Jesus said unto them, Verily, verily, I say unto you, Moses gave you not that bread from heaven; but my Father giveth you the true bread from heaven. 33 For the bread of God is he which cometh down from heaven, and giveth life unto the world. 34 Then said they unto him, Lord, evermore give us this bread. 35 And Jesus said unto them, I am the bread of life: he that cometh to me shall never hunger; and he that believeth on me shall never thirst.

This is what Melchizedek offered Abram. HE offered Abram himself. HE offered Abram, Christ. HE offered Abram a version of himself, covered in symbolism, hidden in time, in a meal. Notice how Melchizedek brought him bread and wine even though Abram only took food from the spoils of war. Why would HE bring Abram something he already won plenty of in war? Because the food that Abram took would last for a short time. The food Melchizedek brought him would last forever! That's what Jesus is speaking about in John 6. Hallelujah! Only God could do this. Only God can know this. Only God could reveal this throughout the generations and different writers to mean the same thing for the same being. Only God can hide HIMself in time yet continue HIS functions to leave traces for those who seek HIM, to find HIM, as you have here. This is truly remarkable when you really take a second and look at the mastery of this throughout the generations. Wow.

The following is an answer for those who question the identity of Melchizedek from another scriptural perspective. They would argue that Melchizedek and Shem were the same person based on the verse in Jasher 16:11. Let's read..

Jasher 16:11

And Adonizedek king of Jerusalem, the same was Shem, went out with his men to meet Abram and his people, with bread and wine, and they remained together in the valley of Melech.

In this verse the name Adonizedek is more of a title rather than a name, which means 'lord of righteousness'. We know that the descriptions of Melchizedek is that he is ageless, without father or mother, etc. No human can have these attributes, only God. Whereas many scholars interpret this verse of Adonizedek to be Shem, who doubles as Melchizedek, we understand it differently for 2 key reasons:

1. We know Shem's father is Noah, which disqualifies him from being Melchizedek (Gen. 5:32). Instead, we see Adonizedek as a title for Shem, being that he too was a leader in the then world known for following after the righteousness of his father Noah who worshipped Elohim, God. Keep in mind, Abram lived in the house of Noah and Shem while he was in hiding from Nimrod early in his life, so seeing Shem would not have been a new or unique thing for him. Which leads us to point #2.

2. Abram (Abraham) considered the greatness of Melchizedek so much so that he obviously saw the uniqueness of this man in his physical form to the point that he in no way gave away a sense of comeliness of kin. He clearly observed the higher sense of presence within Melchizedek which in turn he gave him a 10th of his possessions, which we have come to learn was the food that he ate during the raid on the four Elamite kings to restore Lot. The presence of Melchizedek was different, historically different, even for Abram.

Hebrews 7:4

Now consider how great this man was, unto whom even the patriarch Abraham gave the tenth of the spoils.

To finalize one's mind around what we have learned, one must understand that we have 1 God with many diversities or functions. HE has many descriptions that serve as a name, but 1 name. HE will show HIMself in different ways, which speaks to HIS different abilities as God, which is the very definition of diversities. With that said, we will give you the verses that align HIS diversities with how HE chooses to display HIMself, then you will understand how and why HE decided to show HIMself as a man who was king and high priest of Salem, Melchizedek.

Diversities of God
1 Corinthians 12:6

And there are diversities of operations, but it is the same God which worketh all in all.

Examples of those Diversities:

God as an Angel
Exodus 3:2

And the angel of the LORD appeared unto him in a flame of fire out of the midst of a bush: and he looked, and, behold, the bush burned with fire, and the bush was not consumed.

God as a Mighty Man of War (Commander of the Army of God)
Joshua 5: 13-15

And it came to pass, when Joshua was by Jericho, that he lifted up his eyes and looked, and, behold, there stood a man over against him with his sword drawn in his hand: and Joshua went unto him, and said unto him, Art thou for us, or for our adversaries? 14 And he said, Nay; but as captain of the host of the LORD am I now come. And Joshua fell on his face to the earth, and did worship, and said unto him, What saith my lord unto his servant? 15 And the captain of the LORD'S host said unto Joshua, Loose thy shoe from off thy foot; for the place whereon thou standest is holy. And Joshua did so.

God as a Pillar of Fire and a Cloud
Exodus 13:21

And the LORD went before them by day in a pillar of a cloud, to lead them the way; and by night in a pillar of fire, to give them light; to go by day and night:

God has a name that describes these diversities, Elohim, which means God in the plural sense. Whereas many people have taken this to mean God is multiple or many, it really only means that God has different functions and or roles (diversities) even though HE is One, THE 1. By the name Melchizedek, HE is the King of Righteousness. By the position of the King of Salem, HE is the King of Peace. By instituting the tithe, HE is the God of order and sustenance in the Earth (Malachi 3:10). By bringing Abram bread and wine, HE is the Christ. By choosing to appear to Abram in this form, HE is showing how relatable and personal HE is willing to be with us. HE is the 1 and there is none beside or like HIM.

Hebrews 7: 14-16

For it is evident that our Lord sprang out of Juda; of which tribe Moses spake nothing concerning priesthood. 15 And it is yet far more evident: for that after the similitude of Melchisedec there ariseth another priest, 16 Who is made, not after the law of a carnal commandment, but after the power of an endless life.

And

John 10:30

I and my Father are one.

M.I.P.
Melchizedek = God

Covenant and Confirmation

Genesis 15:1

After these things the word of the LORD came unto Abram in a vision, saying, Fear not, Abram: I *am* thy shield, *and* thy exceeding great reward.

When God sends for you, go. It is the only answer you can really have. Better yet should I say, it's the only answer you should have. HE gives us all the option to obey HIM or not. Obedience or sacrifice. Life or death. It's a choice. It's all a choice. This is the gift of God given to humanity. God himself has choices, options. HE allowed HIS image, humans, the ability to choose with intelligence, which is one of the many things that separate us from the animal kingdom. HE is, therefore we are.

The LORD sees all. HE is vision. I'm not talking about sight, which some people have and some people don't. Vision is different. Vision is the unseen, seen. Sight is the seeing, seen. When God chooses to use vision to get our attention or make a point, it's hard for others to understand. Why? Because they are looking to use sight to accept vision. In most cases, that will never be the case. Vision is for the few, uncommon. Sight is for the many, common. This was the case with Abram and his life story, uncommon.

After everything Abram had accomplished in his life that he could testify to, God chose to come to him in a vision when Abram least expected it, unguarded in his thoughts and routine. HE wanted Abram to see what couldn't be seen by others even though the way HE interacted with Abram was seen by all. The LORD showed himself to Abram in the form of Melchizedek, for his sight to behold, as the king of peace. Now it was time for HIM to show HIMself to Abram in a spiritual sense, using a vision to showcase HIS ability to create Abram's legacy within the Earth and throughout history. When the KING of PEACE tells you to fear not, history and legacy will bend to your will. This is the power and genius of God.

The most stated phrase in all scripture is 'fear not.' Several biblical studies proclaim that it is used 365 times in the bible! How ironic is that it matches the total amount of days we have in the modern calendar year, which translates to God reinforcing the idea to 'fear not' every day of the year. How incredible! Again, the power and genius of God.
In understanding what HE was about to do, for history' sake, God wanted Abram not to fear the next. HE knew the attacks that would be sent Abram's way and those who follow and believe the way Abram would. Therefore, HE told Abram that HE, God, would be his shield, to protect him against all attacks. This is why the apostle Paul, when describing the full body armor of God, called the shield of faith a tool for which we quench all the fiery darts of the enemy (Ephesians 6:16). With that mindset, HE also knew that Abram taking on HIS belief structure and vision would come with a cost. That cost would be offset with a reward, the promise of eternity with the LORD of Lords. Therefore, God told Abram that HE was his reward. Think of it. If the LORD of ALL says fear not, HE'll protect you as a shield and in the end, HE'll be your reward, what else could you want? God covers all bases and reinforces HIS power over all power. HE is God, and there is no other. This is what God offered Abram.

Observe the strategy of God. Once HE established peace within Abram to receive the vision, it was now time to take Abram to a place where he could see the vision.

Genesis 15: 2-7

And Abram said, Lord GOD, what wilt thou give me, seeing I go childless, and the steward of my house *is* this Eliezer of
Damascus? 3 And Abram said, Behold, to me thou hast given no seed: and, lo, one born in my house is mine heir. 4 And, behold,
the word of the LORD *came* unto him, saying, This shall not be thine heir; but he that shall come forth out of thine own bowels
shall be thine heir. 5 And he brought him forth abroad, and said, Look now toward heaven, and tell the stars, if thou be able to
number them: and he said unto him, So shall thy seed be. 6 And he believed in the LORD; and he counted it to him for
righteousness. 7 And he said unto him, I *am* the LORD that brought thee out of Ur of the Chaldees, to give thee this land to inherit
it.

A man can have his reasons, but God has resolve. Abram was correct in his assessment of his life situation, but it wasn't complete. Therefore, God had to show Abram through sight how HIS will would be manifested in the Earth through Abram. On the surface, Abram couldn't see it, as he alluded to Eliezer being his heir because he had no children. But God saw through the lens of time, through Abram's own bowels, which no man can see on the surface. The LORD knew what He was going to do, Abram didn't. HE then used the heavens to declare HIS will by asking Abram to count the stars, which no man can, neither then or now, even with all the technology we have today. No one can count how many people who have or has learned to follow the way of Abram, which modern scholars call the monotheistic faiths (Christianity, Judaism, Islam), to this day as well. That's incredible!

Reader, please note the hidden gem in verse 5. God told Abram to tell the stars. Tell the stars? Yes. Speak to them. How so? HE's speaking in terms of calling them, naming them to show distinction, and keep record of them to prove HIM as LORD of Hosts. If Abram could do that, he'd be able to fully see the vision of God, which he couldn't. God wasn't asking Abram to study the stars, as people have done over the millenniums. HE's asking Abram, and us, to try HIM and see if HE's true. The moment you see that, belief happens that no one can take away. This is why the very next verse, 6, says that Abram believed in the LORD. This is also the numbered day mankind was made on, the 6th. This is righteousness ladies and gentlemen. God is allowing us to see and understand how to get to righteousness in your life. It's not about the perfection of a person, but the willingness to try God and resolve yourself to believing in HIM because HE is tried and true. By the way, only HE knows the names and number of stars in the universe, beyond what we can see.

NASA (estimates) up to one septillion stars (1 followed by 24 zeros)...they think.
Scripture doesn't estimate...

Psalms 147:4

He telleth the number of the stars; he calleth them all by *their* names.

And...

Isaiah 40:26

Lift up your eyes on high, and behold who hath created these *things*, that bringeth out their host by number: he calleth them all by names by the greatness of his might, for that *he is* strong in power; not one faileth.

Who knew this?

God did.

HE knew this before Abram. HE knew this before Adam. HE knew this before the vision. HE knew this before there was a before. Scientists, every day, are studying the blueprint of God throughout the universe trying to determine whether they want to acknowledge him or not. The more they find, the more they acknowledge his majesty and power, even when they deny his presence.

As God revealed HIS will to Abram in the form of vision, it was now time for Abram to understand how his covenant with the LORD will bring forth the Christ. Pay close attention to the details and they will show us the amazingness of God, THE Prophet through whom all prophets would come. Scripture says the testimony of the Christ is the very spirit of prophecy (Rev. 19:10).

Genesis 15: 8-17

And he said, Lord GOD, whereby shall I know that I shall inherit it? 9 And he said unto him, Take me an heifer of three years old, and a she
goat of three years old, and a ram of three years old, and a turtledove, and a young pigeon. 10 And he took unto him all these, and divided
them in the midst, and laid each piece one against another: but the birds divided he not. 11 And when the fowls came down upon the
carcases, Abram drove them away.12 And when the sun was going down, a deep sleep fell upon Abram; and, lo, an horror of great darkness
fell upon him. 13 And he said unto Abram, Know of a surety that thy seed shall be a stranger in a land *that is* not theirs, and shall serve them;
and they shall afflict them four hundred years; 14 And also that nation, whom they shall serve, will I judge: and afterward shall they come out
with great substance. 15 And thou shalt go to thy fathers in peace; thou shalt be buried in a good old age. 16 But in the fourth generation they
shall come hither again: for the iniquity of the Amorites *is* not yet full.17 And it came to pass, that, when the sun went down, and it was dark,
behold a smoking furnace, and a burning lamp that passed between those pieces.

Amazing! This is so powerful! We will break it down for you or as we say, *Make It Plain*, so you can understand why God used the words HE used, specific animals, and concepts to point to the HOLY ONE through the covenant with Abram.

The Heifer

A heifer is a female cow, the one we most commonly learn and know about growing up as children. The heifer is a giver of life and milk. It feeds and nurtures. The heifer is representative of several biblical concepts, worshipped in many different cultures throughout history, but here, especially when connected to the age of 3 years, we have 3 concepts. The 1st is Abraham, Isaac, and Jacob, through whom the Christ would be produced, as a heifer produces offspring. The 2nd, is the 42 generations from Abraham to Christ, 14 generations x 3 different ages, which leads to the birth of Christ. The final connection is the 3-year ministry of Christ, feeding HIS disciples the milk of the WORD in prep for them to bring others to the meat of the WORD, HIMself.

Hebrews 5: 12-13

For every one that useth milk *is* unskilful in the word of righteousness: for he is a babe. 14 But strong meat belongeth to them that
are of full age, *even* those who by reason of use have their senses exercised to discern both good and evil.

The She Goat

A she goat is called a doe or nanny. The lead she goat is called a flock queen. They are responsible for leading the herd to better grazing areas, which means they are leaders in nature. They lead, testing the grazing plants to see if they are consumable by the herd. They lead the baby goats as well. It is from this concept that we get the word kid or kids, which we all have used at some point in our lives when speaking or referencing children. The term kid literally means baby goat, which is not possible without a nanny, or she goat.

The she goat is connected to the Christ through Abraham in 3 more ways. First, from the line of Abraham, Isaac, and Jacob, comes the first belief structure in the world that smelt or tasted of the world and denied it, just like the flock queen when grazing and finding bad or poisonous plants for the herd. She sends a signal to the rest of the herd that this plant or plants are not to be consumed. Abram tried idolatry and turned away, thus leading others in a new way back to the LORD. His act of turning away from the world created the term Hebrew, by which Abram was called the first. Through him would come the Christ, the ultimate pastor, leader of the flock and his WORD deters us from the poisonous plants of the world.

Secondly, the she goat represents the wandering nature of the church, as the flock will act in a state of confusion until they have a she goat to lead them. The world is in confusion when the church doesn't lead correctly, which it is currently in the state of now. This is why our children or kids have gone astray. The church has not led them into better grazing or feeding areas to feast in the fields of the LORD.
Thirdly, the she goat is a flat-out leader but knows that it is not in charge. There is a difference. The male goat, or top buck, leads the herd from behind. When the top buck sees the plants that aren't good for the herd by the flock queen's dissatisfied gestures, he tramples it. He's responsible for the herd's protection as it overlooks the herd and makes sure all stragglers are sternly redirected back to the flock. This is Christ. HE came at the end of scripture to redirect us in the end times how to stay in the flock for which HE leads. HE's in charge but we must lead as the she goat of the worldly herd. HE does it sternly, not softly, like a top buck. The she goat, which is supposed to be the church, job is the lead the flock from the front, go away from sin (poisonous plants/bad grazing areas), declare it to the LORD (top buck) so HE can execute judgement (stomp out the plant[s]). This is why the reward or digesting of sin (bad or poisonous plants) equals death. The gift of good pasture is eternal life.

Romans 6:23

For the wages of sin *is* death; but the gift of God *is* eternal life through Jesus Christ our Lord.

The Ram

The ram is the male sheep, known for its horns and fighting capabilities. Rams are historically associated with strength, creativity, leadership, and protectorship. The role of Abraham and his seed is to be the ram within the Earth. Christ was the living example of the ram. He showcased strength to hold back wrath and give mercy, creativity as HE was the WORD that created the world, HE leads us all down the path of righteousness, and HE is the protector of the saints who are the hearers and doers of HIS Word. Christ is the ram and we are to be HIS followers. Rams are known for their fighting abilities as well, so don't buy into that passive nonsense that people place on believers. We are not that, even when we pass on things. Christ was not passive or soft. Scripture verifies that. Rams often battle one another alongside steep mountainous slopes, seeking to prove their point of domination as they oversee the world from the top of a mountain.

This is why scriptural debate is good. This is why you must be ready to defend the faith. This is why studying scripture is vital to your horn development. Horn development? Yes. The horns are used as weapons when rams clash. They have also been used as tools to make announcements and proclamations for thousands of years. These are all descriptions of the HOLY ONE, HE who sits high and looks low, whose WORD makes announcements and proclamations of HIS will, whose WORD combats the sin of our lives from the mountaintop, declaring HIMself to be the only one we need to lead, as the leader of the flock.

The last characteristic of a ram that is relatable to the power of Christ is virility, which means the quality of having strength, energy, and a strong sex drive, or manliness. This is why Christ came as a man. Full of strength. Full of energy to handle the perils of the world, as a man who leads. As for the sex drive, the goal of the believer is to reproduce more believers, more Christ-like offspring. All of which comes through the seed of Abraham, as Christ did. From a 3-year ministry to today, the WORD showcases virility to the ends of the Earth and shows us how God defines manliness, fruitfully and multiplying HIS kingdom in the WORD through intentional obedience. This is why rams are called commissioners of the herd. True Manliness is a commission, the Great Commission.

Matthew 28: 18-20

And Jesus came and spake unto them, saying, All power is given unto me in heaven and in earth. 19 Go ye therefore, and teach all
nations, baptizing them in the name of the Father, and of the Son, and of the Holy Ghost: 20 Teaching them to observe all things
whatsoever I have commanded you: and, lo, I am with you alway, *even* unto the end of the world. Amen.

The Turtledove

The turtledove is a bird renown for being a symbol of peace. It is a migratory bird that chooses thorny plants to put their nests. They usually eat among the weeds or in places that are low cut so they can see what's in the grass where they feed. It is known as a wedding or marriage symbol of love as it is known for mating with one partner for life. They even mourn when the mate dies.

Ladies and gentlemen, Christ is the Prince of Peace. HIS message and purpose has been traveling or migrated from HIS birth to every corner of the Earth. While HE lived, HE made his resting place among the unwanted. HE hung out with the unwanted. HE was the unwanted. These places would be considered thorny. HE was born in a barn, on hay, which is thorny. The crown placed on HIS head by the Romans was made of thorns. HE teaches us to see the serpent, who cannot hide in the short grass, as HIS Word is a doubled edged sword that cuts down the tall grass so we can see what we are dealing with. HIS Word lives forever as we are bound to HIM forever. HE chose us for all eternity. We are to choose HIS way for all eternity. As for mourning the loss of a loved one, HE identifies with us. Christ mourned the loss of a loved one, Lazarus. HE is the turtledove that feels our pain and subjugated HIMself to it in order to be with us, to understand us, as love with a sweet-sounding voice, as turtledoves are known to have.

John 11: 31-35

The Jews then which were with her in the house, and comforted her, when they saw Mary, that she rose up hastily and went out,
followed her, saying, She goeth unto the grave to weep there. 32 Then when Mary was come where Jesus was, and saw him, she fell
down at his feet, saying unto him, Lord, if thou hadst been here, my brother had not died. 33 When Jesus therefore saw her
weeping, and the Jews also weeping which came with her, he groaned in the spirit, and was troubled, 34 And said, Where have ye
laid him? They said unto him, Lord, come and see. 35 Jesus wept.

The Young Pigeon

The pigeon is a bird that is known worldwide as having great skills as a navigator, fast, strong, and understands directives accurately. This is why for thousands of years pigeons have been used as mail carriers. They understand the assignment given to them when trained to deliver a message. They can carry 10% of their body weight over vast distances precisely. They are believed to be the 1st domesticated birds in nature. They can sense weather change patterns before the weather actually happens. That same distinction gives them the ability to sense sickness in the body, like cancer. They also recognize themselves whereas most other birds cannot identify their own image when looking at a reflection.

The WORD, which is Christ, was a message. HE is the mail and the mail carrier. HE doeth the work (John 14:10). The gospel is the message, HE gave it to us. We are supposed to spread it to the world, like the pigeon. We are to navigate the world, in a timely manner, stronger in HIS WORD, understanding how to precisely hit the mark to destroy the strongholds of sin in an accurate way. Pigeons are sent out with a message to a receiver. When received, the message is deemed important and vital. This is why the gospel is important when we deliver it to others. We must navigate correctly so HIS WORD can be delivered precisely. Through Abraham would come the Christ, preaching and being the gospel. Acceptance would have to come via faith.

See how it all connects?

Genesis 15: 10-11

And he took unto him all these, and divided them in the midst, and laid each piece one against another: but the birds divided he
not. 11 And when the fowls came down upon the carcases, Abram drove them away.

This is why God divided the birds from the four-legged animals but kept them together. The birds represent the spiritual element of Christ. The four-legged animals represent the physical elements of Christ. They were all sacrificed at the same place, just as Christ was sacrificed on the cross. Take a look and see if you see what I see....

Ram

Turtledove — She Goat — Pigeon

Heifer

<u>...a cross.</u>

Just as the fowls came down to feast on the flesh of the sacrifice, so did the evil one when Christ died. Satan thought that he had won at Calvary. This is the same thing with us. When something happens to a believer, you will see the vultures circle around, looking to take a piece out of you. There is a joy that comes over people when a believer falls or fails. That sensation comes from the evil one, who thought he had won when the HOLY ONE was on cavalry's cross.

But God.

Just as Abram chased the fowls away from the sacrifice, so does the grace and power of God chase away the fowlness of sin in our lives. Regardless of how it looks, God always has someone close by to wave the fowls or fouls away. When our faith acts as Abram did, it chases the foul ways of the world away from the sacrifice of obedience to the LORD. Had Satan studied Abram and his story more closely, he would have seen this coming down the pike. But hey, Satan is not all-knowing. He's a created being, just like the rest of God's creation.

Genesis 15: 12-17

And when the sun was going down, a deep sleep fell upon Abram; and, lo, an horror of great darkness fell upon him. 13 And he
said unto Abram, Know of a surety that thy seed shall be a stranger in a land *that is* not theirs, and shall serve them; and they shall
afflict them four hundred years; 14 And also that nation, whom they shall serve, will I judge: and afterward shall they come out
with great substance. 15 And thou shalt go to thy fathers in peace; thou shalt be buried in a good old age. 16 But in the fourth
generation they shall come hither again: for the iniquity of the Amorites *is* not yet full. 17 And it came to pass, that, when the sun
went down, and it was dark, behold a smoking furnace, and a burning lamp that passed between those pieces

God has a tendency to use deep sleep as a tool to pull amazingness from a man. The first time he used deep sleep with man was with Adam. When Adam woke up, woman was standing in front of him.

Genesis 2: 21-22

And the LORD God caused a deep sleep to fall upon Adam, and he slept: and he took one of his ribs, and closed up the flesh
instead thereof; 22 And the rib, which the LORD God had taken from man, made he a woman, and brought her unto the man.

The amazingness of woman was brought forth from man as a gift from God via deep sleep. God does this a few more times in the Bible as well. It's crazy when you think of it. God, in HIS infinite wisdom, tells us why HE does it this way.

Job 33: 14-18

For God speaketh once, yea twice, *yet man* perceiveth it not. 15 In a dream, in a vision of the night, when deep sleep falleth upon
men, in slumberings upon the bed; 16 Then he openeth the ears of men, and sealeth their instruction, 17 That he may withdraw
man *from his* purpose, and hide pride from man. 18 He keepeth back his soul from the pit, and his life from perishing by the
sword.

God uses deep sleep to open up the ears of a man, giving him uninterrupted instructions so we can be purposeful and unprideful. This is what HE did to Adam. This is what HE did to Abram. This is what HE has done to me. The purpose of putting Abram in a deep sleep was to get his attention, discard fear, intentionalize HIS purpose for him, and to verify his historical significance and offspring even though Abram didn't have any children at this point. This was God's way of allowing Abram to see down his own timeline after his belief was cemented, thus causing his faith to blossom.

Genesis 15: 17-21

And it came to pass, that, when the sun went down, and it was dark, behold a smoking furnace, and a burning lamp that passed
between those pieces. 18 In the same day the LORD made a covenant with Abram, saying, Unto thy seed have I given this land,
from the river of Egypt unto the great river, the river Euphrates: 19 The Kenites, and the Kenizzites, and the Kadmonites, 20 And
the Hittites, and the Perizzites, and the Rephaims, 21 And the Amorites, and the Canaanites, and the Girgashites, and the
Jebusites.

God is the Greatest! Reader, notice now how Abram was not in the vision at this point. Verse 17 speaks about the sun and darkness, a smoking furnace and burning lamp. These are all physical world things that can be seen. God was now going to show Abram another aspect of HIS purpose by confirming HIS appointment with Abram's physical eyes. A man without a country, without a people, has now been given both. The beauty of this covenant was not only for Abram within the physical world, but the spiritual one as well.

The LORD is not only giving Abram the blueprint to faith that pleases HIM, but us as well. How so? Abram had no children, yet. Abram had no people to call his own, yet. Abram had no land of his own, yet. So, God told, showed, then promised what HE was going to do for Abram and his unborn offspring in the physical world which has its' roots in the metaphysical world. Abram's focus was physical. God's focus was spiritual. The moment Abram believed HIM, spiritually (metaphysical), God set forth the process of rewarding belief with showing Abram the land his people were going to call home. In a wilderness, God showed himself true. In the wilderness of life, God will show himself true. This is why scripture says in verse 18, the SAME DAY, God made the covenant clear by showing Abram the exact land his children, who haven't been born yet, would have forever. To add precision to HIS promise, HE told Abram exactly who was going to be living in the land prior to their arrival. This is why Moses, the author of Genesis, particularizes the nations that lived in the area so when people throughout history research and study this event, they can find it with precision and make a decision. God is a rewarder of faith, proven by history, believed by the unbelievers, the revealer, and the master of time and its line. None of these things a man can see, yet he must believe. You must believe the source over your sight. From this, you get faith.

Land Promised to Abram by God
© Coeur d'Alene

In conclusion, as a lover of sports, we'll put this covenant in the form of a trade between teams. Pundits and barbershop critics will go on for hours and hours giving different perspectives on major and minor deals that alter teams, organizations, franchises, communities, etc. We will do the same here. We will *Make It Plain* for you as we put this covenant in terms of who won the trade or deal. Debate it as you choose because the whole world has been affected by this deal.

Make It Plain

- *God gets*: a nation that serves HIM
- *Abram gets*: God and ALL of HIS universal/ultimate power **forever**, land **forever**, children **forever**, seed that brings forth the Christ **forever**, a name that lives through the ages **forever**, power **forever**, prestige **forever**, riches **forever**, love **forever**, etc….**forever**

Who do you think won this deal or trade?

God offered.

Abram agreed to the deal.

Deal confirmed.

Hagar

Genesis 16:1

Now Sarai Abram's wife bare him no children: and she had an handmaid, an Egyptian, whose name *was* Hagar.

In order to understand this section, reader, please understand what's going on in this history altering moment. While God was confirming HIS covenant to Abram, spiritually and genetically binding him to the coming Christ and HIS believers, Abram's wife, Sarai, was making a move of her own to invest in the covenant that she wasn't asked to. As a believer, you must understand that when God moves on, to, or for you, everything moves around you. This is no different. The nature of God, man, and woman is about to be put on full display or take off, like a plane. It just so happens that the blessings of the covenant would begin with a woman whose name means exactly that: flight.

Hagar, what a name. It means flight, or one who flees. The bible tells us her role and name, but there's a question, especially for a researcher, that comes to mind. Where did this mystery woman come from and why is she so important? Well, the scripture tells us...

Jasher 15: 31-32

And the king took a maiden whom he begat by his concubines, and he gave her to Sarai for a handmaid. 32. And the king said to his daughter, It is better for thee my daughter to be a handmaid in this man's house than to be mistress in my house, after we have beheld the evil that befell us on account of this woman.

Hagar is Rikayon's daughter. Hagar is the daughter of the first Pharaoh of Egypt. She was a princess, royalty, by the blood of her father. She was a servant, by the blood of her mother, who was a concubine. Concubine means mistress, in today's terminology and lexicon, a side chick. To *Make It Plain*, Hagar was a woman born to serve royalty as royalty. By understanding this part of her story, you can see why she was chosen to be historically one of the most important women to ever live. Let's proceed.

Hagar's biblical story is paralleled with her master, Sarai, Abram's wife. Sarai was a beautiful woman, loved by her husband, adorned by men. Hagar was a young woman, beautiful in her own right, royal in blood. Both women, although different in background upbringing and roles within their families, they both shared one thing, Abram. He was responsible for both women. One as a wife, one as a servant. Sarai was his actual family member, his blood. Hagar was from royalty, a gift, his servant. Sarai was older, wiser, but had no children. Hagar was younger, immature, but fertile. This dynamic will prove to be dynamic.

As time went along, Sarai grew older. Her body was changing, as it does to everyone. As a woman, she was reaching the age when she could no longer have children. A man, until the day he dies, can have children. This difference in our biological nature is very important in understanding the structure of God for the reproduction of humanity and family. Sarai knew this. She loved her husband, dearly. She is regarded throughout history as obedient and loyal to her husband. When you take this into consideration, imagine how she felt at the time about her body's unwillingness to give birth.

This is a woman that the first Pharaoh of Egypt almost gave up his life and kingdom for. Men would see her and want her for themselves. She was loyal to Abram, and he loved her in return. Regardless, the thing she wanted to give him, was children. But she couldn't. Look at it from her perspective: she wasn't present to hear or see what God said to Abram, so she may not have believed what Abram said. However, she loved and believed in her husband, so for the sake of her love, she wanted him to have children. She and Abram had everything that everyone would want or need in those times, except children. As a woman, she felt like she had failed him. It is from this perspective, the story of Hagar unfolds.

Jasher 16: 23-27

And Sarai, the daughter of Haran, Abram's wife, was still barren in those days; she did not bear to Abram either son or daughter.
24. And when she saw that she bare no children she took her handmaid Hagar, whom Pharaoh had given her, and she gave her to
Abram her husband for a wife. 25. For Hagar learned all the ways of Sarai as Sarai taught her, she was not in any way deficient in
following her good ways. 26. And Sarai said to Abram, Behold here is my handmaid Hagar, go to her that she may bring forth
upon my knees, that I may also obtain children through her. 27. And at the end of ten years of Abram's dwelling in the land of
Canaan, which is the eighty-fifth year of Abram's life, Sarai gave Hagar unto him.

This is the nature of woman, especially when she is submissive, loves her man, and wants the best for him. Sarai was the very definition of that type of woman. In fact, she is the biblical standard of what that type of woman is. Her love of Abram, regardless of the vision he had, made her ambitious. She wanted children for him. Pay close attention to what she did. She didn't get emotional and lash out or other none rationally minded things. Instead, she planned, plotted, and schemed. In knowing her husband and looking at the options available, she noticed Hagar, a young girl at the time, and considered her youth and possible fertility. She knew that Hagar was Pharaoh's daughter, so if she could have children, she would serve as the mother of the child, who would have royal blood plus the gift of God through Abram. But first, she would need to prep Hagar in the ways of how to please Abram.

Sarai went into teacher mode, and as verse 25 says, Hagar was a great student. For 10 years, Hagar learned. She learned Abram from Sarai. She knew him well, very well. She learned Abram so well that at the end of 10 years, Sarai felt comfortable in giving Hagar to Abram. Keep in mind, Hagar's father, Pharaoh Rikayon, had previously told his daughter it was better for her to go with Abram than be a mistress in his house than to stay in Egypt and be a mistress to others. In his own way, Rikayon blessed his daughter beyond what he even knew. This was a God thing.

Genesis 16: 2-3

And Sarai said unto Abram, Behold now, the LORD hath restrained me from bearing: I pray thee, go in unto my maid; it may be
that I may obtain children by her. And Abram hearkened to the voice of Sarai. 3 And Sarai Abram's wife took Hagar her maid the
Egyptian, after Abram had dwelt ten years in the land of Canaan, and gave her to her husband Abram to be his wife.

Reader, please note Abram in these verses. Note his nature. He didn't search for another woman. He didn't ask his wife for children. He didn't seek a concubine or other women. He wasn't eyeing Hagar and it just so happen that Sarai groomed her for his taking. No. Abram, the person God revealed the vision to, was content in what he was shown. For 10 years, Abram lived. He didn't question God, he didn't try to scheme, plot, or figure out a way to make the vision work. No. He lived. This is priceless in understanding the true nature of a believer. Stay the course and wait on the revelation of the LORD. Abram didn't doubt God, even after 10 years. He stayed the course. The believer's nature.

On the flip side of things, take note of Sarai. Note her nurture. She did search for another. She wanted to please her husband. She sought a surrogate mother to give her husband the child she wanted. She looked outside of herself for validation. For 10 years, she planned and trained another woman to please her husband. This is the true nature of a nurturer. The nurturer bends and alters to please. Whereas this seems all and well on the surface and it certainly has its place, it often overlooks nature, even when nature is involved.

In flys Hagar.

Abram had to be convinced to take Hagar as his wife. He didn't have pre-marital relations with Hagar to have children. He married her in agreement with his wife. This is very important to know in understanding the chaos of what happens when nature and nurture meet God's will. Better yet, let's *Make It Plain*.

Genesis 16:4

And he went in unto Hagar, and she conceived: and when she saw that she had conceived, her mistress was despised in her eyes.

Scripture says...

Jasher 16: 28-30

And Abram hearkened to the voice of his wife Sarai, and he took his handmaid Hagar and Abram came to her and she conceived.
29. And when Hagar saw that she had conceived she rejoiced greatly, and her mistress was despised in her eyes, and she said
within herself, This can only be that I am better before God than Sarai my mistress, for all the days that my mistress has been with
my lord, she did not conceive, but me the Lord has caused in so short a time to conceive by him. 30. And when Sarai saw that
Hagar had conceived by Abram, Sarai was jealous of her handmaid, and Sarai said within herself, This is surely nothing else but
that she must be better than I am.

Facts vs. Feelings. Nature vs. Nurture. This is what you are looking at. Let's discuss the facts first. Abram listened to his wife, took Hagar as his 2nd wife and got her pregnant pretty quickly. Sarai did a great job of preparing Hagar for her husband. Hagar became more than a mistress, more than her father's blessing on her life, she was now a mother and wife to one of the richest men on the planet. More importantly, she learned the God of the man she married.

Now, for the feelings. Abram had to be a happy man. He finally had the chance to become a father, especially in his older age. Sarai, the matchmaker, initially was happy to see her husband happy. She was the one who set this whole thing up. She went out of her way to try to make her husband happy and give him children, in a way trying to do God's job of giving Abram children. Hagar, of course was happy. She was winning on all fronts! But with all of this happiness of a child coming into the family picture, the two feelers in this equation began to look away from the facts. This is dangerous territory. Why? Because it turns into the game of perception, pride, and the value system concepts of worth. It's such a dangerous game, one in which delusion can play a huge factor. Let's read Jasher...

Jasher 16: 29-30

29. And when Hagar saw that she had conceived she rejoiced greatly, and her mistress was despised in her eyes, and she said
within herself, This can only be that I am better before God than Sarai my mistress, for all the days that my mistress has been with
my lord, she did not conceive, but me the Lord has caused in so short a time to conceive by him. 30. And when Sarai saw that
Hagar had conceived by Abram, Sarai was jealous of her handmaid, and Sarai said within herself, This is surely nothing else but
that she must be better than I am.

See what happens when feelings get in the way? See what happens when facts get pushed to the side? Fight or flight sets in. Delusion sets in. False self-worth evaluation comes forth. Shame and blame. Jealousy and or envy rears its' head to speak. Pride becomes blood and the heart changes. Chaos usually ensues.

Instead of Hagar focusing on the joy of her pregnancy, the allowance of Sarai to wed Abram, and her new status as wife to a man of destiny, Hagar chose to entertain the lower energy of outside perception and validation, which caused internal conflict. Sarai, the one who orchestrated all of this, did the exact same thing. Instead of her being happy for all parties involved, herself included, she decided to despise the very opportunity she created, because of her feelings. Her feelings. Not facts, but feelings.

Hagar picked up on that. She ignored the fact that she was a gift given by her father, given to serve, chosen to be a 2nd wife, was taught how to serve by the 1st wife, was chosen to be a surrogate mother. She chose her feelings. She didn't choose better or positive energy, she internalized non-progressive lower energy. Hagar actually went lower. She said to herself that she was better than Sarai. Not only better than Sarai, but better in the eyes of God.

Delusion. False self-worth evaluation. Pride.

Sarai did the same thing, just in a different way. She ignored the fact that she was barren, completely abandoned it. Instead, she became jealous because her husband got Hagar pregnant, a younger, more fertile woman whom SHE personally picked to be the surrogate mother. She even said to herself the same things that Hagar internally said, which is even worse, especially as the older and wiser woman.

Delusion. False self-worth evaluation. Pride.

Sarai could no longer take it. Fight or flight came forth in her mind. The pain and agony, feelings, stirred her to try to come to a resolution for the opportunity she created. Yes, the mastermind behind this pregnancy was now in such conflict and emotional chaos that she went to her husband to voice her opinion and give another strategy for how to bring peace to their family....because of her feelings.

Genesis 16:5

And Sarai said unto Abram, My wrong *be* upon thee: I have given my maid into thy bosom; and when she saw that she had conceived, I was despised in her eyes: the LORD judge between me and thee.

There's more....

Jasher 16: 31-32

And Sarai said unto Abram, My wrong be upon thee, for at the time when thou didst pray before the Lord for children why didst thou not pray on my account, that the Lord should give me seed from thee? 32. And when I speak to Hagar in thy presence, she despiseth my words, because she has conceived, and thou wilt say nothing to her; may the Lord judge between me and thee for what thou hast done to me.

I told you. You can anticipate it. When feelings get in the way, chaos ensues. Instead of Sarai looking at her own decision and take accountability, accept both the reward and consequence of being a matchmaker, and more importantly, stepping in the way to speed up or amend God's will for her husband, she blamed him. Yes, you are reading this right. She blamed Abram. She even blamed him for not stopping Hagar for speaking to her in a disrespectful way in his presence. Nevermind Hagar was trained by her. That part was conveniently left out. In essence, she blamed Abram for listening to her, which is crazy when you think about it. Not only did she blame him, she said his prayer for children was errant, saying he should have prayed for her to be pregnant, not Hagar. Again, feelings. Imagine what Abram was thinking, how confused, possibly offended, etc. he was at that moment.

Delusion. False self-worth evaluation. Pride. Blame.

After spewing her feelings, Sarai did come back to a fact, which you must see in the language of Abram's response.

Genesis 16:6

But Abram said unto Sarai, Behold, thy maid *is* in thy hand; do to her as it pleaseth thee. And when Sarai dealt hardly with her, she fled from her face.

Abram didn't address her feelings. Look again at verse 6. He did not address her feelings. Not at all. Instead, he addressed the situation, factually. Even though Hagar was his 2nd wife, she was Sarai's servant. She was given as a gift and thus Abram saw the situation from that perspective. Culturally, as the 1st wife, she owned the rights and privileges that the 2nd wife doesn't. However, if you look closely, you'll gain wisdom from the 14 words Abram used. He saw the key things that Sarai wanted that usually gets overlooked when someone is telling this story: pleasure and control. Pleasure and control. In the end, Sarai wanted pleasure. Did you catch that? Read verse 6 again. That's what all this was about, self-pleasure and validation disguised as wanting for her husband. This wasn't about Abram. He prayed for kids and moved on. His mind wasn't on surrogacy. It was on obedience. This was about Hagar, a younger more fertile woman who was doing what she was trained to do. This was about Sarai, trying to manipulate a situation so she can gain the pleasure from it. How so? Seeing Abram have children would give her pleasure. Training Hagar the way of Abram and how to be a wife gave her pleasure. The idea of being a mother, even though the child wouldn't come from her womb, gave her pleasure. Think of it. Sarai was a nurturer who wanted to experience pleasure from a position of control. When she could no longer control the situation, she freaked out. Does any of this sound familiar? I digress.

As we mentioned earlier, this is a dangerous game when feelings are being used to make decisions. It's chaotic and has a low chance of being received well. By Abram giving Sarai the control she wanted to make things right with Hagar, chaos ensued. A peaceful home turned into a mini-war zone of emotional imbalance. Sarai took this opportunity to show Hagar she was boss, 1st wife, and in control. Even though Hagar was the mother of the child, she hit the wall of facts of her situation. She was not Sarai. She did not have the rights and privileges of the 1st wife. She could not operate in disrespect towards Sarai, who to this point had been good to her. Now, after Abram's response, Sarai was more harsh with Hagar than ever before. So harsh, that human nature kicked in. Hagar was forced to a decision, the same expression we've used several times in this section, fight or flight. Well, sticking true to her name meaning, Hagar took flight. She left, pregnant and alone, emotionally charged, irrational, gone.

This makes no sense at all. The danger of doing something like this is through the roof. These people lived in the wilderness where men had to hunt for food while competing with wild predators for the same meal. The idea of a pregnant woman, walking in the wilderness, by herself, while predators roamed looking for an easy meal. Why? Because her feelings were hurt. This is an example of what making emotional decisions look like and how dangerous this is. We may sit and say yes, Hagar was out of her mind and there's no way I would do that, but think carefully about your assessment. We all have made emotional decisions at some point that was just as irresponsible and dangerous as this. I know, it's our time to speak on her, but keep in mind, one day it'll be someone else' turn to speak on you or I and our ill-advised decisions. I digress.

In the midst of Hagar wandering in her feelings, God was watching. HIS plan was in place, the course was set. It wasn't her feelings that covered her while she wandered, it was the fact that the covering of Abram covered her and her unborn child. This is a power given to men by God to cover feelings. This is why facts cover feelings. To be clear, we all have feelings, everyone. As a husband, it's a very unappreciated gift, especially in today's time. God honors coverage. HE orders man to protect woman. HE, in turn, protects man and woman. It's an identity thing. When a man is operating the way God wants him to, he gets the benefit of bonus coverage for his family, even when he's not present or aware, even when they leave, even when they're in their feelings. That's a fact. What do we mean by bonus coverage?

Genesis 16: 7-10

And the angel of the LORD found her by a fountain of water in the wilderness, by the fountain in the way to Shur. 8 And he said,
Hagar, Sarai's maid, whence camest thou? and whither wilt thou go? And she said, I flee from the face of my mistress Sarai. 9 And
the angel of the LORD said unto her, Return to thy mistress, and submit thyself under her hands. 10 And the angel of the LORD
said unto her, I will multiply thy seed exceedingly, that it shall not be numbered for multitude.

See what we mean? The angels fill in when a man of God isn't present. That's bonus coverage. Initially, Hagar didn't know this was an angel. The appearance of the speaker was that of a man. It was the words of the man that let her know that this had to be the LORD or angel of the LORD that was speaking to her. Remember, Hagar learned the ways of Abram, it was a part of her 10-year training. When she heard the words "I will multiply thy seed...", she immediately knew this person was not human. Couldn't be. Only God speaks in terms like this. Who else could find her in a place like this and say something like that? Keep in mind that Hagar was a beautiful woman. This man didn't make an advance towards her, in any way. Instead, he spoke to her about things only she would know, who her master was, and what their issue was with one another. Only God could know that. Hagar knew it.

To my ladies, please take careful note in verse 9. Notice how the angel of God responded when Hagar started to express how she felt. HE didn't coddle her. HE didn't 'yeah girl, I understand.' HE didn't rub her on the back, appease her feelings, or anything like that. Instead, HE immediately gave her an action word: return. How amazing! Return. See the difference?

Direct, stern, deliberate, focused. HE told her to return and submit. WOW! I know this is hard for many ladies in today's world, but this is bible, this is scripture. The LORD said to return, and submit. In the midst of our thoughts, anger, emotions, our feelings, we tend to overlook this very simple directive from the LORD. Return and submit. That's all HE asks of us when we venture away from HIM. Return and submit. That's all HE has asked mankind since Adam's fall. Return and submit. For example....Most marriages end today in divorce. The rate of those divorces are increasing and decreasing at the same time. How so? More marriages are breaking up, even after longer times together. On the flip side, more younger people are choosing not to marry so they don't have to be left in marriage later. Increase and decrease. Why? Because people lost the art of returning and submitting. Ironically, most divorces are filed by women, especially in the western world, which is labeled in the court system as a 'no fault divorce', meaning they just didn't agree or get along. It's not a coincidence. More ladies think nowadays that they are Sarai, positioned for prestige and empowered to lead with control while seeking pleasure for themselves plus claiming that they are help-meets according to the scriptures. What we really have is a lot of Hagar's, those seeking to leave, because their feelings got hurt at some point. The enemy knows this as well. So, what does he do? He sends an evil spirit to take the place of the angel of God because there are so many Hagar's. Instead of telling you to return and submit because GOD is going to increase you when you do, the evil spirits tell you that it's okay to be out here in the wilderness by yourself, it's someone else' fault, appeasing your feelings, telling you all kinds of things that violate God's WORD. The whole time it knows that there are predators waiting to harm you, but because of your feelings, you can't see through it. It's a trick, a sweet-smelling savor that tickles the ear, boost the ego, and grooms the pride. The whole time you're looking for someone to agree with you, the predators are looking to get meat from you. It's a simple concept when you think about it. So ladies, please understand that your feelings are precious and you have a right to them, just as men do. You have to know that God responds to feelings with action. When HE does, you must obey. If you don't, the predators will eventually find you and have the meal they wanted: you. If you do return and submit, blessings on blessings are coming your way. Guess what Hagar did?

Genesis 16: 11-16

And the angel of the LORD said unto her, Behold, thou *art* with child, and shalt bear a son, and shalt call his name Ishmael; because the LORD
hath heard thy affliction. 12 And he will be a wild man; his hand *will be* against every man, and every man's hand against him; and he shall
dwell in the presence of all his brethren. 13 And she called the name of the LORD that spake unto her, Thou God seest me: for she said, Have I
also here looked after him that seeth me? 14 Wherefore the well was called Beerlahairoi; behold, *it is* between Kadesh and Bered. 15 And
Hagar bare Abram a son: and Abram called his son's name, which Hagar bare, Ishmael. 16 And Abram *was* fourscore and six years old, when
Hagar bare Ishmael to Abram.

This is what returning and submitting does. Blessings on blessings on blessings!

Hagar, in the wilderness, learned her connection to the LORD. Remember, this young lady comes from Egypt, a princess from a polytheistic culture. Sarai will never get credit for this interaction, but she's the one who prepared Hagar for an encounter with God. Abram prepared Sarai. It's amazing to see how God covers the branches of a tree because of the root. Hagar was covered because of Abram. This is what obedience and hard truth does. The blessing was born.

After all this time and dysfunction, a child was born and it's a boy!
Ishmael. What a name! Most people discuss the name of their child with their spouse, family members, friends, historical figures, etc. This is different. Hagar had an angel tell her that she was going to have a son and specifically told what his name was going to be. Now, look close to why he gave Hagar that name of all names; because the LORD heard her affliction. Wow! This is incredible. God heard her. HE heard her. I hope this is a lesson to us all, especially the ladies who may be reading this. God will hear you. All that HE requires is that you be obedient. If you are willing to listen, HE is willing to speak and do. The angel of the LORD gave her the name of her unborn child, told Hagar what type of man he would be, how people will view him, and that he will be constantly at war with his brethren. Reader, keep in mind that she nor Abram had no other children. HE is speaking in advance, down the line of time, giving both her and us revelation of who this young man would become. This is profound because Ishmael and his offspring would become exactly what the angel told Hagar, literally, to this very day. None of this happens, however, without Hagar being open to listen, willing to return and submit. See how it all works!
Because of this special encounter, Hagar is the first woman in biblical literature to name a landmark in the Earth. The very place she encountered God, she was allowed to name. The place has even been honored in the WORD of God. How special is that! Not Sarai, not Eve, no woman before has this honor. Hagar is the first. The name of the place she encountered God and served HIM, which is what she means when the she said she looked after the one who sees her. The well is named Beer-Lahai-Roi, which can be interpreted as the 'the well of the vision of life.' How fitting of a title for a place to draw water from, being that Christ is the well from which the believer drinks. This well is a representative of how God sees down the line of time for our sake to return and submit to HIM. God is the Greatest!

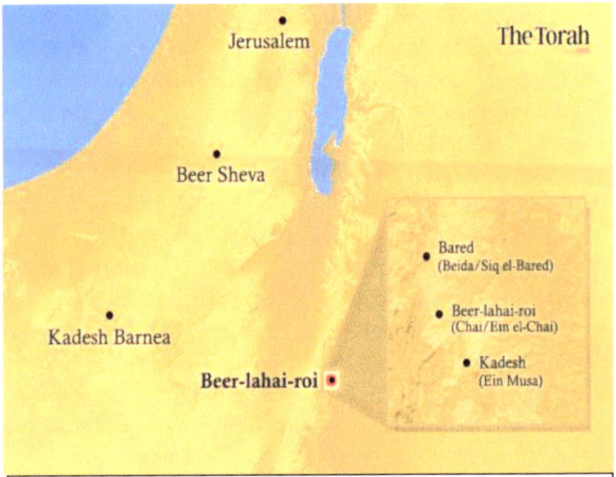

Beer-lahai-roi
© Torah.com

After this encounter, Hagar returned and submitted.
From that submission, Ishmael was born. One of the things you must pay attention to is what happens when obedience is the order of the day. Hagar let her emotions fall to the side, and obeyed. From that submission came Ishmael. What's interesting is the belief structure that came from Ishmael that is the fasting growing "religion" on Earth, which means submission. The irony. Only a fool in his heart believes that there is no God (Psa. 14:1).

Abram was quiet in all of this, as a believer and man of God should. He understood the assignment. Normally, a man names his children, especially his firstborn son. But Abram didn't, the angel of the LORD did. That's a different type of power and appointment and Abram knew it. As an 86-year-old man, he had his first child. Because Abram submitted to God, Hagar submitted to God. Which in turn, Abram accepted the name of Ishmael for his son.
All of this because Hagar took flight. It is here that the story of the Abram everyone knows takes off. Like Hagar, everything begins with a name.

This is just Part 1 of the Hagar story.

Abram to Abraham

Genesis 17: 1-5

And when Abram was ninety years old and nine, the LORD appeared to Abram, and said unto him, I *am* the Almighty God; walk before me, and
be thou perfect. 2 And I will make my covenant between me and thee, and will multiply thee exceedingly. 3 And Abram fell on his face: and
God talked with him, saying, 4 As for me, behold, my covenant *is* with thee, and thou shalt be a father of many nations. 5 Neither shall thy
name any more be called Abram, but thy name shall be Abraham; for a father of many nations have I made thee.

Abraham. Father Abraham.

It took 99 years for Abram to receive the name the world knows him as.
His original name Abram meant exalted father. Exalted means to be held in high regard.
Abraham, his new name, means father of a nation.

As Abram, he was chosen to be a father who was to be held in high regard, even without children. After Ishmael was born, making him a father, singular, it was time for God to make him into a nation, plural. Again, this is God looking down the line of time, revealing HIS power and promise of anointment and appointment. But wait, there's more...

Genesis 17: 7-8

And I will make thee exceeding fruitful, and I will make nations of thee, and kings shall come out of thee. 7 And I will establish my
covenant between me and thee and thy seed after thee in their generations for an everlasting covenant, to be a God unto thee, and
to thy seed after thee. 8 And I will give unto thee, and to thy seed after thee, the land wherein thou art a stranger, all the land of
Canaan, for an everlasting possession; and I will be their God.

New name, new proclamation, new nations, same God.

Circumcision

Genesis 17: 9-14

And God said unto Abraham, Thou shalt keep my covenant therefore, thou, and thy seed after thee in their generations. 10
This *is* my covenant, which ye shall keep, between me and you and thy seed after thee; Every man child among you shall be
circumcised. 11 And ye shall circumcise the flesh of your foreskin; and it shall be a token of the covenant betwixt me and you. 12
And he that is eight days old shall be circumcised among you, every man child in your generations, he that is born in the house, or
bought with money of any stranger, which *is* not of thy seed. 13 He that is born in thy house, and he that is bought with thy money,
must needs be circumcised: and my covenant shall be in your flesh for an everlasting covenant. 14 And the uncircumcised man
child whose flesh of his foreskin is not circumcised, that soul shall be cut off from his people; he hath broken my covenant.

Respect. God wants HIS people to be set apart from the world, Hebrew. This marked a new beginning in the Earth. When you look at mankind dating back to Adam, God set man to be HIS reflection in the Earth. Man has always struggled with this concept because he didn't understand his own reflection. As Michael Jackson would say, the man in the mirror. Because of this lack of understanding and acceptance, man has drifted away from the LORD. This is why Abraham and the covenant he made with God was so important. This was God's way of reconnecting to man, marking a new beginning and restart in relationship with mankind.

When we speak of new beginning, verse 12 validates the genius of God. Through science and mathematics, the number 8 means 'new beginning'. The sign of cycle and infinity as a constant restart is the number 8. This is why a male child is circumcised on the eight day of life. This is also the day that a child is supposed to receive their name. A new beginning keeps the covenant with the LORD as a new beginning in relationship with the LORD. This counts for actual blood relatives of Abraham, servants of his family, and those who follow the way of the Abraham. This is the blessing that overflows the cup of grace into the Earth. The cutting of the foreskin was an external agreement with God for an eternal appointment.

Scientifically, the cut foreskin has many different uses after removal. Scientists have discovered that the foreskin cells help with stem cell research, skin damage drafting, and neurodegenerative diseases. To *Make It Plain*, the foreskin lives, expands, and helps heal the body. Who would have ever thought? From a cut to the thing that can heal a cut, internally and or externally, circumcision is a game changer. A new name, a new aim. God is the Greatest!

In the end, the circumcision set up a new beginning of relationship between God and man. The Flood with Noah was a restart. The sons of Noah understood the power of God, but even they were influenced by the knowledge of the fallen angels ones, from which giants were born. They were living in the Earth, especially in Canaan at the time of Abraham. This type of contamination of humanity was a disgrace to the LORD because the giants were not made in the image of God. They were a mix of humanity and created beings who intentionally disobeyed God by coveting the creation of God. This sent a ripple effect through the universe as all of the heavenly hosts were witnesses to this blatant disrespect of God. This is all detailed in the Book of Enoch and the biblical book of Jude. The circumcision was a way for God to reconnect to humanity from a physical and spiritual perspective, unlike Noah's Flood. This is how amazing and itemized God is when it comes to connection. Circumcision is the way God chose to physically set HIS people apart from the world. This is why Christ came to circumcise our hearts, not literally, but spiritually, which sets us apart from the world for HIS final call back to holiness. From this separation physically and spiritually comes eternal life for all. All praise be to the LORD God of Heaven and Earth!

This is why Abraham means father of nations. Not one nation, but many, under the circumcision of the LORD.

Romans 4: 11-12

And he received the sign of circumcision, a seal of the righteousness of the faith which *he had yet* being uncircumcised: that he
might be the father of all them that believe, though they be not circumcised; that righteousness might be imputed unto them
also: 12 And the father of circumcision to them who are not of the circumcision only, but who also walk in the steps of that faith of
our father Abraham, which *he had* being *yet* uncircumcised.

Sarai to **Sarah**

Genesis 17: 15-22

And God said unto Abraham, As for Sarai thy wife, thou shalt not call her name Sarai, but Sarah *shall* her name *be*. 16 And I will bless her, and
give thee a son also of her: yea, I will bless her, and she shall be *a mother* of nations; kings of people shall be of her. 17 Then Abraham fell
upon his face, and laughed, and said in his heart, Shall *a child* be born unto him that is an hundred years old? and shall Sarah, that is ninety
years old, bear? 18 And Abraham said unto God, O that Ishmael might live before thee! 19 And God said, Sarah thy wife shall bear thee a son
indeed; and thou shalt call his name Isaac: and I will establish my covenant with him for an everlasting covenant, *and* with his seed after
him. 20 And as for Ishmael, I have heard thee: Behold, I have blessed him, and will make him fruitful, and will multiply him exceedingly; twelve
princes shall he beget, and I will make him a great nation. 21 But my covenant will I establish with Isaac, which Sarah shall bear unto thee at
this set time in the next year. 22 And he left off talking with him, and God went up from Abraham.

A husband's coverage extends into the heavens. I'll say that again, ladies and gentlemen. A husband's coverage extends into the heavens. Not only was Abraham blessed to have his name changed, but his wife's name was changed as well. Humbling. When a man's name changes in the LORD, so does his wife. Why? Oneness. When a man is joined in the right union under God's provision, anointment changes everything for everyone underneath their coverage.

Sarai originally meant my princess, a beautiful name with significant meaning. Sarah, although it means the same thing, it has an exalted meaning, given by God himself, meaning mother of nations. Mother of nations? To a 90-year-old woman without kids? How? God.

If you were to tell someone that a 90-year-old woman would have a child, they would probably laugh, hysterically. This is exactly what Abraham did. Keep in mind, Sarah was not around for this conversation. This is just God and Abraham talking. Abraham remarked and laughed to himself about Sarah's age in relation to childbirth, then he tried to flip the conversation towards 13-year-old Ishmael being seen before God. The intelligence of the LORD saw right through it.

For some strange reason, even the most faithful of us forget the true power of God in our thoughts. We are all guilty of this, the same as Abraham. God, knowing our words, feelings, and thoughts, speaks directly to Abraham's words, feelings, and thoughts. Let's look at it closely...

Abraham Thoughts = God particularizes not only that he and Sarah would have a child, but a son, and his name would be Isaac. He then tells him that Isaac is through whom his previous covenant would be established. Not only would he be the child of the promise, but that he would have children after him, previewing to Abraham his grandchildren.

Abraham Feelings = God doesn't see age. Abraham was thinking about Sarah being 90 and himself being almost 100 years old. God didn't care about that. Why should he. He's ageless, timeless, all powerful, having the ability to look backward and forward down the line of time, having to ability to do ALL. Why would he look at life from the same perspective as his creation? Abraham's feelings had 0% to do with the fact of God. Period.

Abraham's Words = *God reinforces to Abraham that he was going to bless Ishmael. HE then tells him that he was going to bless Ishmael with 12 sons, 12 princes or rulers, which would be Abraham's grandsons. This would not just be by the hand of Ishmael, but by God himself. This is amazing when you think of it because this shows more extension of coverage because of Abraham. Regardless, HIS WORD would come through Isaac.*

After this, God left the discussion. No need to say anything else. God spoke, Abraham did.

Genesis 17: 23-27

And Abraham took Ishmael his son, and all that were born in his house, and all that were bought with his money, every male
among the men of Abraham's house; and circumcised the flesh of their foreskin in the selfsame day, as God had said unto him. 24
And Abraham *was* ninety years old and nine, when he was circumcised in the flesh of his foreskin. 25 And Ishmael his
son *was* thirteen years old, when he was circumcised in the flesh of his foreskin. 26 In the selfsame day was Abraham circumcised,
and Ishmael his son. 27 And all the men of his house, born in the house, and bought with money of the stranger, were circumcised
with him.

Done and done. No need to wait and deliberate. It had to be done. This is an example to us all, to be not just hearers but doers of God's WORD (James 1:22). This is a lesson that I have struggled with. The writing of this book was a struggle as this is the longest writing of work I have done as an author. But I digress. Abraham taught us to act when we hear the WORD of the LORD, especially when HE is speaking directly to us. He circumcised all of the men under his coverage, beginning with himself, his son Ishmael, every man. This was an outwardly sign of the inwardly connection to the LORD. Verse 26 said it happened the selfsame day, which means that day, they were all circumcised. This is submissive obedience, on the spot, done. The sacrifice of the foreskin is one thing, but the obedience to the LORD supersedes all. Lesson learned LORD, lesson learned.

It is through Sarah that all of this would be verified and validated. When it comes down to nation building, it begins with woman, who she is, what she means to the family, how she teaches, lives and loves, submits, and helps the man meet his placement with God. This is why Sarah is called the mother of those who ascribe to the faith and exemplifies what a wife should be. She is the mother of nations. She is the princess that gave birth to kings and queens. She did all of this against the odds, who believed in her husband, believed in his God, and set herself accordingly. She, ladies and gentlemen, is the standard.
Sarai to Sarah, done.

1 Peter 3: 5-6

For after this manner in the old time the holy women also, who trusted in God, adorned themselves, being in subjection unto their
own husbands: 6 Even as Sara obeyed Abraham, calling him lord: whose daughters ye are, as long as ye do well, and are not afraid
with any amazement.

God Visits Mamre

Jasher 18:3

And in the third day Abraham went out of his tent and sat at the door to enjoy the heat of the sun, during the pain of his flesh.

There is a funny meme and gif that perfectly exemplifies these three words: three days later...

Three days after all the men in Abraham's home were circumcised, Abraham got up to feel the heat of the day, during the pain of his circumcision. While standing there, Abraham sees something, or better yet, someone, on the horizon.

Genesis 18: 1-2

And the LORD appeared unto him in the plains of Mamre: and he sat in the tent door in the heat of the day; 2 And he lift up his eyes and looked, and, lo, three men stood by him: and when he saw *them*, he ran to meet them from the tent door, and bowed himself toward the ground,

The LORD God, the master of the universe, came to Abraham, in person. Not in the form of his majesty and glory, but in the form of a man. HE brought with HIM 2 angels who also appeared as men. To be clear, Abraham didn't know that this was God and HIS angels. All Abraham knew was that he saw three visitors coming, in the middle of Canaan, in the Plains of Mamre. This is one of the legends of Abraham and his hospitality. He was well known for how he would provide safety, water, and food for all strangers passing by in the wilderness. He would entertain people under the shade trees of Mamre. This visit would be different.

Genesis 18: 3-8

And said, My Lord, if now I have found favour in thy sight, pass not away, I pray thee, from thy servant: 4 Let a little water, I pray you, be fetched, and wash your feet, and rest yourselves under the tree: 5 And I will fetch a morsel of bread, and comfort ye your hearts; after that ye shall pass on: for therefore are ye come to your servant. And they said, So do, as thou hast said. 6 And Abraham hastened into the tent unto Sarah, and said, Make ready quickly three measures of fine meal, knead *it*, and make cakes upon the hearth. 7 And Abraham ran unto the herd, and fetcht a calf tender and good, and gave *it* unto a young man; and he hasted to dress it. 8 And he took butter, and milk, and the calf which he had dressed, and set *it* before them; and he stood by them under the tree, and they did eat.

Hospitality. This is a rich man, asking people if he can serve them, calling himself a servant. He offered bread and water in the wilderness. Even in his pain, he was hospitable. After the three men agreed to the bread and water, Abraham went into his tent and told Sarah to make a meal for his visitors. This wasn't planned, it was on the spot. Then, in his pain, he ran to his herdsmen and asked them to prepare meat from a calf.

Jasher 18:6

And Abraham ran and took a calf, tender and good, and he hastened to kill it, and gave it to his servant Eliezer to dress.

Abraham's Oak
© Jewish Community of Hebron

All of this was done, on the spot, for three random visitors, underneath this tree, which later became known as The Oak of Mamre or Abraham's Oak. It is under this tree that the LORD, his two angels, and Abraham sat and ate a meal prepared by Sarah. The current Jewish and Christian community that live around this area near Hebron have a long tradition of stating that the tree was supposed to die before the AntiChrist comes. In 1996, the tree dried up and died. Two years later, root sprouts appeared around the tree at its base. Perhaps the legend is true, maybe not. Regardless, God is the Greatest!

Genesis 18: 9-15

And they said unto him, Where *is* Sarah thy wife? And
he said, Behold, in the tent. 10 And he said, I will
certainly return unto thee according to the time of life;
and, lo, Sarah thy wife shall have a son. And Sarah
heard *it* in the tent door, which *was* behind him. 11
Now Abraham and Sarah *were* old *and* well stricken in
age; *and* it ceased to be with Sarah after the manner of women. 12 Therefore Sarah laughed within herself, saying, After I am waxed old shall I
have pleasure, my lord being old also? 13 And the LORD said unto Abraham, Wherefore did Sarah laugh, saying, Shall I of a surety bear a child,
which am old? 14 Is any thing too hard for the LORD? At the time appointed I will return unto thee, according to the time of life, and Sarah
shall have a son. 15 Then Sarah denied, saying, I laughed not; for she was afraid. And he said, Nay; but thou didst laugh.

Before you criticize Sarah for laughing, Abraham did it first. Remember? When God came to Abraham and revealed to him the covenant, circumcision, and promise of Isaac being born in his old age, Abraham laughed to himself (Gen. 17:17). I know, for years and in many pulpit sermons and Sunday School lessons Sarah has taken the heat for laughing after hearing God speak of her giving birth. After the men ate the meal prepared for them, they stood in the doorway of the tent as they were on a mission, not just a visit. Sarah didn't eat with the men, only Abraham, which is customary when welcoming guest. The wife is in the other room unless there is a woman present. Sarah was standing behind them inside the tent. She heard the words but began to think of their age, how the pleasure of sex had gone from them as age limited their ability to have children. Regardless, God spoke to her, questioning if anything is too hard to God. Sarah, like most people would do, denied that she did. So God, showcasing HIS power to hear and see all, including our thoughts and feelings, told her HE did hear her laugh. HE also told Abraham that HE would return to him in the process of time of life, 9 months, at which Sarah would have a child.

Genesis 18:16

And the men rose up from thence, and looked toward Sodom: and Abraham went with them to bring them on the way.

The visit was over. After the meal, it was time to resume the mission. The three men, with only one of them speaking, were ready to go. Abraham, showing his hospitality even more, walked with the men on their way as they headed in the direction of Sodom, which was 50 miles southeast of Mamre in the Valley of Shittim. This is also the same area that Lot, Abraham's nephew, settled with his flocks and family.

It was the main speaker, the LORD of Heaven HIMself that walked alongside Abraham at Mamre.

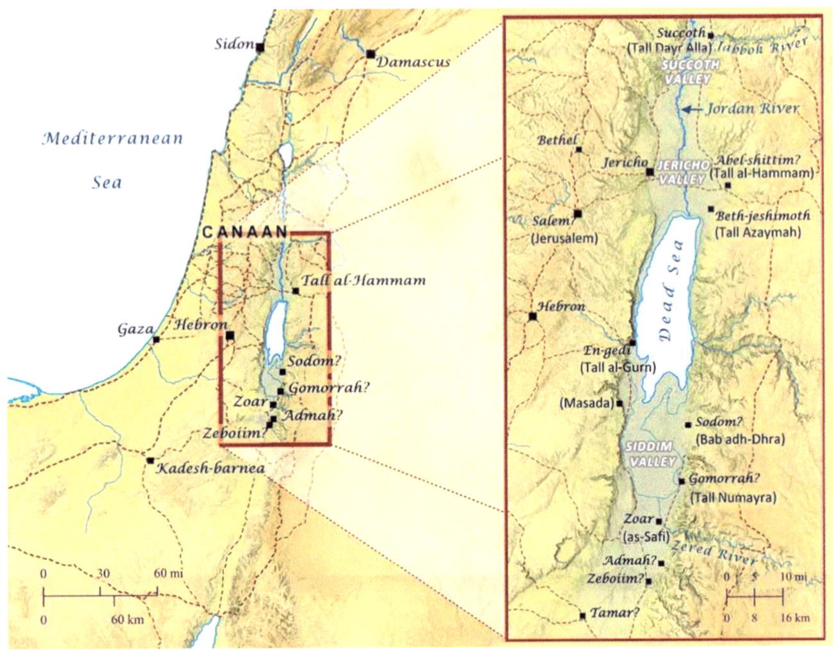

© Patterns of Evidence

SODOM and Gomorroh

Isaiah 3:9

The shew of their countenance doth witness against them; and they declare their sin as Sodom, they hide *it* not. Woe unto their soul! for they have rewarded evil unto themselves.

The story of Sodom and Gomorroh is more than what you and I have been told. It's way more impactful and eye-opening than what we were taught. I'm pretty sure that we probably heard some of the same things, a story of dread, a story of anger, a story of the wrath of God. Regardless of what we may have heard or read, ladies and gentlemen, we didn't really get the perspective and details needed to understand why this story is placed in the Bible. But here, we will *Make It Plain* for you to understand the depth of the perception of God in sending the message HE sent to the world regarding Sodom and Gomorroh type behavior which is running wild in today's world.

Buckle up.

To begin, the story of Sodom and Gomorroh begins with love. Real love. Considerate love. Compassionate love. Forgiving love. Graceful love. Friendly love. Godly, love.

Genesis 18: 16-21

And the men rose up from thence, and looked toward Sodom: and Abraham went with them to bring them on the way. 17 And the LORD said,
Shall I hide from Abraham that thing which I do; 18 Seeing that Abraham shall surely become a great and mighty nation, and all the nations of
the earth shall be blessed in him? 19 For I know him, that he will command his children and his household after him, and they shall keep the
way of the LORD, to do justice and judgment; that the LORD may bring upon Abraham that which he hath spoken of him. 20 And the LORD
said, Because the cry of Sodom and Gomorrah is great, and because their sin is very grievous; 21 I will go down now, and see whether they
have done altogether according to the cry of it, which is come unto me; and if not, I will know.

The LORD of the Universe really thought about Abraham and his feelings. Think about that for a second. HE actually took a few seconds to consider Abraham, his future, us, and how we should operate in the Earth as doers and keepers of HIS will. How humbling. God didn't say these things aloud, but in HIS mind, in HIS heart. Even the two men who were with HIM, angels, didn't know what God was doing, saying, or thinking. They had already turned, looked, and began to head in the direction of Sodom. God, however, considered these things after the meal Abraham and Sarah prepared for them. HE then openly told Abraham what HIS plans were (v.20-21). It was at this moment, after HIS thinking and consideration, that the LORD spoke. This is a lesson to us all. HE didn't just say whatever HE was going to do. Instead, HE considered HIS friend, not just in the moment, but his bloodline and belief structure throughout the generations. God0 showed Abraham love. HE showed Abraham HIMself.

Genesis 18: 22-31

And the men turned their faces from thence, and went toward Sodom: but Abraham stood yet before the LORD. 23 And Abraham
drew near, and said, Wilt thou also destroy the righteous with the wicked? 24 Peradventure there be fifty righteous within the city:
wilt thou also destroy and not spare the place for the fifty righteous that *are* therein? 25 That be far from thee to do after this
manner, to slay the righteous with the wicked: and that the righteous should be as the wicked, that be far from thee: Shall not the
Judge of all the earth do right? 26 And the LORD said, If I find in Sodom fifty righteous within the city, then I will spare all the
place for their sakes. 27 And Abraham answered and said, Behold now, I have taken upon me to speak unto the Lord, which *am*
but dust and ashes: 28 Peradventure there shall lack five of the fifty righteous: wilt thou destroy all the city for *lack of* five? And he
said, If I find there forty and five, I will not destroy *it*. 29 And he spake unto him yet again, and said, Peradventure there shall be
forty found there. And he said, I will not do *it* for forty's sake. 30 And he said *unto him*, Oh let not the Lord be angry, and I will
speak: Peradventure there shall thirty be found there. And he said, I will not do *it*, if I find thirty there. 31 And he said, Behold now,
I have taken upon me to speak unto the Lord: Peradventure there shall be twenty found there. And he said, I will not destroy *it* for
twenty's sake. 32 And he said, Oh let not the Lord be angry, and I will speak yet but this once: Peradventure ten shall be found
there. And he said, I will not destroy *it* for ten's sake.

As a friend, HE gave Abraham a conversation. HE gave Abraham a conversation, which has become a lost art and skill amongst friends. With the Abraham knowing who he was speaking to, the Judge of all the Earth (v25), God gave him HIS ear with the ability to have a different perspective. God was open, willing to listen. Abraham was open, willing to speak. What makes this story beautiful is that Abraham didn't deserve this spacing and placing with the LORD, but God gave him HIS time and attention. Friendship.

The reality of what was at stake made this a hard conversation. I know, we kind of gloss over this when looking at this story, but Abraham was pleading on the behalf of people he didn't know, giving us the blueprint of the believer. It's a hidden gem in plain sight. Abraham was considering a people that he had previous knowledge of, battle of the kings, which he won even though he wasn't a king. For future reference, this is why the Israelites didn't need a king because people could kill kings yet the King of Kings could never be killed or overthrown. That same King of Kings was in Abraham's tent, having a conversation about kingdom policy, which would stretch down the line of time to this very day.

Abraham knew of these people and how they acted. Again I say, Abraham knew of these people and their actions. How? One must consider the reputation of Abraham. He lived in the Plain of Mamre, about 50 miles from the fertile plains of Sodom and Gomorroh. They were in a valley, east of where Abraham was, so he could see over the cities in the valley on the horizon. When people would travel in the wilderness, Abraham, a wealthy man, would gain information about what was going on in the world because of what he offered the public. By giving shelter, a friendly meal, hospitality, and water to strangers in good faith, Abraham knew what was going on around him. Hotels and gas stations operate the same way. Also, keep in mind and perhaps more importantly, his nephew Lot had settled near Sodom with his family and livestock. So again, Abraham knew this area, the people who lived in it, and the reputation of what was going on there.

When we look at Abraham asking for leniency, look closely at what he was asking mercy for. Zoom in on the actual words of Abraham and you can see the love language God desires us to have. Do not take these verses out of context, seeking to justify and minimize things that God did not. First, Abraham asked for grace for the people, not the city nor the actions of the people in the city. Did you catch that? He considered the people themselves, separate from what they do. Abraham considered their life, not their lives. He considered their life, not their lifestyle. God, in HIS infinite wisdom, listening as a friend, heard Abraham and yielded to his perspective.

Secondly, God played the numbers game with Abraham to increase the chances of grace, trying not to administer wrath. Reader, this is truly amazing and humbling at the same time if you see it. Please understand what you are reading and the impact thereof. God, knowing Abraham didn't know what HE knew about the cities of the plain, was willing to be talked down from wrath because of their relationship. HE allowed Abraham the opportunity to walk his number of mercy to drop from 50 to 10. Six times did Abraham reduce the number, and six times God obliged him. Six times! Six times Abraham pleaded for mankind. Six times he asked for mercy for the righteous' sake. The judgement of the LORD was being negotiated for the sake of the righteous by a righteous man. This is the amazingness of the God in HIS desire of relationship with HIS creation, us. For the sake of the righteous, God is willing to delay or abandon judgement. This is a lesson for the world today. This very same reasoning is why God hasn't destroyed the world yet. The prayers of the righteous for the sake of the possibility of other righteous people in places we don't know or haven't been yet. Now you should understand the current and end times a little bit better. We are still here because of Abraham and those praying on your behalf to the HOLY ONE to delay or reduce HIS judgement. Depending on where you fit in those numbers, mercy could be given or taken.

Thirdly, and we cannot overlook this, but the six times Abraham asked for grace is the exact number of mankind. It is not a coincidence. God made man on the 6th day. Remember that? For that reason, six times did God consider man, the image of the LORD HIMself in the Earth. HE is HOLY, righteous in all that HE does. Mankind was created to reflect that. This is why Abraham pleaded with the intentionality of righteous as the buzz word to tug at the heart of the Righteous One. It worked, as God was listening. From 50 to 10, six times, did the LORD look to show mercy. All HE needed was a few good men.

When we consider the perspective above, we arrive at the question that I'm sure you have been asking since coming to this section: what was it about Sodom and Gomorroh that made God come down from heaven with two angels, personally? What was it about these people that the angels immediately headed in their direction after a hospitable visit with Abraham in the presence of the LORD? For God to consider removing HIS wrath, what were they doing to provoke HIM to leave HIS heavenly dwelling? Well, ladies and gentlemen, it's beyond what we were told. Brace yourself.

Parental Discretion Advised:

Jasher 18: 11-17

In those days all the people of Sodom and Gomorrah, and of the whole five cities, were exceedingly wicked and sinful against the Lord and they provoked the Lord with their abominations, and they strengthened in aging abominably and scornfully before the Lord, and their wickedness and crimes were in those days great before the Lord. 12. And they had in their land a very extensive valley, about half a day's walk, and in it there were fountains of water and a great deal of herbage surrounding the water. 13. And all the people of Sodom and Gomorrah went there four times in the year, with their wives and children and all belonging to them, and they rejoiced there with timbrels and dances. 14. And in the time of rejoicing they would all rise and lay hold of their neighbor's wives, and some, the virgin daughters of their neighbors, and they enjoyed them, and each man saw his wife and daughter in the hands of his neighbor and did not say a word. 15. And they did so from morning to night, and they afterward returned home each man to his house and each woman to her tent; so they always did four times in the year. 16. Also when a stranger came into their cities and brought goods which he had purchased with a view to dispose of there, the people of these cities would assemble, men, women and children, young and old, and go to the man and take his goods by force, giving a little to each man until there was an end to all the goods of the owner which he had brought into the land. 17. And if the owner of the goods quarreled with them, saying, What is this work which you have done to me, then they would approach to him one by one, and each would show him the little which he took and taunt him, saying, I only took that little which thou didst give me; and when he heard this from them all, he would arise and go from them in sorrow and bitterness of soul, when they would all arise and go after him, and drive him out of the city with great noise and tumult.

Nasty. I hope you didn't think we were going to keep this politically correct, but what word is better than this one? Nasty. Scripture tells us that these people had a custom, a ritual if you will, of anti-God behavior that became their reputation. Scripture even tells us that they went to what seems like a beautiful setting of nature just to indulge in great sin. They violated the natural law of God with celebration. Men would give their wives and daughters to other men, just because, sexually, while enjoying another man's wife and daughters, just because. From sun up to sun down, debauchery. Then, the women would return home, with another man's or men seed in them, including the virgins. Everyone would go along, business as usual. Intentional disrespect of God, the body, the vow of marriage, mixing of seed (sperm) in a woman, and the violation of the purity of virginity. This actually happened ladies and gentlemen, 4x a year, in celebration, in a beautiful place.

To add insult to injury, they would rob the goods of guests who would come to the city. This is the total opposite of what Abraham was known for. Think about that for a second. People would pass through Mamre, near modern-day Hebron, and Abraham would offer people the best of what he had so they can travel in peace. Not in Sodom and Gomorroh. They would allow people to come in, do business, then rob them, bit by bit, piece by piece. When people would look to get justice, the people would kick them out of the city, taunting them of what they took, and send the visitor off in anger. This gave the people of the city great joy. Again, they didn't just violate themselves against God, they violated strangers and visitors to their city. This is disgraceful!

But wait….there's more nasty coming up…

Jasher 1: 1-7

And the cities of Sodom had four judges to four cities, and these were their names, Serak in the city of Sodom, Sharkad in Gomorrah, Zabnac in Admah, and Menon in Zeboyim. 2. And Eliezer Abraham's servant applied to them different names, and he converted Serak to Shakra, Sharkad to Shakrura, Zebnac to Kezobim, and Menon to Matzlodin. 3. And by desire of their four judges the people of Sodom and Gomorrah had beds erected in the streets of the cities, and if a man came to these places they laid hold of him and brought him to one of their beds, and by force made him to lie in them. 4. And as he lay down, three men would stand at his head and three at his feet, and measure him by the length of the bed, and if the man was less than the bed these six men would stretch him at each end, and when he cried out to them they would not answer him. 5. And if he was longer than the bed they would draw together the two sides of the bed at each end, until the man had reached the gates of death. 6. And if he continued to cry out to them, they would answer him, saying, Thus shall it be done to a man that cometh into our land. 7. And when men heard all these things that the people of the cities of Sodom did, they refrained from coming there.

Rape. You wanted to know why Sodom and Gomorroh is historically viewed as a terrible place, here it is. Rape. Even with judges, no law, rape. Men forcing themselves on men. Men built beds in the streets for people passing through to rest. Like a trap. The moment a man would take a break and rest in one of these beds, he would either be gang raped or killed, depending on his size. Verse 4 tells you that even if a man screamed in horror, pain, or terror, the men wouldn't answer him that was raping him. The reputation of Sodom spread throughout the land so people knew not to pass through Sodom or risk being violated, viciously, and violently. Sodomy. Rape.

We're not done…

Jasher 19: 8-10

And when a poor man came to their land they would give him silver and gold, and cause a proclamation in the whole city not to give him a morsel of bread to eat, and if the stranger should remain there some days, and die from hunger, not having been able to obtain a morsel of bread, then at his death all the people of the city would come and take their silver and gold which they had given to him. 9. And those that could recognize the silver or gold which they had given him took it back, and at his death they also stripped him of his garments, and they would fight about them, and he that prevailed over his neighbor took them. 10. They would after that carry him and bury him under some of the shrubs in the deserts; so they did all the days to any one that came to them and died in their land.

Poor people aren't safe. They would do them dirty, shamefully. Despite giving a poor man silver and gold, they wouldn't allow him to buy bread, meaning he had money but couldn't eat. If the man didn't leave the city, they would allow the man to die from starvation, with his money, then take his money back after he died and buried him in the desert, alone. They even took the man clothing, putting him in a hole in the desert, naked. The people would then fight one another over the dead man's belongings. Yes, you are reading this correctly. No one was exempt, no one.

There are three examples we want to share with you to express how wicked of a place this was. Bare with us, it's about to get even crazier...

A Welfare Check Almost Ended In Murder

Jasher 19: 11-22

And in the course of time Sarah sent Eliezer to Sodom, to see Lot and inquire after his welfare. 12. And Eliezer went to Sodom, and he met a man of Sodom fighting with a stranger, and the man of Sodom stripped the poor man of all his clothes and went away. 13. And this poor man cried to Eliezer and supplicated his favor on account of what the man of Sodom had done to him. 14. And he said to him, Why dost thou act thus to the poor man who came to thy land? 15. And the man of Sodom answered Eliezer, saying, Is this man thy brother, or have the people of Sodom made thee a judge this day, that thou speakest about this man? 16. And Eliezer strove with the man of Sodom on account of the poor man, and when Eliezer approached to recover the poor man's clothes from the man of Sodom, he hastened and with a stone smote Eliezer in the forehead. 17. And the blood flowed copiously from Eliezer's forehead, and when the man saw the blood he caught hold of Eliezer, saying, Give me my hire for having rid thee of this bad blood that was in thy forehead, for such is the custom and the law in our land. 18. And Eliezer said to him, Thou hast wounded me and requirest me to pay thee thy hire; and Eliezer would not hearken to the words of the man of Sodom. 19. And the man laid hold of Eliezer and brought him to Shakra the judge of Sodom for judgment. 20. And the man spoke to the judge, saying, I beseech thee my lord, thus has this man done, for I smote him with a stone that the blood flowed from his forehead, and he is unwilling to give me my hire. 21. And the judge said to Eliezer, This man speaketh truth to thee, give him his hire, for this is the custom in our land; and Eliezer heard the words of the judge, and he lifted up a stone and smote the judge, and the stone struck on his forehead, and the blood flowed copiously from the forehead of the judge, and Eliezer said, If this then is the custom in your land give thou unto this man what I should have given him, for this has been thy decision, thou didst decree it. 22. And Eliezer left the man of Sodom with the judge, and he went away.

Reader, this happened BEFORE Abraham saved Lot during the Battle of the Kings. This is how Lot became a captive in the war. Remember, Eliezer was the one who ran and told Abraham what happened to Lot. Soon after his deliverance, Lot had a daughter with his wife.

Lot's Daughter Killed

Jasher 19: 24-35

At that time the wife of Lot bare him a daughter, and he called her name Paltith, saying, Because God had delivered him and his whole household from the kings of Elam; and Paltith daughter of Lot grew up, and one of the men of Sodom took her for a wife. 25. And a poor man came into the city to seek a maintenance, and he remained in the city some days, and all the people of Sodom caused a proclamation of their custom not to give this man a morsel of bread to eat, until he dropped dead upon the earth, and they did so. 26. And Paltith the daughter of Lot saw this man lying in the streets starved with hunger, and no one would give him any thing to keep him alive, and he was just upon the point of death. 27. And her soul was filled with pity on account of the man, and she fed him secretly with bread for many days, and the soul of this man was revived. 28. For when she went forth to fetch water she would put the bread in the water pitcher, and when she came to the place where the poor man was, she took the bread from the pitcher and gave it him to eat; so she did many days. 29. And all the people of Sodom and Gomorrah wondered how this man could bear starvation for so many days. 30. And they said to each other, This can only be that he eats and drinks, for no man can bear starvation for so many days or live as this man has, without even his countenance changing; and three men concealed themselves in a place where the poor man was stationed, to know who it was that brought him bread to eat. 31. And Paltith daughter of Lot went forth that day to fetch water, and she put bread into her pitcher of water, and she went to draw water by the poor man's place, and she took out the bread from the pitcher and gave it to the poor man and he ate it. 32. And the three men saw what Paltith did to the poor man, and they said to her, It is thou then who hast supported him, and therefore has he not starved, nor changed in appearance nor died like the rest. 33. And the three men went out of the place in which they were concealed, and they seized Paltith and the bread which was in the poor man's hand. 34. And they took Paltith and brought her before their judges, and they said to them, Thus did she do, and it is she who supplied the poor man with bread, therefore did he not die all this time; now therefore declare to us the punishment due to this woman for having transgressed our law. 35. And the people of Sodom and Gomorrah assembled and kindled a fire in the street of the city, and they took the woman and cast her into the fire and she was burned to ashes.

Doing a good deed, feeding a starving man, is worthy of death? Consider what Abraham did for the whole city of Sodom. He saved them. You would think that the gratitude of the people for Abraham towards his nephew Lot would be tremendous, but no. Their wickedness knew no boundaries. They literally burned a woman to death in the streets for being a good Samaritan, which hadn't been created yet.

A Woman Stung To Death

Jasher 19: 36-43

And in the city of Admah there was a woman to whom they did the like. 37. For a traveler came into the city of Admah to abide there all night, with the intention of going home in the morning, and he sat opposite the door of the house of the young woman's father, to remain there, as the sun had set when be had reached that place; and the young woman saw him sitting by the door of the house. 38. And he asked her for a drink of water and she said to him, Who art thou? and he said to her, I was this day going on the road, and reached here when the sun set, so I will abide here all night, and in the morning I will arise early and continue my journey. 39. And the young woman went into the house and fetched the man bread and water to eat and drink. 40. And this affair became known to the people of Admah, and they assembled and brought the young woman before the judges, that they should judge her for this act. 41. And the judge said, The judgment of death must pass upon this woman because she transgressed our law, and this therefore is the decision concerning her. 42. And the people of those cities assembled and brought out the young woman, and anointed her with honey from head to foot, as the judge had decreed, and they placed her before a swarm of bees which were then in their hives, and the bees flew upon her and stung her that her whole body was swelled. 43. And the young woman cried out on account of the bees, but no one took notice of her or pitied her, and her cries ascended to heaven.

Shame. Again, a person doing a good deed to another human being was worthy of death. Lot's daughter was burned in the streets, to death. This woman had honey poured on her, openly, then had bees sting her to death! No one helped her, no one stopped it, no one had mercy. Her cry was so intentional that it ascended into Heaven, to the throne of the LORD of the Universe HIMself.

While you are pondering what you just read, let us address a common question from my analytical peers who read this section:

Was Sodom a poor city or did it lack resources to feed their people?

Answer:

Jasher 19:44

And the Lord was provoked at this and at all the works of the cities of Sodom, for they had abundance of food, and had tranquility amongst them, and still would not sustain the poor and the needy, and in those days their evil doings and sins became great before the Lord.

So now do you understand why Sodom and Gomorroh has the reputation it has? Can you see why God had to come down? These people provoked God to wrath, not understanding what and who the real God of the Universe is. God is love, but HE is also wrath. Abraham chose the former, the world chooses the latter.

The acts of Sodom and Gomorroh is beyond homosexuality...it's outright rebellion against good...and there is no such thing as good without God.

The Two Messengers of Wrath

Genesis 19:1

And there came two angels to Sodom at even; and Lot sat in the gate of Sodom: and Lot seeing *them* rose up to meet them; and he bowed himself with his face toward the ground;

Abraham, while standing in the doorway of his tent, saw three men coming. He spoke to one while the other two sat quietly. Lot, while sitting in the doorway of the city, saw two men, not three. This is very important to understand going forward. The two angels, which appeared as men, came to Sodom the same way they came to Abraham's tent. The only difference was that one person was missing. Where was the other man? Where was the person Abraham spoke to?

The LORD hung back to have the conversation with Abraham. Thereafter, HE went back to HIS place in heaven. I know, this sounds odd, but let's make it clear why HE left Abraham, his follower, and not go to Sodom and Gomorrah.

Habakkuk 1:13

Thou art of purer eyes than to behold evil, and canst not look on iniquity: wherefore lookest thou upon them that deal treacherously, *and* holdest thy tongue when the wicked devoureth *the man that is* more righteous than he?

God cannot be in the presence of sin. HE looks upon sin from wherever HE chooses, but HE cannot be in its presence. HE abhors it. HE could visit Abraham, who was standing in obedience to HIM. HE could not visit Lot, who was sitting in disobedience in Sodom. Therefore, HE sends HIS messengers, angels, to Lot with a safety plan as HE considers the words of Abraham and his requests for at least 10 righteous men in not only Sodom but Gomorroh and the 5 cities of the plain. When you think of it, if there were 2 righteous men in each city, God would not destroy the cities. That's not much. However, as we have learned of the reputation of the cities of sin, finding two men per city would be hard. Therefore, God, in HIS infinite wisdom, sent two angels to balance the scene. Amazing!

Now, back to Lot and Sodom. How interesting is it that both Lot and Abraham both were in the doorway to their homes and both men were humble and serving to the visitors? This shows the character of both men, regardless of where they lived. You can tell that Lot was raised right and attempted to live right.

Genesis 19: 2-3

And he said, Behold now, my lords, turn in, I pray you, into your servant's house, and tarry all night, and wash your feet, and ye shall rise up early, and go on your ways. And they said, Nay; but we will abide in the street all night. 3 And he pressed upon them greatly; and they turned in unto him, and entered into his house; and he made them a feast, and did bake unleavened bread, and they did eat.

Lot knew the reputation of the city he was living in. This was the same city and streets where his oldest daughter was taken and burned to death because she helped feed a starving man in the street. He knew these men were in danger if they stayed in the city. Remember, it was evening time, which meant it was getting close to the time when the men wouldn't be able to travel. Staying in Sodom at night time was a threat of rape, gang rape, in one of the beds that were placed in the streets for those passing through. Sodomy, ladies and gentlemen. This is where it began, openly, disgustingly, wrong. Lot knew this, which is why he pleaded with the men to come to his home and be treated with friendly hospitality. Even though the angels told him they would stay in the street all night, knowing they would be approached by the men of the city, Lot persuaded them to come to his home. Afterwards, he fed them, just as Abraham did. Again, Lot was a good man living in an evil city. That's a message all unto itself.

But evil doesn't rest…

Genesis 19: 4-10

But before they lay down, the men of the city, *even* the men of Sodom, compassed the house round, both old and young, all the
people from every quarter: 5 And they called unto Lot, and said unto him, Where *are* the men which came in to thee this night?
bring them out unto us, that we may know them. 6 And Lot went out at the door unto them, and shut the door after him, 7 And
said, I pray you, brethren, do not so wickedly. 8 Behold now, I have two daughters which have not known man; let me, I pray you,
bring them out unto you, and do ye to them as *is* good in your eyes: only unto these men do nothing; for therefore came they
under the shadow of my roof. 9 And they said, Stand back. And they said *again*, This one *fellow* came in to sojourn, and he will
needs be a judge: now will we deal worse with thee, than with them. And they pressed sore upon the man, *even* Lot, and came near
to break the door. 10 But the men put forth their hand, and pulled Lot into the house to them, and shut to the door.

Don't do so wickedly. When the question of homosexuality and God comes up when relating to Sodom and Gomorroh, quite often this quote is never discussed. Don't do so wickedly. People look everywhere else except for the words of Lot. This is a man who lived in this city, with a wife and daughters. He lost a daughter to the 'anything goes' laws of the city. The acts they performed on themselves, one another, the passing around of the women 4x a year during a sex celebration, gang raping men visitors who didn't know the outside beds were traps, etc. were all things Lot knew too well. He had seen it. From seeing Nimrod in Babel to Sodom and Gomorroh, Lot had seen some things. Sodom and Gomorroh was on a different level. Think of it. For him to beg and plead for these two men to come to his home for safety, to have his door knocked on by the men of the city so they could sexually abuse these men, is wild! Well, in Sodom, it was normal, especially in the evening. When they said in verse 5 that they wanted to "know them", they didn't mean conversation. That's not what they did in Sodom. They wanted to sexually "know them". How do we know this?

When scripture is speaking that someone wanted to "know" someone else in a biblical way, that means sexually. The men of Sodom did not want to know the two men visiting Lot no different than any other man that went through the cities of Sodom and Gomorroh. They weren't trying to philosophy with these men to see where they stand intellectually. They observed these new men who entered the city, and how they looked. Lustful and covetous is an understatement! Strong desire and inordinate affection. The appearance of these men had to be so striking to the eye that the bible says all the men from every quarter (1/4) of the city came to Lot's door. Imagine that. An entire city, coming to one man's house, just to "speak" or know these two men? Come on now. To add insult to injury, they called Lot out of the house. When Lot went to the door, he had to shut the door behind him. Why? Because the men were so aggressive in behavior and demeanor. Lot, respectively, asked the men not to do so wickedly. Why would he say such a thing for men who wanted to talk? These are the same men who killed his oldest daughter for helping a starving man in the street. Keep that in perspective. Lot didn't say that when his daughter was killed, so please don't underestimate what "don't do so wickedly" really mean. These men were looking to sexually violate, rape, and then gang rape these men. The whole city of men came to both see and be a part of the festivity. Evil. The disrespect was so great, that the men threatened to do worse things to Lot than the two men. Still think they were talking about a conversation? This is why the angels pulled Lot back inside the house, to save him, which is a clear indicator of how righteousness views this type of behavior.

Jasher 19: 48-50

And the angels said to Lot, Arise, go forth from this place, thou and all belonging to thee, lest thou be consumed in the iniquity of
this city, for the Lord will destroy this place. 49. And the angels laid hold upon the hand of Lot and upon the hand of his wife, and
upon the hands of his children, and all belonging to him, and they brought him forth and set him without the cities. 50. And they
said to Lot, Escape for thy life, and he fled and all belonging to him.

And…

Genesis 19: 12-17

And the men said unto Lot, Hast thou here any besides? son in law, and thy sons, and thy daughters, and whatsoever thou hast in the city,
bring *them* out of this place: 13 For we will destroy this place, because the cry of them is waxen great before the face of the LORD; and the
LORD hath sent us to destroy it. 14 And Lot went out, and spake unto his sons in law, which married his daughters, and said, Up, get you out of
this place; for the LORD will destroy this city. But he seemed as one that mocked unto his sons in law. 15 And when the morning arose, then the
angels hastened Lot, saying, Arise, take thy wife, and thy two daughters, which are here; lest thou be consumed in the iniquity of the city. 16
And while he lingered, the men laid hold upon his hand, and upon the hand of his wife, and upon the hand of his two daughters; the LORD
being merciful unto him: and they brought him forth, and set him without the city. 17 And it came to pass, when they had brought them forth
abroad, that he said, Escape for thy life; look not behind thee, neither stay thou in all the plain; escape to the mountain, lest thou be
consumed.

Wow. Warning always come before destruction. After being pulled into the house by the angels, Lot was put on notice. Not only were these men evil, they were willing to sexually abuse angels. I'll stop there, the idea of that is too wild to explain.

Let's take a closer look at the grace of God that was given to Lot. The angels gave Lot a chance, the same type of chance God gave Noah, but under different conditions. With Noah, the evil of the world moved God to wrath. With Lot, the evil of the Sodom and Gomorroh moved God to wrath. Noah lived in the middle of an evil world. Lot was living in the middle of an evil city. With Noah, there was a chance given to Noah to have both his sons and their wives on the ark, along with his wife. With Lot, there was a chance given to Lot to have his daughters and their husbands to flee Sodom and Gomorroh, along with his wife. There were 8 people allowed to survive the Flood. There were 7 people allowed to survive Sodom and Gomorroh (Lot's eldest daughter was killed, her husband survived). Noah's family was allowed to live because of his righteousness. Lot's family was allowed to live because of his righteousness.

Noah and Lot have a lot in common, perspectively, when it comes to righteousness, responsibility of family, and God's wrath. Just like the world laughed at Noah for his warnings about destruction, so did the son-in-laws for his 3 daughters. In verse 14, the bible tells us that the sons-in-law laughed at him. Even though the whole city was made blind because of their lustfulness and evil against the angels of the LORD, Lot was allowed to spare his son-in-laws if they chose to trust righteousness and follow Lot. They did not. They too had been infected, like a virus, with the spirit of the city of sin. This is what separated Noah and Lot. The men of Noah's family chose to follow righteousness. The men of Lot's family chose to follow sin. What they didn't see was that God was trying to boost the chances of survival of those in the city because of the righteousness of Abraham. Noah was given the same grace because of Methuselah, the oldest man to ever live and living ancestor of Noah. Even though the angels were sent to destroy the cities, God still tried to give the people a chance. Now, I hope you see why God has spared our world and not come back yet despite the copied behaviors of Sodom and Gomorroh being accepted worldwide as an expression of love for humanity. It's wild! But in the end, never forget, the LORD always send a warning before destruction because of HIS love for us even if HE hates our behavior. HE is so amazing!

Genesis 19: 18-23

And Lot said unto them, Oh, not so, my Lord: 19 Behold now, thy servant hath found grace in thy sight, and thou hast magnified thy mercy,
which thou hast shewed unto me in saving my life; and I cannot escape to the mountain, lest some evil take me, and I die: 20 Behold now, this
city *is* near to flee unto, and it *is* a little one: Oh, let me escape thither, (*is* it not a little one?) and my soul shall live. 21 And he said unto him,
See, I have accepted thee concerning this thing also, that I will not overthrow this city, for the which thou hast spoken. 22 Haste thee, escape
thither; for I cannot do any thing till thou be come thither. Therefore the name of the city was called Zoar. 23 The sun was risen upon the
earth when Lot entered into Zoar.

Lot did what Abraham did, but in a different way, with a different grace. Abraham asked the LORD HIMself for the opportunity for Sodom and Gomorroh to be spared, for the people's sake. Lot asked the angels of the LORD for the opportunity for himself to be spared, for his own sake. Abraham was asking for the people in the valley to be spared. Lot was asking for himself to be spared from a mountain. Both men had interactions with the grace of God, both men seeking different outcomes. Both men wanted the mercy of the LORD. Both, however, due to the wickedness of mankind, witnessed God's judgment both in the present and future.

Genesis 19: 24-25

Then the LORD rained upon Sodom and upon Gomorrah brimstone and fire from the LORD out of heaven; 25 And he overthrew those cities, and all the plain, and all the inhabitants of the cities, and that which grew upon the ground.

Raining brimstone and fire. Imagine that. Brimstone, and fire, raining. To paint the picture, the LORD allowed the sun to rise. That's very important to understand. Why? God wanted the known world and those that were spreading out into it to look up and see HIS judgment raining down on sin. HE didn't want anyone to have any excuse. Think of it. When we get the news of a passing comet, bright planets in the night sky, or even an eclipse, all you would need to do is look up in the sky and you could see it. That's power! The idea of brimstone and fire raining down specifically on this area would have been a sight to behold, humbly. The anger of the LORD outweighed HIS grace and mercy due to the wickedness of Sodom and Gomorroh. HIS judgment even changed the ground, as verse 25 states. With that said, Lot and his family were on their way to Zoar, which means 'little' or 'insufficient'. Because of Lot, Zoar was spared from the fire of the LORD. Meanwhile, the world watched in horror as the LORD allowed the sun to be up in the sky as HE rained hell down on Sodom and Gomorroh. All God wanted Lot and his family to do was go, and don't look back. HE granted them grace, allowed them to leave, just don't look back.

But as always, trauma, drama, doubt, and PTSD curves obedience to unnecessary sacrifice.

Genesis 19:26

But his wife looked back from behind him, and she became a pillar of salt.

And...

Jasher 19: 51-53

Then the Lord rained upon Sodom and upon Gomorrah and upon all these cities brimstone and fire from the Lord out of heaven. 52. And he overthrew these cities, all the plain and all the inhabitants of the cities, and that which grew upon the ground; and Ado the wife of Lot looked back to see the destruction of the cities, for her compassion was moved on account of her daughters who remained in Sodom, for they did not go with her. 53. And when she looked back she became a pillar of salt, and it is yet in that place unto this day.

Ado. Ado. Trauma, drama, doubt, and PTSD. She turned around because of her past. Nevermind the future God was giving her and her family. Nevermind the new start. Nevermind the WORD given to them and grace that was made sufficient for them. She couldn't let go of people who didn't want to let go themselves. I'll say it again. She didn't want to let go of people who didn't want to let go themselves. The trauma of her history, the drama of family choosing to stay in sin, doubting the direction and protection of God, this is all the main ingredients of a PTSD cocktail. Sounds crazy right? Her name, Ado, means a state of agitation or fuss, especially about something unimportant. She turned around, because of her feelings. She lost her life, because of her feelings. She abandoned her family, because of her feelings. She didn't follow her husband, because of her feelings. She went against the WORD of God, because of her feelings. She turned into a pillar of salt, because of her feelings. She turned into a sign of bitter obedience, because of her feelings. This is the danger of being agitated to disobedience for no reason, because of your feelings. It amounts to 'much Ado about nothing.' That term has a whole new meaning now.

One more thing before we move on. Did you notice how the Bible tells us that she looked back from "behind" her husband? This means that Lot was leading. He was doing what he was supposed to do. She, on the other hand, turned back behind his back. Please, go and get our book *Lot's Wife* to get further detail on how we breakdown the modern-day dating game, relationships, role play, role reversal, and how what we call modern isn't modern at all. It failed with Lot's wife thousands of years ago, and it is a failed experiment now. Again, from behind her husband, she turned back. He didn't even see her turn back because he was pressing forward with his family. Her feelings turned her salty.

Jasher 19: 53-55

And when she looked back she became a pillar of salt, and it is yet in that place unto this day. 54. And the oxen which stood in that place daily licked up the salt to the extremities of their feet, and in the morning it would spring forth afresh, and they again licked it up unto this day. 55. And Lot and two of his daughters that remained with him fled and escaped to the cave of Adullam, and they remained there for some time.

See what looking back does in a relationship? See how the bitterness is renewed, everyday? See how the animals who look for salty things to eat look for you? The oxen or animals can be symbolic of people who seek bitter people to use for the taste or talk of the day. Why? Because your bitterness is restored. Meanwhile, her husband and surviving two daughters escaped to the cave of Adullam. They made it to Zoar, but just for a short while.

Genesis 19: 27-29

And Abraham gat up early in the morning to the place where he stood before the LORD: 28 And he looked toward Sodom and Gomorrah, and toward all the land of the plain, and beheld, and, lo, the smoke of the country went up as the smoke of a furnace. 29 And it came to pass, when God destroyed the cities of the plain, that God remembered Abraham, and sent Lot out of the midst of the overthrow, when he overthrew the cities in the which Lot dwelt.

Thanks to Abraham, God spared Lot. Early in the morning, walking to the same spot he spoke to the LORD God, Abraham saw the aftermath of the wrath of the Holy One. The wrath of the message of God was served by the two messengers of God. To be clear, God offered mercy and grace, first. Quite often critics and or the blind accusers of God forget, overlook, or intentionally ignore what HE offers first. Six times HE reduced HIS initial number of wrath for Abraham. No one speaks about the rampage and rape of Sodom and Gomorroh. No one speaks about the sexual violations men had on men, women on women, adults on children (pedophilia), etc. No one speaks on how the violation of reproduction being hindered by such acts and the DNA memories of trauma that was passed on those that were violated and allowed to leave the city in shame. No one speaks about any of these things when God's wrath on Sodom and Gomorroh is concerned. Instead of choosing HIS grace and mercy, man chooses HIS wrath. This is why God sent two messengers, to exact punishment on both violators of HIS natural law. The next time you hear someone talking about God's wrath, especially concerning Sodom and Gomorroh, homosexuality, etc., just know that there is an Abraham for them, that someone praying for their deliverance and repentance. That person may never be seen by those who speak of God's wrath, not realizing God's ear is being bent for the sake of those that care more about them as a person than their lifestyle or thought processes. God showed us that HIS love and wrath are identical in fire, ready to burn away the sin of the world from the inside out.

So, who were the two messengers?
Look closely, God tells us exactly who they were...

1. Abraham pleaded with God to spare Sodom and Gomorroh. That's **love**.
2. Lot pleaded with the angels to stay at his home instead of the streets. That's **love**.
3. One angel pulled Lot back into the house so the men wouldn't kill him. That's **love**.
4. The angels blinded the men instead of killing them. That's **love**.
5. Lot was allowed to leave the city with his family, including those that stayed behind. That's **love**.
6. Abraham was allowed to see the smoke rise from the choices of Sodom and Gomorroh. That's **love**.

---

1. Sodom and Gomorroh was utterly, destroyed. That's **wrath**.
2. Lot's wife was turned into a pillar of salt for looking back instead of moving forward. That's **wrath**.

You see the common theme? Love and wrath. 6 loves, 2 wraths.
Ironically, Abraham pleaded 6x for God to have mercy.
Ironically, Lot pleaded for 2x escape destinations for mercy (Zoar, cave of Adullum).
Intentionally, God gave them both what they wanted. Why? Because he is BOTH **love** and **wrath**!

1 John 4:8

He that loveth not knoweth not God; for God is **love**.

Romans 1: 18-19

For the **wrath** of God is revealed from heaven against all ungodliness and unrighteousness of men, who hold the truth in
unrighteousness; 19 Because that which may be known of God is manifest in them; for God hath shewed *it* unto them. 20 For the
invisible things of him from the creation of the world are clearly seen, being understood by the things that are made, *even* his
eternal power and Godhead; so that they are without excuse:

Now you understand why the two visitors didn't speak at Abraham's home. Now you know who spoke to Lot and gave him a chance to leave with his family, love. Now you know who called down fire and brimstone from heaven, wrath. These are the two messengers of the LORD that went into Sodom and Gomorroh.

Love and **WRATH**

2 Peter 2: 4-9

For if God spared not the angels that sinned, but cast *them* down to hell, and delivered *them* into chains of darkness, to be reserved unto
judgment; 5 And spared not the old world, but saved Noah the eighth *person*, a preacher of righteousness, bringing in the flood upon the
world of the ungodly; 6 And turning the cities of Sodom and Gomorrha into ashes condemned *them* with an overthrow, making *them* an
ensample unto those that after should live ungodly; 7 And delivered just Lot, vexed with the filthy conversation of the wicked: 8 (For that
righteous man dwelling among them, in seeing and hearing, vexed *his* righteous soul from day to day with *their* unlawful deeds;) 9 The Lord
knoweth how to deliver the godly out of temptations, and to reserve the unjust unto the day of judgment to be punished:

Lot and His Daughters

Genesis 19: 30-31

And Lot went up out of Zoar, and dwelt in the mountain, and his two daughters with him; for he feared to dwell in Zoar: and he
dwelt in a cave, he and his two daughters. 31 And the firstborn said unto the younger, Our father *is* old, and *there is* not a man in
the earth to come in unto us after the manner of all the earth:

This is the danger of ignorance if it is the lead perspective. These two young ladies, who had witnessed the death of all they knew in Sodom, the pillaring of salt of their mother in the wilderness, and the isolation from the world with their father in a cave, had come to conclude that the world was lost. I know, this sounds ridiculous to you and I, but these young ladies were convinced that the world had ended and they were the only ones left and their father was the only man left alive. It was the oldest that decided to act on their ignorance.

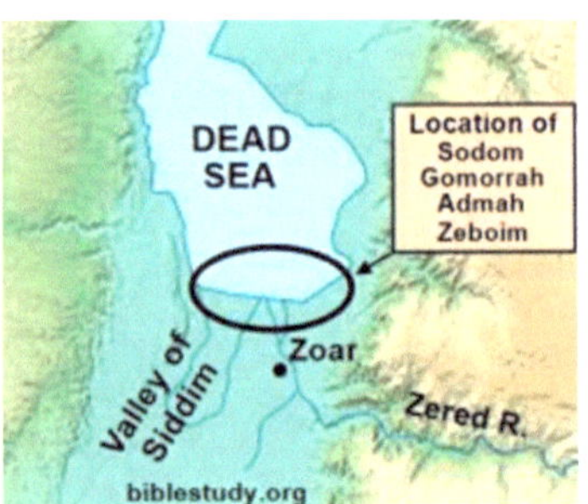

Was it true that they were the only people on the planet? No, absolutely not. In fact, they had just left Zoar, a small village that was spared from the wrath of the LORD at Lot's request. They passed through the town, which had people, but they continued on to the mountains, to the cave of Adullam. Is it possible that they feared that Zoar had been destroyed behind them in their haste to pass through? Maybe. But this also points to their lack of awareness of what was going on around them, similar to what was going on in Sodom and Gomorroh. They grew up in a city of abomination, so to be isolated from that while losing everyone you ever knew, including your mother, had to be traumatizing. Running away from the destruction of your past into the mercy of your future had to be life changing and very dramatic. However, you cannot help but imagine them running from what was behind them, not to what was in front of them. God destroyed Sodom and Gomorroh, not the world. Had HE actually did that, they would have nowhere to run to. Lot knew that, he had to, especially as an older man with the experience of life knowing the God of Abraham. His daughters, however, did not. They, like their mother, began to identify with their feelings to the point of making a choice. What happens next could be a whole book unto itself.

Genesis 19: 32-38

Come, let us make our father drink wine, and we will lie with him, that we may preserve seed of our father. 33 And they made
their father drink wine that night: and the firstborn went in, and lay with her father; and he perceived not when she lay down, nor
when she arose. 34 And it came to pass on the morrow, that the firstborn said unto the younger, Behold, I lay yesternight with my
father: let us make him drink wine this night also; and go thou in, *and* lie with him, that we may preserve seed of our father. 35 And
they made their father drink wine that night also: and the younger arose, and lay with him; and he perceived not when she lay
down, nor when she arose. 36 Thus were both the daughters of Lot with child by their father. 37 And the firstborn bare a son, and
called his name Moab: the same *is* the father of the Moabites unto this day. 38 And the younger, she also bare a son, and called his
name Benammi: the same *is* the father of the children of Ammon unto this day.

LORD help us. Yes, ladies and gentlemen, you read that right. Lot's daughters did the unthinkable. In no way is this honorable, at all. Maybe they were thinking that they were being honorable to their father by carrying on his name if they had sex with him because all the men of Earth, they thought, was dead. By having children by him, they could have companionship and children to replenish the Earth. So, from their perspective, in thought, they were doing a pro-human thing.

Nonsense, utter nonsense. In fact, with respect to that perspective, scripture shows us that even if they believed their father was the only man on the planet, they knew that having sex with him was wrong. How so? They got him drunk. Why would you need to get your parent tipsy or drunk just to take advantage of them? How deceitful is that? How demonic is that? They knew it was wrong, and they knew Lot was going for it. This is why they took turns on their father in back to back nights, getting him drunk so they could do their dirt, for lack of a better term. I know, sounds wild, but I hope you see the after effects of Sodom and Gomorroh. This is the after effect of sexual dysfunction that children should never experience. Imagine seeing the original Sodom and Gomorroh, every day, then coming home to a God-fearing father that wasn't accepting the ways of the world. Lot did not agree with what was going on around him. He would not have agreed with what his daughters were thinking, which is why they conspired without telling him. Instead, they made decisions with their feelings instead of following their father to a better place. Parents, see how trauma effects the mind of children, especially those that have been exposed to highly traumatic and or dramatic experiences of their surrounding environment?

To be fair, we are not absolving Lot from the responsibility of what happened. He too chose the greener pastures for his flock instead of staying with Abraham. He chose to live in Sodom. He chose the wife he married. He chose to go to Zoar then leave for a cave in the mountain. Those were his choices. It doesn't take away from the fact that God considered him a righteous man, in fact he was, just made some questionable choices. But again, we must look at Lot's situation similar to Noah.

Make It Plain

Post Flood = Noah leaves with sons, he gets drunk
Post Sodom and Gomorroh = Lot leaves with daughters, they get him drunk
Noah gets drunk, falls asleep = Ham looks upon Noah's nakedness, grandson Canaan is cursed
Lot gets drunk, falls asleep = daughters get pregnant by Lot, children are cursed

Even the righteous can fall into distress. Solomon said time and chance happens to every man. If nothing else, reader, please understand that being a good man or woman, righteous before the LORD, doesn't guarantee that your children will act in accordance. These stories of Noah and Lot are no different. This is why we must pay close attention to what the scripture is telling us. This is why we must pay close attention to the trauma and drama of our children's lives even if we are dealing with it ourselves. It's an ongoing lesson that sometimes drive a righteous parent crazy! God is The Father, the Holy One, perfect in All. HE is righteousness. We are HIS children. Consider the ridiculousness of our actions throughout our lives, even if we are on the path of righteousness now. This is why we can't look past this story as if it's on the other side of the moon and so far removed from us. We all have sinned, thinking we are doing good, but God sees through it all. We must be sober minded to increase our chances of making sound and God approved decisions. Adding wine to the equation made the situation even worse. This is not to say wine is bad, because scripture says that a little wine is good for you for reasons specified (1 Tim. 5:23). But the way it was used to manipulate a situation is never good.

In closing, when one considers Noah and Lot, the question arises: why did they get drunk in the first place? Well, the concept of drinking wine when you are in misery is not new nor non-biblical. When a person is in misery, wine is also a quick remedy but not the cure. Scripture tells us...

Proverbs 31: 6-7

Give strong drink unto him that is ready to perish, and wine unto those that be of heavy hearts. 7 Let him drink, and forget his poverty, and remember his misery no more.

See, there must be understanding to the 'why drink the wine' for both Noah and Lot. As we have discussed, both of these men witnessed catastrophic and intentional wrath by God on humanity that no one else can say they saw. They wanted to forget their misery, the poverty of their spirit after seeing obliteration. Sure, Noah's wife and sons can say they witnessed the Flood, but they didn't have conversations with God personally about it and then be tasked to carry out the plan for a global reset. I would say that man need a drink to deal with the misery of seeing what he saw. As for Lot, I would say the same thing even though his situation was different. Does that mean that it's okay to get drunk? No. All things must be done in moderation. Even these righteous men who drank too much were taken advantage of by their children while in the state of drunkenness. When we are not in our right mind because we succumb to an escape from reality, opportunity for dysfunction and curse comes in. Both men offspring were cursed because of it. It didn't diminish their righteousness, but it did bring them into judgment. Not only judgment, but in the wisdom of God, it brought them into judgment, together. Abraham, Lot's uncle, is connected to them as well. How so?

Make It Plain

Lot now had 2 sons from his 2 daughters: Moab and Ammon
Moab and Ammon would later come to be major players in the history of the Israelites in their conquest of the Promised Land. Israel is Jacob, the son of Isaac, the grandson of Abraham. The Moabites and Ammonites were fiercely known warriors whose offspring included giants that even King David had to contend with.
The Promised Land is located in Canaan, the cursed grandson of Noah.
Noah, Abraham, and Lot are all connected. All flawed men. All righteous men.

Please allow the lesson of Lot and his daughters to serve as a reminder that our children must be made aware of the world around us and that God requires obedience. We must follow HIS plan, not our perspective. We cannot lean to our own understanding of what the world is. We cannot assume from our children that they will see God as we do. We need to learn from these men of God so our sons and daughters don't sin due to our misery. If we are not careful, giants will emerge on our timeline that could prohibit us from having a smooth transition into the Promised Land of our lives.

Mark 10: 13-16

And they brought young children to him, that he should touch them: and *his* disciples rebuked those that brought *them*. 14 But
when Jesus saw *it*, he was much displeased, and said unto them, Suffer the little children to come unto me, and forbid them not:
for of such is the kingdom of God. 15 Verily I say unto you, Whosoever shall not receive the kingdom of God as a little child, he
shall not enter therein. 16 And he took them up in his arms, put *his* hands upon them, and blessed them.

Abimelech, pt. 1

Jasher 20:1

And at that time Abraham journeyed from the plain of Mamre, and he went to the land of the Philistines, and he dwelt in Gerar; it was in the twenty-fifth year of Abraham's being in the land of Canaan, and the hundredth year of the life of Abraham, that he came to Gerar in the land of the Philistines.

Abraham was done at Mamre after seeing the smoke of Sodom and Gomorroh. He didn't know the status of his nephew Lot, who went in the opposite direction of Abraham after the destruction of the cities of the valley and fled to Zoar then the cave of Adullam. Abraham was ready to grow and expand into another place to live out the covenant he made with the LORD. The last time Abraham made a move from one place to another was when he entered into Egypt. That journey began with a lie and ended with a whole nation of people, including pharaoh, getting sick, then having to expel Abraham. Let's see if Abraham had learned his lesson yet, especially as a 100-year-old man.

Genesis 20: 2-7

And Abraham said of Sarah his wife, She *is* my sister: and Abimelech king of Gerar sent, and took Sarah. 3 But God came to Abimelech in a dream by night, and said to him, Behold, thou *art but* a dead man, for the woman which thou hast taken; for she *is* a man's wife. 4 But Abimelech had not come near her: and he said, Lord, wilt thou slay also a righteous nation? 5 Said he not unto me, She *is* my sister? and she, even she herself said, He *is* my brother: in the integrity of my heart and innocency of my hands have I done this. 6 And God said unto him in a dream, Yea, I know that thou didst this in the integrity of thy heart; for I also withheld thee from sinning against me: therefore suffered I thee not to touch her. 7 Now therefore restore the man *his* wife; for he *is* a prophet, and he shall pray for thee, and thou shalt live: and if thou restore *her* not, know thou that thou shalt surely die, thou, and all that *are* thine.

Nope! Abraham was back at it again. He did the exact same thing he did years earlier when they entered Egypt. He misled, again, to protect his life at the expense of Sarah, his beautiful wife. Yes, even in her older age, Sarah was regarded as a beautiful woman. So much so that Abimelech, the king of Gerar, a land later to be called the land of the Philistines, saw her and had to have her for himself, just as Rikayon the first pharaoh of Egypt ventured to do. Just like Pharaoh, it didn't end well.

Jasher 20: 3-12

And as Abraham was dwelling in the land of the Philistines, the servants of Abimelech, king of the Philistines, saw that Sarah was exceedingly beautiful, and they asked Abraham concerning her, and he said, She is my sister. 4. And the servants of Abimelech went to Abimelech, saying, A man from the land of Canaan is come to dwell in the land, and he has a sister that is exceeding fair. 5. And Abimelech heard the words of his servants who praised Sarah to him, and Abimelech sent his officers, and they brought Sarah to the king. 6. And Sarah came to the house of Abimelech, and the king saw that Sarah was beautiful, and she pleased him exceedingly. 7. And he approached her and said to her, What is that man to thee with whom thou didst come to our land? and Sarah answered and said He is my brother, and we came from the land of Canaan to dwell wherever we could find a place. 8. And Abimelech said to Sarah, Behold my land is before thee, place thy brother in any part of this land that pleases thee, and it will be our duty to exalt and elevate him above all the people of the land since he is thy brother. 9. And Abimelech sent for Abraham, and Abraham came to Abimelech. 10. And Abimelech said to Abraham, Behold I have given orders that thou shalt be honored as thou desirest on account of thy sister Sarah. 11. And Abraham went forth from the king, and the king's present followed him. 12. As at evening time, before men lie down to rest, the king was sitting upon his throne, and a deep sleep fell upon him, and he lay upon the throne and slept till morning.

Sounds like the same story from before. The integrity of a man is always a question for the righteous. This was the question for Abimelech. This is why in Genesis 20: 4-7, God talks to Abimelech through a dream, validating to him that righteousness is attached to life and death. Had Abimelech taken Sarah and slept with her, had he touched her, he and all that he had would have died. A city, nation, would have perished on the account of a good man that was anointed. God himself called Abraham his prophet. Yes, even though Abraham misled Abimelech, he still had an anointing on his life and those that was under his coverage. He and Sarah both. Although this sounds unjust to possibly punish everyone else and not Abraham and Sarah for their manipulation, God is faithful and just. Both Abraham and Sarah' day to atone for their actions was coming, in due time. But as for now, Abimelech had to make a move. Keep this woman and suffer the consequences, or let her go and be blessed for it. While he was deciding on this issue, God send an angel into the land to send a physical message to Abimelech beyond the dream he was having so he couldn't awake and say 'it was all a dream' like Notorious B.I.G.

Jasher 20: 15-19

And on that night there was a great outcry in the land of the Philistines, and the inhabitants of the land saw the figure of a man
standing with a drawn sword in his hand, and he smote the inhabitants of the land with the sword, yea he continued to smite
them. 16. And the angel of the Lord smote the whole land of the Philistines on that night, and there was a great confusion on that
night and on the following morning. 17. And every womb was closed, and all their issues, and the hand of the Lord was upon
them on account of Sarah, wife of Abraham, whom Abimelech had taken. 18. And in the morning Abimelech rose with terror and
confusion and with a great dread, and he sent and had his servants called in, and he related his dream to them, and the people
were greatly afraid. 19. And one man standing amongst the servants of the king answered the king, saying, O sovereign king,
restore this woman to her husband, for he is her husband, for the like happened to the king of Egypt when this man came to Egypt.

You see what we mean? Same story. Even a random man in the land was willing to tell the king that he had heard this same story had occurred in Egypt with this same man and his wife. The moment Abimelech took Sarah in and paid what seems to be a dowry for the "sister" of Abraham, chaos broke loose in the land. The dream the king had was over and the reality of the horror in the land was now very real. The angel of the LORD was seen by the eyes of men, striking men and shutting up the womb of every woman! That had to be wild! While the men were trying to fight this angel, the women's womb was being closed to the point that no one could have children, including the king's wife. Yes, Abimelech had a wife. Sarah was going to be added to the list or made a concubine, even though she was the wife of Abraham. This was not what God wanted. This is why HE allowed the angel to stand in the land and be seen by men. For future reference, this land became known for its giants. None of them could withstand the angel of the LORD, who was seen as a "man of war." This same man with a sword was later seen in the land when Joshua came to Jericho.

Joshua 5: 13-15

And it came to pass, when Joshua was by Jericho, that he lifted up his eyes and looked, and, behold, there stood a man over
against him with his sword drawn in his hand: and Joshua went unto him, and said unto him, *Art* thou for us, or for our
adversaries? 14 And he said, Nay; but *as* captain of the host of the LORD am I now come. And Joshua fell on his face to the earth,
and did worship, and said unto him, What saith my lord unto his servant? 15 And the captain of the LORD'S host said unto Joshua,
Loose thy shoe from off thy foot; for the place whereon thou standest *is* holy. And Joshua did so.

So yes, the angel of LORD, the captain of the host, the mighty man of war, the same person. In Exodus 3:5, God told Moses the exact same thing. Joshua, knowing the story of Moses meeting God at the burning bush, knew immediately who this mighty man of war was by the statement of him standing on holy ground, which is why he took off his shoes and bowed down. In the land of the giants, there is one that stands above them all and even ties the womb of the women to the point that they couldn't have children. Only the Holy One could do that. This person, this mighty man of war, is none other than ***Jesus***. So yes, Joshua met Jesus but only saw him as a mighty man of war. Moses saw him as man of war. The people of Gerar saw him on the account of Abraham, as a man with a sword in his hand, a man of war.

Exodus 15:3

The LORD *is* a man of war: the LORD *is* his name.

The anointed has this type of covering. Again, this is not to atone for their wrong, but this is to set a boundary between righteous and unrighteous, the called and uncalled. Abraham was righteous and the LORD's plan superseded this moment of mishap.

With that said, let's take a look at what made Abraham in this situation. Did he really lie about Sarah being his sister? Where was he wrong?

Genesis 20: 8-13

Therefore Abimelech rose early in the morning, and called all his servants, and told all these things in their ears: and the men were
sore afraid. 9 Then Abimelech called Abraham, and said unto him, What hast thou done unto us? and what have I offended thee,
that thou hast brought on me and on my kingdom a great sin? thou hast done deeds unto me that ought not to be done. 10 And
Abimelech said unto Abraham, What sawest thou, that thou hast done this thing? 11 And Abraham said, Because I thought, Surely
the fear of God *is* not in this place; and they will slay me for my wife's sake. 12 And yet indeed *she is* my sister; she *is* the daughter
of my father, but not the daughter of my mother; and she became my wife. 13 And it came to pass, when God caused me to wander
from my father's house, that I said unto her, This *is* thy kindness which thou shalt shew unto me; at every place whither we shall
come, say of me, He *is* my brother.

There you have it, ladies and gentlemen. It was fear of losing his life in an evil land that made Abraham wrong in this sense. Yes, even though he was chosen, knew that LORD God personally and all of human history would be changed through him, he still was human and had a fear of losing his life. Do not consider this to be strange, even the profit Elijah, who called down fire from heaven, caused it not to rain for years, healed people, and was taken (translated) to the LORD in a chariot of fire, ran and hid for his life on the account of Jezebel, the evil queen of Israel. All men, including righteous ones, have a flaw and this was Abraham's. He thought the fear of God was not in Gerar (v.11) so he would be killed so Abimelech could have Sarah. This is predatory. Throughout history, men would kill other men for access to their women. Abraham knew this all too well thousands of years ago, especially in the land of Canaan. He knew this people did not fear the ways of the living God so his fear crept in. Again, this was Abraham's flaw.

As for telling Abimelech that Sarah was his sister by being the daughter of his father, but not the daughter of his mother, is somewhat true. Sarah was his cousin and wife, true. But as the niece and daughter-in-law of his father, it was also true. Sarah's father, Haran, was killed in the same fire Abraham walked, back in Ur, by Nimrod. Terah, Abraham's father, took Haran his son's children to be his own (adoption), and gave Haran's daughters (Milca and Sara[i]h) in marriage to both Nahor and Abraham (Jasher 12:44). Abraham's mother had nothing to do with this, which verifies Abraham's story. This is why Abraham told Sarah to call him her brother.

Genesis 20: 14-18

And Abimelech took sheep, and oxen, and menservants, and womenservants, and gave *them* unto Abraham, and restored him
Sarah his wife. 15 And Abimelech said, Behold, my land *is* before thee: dwell where it pleaseth thee. 16 And unto Sarah he said,
Behold, I have given thy brother a thousand *pieces* of silver: behold, he *is* to thee a covering of the eyes, unto all that *are* with thee,
and with all *other*: thus she was reproved. 17 So Abraham prayed unto God: and God healed Abimelech, and his wife, and his
maidservants; and they bare *children*. 18 For the LORD had fast closed up all the wombs of the house of Abimelech, because of
Sarah Abraham's wife.

See what happens when a man of God operates in his gift? Gifts come from what appears to be a curse. Not only gifts, but riches and the necessary supplies to continue to do the will and work of the Holy One. Abimelech and all of his people, including his wife, we allowed to have children that they couldn't have before. This was done on the account of Sarah, who was under the coverage of Abraham. This, ladies, is a direct message to you as well to seek and accept the coverage of a good man, a Godly man. You have more than just that man covering you, but the LORD himself will stand in the land on your behalf if you trust the LORD and follow a Godly man. Sarah did, and look what came with it. If you notice, she wasn't in her feelings, saying all kinds of things that could have caused a reaction, etc. She was steadfast, submissive, in alignment. In return, again and again, God himself stood in the gap for her and blessed her tremendously.

Also, and this cannot be overlooked, her beauty was preserved, even in her old age. She was 90 years old at this point. Abimelech still saw her as a beautiful woman and took her as his wife. Imagine how stunning she had to be to see. More importantly than that, her demeanor and presence was so beautiful that Abimelech chose her over his own wife and maidservants, all younger women. You see ladies, there are levels to beauty. Who Sarah was internally flowered through her external shell, that even age and wilderness lifestyle couldn't change. If you notice, it has never been said that she wore makeup, dressed herself up to appear as anything other than who she was. That, ladies, is a true sign of beauty, self-acceptance and confidence. This type of thought process can take a culturally covered woman, 90 years old, and make her the desired taste of kings of world renown kingdoms. That's something you can't take off or put on, it's in you. That's Sarah.

In conclusion, consider Abimelech for a second. He was chosen for such a time as this, for a story such as this. A king in a land of people who did not fear or obey God. A family man. A king with wealth to spare. He will go down in history for many things, but the greatest of them will be for his decision to go away from his pride and do what's right. God chose him for this purpose. Yes, even a man who ruled a land that did not follow God was used by the LORD himself to show a standard of righteousness will be upheld and the righteous will never be forsaken. Abimelech had a choice and he could have chosen death, but he didn't. He chose life. He, unlike most rulers throughout history, had a one on one with the LORD himself in a dream. After the dream, he saw the ill effects of going against HIS will. The people of Gerar saw Jesus, the mighty man of war, the LORD himself. Think about that, literally. They couldn't stand against HIM then, they can't stand against HIM now. The LORD shows HIMself as HE pleases and Abimelech witnessed the power of HIS presence. But why Abimelech, of all people, would God do this to?

It's all in a name. What do we mean? His name, Abimelech, means 'the divine Father is King.' His name means the exact reason why God had to show up and show out as both A Father to Sarah in protection, but The Father to Abraham and his promise. A good father will keep his word to his children and God had a promise to fulfill. He had just previously told Abraham that at the appointed time Sarah would have a child. Months had gone by since then. Sodom and Gomorroh had been destroyed and Abraham was no longer living in the plains of Mamre. HIS WORD, however, showed up, as a mighty man of war. This is HIS divinity, showcasing itself, even in a land that didn't respect the LORD as God. HE is who HE is, regardless of who you think HE is. That's what a real father is. He doesn't need to be validated by whether or not his children know him. He is because he is. Abimelech proved this, which is why he was honored to see the Holy One appear in his land, sword in hand, as a father protects his children. Abraham and Sarah were saved by HE WHO SAVES, which means Jesus.

1 Corinthians 8:6

But to us *there is but* one God, the Father, of whom *are* all things, and we in him; and one Lord Jesus Christ, by whom *are* all things, and we by him.

Isaac

Jasher 21:1

And it was at that time at the end of a year and four months of Abraham's dwelling in the land of the Philistines in Gerar, that God visited Sarah, and the Lord remembered her, and she conceived and bare a son to Abraham.

God is the Greatest! Amen, amen. How amazing is our God and here, HE displays HIS power to fulfill HIS WORD. When the LORD visited Abraham to tell him about Sodom and Gomorroh on the plains of Mamre, HE made a promise. That promise was that HE would revisit Sarah at that same time the following year and she would have a child. When HE said that, Sarah laughed. Prior to that, when God first told Abraham about him having a child through whom the promise of the coming Christ would come, Abraham laughed as well. The idea of a 90-year-old woman having a baby was funny in the mind of Sarah, especially with a 100-year-old husband. When that time had come, after the destruction of Sodom and Gomorroh and moving to the land of the Philistines, Abraham and Sarah were operating business as usual. While they were living in the peace of the land, God came to Sarah and fulfilled HIS promise at the end of the year, four months into living in the land of the Philistines. She conceived and had a son, the son she laughed at having a year prior to date. The LORD is a keeper of HIS WORD, especially to HIS own. HE is HIS WORD, Sarah and Abraham were now witnesses.

Numbers 23:19

God *is* not a man, that he should lie; neither the son of man, that he should repent: hath he said, and shall he not do *it*? or hath he spoken, and shall he not make it good?

Amen.

Genesis 21: 2-3

For Sarah conceived, and bare Abraham a son in his old age, at the set time of which God had spoken to him. 3 And Abraham called the name of his son that was born unto him, whom Sarah bare to him, Isaac.

Who's laughing now? Who's laughing now? Our God cannot be mocked! I repeat, our God cannot be mocked! Abraham and Sarah both laughed at the idea of themselves having a child in their old age and how it would look like to everyone who would hear about it. Jokes on them now. A 100-year-old man and 90-year-old woman could now say it was so. Because they laughed to themselves when God told them about this child to be, it was with this same fulfilling smile of God's promise fulfilled we get Isaac, the son of the promise, which means laughter. Yes ladies and gentlemen, Isaac is the original LOL.

Genesis 21: 4-7

And Abraham circumcised his son Isaac being eight days old, as God had commanded him. 5 And Abraham was an hundred years old, when his son Isaac was born unto him. 6 And Sarah said, God hath made me to laugh, *so that* all that hear will laugh with me. 7 And she said, Who would have said unto Abraham, that Sarah should have given children suck? for I have born *him* a son in his old age.

LOL! Our God is God, alone. There is none with HIM. There is none beside HIM. Who can tell HIM no? Restrict HIM? Tell HIM what cannot be done? Even those who follow HIS will are amazed at HIM. Even Abraham had to chuckle at the idea of God doing such a thing. HE amazes us with the things HE's done. For Sarah, a now 90-year-old woman, breastfeeding a child seemed ridiculous and humanly impossible. But God.

Genesis 21:8

And the child grew, and was weaned: and Abraham made a great feast the same day that Isaac was weaned.

It's time to celebrate! After everything they have been through, Abraham and Sarah deserved to celebrate. God is the Greatest! It was time to share the gift with their loved ones so they could all see the glory of the gift of the Holy One. In the process of about two years, Isaac was finally weaned from Sarah, which means he had finally reached the age and maturity to move on from breastfeeding to solid food. Historically, this is a day that means that a child is ready to enter community life. The very same day Isaac was weaned, Abraham had the party set for a celebration. It's time to share the laughter with everyone! The guest list for this party showcased the influence and power of the good name of Abraham.

Jasher 21: 5-8

And Shem and Eber and all the great people of the land, and Abimelech king of the Philistines, and his servants, and Phicol, the captain of his host, came to eat and drink and rejoice at the feast which Abraham made upon the day of his son Isaac's being weaned. 6. Also Terah, the father of Abraham, and Nahor his brother, came from Haran, they and all belonging to them, for they greatly rejoiced on hearing that a son had been born to Sarah. 7. And they came to Abraham, and they ate and drank at the feast which Abraham made upon the day of Isaac's being weaned. 8. And Terah and Nahor rejoiced with Abraham, and they remained with him many days in the land of the Philistines.

LOL! Wow, what a guest list. Shem, the son of Noah, father of the Semitic language, ancestor through who the Christ would come, post-flood the world spoke his language, and teacher of Abraham in the ways of the LORD, was at the party. Eber, father of Peleg and Joktan, name translates to what Abraham did by standing against the world which means Hebrew. It was symbolized through his sons Peleg and Joktan that the original formation of the continents, Pangea as scientists call it, was split into what we know and see it as today (Gen. 10:25). Abimelech was the king of the Philistines, a man that had seen the LORD as a mighty man of war, the coming Christ, even though Jesus wouldn't be born for a few thousand years. Phicol, his captain, actually fought against the man of war and survived to bare witness. Terah, Abraham's father and his brother Nahor came to the party. Wow! Cheers to all! God is the Greatest!

After the party was over, Terah and Nahor stayed with Abraham in the land of the Philistines for many days to keep the party going! Celebrating with family always make the moment sweater. You see, God has a great sense of humor and HE allows a good celebration, especially in HIS honor after doing such an amazing feat. It's not that HE couldn't do it, it's that HE did do it. Again I say, it's not that HE couldn't do it that makes it a special moment, it's that HE did do it.

This moment changed human history, forever. What makes it even crazier is that HE did this after his two servants Abraham and Sarah laughed to themselves about HIS ability to be HIMself. Nothing is too hard for God. To think that something is too hard for God is a joke, LOL!

This is the meaning of Isaac.

Jeremiah 32:27

Behold, I *am* the LORD, the God of all flesh: is there any thing too hard for me?

Hating

Jasher 21: 11-14

And Ishmael the son of Abraham was grown up in those days; he was fourteen years old when Sarah bare Isaac to Abraham. 12. And God was with Ishmael the son of Abraham, and he grew up, and he learned to use the bow and became an archer. 13. And when Isaac was five years old he was sitting with Ishmael at the door of the tent. 14. And Ishmael came to Isaac and seated himself opposite to him, and he took the bow and drew it and put the arrow in it, and intended to slay Isaac.

Hating.

Flat out, unapologetic, hatred. Not from a stranger. Not from an enemy. Not from an opponent. But from a family member. Someone in your own home. Someone close to you.
Hating.

14-year-old Ishmael, the son of a princess and the firstborn child of Abraham, hating. Even though God was with him, as HE told Hagar HE would, there was still a problem. Ishmael saw all the attention of his little brother and it didn't sit well with him. From his perspective, what about me? Wasn't he special too? Why wasn't he celebrated like Isaac? Wasn't he the oldest? Didn't he make Abraham a father, first? Why didn't all the people from around the known world come to his weaning ceremony? Why didn't his grandfather, Terah, and uncle Nahor come to see him?

Ladies and gentlemen, it's understandable for Ishmael to feel some type of way. When you look at it from his perspective, he has a case to ask questions to his parents. He would have a case. He had to feel some type of way because his other grandfather, Rikayon, the pharaoh of Egypt, didn't show up for him as Terah did for Isaac. Again, you have to see things from his perspective to understand the depth of this story.

With that being said, he's still hating.

Ishmael was a gifted archer. For scripture to say he was an archer gives us reason to understand that he was skilled in the art of archery with bow and arrow. For him, as a 14-year-old boy, to use his bow and arrow to try to kill his own little brother is wild. To see his 5-year-old little brother, standing in the doorway of his tent, aligning himself in the direct line of sight for an easy shot, to pick up his bow and arrow to shoot and kill his brother, is savage, 100% savage. This is not the normal thinking of a 14-year-old kid. Sure, those who have brothers and or sisters understand sibling rivalry. That's normal. Doing this, however, is on a whole other level. This is premeditated. Deep hatred. Envy.

To be clear, that doesn't mean Ishmael hated Isaac. I know, sounds crazy right? Yes, I get it but please look at the situation a little bit closer. Ishmael killing Isaac was an attention issue, not a direct hatred of Isaac issue. Consider the envy of Ishmael towards Isaac being accepted in a way he never did. How that made him feel as a kid. This is in no way an excuse. It's still attempted murder. But you have to look at the situation and see through it. Ishmael wanted what Isaac had, as any child would. When he didn't get it, he went to an extreme to try to receive it. He wanted Isaac's situation, not the actual death of Isaac. The death of Isaac would be a byproduct of his desire to be desired. This may be tough to understand now, but as we progress through this work and you get the story of Ishmael and Isaac, you will see that it was never really about Isaac as a person, but as a position desired, even to this day.

Until that time comes....he's still hating....and something needed to be done.

Genesis 21: 9-14

And Sarah saw the son of Hagar the Egyptian, which she had born unto Abraham, mocking. 10 Wherefore she said unto Abraham,
Cast out this bondwoman and her son: for the son of this bondwoman shall not be heir with my son, *even* with Isaac. 11 And the
thing was very grievous in Abraham's sight because of his son. 12 And God said unto Abraham, Let it not be grievous in thy sight
because of the lad, and because of thy bondwoman; in all that Sarah hath said unto thee, hearken unto her voice; for in Isaac shall
thy seed be called. 13 And also of the son of the bondwoman will I make a nation, because he *is* thy seed. 14 And Abraham rose up
early in the morning, and took bread, and a bottle of water, and gave *it* unto Hagar, putting *it* on her shoulder, and the child, and
sent her away: and she departed, and wandered in the wilderness of Beersheba.

Sarah saw and felt the hating. She saw the bow and arrow event beyond sibling rivalry. She saw something that was troubling to the future of their family unit. Instead of her acting on it, she went to her husband to voice her concern. When you look at it, notice how it wasn't a long, drawn out conversation. Even though it contained emotion, the complaint wasn't consumed with emotion. She was clear, concise, and to the point. This gave Abraham a chance to assess the situation, process it, and make the decision for the family. Ladies and gentlemen, please take note of the structure of the family decision making process. As head of the house, Abraham was offered information, communicated to with directness and concern, then left alone to make the decision. This is God's design. Therefore, when we use this structure, God allows HIS wisdom to step in to help the head of the household to make the decision, which is exactly what Abraham did.

To be clear, Abraham did not want to send his son away. He did not. So much so, that God HIMself had to tell Abraham to send Ishmael away. Not because of the act, but because of his mother. Quite often this is missed when people read this story. It's overlooked. God wanted Ishmael gone because of the influence of his mother. Why? Egypt.

Hagar represents Egypt, the country of her origin. Ishmael represents Arabia. Sarah represents Israel. Abraham represents the faith. Isaac represents God having the last laugh, which is exactly what the name Isaac means. This is why Ishmael had to go, because of his mother, the bondwoman. Egypt would later hold Israel in bondage. By faith, God would release the Hebrews from bondage, crossing through Arabia into the Promised Land. All parties involved. See how God gets the last laugh, in the beginning?

When God spoke to Abraham, the decision to make the move was immediate. In fact, it was early the next morning. With bread and water, Abraham sent his 2nd wife away in separation. Again, pay close attention to verse 14. Although it looks like a divorce, as some would suspect, Abraham sent them away into the wilderness of Beersheba, south of where they were located. By sending her south, she was sent in the direction of her father and home country, Egypt. To comfort Abraham, God reassured him that HE would make a great nation of Ishmael, so don't worry. This is the compassion and love of God, not always easy to take, but must be trusted and obeyed. This is the formula for how to put out the fire of hating.

Genesis 21: 15-19

And the water was spent in the bottle, and she cast the child under one of the shrubs. 16 And she went, and sat her down over against *him* a
good way off, as it were a bowshot: for she said, Let me not see the death of the child. And she sat over against *him*, and lift up her voice, and
wept. 17 And God heard the voice of the lad; and the angel of God called to Hagar out of heaven, and said unto her, What aileth thee, Hagar?
fear not; for God hath heard the voice of the lad where he *is*. 18 Arise, lift up the lad, and hold him in thine hand; for I will make him a great
nation. 19 And God opened her eyes, and she saw a well of water; and she went, and filled the bottle with water, and gave the lad drink.

See what hating does? This is the side of jealousy that no one sees. The brokenness. The desperation. The tears. The fear. Do not be fooled, even Jesus said that a man's enemies will be from within his own household (Matt. 10:36). Hagar is the perfect example of this concept. Hating is real. Despite the life and positioning she and Ishmael had, the jealousy eye was strong and it led her into a situation that was desperate. What makes this story even crazier is that all this happened pretty quickly. After being sent away into the wilderness, the bread and water was used up. Ishmael was on the verge of dying and Hagar couldn't stand to see it. She sat him underneath a few shrubs so he can die in the shade. This is when the tears began to roll. This same woman, who was hating on Sarah, was now in distress, because of her hating. Ishmael, who didn't hate his brother, but was hating on Isaac' situation, was dying of dehydration and starvation. Granted, the love Hagar had for Ishmael allowed her to lay him under a shrub, but in a wilderness, a shrub is a dangerous place to be. Why? It's the place where predators, like snakes and scorpions, choose to cool themselves from the heat of the day. But again, just like she did when she ran away into the wilderness when she was pregnant with Ishmael, Hagar wasn't thinking about predators. This is the blinding delusion of hating while being covered by a man of God, which Hagar and Ishmael both were still under, even in the wilderness. But how so, when Abraham sent them away?

The coverage of a Godly man is universal, not emotional. The LORD allows those under their coverage to do things, but HE always has an angel waiting to attend to their needs on behalf of the righteous man. The first time Hagar ran away, an angel came and redirected her back to Abraham. This time, as verse 17 says, an angel called to her from heaven to redirect her mind and remind her that Ishmael will live to become a great nation. Even in her distress, the LORD is there. HE sends HIS reminder, then makes a way. After making the way, you must move on HIS WORD. That's exactly what Hagar did. But she first had to have her eyes opened. She was a victim of blinding delusion. Blinding delusion. It wasn't until God, not Abraham, opened her eyes, she was walking blind, in her jealousy and wide range of feelings, in a wilderness, on the verge of death. When HE opened her eyes, she saw a well of water, a restorer of life and reassurance of promise. Why the well of water? HE was and still is the well of water that never runs dry.

John 4: 13-14

Jesus answered and said unto her, Whosoever drinketh of this water shall thirst again: 14 But whosoever drinketh of the water that I shall give him shall never thirst; but the water that I shall give him shall be in him a well of water springing up into everlasting life.

This is a lesson to us all.

Genesis 21: 20-21

And God was with the lad; and he grew, and dwelt in the wilderness, and became an archer. 21 And he dwelt in the wilderness of Paran: and his mother took him a wife out of the land of Egypt.

When we move past the emotions. When we move past the feelings. When we move past the traumas and dramas of our past. There is life. There is love. This is providence and promise. God never promised us easy. HE only promised us HIM. Somewhere along the way we have become blinded in our delusions of self this, self that, calling it self love. It's a delusion of this world, a strategy of the evil one that has led to a world full of 'self-loving haters'. That's how he fell from heaven. That's how we fall from grace. The greatest self-love is God, not self, because self isn't God, even though God resides in self.

In conclusion, it is necessary that we send haters away, at the right time. It is necessary that we are sent away, at the right time. It is necessary that we separate from the separable, at the right time. It is necessary that we separate from those who choose separation, at the right time. From this separation, you get connection and closure. You get clarity. You get chance. Ultimately, you're supposed to get Christ. When Hagar and Ishmael recovered at the well, from it came a whole new world of opportunity and vision. Hagar went back to Egypt, the land of her father, and found a wife for her son to start his own family. Ishmael thrived in the desert as an archer, a hunter, a man's man. God blessed him, as HE said HE would. Ishmael needed the space to grow, which God gave him. When the hating stopped, the blessings increased. Through his blessings, Hagar's hating decreased as well.

From this story, we learn the intention of God in relational matters of family. HE intends for us to operate in love, for better or for worse, in sickness and in health, until death do we part, especially in matters related to marriage. However, we must view our independent relationship with HIM the same, which is why we can't be Hagar in relation to God, a person HE deems separating from. We can't hate on someone else's progress or process because ours isn't going the way we want it to. We can't operate in blind delusion as she did, needing an angel to save us multiple times because of the coverage of a righteous person who covers us. Going back to the land of our father is not always good, depending on who our father truly is. Hagar's father was the first Pharaoh of Egypt, true, but he was also a cunning and deceptive man. He was wise in his own eyes. He gave his daughter away to a stranger to save his own self. See how "self-love" can be deceptive? See how character flaws can be passed down to our children indirectly, costing them more than they have to spend? By returning to her father's land, she found a wife for her son that would come forth to be a gift and a curse, a reward of her hating, the judgment of her return to the place of the origin of her trauma. This is a common theme for today's Hagar, the person who returns to the place of their trauma and drama thinking that a return will make things better. Most of the time it makes life worse. The key in this case was the perspective of Hagar in relation to her father. Instead of looking at him for who he truly was, she looked at him for who he was to people. Instead of seeing her position for what it was in Abraham's home, she saw Ishmael's birth as a positioning in Abraham's eyes for what people would see. This is why she returned to Egypt to find a wife for Ishmael. It wasn't to find a woman who would be a helpmeet to Ishmael from the foundation of who his father truly was, but she wanted to find a woman who would satisfy her and who people would see her as. Ladies and gentlemen, even out of love, you can get someone hating. Usually, it's your own people. In this case, it's his own people. Hating.

John 13:18

I speak not of you all: I know whom I have chosen: but that the scripture may be fulfilled, He that eateth bread with me hath lifted up his heel against me.

 A Good Nail 

Jasher 21:17

And he and his mother afterward went to the land of Egypt, and they dwelt there, and Hagar took a wife for her son from Egypt, and her name was Meribah.

Danger. When we return to our trauma in search of a good thing, danger lurks in all midst. To be clear, the intentions of Hagar was good. She was taught how to be a wife by the most respected woman in biblical history, firsthand, for a decade. Her husband was Abraham, the greatest man in the known world, the man who stood against the world ruler Nimrod, the man who God and the angels guarded and spoke to, regularly. She was the daughter of Rikayon, the first Pharaoh of Egypt. Hagar wanted to find a good wife for her son. Although the idea is noble and nurturing, but there is a problem. When she left Egypt, it was as a bondwoman. When she returned, it was as a woman sent away from her husband, a bondwoman to her pain, her perspectives, her past. She was not the person to look to find a wife. Again, her intentions were good, but Hagar was not in the position to find the best helpmeet for Ishmael. But, as in most situations with people who convince themselves that there is better back where their trauma began, Hagar did what she desired. She found a woman, Meribah, an Egyptian, and brought her to Ishmael to marry. Danger alert!

Jasher 21: 18-21

And the wife of Ishmael conceived and bare four sons and two daughters, and Ishmael and his mother and his wife and children afterward went and returned to the wilderness. 19. And they made themselves tents in the wilderness, in which they dwelt, and they continued to travel and then to rest monthly and yearly. 20. And God gave Ishmael flocks and herds and tents on account of Abraham his father, and the man increased in cattle. 21. And Ishmael dwelt in deserts and in tents, traveling and resting for a long time, and he did not see the face of his father.

When you are covered by a good man, provisions await you. God is the Greatest! Ishmael was blessed. Not only was he blessed, but he began to expand in wealth the same way his father Abraham did, with tents and livestock. As an archer and master of the wilderness, Ishmael was establishing himself in the world as his own man, a builder, a hammer. With Meribah in the wilderness of Paran, Ishmael had four sons and two daughters, six children. Below are their names (Gen. 25:13, 28:9).

Children of Ishmael and Meribah

Son	Daughter
Nebajoth	Mahalath
Kedar	?
Adbell	
Mibsam	

As time passed on, in the middle of child bearing, traveling, and expanding, Ishmael had not seen his father since he left with his mother into the wilderness. This is very important to understand. Ishmael the archer and hammer, was loved by his father. Remember, Abraham had to be told by God himself to send Ishmael away with Hagar. He did not want to do it and scripture says that it grieved Abraham to do so. Father and son loved one another despite the circumstances. It was from this bond that the rest of this story takes off.

Jasher 21: 22-24

And in some time after, Abraham said to Sarah his wife, I will go and see my son Ishmael, for I have a desire to see him, for I have not seen him for a long time. 23. And Abraham rode upon one of his camels to the wilderness to seek his son Ishmael, for he heard that he was dwelling in a tent in the wilderness with all belonging to him. 24. And Abraham went to the wilderness, and he reached the tent of Ishmael about noon, and he asked after Ishmael, and he found the wife of Ishmael sitting in the tent with her children, and Ishmael her husband and his mother were not with them.

A good father always seeks time with his children. Even in the midst of disagreement, a father wants that connection that cannot be broken. Abraham handled his business in a way that is respectable of both of his wives. He let Sarah know what he was going to do. She was honorable in not making a fuss and allowing him to go and see his son in peace.

No static.

When Abraham arrived where he had been told Ishmael tents were, he found Meribah sitting in the tent with her children. Ishmael and Hagar were gone. The irony is outstanding. A father-in-law meets his daughter-in-law for the first time with the grandchildren Abraham never knew he had, all in one place. Imagine the emotion of Abraham, a 100+ year old man who didn't have a child until he was 86, which was Ishmael, then Isaac when he was 100. Now, after a camel ride in the desert, he comes to a tent that was believed to be his son', then he sees 6 children. He didn't know he had any grandchildren. To find out this way and keep his composure had to be other worldly! That's a story all unto itself. Meanwhile, we have a monumental meeting here that will teach us all a lesson in how to choose a good helpmeet. Let's take note...

Jasher 21: 25-29

And Abraham asked the wife of Ishmael, saying, Where has Ishmael gone? and she said, He has gone to the field to hunt, and Abraham was still mounted upon the camel, for he would not get off to the ground as he had sworn to his wife Sarah that he would not get off from the camel. 26. And Abraham said to Ishmael's wife, My daughter, give me a little water that I may drink, for I am fatigued from the journey. 27. And Ishmael's wife answered and said to Abraham, We have neither water nor bread, and she continued sitting in the tent and did not notice Abraham, neither did she ask him who he was. 28. But she was beating her children in the tent, and she was cursing them, and she also cursed her husband Ishmael and reproached him, and Abraham heard the words of Ishmael's wife to her children, and he was very angry and displeased. 29. And Abraham called to the woman to come out to him from the tent, and the woman came and stood opposite to Abraham, for Abraham was still mounted upon the camel.

A good man, a godly man, a father, father-in-law, grandfather. Abraham honored his wife by not getting off the camel, showing respect to Sarah in allowing her to take comfort in knowing that Abraham would not go in to Hagar if she was there. Honorable. When he asked Meribah about Ishmael's location, she told Abraham that he was out hunting, which would please any father, knowing his son was out working to provide for his family. The key here is what happens next.

When Abraham said daughter, when asking for water, Meribah showed no respect to the word and presence of Abraham. She kept on beating and cursing her children, Abraham's grandchildren that he just found out that he had, while in his presence, which indicates a total lack of respect for authority and elders. She paid no attention to the fact that Abraham had just revealed to her who he was by calling her daughter. Not only was she cursing the children while beating them, she was cursing Ishmael, his son, who wasn't present. This is vile on so many levels. She was not only beating her children and cursing them, but she was indirectly teaching her children how to disrespect their father, which was a major offense. Reader, please keep in mind that Abraham was known for being a gracious host. Meribah was the opposite of that. She operated in total disrespect of her husband. This was too much for Abraham, as scripture says he became angry and displeased. All of this happened with Abraham staying on his camel, keeping his word to Sarah. Instead of breaking his word and losing his cool, he called Meribah to him outside of the tent. It was time for Abraham to leave. But first...

Jasher 21: 30-32

And Abraham said to Ishmael's wife, When thy husband Ishmael returneth home say these words to him, 31. A very old man from the land of the Philistines came hither to seek thee, and thus was his appearance and figure; I did not ask him who he was, and seeing thou wast not here he spoke unto me and said, When Ishmael thy husband returneth tell him thus did this man say, When thou comest home put away this nail of the tent which thou hast placed here, and place another nail in its stead. 32. And Abraham finished his instructions to the woman, and he turned and went off on the camel homeward.

A report and a nail. A report. A nail.

The report, an old man from the land of the Philistines came and was disrespected. That same old man was from the same area where his father was from. Meribah didn't care, she was operating in disrespect, open disrespect. Either she didn't know or didn't care to know for a stranger to be treated with such disrespect is ungodly and speaks to how a man represents his family. That's not a good report.

The nail is the one who keeps the home stable. It keeps the home, stable. One more time, it keeps the home, stable. Regardless of the weather, it keeps the home stable. Regardless of what happens inside or outside the home, it keeps it stable. When the home needs to be moved, the nail has to be moved. It is the hammer that must be in connection with the nail in order for it to be an effective tandem to create structure. The hammer does its' work then leaves, but it is the nail that remains. It is the nail that remains stable. It is the nail.
Abraham's summary after the report: move the nail and get another one.

Not long after Abraham leaves to go back home, Ishmael and Hagar returns.

Jasher 21: 33-36

And after that Ishmael came from the chase he and his mother, and returned to the tent, and his wife spoke these words to him, 34. A very old man from the land of the Philistines came to seek thee, and thus was his appearance and figure; I did not ask him who he was, and seeing thou wast not at home he said to me, When thy husband cometh home tell him, thus saith the old man, Put away the nail of the tent which thou hast placed here and place another nail in its stead. 35. And Ishmael heard the words of his wife, and he knew that it was his father, and that his wife did not honor him. 36. And Ishmael understood his father's words that he had spoken to his wife, and Ishmael hearkened to the voice of his father, and Ishmael cast off that woman and she went away.

The report, then the nail. The report. Then the nail.

The report, delivered just as Abraham requested. Ishmael received it. While his wife was telling him what happened, Ishmael used discernment to understand what was being said and who the man from the land of the Philistines was: his father, Abraham. Ishmael grew up watching his father entertain strangers with humility and respect. He knew how to be hospitable and graceful, especially with the elderly, like his father was. He knew his father was dishonored by the report of his visit. In hearing this, Ishmael knew what to do. He did the EXACT same thing to his wife that his father did to his mother, who just so happen to not be in the tent when the report was given (v33). Notice the wisdom of Ishmael here. He had the conversation with his wife Meribah, the woman chosen by his mother Hagar, alone. He gave interpretation of the report, alone. He did what a man should do. He did what his father did.

The nail, Meribah. She was the nail. The wife is the nail. The wife is the one who must be stable. She balances the home. She must be tough, dependable, and stable. Meribah, however, was not. Her name means quarrel, contention, or strife. It would later be used by Moses to name a place in the wilderness where there was no water while the people were complaining (Exo. 17:7). She was the nail that Abraham said needed to be removed and replaced. She said it with her own mouth. She put the nail in the coffin with her own words.

Ishmael sent his wife away, separating from her.

Jasher 21:37

And Ishmael afterward went to the land of Canaan, and he took another wife and he brought her to his tent to the place where he then dwelt.

Ishmael went and found another wife on his own. He didn't use the services of his mother Hagar this time. Again, he found what he was looking for, not his mother, who was looking for what she likes that she thought he would like. Ishmael went to the land of Canaan, the future Promised Land, to find his wife.

Jasher 21: 38-44

And at the end of three years Abraham said, I will go again and see Ishmael my son, for I have not seen him for a long time. 39. And he rode upon his camel and went to the wilderness, and he reached the tent of Ishmael about noon. 40. And he asked after Ishmael, and his wife came out of the tent and she said, He is not here my lord, for he has gone to hunt in the fields, and to feed the camels, and the woman said to Abraham, Turn in my lord into the tent, and eat a morsel of bread, for thy soul must be wearied on account of the journey. 41. And Abraham said to her, I will not stop for I am in haste to continue my journey, but give me a little water to drink, for I have thirst; and the woman hastened and ran into the tent and she brought out water and bread to Abraham, which she placed before him and she urged him to eat, and he ate and drank and his heart was comforted and he blessed his son Ishmael. 42. And he finished his meal and he blessed the Lord, and he said to Ishmael's wife, When Ishmael cometh home say these words to him, 43. A very old man from the land of the Philistines came hither and asked after thee, and thou wast not here; and I brought him out bread and water and he ate and drank and his heart was comforted. 44. And he spoke these words to me: When Ishmael thy husband cometh home, say unto him, The nail of the tent which thou hast is very good, do not put it away from the tent.

New wife, new visit, new report, new nail.

New report reads: honor, honor, honor. Abraham was welcomed, fed, and given drink for his journey. After three years, Abraham returned to be honored by a woman he didn't know in the absence of his son. This new wife was open and willing to serve, respectable. Abraham was pleased. As for the nail, the one that is in this tent is very good. It's a keeper.

New nail, new wife. She was stable. She was dependable, respectable, and honorable. She was comforting, a server, one who took the honor of her husband seriously. She was the nail. She was the one who was a keeper of the home despite the weather, despite the world, despite the circumstances. So much so that the old man from the land of the Philistines said she was a keeper. Not just a nail, but the nail.

So, what did Ishmael do when he heard the report?

Jasher 21: 45

And Abraham finished commanding the woman, and he rode off to his home to the land of the Philistines; and when Ishmael came to his tent his wife went forth to meet him with joy and a cheerful heart. 46. And she said to him, An old man came here from the land of the Philistines and thus was his appearance, and he asked after thee and thou wast not here, so I brought out bread and water, and he ate and drank and his heart was comforted. 47. And he spoke these words to me, When Ishmael thy husband cometh home say to him, The nail of the tent which thou hast is very good, do not put it away from the tent. 48. And Ishmael knew that it was his father, and that his wife had honored him, and the Lord blessed Ishmael.

She's a keeper! God is the Greatest! She's a keeper! Ladies and gentlemen, notice how she met Ishmael with good news and a cheerful heart. This is a secret to holding a man's mind and attention, especially after a long day's work as Ishmael had just completed. He didn't even make it to the tent to get the news, she met him, with a cheerful heart and a smile. Imagine what that did to Ishmael! Moments like so remove the wear and tear of the day from a man when he's met with good news and a cheerful heart. When she told him the story of the visit and how she served the man from the Philistines, imagine how Ishmael felt. Relief and pride. A good man wants to be represented as such. Just as she was allowed to stay put while he worked to feed their family, which is honorable, she in turn honored her husband by representing the peace and respect of their home. This is teamwork, relational teamwork, working hand in hand. The happiness came in the end, not the beginning. This is a lesson we all need to learn. The new nail allowed Ishmael to be blessed by the LORD! This is why scripture says that....

Proverbs 18:22

Whoso findeth a wife findeth a good *thing*, and obtaineth favour of the LORD.

Ishmael had found favor. He found his wife. He found the nail, his nail. Finding that nail will change a man, open him up for lack of a better term. Because she honored her husband and gave a positive and cheerful report, Ishmael experienced one of the greatest gifts any man could have: a good thing. That's so rare to find nowadays. People are so caught up in value systems, schemes, and selfishness unlike anything the world has ever seen, we don't really know what a good thing is anymore. It's not being taught anymore. But Ishmael had it with his 2nd wife. Because of that, look what happens next, when a man has clarity and connection with a cheerfully hearted woman of good report....

Jasher 22: 1-3

And Ishmael then rose up and took his wife and his children and his cattle and all belonging to him, and he journeyed from there and he went to his father in the land of the Philistines. 2. And Abraham related to Ishmael his son the transaction with the first wife that Ishmael took, according to what she did. 3. And Ishmael and his children dwelt with Abraham many days in that land, and Abraham dwelt in the land of the Philistines a long time.

Ishmael went to his father. Not only did he go back to his father, but he took his children and everything belonging to him. His children was with him, not the wife that was sent away. Ishmael went back to his father in peace, allowing Abraham to enjoy being a grandfather. He allowed Sarah to see his children, in peace. He allowed Isaac to see his nephews and nieces, in peace. In peace, with a cheerful heart, reflective of his new wife, his new nail.

Reader, did you notice who was missing in the second nail story? Hagar. Guess who was not present for Abraham's visit the second time to the second wife? Hagar. Guess who didn't share in the good report? Hagar. Guess who didn't go back with Ishmael to Abraham in the land of the Philistines? Hagar. The woman who chose the first wife was not allowed to impact the second wife. The woman who separated herself from her family because of her feelings and wanted to be seen was no longer in sight. The woman who returned to the land of her father and trauma, who found a woman for her son who was dishonorable, was not a part of the traveling party back to Abraham.

Well, when we look at Hagar and Ishmael, what did you notice that was similar? They both went back to the land where their father lived. Both were sent away. Both were looking for acceptance. What was the difference? Hagar's father was not honorable. Ishmael's father was honorable. Hagar returned to the origin of her trauma. Ishmael returned to the origin of his blessings. Hagar ran away from her covering. Ishmael returned to his covering. Hagar wanted to be seen. Ishmael wanted to be felt. Hagar had FOMO (fear of missing out) and didn't want to miss out on the perks and positioning of wife and motherhood to Abraham. Ishmael didn't want to miss out on the duty and honor of being a respectable family man to his father Abraham. Hagar wanted adoration for her position. Ishmael gave adoration to his wife for her positioning. Hagar dishonored Abraham. Ishmael honored Abraham.

In choosing a nail, an instrument used to help connect and build things, we must be clear. It is meant to help a builder or user meet an expectation or assignment. That is the purpose of a nail. This is the purpose of a wife, a helpmeet. The role and position of a wife is to help her husband meet an expectation or assignment. It is God who gives the vision for the family to husband. It is his responsibility to meet that expectation or assignment. His wife's role is to help him meet and or complete that expectation or assignment. This is what Sarah did with Abraham, even when she errored. She errored in helping Abraham complete the assignment of being a father of many nations. This is what Ishmael's second wife did, by honoring her husband, by serving Abraham when Ishmael was away working. This is not what Hagar did, who left her family because of her feelings, causing an angel from heaven to come and redirect her back to Abraham. Mind you, she didn't return because it was the right thing to do, she returned because the angel told her 12 princes would come from Ishmael. This is not what Meribah did, by dishonoring and not serving Abraham when he came to see Ishmael. The honorable wife experiences blessings and honor. The dishonorable wife experience self-inflicted separation and the harsh realities of life without covering.

A nail, ladies and gentlemen, without a covering, will rust in the open weather. In time, it will decay and break with little resistance. Its strength will be broken. However, a nail that is attached, connected, and serving its role in helping a structure meet its purpose, stays intact and increases the value of the overall unit, home, or family. There are homes that are still in tack that are thousands of years old. From the Gobekli Tepe in Turkey to the Pyramids of Egypt and Meroe, nails are still holding these structures together. Thousands and thousands of years, weather pattern changes, wars, life, death, etc., they are still standing, still strong, still standing. The builders are dead. The hammers are gone, but the buildings still stand. Why? The nails.

Ladies, if you get nothing from this section, please understand how God views you in relation to the concept of a wife. We use this story of Ishmael and the three women in his life to teach the value of a wife, perspectively, through the wisdom of Abraham. To understand that God sees a wife as a connector, not a ruler, is very important. A ruler measures, that's God. A husband is a hammer, a tool used to perform as a builder and destroyer. He must be able to do both, just as God does, who was the first husband. A wife that is dishonorable to her husband first dishonors God, whether she intends to or not. There is a consequence for that, which directly falls at the feet of her husband, the one responsible for her. A wife that is honorable to her husband first honors God, whether she intends to or not. There is a reward for that, which directly falls at the feet of her husband as well, because he is responsible for her. This is why, ladies and gentlemen, as you check your own inventory of who and where you are relationally, we must understand there is no accountability without consequence and reward. Society likes to throw that word around with loose meaning. Most people think acknowledgement and responsibility is accountability. No, these are components of accountability, but incomplete without consequence and reward. This is why becoming a nail is so important. This is why understanding what nail you're getting for a family building project is so important. The strength and length of the nail, how it was made, fashioned, reinforced, stored, and used is crucial in every building project. Get a cheap made, poorly stored, irregularly fashioned nail, and the building project will end with a constant need of repair. It'll look good, but it won't stand the test of time. On the contrary, if you get sure made, precise, reinforced, properly kept, unused nail, then the project has a higher percentage chance of succeeding. This is the mistake of Hagar. She was a nail that wanted to be seen, not realizing that any home that has nails showing can be disassembled due to exposure to the elements. Ishmael's second wife wanted to cover her covering by being honorable, the same way a nail is covered from the elements, fitting in tight space, doing their job, sacrificing being seen now for being seen throughout the ages.

Ezra 9: 8-9

And now for a little space grace hath been *shewed* from the LORD our God, to leave us a remnant to escape, and to give us a nail in his holy place, that our God may lighten our eyes, and give us a little reviving in our bondage. 9 For we *were* bondmen; yet our God hath not forsaken us in our bondage, but hath extended mercy unto us in the sight of the kings of Persia, to give us a reviving, to set up the house of our God, and to repair the desolations thereof, and to give us a wall in Judah and in Jerusalem.

A nail ladies and gentlemen, a nail.

Abimelech, pt.2

Jasher 22: 4-5

And the days increased and reached twenty six years, and after that Abraham with his servants and all belonging to him went
from the land of the Philistines and removed to a great distance, and they came near to Hebron, and they remained there, and the
servants of Abraham dug wells of water, and Abraham and all belonging to him dwelt by the water, and the servants of Abimelech
king of the Philistines heard the report that Abraham's servants had dug wells of water in the borders of the land. 5. And they
came and quarreled with the servants of Abraham, and they robbed them of the great well which they had dug.

As the years go forth, so does the favor of Abraham. Now that Ishmael is living alongside Abraham and his servants, Abraham was a father's father, a happy man. After living in the land of the Philistines for several years, it was time to move on to Hebron, a place he knew all too well. In the midst of the wilderness, Abraham and his servants began to build wells of water to feed their families and flocks. It was during this time, some of the Philistines came and took over the big well that Abraham's servants had dug. Why is this important? For many years Abimelech and Abraham had an agreement that allowed Abraham to have residence grace and the best land in Abimelech's kingdom. This robbery, even though Abraham had moved away, was still a violation of their previous agreement. When Abimelech heard about what happened, the king himself took a trip to see his friend.

Genesis 21: 22-26

And it came to pass at that time, that Abimelech and Phichol the chief captain of his host spake unto Abraham, saying, God *is* with thee in all
that thou doest: 23 Now therefore swear unto me here by God that thou wilt not deal falsely with me, nor with my son, nor with my son's
son: *but* according to the kindness that I have done unto thee, thou shalt do unto me, and to the land wherein thou hast sojourned. 24 And
Abraham said, I will swear. 25 And Abraham reproved Abimelech because of a well of water, which Abimelech's servants had violently taken
away. 26 And Abimelech said, I wot not who hath done this thing: neither didst thou tell me, neither yet heard I *of it*, but to day.

Abraham rebuked the king. Yes, you read that right. Even though they were friends, Abraham still rebuked Abimelech. This is the kind of favor God can give you if you walk in his light, in the presence of both enemies and friends. Abraham was not having it and he meant business, respectively.

Genesis 21: 27-34

And Abraham took sheep and oxen, and gave them unto Abimelech; and both of them made a covenant. 28 And Abraham set
seven ewe lambs of the flock by themselves. 29 And Abimelech said unto Abraham, What *mean* these seven ewe lambs which thou
hast set by themselves? 30 And he said, For *these* seven ewe lambs shalt thou take of my hand, that they may be a witness unto me,
that I have digged this well. 31 Wherefore he called that place Beersheba; because there they sware both of them. 32 Thus they made
a covenant at Beersheba: then Abimelech rose up, and Phichol the chief captain of his host, and they returned into the land of the
Philistines. 33 And *Abraham* planted a grove in Beersheba, and called there on the name of the LORD, the everlasting God. 34 And
Abraham sojourned in the Philistines' land many days.

Done and done. To settle a quarrel, two good men made another agreement in the presence of God as an example of how to handle disputes between men. This could have gotten ugly, but it didn't. One man honored the other even though one man's honor had been violated. Instead of fighting, they resolved their issues with dignity and respect. The man who was violated, Abraham, gave not only his word, but livestock, as a token of his word and willingness to work things out in peace. Upon accepting this gift, Abimelech left and went back home, in peace, with his men. No harm was to come to Abraham and all that was his.

In the meantime, Abraham built a grove, which in Hebrew means place of trees, similar to an orchard. He planted trees to symbolize his roots in that place. The trees would need water to sustain themselves, which would come from the underwater springs that fed the water wells that Abraham had dug. In a wilderness, God provided what was needed to produce plenty for his chosen.

Jasher 22: 11-14

And Abraham planted a large grove in Beersheba, and he made to it four gates facing the four sides of the earth, and he planted a vineyard in it, so that if a traveler came to Abraham he entered any gate which was in his road, and remained there and ate and drank and satisfied himself and then departed. 12. For the house of Abraham was always open to the sons of men that passed and repassed, who came daily to eat and drink in the house of Abraham. 13. And any man who had hunger and came to Abraham's house, Abraham would give him bread that he might eat and drink and be satisfied, and any one that came naked to his house he would clothe with garments as he might choose, and give him silver and gold and make known to him the Lord who had created him in the earth; this did Abraham all his life. 14. And Abraham and his children and all belonging to him dwelt in Beersheba, and he pitched his tent as far as Hebron.

Four gates. North, south, east, and west. Four gates to see all directions. Four gates to welcome all visitors. Four gates to welcome the four winds. Four gates to showcase the grace of God going forth throughout all the Earth. The grove allowed peace and shade in the wilderness, a place to eat and relax, a place to showcase the love of God to all men. Abraham didn't know what type of men would come by, as scripture said even naked people would come and he would clothe them. Abraham even gave them money to help them along their way. This is the legacy of Abraham that would spread throughout the known world. At that place, where Abraham built the groves and established a peaceful home in the midst of a Nimrod-ran world, became known as Beersheba, the well of the Oath.

The LORD Was Listening…

Jasher 22: 40-41

And Isaac the son of Abraham was growing up in those days, and Abraham his father taught him the way of the Lord to know the Lord, and the Lord was with him. 41. And when Isaac was thirty-seven years old, Ishmael his brother was going about with him in the tent.

Isaac learned the ways of God from his father. From his celebratory birth to being a 37-year-old man, Isaac knew God. He knew that the LORD was with him because God was with his father. After all this time had passed, Isaac was still covered, blessed. He was no longer a child, but a man, a 37-year-old man. His estranged brother was now living alongside him. They grew together, with their father, with Sarah watching and living with them in peace. Amen.

One day, while Isaac and Ishmael were in the tent together, something happened. This following story is the forgotten one that spearheaded one of the greatest sagas in the history of the world. It didn't begin in dramatic fashion, but very subtly. Two brothers, just talking, hanging out in the house, or in their day, a tent. Nothing much, but everything major. What happened in this tent sent ripple effects down the line of time to Jesus the Christ himself.

Jasher 22: 42-45

And Ishmael boasted of himself to Isaac, saying, I was thirteen years old when the Lord spoke to my father to circumcise us, and I did according to the word of the Lord which he spoke to my father, and I gave my soul unto the Lord, and I did not transgress his word which he commanded my father. 43. And Isaac answered Ishmael, saying, Why dost thou boast to me about this, about a little bit of thy flesh which thou didst take from thy body, concerning which the Lord commanded thee? 44. As the Lord liveth, the God of my father Abraham, if the Lord should say unto my father, Take now thy son Isaac and bring him up an offering before me, I would not refrain but I would joyfully accede to it. 45. And the Lord heard the word that Isaac spoke to Ishmael, and it seemed good in the sight of the Lord, and he thought to try Abraham in this matter.

The LORD heard that.

The LORD heard that.

Two brothers, just talking, doing what brothers do, even there, God was listening. This is amazing!

Big brother Ishmael was boasting about himself to his little brother. A 50-year-old man, boasting to his 37-year-old younger brother. This is amazing in so many ways, namely because it makes scripture personal, something we all can relate to, especially if you have brothers. Well, what was Ishmael boasting about? His obedience to God's law of circumcision. To be honest, that was not his brag moment, it was Abraham's brag. Ishmael was a boy who had to do the will of his father because his father was doing the will of his FATHER. To give himself to the LORD is honorable, which he was raised to be. Ishmael wanted Isaac to know that he mattered too in the grand scheme of God's providence. This type of banter happens amongst brothers all the time, and right on que, Isaac the younger brother responds in typical younger brother fashion, not to be undone or outmatched.

Isaac dismissed the flesh cutting of circumcision as a small thing. Instead, he jabbed back at his brother with a challenge. A wild challenge. A life changing challenge. An immature challenge. A prideful challenge. A nonsensical challenge. But a challenge nonetheless. Let's read what little bro said again.

Jasher 22:44

As the Lord liveth, the God of my father Abraham, if the Lord should say unto my father, Take now thy son Isaac and bring him up an offering before me, I would not refrain but I would joyfully accede to it.

Why? Why Isaac? Why? Why do this? Why say this? It makes no sense. I get it, I assure you, I get it. I'm the youngest of my brothers so I understand. But Isaac, really? He didn't just speak on himself or Abraham, but God's life. As the LORD liveth! Really? This is dangerous on so many levels that Isaac clearly didn't understand. To say that if the LORD told Abraham to sacrifice him as an offering, he would with joy. What? Isaac really said this. Two brothers, just talking, jabbing at one another and boasting as privileged men is a problem and their age had nothing to do with it. Physical maturity is way different than spiritual maturity. Here, even though both men were physically mature, Isaac showcased his spiritual immaturity in making such a statement. Now, had this statement been made between brothers in jest or fun, then this wouldn't be that big of a deal. But Isaac used the LORD's power in vain and attached his willingness to be a sacrifice to prove a point of loyalty to outdo his older brother. We must be careful in all of our statements, both inwardly and outwardly, publicly and privately. Why?

The LORD is listening.

Even though Isaac was raised to know the LORD by his father Abraham, just as Ishmael was, he needed to learn a valuable lesson in understanding that words mean something to the WORD. Again....

The LORD was listening.

Jasher 22:45

And the Lord heard the word that Isaac spoke to Ishmael, and it seemed good in the sight of the Lord, and he thought to try Abraham in this matter.

Physical and spiritual ears hear things. The physical ears of Ishmael and Isaac heard one another, but the spiritual ears of the LORD was present. Reader, please be aware of the following: God, who's omnipresent, was listening, but someone else was paying attention to the sons of the most righteous man on Earth. Buckle up, we're about to go on a wild ride...

Jasher 22: 46-55

And the day arrived when the sons of God came and placed themselves before the Lord, and Satan also came with the sons of God before the Lord. 47. And the Lord said unto Satan, Whence comest thou? and Satan answered the Lord and said, From going to and fro in the earth, and from walking up and down in it. 48. And the Lord said to Satan, What is thy word to me concerning all the children of the earth? and Satan answered the Lord and said, I have seen all the children of the earth who serve thee and remember thee when they require anything from thee. 49. And when thou givest them the thing which they require from thee, they sit at their ease, and forsake thee and they remember thee no more. 50. Hast thou seen Abraham the son of Terah, who at first had no children, and he served thee and erected altars to thee wherever he came, and he brought up offerings upon them, and he proclaimed thy name continually to all the children of the earth. 51. And now that his son Isaac is born to him, he has forsaken thee, he has made a great feast for all the inhabitants of the land, and the Lord he has forgotten. 52. For amidst all that he has done he brought thee no offering; neither burnt offering nor peace offering, neither ox, lamb nor goat of all that he killed on the day that his son was weaned. 53. Even from the time of his son's birth till now, being thirty-seven years, he built no altar before thee, nor brought any offering to thee, for he saw that thou didst give what he requested before thee, and he therefore forsook thee.

Uh oh! Yes, ladies and gentlemen, you read that right. Satan was paying attention to what was going on too. He was watching Abraham. By watching Abraham, he had a chance to watch his sons as well. The most righteous man on Earth at the time was Abraham, who by default became the enemy of Satan. Nimrod allowed Satan to establish himself as the ruler of the known world. Abraham was an enemy of everything Nimrod stood for, thus putting Satan as his spiritual enemy because Nimrod served Satan and his agenda. As a restless spirit Satan spent and to this day, spends time traveling to and fro in the Earth, always on the move, unsettled. With the fall of Babel and Nimrod's solo seat as world leader changed, Satan now had mini kingdoms sprouting up all over the world as mankind began to travel and spread out over the continents. Although his kingdom was spreading like a virus over the planet, it was Abraham that he watched the most. Reader, please make note: even though his kingdom spread over the Earth, the person he watched the most wasn't his own, but his enemy, Abraham. This should open your eyes to the strategy and thought process of the evil one.

Satan was not privy to the conversation between Ishmael and Isaac in the tent. How do we know that? Satan is NOT omnipresent, meaning he cannot be everywhere at one time. Only God is omnipresent. The word omnipresent has one owner, the LORD God Almighty. That's important to comprehend in order to understand the conversation and relationship between God and Satan. Satan has to report to the LORD, daily, to give details of his doings. Whenever God requires him, he has to give an account, and when he does, it is always accurate. Yes, reader, understand the evil one's relationship with the LORD. He knows he cannot lie to God because he knows the real God that we are attempting to know. He knows God to be true, knowing all and seeing all, so therefore he doesn't lie to the One True God because he knows HIS power. We, as humans, don't really know the power of the LORD to the degree that Satan does. We'll lie to God. Satan won't. This should humble you as it did me when we really look at the conversation between the LORD and Satan. It should also remind you of another conversation similar to this one. There was another conversation made about another righteous man in the Earth that Satan desired to change how they viewed God:

Job.

Job 1: 6-12

Now there was a day when the sons of God came to present themselves before the LORD, and Satan came also among them. 7
And the LORD said unto Satan, Whence comest thou? Then Satan answered the LORD, and said, From going to and fro in the
earth, and from walking up and down in it. 8 And the LORD said unto Satan, Hast thou considered my servant Job, that *there*
is none like him in the earth, a perfect and an upright man, one that feareth God, and escheweth evil? 9 Then Satan answered
the LORD, and said, Doth Job fear God for nought? 10 Hast not thou made an hedge about him, and about his house, and about
all that he hath on every side? thou hast blessed the work of his hands, and his substance is increased in the land. 11 But put
forth thine hand now, and touch all that he hath, and he will curse thee to thy face. 12 And the LORD said unto Satan, Behold, all
that he hath *is* in thy power; only upon himself put not forth thine hand. So Satan went forth from the presence of the LORD.

Amen.

Just like the story of Job that came later in history, Abraham was viewed as privileged in the eyes of the evil one. Satan's whole plan was to get the righteous to go against the LORD, to curse HIM and or HIS name. That's the plan. Simple. How he does it is very complicated, but the plan itself is simple. Keep in mind, Satan doesn't do this for everyone, just the righteous. He didn't have this conversation about Nimrod and those that follow him. Only the righteous. Only those that really serve the LORD is within his sight and worthy of conversation with the LORD. Please keep this in mind as we progress forward.

One of the other things to take note when reading about Satan's observation of Abraham is how much he worshipped the LORD. He knew when Abraham sacrificed, built altars, had celebrations, etc. He was watching Abraham closely. Again, being righteous comes with eyes that watch even when we are not. For 37 years, according to the evil one, Abraham abandoned worship of God.

While Satan was doing what he does best, God was doing what he does most, considering us...

Jasher 22: 54-55

And the Lord said to Satan, Hast thou thus considered my servant Abraham? for there is none like him upon earth, a perfect and an upright man before me, one that feareth God and avoideth evil; as I live, were I to say unto him, Bring up Isaac thy son before me, he would not withhold him from me, much more if I told him to bring up a burnt offering before me from his flock or herds.
55. And Satan answered the Lord and said, Speak then now unto Abraham as thou hast said, and thou wilt see whether he will not this day transgress and cast aside thy words.

While Satan was hating, God was deliberating. There in none like Abraham upon the Earth! Wow, what a compliment! There is none like him, perfect and upright before me, one that respects God and avoids evil. Amen, amen, amen. This is how our mindset should be when someone starts hating. We should look through the higher energy of the lens of God and see the truth of a man as opposed to giving in to the lower energy of hating.

God did.

The LORD set a cunning trap for the cunning trapper. The LORD wanted to show Satan that there are levels to this spiritual thing and he ain't close to understanding humanity as HE does. HE set the bait and Satan jumped on it, claiming that Abraham will bring Isaac as a human sacrifice, beyond an animal sacrifice. Satan, seeing a possible kink in the armour of God in relation to human sacrifice, accepted the opportunity and even said the very day God speaks to Abraham about it that he will curse God. Even though they were talking, Satan forgot something very important....

The LORD was listening.

Let the games begin....

Jeremiah 23:24

Can any hide himself in secret places that I shall not see him? saith the LORD. Do not I fill heaven and earth? saith the LORD.

Standing on *Business*

Genesis 22: 1-2

And it came to pass after these things, that God did tempt Abraham, and said unto him, Abraham: and he said, Behold, *here* I *am*. 2 And he said, Take now thy son, thine only *son* Isaac, whom thou lovest, and get thee into the land of Moriah; and offer him there for a burnt offering upon one of the mountains which I will tell thee of.

It's time to stand on business. The LORD had HIS conversation with Satan, said what HE was going to do, and now it was time to stand on the business of that conversation. The LORD didn't wait to get things going, HE immediately set the event into play, which began with a simple call of a name, Abraham.

Here I am. What a response! Here I am. This should be our name, as a believer. Here I am. The concept of this verbiage means wherever I am, regardless of where I am, what I'm doing, where I'm going, etc., is I am available LORD. Here I am. Amazing, amazing, amazing response and lesson for the believer and doer of God's call.

When God told Abraham to take Isaac, the child of the promise, to the land of Moriah and give him as a burnt offering upon a yet to be named mountain, two things occurred that goes beyond the surface that even Satan didn't see. God is so amazing. Allow us to *Make It Plain* for you and give you a mystery of the WORD before we go forward:

Make It Plain

1. Since when has God not been specific? In verse 2, HE told Abraham to go to one of the mountains that HE would tell him, later. What? God didn't know at the time? Was HE not ready to reveal it? God, none direct? Come on now, let's be for real. Abraham didn't catch it neither did Satan. This should have been a dead giveaway that the LORD was cunning the cunner, out-hustling the hustler, outplaying the player, for lack of better terms. Abraham was listening to be obedient, Satan was watching to set a trap to offset righteousness in the Earth and possibly destroy the bloodline that gave birth to the future Christ. God had them both right where HE wanted them.

2. Since when did God become okay with human sacrifice? Put aside what Isaac said to Ishmael in the tent for a second, reckless talking between brothers. Remember, God heard that conversation, not Satan. That's very important to keep in mind. Satan, the accuser and hater of all mankind, loved and continues to love the idea of humans killing humans, especially with fire, since we are the image of the living God and he is not. He knows that he can't hurt God, but showing us how to hurt ourselves hurt God. That's his strategy. Human sacrifice is not a God thing. In fact, HE later outlawed it with Moses and the children of Israel because some of them start practicing what the surrounding nations were doing (Lev. 18:21, Duet. 18:10). It's abominable to God. With that said, why would HE not only tell Abraham to sacrifice his son, but to do it as a burnt offering? When you bring back into play what Isaac said to Ishmael, Isaac was talking about giving his life, such as a regular sacrifice of killing by knife with bloodshed, meaning the death would be quick, no extended pain. But God added the concept of fire to the plan, which is pain on a whole different level. That's long, extended, soul changing pain. Not only would Isaac feel it, so would his father Abraham, the one who was set to offer the sacrifice. The scream alone would kill Abraham, a 137-year-old man at the time. Heaven forbid.

But again...Abraham and Satan didn't see what God was doing.

The test wasn't really just for Abraham....it was for Satan as well.

When we look at God's request, we have to look at Abraham from a human point of view. God asking a man to give his son away to be killed as a sacrifice is cruel, very unusual punishment. I'm sorry, it just is. It's like asking a person to burn or kill a portion of themselves, as children are an expression of their parents. For 87 years, Abraham waited to be a father, then Ishmael was born. For 100 years, Abraham waited to be a father, then Isaac was born. To ask him at 137 to sacrifice his youngest son in his old age is a problem.

In most sermons and lessons taught on Abraham and this request from God, we always see Isaac as a child, but he was not. He was 37. We always read the next verses and assume that Abraham just did what he was told without emotion and feeling, robotic. That's not true either. Let's read...

Jasher 23: 1-7

At that time the word of the Lord came to Abraham, and he said unto him, Abraham, and he said, Here I am.2 And he said to him, Take now thy son, thine only son whom thou lovest, even Isaac, and go to the land of Moriah, and offer him there for a burnt offering upon one of the mountains which shall be shown to thee, for there wilt thou see a cloud and the glory of the Lord. 3 And Abraham said within himself, How shall I separate my son Isaac from Sarah his mother, in order to bring him up for a burnt offering before the Lord? 4 And Abraham came into the tent, and he sat before Sarah his wife, and he spoke these words to her, 5 My son Isaac is grown up and he has not for some time studied the service of his God, now tomorrow I will go and bring him to Shem, and Eber his son, and there he will learn the ways of the Lord, for they will teach him to know the Lord as well as to know that when he prayeth continually before the Lord, he will answer him, therefore there he will know the way of serving the Lord his God. 6 And Sarah said, Thou hast spoken well, go my lord and do unto him as thou hast said, but remove him not at a great distance from me, neither let him remain there too long, for my soul is bound within his soul. 7 And Abraham said unto Sarah, My daughter, let us pray to the Lord our God that he may do good with us.

Ladies and gentlemen, this is a father, a real father. He was hurt, broken, undone. The narrative of this story has always been told wrong. Abraham was devastated. It was as if Isaac had died already, in his mind. Why? Because when the LORD spoke, Abraham knew to do. It was who he was as a man. This request was catastrophic and cringe-worthy. He knew this request was on a whole different level of commitment. Undone is an understatement. Not only did Abraham think about what he was feeling, he considered Sarah, his wife, who had Isaac at 90. She was 127 at this time. The news of this would kill her and he knew it. A broken heart for a woman of this age would be too much to bear. Again, this was a father, a man who loved his family.

With Sarah' life in mind, he went in to speak to her. Instead of telling her exactly what God said, he did what Abraham had done several times in his past, not tell the whole truth. The half truth was that he was going to take Isaac to learn the ways of God. He was going to take him to Shem, Noah's son, and Eber, Shem's son, to teach Isaac. That was not a part of the equation nor was that what God said to him. Abraham couldn't bring himself to hurt or kill the heart of his wife, so he told her a half truth. By saying it the way that he did, Sarah's only concern would be with the distance from Isaac, not the departure of Isaac. That's key in understanding the heart of a mother. Abraham knew how Sarah would take the news if he was direct with her. She probably would have fought Abraham tooth and nail to get him to stay and not take Isaac. Abraham knew that.

After hearing the news, Abraham had to prepare to travel the following morning. He had to think through who he was taking with him, how the process would go, all while remaining obedient to the LORD. Meanwhile, the mother in Sarah kicked in. Even though Isaac was 37 years old, she went into mother mode, indicating that no matter how old we get, true mothers will always look at their children as their babies, observe...

Jasher 23: 8-13

And Sarah took her son Isaac and he abode all that night with her, and she kissed and embraced him, and gave him instructions till morning. 9 And she said to him, O my son, how can my soul separate itself from thee? And she still kissed him and embraced him, and she gave Abraham instructions concerning him. 10 And Sarah said to Abraham, O my lord, I pray thee take heed of thy son, and place thine eyes over him, for I have no other son nor daughter but him. 11 O forsake him not. If he be hungry give him bread, and if he be thirsty give him water to drink; do not let him go on foot, neither let him sit in the sun. 12 Neither let him go by himself in the road, neither force him from whatever he may desire, but do unto him as he may say to thee. 13 And Sarah wept bitterly the whole night on account of Isaac, and she gave him instructions till morning.

Tell me that's not a mother? Let's *Make It Plain*, that's a mama!!

Mama's have instructions for everybody! She wasn't Abraham's mama, but she was giving him instructions like she was. As the lingo goes, everybody can get it! That's what Sarah was doing. She knew Isaac would be away for a while, and as an old woman, she wasn't sure if she would ever see him again. There was no guarantee. This is why she cried all night and gave instructions like she did. A bit over dramatic? Yes. A bit over bearing? Yes. A bit over protective? Yes. But what mama isn't? Even after crying all night, everyone woke up to instructions. That's a mama. That was Sarah.

She wasn't done.

Jasher 23: 14-19

And in the morning Sarah selected a very fine and beautiful garment from those garments which she had in the house, that Abimelech had given to her. 15 And she dressed Isaac her son therewith, and she put a turban upon his head, and she enclosed a precious stone in the top of the turban, and she gave them provision for the road, and they went forth, and Isaac went with his father Abraham, and some of their servants accompanied them to see them off the road. 16 And Sarah went out with them, and she accompanied them upon the road to see them off, and they said to her, Return to the tent. 17 And when Sarah heard the words of her son Isaac she wept bitterly, and Abraham her husband wept with her, and their son wept with them a great weeping; also those who went with them wept greatly. 18 And Sarah caught hold of her son Isaac, and she held him in her arms, and she embraced him and continued to weep with him, and Sarah said, Who knoweth if after this day I shall ever see thee again? 19 And they still wept together, Abraham, Sarah and Isaac, and all those that accompanied them on the road wept with them, and Sarah afterward turned away from her son, weeping bitterly, and all her men servants and maid servants returned with her to the tent.

Mamas. Again, she didn't know if she was going to see Isaac again. The whole camp was up to see Abraham and this crew off. Keep in mind, Abraham didn't say they were going to be gone forever, just a short time. He said Isaac was going so he could learn the way of the LORD. Sarah bypassed all of that information and maintained her position of possibly not seeing Isaac again. She even dressed Isaac with clothing she received from king Abimelech. She put a turban on his head which had a precious jewel in it, indicating that he was a man of prestige.

When they began to leave the camp and go down the road, Abraham and Isaac told her to go back home, to the tent, as men do. After hearing this, she lost her cool, and began to weep. She wasn't surprised to hear Abraham say this. Husbands leave and go all the time (work, hunting, protecting, etc.). It was Isaac's words that pierced her heart to begin crying. When Abraham saw this, he too was broken hearted. Not just because Sarah was crying, but because he was the only one in the group that really knew that this would be their last time together. He didn't want to rob Sarah of her moment, so he allowed them to come together one last time as a family. A father being a father, a mother being a mama.

After the last embrace and tears shed, it was time to get back to business.

Genesis 22:3

And Abraham rose up early in the morning, and saddled his ass, and took two of his young men with him, and Isaac his son, and clave the wood for the burnt offering, and rose up, and went unto the place of which God had told him.

4 men left on this journey. Abraham, Isaac, and two other young men. Who were these two men? Why would the bible include them in this story? Because they have always been a part of the Abraham story.

Jasher 23:21

And Abraham took two of his young men with him, Ishmael the son of Hagar and Eliezer his servant, and they went together with them, and whilst they were walking in the road the young men spoke these words to themselves,

Abraham, Isaac, Ishmael, and Eliezer. A father, two sons, and a servant. These four men represent the four phases of faith. The origin or source from which you discover your father, that's Abraham. The promise of your faith, that's Isaac. The force of your faith, that's Ishmael. Last but certainly not least is the service of your faith, that's Eliezer. Let's proceed.

Jasher 23: 22-24

And Ishmael said to Eliezer, Now my father Abraham is going with Isaac to bring him up for a burnt offering to the Lord, as He commanded him. 23 Now when he returneth he will give unto me all that he possesses, to inherit after him, for I am his first born. 24 And Eliezer answered Ishmael and said, Surely Abraham did cast thee away with thy mother, and swear that thou shouldst not inherit any thing of all he possesses, and to whom will he give all that he has, with all his treasures, but unto me his servant, who has been faithful in his house, who has served him night and day, and has done all that he desired me? to me will he bequeath at his death all that he possesses.

Ishmael was still hating. You would think, after all this time, Ishmael would have learned his lesson. All that hating, for what? He clearly had learned from his father what the purpose of the mission was for the day. Instead of looking at the moment as the last time he would get to spend with his brother, he was riding with Eliezer talking about himself becoming the heir to everything once Isaac dies. This was wild! Not to be undone, Eliezer, Abraham's most trusted servant, chimed in and put his bid in to be the beneficiary of Abraham's estate once Isaac dies. He gave Ishmael a dosage of reality by sending him a reminder of what Abraham did and said in revoking Ishmael from heirship when he sent Hagar and Ishmael away. No lies were told, so Eliezer would have the last say on the matter while Ishmael had to come to reality that he wasn't in the position that he thought he was in for Abraham's blessings. What a reality check.

Meanwhile, Satan was watching.

God had already listened, but it was now time for Abraham and his 3 young men to face the real test of the journey, Satan himself.

Reader, before we move forward, please prepare yourself to take notes of the enemy and how he operates. What you are about to read and learn will help you understand the sheer power, skill, and will of the enemy we face. Do not be deceived, Satan is a very powerful entity that really exists in this world. Don't let anyone tell you he isn't. That doesn't mean to fear him, but you must respect what he can do. Again, he wasn't privy to the conversation between Ishmael and Isaac, but he was watching these four men out on the road, namely Abraham. His strategy was to go at the head of the group to cause doubt. If he could get Abraham to doubt, the other three would be easy work. Again, please take note.

Jasher 23: 25-27

And whilst Abraham was proceeding with his son Isaac along the road, Satan came and appeared to Abraham in the figure of a very aged man, humble and of contrite spirit, and he approached Abraham and said to him, Art thou silly or brutish, that thou goest to do this thing this day to thine only son? 26 For God gave thee a son in thy latter days, in thy old age, and wilt thou go and slaughter him this day because he committed no violence, and wilt thou cause the soul of thine only son to perish from the earth? 27 Dost thou not know and understand that this thing cannot be from the Lord? for the Lord cannot do unto man such evil upon earth to say to him, Go slaughter thy child.

Satan can appear as the contrite, humble, meek man that is very unassuming. In this case, an old man, which represents wisdom and respect. But, just as his nature is, he eventually shows his true self. He actually showed his hand by telling Abraham information about Isaac and his birth conditions. How could an old man on the road to a random mountain know that? How could he know the intent of the trip? Sarah didn't even know the intent of the trip! Neither did Isaac. To add more ridiculousness to this equation, and to prove the true relationship between Satan and God, the evil one told the truth. Did you catch that, in verse 27? Satan told the truth! Even as the father of lies, he has to tell the truth when it comes to God and his will. Satan is no fool, in fact, he's very wise. He told Abraham that a man killing his own son cannot be a God thing. Imagine that. He is telling Abraham and us, right here and now, that God himself doesn't condone the killing of children by a parent. What's interesting is how we debate about abortion and whether or not it is evil but we get a direct answer from Satan himself about the issue saying what is from God and what isn't from God. Can this be any clearer? I digress.

I told you to buckle up, this ride is just getting started....

Jasher 23:28

And Abraham heard this and knew that it was the word of Satan who endeavored to draw him aside from the way of the Lord, but Abraham would not hearken to the voice of Satan, and Abraham rebuked him so that he went away.

Father Abraham, thank you! Thank you, thank you, thank you. Thank you for showing us how to respond to the fallen one. Notice how he responded to the contrite, humble, meek, respectable old man that met him on the way to the LORD's will. Abraham saw right through it. Notice how he didn't argue with Satan? How he didn't throw words at the enemy? All he did was disregard the voice of Satan, meaning his focus was on being obedient to the voice of God, who told him to go on this mission. Abraham chose. In his choosing, which was a denial, he rebuked the devil and moved on. After the rebuke, Satan moved on as well. Remember, he is a restless spirit. Disregard his words, stay focused on the mission at hand, rebuke him and move on. He will. What a lesson for us all. Boom!

Jasher 23: 29-31

And Satan returned and came to Isaac; and he appeared unto Isaac in the figure of a young man comely and well favored. 30 And he approached Isaac and said unto him, Dost thou not know and understand that thy old silly father bringeth thee to the slaughter this day for naught? 31 Now therefore, my son, do not listen nor attend to him, for he is a silly old man, and let not thy precious soul and beautiful figure be lost from the earth.

See how Satan works? Abraham rebuked him, so he moved on. When he can't get to you, he will move on to the ones you love to see if he can get them. In this case, it was Isaac. Not only did he move on to Isaac, but he transformed how he looks. Different look, same devil. He appealed to Isaac's flight or fight sense of human survival response first. Not only that, he appealed to the youthful mind of Isaac, trying to get him to think of his "precious" soul and "beautiful" figure. This is nuts! Think of it. He literally said that Isaac should consider what's going on because of his figure, his handsomeness, which would be lost from the Earth, as if that was that important of a thing. It's ridiculous! Now, don't be fooled. How many people has he said this same thing to and they listened, on the account of their "precious" and "beautiful" figure. This is a very real trap of the mind that people even to this day fall for. Understand your enemy and his tricks. With Abraham, an old man. With Isaac, a young man. His appeal is to your nature, your selfish mind, the part of you that he identifies with, self-preservation and self-elevation. We know how Abraham handled Satan, all business. So how did Isaac handle Satan?

Jasher 23: 32-33

And Isaac heard this, and said unto Abraham, Hast thou heard, my father, that which this man has spoken? even thus has he spoken. 33 And Abraham answered his son Isaac and said to him, Take heed of him and do not listen to his words, nor attend to him, for he is Satan, endeavoring to draw us aside this day from the commands of God.

Ladies and gentlemen, forget what society has told you that makes a good man, a good father. If you are in question of what it looks like as a good man and father, look at Abraham, particularly in this situation. Isaac, in the presence of Satan himself, asked his father to help him understand how to answer and deal with a situation like so. Abraham was direct and intentional. He told Isaac to be careful in how you hear him, don't listen to him, don't entertain him. More importantly, he defined exactly who Satan was, the one whose job was to draw you away from the commands of God. It doesn't get any simpler than this. For his son, he was concise, simple, plain, and direct. A good man is concise, simple, plain, and direct. A good father is concise, simple, plain, and direct. A good husband is concise, simple, plain, and direct. They all go hand in hand. Abraham handled the situation for his son, then, as a lesson for us all now.

So how did Satan respond to Abraham and Isaac's response?

Jasher 23: 34-36

And Abraham still rebuked Satan, and Satan went from them, and seeing he could not prevail over them he hid himself from them, and he went and passed before them in the road; and he transformed himself to a large brook of water in the road, and Abraham and Isaac and his two young men reached that place, and they saw a brook large and powerful as the mighty waters. 35 And they entered the brook and passed through it, and the waters at first reached their legs. 36 And they went deeper in the brook and the waters reached up to their necks, and they were all terrified on account of the water; and whilst they were going over the brook Abraham recognized that place, and he knew that there was no water there before.

Wow. Don't you ever think or let someone tell you that Satan is not a powerful entity and enemy. This was his response. He transformed from an old man to a young man to a whole brook of water! All three transformations were real. These were not delusions, these were real. When he saw that he could not prevail against Abraham and Isaac, the two men of promise, he transformed into a large raging water in the middle of the road. Yes ladies and gentlemen, this is real. But why raging water? Raging water is a deterrent for travelers, even to this day with all the technology we have. It's hard for any boat or submarine to navigate raging water, which is one of the most destruction forces on this planet. Abraham, Isaac, Ishmael, and Eliezer didn't have a boat, so imagine how discouraging this would have been for them to see this raging water. Satan knew that too.

But God.

Abraham, even with the discouragement of this 'new' raging brook of water, stayed focused on the mission. Reader, this is a lesson for us all. Abraham, regardless of what was said and done, stayed focused. Instead of turning around, he went into the water. Those who followed him, went in as well. Why? Because of the orders he received from God before all of this happened. He knew something that we all need to keep in mind. It's a mystery of the faith that I need you to keep in your heart from this day forward:

When God gives you a command, it's HIS responsibility to protect you through whatever comes. Your responsibility is to do as HE commands. Period.

Abraham knew this. He knew God was bound to HIS word. His trust and faith in God Almighty superseded the raging water. He served, when provoked, a raging God. He served the God that made water. Also, Abraham walked around in a raging fire, protected by the LORD God HIMself, in the presence of the whole known world and Nimrod. Being that God brought him through the fire, why wouldn't HE bring him through water? See, a true believer has a faith in God that supersedes the understanding of the elements. The God we serve is the element. The God we serve created the elements.

To be clear, Abraham and his followers dealt with the human nature side of it. When the water came to their legs, Abraham went forward. When the water came to their necks, Abraham went forward. The others with him followed him and his focused demeanor. In the midst of the raging water, his human side of terror came into play, until he remembered something very important. This is another lesson to us all. In the midst of the raging waters of our lives, we need to take a second and remember our past experiences and be aware at all times of our surroundings.

Abraham, a man that had traveled through this area before, remembered that there was no brook of water here, especially a raging brook of water. He remembered. That's what we have to do that quite often we forget in the midst of a raging situation. If I'm obedient and aware, God will allow for you to notice the little things that perhaps you weren't paying attention to as much at the time. If you are connected and tuned in, you will remember some things, little things, that could save your life and shame the devil. Guess what happened when Abraham remembered this place for what it was as opposed to what it was showing itself to be?

Jasher 23: 37-40

And Abraham said to his son Isaac, I know this place in which there was no brook nor water, now therefore it is this Satan who does all this to us, to draw us aside this day from the commands of God. 38 And Abraham rebuked him and said unto him, The Lord rebuke thee, O Satan, begone from us for we go by the commands of God. 39 And Satan was terrified at the voice of Abraham, and he went away from them, and the place again became dry land as it was at first. 40 And Abraham went with Isaac toward the place that God had told him.

Amen!! We could stop here with the work and this would be enough. God is the Greatest! Abraham, thank you so much for remembering. Not only did Abraham remember from his awareness, but he had the wherewithal to let his son Isaac know that this was Satan, trying to deter them from the command of God. Boom! Salute to the courage of Abraham to rebuke Satan in the middle of raging water up to his neck. Now, reader, look closer at verse 39. There's something about Satan you need to know:

:39 And Satan was terrified at the voice of Abraham, and he went away from them, and the place again became dry land as it was at first.

Terrified!!! Yes, you read that right, terrified!! It didn't say he was terrified of Abraham. It said he was terrified at the voice of Abraham! Abraham commands his own voice, so how much do you think he really was terrified of Abraham who was standing on the business of God! Abraham rebuked Satan in confidence, causing the devil himself to be terrified. Keep in mind, Satan had a conversation with God without Abraham being present. He had the upper hand, or so he thought. The lesson for us here is that your voice, if you stand on the business of God, is enough to terrify the devil himself to the point that he will flee from you if you rebuke him. Think about this for a moment or two. You are that powerful when you speak with the command and confidence of the LORD God himself if you are willing to operate in obedience. This is incredible!

Standing on business is key in the kingdom of the GOD. Not just business, but the Father's business. Jesus said...

Luke 2: 49-51

And he said unto them, How is it that ye sought me? wist ye not that I must be about my Father's business? 50 And they understood not the saying which he spake unto them. 51 And he went down with them, and came to Nazareth, and was subject unto them: but his mother kept all these sayings in her heart.

Jesus stood on business. Even HIS earthly parents didn't understand, but God did. Sometimes, your loved ones won't understand what and why you stand on business. They don't have to. Again I say, they don't have to. It's not about whether or not someone sees, agrees, or understands what you are doing or saying. Jesus proves this, and so does Mary. Notice how in verse 51 that Mary kept what Jesus said in her heart. It wasn't a conversation, it was a moment. She understood that she didn't understand, which is what we must do sometimes. The power and wisdom of God doesn't require our understanding, just our obedience. We must have confidence, trust, and faith in HIS WORD, not just ours. Our confidence must be in HIM.

This is what Abraham did. He stood on the business of God. He chose obedience. He used his voice to stand on business. He used his position as father and leader of his family to walk into the raging water, just to be obedient. Just as Jesus stood on HIS Father's business in the temple, so did Abraham in the wilderness. It didn't matter what Satan said, he stood on business. It didn't matter whether it was an old or young man, meek, mild, and otherwise, Abraham knew the assignment. He taught us that the assignment is the assignment. He used his voice to showcase to us that deterring the devil can be done with your voice, rooted in the WORD of God. He has to obey the LORD, by voice, the same way we do. When we accept the power of God, and do HIS work, rebuking the devil is a word. Not an argument. No ego necessary. Just word, God's WORD. HE has given us a blueprint of how to stand on HIS WORD when facing the enemy. Abraham submitted to God's will. He resisted the devil. And Satan fled.

James 4:7

Submit yourselves therefore to God. Resist the devil, and he will flee from you.

This is the Standing on Business blueprint.

Offering Isaac

Genesis 22: 4-5

Then on the third day Abraham lifted up his eyes, and saw the place afar off. 5 And Abraham said unto his young men, Abide ye here with the ass; and I and the lad will go yonder and worship, and come again to you.

Amen. On the third day. Amen, on the third day. Amen, on the third day.

On the third day God made vegetation and the seas.

Jesus, on the third day, got up after preaching to the captives of death in hell.

There are so many things that happened on the third day. Amen, amen, the third day.

After the run in with the devil himself, Abraham and his young men looked up and saw the place that the LORD had preserved for Isaac's sacrifice. They certainly had a testimony for the ages, but what was about to happen was God showing HIMself in HIS simple power. I mean this constructively, not comedically. To be clear, Abraham and the men didn't just see a mountain, but something else. Genesis 22 verse 4 tells us that Abraham saw the place from afar. That could mean a mountain, but it was more, much more.

Jasher 23:42

And a pillar of fire appeared to him that reached from the earth to heaven, and a cloud of glory upon the mountain, and the glory of the Lord was seen in the cloud.

God marked the place in the heavens and the Earth! Wow! This is a multi-layered showcase by the LORD that we must appreciate before moving forward. First, the LORD demonstrated with a pillar of fire the location of the sacrifice. The pillar which stretched from the Earth to Heaven was a literal sign of HIS appointment and attention, like a precise laser beam. Two, HE had a cloud of glory on the exact mountain and place which allowed for HIS holiness to be seen in the cloud, like a picture of HIS majesty that proves or stamps that this was HIM. Third, and perhaps the most amazing of this display of awesomeness, is that God allowed this to be seen by both physical and spiritual eyes. However, not everyone could see it. What do we mean? Read...

Jasher 23: 43-48

And Abraham said to Isaac, My son, dost thou see in that mountain, which we perceive at a distance, that which I see upon it? 44 And Isaac answered and said unto his father, I see and lo a pillar of fire and a cloud, and the glory of the Lord is seen upon the cloud. 45 And Abraham knew that his son Isaac was accepted before the Lord for a burnt offering. 46 And Abraham said unto Eliezer and unto Ishmael his son, Do you also see that which we see upon the mountain which is at a distance? 47 And they answered and said, We see nothing more than like the other mountains of the earth. And Abraham knew that they were not accepted before the Lord to go with them, and Abraham said to them, Abide ye here with the ass whilst I and Isaac my son will go to yonder mount and worship there before the Lord and then return to you.48 And Eliezer and Ishmael remained in that place, as Abraham had commanded

Not everyone can see what God has in store for you. Not everyone can see the place appointed for you. Not everyone can see what God ordained for and in you. Not everyone can accept that they aren't the one. The anointing of God is not for everyone, even if that someone is abundantly blessed. Anointment is appointment.

When God decided to mark this spot on Earth, HE sent out a signal to the heavens as well, getting Satan's attention and every spirit in the universe. How do we know this? Remember the conversation that God had with Satan about Abraham possibly cursing HIM? Remember what God said? Now, remember the conversation Isaac and Ishmael had in the tent that God heard but Satan didn't? By allowing a pillar of fire to be seen going from Earth to Heaven, the LORD was showing HIS intent to purify from Earth to Heaven! The coming sacrifice was more than words, but a connection to the WORD, the purifier, Esh Oklah, the coming Christ. The conversation between the brothers are more than just words in a tent. It was a connection from Earth to Heaven.

When Abraham asked Isaac if he saw the glory of the LORD, Isaac said yes and described what he saw. Abraham knew then that Isaac had the gift of God. Not that he needed to be convinced, but it was validation of the promise of the LORD via the covenant made between Abraham and the LORD God of Heaven. Isaac was accepted by the LORD, which was both a gift and a curse. How so? It was a gift because Abraham could see that Isaac had a spiritual eye that saw beyond the physical, which is a rare gift of God. On the contrary, it was a curse because Isaac was set to be sacrificed to the LORD despite his gift.

When Abraham asked Eliezer and Ishmael if they saw what he saw, they said no. They saw what any human being would see. They did not have the gift of the spiritual eye of God's anointment. This is not a knock to either man, by the way. Eliezer was a man trusted above all other men in Abraham's life, so much so that he was chosen to go on this trip with Abraham and his sons as a servant and son, one who had a right to claim an inheritance from Abraham, one of spiritual significance as he learned to follow God as Abraham taught. Ishmael, the firstborn son of Abraham, was protected by the angels of the LORD, spoken of directly by God HIMself, and blessed abundantly. His sons, even to this day, are some of the wealthiest families on the planet, the pre-Islamic Arabs. From him would come Muhammed, the creator of Islam, the fastest-growing religion in the world today. With that said, Ishmael was not privy to see the glory of the LORD on the mountain as his brother and father did. Again, this wasn't a knock to him either. This is why Abraham told both Eliezer and Ishmael to stay behind and watch the ass, or donkey, while he and Isaac go forward to worship the LORD. Sacrifice, ladies and gentlemen, is worship too. Please keep this in mind.

Genesis 22: 6-8

And Abraham took the wood of the burnt offering, and laid *it* upon Isaac his son; and he took the fire in his hand, and a knife; and
they went both of them together. 7 And Isaac spake unto Abraham his father, and said, My father: and he said, Here *am* I, my son.
And he said, Behold the fire and the wood: but where *is* the lamb for a burnt offering? 8 And Abraham said, My son, God will
provide himself a lamb for a burnt offering: so they went both of them together.

It's time for business. Abraham found the wood needed for the sacrifice. Why? Because God had provided the fire. He gave it to Isaac as he took the fire and knife in his hand. Why the fire and the knife? The fire represents the commitment to the WORD, the knife represents the willingness to be obedient as the sacrifice is a byproduct of the act of obedience. The wood that was given to Isaac represents the willingness to be used. Remember what Isaac said to Ishmael in the tent? His willingness to give his life in joy to the LORD? Well, here it is.

If wood could speak, especially in its usage in the ancient and modern world, can you imagine what story it would tell of the universe? What is was a witness to on the dark nights around a fire around the world. The conversations from kings to kids being told while the wood itself is burning. It would be incredible! Wood is symbolic of usage to serve. From day to day tasks such as fuel for fire or generational usage for the building of structures, homes, etc., wood is a servant. In this allegory, Isaac was the servant, wood for the flame of fire of the LORD.

When everything was set and ready, Isaac asked his father what was being sacrificed. Even though they had heard from Satan that he, Isaac, was going to be sacrificed by Abraham, Isaac wasn't thinking of those words in the moment. Do not consider this to be strange. Why? Because Abraham told him to disregard the words of Satan (Jasher 23:33). Now that he was in the moment of truth, Isaac was open to whatever his father told him. This is why Isaac asked about a lamb for the sacrifice, a symbol of purity. Abraham told him that God would provide the lamb, a truth that would stretch thousands of years to the birth of the Lamb of God, a willing sacrifice for the sins of the world, The Purifier, the Christ.

But the moment of truth was at hand, when Abraham the father was about to be tested. This moment was about to bring forth the culmination of everything that had happened in the life of Abraham. Every amazing and humbling experience he had was about to come full circle.

Jasher 23: 52-59

And Abraham answered his son Isaac, saying, The Lord has made choice of thee my son, to be a perfect burnt offering instead of the lamb. 52
And Isaac said unto his father, I will do all that the Lord spoke to thee with joy and cheerfulness of heart. 53 And Abraham again said unto
Isaac his son, Is there in thy heart any thought or counsel concerning this, which is not proper? tell me my son, I pray thee, O my son conceal it
not from me. 54 And Isaac answered his father Abraham and said unto him, O my father, as the Lord liveth and as thy soul liveth, there is
nothing in my heart to cause me to deviate either to the right or to the left from the word that he has spoken to thee. 55 Neither limb nor
muscle has moved or stirred at this, nor is there in my heart any thought or evil counsel concerning this. 56 But I am of joyful and cheerful
heart in this matter, and I say, Blessed is the Lord who has this day chosen me to be a burnt offering before Him. 57 And Abraham greatly
rejoiced at the words of Isaac, and they went on and came together to that place that the Lord had spoken of. 58 And Abraham approached to
build the altar in that place, and Abraham was weeping, and Isaac took stones and mortar until they had finished building the altar. 59 And
Abraham took the wood and placed it in order upon the altar which he had built. 60 And he took his son Isaac and bound him in order to place
him upon the wood which was upon the altar, to slay him for a burnt offering before the Lord.

Humbling. Isaac was willing to stand of business. Everything he said to his brother in the tent, in the moment of truth, he stood on. He could have ran, begged, screamed, etc., but he didn't. He did not. He stood on business, God's business. Not only did he stand on business, he laid on wood, with a cheerful heart, ready to be sacrificed to the glory of God! Isaac understood the moment. He understood that regardless of his feelings, the fact that God set this place for him was beyond his understanding. Can you, reader, understand this moment? Can you get a grasp of this? Imagine laying on wood, looking at your father, on a mountain, with a pillar of fire surrounding you, stretching to heaven itself with the glory of the LORD around you?!?! To know that HE showed up just for you!?!? It's beyond awesomeness. It's humbling. Isaac, the 37-year-old man, understood the assignment. He understood his anointment. He understood the stage. This is amazing!

Abraham, on the other hand, was in dad mode. He was looking at his son, nearly undone. Scripture said he was crying, but you have to understand the father element of this. To be asked to sacrifice your child is one thing, but to actually be in the moment to do it is another. But obedience trumps all of that. Abraham was there, knife in hand, fire ready to consume the body of Isaac. I wouldn't wish this moment on anyone. Heartbreaking is an understatement. But wait, there's more...

Jasher 23: 61-65

And Isaac said to his father, Bind me securely and then place me upon the altar lest I should turn and move, and break loose from the force of
the knife upon my flesh and thereof profane the burnt offering; and Abraham did so. 62 And Isaac still said to his father, O my father, when
thou shalt have slain me and burnt me for an offering, take with thee that which shall remain of my ashes to bring to Sarah my mother, and
say to her, This is the sweet smelling savor of Isaac; but do not tell her this if she should sit near a well or upon any high place, lest she should
cast her soul after me and die. 63 And Abraham heard the words of Isaac, and he lifted up his voice and wept when Isaac spake these words;
and Abraham's tears gushed down upon Isaac his son, and Isaac wept bitterly, and he said to his father, Hasten thou, O my father, and do with
me the will of the Lord our God as He has commanded thee. 64 And the hearts of Abraham and Isaac rejoiced at this thing which the Lord had
commanded them; but the eye wept bitterly whilst the heart rejoiced. 65 And Abraham bound his son Isaac, and placed him on the altar upon
the wood, and Isaac stretched forth his neck upon the altar before his father, and Abraham stretched forth his hand to take the knife to slay
his son as a burnt offering before the Lord.

Humbling. The emotions here had to be unbearable for both men. Lord, have mercy. The commitment was that deep. Isaac didn't want any excuses as he was fully committed to the LORD to being a sacrifice. Telling his father to bind him tightly so he can't escape, is surreal. For him to tell his father to keep his ashes for his mother, thinking with respect to her located when Abraham would tell her, proves the love and connection between mother and son. For Isaac to use his last words to be considerate of his mother is outstanding and honorable, especially in the presence of his father. This was crazy! For Abraham to hear his son say these things while being the one who was going to sacrifice him is gut-wrenching. The mix bag of emotions and shedding of tears fell on Isaac, causing him to cry on the altar.

The greatest aspect of this situation is mentioned in verse 64:

Even though they cried bitterly, they rejoiced greatly because they were doing what the LORD commanded them.

This is very important to keep in mind and focus. Despite the situation, in consideration of their feelings and everything that could devastate a man, these two men rejoiced in the LORD because they were being obedient. They didn't ignore the sacrifice, they embraced it, regardless of how they felt. They saw with both the physical and spiritual eye that obedience supersedes sacrifice.

The altar was set. Abraham was ready to fulfill his word to the LORD. Isaac was ready to be given to the LORD. So much so that he stretched forth his neck on the altar so his father could cut it. When he saw this, Abraham took the knife, and extended it into the air. It was time to obey God.

But the angels of mercy....

Jasher 23:66

At that time the angels of mercy came before the Lord and spake to him concerning Isaac, saying,

Uh oh...

Jasher 23: 67-68

O Lord, thou art a merciful and compassionate King over all that thou hast created in heaven and in earth, and thou supportest them all; give therefore ransom and redemption instead of thy servant Isaac, and pity and have compassion upon Abraham and Isaac his son, who are this day performing thy commands. 68 Hast thou seen, O Lord, how Isaac the son of Abraham thy servant is bound down to the slaughter like an animal? now therefore let thy pity be roused for them, O Lord.

The angels of mercy spoke to God on behalf of Isaac and Abraham. Wow! Amazing, amazing, amazing! Reader, please reread the words of the angels of mercy, the angels created for this cause, who speak to God on the behalf of mankind. Notice how they honored God in truth, appealing to HIS compassion for Abraham and Isaac's obedience. The part I really like is how they said that Isaac was bound like an animal, appealing to the imagery of Isaac being animal-like instead of God-like. Keep in mind, God made man in HIS image, in spirit and truth, which is what Isaac was operating in. The mere fact that Isaac was a willing sacrifice to please the LORD roused the pity of God even though Isaac volunteered himself.

The LORD heard them.

The angels of mercy did their job. The LORD heard them and his compassion was moved for Isaac and Abraham. At that moment, with the pillar of fire stretching from Earth to Heaven, the glory of the LORD in the mountain, every spirit being able to see this place at this moment, and the bloodline to the coming Christ about to be cutoff, the LORD heard them. HE saw Abraham and Isaac, but HE heard the angels of mercy.

While this is happening, please keep in mind that Satan was on the verge of victory. Even though Abraham didn't curse God, Isaac was the child of the promise that would eventually bring forth the Christ, Jesus, the savior of the world. If Abraham went ahead and killed Isaac, then the promise would be dead. Ishmael was not it. Even though he was blessed, and would continue to be blessed, he wasn't the promised child through whom the LORD HIMself would come. Eliezer was a trusted servant, a favorite of Abraham's house, but he wasn't the one. Satan wasn't available to hear the plea of the angels of mercy to God, again proving that he's not omnipresent. There's another perspective related to this story that cannot be overlooked: scripture. With the death of Isaac, there would be no scripture, no Bible. Christ is the fulfillment of ALL scripture. The Bible is the book that contains the information that God allowed to be passed through the generations as a road map to HIM, HIS will, and HIS way. Without Isaac, the covenant between God and humanity would be broken, by the covenant acceptor, Abraham. With one blow, there would be no real story of glory to tell. Satan was on the verge of spiritual and physical victory over mankind. Victory was on his mind and within the fall of a knife, it was almost done.

But God.

Genesis 22: 11-12

And the angel of the LORD called unto him out of heaven, and said, Abraham, Abraham: and he said, Here *am* I. 12 And he said, Lay not thine hand upon the lad, neither do thou any thing unto him: for now I know that thou fearest God, seeing thou hast not withheld thy son, thine only *son* from me.

Amen, Amen! God is the Greatest! God is the Greatest!

Ladies and gentlemen, God did!

From heaven, HE speaks. The angels of mercy did what they were supposed to do. Abraham did what he was supposed to do. Isaac did what he was supposed to do. Eliezer and Ishmael did what they were supposed to do. Also, Satan did what he was supposed to do. Everyone involved did what they were supposed to do. God is the Greatest! Why? Because, no matter happens, HE always has the first and last say. HE is the alpha and omega, the beginning and the end, the first and the last. HE is, period.

When the LORD spoke from heaven, it was through the pillar of fire, the cloud of glory, over the mountain, through the heavens, both in the physical world and the spiritual one. This was a signal to All that was blessed to see and know what was going on that HE is God Almighty. By using one of HIS angels to speak through, HE stopped Abraham from sacrificing Isaac. With a few words, The Father validated the father for not withholding his son from him. This event was a precursor to Christ. How so?

Let's Make It Plain:

Son means servant.
Isaac was the son of Abraham, the father of the faith.
Isaac means laughter. Christ means anointed one.
Christ was known as the son of man and the son of God.
Son of man = servant of man(kind), Son of God = servant of God
Having faith (Abraham) in God versus the world allows YOU to have the last laugh (Isaac), that's Christ.

Satan was defeated. Abraham didn't curse God that day, the other three days journey, or any day thereafter. Isaac didn't die. The covenant wasn't broken. Scripture was written, so was the Bible. The chain that connects to the Christ is unbroken! Just as Christ was the sacrifice for all mankind, so was Isaac for the covenant of mankind being connected to the LORD HIMself.

Isaac showed us how to be obedient in the midst of adversity. He showed us how to be cheerful in doing the will of God, regardless of what happens to us. He also showed us how to stand on business, both publicly and privately. Amen, amen. Abraham showed us how to be faithful to our belief, trusting in God and being a man of your word. He taught us how to be steadfast in our belief in God, rebuking the devil, and remaining true to who we are in HIM. We should be grateful to God for this example of diligence and faith. God is the Greatest, servant and master! Sacrificing Isaac was an example of God's triumph over evil, mediocrity, and the Satanic plan for man to curse God. Abraham's words made the devil go away. God spoke to Abraham and made death go away. God requires obedience, which is a sacrifice within itself. Abraham and Isaac obeyed, the angels of mercy spoke up about it, and God moved on their behalf. So reader, regardless of what happens, always remember...

Obedience is better than sacrifice!

The Ram In The Bush

Genesis 22:13

And Abraham lifted up his eyes, and looked, and behold behind *him* a ram caught in a thicket by his horns: and Abraham went and took the ram, and offered him up for a burnt offering in the stead of his son.

In most cases whenever this story is told, there is less attention paid to the ram caught in the thicket by the horns. The lessons and attention is usually placed on Abraham, his patience and willingness to follow God's Word, the LORD's timing for mercy, and the sacrifice the LORD substituted for Isaac. To be clear, we are not overlooking these concepts because they are very important to listen and learn about. However, the ram, the ram, is so important that we need to highlight it as it deserves its own lesson.

This ram was not just a random animal roaming the mountain, that just happened to be on the mountain that day. It was not an animal that Abraham brought with him. In fact, the only animal mentioned in scripture that Abraham and his crew had was an ass (donkey) that he left behind with Ishmael and Eliezer. A donkey and a ram are two completely different animals with two completely different purposes in the story of Abraham. Both animals, in the grand scheme of things, are attributed to the story of the Christ. The donkey was ridden by Jesus into Jerusalem on Palm Sunday (Luke 19: 28-38), fulfilling the prophecy of Zechariah the prophet (Zech. 9:9), which pronounced the coming of Zion's King. That donkey, as Jesus told the disciples, had never been ridden (Luke 19:30). I wonder why? It's interesting. Why is that? Because the donkey Abraham told Ishmael and Eliezer to watch over hadn't been rode either (Gen. 22:5), even though it made the journey to the mountain where God marked in both the heavens and the Earth as the place where the promised child was set for the sacrifice. The donkey that Jesus rode was set to carry the Christ into Jerusalem for the sacrifice on the cross. Same concept. So again, the donkey is very important in the story. But the ram, the ram, was different.

A ram is a male lamb. They are the leaders of sheep herds and are some of the most dominant male species on the planet. Whenever there is an issue within the herd, they battle by ramming their horns against one another at high rates of force and speed. These fights could go on for hours, until the dominant one emerges victorious. Rams are very nimble and balanced animals as they often have to climb very steep mountains to find food or to escape enemies. Rams do not make the mistake of leading their herd into traps of mountain predators. They are well known for their intellect and power, for thousands of years, as nearly every ruler of every major kingdom in world history consider themselves as the ram of their people.

Many of these leaders wear crowns with ram horns, representing their ability to lead their people, intellectually spar with the best minds on the planet, and balance out any issue that seems too steep for others to understand. Therefore, the ram, this ram, that was on the mountain this day, was no ordinary ram. This is not typical ram behavior, to walk up to a scene such as this, and get its horns caught in a bush. They are too intelligent for that.

So......what's so special about this ram?

Let's read:

Jasher 23: 70-71

And Abraham lifted up his eyes and saw, and behold, a ram was caught in a
thicket by his horns; that was the ram which the Lord God had created in the
earth in the day that he made earth and heaven. 71 For the Lord had
prepared this ram from that day, to be a burnt offering instead of Isaac.

God is the Greatest! This is why we should talk about this ram! This is why the ram was on the mountain that day. The same mountain that was marked in fire, with the glory of God in a cloud, with Satan the predator roaming around, seeking Abraham and Isaac to devour. This ram had been created in the day God made the Earth and heaven, which was day 1.

Genesis 1: 1-5

In the beginning God created the heaven and the earth. 2 And the earth was without form, and void; and darkness *was* upon the face of the
deep. And the Spirit of God moved upon the face of the waters. 3 And God said, Let there be light: and there was light. 4 And God saw the
light, that *it was* good: and God divided the light from the darkness. 5 And God called the light Day, and the darkness he called Night. And the
evening and the morning were the first day.

Did you catch that? Do you see what God did? Look closer, read the verses again. In the day HE created the heaven and the earth, there were no animals created. Outside of God HIMself, there was heaven, Earth, and waters. When HE spoke, HE created light. That was the only thing HE created day one. So, where does the ram come into play? The ram was the light! Sounds crazy right? No way. How can this be? The apostle John, writer of both the epistle of John and the book of Revelation told us...

John 1: 1-5

In the beginning was the Word, and the Word was with God, and the Word was God. 2 The same was in the beginning with God. 3 All things
were made by him; and without him was not any thing made that was made. 4 In him was life; and the life was the light of men. 5 And the light
shineth in darkness; and the darkness comprehended it not.

Tell me God ain't the Greatest! Excuse my lingo, but this is incredible! Jesus is the light of men, the one that shined in the darkness and darkness couldn't understand, which scientists verify to this day that darkness still can't quantify or explain. John testifies even more about this light we read about in Genesis 1.

John 1: 6-9

There was a man sent from God, whose name *was* John. 7 The same came for a witness, to bear witness of the Light, that all *men* through him
might believe. 8 He was not that Light, but *was sent* to bear witness of that Light. 9 *That* was the true Light, which lighteth every man that
cometh into the world.

Boom! John also said...

John 1:36

And looking upon Jesus as he walked, he saith, Behold the Lamb of God!

The Lamb of God! John told us who HE was, from the beginning, the light of life. He also told us that Jesus is the Lamb of God. There were others who told us about this lamb of God. The prophet Isaiah said...

Isaiah 53:7

He was oppressed, and he was afflicted, yet he opened not his mouth: he is brought as a lamb to the slaughter, and as a sheep before her shearers is dumb, so he openeth not his mouth.

The lamb for the slaughter. The lamb for the slaughter. Thank you, Isaiah, for your testimony. Now, in the presence of two witnesses (Isaiah and John, old and new testament), the question remains: what type of lamb were Isaiah and John speaking about? Well, let's see what God HIMself told Moses, another witness:

Exodus 12:5

Your lamb shall be without blemish, a male of the first year: ye shall take *it* out from the sheep, or from the goats:

A male sheep! What is a male sheep? A ram!!!

Why a male of the first year? Because this ram was made on the first day of creation. Unblemished, made to be sacrificed, pure in heaven and Earth.

Before we move forward, John had something else to say about the lamb of God, the Holy Lamb of God..

Revelation 5: 6-10

And I beheld, and, lo, in the midst of the throne and of the four beasts, and in the midst of the elders, stood a Lamb as it had been
slain, having seven horns and seven eyes, which are the seven Spirits of God sent forth into all the earth. 7 And he came and took
the book out of the right hand of him that sat upon the throne. 8 And when he had taken the book, the four beasts and
four *and* twenty elders fell down before the Lamb, having every one of them harps, and golden vials full of odours, which are the
prayers of saints. 9 And they sung a new song, saying, Thou art worthy to take the book, and to open the seals thereof: for thou
wast slain, and hast redeemed us to God by thy blood out of every kindred, and tongue, and people, and nation; 10 And hast made
us unto our God kings and priests: and we shall reign on the earth.

The lamb is worthy! Not only is HE worthy, but HE is to be exalted!

Revelation 5: 11-14

And I beheld, and I heard the voice of many angels round about the throne and the beasts and the elders: and the number of them was ten
thousand times ten thousand, and thousands of thousands; 12 Saying with a loud voice, Worthy is the Lamb that was slain to receive power,
and riches, and wisdom, and strength, and honour, and glory, and blessing. 13 And every creature which is in heaven, and on the earth, and
under the earth, and such as are in the sea, and all that are in them, heard I saying, Blessing, and honour, and glory, and power, *be* unto him
that sitteth upon the throne, and unto the Lamb for ever and ever. 14 And the four beasts said, Amen. And the four *and* twenty elders fell
down and worshipped him that liveth for ever and ever.

Wow! John spoke presently of something in Revelation that happened prior to the creation of the universe. Jesus is the Lamb, the ram, that was stuck in the bush that Abraham saw. God made this ram specifically for this day, for this time, to fulfill HIS covenant with Abraham for all future believers to have faith in HIM, calling us to be holy before HIM, like the lamb, the ram. The lamb seen in heaven by John was the same ram made and held for this day on the mountain the day of the sacrifice of Isaac. Again, God is the Greatest!

Before we move forward with the ram, let's go back to the bush that the ram was caught in. God allowed another prophet to experience the LORD in a way that supersedes the natural eye. Just as the ram was caught in the bush, symbolizing God's willingness to be the sacrifice for mankind to return unto HIM, the bush was symbolic as well. Moses, when meeting God, saw HIM in fire, similar to what Abraham and Isaac saw reaching from the Earth to heaven. Moses saw a bush on fire, but it wasn't consumed. Moses saw the same fire as Abraham, on a mountain, herding sheep and goats.

Exodus 3: 1-6

Now Moses kept the flock of Jethro his father in law, the priest of Midian: and he led the flock to the backside of the desert, and
came to the mountain of God, *even* to Horeb. 2 And the angel of the LORD appeared unto him in a flame of fire out of the midst of
a bush: and he looked, and, behold, the bush burned with fire, and the bush *was* not consumed. 3 And Moses said, I will now turn
aside, and see this great sight, why the bush is not burnt. 4 And when the LORD saw that he turned aside to see, God called unto
him out of the midst of the bush, and said, Moses, Moses. And he said, Here *am* I. 5 And he said, Draw not nigh hither: put off thy
shoes from off thy feet, for the place whereon thou standest *is* holy ground. 6 Moreover he said, I *am* the God of thy father, the God
of Abraham, the God of Isaac, and the God of Jacob. And Moses hid his face; for he was afraid to look upon God.

Same God, same fire, same glory, same purpose: to save by sacrifice. This is why Isaac couldn't be the sacrifice for the faith, only the ram. Regardless of the conversation between Isaac and Ishmael in the tent, the plan of God predates human existence. This is also why Satan had no chance of being successful with his schemes to deter Abraham and Isaac. Before the conversation about Abraham cursing and or abandoning his worship of God, the LORD had already planned this out prior to the creation of Satan himself. Wow!

Speaking of Satan, he was there, on the mountain, looking at what was happening, seething! He's a real hater, the hater, the accuser of mankind or the brethren, which is what the word or name Satan means. Instead of him bowing out and going away, accepting his defeat and moving on, he was there, turning his attention on the ram.

Jasher 23: 72-73

And this ram was advancing to Abraham when Satan caught hold of him and entangled his horns in the thicket, that he might not advance to Abraham, in order that Abraham might slay his son.73 And Abraham, seeing the ram advancing to him and Satan withholding him, fetched him and brought him before the altar, and he loosened his son Isaac from his binding, and he put the ram in his stead, and Abraham killed the ram upon the altar, and brought it up as an offering in the place of his son Isaac.

See, we told you! This guy. Satan is so disappointing in his approach. Again, he could have just went away, left things as they were, and that would have been it. Instead, he's the one who entangled the horns of the ram in the thicket of the bush. That's crazy! This move was to deter Abraham to use his manly wisdom, which is inferior to God's, and go ahead and sacrifice Isaac because the ram was delayed. This, ladies and gentlemen, is the purpose of the stories of scripture. How so? We will reveal a mystery of the scripture here for you to understand that we hope clarify God's Word for you.

Let's Make It Plain

The ram of God could have been sacrificed in the garden after the fall of Adam, thus rescuing us from a history of failing to be holy before the Holy One. HE could have been sacrificed for the sake of the world with Noah's flood. From Genesis to Matthew, HE could have come, but HE didn't. HE waited, patiently, allowing obedience and sacrifice to run its course, waiting to see who are the true Hebrews, the ones who stand opposite of the world. This is why Abraham was chosen, the first Hebrew, who stood against Nimrod, Satan, and the world. Instead, HE came to Mary and Joseph, during the time of Roman rule, through the prophets. Just as Satan attempted to delay the ram with Abraham, he attempted to delay the Christ through the ages. How so?

- Trying to kill Abraham, Isaac, and Jacob
- Killing the Hebrew males in Egypt
- Pharaoh and his army in the Red Sea
- The giants in Canaan
- The Philistines
- The Kings and their idols
- The killing of the prophets
- The Assyrian and Babylonian captivities
- Roman rule

All of these things delayed the Christ, but it didn't stop HIM. It really wasn't a delay, it was a plan of God, which happened perfectly and on time. Satan's attempt to delay, spontaneously, has always been pre-prepped by God to be on the gameplan list of time. There are no surprises to God. If there was, he wouldn't be God, just a good planner. God has no equal and this story proves it.

This is also why Abraham, operating in obedience, had the power to go to that same bush and take the ram out of the hands of Satan, and handle his business. Notice how Satan could not dispute Abraham. He was already terrified of the voice of Abraham. Now, he had the ram of God taken out of his hands and given in sacrifice against his will. This is the power of God working through Abraham because he was willing to be obedient to the end, something Satan was unwilling to do. The moment we begin to understand what obedience can do for you, we can understand that the plans and plots of the evil one has no power to delay or deter you. In fact, any perceived delay or deterrence is really a determined time for God to show HIMself true and proven. Satan holding back the ram was meant for bad, but God meant it for good.

Jasher 23: 74-75

And Abraham sprinkled some of the blood of the ram upon the altar, and he exclaimed and said, This is in the place of my son, and may this be considered this day as the blood of my son before the Lord. 75 And all that Abraham did on this occasion by the altar, he would exclaim and say, This is in the room of my son, and may it this day be considered before the Lord in the place of my son; and Abraham finished the whole of the service by the altar, and the service was accepted before the Lord, and was accounted as if it had been Isaac; and the Lord blessed Abraham and his seed on that day.

The blood of the ram was the purifier, the saving grace, the substitute. Abraham understood this and was grateful for the way and will of the LORD. He understood and exclaimed that the substitute for his son was the ram, the lamb of God. He acknowledged it and God acknowledged him. The LORD is worthy to be praised. Abraham, in his service to the LORD, used his voice, the same voice that terrified Satan, renamed the place that event happened. It just so happens that the name of this place is also one of the names of God, Jehovah Jireh.

Genesis 22:14

And Abraham called the name of that place Jehovahjireh: as it is said *to* this day, In the mount of the LORD it shall be seen.

To Abraham, jehovahjireh was a place, meaning in the mountain of the LORD, it shall be seen. To the Hebrews and later, the Jews, Jehovah Jireh means the LORD will provide. You see, Abraham didn't know God as Jehovah Jireh. He didn't know HIM as Jehovah. If you would have gone to Abraham and ask him who Jehovah was, he wouldn't know. Really? How do we know that? God told Moses...

Exodus 6: 2-3

And God spake unto Moses, and said unto him, I *am* the LORD: 3 And I appeared unto Abraham, unto Isaac, and unto Jacob, by *the name of* God Almighty, but by my name JEHOVAH was I not known to them.

You see, Abraham named a place of the LORD, not knowing one of the names of the LORD is the name of the place that the LORD provided the ram. Abraham only knew HIM as God Almighty, which is pronounced *El Shaddai* in Hebrew. This is the wisdom of the LORD, allowing HIMself to be known in phases throughout the ages for HIS many different operations, even though HE's the same God.

Genesis 22: 15-18

And the angel of the LORD called unto Abraham out of heaven the second time,
16 And said, By myself have I sworn, saith the LORD, for because thou hast done this thing, and hast not withheld thy son, thine only *son*:
17 That in blessing I will bless thee, and in multiplying I will multiply thy seed as the stars of the heaven, and as the sand which *is* upon the sea shore; and thy seed shall possess the gate of his enemies;
18 And in thy seed shall all the nations of the earth be blessed; because thou hast obeyed my voice.

God verifies HIS why after the sacrifice of the ram. The purpose of the ram was to substitute hopelessness for holiness. Our mission as believers in God via the faith is to be obedient to God, period, just as Abraham was. It's not about perfection, but the process. Abraham wasn't perfect. The devil himself reminded God about it. Abraham would've told you that. But he didn't care about that and neither should we. Why? Because God knew of our fall prior to the creation of the foundation of the world. HE knew, which is why the ram was set to be put on that mountain, on that day, as a substitute for the Isaac. There is a process to getting back to God and holiness is that process. The lamb of God, the male lamb, the ram, is meant to be our substitute as God provides for us. HE is Jehovah Jireh, our provider.

John 1:29

The next day John seeth Jesus coming unto him, and saith, Behold the Lamb of God, which taketh away the sin of the world.

Death of Sarah

Genesis 22:19

So Abraham returned unto his young men, and they rose up and went together to Beersheba; and Abraham dwelt at Beersheba.

After the sacrifice of the ram, Abraham and Isaac returned to Ishmael and Eliezer. It was now time to go back home. What a journey! To this point, they had witnessed the power and majesty of the LORD God Almighty, El Shaddai, live and in living color. They had rebuked the devil, forcing him to flee away from them, giving us the blueprint for how to deal with Satan. These men had a testimony that stretched into the heavens for all to see and know. The same devil that lost, however, wasn't done. He could have quit, but that's not what the ultimate hater does. He was there to witness the words of Isaac, his so-called last words. Remember this, while Isaac was on the altar, his deathbed confession to his father:

Jasher 23: 62-63

And Isaac still said to his father, O my father, when thou shalt have slain me and burnt me for an offering, take with thee that which shall remain of my ashes to bring to Sarah my mother, and say to her, This is the sweet smelling savor of Isaac; but do not tell her this if she should sit near a well or upon any high place, lest she should cast her soul after me and die. 63 And Abraham heard the words of Isaac, and he lifted up his voice and wept when Isaac spake these words; and Abraham's tears gushed down upon Isaac his son, and Isaac wept bitterly, and he said to his father, Hasten thou, O my father, and do with me the will of the Lord our God as He has commanded thee.

Sarah. That's the soft spot, Sarah. Not Sarah the wife, but Sarah the mother, who was also Sarah the wife. Isaac and his mother had a tight bond, and rightfully so. Satan heard these words of Isaac and knew that his only chance of breaking this family was to go at both Abraham and Isaac's soft spot, Sarah. So, while Abraham and his crew were leaving the mountain to return to Sarah with a testimony of testimonies, Satan took a quick trip to see the soft spot. What would happen next is like what happens when a virus, bacteria, or disease sees an open wound: deceive, infiltrate, and destroy, in hopes that medicine doesn't arrive in time to dispel it.

Jasher 23:76

And Satan went to Sarah, and he appeared to her in the figure of an old man very humble and meek, and Abraham was yet engaged in the burnt offering before the Lord.

To all leaders of families, myself included, we must understand what we are reading. While we are out here doing what we are called to do, be mindful of your other. Consider the scheme of the enemy. He may not be able to get to you, as the case with Abraham and Isaac. He may not be able to deceive you, just like he couldn't deceive Adam. But your other is your soft spot. All wives and children need to read this section to understand the importance of the coverage of a Godly man and how the enemy chooses to attack them by getting at you. Satan tried his old man scheme on Abraham and Isaac and was rebuked, meaning he lost. But now, he was about to try the same trick on Sarah. He came to Abraham as an old man, a symbol of wisdom and respect. He has now showed up in front of Sarah, as an old man, a symbol of wisdom and respect.

Jasher 23:77

And he said unto her, Dost thou not know all the work that Abraham has made with thine only son this day? for he took Isaac and built an altar, and killed him, and brought him up as a sacrifice upon the altar, and Isaac cried and wept before his father, but he looked not at him, neither did he have compassion over him.

Wow. The accuser of the brethren. A 3-day's journey from home, Sarah is met by a random old man, a symbol of wisdom and respect. Lies, all lies. Ladies, please read this section very carefully, please. Married, single, mother, sister, cousin, daughter, aunt, etc. Please read this very carefully. Satan came to Sarah in a weakened state of mind, appearing as a man of respect, speaking softly and unalarmingly to a mother who was missing her only child. We know how she had a meltdown when Isaac left, so she was an emotional rollercoaster at the time. Feelings, ladies, feelings. He targeted her feelings.

Satan told Sarah what happened with Abraham and Isaac. In the midst of the story, look at the strategy of the evil one. He told a half truth, which always ends as a whole lie. This is the same strategy he used with Eve in the garden. He told Sarah that Abraham took Isaac for a sacrifice, put him on an altar, Isaac cried (emotional heart string), but Abraham had no compassion on him. Even though we know the truth of the matter, Sarah didn't. She was caught in the moment, hearing news that pulled at her heart strings. Regardless of what Satan said, Sarah heard with her mother/mama ears, not her wife ears. Satan knew this. This is why he painted a picture of murder and not mercy. He knows how to plant seeds of doubt that cause division. Imagine what Sarah really heard.

What Sarah heard...

This man took my baby, lied to me, took my baby (even though he was 37 years old), he lied to me, took my baby away saying he was going to show him the ways of God with Shem and Eber (Jasher 23:5), and he killed my baby! My baby is dead, my child is gone, my baby is dead. That man (Abraham) lied to me and killed my baby! This cannot be!!!

While Sarah is falling into an emotional sunken place, Satan continues...

Jasher 23: 78-80

And Satan repeated these words, and he went away from her, and Sarah heard all the words of Satan, and she imagined him to be an old man from amongst the sons of men who had been with her son, and had come and told her these things. 79 And Sarah lifted up her voice and wept and cried out bitterly on account of her son; and she threw herself upon the ground and she cast dust upon her head, and she said, O my son, Isaac my son, O that I had this day died instead of thee. And she continued to weep and said, It grieves me for thee, O my son, my son Isaac, O that I had died this day in thy stead. 80 And she still continued to weep, and said, It grieves me for thee after that I have reared thee and have brought thee up; now my joy is turned into mourning over thee, I that had a longing for thee, and cried and prayed to God till I bare thee at ninety years old; and now hast thou served this day for the knife and the fire, to be made an offering.

Sarah was undone. Undone. Satan said what he said and left, watching Sarah fall into a sunken place. He lost at Mt. Moriah with Abraham, but he was winning with his wife Sarah. He planted the seeds of doubt then let Sarah water it. It's crazy. Sarah started thinking that this was an actual old man, even though he disappeared after telling her what he told. Old men don't disappear anywhere that fast, especially in an open wilderness where they lived. This part didn't enter into her mind, at all. She was too consumed to see that. Ladies, please read this again, especially for those that jump to conclusions easily, gets angry easily, or tends to wonder mentally when told something that can disturb your peace. This is a trick of Satan that hasn't been studied or taught enough to us as children so we don't make these mistakes in our adulthood. There are millions of people and families that have been damaged or broken up as a result of falling into this sunken place of Satan's seeding, while we feed it instead of leaving it. This same trick is still working today. While Sarah was crying, Satan was enjoying himself, watching the wife of the man he was terrified of, weeping in terror of the thought of losing her son. See how he works? Ladies and gentlemen, study this strategy closely.

Jasher 23: 81-83

But I console myself with thee, my son, in its being the word of the Lord, for thou didst perform the command of thy God; for who can transgress the word of our God, in whose hands is the soul of every living creature? 82 Thou art just, O Lord our God, for all thy works are good and righteous; for I also am rejoiced with thy word which thou didst command, and whilst mine eye weepeth bitterly my heart rejoiceth. 83 And Sarah laid her head upon the bosom of one of her handmaids, and she became as still as a stone.

Poor Sarah. She was undone. You have to give Sarah your heart in a situation like this, even though she was wrong for listening to Satan. Again, she was wrong for listening to Satan, no excuses. But you have to have compassion on Sarah for what she was going through, especially as a 127-year-old woman. The crying she did was so stressful for her that she became as stiff as a stone! She began to console herself by speaking in obedience to God in acceptance of his decision, which was a "perceived" decision. Now, let's address something that may be hard for many people so...

Let's Make It Plain

We have to stop saying and doing what Sarah did here, orally, in relation to God. We have to, we have to, we have to do better. God deserves better. To be clear, we are not talking about her emotions here, which is understood and can be understood, but her actual words are a concern. Again I say, we need to look at her actual words. First, God did not tell Sarah anything in this situation, Satan did. Sarah didn't know it, all she knew was that an old man told her something about her son and husband that broke her heart. As she began to console herself, she brought God into the picture because of what she felt. Not a fact, but what she felt. Feelings and faith are not the same. That is not God's, doing it is Satan's. Second, at no point during her self-consoling process did she consider the information false. The same God that told Abraham she was going to be pregnant, the same God that allowed her to give birth at 90 years old, that told her that her son would be a son of promise that will bless the whole world, the same God was not consulted. The same woman who had been through so much with Abraham that she was way more real because she had seen it or experienced it personally, in this moment of weakness, took no time to consult with the God that had brought her through it all. Next, and perhaps the most simple, is why didn't Sarah just wait on Abraham to return? Whatever question she had, could have been answered in a short time, a matter of days. That would have solved everything. Finally, and perhaps the most troubling, is that she didn't ask any questions to the 'old man' who disappeared after giving her this news.

In the end, God deserves better than this, way better than this. Why are people teaching people that it's okay to throw HIS name into so much stuff that HE isn't involved in? Since when did God become so available yet not be available? It's ridiculous. God literally had nothing to do with the interaction between Satan and Sarah. She had the same opportunity to disregard Satan as Abraham did. She knew God enough to know better. This is not to throw stones at Sarah as she is forever engraved as the mother of all those that are faithful to God through Abraham as well as the mother of all noble wives from a biblical point of view. She is outstanding and amazing, no doubt. But her choice to self-console and add God into a situation HE wasn't was irresponsible. We must either stop listening or speaking on HIM in situations that is rooted in feelings! That is not our God, but it has become the God of so many people looking for God, or a god.

There are so many people that have done this for so long, which LORD knows is being preached from pulpits and online ministries, that this message is already causing them to become uncomfortable. Reader, let's be clear, this is not to pick at a person, but to pick up a person, to get us all to reconsider how we treat God in our simple conversations the same way we do our complex ones. God' Word is a foundation for us all that if we search the scriptures, we can find consolation in them. When there is no scripture for what we feel, HE is a simple thought away. Conscience and Christ are two different things. Our conscience is a gift from God, given to help with the resolve of the mind. Christ too is a gift of God, given to resolve the whole body. What's wrong with just saying 'I feel' or 'I think' this is something or another and stand on that? Instead, we bring God into it. Why not be more aware? Perhaps Sarah would have said something different if she was more aware, even in the middle of her emotional state. So, for one last time, we must be better.

Even though this was a lot on Sarah and those around her, she wasn't done.

Jasher 23: 84-85

She afterward rose up and went about making inquiries till she came to Hebron, and she inquired of all those whom she met walking in the road, and no one could tell her what had happened to her son. 85 And she came with her maid servants and men servants to Kireath-arba, which is Hebron, and she asked concerning her Son, and she remained there while she sent some of her servants to seek where Abraham had gone with Isaac; they went to seek him in the house of Shem and Eber, and they could not find him, and they sought throughout the land and he was not there.

Another mistake made by Sarah: acting and making decisions when in a highly emotional state. Sarah was not supposed to leave home, looking for her husband and his crew. When Abraham left her, he left her in a safe place. She had now ventured into an unsafe place, which puts the whole family at risk. She traveled from their home in the groves in Beersheba to Hebron, a 54km trek or 33.5 mile journey.

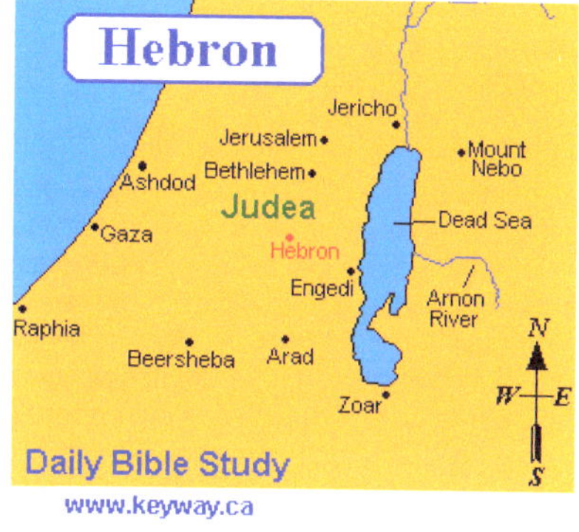

When she didn't find Abraham and Isaac in Hebron, she sent her servants into the wilderness to find and ask about their whereabouts. At this point, she started to think about what Abraham told her. She remembered that he said he was taking Isaac to see Shem and Eber. So, she went to them, looking to see if they had seen Abraham and Isaac. When they said they hadn't, they all went into search mode in the countryside looking and asking questions. Reader, keep in mind, Abraham was not lost, he was busy. His crew was on the way back from the journey on the mount. The anxiety is increasing for Sarah, especially since they couldn't find them. Not only was she now concerned with the absence of Isaac, but Abraham as well.

The biggest problem in all of this is Sarah listening to Satan. This doesn't look good nor does end well for anyone, ever.

While everyone was in search mode for Abraham and the crew, Satan was watching, enjoying himself. He was finally winning at something and he knew it. When he noticed that Sarah was starting to think about what Abraham told her about the trip plans, he knew it was time to act. Why? He knew the moment she started to come down off her emotions, he was in trouble and ran the risk of her coming to her senses and returning home. He would lose. The last thing he wanted was for her to become aware and think about facts. So, what did he do?

Jasher 23:86

And behold, Satan came to Sarah in the shape of an old man, and he came and stood before her, and he said unto her, I spoke falsely unto thee, for Abraham did not kill his son and he is not dead; and when she heard the word her joy was so exceedingly violent on account of her son, that her soul went out through joy; she died and was gathered to her people.

Wow! Stunning, shocked, hurt, disheartened.

This is so disgusting, hurtful, and sad.

Satan got her. He didn't kill her, but he got her. How did he do it? He got her to do it to herself. Satan came back to her in the form of an old man again, and told her the whole truth. Remember, in the form of an old man, he told her a half truth, the first part being true, the second part being false. Now he returns, because he has to tell the truth even as the father of lies, because of the order of the universe that God made. When he came back and told Sarah the whole truth, that Abraham didn't kill Isaac, she ended up having a heart attack from the joy of the news she received, and she died on the spot. This was a very cruel thing to do to a woman, any person honestly, but especially to a weary mother, who on top of everything was a 127 year-old-woman. Satan didn't care, he didn't then, and he doesn't now.

Ladies and gentlemen, especially ladies, Sarah is a lady that we must study and admonish for her character, commitment, and willingness to be what God called her to be. Do not mistake how her story ended with her life story. Sarah is arguably the highest respected woman in biblical history. She is admired and loved throughout the ages as there have been millions of women named after her. Even in the midst of her sadness, she found a way to credit God for being sovereign and LORD over all. She didn't handle her last situation in the right way by listening to Satan, but God, in HIS amazing wisdom, allowed for her to know the truth of Abraham and Isaac, allowing her to die with joy in her heart. This is the wisdom and compassion of God, even when we are listening to the wrong voices. HE finds different ways to allow us to experience good, even in judgment, if you are a willing follower of HIS.

Sarah should always be held in high regard. She is considered the first woman in biblical literature that was considered faithful. This is an honor above honors.

Hebrews 11: 11-12

Through faith also Sara herself received strength to conceive seed, and was delivered of a child when she was past age, because
she judged him faithful who had promised. 12 Therefore sprang there even of one, and him as good as dead, *so many* as the stars of
the sky in multitude, and as the sand which is by the sea shore innumerable.

Faithful. Not perfect, but in the process, faithful. That's a compliment that recognizable before both man and God. Satan knew this about Sarah and decided to attack her weakness, a mother's bond with her children. Even though she laughed when she overheard what God said to Abraham about the birth of Isaac, she was faithful to believe God from that point forward. She judged God, concluding HE was faithful. Through Sarah came the stars of the sky in multitude. What stars are verse 12 speaking about? The saints. All those that are believers can accredit Sarah as their mother in the faith. She believed God in faith that HE was going to do what HE said HE was going to do. The story of Abraham doesn't happen without her. It is impossible for Abraham to become the father of so many people and nations without Sarah. She is synonymous with Abraham and honorable character as a woman and wife. This is what we must remember about Sarah. It's sad that she died this way, which could have been avoided had she stayed where her husband left her and not listen to anyone else.

1 Peter 3: 1-6

Likewise, ye wives, *be* in subjection to your own husbands; that, if any obey not the word, they also may without the word be won
by the conversation of the wives; 2 While they behold your chaste conversation *coupled* with fear. 3 Whose adorning let it not be
that outward *adorning* of plaiting the hair, and of wearing of gold, or of putting on of apparel; 4 But *let it be* the hidden man of the
heart, in that which is not corruptible, *even the ornament* of a meek and quiet spirit, which is in the sight of God of great price. 5 For
after this manner in the old time the holy women also, who trusted in God, adorned themselves, being in subjection unto their own
husbands: 6 Even as Sara obeyed Abraham, calling him lord: whose daughters ye are, as long as ye do well, and are not afraid with
any amazement.

Mother Sarah, we salute you. We love you, we thank you, we honor you. Thanks for being the model of commitment of faithfulness that you were. She was the first biblical character as a woman who considered holy. That's the highest honor any of us can achieve, to be considered holy, is sacred to the LORD. She called her husband lord, lowercase, meaning ruler. She didn't call Abraham lord meaning God, but lord meaning her ruler. This, ladies and gentlemen, is considered honorable to God when you submit to your husband as Sarah did. When she operated outside of this placement, the results didn't go the way she wanted. Again, this is not about perfection but the process, and she is the model that God used to let the world know that it is good for a believing man to have as his wife. HE could have used Eve, Noah's wife, etc., but HE didn't. HE used Sarah, intentionally. So, ladies and gentlemen, let us give queen mother Sarah her just due.

Rest In Peace Sarah.

Machpelah

Genesis 23: 1-2

And Sarah was an hundred and seven and twenty years old: *these were* the years of the life of Sarah. 2 And Sarah died in Kirjatharba; the same *is* Hebron in the land of Canaan: and Abraham came to mourn for Sarah, and to weep for her.

Sarah died in Hebron at 127 years old. This great woman, faithful and honorable, was now dead and the word was spreading of what had happened. No one saw the old man again that she spoke to that caused her heart attack, who was Satan disguised as an old man. Regardless, this great woman of history passed away and it was now time to bury and mourn her. While all of this was going on, the question comes to mind, where was Abraham and how would he react to her death? Even more heart aching would be the response of Isaac. How would he respond?

Jasher 23: 87-90

And when Abraham had finished his service he returned with his son Isaac to his young men, and they rose up and went together to Beersheba, and they came home. 88 And Abraham sought for Sarah, and could not find her, and he made inquiries concerning her, and they said unto him, She went as far as Hebron to seek you both where you had gone, for thus was she informed. 89 And Abraham and Isaac went to her to Hebron, and when they found that she was dead they lifted up their voices and wept bitterly over her; and Isaac fell upon his mother's face and wept over her, and he said, O my mother, my mother, how hast thou left me, and where hast thou gone? O how, how hast thou left me! 90 And Abraham and Isaac wept greatly and all their servants wept with them on account of Sarah, and they mourned over her a great and heavy mourning.

Broken men, broken hearts.

The last time Abraham and Isaac saw Sarah, she was crying because she didn't want to be separated from Isaac. Now, they find out that she died in search of them. Abraham, her husband and love of her life, wept bitterly. This was not the way he imagined her dying. Most men, godly men, husbands, want to die before their wives, leaving a legacy they and their children can live on in approval of God. Accepting Sarah' death before his hurts, but the way she died made it even more bitter. Isaac, with his connection to his mother being so tight, was completely hurt and dismantled over the passing of his mother. To know that she took this trip from their home in search of him had to be hard to accept. Isaac immediately felt alone without his mother who had him when she was 90 years old, a feat within itself that's unheard of. Not only were Abraham and Isaac broken because of Sarah's death, but also all of the servants of the household of Sarah wept bitterly over her death. This woman who had kings willing to risk their lives and kingdoms for, even as an elderly woman, was now dead. Mourning and loss were definitely in order. It was now time to bury Sarah.

Genesis 23: 3-16

And Abraham stood up from before his dead, and spake unto the sons of Heth, saying, 4 I *am* a stranger and a sojourner with you:
give me a possession of a buryingplace with you, that I may bury my dead out of my sight. 5 And the children of Heth answered
Abraham, saying unto him, 6 Hear us, my lord: thou *art* a mighty prince among us: in the choice of our sepulchres bury thy dead;
none of us shall withhold from thee his sepulchre, but that thou mayest bury thy dead. 7 And Abraham stood up, and bowed
himself to the people of the land, *even* to the children of Heth. 8 And he communed with them, saying, If it be your mind that I
should bury my dead out of my sight; hear me, and intreat for me to Ephron the son of Zohar, 9 That he may give me the cave of
Machpelah, which he hath, which *is* in the end of his field; for as much money as it is worth he shall give it me for a possession of a
buryingplace amongst you. 10 And Ephron dwelt among the children of Heth: and Ephron the Hittite answered Abraham in the
audience of the children of Heth, *even* of all that went in at the gate of his city, saying, 11 Nay, my lord, hear me: the field give I
thee, and the cave that *is* therein, I give it thee; in the presence of the sons of my people give I it thee: bury thy dead. 12 And
Abraham bowed down himself before the people of the land. 13 And he spake unto Ephron in the audience of the people of the
land, saying, But if thou *wilt give it*, I pray thee, hear me: I will give thee money for the field; take *it* of me, and I will bury my dead
there. 14 And Ephron answered Abraham, saying unto him, 15 My lord, hearken unto me: the land *is worth* four hundred shekels
of silver; what *is* that betwixt me and thee? bury therefore thy dead. 16 And Abraham hearkened unto Ephron; and Abraham
weighed to Ephron the silver, which he had named in the audience of the sons of Heth, four hundred shekels of silver,
current *money* with the merchant.

Spare no expense. That's what all this means. Ladies and gentlemen, please read this carefully. Abraham didn't want a cheap burial for his wife, he didn't ask for a discount, he didn't want it done free. He wanted to pay full and fair price for her burial. Why? Because the memory of Sarah needs to be done in full as she was a full member of his life, a full representation of himself as one flesh, the full love of his life. I hope and pray that we really pull and understand this statement as Abraham showed honor and respect to not only Sarah but Ephron, the owner of the land and cave Abraham wanted to bury Sarah in.

For the record, Sarah was buried quickly, as the custom with the Hebrews both then and now. She was buried within 24 hours of her death. As you read in verse 3, Abraham was in mourning over Sarah, standing over her dead body. He rose up from his crying to go and acquire of the cave from Ephron to bury her. As people were running in different directions to spread the word of Sarah's death, Abraham had to handle the business of burial. The basis of this law was practiced by Moses and later adopted by the Hebrews in the wilderness when Moses made it a law (Deut. 21:23), even though the context of this law was for those hung on a tree and how they should be buried. The land would be cursed if you don't bury the person the day they died, which is why this belief has been copied throughout the generations to this day. So yes, Sarah was set for burial within 24 hours and it was the responsibility of Abraham to take care of it.

Ephron and Abraham made an agreement for the Cave of Macpelah. For 400 shekels of silver, the land was purchased, in the presence of witnesses. In fact, there were 4 witnesses, one for each corner of the Earth.

Jasher 24: 7-8

And Ephron and all his brethren heard this, and Abraham weighed to Ephron four hundred shekels of silver in the hands of Ephron and in the
hands of all his brethren; and Abraham wrote this transaction, and he wrote it and testified it with four witnesses. 8 And these are the names
of the witnesses, Amigal son of Abishna the Hittite, Adichorom son of Ashunach the Hivite, Abdon son of Achiram the Gomerite, Bakdil the son
of Abudish the Zidonite.

Amen. Abraham sealed the deal to bury Sarah, fair and square. These are the men who were considered the sons of Heth. As a receipt and tribute to Sarah so her placement will be known for history's sake, Abraham wrote words that was placed in the book of the children of Heth for those to know who may come to see or question in the future.

Jasher 24: 9-11

And Abraham took the book of the purchase, and placed it in his treasures, and these are the words that Abraham wrote in the book, namely: 10 That the cave and the field Abraham bought from Ephron the Hittite, and from his seed, and from those that go out of his city, and from their seed for ever, are to be a purchase to Abraham and to his seed and to those that go forth from his loins, for a possession of a burial place for ever; and he put a signet to it and testified it with witnesses. 11 And the field and the cave that was in it and all that place were made sure unto Abraham and unto his seed after him, from the children of Heth; behold it is before Mamre in Hebron, which is in the land of Canaan.

Not only the cave belonged to Abraham, but the field around it. It was purchased to be a burial place for the children of Abraham forever.

Genesis 23: 17-20

And the field of Ephron, which *was* in Machpelah, which *was* before Mamre, the field, and the cave which *was* therein, and all the trees that *were* in the field, that *were* in all the borders round about, were made sure 18 Unto Abraham for a possession in the presence of the children of Heth, before all that went in at the gate of his city. 19 And after this, Abraham buried Sarah his wife in the cave of the field of Machpelah before Mamre: the same *is* Hebron in the land of Canaan. 20 And the field, and the cave that *is* therein, were made sure unto Abraham for a possession of a buryingplace by the sons of Heth.

Amen. Now that the field and cave had been secured, Abraham and family could now proceed with the actual funeral. Remember, Abraham had a reputation around the known world for being a man guarded by God, untouchable because of God, and even Nimrod couldn't touch him. His wife, Sarah, was regarded in the same light. The moment the word spread that she had died, as far and fast as the messengers could go, people left what they were doing and immediately traveled to Hebron to pay homage to Sarah and pay their respects to Abraham for the loss of his love in life.

Jasher 24: 12-16

And after this Abraham buried his wife Sarah there, and that place and all its boundary became to Abraham and unto his seed for a possession of a burial place. 13 And Abraham buried Sarah with pomp as observed at the interment of kings, and she was buried in very fine and beautiful garments. 14 And at her bier was Shem, his sons Eber and Abimelech, together with Anar, Ashcol and Mamre, and all the grandees of the land followed her bier. 15 And the days of Sarah were one hundred and twenty-seven years and she died, and Abraham made a great and heavy mourning, and he performed the rites of mourning for seven days. 16 And all the inhabitants of the land comforted Abraham and Isaac his son on account of Sarah.

Sarah was honored in death, and rightfully so. Abraham buried her with pomp, which means extravagance. The word interment, as written in verse 13 above, means to place a corpse in a grave inside the Earth while allowing others to come by and bid a farewell. This was done for kings, not commoners. Again, this was done for kings, not commoners. This is the type of funeral Abraham had for Sarah. She was buried in very fine and beautiful garments, showcasing beauty as a byproduct of who and how amazing Sarah was a woman, wife, mother, and person.

Shem, the originator of the Semitic language and son of Noah, attended the funeral, as did his sons Eber and Abimelech. The whole world spoke the language of Shem after the flood. It wasn't until God confused the languages at the Tower of Babel with Nimrod that everyone spoke the same language, the Semitic language, Shem's way of saying things. Anar, Ashcol, and Mamre, the one whom the plains of Mamre where Abraham had lunch with God and was told that Isaac would be born the next year, also attended the funeral. There were so many elders and rulers who came quickly to this funeral that scripture quite simply called them grandees.

When the funeral ended, Abraham performed the rites of mourning for seven days. The area went into mourning, the same as if a king had died. This shows the amount of respect Sarah garnered by everyone. Please keep in mind, Abraham was Hebrew, meaning he stood on the other side of the world. Most of these people who attended the funeral and or paid respects to Abraham weren't worshippers of God. They were accepting of the teachings of Nimrod. For them to go into mourning shows the respect of Abraham and Sarah throughout the world. Even his enemies felt his pain. Abraham and Isaac were comforted by friends and enemies on the behalf of Sarah.

Cave of Macpelah/Ibrahimi Mosque
© Daily Sabah

The Cave of Macpelah is a place that should be known worldwide, even to this day. Most people have never heard of it. This place is regarded as one of the most sacred places on the planet for Jews and Muslims, but the other monotheistic religion, Christianity, doesn't speak or teach about it. Judaism, Christianity, and Islam, the three major monotheistic belief structures, all accredit Abraham with being their father. By default, they have to accredit Sarah with being their mother. The Cave of Macpelah and the field surrounding it was purchased so all the children of Abraham could be buried there. The Jews and Muslims actively and opening respect this place of burial. In fact, it is called the Ibrahimi Mosque today.

In conclusion, anything that is faith related has been questioned throughout the ages. People literally risk their eternal life on such issues. One of the easiest things to do when beginning your search of the truth of faith in God begins with Abraham. Even he, and whether or not he was an actual person, has been a real discussion and debate among academics for years. The question of his birth and life can be questioned, but you can conclude many things by going to this cave to see whether or not there are bodies and bones there that go back to the time that the bible says that he lived. Before you find him, you'll find her, Sarah. No one questions whether or not Sarah lived, but they question her husband because of his significance, which is asinine without Sarah. There is no Isaac without Sarah. She wasn't married to a ghost, so she had to be a married to a man, who just so happen to have written record and oral tradition of existing. Abraham's name was changed the same day Sarah name changed. Sarah and Abraham go hand in hand.

To add to the intrigue of the Cave of Macpelah, is the two bodies that Jewish tradition speak to was buried there first. In Genesis 23:2, the word "kirjatharba" is used to describe the Cave of Macpelah. What does this word mean? In Hebrew, it means the city of four. There are two meanings that are attached to this name. First, Hebron was believed to be one city divided into 4 quarters in its earliest days. Second, after the deaths of Abraham, Isaac, and Jacob, along with their wives, four couples were discovered to be buried in that cave, with one couple being older than the others. That couple, according to Jewish traditions, state that the original couple buried in that cave was none other than the original created humans, Adam and Eve. Yes, ladies and gentlemen, the actual burial place of the father and mother of us all is believed and enshrined at the Cave of Macpelah. Sarah would have been the third person buried here, which adds to the significance of the burial of Sarah and how impactful she was to human history. The Cave of Macpelah is a place where 4 couples are buried, one of those people being Sarah, the mother of the promised son to come, Isaac. Had it not been for Abraham, we would not have known about this cave and the significance of those being buried there. His son Isaac and unborn grandson Jacob would solidify this place as a place of honor and respect. Sarah is the first post-flood person to be buried here. The Cave of Macpelah is a place of study and respect that shows the allowance of God for the patriarchs and matriarchs to be examples and proof of his benevolence. God is the Greatest!

Cave of Macpelah/Cave of the Patriarchs
© Jewish Virtual Library

Shalom and blessings to mother Sarah and father Abraham. May peace rest on them in the presence of God. May the Cave of Macpelah serve as a marker of the faith for all of us to serve the LORD always, even unto death.

Keeping His Word

Jasher 24:17

And when the days of their mourning passed by Abraham sent away his son Isaac, and he went to the house of Shem and Eber, to learn the ways of the Lord and his instructions, and Abraham remained there three years.

After 7 days had passed, Abraham and Isaac were still at Hebron, mourning Sarah. While being there, Abraham decided to send Isaac to Shem and Eber. If you can remember, Abraham told Sarah that he was going away to take Isaac to the house of Shem and Eber so Isaac can learn the ways of God (Jasher 23: 1-5). That would have been approximately 14-15 days prior to this moment, as the journey to the mountain took 3 days for Abraham and Isaac to make. It would have taken 3 days to return, as he had to leave Beersheba and go 30+ miles to Hebron to find Sarah dead. Add a day to set up the funeral for burial, then add 7 days of mourning. Both men whole world had changed in a matter of two weeks. With Sarah' passing and mourned complete, Abraham knew it was time to move forward in life. So, he did.

Abraham sent Isaac to Shem and Eber, the same way his father and mother sent him to Noah and Shem to learn the ways of the LORD for himself. After sending Isaac away, Abraham remained in Hebron for 3 years, at the same place Sarah was buried. From death, both men would receive life and a different perspective of it to the glory of God! Amen.

DEATH OF ABIMELECH

Jasher 24:18

At that time Abraham rose up with all his servants, and they went and returned homeward to Beersheba, and Abraham and all his servants remained in Beersheba.

Three years after Isaac left to go learn the ways of God from Shem and Eber, Abraham decided it was now time to return to the groves of Beersheba, his home. The people of Hebron had been good to him while mourning the death of Sarah. Abraham was now 140 years old, still an able-bodied man. I know that sounds crazy in today's world, but people in those days lived long ages like so.

Ancient City of Beersheba
© Bible Places

Prior to Abraham's time, people lived much longer than 100-200 years, they lived well into the 7, 8, 900-year range. I know people doubt this concept, but you must understand that the Earth, atmosphere, vegetation, climate, diet, and daily exercise of the average human being was much different than today. God allowed those people to live longer to have more children in a climate that produced more oxygen, which even plants grow bigger and live longer in, with humans who strictly lived on natural food. There was no such thing as preservatives, GMOs, etc., or any anti-human initiatives that kill people through food. Therefore, people could live longer lives, especially with the amount of exposure to the elements, the amounts of walking they did, the access to clean water, etc. Science aside, God allowed it, which means if God willed or said it, I believe it. Also, the most important detail about man and time is that mankind was not made to die, but to live forever. It was through sin that we experience death, which outside public speaking, is still the number one fear of most humans on this planet and throughout history.

Wisdom of Solomon 2:23

For God created man to be immortal, and made him to be an image of his own eternity.

But again, I digress.

As Abraham had settled back in his home in Beersheba, he got news that he didn't want to hear. Death struck close to home for the 2nd time.

Jasher 24: 18-21

And at the revolution of the year Abimelech king of the Philistines died in that year; he was one hundred and ninety-three years old at his death; and Abraham went with his people to the land of the Philistines, and they comforted the whole household and all his servants, and he then turned and went home. 20 And it was after the death of Abimelech that the people of Gerar took Benmalich his son, and he was only twelve years old, and they made him lying in the place of his father. 21 And they called his name Abimelech after the name of his father, for thus was it their custom to do in Gerar, and Abimelech reigned instead of Abimelech his father, and he sat upon his throne.

The Philistine king was dead. The man that shared good and bad times with Abraham, the man who allowed him to live in his land, created a safe space for all travelers in the desert, had now passed away at the age of 193. Abraham journeyed to place of Abimelech's death and showed his respects to the family, just as Abimelech had done when Sarah died. He returned the consolation to the family the same way Abimelech had done his family.

Abimelech's son, Benmalich, became king in Gerar. As their tradition, Benmalich took on his father's name, Abimelech, which became a common custom to most ancient kingdoms in world history. Many rulers would either take the name of their ancestor or royal name of their father to honor them by keeping their name alive, especially if they were worshipped as a god among their people. At 12 years old, Benmalich was now king in the place of his father. Abimelech means 'my father is king.'

Abraham had lost another friend.

The king is dead, long live the king.

Death of Lot

Jasher 24.22

And Lot the son of Haran also died in those days, in the thirty-ninth year of the life of Isaac, and all the days that Lot lived were one hundred and forty years and he died.

More sad news for Abraham.

Two years after the death of Sarah, Abraham received news that his beloved nephew Lot had died while Isaac was away learning about God with Shem and Eber. He was 140 years old when he died.

Kingdoms of Moab and Ammon, Sons of Lot

Jasher 24: 23-24

And these are the children of Lot, that were born to him by his daughters, the name of the first born was Moab, and the name of the second was Benami. 24 And the two sons of Lot went and took themselves wives from the land of Canaan, and they bare children to them, and the children of Moab were Ed, Mayon, Tarsus, and Kanvil, four sons, these are fathers to the children of Moab unto this day.

The salting of Lot's wife was not the end of Lot, but a restart. Even though his daughters took advantage of their father and had two sons by him, his sons had several children that became a nation unto themselves in Canaan. Moab, the son of Lot's eldest daughter, name means 'he is of my father', giving an admission of incest. The second son Benami, the son of Lot's youngest daughter, name means 'son of my people.' Moab became a nation named after himself as his younger brother is the father of the Ammonite nation, both well documented in both biblical and academic history.

Jasher 24: 25-26

And all the families of the children of Lot went to dwell wherever they should light upon, for they were fruitful and increased abundantly. 26 And they went and built themselves cities in the land where they dwelt, and they called the names of the cities which they built after their own names.

Rest in peace to Lot, a good man before the LORD. Abraham lost another loved one.

Death of Nahor

Jasher 24:27

And Nahor the son of Terah, brother to Abraham, died in those days in the fortieth year of the life of Isaac, and all the days of Nahor were one hundred and seventy-two years and he died and was buried in Haran.

The sad news keeps coming.

A year after Lot passed away, Nahor, Abraham's older brother and Lot's uncle, died. For many years, Abraham didn't have to deal with the pain of losing loved ones to death. But now, especially since the death of Sarah, it has been a falling domino effect of death around him. First, Sarah. Then Abimelech, Lot, and now Nahor, his brother, whom Abraham loved dearly. Nahor came and mourned with his brother at the death of Sarah, celebrated with Abraham with the birth of Isaac, and left Ur of the Chaldees with his brother to start a new life.

Jasher 24:28

And when Abraham heard that his brother was dead he grieved sadly, and he mourned over his brother many days.

Broken heart.

To be a believer as Abraham was, we must embrace loss. We must understand that we will have to endure broken-heartedness. It's a requirement, beyond others in the world who don't believe as we do. Everyone experiences loss, but the believer must endure. Why? Because the ONE in whom we believe is endurance. Before the creation of the universe, God knew all this was going to happen, HE foresaw it, thus making HIM the most broken-hearted being in the universe. Think of it, every human being that has lived, currently lives, and will be born, will pass away. We think of it on a human level, but if you can, just for a moment, look at the concept of a human passing through the lens of God. HE loses all! We may lose one, two, ten, or even a nation. But not all. Even if we feel like it's all, it's not all. HE, however, experiences EVERY loss, whether we see it or not, know it or not, feel it or not. HE does. Therefore, HE is the comforter above all comforters, which is why Jesus told us that HE is and always have been the comforter. The book of Psalms, Proverbs, Song of Solomon, Ecclesiastes, the prophets, etc., all testify of HIM comforting us despite our actions discomforting HIM.

M.I.P.

God is the most uncomforted, unappreciated, unthought of being in the universe. Yet, he is the most comforting, appreciative, and thoughtful being in the universe.

There is none like HIM.

The loss of Nahor really hit Abraham because now, outside of Ishmael and Isaac, he was alone in the world. Terah, his father, was dead. His mother, Amthelo, dead. His wife, Sarah, dead. Haran, his eldest brother, dead. Abimelech, the Philistine king that was a friend of Abraham, dead. Noah, the one who taught him the ways of God, dead. Now, his older brother Nahor, had now passed. Most of these deaths happened in short order, so the impact of Nahor's death brought everything full circle for Abraham.

However, instead of drowning in his sadness, he took a good look around him and noticed that his time had to be coming as well as he was one of the last of a dying breed of righteousness in the Earth. He properly mourned his brother, many days, but he knew life was moving on. It's the penalty of old age, seeing loved ones die. For many, it creates survivor's remorse. For Abraham, it created focus. The remaining remnant that connect all of these loved ones that passed was Isaac. It was time to focus on him as the legacy God gave Abraham to be a gift to the world. Abraham was now ready to restart life with an intentional focus on his now 40-year-old son who was returning from the house of Shem and Eber, Isaac.

Finding A Submissive Woman

Genesis 24: 1-4

And Abraham was old, *and* well stricken in age: and the LORD had blessed Abraham in all things. 2 And Abraham said unto his
eldest servant of his house, that ruled over all that he had, Put, I pray thee, thy hand under my thigh: 3 And I will make thee swear
by the LORD, the God of heaven, and the God of the earth, that thou shalt not take a wife unto my son of the daughters of the
Canaanites, among whom I dwell: 4 But thou shalt go unto my country, and to my kindred, and take a wife unto my son Isaac.

Refocused and intentional. Abraham, in the midst of losing Nahor, was ready to take the next step in obeying God: family planning. As a father, he knew that Isaac was still dealing with the death of his mother Sarah. Even though Isaac was off learning about God with Shem and Eber, he had no family of his own. After loss must come gain. Abraham understood this.

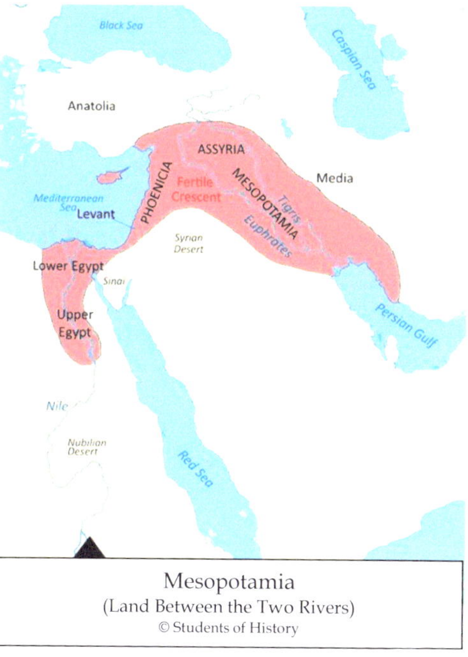

Mesopotamia
(Land Between the Two Rivers)
© Students of History

The eldest servant of Abraham's house was Eliezer, his most trusted servant. Abraham called Eliezer to him, asking him to make a vow by placing his hand underneath Abraham's thigh, a ritual signifying that Eliezer's hand and word was under Abraham's authority to fulfill his wishes. Abraham's desire was for Eliezer to go to the land of Mesopotamia to find Isaac a wife, from among Abraham's people. He did not want Isaac to marry a Canaanite woman. Why? Two reasons. First, Abraham knew that Canaan was cursed by Noah because of the sin of his father Ham, who looked upon the nakedness of his father, violating the law of God of honoring our parents. The curse was that Canaan would be a servant to his brothers, not a ruler. Abraham's covenant with God was one of rulership. Therefore, marrying a woman that comes from Canaan would be counterculture to the promise of God. Secondly, Abraham wanted a sense of purity of a wife for Isaac. The women and customs of Canaan were well known by Abraham as unpure. He knew from the time of his homesteading at Haran, Mamre, Egypt, and now Beersheba, the reputation of the people of the known world. Abraham had access to knowledge of cultures as he allowed his home to be a safe space in a wilderness for travelers. The idea of marrying a woman from the place of Abraham's birth was also a reminder of Sarah. Sarah, Abraham's younger cousin and deceased wife, was from Abraham's birthplace and kindred. Abraham knee that Isaac would feel a real connection in honor of his mother if a wife was found from among his own people like Abraham did with Sarah.

Jasher 24: 29-31

And Abraham called for Eliezer his head servant, to give him orders concerning his house, and he came and stood before him. 30
And Abraham said to him, Behold I am old, I do not know the day of my death; for I am advanced in days; now therefore rise up,
go forth and do not take a wife for my son from this place and from this land, from the daughters of the Canaanites amongst
whom we dwell. 31 But go to my land and to my birthplace, and take from thence a wife for my son, and the Lord God of Heaven
and earth who took me from my father's house and brought me to this place, and said unto me, To thy seed will I give this land for
an inheritance for ever, he will send his angel before thee and prosper thy way, that thou mayest obtain a wife for my son from my
family and from my father's house.

Amen. Eliezer had his orders. He agreed to the conditions of Abraham. In the midst of the agreement, Eliezer had a question, a very important one that answers the dating question that can help people marry the right person if you do the due diligence required. What was his question?

Genesis 24:5

And the servant said unto him, Peradventure the woman will not be willing to follow me unto this land: must I needs bring thy son again unto the land from whence thou camest?

What if the woman is unwilling to follow you? Should Isaac go to your hometown and pursue a woman? The first question is the big one! Should a man date or marry a woman that is unwilling to follow? That question simplifies the concept of the wedding vow and purpose of dating with intent. The answer, relative to the order of God, is no. HIS way is a matter of accountability and responsibility that falls to a man first, as man was created in God's image, not woman. The woman was made from man, not God, to be a mate for man. A woman was made for a man, not a man made for a woman. Therefore, a woman suitable for marriage is a woman that is willing to follow. If she is not willing to follow, she is not marriage material. It's that simple.

1 Corinthians 11: 8-9

For the man is not of the woman; but the woman of the man. 9 Neither was the man created for the woman; but the woman for the
man.

This is incredible! Sarah showed us all, male and female, that following your man, a good man, a Godly man, comes with promises and perks. Kings, even in her old age, almost risked their kingdoms just to have a night with her regardless of the fact that she was married to Abraham, a man revered throughout all of history. She didn't do anything special other than follow her man, even when he was in error. God disciplined her husband while she remained blessed. That's the beauty of followship. The concept of Christ marrying the Church is based in us all understanding the role of both woman and wife, even if we are a man and husband. She, the real Church, is the beneficiary of the promises of God that stretch into eternity. Most women nowadays don't understand this concept as they associate ordinary men with Godly men, thinking that they should be entitled to the benefits of a Godly man while being passed around by ordinary men. Following a man who's in the world has a different grading scale than that of a Godly man. How so? What makes them different?

A Godly man sees a woman through the value of the lens of God. A man of this world sees a woman through the value of the lens of the world. Godly men date and marry through the lens of God, understanding the vow is to God not the woman, and it is until death do we part. The man of the world dates and marry through the lens of the world, not understanding the vow is to God but instead makes the vow to the woman or their own thoughts, feelings, emotions, agendas, etc. This is a large reason why divorce rates are as high as they are. Clarity on the purpose of the vow is missing. But wait, aren't women the one filing for divorce at an all-time high rate? Yes. But that too is explainable.

Both men and women are not being taught the way of God. They are being taught the way of the world, the way of themselves. The world teaches that it's okay to "upgrade" or get another spouse if you are not happy. Fulfill yourself, not your vow. It's transactional, even at the expense of children and families. The easiest example to use is that of a business or job, work that relationship for a while and then move on, always being in the pursuit of self-satisfaction and or happiness. To be truthful, it's an indirect way of turning to idolatry. Your own thoughts and feelings become God, which leaks into the mental health crisis going on in the world. It's like a program. Its purpose is to un-program us from the natural law of God to accept the unnatural law of the world that says do what you want with who you want for your own gain. Breaking the law of God is so common place in marriage by divorcing for various reasons that aren't scriptural or biblical. The leading reason is 'irreconcilable differences', which means we don't get along. To be clear, Abraham sent Hagar away in separation, not divorce, because of irreconcilable differences. Even though he had another wife in Sarah, he still kept his vow to God. Hagar did the same.

The teachings of the elders whom God considered holy in his own eyes taught that a woman should embrace following a Godly man because she benefits from a version of God himself through her husband. That doesn't mean that a husband is God, by no means, but he is a representation of the first husband, God. A man is made in the image of God. When a woman understands that, she understands that following a Godly man is likened to following God himself. She, following her husband, teaches him how to follow God from a perspective that's different than the one he previously had. It's a whole new world and relationship a man garners with God that speaks for the duration of a lifetime. Both people teach one another for the uplift of the overall unit. It is the man that is seen by God as the leader and the one responsible for the overall relationship, being that you both are one flesh. The lens of a Godly man will love his wife as God loves, not how a man or woman loves, which is a dangerous concept if not properly understood. Women, who are more natural in expressing their emotions, quite often misappropriate their love, comparatively, with God's love. They are not the same. God's love is not emotional even though it contains emotion. Godly men operate more from this space which can seem like it's distant, but it is not. This is not the case for all men, but it is for a Godly man, who seeks balance, which is how God loves, present yet distant at all times.

A common complaint of women in the dating or marital world is that a man doesn't love them the way they love or that their love isn't being reciprocated, which definitely can be true. However, there is a question that stretches beyond the surface of reciprocation, and that's this: are you loving him as God does? Consider it. God allows us to have free will, the option to do as we please to an extent, live, learn, bump our heads, experience pain and pleasure, etc. In that process, HE doesn't jump in and or interfere at every beckoning call. Does that mean HE doesn't love us? No. Again, HE's present yet distant, interacting depending on the situation. We wouldn't dare say that God doesn't love us because he allows us to live and be. Instead, we embrace this as life and move forward with his providence. Why is this not the same for a husband's love? The real question is how do we interact with God, HIS presence, and HIS will for our lives? Understanding that a Godly man seeks to live according to God's will and way can open the relationship to a higher level of understanding one another' humanity beyond emotions and actions into a representation of God's relationship with the Church HE is coming back for. There was a joke I heard a comedian on television say years ago in relation to this topic that always stuck with me, which she posed to the crowd and I will pose to you below:

*Ladies, what if God was a man? Would he be enough for us? Seriously, think about that for a second. We know us and how we are, like how we really are, you know? I mean, the God of the universe, the creator of all, if he was your man, would you listen to him? **** no! We'd be doing the same thing we do to our men now! (the crowd laughs). I'd actually say we'd be worse! Think about it, we'd be like…girl, I can't stand his ***. He always think he right. Well, he is right, but he wrong because he right! Like, he loves me, treat me right, always on time, makes sure I'm good, you know? Why can't he be like Ray or John? Like he's a good man but dang, why can't I have a little spice sometime? Like why can't he just come home upset sometimes? He always so calm and cool and under control? I don't know girl, you know what I'm saying? Is it me? (the crowd is hysterically laughing).*

She continues…

*I'm just saying y'all, you know? You can't even argue with him. Like, you know he right, every time, but you like, he gonna be wrong one time and I'ma be like **** naw, you wrong, you wrong, you wrong, I knew it! You always think you're right! Ain't nobody perfect! Ain't nobody perfect! I knew it, I knew it! (she paused, watching the crowd laugh). Now, while I'm saying all this, I stop and think….he's actually right. He's actually right. Dang, he got me again. Should I tell him? **** naw. Now he knows how I feel, well not really because he right and perfect, but I gotta win atleast one argument, he like 1,000,000 – 0. What am I gonna say?….(she pauses, the crowd gets quiet as the laughter dies down….then she says with a playful smile)…you know I'm so crazy! I love you boo! Let's go on vacation or something. Tell Michael to get the jet ready. Oh, I gotta tell you about this new girl Sarah at work, she be getting on my nerves!*

(every woman in the room stands, applauds, laughs)

Y'all know I ain't lying!!! That's exactly how we would be if God was our man. He could never be right. We'd be trying to compete with him and say he's the one competing!?!?!? Tell me I'm lying?

(the crowd erupts in laughter)

No one disagrees.

She walks off stage to a standing ovation.

Perspective is key.

This doesn't mean it will be easy, in fact, it will be harder. The commitment of the marriage bond is a heavenly gift that supersedes the superficiality of this world, whose reward is God blessed and God ordained. Gentlemen, if you don't take anything else from this section, get this: you can learn a lot about a woman's personal relationship with God through her willingness to follow her husband, as Sarah did. Ladies, if you don't take anything else from this section, get this: you can learn a lot about a man's personal relationship with God through his willingness to listen to his wife, as Abraham did. I don't mean pandering, I mean commitment to the cause, which is bigger than both parties. Vow supersedes all, the commitment to the work that God has called you both to do, which is the purpose of the yoke of marriage. It's more than a feeling, that comes and goes. Feelings can lie to us. God is not a man, that HE should lie (Num. 23:19). God is purposeful and intentional. HE has order and structure.

Following is not always agreement. Listening is not always doing as told. Following and listening have one thing in common: commitment beyond self. This is the true essence of relationship within the confines of intentional dating and marriage. This is why the church is biblically regarded to as a she. When you parallel this concept relationally, both husband and wife teach one another submission, the word that scares most people in relationships. Why? Because we don't understand it. The moment we take some time and learn it, the vision of marriage is simplified and given its true placement in relationships. The word submissive is the modern word that categorizes the questions Eliezer had for Abraham and how he should identify the woman Abraham wanted for his son. Do not consider this strange, Abraham did the same for Ishmael. The concept is the same for all of us.

Ephesians 5: 21-25

Submitting yourselves one to another in the fear of God. 22 Wives, submit yourselves unto your own husbands, as unto the Lord. 23 For the husband is the head of the wife, even as Christ is the head of the church: and he is the saviour of the body. 24 Therefore as the church is subject unto Christ, so *let* the wives *be* to their own husbands in every thing. 25 Husbands, love your wives, even as Christ also loved the church, and gave himself for it;

This is what Abraham wanted for Isaac. This is what Abraham wanted for Ishmael. This is what Abraham wants for all of his children. If you are a believer, this is what he wants for you. This was the mission for Eliezer.

Genesis 24: 6-9

And Abraham said unto him, Beware thou that thou bring not my son thither again. 7 The LORD God of heaven, which took me
from my father's house, and from the land of my kindred, and which spake unto me, and that sware unto me, saying, Unto thy
seed will I give this land; he shall send his angel before thee, and thou shalt take a wife unto my son from thence. 8 And if the
woman will not be willing to follow thee, then thou shalt be clear from this my oath: only bring not my son thither again. 9 And
the servant put his hand under the thigh of Abraham his master, and sware to him concerning that matter.

Find my son a submissive woman.

- Abraham to all his children.

Finding The One

Genesis 24: 10-11

And the servant took ten camels of the camels of his master, and departed; for all the goods of his master *were* in his hand: and he
arose, and went to Mesopotamia, unto the city of Nahor. 11 And he made his camels to kneel down without the city by a well of
water at the time of the evening, *even* the time that women go out to draw *water*.

Eliezer had his orders. Abraham instructed him to find a submissive woman, one from the land of his kindred, which was in Mesopotamia, which means the land between the two rivers (Tigris and Euphrates). Abraham knew where to find a good woman, the people from whom he wanted his son to marry, and he sent a trusted man of his own to ensure that this woman be found. Eliezer left Beersheba and headed north to the city of Nahor, which was in Haran, a city lived in by Abraham and Nahor which is in Mesopotamia.

Jasher 24:34

And Eliezer did as Abraham ordered him, and Eliezer swore unto Abraham his master upon this matter; and Eliezer rose up and took ten camels of the camels of his master, and ten men from his master's servants with him, and they rose up and went to Haran, the city of Abraham and Nahor, in order to fetch a wife for Isaac the son of Abraham; and whilst they were gone Abraham sent to the house of Shem and Eber, and they brought from thence his son Isaac.

When Eliezer left with the 10 camels and 10 men to find a wife for Isaac, Abraham sent a different servant to the house of Shem and Eber to bring his son back home. For three years, Isaac was away, learning what he needed to learn about the LORD. The time to return was at hand.

When Isaac returned home, Eliezer arrived at Nahor in the land of Haran.

Beersheba to Haran
(the city of Abraham and Nahor)
© The History of Ancient Israel

Jasher 24:35

And Isaac came home to his father's house to Beersheba, whilst Eliezer and his men came to Haran; and they stopped in the city by the watering place, and he made his camels to kneel down by the water and they remained there.

Strategy. Eliezer was a strategist, which makes him the perfect man to find the wife for Isaac. When he came to the city, he purposely went to the water during the time of day when women would go to get what they needed for their families for the night. This was the perfect place to find a woman who was responsible, family oriented, and a server. He made the camels lie down and rest, which gives the imagery of men passing by, being responsible workers and keepers, which is attractive to any working woman. The camels represented wealth. Making them kneel represented power. Resting them at the water represented intentionality. Perspective matters when finding the one comes into play. This place was perfect for both parties to see what the other needed to see.

When women came out to do what they needed to do, it would be impossible to distinguish between them all. Eliezer wasn't tasked to find some women, but a woman, the right woman, the one. With that in mind, Eliezer knew that only God could show him the one that he was tasked to bring to his master. So, he did what any good or Godly man should do when looking for the one: he prayed.

Genesis 24: 12-14

And he said, O LORD God of my master Abraham, I pray thee, send me good speed this day, and shew kindness unto my master
Abraham. 13 Behold, I stand *here* by the well of water; and the daughters of the men of the city come out to draw water: 14 And let
it come to pass, that the damsel to whom I shall say, Let down thy pitcher, I pray thee, that I may drink; and she shall say, Drink,
and I will give thy camels drink also: *let the same be* she *that* thou hast appointed for thy servant Isaac; and thereby shall I know that
thou hast shewed kindness unto my master.

Intentional prayers are powered in the eyes of God. Eliezer knew he needed help in the process and he knew to ask The ONE to help him find the one for Isaac. His prayer was that the woman that specifically answered the way he prayed be the one. While Eliezer was doing his work and asked the LORD to help him in the process, the request of finding a woman that was of his family was not in the prayer. Eliezer didn't remember this part, but God did. He asked God for speed in this process, and guess what happened?

Genesis 24: 15-21

And it came to pass, before he had done speaking, that, behold, Rebekah came out, who was born to Bethuel, son of Milcah, the
wife of Nahor, Abraham's brother, with her pitcher upon her shoulder. 16 And the damsel *was* very fair to look upon, a virgin,
neither had any man known her: and she went down to the well, and filled her pitcher, and came up. 17 And the servant ran to
meet her, and said, Let me, I pray thee, drink a little water of thy pitcher. 18 And she said, Drink, my lord: and she hasted, and let
down her pitcher upon her hand, and gave him drink. 19 And when she had done giving him drink, she said, I will draw *water* for
thy camels also, until they have done drinking. 20 And she hasted, and emptied her pitcher into the trough, and ran again unto the
well to draw *water*, and drew for all his camels. 21 And the man wondering at her held his peace, to wit whether the LORD had
made his journey prosperous or not.

Done. God is always God, and speed is not fast enough to race HIM or HIS timing. HE adjusts what HE does to put on the line of time. Here, not only did God hear Eliezer, but HE sent a young lady out before the prayer was done. Look at God! It was a young lady by the name of Rebekah.

When Eliezer saw her, he noticed her actual features described as her being fair, a virgin, with a pitcher on her shoulder. Fair means attractive or good looking. A virgin means she hadn't had sex with a man yet, purity. The pitcher on the shoulder is the greatest feature of all. This is the God part. Let's *Make It Plain...*

Make It Plain

The pitcher on the shoulder is symbolic of a divine combination of choice. The pitcher represents redemption, filled with water, a cleanser and purifier. Holding it above the shoulder means that redemption and purity comes from above.

Eliezer ran to meet her. He asked her if she would give him water to drink, and she did. She dipped down to give him water, showing her ability to serve gracefully. After Eliezer finished drinking, Rebekah volunteered to water the camels as well. When she ran to refill her pitcher of water, Eliezer stood wondering and asked the LORD if this was the one. While he wondered about Rebekah, the family connection question finally came back to his mind when she returned to him.

Genesis 24: 22-27

And it came to pass, as the camels had done drinking, that the man took a golden earring of half a shekel weight, and two bracelets for her
hands of ten *shekels* weight of gold; 23 And said, Whose daughter *art* thou? tell me, I pray thee: is there room *in* thy father's house for us to
lodge in? 24 And she said unto him, I *am* the daughter of Bethuel the son of Milcah, which she bare unto Nahor. 25 She said moreover unto
him, We have both straw and provender enough, and room to lodge in. 26 And the man bowed down his head, and worshipped the LORD. 27
And he said, Blessed *be* the LORD God of my master Abraham, who hath not left destitute my master of his mercy and his truth: I *being* in the
way, the LORD led me to the house of my master's brethren.

She's the one! Who would have known?

God did.

Eliezer thanked this young lady by paying her for her services with an earring and two golden bracelets. When he asked her who her parents were, she claimed to be the daughter of Bethuel, the son of recently deceased Nahor. To *Make It Plain*, she was Nahor's granddaughter. The moment she said that, Eliezer immediately went into worship mode! He had a chance to see, learn, and experience God at work for himself. Only God could have done something like this, exactly like this, specifically like this.

Now, it was time to handle the business of the trip.

Genesis 24: 28-41

And the damsel ran, and told *them of* her mother's house these things. 29 And Rebekah had a brother, and his name *was* Laban: and Laban
ran out unto the man, unto the well. 30 And it came to pass, when he saw the earring and bracelets upon his sister's hands, and when he
heard the words of Rebekah his sister, saying, Thus spake the man unto me; that he came unto the man; and, behold, he stood by the camels
at the well. 31 And he said, Come in, thou blessed of the LORD; wherefore standest thou without? for I have prepared the house, and room for
the camels. 32 And the man came into the house: and he ungirded his camels, and gave straw and provender for the camels, and water to
wash his feet, and the men's feet that *were* with him. 33 And there was set *meat* before him to eat: but he said, I will not eat, until I have told
mine errand. And he said, Speak on. 34 And he said, I *am* Abraham's servant. 35 And the LORD hath blessed my master greatly; and he is
become great: and he hath given him flocks, and herds, and silver, and gold, and menservants, and maidservants, and camels, and asses. 36
And Sarah my master's wife bare a son to my master when she was old: and unto him hath he given all that he hath. 37 And my master made
me swear, saying, Thou shalt not take a wife to my son of the daughters of the Canaanites, in whose land I dwell: 38 But thou shalt go unto my
father's house, and to my kindred, and take a wife unto my son. 39 And I said unto my master, Peradventure the woman will not follow me. 40
And he said unto me, The LORD, before whom I walk, will send his angel with thee, and prosper thy way; and thou shalt take a wife for my son
of my kindred, and of my father's house: 41 Then shalt thou be clear from *this* my oath, when thou comest to my kindred; and if they give not
thee *one*, thou shalt be clear from my oath.

Big brother Laban stepped up to see what was going on, serving as his sister's protector until his father Bethuel showed up. Honorable. He wanted to know who was this man that came to their home with his little sister Rebekah. They offered to feed Eliezer, his camels, wash his feet, along with the 10 men that came with him. Eliezer decided not to accept any of these gifts as a visitor until he explained why he was there, so he did. When he expressed why he was there, Eliezer made sure to give both oral and mental details of how the LORD made this possible and how it has and will bless the spirit of his master Abraham and strengthen the family connection between both brothers, Abraham and Nahor, especially with Nahor recently dying. The purpose of the trip was to find a wife for Isaac, the one. Having been led by an angel, Eliezer was bound by oath to complete this work for his master and cannot return until he does.

Genesis 24: 42-49

And I came this day unto the well, and said, O LORD God of my master Abraham, if now thou do prosper my way which I go: 43Behold, I stand
by the well of water; and it shall come to pass, that when the virgin cometh forth to draw *water*, and I say to her, Give me, I pray thee, a little
water of thy pitcher to drink; 44And she say to me, Both drink thou, and I will also draw for thy camels: *let* the same *be* the woman whom the
LORD hath appointed out for my master's son.45And before I had done speaking in mine heart, behold, Rebekah came forth with her pitcher on
her shoulder; and she went down unto the well, and drew *water*: and I said unto her, Let me drink, I pray thee. 46And she made haste, and let
down her pitcher from her *shoulder*, and said, Drink, and I will give thy camels drink also: so I drank, and she made the camels drink also. 47And
I asked her, and said, Whose daughter *art* thou? And she said, The daughter of Bethuel, Nahor's son, whom Milcah bare unto him: and I put the
earring upon her face, and the bracelets upon her hands. 48And I bowed down my head, and worshipped the LORD, and blessed the LORD God
of my master Abraham, which had led me in the right way to take my master's brother's daughter unto his son. 49And now if ye will deal kindly
and truly with my master, tell me: and if not, tell me; that I may turn to the right hand, or to the left.

A servant knows how to find a servant. This is a beautiful recount of a love story, given by a servant who understands, respects, submits, and thrives in serving his master. This was the same concept that Sarah thrived at when serving Abraham. Eliezer was not only doing what he was supposed to do, but he was doing it with amazement and accuracy, being careful and fully transparent to Bethuel and Laban so they would know how serious this visit was. This is a beautiful lesson of dating and marriage. Being careful and transparent, both orally and mentally, especially when meeting the family. Eliezer did not want to come across as a man seeking to take a woman from a family as if she was going to be a part of a harem or anything non-honorable. Instead, he led with the LORD and he himself serving his masters, both God and Abraham. By being transparent, there was no hidden agenda or alternative plan. A servant understands what another servant truly looks like and Eliezer knew what he saw. With that said, he told them exactly his purpose for the meeting, refused to accept gifts and food until he made it clear as to why he was there. If what he was seeing wasn't true, as in terms of Rebekah not being what she portrayed herself as, then now was the time for Bethuel and Laban, the protectors of Rebekah, to return the favor of transparency. They knew who Rebekah really was.

Genesis 24: 50-54

Then Laban and Bethuel answered and said, The thing proceedeth from the LORD: we cannot speak unto thee bad or good. 51 Behold,
Rebekah *is* before thee, take *her*, and go, and let her be thy master's son's wife, as the LORD hath spoken.52 And it came to pass, that, when
Abraham's servant heard their words, he worshipped the LORD, *bowing himself* to the earth. 53And the servant brought forth jewels of silver,
and jewels of gold, and raiment, and gave *them* to Rebekah: he gave also to her brother and to her mother precious things. 54And they did eat
and drink, he and the men that *were* with him, and tarried all night; and they rose up in the morning, and he said, Send me away unto my
master.

Laban and Bethuel knew this was a God thing. There was no hidden agenda or game being played. There was no transaction or thought thereof, no scheme, no gimmicks, no lies. All truth. These men understood what Eliezer was saying and that only the LORD could allow something like this to happen. Rebekah was who she portrayed herself to be, a servant, just as Eliezer saw with his own eyes. For her father and brother to validate that and then bless the giving away of her into marriage was also a God thing that neither Laban or Bethuel wanted to get in the way of. The moment they blessed the engagement, it was time to celebrate! Not only did Eliezer immediately go back into worship mode in front of Laban and Bethuel, he blessed them with gifts of silver, gold, and precious clothing! This is known as a dowry, gifts given in exchange for a daughter's hand in marriage to replace the value of a daughter to a family. After the passing out of gifts, they ate and drank all night, partying hard! Yes, all night! Scripture didn't say for a moment or two, but all night! They partied all night into the morning before Eliezer finally had to ask Bethuel if he could leave.

Genesis 24: 55-61

And her brother and her mother said, Let the damsel abide with us *a few* days, at the least ten; after that she shall go. 56And he said unto
them, Hinder me not, seeing the LORD hath prospered my way; send me away that I may go to my master. 57And they said, We will call the
damsel, and inquire at her mouth. 58And they called Rebekah, and said unto her, Wilt thou go with this man? And she said, I will go. 59And
they sent away Rebekah their sister, and her nurse, and Abraham's servant, and his men.60And they blessed Rebekah, and said unto her,
Thou *art* our sister, be thou *the mother* of thousands of millions, and let thy seed possess the gate of those which hate them.61And Rebekah
arose, and her damsels, and they rode upon the camels, and followed the man: and the servant took Rebekah, and went his way.

They didn't want Rebekah to go so soon. To be clear, this all happened in one night, so we must understand the perspective of Laban and Milcah, Rebekah's mother. To be honest, I would have felt some kind of way too had this all happened in one night. I probably would have done the same thing, even if I knew it was from the LORD. Not maliciously, but just a parent. Yes, this is an admission of selfishness on my behalf, but just as they had to defer and get out of the way, so would I. We are just empathizing with Laban and Milcah. Two amazing things happened here that we must pay close attention to. One, mother and brother asked Rebekah what did she want. They didn't force her into a decision on whether or not she wanted to go, they asked her. Granted, her father had already made the decision previously, but they asked her, showing their respect of her as a person. Even though she was a young lady, she had to be trusted by them to manage her own thoughts to make such a decision. How do we know? Her mother wasn't the one bringing water for her family, Rebekah was. For her to do such a thing was a dangerous risk, especially in the evening in this time in the world. Historically, women were the ones who brought water from watering holes to take care of the needs in a family. Many women would be taken or killed doing such as they were unprotected in most cases unless men were sent to guard them, especially in the evening time. Wars have erupted over such cases. Going to go get water for the home left women vulnerable to abuse and families in danger of having their bloodline interrupted or destroyed. For Rebekah to be the one responsible for this task, especially as a young woman, meant that she was well respected and able to take care of herself, trustworthy and strong, and more importantly, aware.

The second thing to observe here is that her father didn't say a word. Bethuel said nothing. His wife and son wanted Rebekah to stay for another 10 days as they prep for her to leave, due to the emotional connection, but her father said nothing. Why? Because he knew that when a thing is from God, you have to let it go. He was emotionally attached to his daughter, but he knew not to get in the way of something God is doing. He had to learn this from his father Nahor, who learned it from his brother Abraham. Being that his father had recently died and Abraham was well known for being a man of divine purpose and protection, the marriage of his daughter to Isaac would be a blessing that extends beyond the 10 days his wife and son wanted. He saw the bigger picture, using a different kind of love, the equivalent of assessing a situation from a macro and micro point of view. This is why when Rebekah did leave, they blessed her and said...

Genesis 24:60

And they blessed Rebekah, and said unto her, Thou *art* our sister, be thou *the mother* of thousands of millions, and let thy seed possess the gate of those which hate them.

You see, blessings on blessings on blessings on blessings! Her father saw this in the big picture, her mother and brother saw it in the smaller picture. The key is that they all came to the conclusion that she must go as Rebekah chose, but blessing her in such a way became a prophetic message that extends to today. All from a remote city in Haran, the city of Abraham and Nahor, in Mesopotamia, in modern-day Turkey. The trip south to Beersheba would be one for the ages.

Genesis 24:61

And Rebekah arose, and her damsels, and they rode upon the camels, and followed the man: and the servant took Rebekah, and went his way.

When it's time to go, it's time to go. One day Rebekah was doing her daily work, taking care of her family, being respectful and hospitable to who she thought were travelers. That night she was gifted with gifts of silver and gold while her parents and brother partied with these travelers. The next morning, she and her maidservants were on camelback riding south to meet her husband to be. All because she was willing to serve.

By Rebekah carrying the pitcher above her shoulder, she was symbolizing her role within the promise of God to Abraham. Through Sarah, the promise of God that would stretch throughout the ages with the birth of Isaac. Now that Sarah was dead and mourned, it was time for God to give Isaac the right woman to serve HIM in the way God chose for the bloodline of the covenant HE made with Abraham. Ishmael had children, which blessed Abraham to become a grandfather several years prior. But it was Isaac, the son of the promise, that the covenant would be passed. Just as Isaac was revered as the one, a child born from his parents old age, his wife would be given to him at 40 years old. She too had to be the one.

Eliezer was an obedient servant, a solid man, a keeper, an example for us all. He served with the agenda of God 1st, as a servant to his master. He understood the assignment and humbled himself to it. He showed us all that a trusted man can see what a good woman looks like. A servant understands service. The society we now live in has shunned this type of outlook. Instead, it's being taught to serve self, not others. When an issue doesn't work the way you want it to and you become distressed, claim mental health or abuse and the world will allow you to be comforted or excused. Even if it's for a short time, you get that excuse. This is a new concept in the world as it makes for a shift in thought and accountability in human history. In essence, people are being taught that if you can't have what you want when you want it, you can play victim, whether it be physically, emotionally, and or mentally, and someone will come to your aid, especially if you are a woman. This is not to bash nor is this a rant, this is reality. Self-elevation and preservation rules the day at someone else' expense. Eliezer served and saw a woman that accepted service. It was an attribute that stood out, so much so that the men in her family concurred with what he saw. How many families say the same thing to men acquiring about the truth of their female family members when a man comes to seek her hand in dating or marriage? How many times has a friend who was the hookup person told the truth about their friend that was potentially about to date or marry someone? It's rare. As a married man myself, I can attest to this, it is rare.

People seek their own agendas to upgrade or enhance themselves. There is so much time, money, and attention paid to weddings and not marriages that divorces are through the roof. People still have the photos and videos to showcase, which go along with the scars. It's a commitment to self that promotes the divorce, which goes against what God stands for. Notice in the section above that Eliezer was committed to the vow he gave. True, finding Rebekah via the angel of the LORD the way that he did was special, along with every detail of this story, but we cannot overlook the commitment to the vow. That's the most honorable element of all of this. The vow. Who is really operating from the perspective and commitment to the vow they made? This is why Eliezer was chosen as the most trusted man of Abraham's home, seen as a son of Abraham, so much so that he was one of the four men that went to Mt. Moriah for Isaac's sacrifice. This same man was trusted to be the one to find the wife of Isaac by father Abraham himself. He is just as crucial to the story of Abraham as Sarah, Terah, Nahor, Ishmael, and Isaac. Just as important, but in a different way. The future of Abraham's seed doesn't happen without Eliezer and his honorable position to serve, not self. He served, not selfish, in truth and transparency. This is the type of way we should be in serving one another. This is how we should operate whenever we make a vow, committed. Even though he wasn't marrying Rebekah, he was the one who was tasked to evaluate her to see if she was marriage material.

God HIMself allowed Eliezer to do such an honorable thing because HE too saw Eliezer as Abraham saw him. He was the one in Abraham's house that served. Rebekah was the one in Bethuel house that served. It was now time to bring both the old and young, male and female servants together to serve one master, Isaac, who was born to serve the LORD in front of the world.

Only the one can find the one.

This same concept applies to marriage. This same concept applies to salvation.

Thanks again to Eliezer and Rebekah for serving! I pray we all learn how to serve as you did.

Rebekah

Genesis 24: 62-63

And Isaac came from the way of the well Lahairoi; for he dwelt in the south country. 63 And Isaac went out to meditate in the field at the eventide: and he lifted up his eyes, and saw, and, behold, the camels *were* coming.

When the one comes, you can remember the moment. No matter where you are, what you are doing, who you are with, you always remember that moment. It's not just you that has had that moment, the universe had that moment as well. The story of creation was that moment. For God to say 'Let there be…', and there was. How amazing that moment had to be? That moment is shared as our personal universe begins when we see the one. A whole new world is created at that moment.

Isaac can testify.

As he had returned from the house of Shem and Eber, getting back into the groove of being at Beersheba was underway. He didn't stay in the area near Abraham, he went a little further south in the countryside. While away for three years learning the ways of God, one of the things he picked up on was meditation. This art of focus, thinking, and contemplating things with the LORD was a learned behavior that the LORD himself enjoys. It's time you give him quietly, humbly, peaceably. He chose to meditate at Lahairoi, or Beer Lahai Roi, the place that the LORD spoke to Hagar when she ran away from Abraham and Sarah, Isaac's mother. As he was there meditating, he looked up and saw camels coming, which meant that someone of importance was heading to the house of Abraham. The place Lahairoi means 'the well of the vision of life.' From this well, a vison of life would be placed in the eye sight of Isaac.

Genesis 24: 64-65

And Rebekah lifted up her eyes, and when she saw Isaac, she lighted off the camel. 65 For she *had* said unto the servant, What man *is* this that walketh in the field to meet us? And the servant *had* said, It *is* my master: therefore she took a vail, and covered herself.

Seeing the one is not a one-sided event. The one always has a one that sees them as well. In order for the moment to be memorable, there has to be a signature sign or event that unites both parties. You know it when you see it. You know it when you feel it. It's beyond a simple rush. That's what Rebekah felt when she saw the man walking in the field to meet them. When she asked Eliezer who was the man, he told her it was his master. To be clear, Abraham was his master, just as Isaac was. The man walking was not Abraham, but Isaac. Eliezer didn't tell Rebekah which one it was walking, so out of respect, Rebekah pulled the vail over her face so she would be covered.

Genesis 24:66

And the servant told Isaac all things that he had done.

Eliezer, "Mr. Hook-up" in this scenario, was now face to face with Isaac for the first time in three years. He not only greeted him, but filled him in on the mission he was sent on. Isaac had no idea what was going on as his father didn't tell him prior to his return from being away with Shem. This is exactly how Abraham wanted it. Eliezer told Isaac everything, including who the young lady was on the camel. What a surprised man Isaac had to be. One minute he was meditating, the next he was looking at his future wife. How wild is that? What a moment! From here, the marriage was setup, arranged, and performed, just as Abraham arranged and Eliezer executed.

For Rebekah, she saw a man walking in a field towards them. A man she was told was the master of the man who brought her to this new land. For Isaac, after meditation with the LORD, it was a young lady riding camelback who was brought to him by his father's most trusted servant. Moments matter. For these two, the individual moments are the ones they keep to themselves and share with their loved ones and us as the plan of Abraham comes together perfectly. However, it is the next moment that allows us to see the bigger picture of God to unite both Isaac and Rebekah for the sake of the future of the promise of the LORD.

Genesis 24:67

And Isaac brought her into his mother Sarah's tent, and took Rebekah, and she became his wife; and he loved her: and Isaac was comforted after his mother's *death*.

God has a way of making sure we are comforted. For Isaac, Rebekah gave him the womanly connection that he craved and waited for since the loss of his mother. Rebekah allowed Isaac to love again, to learn again, to be connected again. After three years since Sarah's death and a chance to learn the ways of God from Shem and Eber, the marriage to Rebekah allowed him to move on correctly, following God 1st as his blueprint in life, a lesson he learned for himself. For Rebekah, Isaac gave her a chance to begin life with a purpose and devoted person with whom her life would be centered. She was a young lady but was trusted by her family to be responsible enough to go and be married. She was a server to her core, so serving and learning to serve in a different place was something the men of her family were okay with. She was in a foreign place and didn't know if she was going to be accepted, so operating in respect from the initial meeting set the tone for her arrival in Abraham's house. For Rebekah, it was respect. For Isaac, it was love. Why is this important?

Ephesians 5:33

Nevertheless let every one of you in particular so love his wife even as himself; and the wife *see* that she reverence *her* husband.

Husbands are to love their wives. Wives are to respect their husbands.

As a husband, you are to love your wife in a way that is beyond the emotion. This is not my opinion, but that of the LORD himself. I cannot stress this enough. The love HE tells the man to have for his wife is the same love HE has for the church, which he gave his life for (Eph. 5:25). Most people have taught men to love as emotion tells them to or in a way that the woman can identify as love. Most counselors teach this to young couples and the internet is flooded with relationship gurus that aren't Godly gurus at all. The way God intended a man to love his wife is the way HE does, being that a husband is a representative of HIM. God was the 1st and last husband and man was made in HIS image. The way that God loves is not emotional even though it has emotion in it. HIS way doesn't react to or make decisions on feelings, but is tactical and objective, open, and dependable. As men, we don't study God enough to know HIS love, therefore, until we study God intimately, we cannot love our wives as we should. Instead, we do the best that we can thinking that this will suffice. Meanwhile, we overlook the childhood trauma of not being able to connect to our feelings as much as we should because little boys are taught they are not supposed to show emotion and be expressive, which is not true. In turn, we become men that aren't open and expressive about our true feelings, which leaves us undeveloped. In turn, our marriages become underdeveloped. What God wants us to be is developed, mature, and balanced, as HE is. Loving as God does means that we act as HE does, giving and restricting, teaching and learning, providing and protecting, overseeing and understanding. Emotion comes as a byproduct of the above, which is why a man is called to love because he is called to lead. The greatest leaders are the greatest lovers. It's not a coincidence.

As a wife, you are to respect your husband in a way that is beyond emotion. This too is not my opinion, but that of the LORD HIMself. I cannot stress this enough. The respect God wants the woman to have for her husband is the same that the church should have for HIM (Eph. 5: 22-24). But just like the modern so-called church, there is a major separation between God's agenda and the church's agenda. God's agenda ends with holiness. The modern church's agenda ends with loneliness. This is the thought process of the modern woman. Modern church seeks membership over salvation. God seeks holiness. It's idolization, a violation of the 1st Commandment. The same is happening with women in today's society in the dating and marriage world. The woman's seeking of happiness and self-fulfillment is a separate agenda than the purpose of marriage. What's being taught on every social media corner you can find is all about her getting what you can get from the relationship more so than committing to the duty of the relationship. This is why the divorce rate is the highest in the history of the planet! To be clear, we are not saying that you should be miserable or anything like that; heaven forbids. What we are saying is duty supersedes feelings. What we are saying is evaluate your base. Were you raised to honor God or yourself? Your culture? Your will? Your way? Your wallet? It's very important to analyze. Still don't agree? Here's a question for you: when was the last time you asked God to make a decision based on what HE's feeling? Better yet, when was the last time you asked HIM how HE feels about anything? See what I mean? We want from HIM without regarding HIM. This is the same thing we do in relationships, wanting without regard.

When we hold someone in high regard, which is the literal meaning of the word respect, then how we feel about them is put to the side. Discipline over desire. This is what a wife is being asked to do. It goes against her nature, being that she is more emotionally expressive than a man. Her subjugating herself to operate from this space of reverence for her husband is NOT a love language. God is love, and while love languages are cool to learn and work through, they are every changing, depending on where a person is on their walk in life. Our God doesn't change. We think that HE has to because we don't know him well enough or study HIM close enough to see why HE said HE's the same today, yesterday, and forever more (Heb. 13:8). Learning and living with respect is the way of the women that God considers righteous, like Sarah, and now Rebekah.

In the end, we must come to understand that God's love is not like ours. HIS ways are not our ways, which is why we must learn HIM. As a husband, I can attest to the fact that I haven't loved my wife the way that I should have. Why? Because I didn't study God as close as I should have early in the dating process to support her the way that I should have when we first got married. It was and is a mistake that I made. Now that I know better, I must now do better, accepting my fault, acknowledging it, ask for forgiveness, and launching into a better and greater version of myself to mend that uncovered area. My concern is not that I get the same in return, which would be transactional, but that I align my ways with the ways of God so that I can love my wife the way HE does. That's the true desire of a man of God for his wife. This is the love that Isaac used with Rebekah. This is the respect that Rebekah used with Isaac.

The blueprint is laid. Now, let' get the tools we need and build the future the way God wants us to in the midst of this chaotic and deceitful world.

Isaiah 55: 6-9

Seek ye the LORD while he may be found, call ye upon him while he is near: 7 Let the wicked forsake his way, and the unrighteous man his
thoughts: and let him return unto the LORD, and he will have mercy upon him; and to our God, for he will abundantly pardon. 8 For my
thoughts *are* not your thoughts, neither *are* your ways my ways, saith the LORD. 9 For *as* the heavens are higher than the earth, so are my
ways higher than your ways, and my thoughts than your thoughts.

Keturah

Genesis 25:1

Then again Abraham took a wife, and her name *was* Keturah.

Now that Isaac was married, it was time for Abraham to move on as well. It has been a few years since the death of Sarah. Ishmael had been married twice, sent his first wife away because she was disrespectful, married another woman who was respectful and pleasing to him, as he had 12 sons to raise. He didn't leave his children with their mother, but kept and raised them himself, as the order of the LORD. Isaac had recently married Rebekah. Each of Abraham's sons were married and not alone. Now that he had secured their future with a companion, it was time for him to move on and find another wife.

In walks Keturah. Scripture tells us that she was from the land of Canaan. We know Abraham wasn't too fond of the women of Canaan, which means she had to be from the Hamite bloodline as a Canaanite woman who worked in the house of Abraham. This is why she is referred to later in the scriptures as his concubine (1 Chron. 1:32). It also means that she had to be an exceptional woman herself to be chosen to marry a worldwide renown man such as Abraham.

Jasher 25:1

And it was at that time that Abraham again took a wife in his old age, and her name was Keturah, from the land of Canaan.

Most historical writings on Keturah claim she was Hagar, but renamed due to character change. This is not true. Hagar went back to the land of her father, Egypt. She was the one who chose the first wife of Ishmael, a bad choice, who Ishmael later separated from. Eventually, Ishmael left her in the wilderness to return to place of choosing and went to live with his father at Beersheba. Hagar's character did not change. This woman, Keturah, was a woman who lived in the house of Abraham as a concubine that Abraham later married, making her his third wife. Each woman's character is different, and from these three women is Abraham blessed to increase in the world.

Of any woman on the planet, Keturah was chosen by Abraham to be his wife. Not only was she chosen to be his wife, but she is the woman that helped Abraham fulfill his name meaning, father of nations. From Keturah we get the peoples that spread throughout the world. One of which is directly connected to the Hebrews and Moses in the Exodus story. One of Abraham's sons became the leader of a people whom the chief of the tribe actually became the father-in-law to Moses, the great lawgiver and leader of the Hebrews. With that said, let's break down who these sons of Abraham and Keturah were, where they settled, and what nations they became.

Genesis 25: 2-4

And she bare him Zimran, and Jokshan, and Medan, and Midian, and Ishbak, and Shuah. 3 And Jokshan begat Sheba, and Dedan.
And the sons of Dedan were Asshurim, and Letushim, and Leummim. 4 And the sons of Midian; Ephah, and Epher, and Hanoch,
and Abida, and Eldaah. All these *were* the children of Keturah.

Jasher 25: 2-5

And she bare unto him Zimran, Jokshan, Medan, Midian, Ishbak and Shuach, being six sons. And the children of Zimran were
Abihen, Molich and Narim. 3 And the sons of Jokshan were Sheba and Dedan, and the sons of Medan were Amida, Joab, Gochi,
Elisha and Nothach; and the sons of Midian were Ephah, Epher, Chanoch, Abida and Eldaah. 4 And the sons of Ishbak were
Makiro, Beyodua and Tator. 5 And the sons of Shuach were Bildad, Mamdad, Munan and Meban; all these are the families of the
children of Keturah the Canaanitish woman which she bare unto Abraham the Hebrew.

6 Sons and 21 Grandsons of Abraham and Keturah

Zimram - Abihen, Molich, Narim
Jokshan - Sheba, Dedan
Medan - Amida, Joab, Gochi, Elisha, Nothach
Midian - Ephah, Epher, Chanoch, Abida, Eldaah
Ishbak - Makiro, Beyodua, Tator
Shuah - Bildad, Mamdad, Munan, Meban

Name = Name meaning (notable information)

Zimram = celebrated (believed to settle Arabian city of Zambran [between Mecca and Medina])
Jokshan = an offense, hardness (ancestor to the Sabeans, Dedanites of southern Arabia)
Medan = to twist, conflict (unknown where descendants settled)
Midian = judgment (father of the Midianite people [**Jethro** {tribal chief} was the father in law to Moses])
Ishbak = he will leave (settled villages in northern Arabia)
Shuah = swimming, sinks down (father of Judah's wife, Job's friend Bildad was a Shuhite)

Even though God blessed Abraham with 6 other sons, bringing his total to 8 sons, his mind was set on his legacy. The number 8 means new beginning, which meant that these sons of Abraham were meant to be a new beginning and connection to God in the world through faith, the way of their father. He knew the LORD's promise and covenant, knowing that through Isaac the world would be blessed. Through his sons he would have a connection with the world to come as these men all influenced the path and story of the future Hebrews. Even though these were his sons, just as Ishmael and Isaac, Abraham also knew that his time to live was coming to an end and he needed to make sure Isaac had what he needed to do the will of the LORD. So, what did he do? He sent his sons away, but with gifts as a reminder of who they were and who their father was.

Genesis 25: 5-6

And Abraham gave all that he had unto Isaac. 6 But unto the sons of the concubines, which Abraham had, Abraham gave gifts, and sent them away from Isaac his son, while he yet lived, eastward, unto the east country.

And...

Jasher 25: 6-13

And Abraham sent all these away, and he gave them gifts, and they went away from his son Isaac to dwell wherever they should find a place. 7 And all these went to the mountain at the east, and they built themselves six cities in which they dwelt unto this day. 8 But the children of Sheba and Dedan, children of Jokshan, with their children, did not dwell with their brethren in their cities, and they journeyed and encamped in the countries and wildernesses unto this day. 9 And the children of Midian, son of Abraham, went to the east of the land of Cush, and they there found a large valley in the eastern country, and they remained there and built a city, and they dwelt therein, that is the land of Midian unto this day. 10 And Midian dwelt in the city which he built, he and his five sons and all belonging to him. 11 And these are the names of the sons of Midian according to their names in their cities, Ephah, Epher, Chanoch, Abida and Eldaah. 12 And the sons of Ephah were Methach, Meshar, Avi and Tzanua, and the sons of Epher were Ephron, Zur, Alirun and Medin, and the sons of Chanoch were Reuel, Rekem, Azi, Alyoshub and Alad. 13 And the sons of Abida were Chur, Melud, Kerury, Molchi; and the sons of Eldaah were Miker, and Reba, and Malchiyah and Gabol; these are the names of the Midianites according to their families; and afterward the families of Midian spread throughout the land of Midian.

Not only did Abraham send his six sons by Keturah away with gifts from their father, but he sent Ishmael away as well with his children. This was not done maliciously, but in a way of a father sending his sons to establish themselves as men in the world, like the creation of a kingdom. Most of his sons and grandsons settled amongst one another and joined up into groups, choosing leaders or elders to represent their people. Shuah, Midian, Zimran, and Jokshan were the most notable sons that established themselves in the new world.

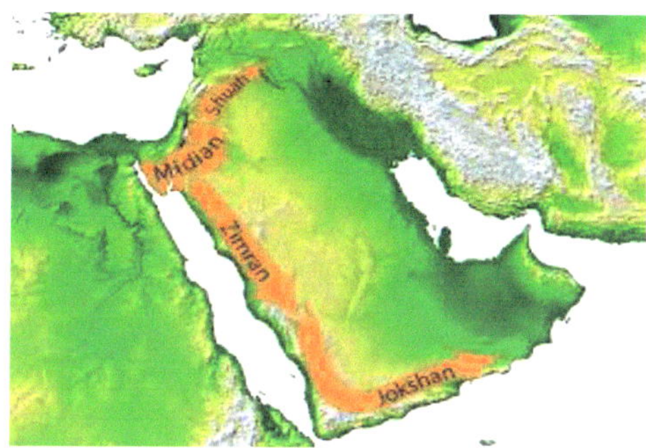

While his little brothers were being sent away with gifts, Ishmael did the same thing at this time, fulfilling the words of the angel of the LORD when he spoke to his mother Hagar at the well in the wilderness when she ran away while pregnant.

Jasher 25: 14-21

And these are the generations of Ishmael the son Abraham, whom Hagar, Sarah's handmaid, bare unto Abraham. 15 And Ishmael took a wife from the land of Egypt, and her name was Ribah, the same is Meribah. 16 And Ribah bare unto Ishmael Nebayoth, Kedar, Adbeel, Mibsam and their sister Bosmath. 17 And Ishmael cast away his wife Ribah, and she went from him and returned to Egypt to the house of her father, and she dwelt there, for she had been very bad in the sight of Ishmael, and in the sight of his father Abraham. 18 And Ishmael afterward took a wife from the land of Canaan, and her name was Malchuth, and she bare unto him Nishma, Dumah, Masa, Chadad, Tema, Yetur, Naphish and Kedma. 19 These are the sons of Ishmael, and these are their names, being twelve princes according to their nations; and the families of Ishmael afterward spread forth, and Ishmael took his children and all the property that he had gained, together with the souls of his household and all belonging to him, and they went to dwell where they should find a place. 20 And they went and dwelt near the wilderness of Paran, and their dwelling was from Havilah unto Shur, that is before Egypt as thou comest toward Assyria. 21 And Ishmael and his sons dwelt in the land, and they had children born to them, and they were fruitful and increased abundantly.

Amazing, simply amazing! Ishmael did what men are supposed to do when a family is broken when children are involved. He took the responsibility of his children and raised them. With his first wife, he had 4 sons and one daughter, Bosmath. He separated from his wife because she was disrespectful, as we have covered in this work. Because of the culture they were in, he was allowed to marry another wife, Malchuch, who gave him 8 sons. All 13 children, 12 of which are sons, grew up with their father close to their grandfather Abraham and uncle Isaac. The wife he separated from went back to live with her father in Egypt, where his mother found her, alone. Because she was married to Ishmael but separated, she could not remarry, a shamed woman, who had 5 children with a man but was dishonorable to him.

Map of Saudi Arabia, Where Ishmael Settled
© Questioning Torah

When the time came, Ishmael left with his wife and children. They found a place in the wilderness of Paran, living between Havilah and Shur, in the wilderness. They became masters of the desert area between Egypt and the rest of the modern Middle East. From that place, they increased in number and his sons became princes and tribal leaders over their children. They grew to the point that they were called Ishmaelites by neighboring nations and historical scholars, thus fulfilling the Word of God and promise made to Abraham.

Keturah is not often spoken of in biblical or historical literature. Yet, she is the woman with whom Abraham had the most children. She is arguably one of the most important women in scriptural history for this reason alone. From her comes the Middle Eastern nations that spread throughout the world in small bands. From her came the Midianites, one of which became the father in law to Moses himself, Jethro. He influenced Moses to create structure of law from which the Jewish people to this day use. From her comes Bildad, who was an advisor to Job, the rich man of the East, which is the same direction the Bible tells us Abraham sent his children, south and eastward. From her comes several Arab tribes. From her comes Sheba, who had a queen that would travel in her great wealth and thirst of wisdom to the Hebrew king Solomon, becoming one of his wives, then giving birth to a son that would become the legendary first king in the Ethiopian Empire, Menelik I. Again, from her come so many more jewels of a people and connection of the Abrahamic brotherhood, worldwide. Ishmael, Isaac, and the sons of Keturah connected the then known world by brotherhood, literally. From this came many nations, which is exactly what God told Abraham many years before he had a child. Hagar began the fulfillment with the birth of Ishmael, Keturah enhanced it. Only Isaac, the son of Sarah, was childless at this point. But that too was about to change. Without Keturah blessing Abraham with so many children, it would have been only Ishmael and later Isaac to spread the seed of Abraham into the world, from a spiritual point of view. This does not happen without queen mother Keturah, whose name means fragrance. She gave Abraham a sweet smell of life in his older age and the world is thankful and forever changed because of it.

Proverbs 19:14

House and riches *are* the inheritance of fathers: and a prudent wife *is* from the LORD.

King Menelik I of Ethiopia
© Britannica

Death of Arphaxad

Jasher 25:28

And Rebecca the daughter of Bethuel, the wife of Abraham's son Isaac, was barren in those days, she had no offspring; and Isaac dwelt with his father in the land of Canaan; and the Lord was with Isaac; and Arpachshad the son of Shem the son of Noah died in those days, in the forty-eighth year of the life of Isaac, and all the days that Arpachshad lived were four hundred and thirty-eight years, and he died.

The first child born in the new world after Noah's Flood was Arpachshad (Arphaxad). His name in Hebrew means 'healer' or 'releaser'. Why this name? Because it means that he was born to both heal and be a symbol of healing in the new world. From him will come a release. His alternate name meaning is 'stronghold of Chaldees'. Why does this name matter? Because he was a ruler in Mesopotamia and is considered the father of the Chaldees. Abraham was from Ur of the Chaldees, meaning that he was the father of the people who lived in that area that were to be called Chaldees. These are the indigenous people of modern-day southern Iraq. These people later became the Babylonians. They were a well-respected group within the nations of people who joined Nimrod at the Tower of Babel. These are the people who maintained this area of the world after God confounded the languages and sent people all over the planet.

Chaldeans

© Chaldean News

Arphaxad's death symbolized the end of an era beyond his loss of life. When Isaac was 48 years old, Arphaxad had lived to be a 438-year-old man. He was meant to heal the world, like a doctor with medicine. But like our modern-day pharmaceutical crisis has shown us, the misuse of a good thing can go bad, quickly.

Medicine for healing is innocent on the surface, a gift of God. However, it is when it is abused or not used as directed that you get a problem. Arphaxad's children fell into that category during the time of Nimrod. They helped him build the Tower of Babel and partake in the foolishness of his kingdom. He may have been meant to heal the world, but too much of his gift ended up being a part of the curse. His death meant that the leader of the Chaldees was gone. From him comes the Babylonian people, which is directly connected to the Hebrew world until the end of time. The world system that birthed the ideology of the Egyptians, Persians, Greeks, and Romans all come from the Sumerians, which later became the Babylonians, a faction of which were the Chaldeans. These ancient people's knowledge was and still remains meant to heal the world, but evil has overtaken it and how it has been distributed, just like Nimrod using the knowledge and wisdom of the Chaldees to do evil. Remember, Nimrod was meant to help people go in the right direction of life under God, as he started out as a beloved one of God, but he chose to go away from the LORD. To *Make It Plain*, Arphaxad's death symbolized that there was a coming shift in the health of the world's spiritual and mental state. As his name means healer on one hand, his name also means releaser, which means a release of something was about to happen that will change the way the world operates from his death forward. Rest in peace, Arphaxad, son of Shem.

From Barren to Blessed

Jasher 26:1

And in the fifty-ninth year of the life of Isaac the son of Abraham, Rebecca his wife was still barren in those days.

After 19 years of being married to Isaac, Rebekah was still barren. It was not from a lack of trying. The opening of the womb for a woman to conceive is a gift of God given unto women. Some women understand this, not all women do. Some abuse the right to have children, some appreciate the opportunity to continue family. On a scientific note, without the blessing of children, there is no human species. So, needless to say, women having the ability to have children is a huge deal for any family, especially a married couple of almost 20 years. For Rebekah, this had to be heartbreaking. As a young woman, wanting to give her husband children had to be a pressing issue. Isaac had to feel the same way but he had close family experience in this area that could help him cope with it: Sarah, his mother. The bond Isaac had with Sarah was so close, primarily because she was barren for 90 years before she had him. As her only child, they were connected in ways that is hard for anyone to understand other than Abraham.

In understanding this, Isaac had a reference point, Abraham, to help him work through the situation. This experience was invaluable in helping Rebekah navigate the mental and emotional agony of not having children at this time. With that said, Rebekah decided to do what any woman of substance would do: she asked for help. Her steps have given us a scriptural blueprint on how to address barrenness.

Jasher 26: 2-5

And Rebecca said unto Isaac, Truly I have heard, my lord, that thy mother Sarah was barren in her days until my Lord Abraham,
thy father, prayed for her and she conceived by him. 3 Now therefore stand up, pray thou also to God and he will hear thy prayer
and remember us through his mercies. 4 And Isaac answered his wife Rebecca, saying, Abraham has already prayed for me to God
to multiply his seed, now therefore this barrenness must proceed to us from thee. 5 And Rebecca said unto him, But arise now thou
also and pray, that the Lord may hear thy prayer and grant me children, and Isaac hearkened to the words of his wife, and Isaac
and his wife rose up and went to the land of Moriah to pray there and to seek the Lord, and when they had reached that place
Isaac stood up and prayed to the Lord on account of his wife because she was barren.

The first step Rebekah took was to go to her husband. She didn't go to her friends, family, social media, doctor, etc. She went to her husband, the one whom she shares the issue with. Also, notice how she addressed him, in respect. She referenced his mother, showing her ability to take interest in Isaac's first love in a woman. Every man's first love is his mother or a motherly figure. In your mother's womb do we form and become human, so our attachment to anything substantial in life begins in the womb of our mother, which is why there's a common theme that dating women learn about men that is commonly true, not always true. That theme is 'watch how a man treats his mother which could show you how he'll treat you.' How Isaac loved his mother was an indicator how he was going to love his wife. Even though Rebekah never knew Sarah, she met her through the impact she had on Isaac, Abraham, and the world that she was married into. The first place Rebekah visited after marrying Isaac was the tent of Sarah, which was Isaac's way of showing his love and reverence to his mother. This was very wise of Rebekah to speak to Isaac from an understanding of his experience with barrenness. By doing so, it allowed Isaac to connect with Rebekah in a more intimate way. Teamwork.

The second thing she did, which is huge, is that she asked for prayer. We cannot overstate this in the process of having children. She asked for a multi-layered prayer. Not a personal prayer, which she had already done for herself, but she asked for a specific prayer from her husband and father-in-law Abraham. When Isaac responded out of love and said Abraham already prayed, but nothing has happened so being barren must be what God wants, Rebekah respectfully asked him to pray on his own behalf and not the behalf of Abraham. That was a grown woman move. She didn't complain and pitch a fit, storm out, answer emotionally or otherwise. She respectfully responded and asked her husband for his direct prayer. Abraham's prayer was good, but she wanted Isaac's prayer, direct to connect. She understood something that Isaac perhaps was missing. Abraham's experience of a barren wife was Abraham's direct experience, not Isaac. Isaac was the result of a prayer answered. Being that she was barren, it was now time for Isaac to do his own prayer and perhaps the LORD would listen to him, directly, allowing him to take a step in life as a man to separate himself from his father even though they were in similar positions. Indirectly, she was helping Isaac establish himself in the eyes of God separately from Abraham. When he obliged her, they both journeyed to Mt. Moriah, to pray to the LORD, together, separate from everyone. A blessing within a blessing on a blessing. Keep in mind, this is the same mountain Isaac was set to be sacrificed on.

Jasher 26: 6-8

And Isaac said, O Lord God of heaven and earth, whose goodness and mercies fill the earth, thou who didst take my father from his father's house and from his birthplace, and didst bring him unto this land, and didst say unto him, To thy seed will I give the land, and thou didst promise him and didst declare unto him, I will multiply thy seed as the stars of heaven and as the sand of the sea, now may thy words be verified which thou didst speak unto my father. 7 For thou art the Lord our God, our eyes are toward thee to give us seed of men, as thou didst promise us, for thou art the Lord our God and our eyes are directed toward thee only.8 And the Lord heard the prayer of Isaac the son of Abraham, and the Lord was entreated of him and Rebecca his wife conceived.

God heard him. Better yet, God heard them. Without Rebekah's respectful plea to her husband, perhaps she stays barren. Even though Isaac loved Rebekah, it was not uncommon for men to marry other women who were fertile for him to have children. Sarah petitioned Abraham to marry Hagar because she was barren, even though Abraham loved Sarah. Rebekah understood the assignment and didn't want to share her husband with any woman. Notice the learned history lesson? Even though Sarah is regarded as the biblical model wife and mother, Rebekah learned from her missteps. Sarah didn't go to Abraham in the same fashion that Rebekah did. This was wisdom on display that Rebekah was showing us all. Abraham couldn't go to his father for prayer, but Isaac could. Sarah tried to speed up God's promise by arranging a marriage of her husband to Hagar, which eventually led to a marital separation after the birth of Ishmael. Rebekah respectfully asked her husband to pray for her, with her. God saw the difference, and according to HIS plan, grace, and mercy, HE opened Rebekah's womb and allowed her to become pregnant.

Genesis 25: 19-21

And these *are* the generations of Isaac, Abraham's son: Abraham begat Isaac: 20 And Isaac was forty years old when he took Rebekah to wife, the daughter of Bethuel the Syrian of Padanaram, the sister to Laban the Syrian. 21 And Isaac intreated the LORD for his wife, because she *was* barren: and the LORD was intreated of him, and Rebekah his wife conceived.

This, ladies and gentlemen, is the blueprint that moved God once. Why can't it move HIM again?

From barren to blessed. Just like that.

Isaiah 66:9

Shall I bring to the birth, and not cause to bring forth? saith the LORD: shall I cause to bring forth, and shut *the womb*? saith thy God.

The Humor of God

Jasher 26:9

And in about seven months after the children struggled together within her, and it pained her greatly that she was wearied on account of them, and she said to all the women who were then in the land, Did such a thing happen to you as it has to me? and they said unto her, No.

From the bliss of a first-time pregnancy to the pains of constant fighting and movement in the womb, Rebekah was vexed. 7 months in and she was going through it! She prayed for the situation but didn't know this was coming with it. The humor of God. The pregnancy bothered her to the point that she went to different women in the land they were living and asked them did this same thing happen during their pregnancy. Everyone told her no. Not some women, but EVERY woman told her no. What a comfort! For no one to be able to relate? That's crazy!

The humor of God, when understood, offers perspective that quite often we never take the next step to see. For example, Abraham had no one to relate to with his struggles from birth. Sure, he learned about God in the house of Noah and Shem, but his walk and journey was his own. It developed his faith and trust in the LORD. This same man became Rebekah's father-in-law. The fact that she was told no by EVERY woman she asked could be looked at the same way Abraham defined Hebrew, which means to stand against the world or on the other side. Perhaps, she was experiencing something no other woman was because she was about to give birth to something that no other woman could.....just a thought, perspective. Who could know the answer?

Only the LORD HIMself, the one who opened her womb to get pregnant. So, she went to her elders Abraham, Shem, and Eber to see if they would ask the LORD on her behalf.

Jasher 26: 10-11

And she said unto them, Why am I alone in this amongst all the women that were upon earth? and she went to the land of Moriah to seek the Lord on account of this; and she went to Shem and Eber his son to make inquiries of them in this matter, and that they should seek the Lord in this thing respecting her. 11 And she also asked Abraham to seek and inquire of the Lord about all that had befallen her.

Another wise move on Rebekah's behalf. Shout out to her for teaching us all how to follow the blueprint to moving the mind and heart of God, even if what's going on is in HIS will. You have to respect her hustle and willingness to ask for help. Just as she asked, when they heard back from the LORD, all three men told her the same thing.

Jasher 26:12

And they all inquired of the Lord concerning this matter, and they brought her word from the Lord and told her, Two children are in thy womb, and two nations shall rise from them; and one nation shall be stronger than the other, and the greater shall serve the younger.

The humor of God, again. Two children, two nations. One will be stronger than the other, and the stronger one will serve the younger. Wow! This is why they were fighting. This is also why to this day, they are still fighting! From barren to blessed, from blessed to stressed. Again, the humor of God!

After hearing this from Abraham, Shem, and Eber, Rebekah wanted to ask God herself what was going on. Not that she didn't believe her elders, but she wanted to hear it from the LORD God with her own ears. Well, God is not bashful, and HE has no secrets or respecter of persons. She asked, HE obliged.

Genesis 25: 22-23

And the children struggled together within her; and she said, If *it be* so, why *am* I thus? And she went to inquire of the LORD. 23 And the LORD
said unto her, Two nations *are* in thy womb, and two manner of people shall be separated from thy bowels; and *the one* people shall be
stronger than *the other* people; and the elder shall serve the younger.

Yes, the exact same message. Nothing to see here, just confirmation that the LORD said what HE said and it's time to move on. She asked, HE responded, time to accept it. 7 months in, 2 months to go, 2 nations to come.

Genesis 25: 24-26

And when her days to be delivered were fulfilled, behold, *there were* twins in her womb. 25 And the first came out red, all over like
an hairy garment; and they called his name Esau. 26 And after that came his brother out, and his hand took hold on Esau's heel;
and his name was called Jacob: and Isaac *was* threescore years old when she bare them.

All praise to the Most High, the LORD God Almighty!! She did it! Rebekah did it! From barren to blessed, from blessed to stressed, and now, from stressed to passing the test! She did it! Twins, two boys, two fighters, two ways in which they entered the world.

How Two Nations Were Born

Esau, the first son, entered the world red, hairy, with all the birth rights given to the eldest son
Jacob, the second son, entered the world holding on to his brother's heel, never conceding

What a way to be born. These two were destined to do something great! The people who witnessed their birth in the land added to their birth story...

Jasher 26: 13-15

And when her days to be delivered were completed, she knelt down, and behold there were twins in her womb, as the Lord had
spoken to her. 14 And the first came out red all over like a hairy garment, and all the people of the land called his name Esau,
saying, That this one was made complete from the womb. 15 And after that came his brother, and his hand took hold of Esau's
heel, therefore they called his name Jacob.

One came out complete looking, the other came out holding on, signifying his effort to be first. Again, they fought one another the entire time in the womb. Regardless of their birth story and how the people of the land saw them when they were born, only four people knew what this meant: Abraham, Shem, Eber, and their mother Rebekah. Isaac was told what it meant but he wasn't told directly from the LORD what it meant. Remember, God told them that the greater shall serve the latter, which meant that the first shall serve the second. So yes, even though Esau was born first with the birth rights of the oldest bestowed upon him, that grabbing of the heel was a signature move by God to show that HIS will remains supreme regardless of what happens. For a 60-year-old Isaac (meaning of threescore [3 x 20 = 60], a score = 20) and first-time father, this had to be a wild event to witness! Again, the humor of God.

Don't think God has a sense of humor? Don't think that HE laughs? Don't think HE'll make you laugh?

Read....

Psalms 2:4

He that sitteth in the heavens shall laugh: the Lord shall have them in derision.

37:13

The Lord shall laugh at him: for he seeth that his day is coming.

59:8

But thou, O LORD, shalt laugh at them; thou shalt have all the heathen in derision.

Job 8:21

Till he fill thy mouth with laughing, and thy lips with rejoicing.

Remember, Isaac's name means.....you guessed it.....laughter!

ESAU and **Jacob**

Genesis 25: 27-28

And the boys grew: and Esau was a cunning hunter, a man of the field; and Jacob *was* a plain man, dwelling in tents. 28 And Isaac loved Esau, because he did eat of *his* venison: but Rebekah loved Jacob.

Two nations came from one womb. Esau and Jacob, twins, two different characters, two different destinies. Esau, the first from the womb, means hairy. This is what the people meant when they said he was born complete. Most children aren't born hairy all over as he was. Most children are born smooth, and the hairs grow as they do with age. That was the case with Jacob, who was known as a plain and smooth boy. His name means to follow or overreach, the identity of him clutching his brother's heel.

These two twin boys were different from birth not only in appearance but in their desires. Esau grew to be an outdoorsman, a man of the field, a very cunning hunter, very skilled, learning how the world works outside of people. Jacob, on the other hand, stayed in the house a lot, learning how things worked around people, more political. This is why the Bible says Isaac loved Esau, but Rebekah loved Jacob. This doesn't mean they hated the other, just that they had a preference of their boys due to their similarities and desires. Isaac was more of an outdoorsman, so he would have had more experiences with Esau than Jacob in that world. Esau had several things in common with Isaac's big brother, Ishmael, who was an expert archer. Jacob, on the other hand, spent more time with his mother, in the tents, learning how people work, how families work, how communication work between people. He would have had more experiences with his mother than his father and brother due to their choices and day to day activities.

Jasher 26: 17-18

And the boys grew up to their fifteenth year, and they came amongst the society of men. Esau was a designing and deceitful man, and an expert hunter in the field, and Jacob was a man perfect and wise, dwelling in tents, feeding flocks and learning the instructions of the Lord and the commands of his father and mother. 18 And Isaac and the children of his household dwelt with his father Abraham in the land of Canaan, as God had commanded them.

When Isaac was 75 years old, and Abraham 175, the boys began to develop their reputation even more amongst the people of the land. This is very important to understand. Esau learned how to be deceitful and an excellent planner or trapper, which is what designing means here. Jacob, on the other hand, was learning how to lead by feeding flocks and learning the ways of God. Two different nations.

When these two were growing up, Ishmael and the other sons of Abraham via Keturah came back to meet their brothers and cousins. The 15-year timeline that we speak of in relations to the birth of Esau and Jacob to this point is highlighted by scripture telling us for the 2nd time that Abraham sent his sons away and Isaac remained (Jasher 26: 19-20). This is very important to understand before we finalize this work. Abraham had his sons know and meet one another, receive gifts, then go back to their respective homes so in the future they or in their travels, they will know one another and so will their children. By him doing this, he created a table of nations of his own children that would be underappreciated in his life story. Meanwhile, it validated the prophecy the LORD given to him of his offspring being many nations. The Bible itself from the birth of Ishmael to the book of Revelations details all kinds of people and various different nations, gentiles as scripture calls them and us, who are intertwined in the story of the Hebrews. Why? Several of those nations are the sons of Abraham that spread out into the world. Why did God do this, outside of HIS promise to Abraham? Look at it this way....

The world was sick. God brought the flood.

Arphaxad was born into the new world, symbolizing healing. He was allowed to live for 400+ years, seeing a nation come from him, that worked with the world leader Nimrod, who turned on God and led the world to go against God.
Nimrod became the first hunter of men and animal flesh. He was the world's first AntiChrist.
Abraham became the first Hebrew amongst men. He was the precursor to the Christ.
God promises a new nation, one that will serve him, through Abraham. Isaac is born.
Arphaxad dies, leaving the world without a healer, leaving it sicker, mentally and spiritually.
Isaac has Esau and Jacob.
The world was sick with an open wound. God sends medicine, one who hunts and one who restores.
God has sent medicine through the form of two boys, Esau and Jacob

Esau was a hunter, a trapper, in the way of his uncle Ishmael, but better.

Jacob was a people person, a restorer, in the way of his grandfather Abraham.

They were the medicine. One's job was to seek and destroy the bacteria in the world. The other's job was to restore the way of the LORD in the world, thus giving the world new life, new blood, a new way. Together, and yet apart, these twins reshaped the world.

To Isaac, My Son…

Jasher 26:21

And Abraham gave all that he had to his son Isaac, and he also gave him all his treasures.

It was time. Abraham was at the end, and he knew it. Most of his loved ones who lived alongside him were dead and gone. He had a new wife, Keturah, and many sons who had children of their own. He went from being a man with no children for 100 years to a father, grandfather, and great-grandfather in a matter of 75 years. It had to be an awesome feeling to see God's plan unfold right before his eyes. God had truly kept his word with Abraham and allowed him to experience the blessings and promises of the LORD in a time of heathenism and idolatry. Abraham was the exception, he was the gift that many people around the world knew existed as the opposite of the way of the world. With his children by Keturah being sent away with gifts and Ishmael leaving again to go back to his home near Havilah, it was now time to bless the one person he hadn't to this point: Isaac.

Jasher 26: 22-27

And he commanded him saying, Dost thou not know and understand the Lord is God in heaven and in earth, and there is no other
beside him? 23 And it was he who took me from my father's house, and from my birth place, and gave me all the delights upon
earth; who delivered me from the counsel of the wicked, for in him did I trust. 24 And he brought me to this place, and he
delivered me from Ur Casdim; and he said unto me, To thy seed will I give all these lands, and they shall inherit them when they
keep my commandments, my statutes and my judgments that I have commanded thee, and which I shall command them. 25 Now
therefore my son, hearken to my voice, and keep the commandments of the Lord thy God, which I commanded thee, do not turn
from the right way either to the right or to the left, in order that it may be well with thee and thy children after thee forever. 26 And
remember the wonderful works of the Lord, and his kindness that he has shown toward us, in having delivered us from the hands
of our enemies, and the Lord our God caused them to fall into our hands; and now therefore keep all that I have commanded thee,
and turn not away from the commandments of thy God, and serve none beside him, in order that it may be well with thee and thy
seed after thee. 27 And teach thou thy children and thy seed the instructions of the Lord and his commandments, and teach them
the upright way in which they should go, in order that it may be well with them forever.

Wow. Humbling. Thank you, father Abraham for this direction. These words are more than a gift, they are the treasure that Abraham kept for Isaac that was different than the gifts he gave his other sons. These words, if you read them correctly, tells his life story, how to follow the LORD, and how to be better than himself at following God. This is a blueprint to faithfulness, a guiding map to holiness. Abraham didn't credit himself for his providence and position in life, but the LORD God HIMself. In essence, Abraham gave Isaac the instructions of life to teach to Esau and Jacob, the future two nations through whom HIS promise of blessings would come.

Jasher 26:28

And Isaac answered his father and said unto him, That which my Lord has commanded that will I do, and I will not depart from the commands of the Lord my God, I will keep all that he commanded me; and Abraham blessed his son Isaac, and also his children; and Abraham taught Jacob the instruction of the Lord and his ways.

Humble and respectful. This is one of the most honorable things a man can do and say to his father at the elder stage in their life. He acknowledged what Abraham told him and assured him that he would follow the LORD. In the process of that promise, he learned the ways of Abraham with God. This had to be a special time in both men's lives as Abraham had a chance to live out his final instructions to his son Isaac while Esau and Jacob were teenagers. It had to be a cool feeling to be there to see such a blessing.

Abraham was a blessed man. In my earlier learnings, I did not know that he saw Esau and Jacob born. I did not know he called all of children together and sent them out again. I did not know that he gave Isaac his last charter and the intimate details of faithfulness as we have learned above. He showed us how a father is supposed to live out his instructions, flaws and all, then pass them to his children as gifts and treasure. Abraham literally gave us the blueprint to please God and live a life as a husband and father in this world. This was his final chance to gift his promise with a promise.

For that, we salute and thank you, father Abraham.

3 John 1:4

I have no greater joy than to hear that my children walk in truth.

Death of Abraham

Genesis 25: 7-8

And these *are* the days of the years of Abraham's life which he lived, an hundred threescore and fifteen years. 8 Then Abraham gave up the ghost, and died in a good old age, an old man, and full *of years;* and was gathered to his people.

At the ripe old age of 175 years old (a hundred threescore and fifteen = 100 + 3 x 20 = 160 + 15 = 175), fully blessed and having seen the promise of the LORD revealed and realized, the great heart of Abraham gave out. He died, in his home, around his family, in the land that the LORD God gave him peace within. Everything he stood for, everything he gave the world, the blueprint he laid for faithfulness to the LORD, was now done. His birth was shown in the stars, prophesied to alter the way men see God, chosen to be the opposite of Nimrod. Only Christ was born with more prophetic revelation in the heaven and Earth than Abraham. He was born with an expectation unlike anyone else prior to him, especially in a paganistic world. Anti-god prophets even saw his birth being their end as they petitioned Nimrod to kill him at birth. 175 years later, Abraham was content with his work and worship of the LORD after doing HIS will for the duration of his life. After giving all of his gifts and treasure to his children throughout the known world, especially teaching Isaac the ways of the LORD personally, Abraham took his last breath, and passed away.

Jasher 26:29

And it was at that time that Abraham died, in the fifteenth year of the life of Jacob and Esau, the sons of Isaac, and all the days of Abraham were one hundred and seventy-five years, and he died and was gathered to his people in good old age, old and satisfied with days, and Isaac and Ishmael his sons buried him.

Isaac, at 75 years old, saw his father Abraham die. His sons, Esau and Jacob, also witnessed their grandfather Abraham pass. This is very important to understand. Why? God blessed Abraham to see them grow to the age that they were regarded as young men, old enough to care for themselves and start a family of their own. Abraham had a chance to see Esau and Jacob grow from their entrance into this world to 15-year-old young men who had developed their own personalities in the world. The blessing of seeing them grow was just as impactful for Abraham as it was for the twins Esau and Jacob. This time with Abraham before his death blessed them for the rest of their lives as these two twins would be the left and right arms of the law of God that would bring the world system to its knees.

When Abraham died, the word spread to the known world that Abraham passed on. When Ishmael heard it, he came immediately to Beersheba to Abraham's home to bury his father with his brother Isaac. While they were consoling one another with their loss, something amazing happened. They lifted up their eyes and looked....

Jasher 26: 30-31

And when the inhabitants of Canaan heard that Abraham was dead, they all came with their kings and princes and all their men to bury Abraham. 31 And all the inhabitants of the land of Haran, and all the families of the house of Abraham, and all the princes and grandees, and the sons of Abraham by the concubines, all came when they heard of Abraham's death, and they requited Abraham's kindness, and comforted Isaac his son, and they buried Abraham in the cave which he bought from Ephron the Hittite and his children, for the possession of a burial place.

They all came. They all came.

The whole land of Canaan came to pay their respect to Abraham. All the kings. All the princes. All their men came. All the people of Haran came. All the families related to Abraham came. All his concubines and their children came.

They all came. They all came.

Imagine the sight of this. All these people, coming on the horizon for the eye to see, great and small, rich and poor, man, woman, and child. All coming to pay their respect to the man who was known for being kind to them all. His travels and tents were welcoming to all. Abraham lived as a man of honor and respect that everyone who heard about his death in the area left what they were doing and came. That shows the maginatude of his life's work, that even those that didn't know him came because of his kindness to any and everyone who passed his way in life. For 175 years, imagine how many people he helped that's not recorded. Again, all of these people came to say their final goodbye. They not only came to pay their respects just cause, but they felt the loss. Not just for the moment, but for an extended period of time.

Jasher 26: 32-33

And all the inhabitants of Canaan, and all those who had known Abraham, wept for Abraham a whole year, and men and women mourned over him.33 And all the little children, and all the inhabitants of the land wept on account of Abraham, for Abraham had been good to them all, and because he had been upright with God and men.

After Ishmael and Isaac buried Abraham in the Cave of Macpelah next to Sarah, the mourning process began. For a whole year, all mourned Abraham. Even the little children mourned him for a year. Think about that for a second, even the little children cried for a year because of the loss of Abraham. Most kids don't cry at a funeral unless they are old enough to understand what is going on. The little children cried, people, wow! Not just for a few minutes or that day, but they too cried for a year. The impact was felt by everyone, young and old. Because Abraham was a good man, upright with God and men, the tidal wave of his death swept through the known and spreading world. Who was like Abraham among men? What words were said that stood for Abraham like words on a tombstone?

Jasher 26: 34-37

And there arose not a man who feared God like unto Abraham, for he had feared his God from his youth, and had served the Lord, and had gone in all his ways during his life, from his childhood to the day of his death. 35 And the Lord was with him and delivered him from the counsel of Nimrod and his people, and when he made war with the four kings of Elam he conquered them. 36 And he brought all the children of the earth to the service of God, and he taught them the ways of the Lord, and caused them to know the Lord. 37 And he formed a grove and he planted a vineyard therein, and he had always prepared in his tent meat and drink to those that passed through the land, that they might satisfy themselves in his house.

Wow. Humbling, very humbling. No one feared God like Abraham. From his youth, all his life, he served the LORD. In essence, his way of life defeated Nimrod and the highly regarded kings of Elam that lived in the ways of Nimrod. Abraham did as God wanted, Nimrod and his followers didn't.

So, what did God say in regards to Abraham to let people know, for all generations, why Abraham should be respected beyond what we know?

Jasher 26:38

And the Lord God delivered the whole earth on account of Abraham.

Abraham's life and dedication was represented on the same level as Noah and the flood. Wow! Think about this for a minute. God destroyed the world via water with the flood but allowed mankind to survive on the account of Noah. With Abraham, HE allowed them to spiritually be delivered from destruction. The whole Earth was delivered because of him. Nimrod ruled the world, evil personified. The world should have been destroyed because of this evil, but Abraham's way of living and faith allowed God to deliver mankind on his behalf. This is amazing!

Jasher 26:39

And it was after the death of Abraham that God blessed his son Isaac and his children, and the Lord was with Isaac as he had been with his father Abraham, for Isaac kept all the commandments of the Lord as Abraham his father had commanded him; he did not turn to the right or to the left from the right path which his father had commanded him.

Isaac took his father's words and ways to heart. He did exactly as Abraham told him, lived as Abraham did, and God accepted him as such. The blessings and covering of the LORD not only was spread to Isaac but his children as well.

To be clear, Abraham was the opposite energy of Nimrod, like faithfulness is the opposite of surety. We must understand this concept. The opposite of the faith is not really doubt, because faith has its doubt. Abraham's life was wrapped in doubt. We know about Abraham' doubts, they are scripturally and biblically documented. So again, we understand doubt as a believer. To be clear, we are not speaking about doubt in God, but doubt in self or situations we place ourselves in. Therefore, doubt is not the opposite of faith, but surety is. Surety sits while faith stands. Surety blocks out what we see while faith widens our view. What's interesting about surety and faith is that by mastering one, you master the other. This is what Abraham did. How so? He was sure in his faith, which is what a believer truly is. The formula that God wants for us is faith plus surety equaling holiness. It's not about perfection, but the process. Faith processed is righteousness. Surety processed is trust. When it is not processed, it becomes idolatry, which is a violation of the first commandment. This too is one of the mysteries of the faith.

When we think faith, we must thank father Abraham. He showed the world that it is okay to follow the way of God your entire life. The concept of faith was put on display with his life and how God delivered the world on his behalf. There has been billions of people born since the creation of man. He is one of one. Through him comes the Christ. Through him comes the Hebrews. Through him comes the end of evil. Through him comes the end of Nimrod.

Nimrod chose surety. Abraham chose faith. From him, we learn how to obey God in holiness, via faith. From him comes the three monotheistic faiths: Judaism, Christianity, and Islam. All three belief structures claim Abraham to be their father. All three are faiths. All three seek to follow one belief: One God. Abraham stood on the other side against evil, becoming Hebrew. From him comes the nation that followed his way to God, later called the Hebrews. What was their qualification? Faith.

Hebrews 11: 8-19

By faith Abraham, when he was called to go out into a place which he should after receive for an inheritance, obeyed; and he went out, not
knowing whither he went. 9 By faith he sojourned in the land of promise, as *in* a strange country, dwelling in tabernacles with Isaac and Jacob,
the heirs with him of the same promise: 10 For he looked for a city which hath foundations, whose builder and maker *is* God. 11 Through faith
also Sara herself received strength to conceive seed, and was delivered of a child when she was past age, because she judged him faithful who
had promised. 12 Therefore sprang there even of one, and him as good as dead, *so many* as the stars of the sky in multitude, and as the sand
which is by the sea shore innumerable. 13 These all died in faith, not having received the promises, but having seen them afar off, and were
persuaded of *them*, and embraced *them*, and confessed that they were strangers and pilgrims on the earth. 14 For they that say such things
declare plainly that they seek a country. 15 And truly, if they had been mindful of that *country* from whence they came out, they might have
had opportunity to have returned. 16 But now they desire a better *country*, that is, an heavenly: wherefore God is not ashamed to be called
their God: for he hath prepared for them a city. 17 By faith Abraham, when he was tried, offered up Isaac: and he that had received the
promises offered up his only begotten *son*, 18 Of whom it was said, That in Isaac shall thy seed be called: 19 Accounting that God *was* able to
raise *him* up, even from the dead; from whence also he received him in a figure.

Thank you, father Abraham, for the blueprint on how to walk in faith. The world has never been the same since you took the approach to show us God's way. Those that taught you had to be proud, in a Godly way, of the path you took. We are thankful, humbled, and amazed at how you stood in faith against Nimrod and the world. God is the Greatest!

Bless you Abraham. Bless you.

Genesis 25: 9-11

And his sons Isaac and Ishmael buried him in the cave of Machpelah, in the field of Ephron the son of Zohar the Hittite,
which *is* before Mamre; 10 The field which Abraham purchased of the sons of Heth: there was Abraham buried, and Sarah his
wife. 11 And it came to pass after the death of Abraham, that God blessed his son Isaac; and Isaac dwelt by the well Lahairoi.

The Shockwave

1 John 3:8

He that committeth sin is of the devil; for the devil sinneth from the beginning. For this purpose the Son of God was manifested, that he might destroy the works of the devil.

When Abraham died, the world changed. As we read, even the little children of the land of Canaan mourned for a year. Isaac and Ishmael buried their father in the Cave of Macpelah next to Sarah while his other children by Keturah and other concubines went back to their respective homes to continue their lives. Eliezer, Isaac, Esau, and Jacob remained in the same place they did prior to Abraham's death. Again, the world changed and the news spread everywhere that the great Abraham had died.

Nimrod, the arch-nemesis and sworn enemy of Abraham was still living in his kingdom. He and his family had taught the world evil in ways that has yet to be duplicated. The kingdoms that came from him even overtook certain areas that he ruled over as expressions of Nimrod but they too were not as powerful as the great Nimrod, neither did they have his age and experience of ruling.
Imagine how Nimrod felt when he heard the word that Abraham had died. He probably was ecstatic! His one and only true enemy, other than God himself, was now dead. Trying to kill Abraham since before he was born was a task that no man on Earth could do, beginning with the world ruler, Nimrod. But now that Abraham was dead, there had to be a sigh of relief and celebrations going on within the mind and heart of the evil king, even if the land mourned. Nimrod was a man a great reputation, so to hear that he had outlived his enemy in Abraham was a great reason to celebrate.

Or so he thought.

Reader, study the ways of the LORD and you can foresee what is about to happen next. When Arphaxad, the healer, died, it sent out a sign of coming change into the Earth. God was not pleased with mankind and the healer himself couldn't help make the world a healthier place, spiritually. Despite the teachings of Noah, Shem, and Eber, the world chose to follow the ways of Nimrod and his family. The Egyptians had emerged as a rulership that followed the ways of the Sumerians. In the far East, the children of Sin, later called the Chinese, were establishing their kingdoms. The sons of Japheth were establishing the European continent. The sons of Ham were establishing Africa. All were following the ways of Nimrod, re-establishing a different way of belief, changing names of their deities, but going against God all the same. This is why you see pyramids all over the world, which look like the famed pyramids of Egypt, who were first implemented in Sumer and Babel (Babylon). Even the pyramids of Meroe, Nubia, are older than the great pyramids of Egypt. Regardless, these large tombs are examples of the teaching of Nimrod.

As spiritual sickness spread, only Abraham and those that followed him gave God reason not to destroy the world once and for all. On the behalf of Abraham, God gave mankind another chance. Through him, the world still spun. When Isaac took on the ways of his father, the LORD allowed the world to do what it was going to do while Isaac was set to be the beacon of light that the world needed to follow in order to find God again. Justice, however, needed to be served for such a cruel time of sin. God is the judge, the final say, HIM, and it was time for change.
It was after the death of Arphaxad that God cut time down for his beloved Abraham, something HE had done before the flood to the righteous so they wouldn't see the horrors of the world, which resulted in the Great Flood of Noah. In that time, God took all sinners to death, all humans, after giving them a chance to repent, in a global baptizing. What HE was about to do now would show justice in a different way. Instead of taking all sinners to death, HE decided to administer justice to the one who called himself justice, the world leader and judge, the one HE once loved, the teacher of sin and antigod behavior, the greatest sinner of them all, the *World's First AntiChrist* himself......

Nimrod.

God considered Nimrod and his path.

1. He tried to kill Abraham as a child.
2. He loved the wilderness, which was a representative of wildness.
3. He loved hunting more than anything, which shows his attempt to control life and death.
4. He created the concept of a crown for the head to show kingship, which every ruler wears.
5. He created evil chaos in a way that the world has never seen before.
6. He was the World's First AntiChrist because he stood against everything God stands for.

So how was God going to administer justice to such a monument of a man???
1....with a child
2....in a place the place that Nimrod loved the most
3....hunting, the thing Nimrod was the best at
4....by taking his crown, and head
5....his death would create chaos amongst sinners
6....the example of what the coming Christ would do to ALL evil, including the AntiChrist.

Court was now in session.

It all began in a field....

Death of Nimrod

Genesis 25: 27-28

And the boys grew: and Esau was a cunning hunter, a man of the field; and Jacob *was* a plain man, dwelling in tents. 28 And Isaac loved Esau, because he did eat of *his* venison: but Rebekah loved Jacob.

Esau and Jacob.

Esau, a cunning hunter, a man of the field. Jacob, a plain man, dwelling in tents. Isaac had more in common with Esau as Rebekah had favor on Jacob. These two twins were the remnant of Abraham, the children of the promise of God, chosen. They were born together, fighting in the womb, two nations. One was chosen to serve the other as Abraham bore witness from the LORD. These two were prophesied to be fighters, from the womb. Esau the hunter, and Jacob the man of the people. Isaac their father, his name meaning laughter, was going to live to see something that not even he could imagine. His birth, name, and presence in the world would be a symbol of God getting the last laugh in regards to sin. His two sons were about to change the world on a grand scale that we still feel the shockwaves of today. But how?

It happened on a random day while everyone was operating business as usual. Esau, the eldest, was out doing what he does best, hunting.

Jasher 27:1

And Esau at that time, after the death of Abraham, frequently went in the field to hunt.

In a field.

A cunning hunter, 15 years old, in a field. After the death of his grandfather, you can imagine how it made Esau feel being in the same place as his grandfather when he died. Most people, when dealing with a major death in the family, take time off to clear their head and or dive deeper into their work. Esau was no different as he had a reputation of being a very skilled hunter, so going more frequently into the field to hunt would have been a natural reaction. He, like his uncle Ishmael, were known in their respective lands as the best of the best hunters. Only one person rivaled their reputation in the world at that time as a hunter: The Great Nimrod. Esau was in Canaan and his uncle Ishmael was in Havilah, to the south, near modern-day Saudi Arabia. Nimrod was far away in Mesopotamia, ruling his kingdom....

....or so they thought.

Jasher 27: 2-3

And Nimrod king of Babel, the same was Amraphel, also frequently went with his mighty men to hunt in the field, and to walk about with his men in the cool of the day. 3 And Nimrod was observing Esau all the days, for a jealousy was formed in the heart of Nimrod against Esau all the days.

Nimrod had eyes on the house of Abraham for many years. He never stopped after Abraham left Ur.

Wow! You didn't see that one coming.

In the midst of detailing the story of Abraham and how the Christ comes through his bloodline, Nimrod was always looking into Abraham's life as well, just from a distance. Even though he was a long way away in Babel, ruling his empire under the name Amraphel, he kept watch on his arch nemesis Abraham. The death of Abraham didn't deter him from his hatred of the man or what he stood for. Instead, it spurred him on, which is how deep his disdain for God and Abraham ran. He could have left his feelings in the grave with Abraham's death but he didn't, he couldn't, because evil doesn't rest or relinquish itself. It churns and turns, always burning, always going, never at rest. This is how Satan works, always burning, always going, never resting. He's a restless spirit, so those that follow him take on his traits. This was Nimrod.

Esau was being watched, all the days of his hunting, as verse 3 says. Nimrod closely watched Esau and how gifted at hunting he was. The great hunter before the LORD was now watching someone who possibly was better than he at hunting. God called Nimrod the 'Great Hunter' (Gen 10:9) before HIMself, which cannot be understated. HE didn't say that about Esau, but at this point it didn't matter. Evil doesn't allow logic and reason to factor into decision making or perspective, only more schemes, only more evil. This studying of Esau caused Nimrod to become jealous, which is a weak and dangerous emotion to operate from if you are not aligned correctly. Jealousy means to want something that you already have. Envy means to want something that someone else has, but you want for yourself. Nimrod had what Esau was trying to learn but he didn't see it that way. His jealous heart blinded him.

Jasher 27: 4-5

And on a certain day Esau went in the field to hunt, and he found Nimrod walking in the wilderness with his two men. 5 And all his mighty men and his people were with him in the wilderness, but they removed at a distance from him, and they went from him in different directions to hunt, and Esau concealed himself for Nimrod, and he lurked for him in the wilderness.

The watcher was being watched, the hunter was now being hunted. In a quick change of events, on this random day, Esau noticed that he was being watched. The reputation Esau developed earlier in his life when he first began to hunt was that of an excellent trapper, meaning that he was good at setting up and or deceiving his prey. He was about to trap the biggest prey of all time, he just didn't know it yet.

On this day, Esau saw a man he didn't know with two other men walking in the wilderness. As Esau watched closer, he noticed that the camp of this man was large, filled with giant men and their people, but they were a long way away from this group of 3 men. Esau also noticed that the giant men ventured in different directions, also hunting. As he looked on, Esau began to stalk the man that the other men were following. He concealed himself to the degree that none of the men, including the main man, could see him. Cunning and deceitful, camouflaged.

Jasher 27:6

And Nimrod and his men that were with him did not know him, and Nimrod and his men frequently walked about in the field at the cool of the day, and to know where his men were hunting in the field.

When scripture says that Nimrod didn't know him, it means that they couldn't find Esau. Nimrod knew who Esau was, but Esau didn't know who Nimrod was. Again, Esau was a 15-year-old boy. Nimrod was a multi-hundred-year-old man whose paths never crossed before. So why did scripture say Nimrod frequently went out in the cool of the day? The cool of the day is 'ruach' in Hebrew, meaning 'at the time of the evening breeze.' By hunting in the evening, Nimrod knew this was a good time to find animals looking for food, water, or shelter before the night comes. Moving around in the heat of the day would put an animal at risk of being seen, killed, or exhausted by the sun. As the Great Hunter, Nimrod thought as the prey he hunted, which is what made him wiser than any other hunter of his time. What also added to his hunting prowess were the garments he wore while hunting. The garments he wore not only made him very successful, but virtually invincible. These garments, made from the hand of God himself, were the same clothes that made Nimrod the Great Hunter and world king he became.

Jasher 7:30

And Nimrod became strong when he put on the garments, and God gave him might and strength, and he was a mighty hunter in the earth, yea, he was a mighty hunter in the field, and he hunted the animals and he built altars, and he offered upon them the animals before the Lord.

The garments.

Hand made by God, given from Cush to Nimrod in secret, which gave Nimrod might and strength, is the most important detail here. What you are about to read cannot be understood properly without knowing the origin of the strength, prowess, and power of Nimrod, which was aided by these garments. The world king started out as a follower of the LORD until fame and power contaminated his mind and heart. In his most comfortable setting, he and the world would be reminded, in secret, of who the LORD of the universe was, publicly, as HE is the king of kings.

Brace yourself...

Jasher 27: 7-11

And Nimrod and two of his men that were with him came to the place where they were, when Esau started suddenly from his lurking place, and drew his sword, and hastened and ran to Nimrod and cut off his head. 8 And Esau fought a desperate fight with the two men that were with Nimrod, and when they called out to him, Esau turned to them and smote them to death with his sword. 9 And all the mighty men of Nimrod, who had left him to go to the wilderness, heard the cry at a distance, and they knew the voices of those two men, an they ran to know the cause of it, when they found their king and the two men that were with him lying dead in the wilderness. 10 And when Esau saw the mighty men of Nimrod coming at a distance, he fled, and thereby escaped; and Esau took the valuable garments of Nimrod, which Nimrod's father had bequeathed to Nimrod, and with which Nimrod prevailed over the whole land, and he ran and concealed them in his house. 11 And Esau took those garments and ran into the city on account of Nimrod's men, and he came unto his father's house wearied and exhausted from fight, and he was ready to die through grief when he approached his brother Jacob and sat before him.

Nimrod the Great Hunter before the LORD...was dead.

Esau didn't see a man walking, he saw what looked like an animal walking. Nimrod was not walking as a normal man. He was walking around with the clothing he always hunted in, the garments that God made for Adam and Eve that gave him might and strength. The appearance of these garments made Nimrod look like a beast of the field. Nimrod didn't know that he had fallen into the trap he thought he was setting on Esau, the child he was stalking that he became jealous of.

Esau saw the chance to strike, moved in, got closer to Nimrod, and when the moment was right, he struck Nimrod with his sword. Not only did he strike and kill Nimrod, but he chopped off his head. The same head that held the world's first crown. The same head that rose from protector to king. The same head that taught the world sin and evil. The same head that conspired to kill Abraham every chance he got. The same head that set himself against the LORD God Almighty. The same head that became the head of the world....was now off. Esau chopped the head of the world's ruler off in a wilderness.

Esau, after chopping off the head of the beast, realized that this was a man. Not just any man, but a man of importance. Keep in mind, Esau was just 15 years old. He was hunter of animals, not men, as Nimrod was. In a moment's notice, he went from being a hunter to a murderer. I know, that's a lot to process, but Esau didn't have time to do so. After killing Nimrod, Esau's life was in immediate danger. There were two men, two of Nimrod's personal bodyguard, coming towards him. In a quick move of self-preservation, Esau turned towards the two men and killed them both. Scripture says he fought desperately, meaning with great fear of death, which indicates that Esau fought with adrenaline and skill to survive. He prevailed.

As Esau looked up, the other men which were giants that Esau had already scouted before the hunt began, heard the voices of the two dying men, came running in that direction. When they got to the spot where the two men were dead, they noticed their leader's body, Nimrod, lifeless, without a head. When they looked up, they could see a boy running with something in his hands. When they looked down at Nimrod, they noticed something missing other than his head: his garments.

When Esau saw the giant men of Nimrod coming, he took the garments off Nimrod. The Great Hunter before the LORD died and was found headless and naked, stripped by a boy on a hunting trip. Wow! After fighting off the two personal guards of the dead king, Esau ran away for his life with the garments of Nimrod in hand. He escaped the giants and ran to his home and hid the garments, knowing that if he is found, the only proof they could have of his killing of a man would be the garments he took. Remember, Esau was a cunning man since birth, so hiding and being deceitful was in his nature and an accepted behavior of his personality. Therefore, he ran away, fearing his life, scared, exhausted, thinking he was about to die. Running scared with adrenaline pumping, once you calm down from it, it will lead you to a real empty feeling. You are burning so much energy at one time, so rapidly, that the body is depleted and needs to refill quickly. This is why when Esau hid the garments, he did what all children do after they get in trouble or experienced some real traumatic event: they go to their parents. In this case, Esau went to his father's tent in hopes that Isaac would be there. Instead, someone else was there: his twin brother, Jacob, who just so happen to be cooking.

Genesis 25:29

And Jacob sod pottage: and Esau came from the field, and he was faint:

Scared to death, depleted of energy, feeling empty. Esau was so scared that all he could think of was being refilled. He knew what he had done. He knew he was being looked for. He knew that at some point someone would come asking to see if someone ran into the tents, a boy, hairy, with some garments in his hand. While he was sitting there, watching his brother cook, he realized that it was a high probability that he was going to die. He knew that he was probably going to be killed because he had killed, 3 men to be exact. While going through this bleak process of thinking, taking into consideration that he was faint now that the desperation had subsided, he chose to do what his body said he needed first: food. But this food, would come with a price.

Jasher 27:12

And he said unto his brother Jacob, Behold I shall die this day, and wherefore then do I want the birthright? And Jacob acted wisely with Esau in this matter, and Esau sold his birthright to Jacob, for it was so brought about by the LORD.

And...

Genesis 25: 30-34

And Esau said to Jacob, Feed me, I pray thee, with that same red pottage; for I am faint: therefore was his name called Edom. 31
And Jacob said, Sell me this day thy birthright. 32 And Esau said, Behold, I am at the point to die: and what profit shall this
birthright do to me? 33 And Jacob said, Swear to me this day; and he sware unto him: and he sold his birthright unto Jacob. 34
Then Jacob gave Esau bread and pottage of lentils; an he did eat and drink, and rose up, and went his way: thus Esau despised his birthright.

Disgraceful. Esau sold his birthright over a pot of lentil stew. This is nuts! A pot of red, lentil, stew. Esau reduced his birthright, which is connected to God, through Abraham his grandfather, over a pot of stew. From Adam to Abraham, from Abraham to Jesus the Christ, reduced....for a bowl of stew. This was the issue at hand. Now, to be clear, regardless of what Esau was thinking or not thinking, this was God at work. The disrespect of his grandfather Abraham was enough, but this was God's doing. How so? Remember, that same Abraham was told to tell Esau and Jacob's mother the significance of how they came out of the womb:

Jasher 26:12

And they all inquired of the Lord concerning this matter, and the brought her word from the Lord and told her, Two children are in they womb, two nations shall rise from them; and one nation shall be stronger than the other, and the greater shall serve the younger.

Prophecy fulfilled. By giving up his birthright, Esau, unknowingly, became the servant to his younger brother Jacob. Perspectively, Esau was thinking he was going to die, so the birthright, in his eyes, was meaningless. Although this was somewhat logical, it is the danger of being sure, which is the opposite of faith, that moved Esau to this conclusion. The man he killed was the king of sure. The man he received his birthright from was the servant of faith. By making this decision to deal with the idea of surety, Esau was choosing his thoughts over God's way. This was the mindset that made Nimrod, Nimrod. This is the opposite thinking of Abraham, the opposite thinking of his father Isaac. Had Esau went to LORD in counsel, his outcome possibly could have been different, as was for his grandfather and father before him. But he didn't. He chose his own way of thinking, just as Nimrod did.

As we analyze this decision closer, reader, please understand the birthright. The birthright belongs to the eldest born child of a family, most commonly a son or male. By being the first birthed, the right and privileges of leader and family responsibility goes to the eldest. Even though Esau and Jacob were twins, Esau was the eldest, being that he came from the womb first. By surrendering his birthright, Jacob was now chosen as the one through whom the LORD would send the Christ. Jacob would now have both leadership and responsibility over the covenant of Abraham in the Earth. Yes, just like that, the birthright was sold, over a bowl of stew.

Jacob, on the other hand, used what scripture called wisdom in his dealings. This seems capitalistic, which to a certain degree, it 100% is, but something bigger was at play. This was the reason Jacob was pulling on the heel of Esau from birth. It was for this cause, the prophecy that followed, the reason for his personality traits. Remember, Jacob stayed amongst the people, in the tents, beloved of his mother. Esau stayed outside, hunting and scheming, beloved of his father. This moment to rise from being 2nd to 1st was something that Jacob had been fighting for since being in the womb with his brother. On another note, Jacob understood the significance of the birthright that his brother Esau didn't. He respected it in a way that Esau didn't. He understood the responsibility of the birthright in the eyes of God and men that Esau was too cunning to see. Esau preferred knowledge, Jacob preferred wisdom. This was the difference between them too. The wisdom to know between the two was God showing us all that HIS will will be done regardless of the situation. Abraham knew this, even though he was now dead, that the younger would lead the elder. He just didn't know how.

God did.

What makes Esau's decision so crazy is that after he ate, had a little time to recover and decompress from the day, the Bible tells us in Genesis 25 verse 34 that Esau ate, got up, and went about his way. Wait, what? Yes, you read that right! All of that panic, fear, emotional decision making, was for a moment. When that moment passed and after he was refilled, he was good to go, business as usual. Esau gave away his birthright, something he would later to regret for the rest of his life, over a bowl of stew, which after a good nap and bowel movement, was gone forever. So was his birthright. Again, prophecy fulfilled.

Jacob, now the keeper of the birthright of his family and the covenant made with the LORD, used more wisdom in his dealings with his brother. Even though the deal was made in secret, he decided to record it so Esau couldn't come back later and say it didn't happen. Even though Esau was known for being a cunning hunter and trapper, Jacob understood people and how people work.

Jasher 27: 13-14

And Esau's portion in the cave of the field of Machpelah, which Abraham had bought from the children of Heth for the possession of a burial ground, Esau also sold to Jacob, and Jacob bought all this from his brother Esau for value given. 14 And Jacob wrote the whole of this in a book, and he testified the same with witnesses, and he sealed it, and the book remained in the hands of Jacob.

Again, Jacob was all business. Whereas his brother despised his birthright, Jacob took it serious. He not only wrote it down but he got witnesses to testify on his behalf that Esau had done this thing. After sealing the deal, he didn't just hide the book. Instead, he kept the book with him, at all times, so no one could take it and dispute it. What I hope you have come to learn about Jacob is that he too was a hunter, like Esau, just in a different way. He too was just as crafty, just as cunning, just as competitive.

Meanwhile....

Nimrod the mighty king of world, the Great Hunter before the LORD, the crown maker, the great idolator, was lying in a wilderness, far from home, headless, lifeless, dead. A child, a 15-year-old boy that he became jealous of, had killed him. Not only killed him, but decapitated him. He was killed as a beast in the field, beheaded like a trophy for a wall, stripped of his precious garments, lying naked as a man of shame. He was killed in the place he loved most, the place he earned his fame, the wilderness. None of his people could save him, none of his power could save him, none of his sin could save him, none of his evil could save him, and the devil himself that he served could not save him. God's judgment had been served on him, but it was only the beginning.

Jasher 27: 15-16

And when Nimrod the son of Cush died, his men lifted him up and brought him in consternation, and buried him in his city, an all the days that Nimrod lived were two hundred and fifteen years and he died. 16 And the days that Nimrod reigned upon the people of the land were one hundred and eighty-five years; and Nimrod died by the sword of Esau in shame and contempt, and the seed of Abraham caused his death as he had seen in his dream.

Remember the Tower of Babel, the thing that Nimrod is most remembered for. It was there that God came down with 70 angels to confuse the languages of men which created the base of world languages from which we get every dialect we speak today. Babel means confusion, which is what Nimrod was responsible for. The confusion caused chaos, which is why the Tower was abandoned. When we read about Nimrod's death, the same thing occurred, just in a different way. The key word in Jasher 27 verses 15-16 is consternation. It means amazement or dismay that hinders or throws into confusion. To *Make It Plain*, it means to be amazed that something happened that in turn causes chaos. This is exactly what happened next.

The giants that were chasing Esau never found him. Instead, they returned to the place where Nimrod lay dead. The rest of the people in his hunting camp came out to the place he was, saw his remains, and carried his body back to his people, headless. He was brought back to his kingdom where the people saw him and went into a full panic! All the nations of the world were in shock, chaotic, wild! The man who ruled the world was now dead. All the kingdoms he created, allowed to ruled, taught evil and everything Anti-God that he could, was now in chaos. Never did they think he would die this way, or die period. Nimrod had that type of appeal. He died as the most powerful man on Earth. When the people found out how he died, at the hands of a 15-year-old boy that Nimrod's best men couldn't find, they absolutely lost it. Scripture says he died in shame and contempt, which is the justice of God. His behavior was shameful as he lived a life of contempt to the LORD. Justice.

As for his family, they endured the shame and pain of Nimrod's decisions. They too deserve justice as contributors and beneficiaries of his fame, fortune, and evil. They too taught the world evil that we still see and operate in today. God had something for them as well...

Jasher 27:17

And at the death of Nimrod his kingdom became divided into many divisions, and all those parts that Nimrod reigned over were restored to the respective kings of the land, who recovered them after the death of Nimrod, and all the people of the house of Nimrod were for a long time enslaved to all the other kings of the land.

Justice. The same people that enabled Nimrod to rule was now in chaos. His house was broken. His kingdom was broken. His law was broken. His reputation was broken. His name was broken.

From this point, the name Nimrod took on a different meaning. If you look up the name Nimrod now, it means idiot, jerk, airhead, birdbrain, blockhead, dum-dum, jackass, meathead, nitwit, pinhead, simpleton, stupid, yahoo, or the opposite of genius. His name originally meant 'Mighty Hunter before the LORD'. Now, it means everything opposite of that. His family, who was regarded as the royal of the royals, were now slaves. His teachings were being extracted and copied, changed, so that others can try to replicate what he did but they would come to change his name again and again so as not to give him credit for their adopted abominations. His kingdom was broken into so many different divisions and kingdoms that even archaeologists struggle putting timelines together to mark his presence in the Earth. Historians question whether or not he even lived, just like they do Abraham. His followers were united in evil, from which he was the most evil. When he died, they did what evildoers do, they panicked and looked for better ways to become as evil. They destroyed what he built, and as history would prove, every evil ruler after him tried to copy him in some way to achieve the world leader status that only he has achieved.

In the end, no man has ever achieved the position as ruler of the world as Nimrod did. No one. Just as there has been no man like Abraham, there has been no man like Nimrod. Just as Abraham was a precursor to the Christ, so was Nimrod to the coming AntiChrist. The land of Canaan mourned when Abraham died. The land of Mesopotamia went into chaos when Nimrod died. Abraham united people for the cause of bringing people to the LORD God in faith. Nimrod united people for the cause of pulling people away from the LORD God in the surety of idolatry. Abraham died in peace. Nimrod died in panic. Abraham lived as a servant. Nimrod lived as a tyrant. What's crazy is both men started out the same. Nimrod lived for 215 years. He ruled for 185 years. He had at least 185 years to repent and come back to God, which is where he began. But his desire for evil almost pushed the world into the final destruction. That's how epically vile this man was. From him, we learned that there is always a greater evil in human form to come because there has never been a more evil man this him. Everything faith, holiness, and righteousness stands for, he was against. By killing Abraham, he would have killed the bloodline through whom Jesus the Christ would come. Think about how powerful that is and how powerful Nimrod had to be to try to kill a man that had this promise of salvation marked on his life in the heavens. Who would want to kill or cut off the path to the savior? Nimrod. His death ended his reign and the position of global ruler. Others who history has shown us were terrifying to live with during their reign and or learn about, none can touch this man. He started out straight, with a good head on his shoulders, a man of color, the grandson of Cush. He died a man with no head on his shoulders, a man of sin, the son of the devil. He died one of one, and until THE AntiChrist comes, there will be none like him.

This is the shame and contempt that scripture spoke about.

This is Nimrod....

The World's First AntiChrist

Christ and the AntiChrist

Blasphemy! That's the best way we can describe this term or person, blasphemy! There is no other explanation that can summarize who this man will be. Blasphemy! To the one whose spirit or likeness has been in the world for thousands of years, beginning with Nimrod, blasphemy! This spirit is the same spirit that ruled Nimrod. To the rulers of vast empires who invoked and still try to summon the spirit of the AntiChrist, blasphemy!

Anti-Christ is a hot topic when discussing the future of humanity. Saying the term Anti-Christ draws a lot of attention, even with atheists, and rightfully so. Before we get into how the Anti-Christ is connected to the Christ, we must define some terms for foundational purposes.

Blasphemy = the act of insulting or showing contempt or lack of reverence for God
Christ = the anointed one
Perdition = eternal damnation, utter destruction

We'll begin by facing a fact: the AntiChrist will come. It's not negotiable. Regardless of what you think, he is set to come although he has yet to be revealed. This man will be several things, do amazing things, but good will not be one of them. There are whole books written about the AntiChrist and how he will impact the world. Our focus in this section will be to cover the biblical aspect of him and how he is connected to Christ. With that said, we have some simple questions to ask and then answer to *Make It Plain* for you to prove how real and devastating this man will be, Nimrod 2.0.

1. Who is the AntiChrist and has he been revealed?

2 Thessalonians 2:6
And now ye know what **withholdeth** that he might be **revealed in his time**.

Answer: We don't know yet and no, he hasn't been revealed.

2. What is an antichrist?

1 John 2:22
Who is the **liar**, but the **one who denies that Jesus is the Christ**? This is the antichrist, the **one who denies the Father and the Son**.

Answer: A liar who denies Jesus is the Christ, denying both the Father and the Son.

3. Is it possible to be "an" antichrist and not "THE" AntiChrist?

2 John 1:7
For many **deceivers** are entered into the world, who **confess not that Jesus Christ is come in the flesh**. This is a deceiver and an antichrist.

Answer: Yes.

4. What are some characteristics of the AntiChrist?

1 John 4:3

And very spirit that **does not confess Jesus** is not from God; this is the spirit of the antichrist, of which you have heard that it is coming, and now it is already in the world.

Answer: He will not confess Jesus is from God.

5. Is there another name we can find in scripture that describes the AntiChrist, like a nickname?

2 Thessalonians 2:3

Let no man deceive you by any means: for that day shall not come, except there come a falling away first, and that **man of sin** be revealed, the **son of perdition**.

:8

Then that **lawless one** will be revealed whom the Lord will slay with the breath of His mouth and bring to an end by the appearance of His coming.

Answer: Man of sin, son of perdition, lawless one.

6. How much influence will the AntiChrist have on the world?

Daniel 8:25

"And through his shrewdness He will cause deceit to succeed by his influence; And he will magnify himself in his heart, **And he will destroy many** while they are at ease. **He will even oppose the Prince of princes**, But he will be broken without human agency.

Answer: He will have leading influence on the world to the point that all things will be impacted by him and his ways.

7. What will he do while here on Earth?

2 Thessalonians 2:4

Who opposeth and **exalteth himself above all that is called God**, or that is worshipped; so that **he as God sitteth in the temple of God, shewing himself that he is God**.

Answer: He's going to set himself up as God, even going as far as setting up office in the temple of God in Jerusalem in the 3rd Temple.

2020 Mock Architecture of 3rd Temple

© Construction of 3rd Temple

The term Christ, as we have learned, means the anointed one. By default, the term AntiChrist really means the un-anointed one. The concept of what he represents is the ultimate evil just as the Christ represents the ultimate good. There have been many versions of him throughout the ages, but none in a manifested form of the actual being yet to come. The verses above explain how the spirit of the AntiChrist has been here on this planet, but the actual AntiChrist has yet to be revealed. Why? Because of the love of God, which allows HIS grace to abound for us, the believer, for our sake. There is an appointed time before the AntiChrist comes that we shall exist and serve God before all hell breaks loose. What's important to know is that the AntiChrist will get his power from the dragon, Satan himself. He will be Nimrod 2.0. And yes, dragons do exist, but that's a different book for a different day.

Revelation 13:2

And the beast which I saw was like unto a leopard, and his feet were as the feet of a bear, and his mouth as the mouth of a lion: and the dragon gave him his power, and his seat, and great authority.

Reader, please understand that the AntiChrist will not be a slouch or pushover! By no means! He will not be just another political figure with territorial power. He will be the most powerful ruler to live in world history! When Nimrod ruled the planet as the *World's First AntiChrist*, there was less than 20 million people on Earth. We now have cities like Tokyo, Japan, that has over 20 million people living in it. Earth now has billions of people, spread across 7 continents, who will be governed by 1 person. Think about that for a second. Billions of people, ruled by 1 man. Wow! Imagine the amount of power that will be in his hands! All governments of the world will unite under one ruler, him, as he will draw his power from the ruler of this world, Satan. A satanic power-backed world without restraints will be hell on Earth. There will be resistance, but it will fail.

Revelation 13:7

It was granted to him to make war with the saints and to overcome them. And authority was given him over every tribe, tongue, and nation.

Similar to the godhead which consists of God as the Father, Son, and Holy Spirit as ONE, Satan has a replicant of his own. This is why he's pushing the agenda of trinity so he can introduce his to the world and it'll be accepted by so-called Christians. He began this with Nimrod and his family, the first "trinity".

For the record reader, I bear witness to the fact that our God is ONE. He has several roles and responsibilities, but HE is yet ONE. Satan cannot be multiple as one but his evil empire will operate as one. He was made an angel in his creation which means he has an origin. Anything that has a birth date also has a death date. Needless to say, he has a bucket list before his name gets called into final judgement. So yes, Satan has an agenda to copycat what God has ordained and soon it will be unraveled in the Earth. It has already been revealed.

Satan = dragon
AntiChrist = beast
False Prophet = same

Jesus himself told the disciples about the kingdom of Satan and how it is united.

Matthew 12: 25-26

And Jesus knew thei thoughts, and said unto them, Every kingdom divided against itself is brought to desolation; and every city or house divided against itself shall not stand: 26 And if Satan cast out Satan, he is divided against himself; how shall then his kingdom stand?

Now that we have a foundation in the scripture for the AntiChrist, let's analyze and compare the roles and responsibilities of Jesus the Christ vs. the AntiChrist.

Jesus the Christ

Son of God

John 1:34

And I saw, and bare record that this it the Son of God.

Seed of Woman

Genesis 3:15

And I will put enmity between thee and the woman, and between they seed and her seed; it shall bruise they head, and thou shalt bruise his heel.

Holy One

Mark 1:24

Saying, Let us alone; what have we to do with thee, thou Jesus of Nazareth? Art thou come to destroy us? I know thee who thou are, the Hoy One of God.

Prince of Peace

Isaiah 9:6

For unto us a child is born, unto us a son is given: and the government shall be upon his shoulder: and his name shall be called Wonderful, Counsellor, The mighty God, The everlasting Father, The Prince of Peace.

Good Shepherd

John 10:11

I am the good shepherd: the good shepherd giveth his life for the sheep.

The Christ

Matthew 16:16

And Simon Peter answered and said, Thou are the Christ, the Son of the living God.

Man of Sorrows

Isaiah 53:3

He is despised and rejected of men; a man of sorrows, and acquainted with grief: and we hid as it were our faces from him; he was despised, and we esteemed him not.

Glorious Branch

Isaiah 4:2

In that day shall the branch of the LORD be beautiful and glorious, and the fruit of the earth shall be excellent and comely for them that are escaped of Israel.

Comes From Heaven

John 3:13

And no man hath ascended up to heaven, but he that came down from heaven, even the Son of man which is in heaven.

Backed by the Holy Spirit

Luke 4:14

And Jesus returned in the power of the Spirit into Galilee: and there went out a fame of him through all the region round about.

Humbled Himself

Philippians 2:8

And being found in fashion as a man, he humbled himself, and became obedient unto death, even the death of the cross.

About His Father's Business

John 6:38

For I came down from heaven, not to do mine own will, but the will of him that sent me.

Ministered to the Needy

John 6: 11-12

And Jesus took the loaves; and when he had given thanks, he distrusted to the disciples, and the disciples to them that were set down; and likewise of the fishes as much as they would. 12 When they were filled, he said unto his disciples, Gather up the fragments that remain, that nothing be lost.

Rejected By His Own

John 1:11

He came unto his own, and his own received him not.

Leads His Flock

John 10:3

To him the porter openeth; and the sheep hear his voice: and he calleth his own sheep by name, and leadeth them out.

Glorifies God

John 17:4

I have glorified thee on the earth: I have finished the work which thou gavest me to do.

Gave Himself For the Nation

John 11:51

And this spake he not of himself: but being high priest that year, he prophesied that Jesus should die for that nation;

Received Back Into Heaven

Luke 24:51

And it came to pass, while he blessed them, he was parted from them, and carried up into heaven.

The Lamb

Isaiah 53:7

He was oppressed, and he was afflicted, yet he opened not his mouth: he is brought as a lamb to the slaughter, and as a sheep before her shearers is dumb, so he openeth not his mouth.

Came In *The Name*

John 5:43

I am come in my Father's name, and ye receive me not: if another shall come in his own name, him ye will receive.

Amen. That was a lot of information, but it is needed and intentional for use. You need to know what Christ represents and the majesty of HIS presence. As a believer or person of interest, you must have a foundation of go-to-information to teach and defend the faith. Meanwhile, the enemy has a counterfeit to everything God has planned for us, for you. We cannot be ignorant of this reality. Many fall by the wayside because they don't have the tools to fight back for their souls. Convenience kills.

Jesus said there are many antichrists that have come into the world, even during HIS time. We have defined what an antichrist is. However, THE ANTICHRIST, will come and he will rule. The world will be taken over by his charismatic leadership and savvy ways. Just as the story of the power of Christ spread throughout the world, so will the power of the AntiChist. Reader, make no mistake about it, he will have power, real power!

The AntiChrist will be fueled by Satan himself. Regardless of what your pastor, teacher, bishop, parent, etc. say about Satan's power, you would be wise to understand that Satan is very powerful. He's not all powerful, only God can say that, but Satan can hold his own. Don't be fooled, he made war in heaven against the LORD himself. Who do you know did that? In heaven? In the presence of God himself? Only Nimrod, at the Tower of Babel. A third (1/3) of the angels were fooled by him and fell alongside him. Jesus himself said that Satan roams the earth like a roaring lion. Have you ever known a roaring lion to be weak? Come on now, think about it. He is the greatest of the evil in the Earth. So, for him to give his power to a human being, it will be like the manifestation of evil incarnated It will be as if we are seeing Lucifer himself, who is only described as a man in the scripture (Isaiah 14: 3-22), living amongst humanity. Just as the scripture tells us that Lucifer got as high as he failed, the plan for godship will fail for the AntiChrist and Satan.

The most important aspect of understanding the relationship between Christ and The AntiChrist is a question of representation. Whose name do you represent? Well, as we will learn, the AntiChrist will come in his own name. In order for him to have a following in the Earth as a political figure, he must have a name that people can say or use that represents the desired highest power as he will come in his own way, in his own name, for his own purpose, to exalt himself, to become an idol to himself...and the people will love it! We already live in an I-society so The AntiChrist will slide right in without detection. Like Nimrod.

What's really amazing is that the same people that have a problem with God existing as ONE will gladly accept the fake godhead of Satan. But the god of this world (2 Cor. 4:4), who will be worshipped, is a fake. And because of that, he will be destroyed, along with the AntiChrist. Let's go to work and give you the counterfeit Christ the same way we gave you the points relating to the Christ.

Brace yourself...

Anti-Christ

Son of Perdition

2 Thessalonians 2:3

Let no man deceive you by any means: for that day shall not come, except there come a falling away first, and that man of in be revealed, the son of perdition;

Seed of the Serpent

Genesis 3:15

And I will put enmity between thee and the woman, and between they seed and her seed; it shall bruise thy head, and thou shalt bruise his heel.

Wicked One

2 Thessalonians 2:8

And then shall that Wicked be revealed, whom the Lord shall consume with the spirit of his mouth, and shall destroy with the brightness of his coming:

Profane Prince

Ezekiel 21:25

And thou, profane wicked prince of Israel, whose day is come, when iniquity shall have an end

Idol Shepherd

Zechariah 11:17

Woe to the idol shepherd that leaveth the flock! The sword shall be upon his arm, and upon his right eye: his arm shall be clean dried up, and his right eye shall be utterly darkened.

AntiChrist

1 John 4:3

And every spirit that confesseth not that Jesus Christ is come in the flesh is not of God: and this is that spirit of antichrist, whereof ye have heard that it should come; and even now already is it the world.

Man of Sin

2 Thessalonians 2:3

Let no man deceive you by any means: for that day shall not come, except there come a falling away first, and that man of in be revealed, the son of perdition;

Abominable Branch

Isaiah 14:19

But thou are cast out of they grave like an abominable branch, and as the raiment of those that are slain, thrust through with a sword, that go down to the stones of the pit; as a carcase trodden under feet.

Comes From the Bottomless Pit

Revelation 11:7

And when they shall have finished their testimony, the beast that ascendeth out of the bottomless pit shall make war against them, and shall overcome them, and kill them.

Backed by Satan/the Dragon

Revelation 13:4

And they worshipped the dragon which gave power unto the beast: and they worshipped the beast, saying, Who is like unto the beast? Who is able to make war with him?

Here To Do His Own Business

Daniel 11:36

And the king shall do according to his will; and he shall exalt himself, and magnify himself above every god, and shall speak marvelous things against the God of gods, and shall prosper till the indignation be accomplished: for that is determined shall be done.

Robs the Poor

Psalms 10:9

He lieth in wait secretly as a lion in his den: he lieth in wait to catch the poor: he doth catch the poor, when he draweth him into his net.

Accepted By Men

Revelation 13:4

And they worshipped the dragon which gave power unto the beast: and they worshipped the beast, saying, Who is like unto the beast? Who is able to make war with him?

Leaves His Flock

Zechariah 11:17

Woe to the idol shepherd that leaveth the flock! The sword shall be upon his arm, and upon his right eye: his arm shall be clean dried up, and his right eye shall be utterly darkened.

Blasphemes God

Revelation 13:6

And he opened his moth in blasphemy against God, to blaspheme his name, and his tabernacle, and them that dwell in heaven.

Slays The People

Isaiah 14:20

Thou shalt not be joined with them in burial, because thou hast destroyed thy land, and slain thy people: the seed of evildoers shall never be renowned

The Beast

Revelation 13:4

And they worshipped the dragon which gave power unto the beast: and they worshipped the beast, saying, Who is like unto the beast? Who is able to make war with him?

Going Into the Lake of Fire

Revelation 19:20

And the beast was taken, and with him the false prophet that wrought miracles before him, with which he deceived them that had received the mark of the beast, and them that worshipped his image. These both were cast alive into a lake of fire burning with brimstone.

Comes In His Own Name

John 5:43

I am come in my Father's name, and ye receive me not: if another shall come in his own name, him ye shall receive.

He Will Be Homosexual or A-Sexual

Daniel 11:37

Neither shall he regard the God of his fathers, nor the desire of women, nor regard any god: for he shall magnify himself above all.

As we have learned, the meaning of Christ is the anointed one. After reading all of this information and Bible verses about the coming AntiChrist, there will be a man that comes into global power that is not of God that will claim to be God. To add insult to injury, he will be accepted as the Christ by all. What does this mean? He will be affiliated with the Jews. How do we know that? Daniel 11:37 tells us that he will disregard the God of his fathers. Only the Jews are not accepting of the Christ among the Abrahamic faiths that believe in an AntiChrist. Muslims have what they call the Mahdi, who is a Christlike figure, but they believe that Jesus was a prophet, so they do not associate Jesus with being God in the flesh bearing his name Jesus. Christians believe in Jesus being the Christ, but there was no such thing as Christianity when Daniel wrote this. The Christ had not yet come. The only belief structure that could or would understand this teaching were the Jews. Therefore, the AntiChrist would be Jewish affiliated. He will have access to the 3rd Temple to be built in Jerusalem because of his Jewish heritage. This is also why Jesus told the Jewish officials who were asking him these questions that another will come in his own name and they will receive him, but Jesus himself they will not accept. Muslims accept that Jesus was special. Christians believe HE was God in the flesh. Only the Jews doubt HIS power and person. Like Nimrod to Abraham.

To be frank, the world, including many in the Jewish community, will see him as the Christ they have been waiting for that the prophets prophesied about since they don't accept Jesus as such. If he was going to be a great ruler that wasn't associated with the Jewish people, he would be given a different reputation and disconnection to the people God designated. The Bible says that he will even make an agreement of peace with the nation of Israel for a week, only to come back and violate that peace treaty and kill many Jews (Dan. 9:27). Regardless, he will be an imposter, a fake, a fraud, yet he will be accepted. The scary part about learning about the AntiChrist is that he will be empowered by Satan, the chief devil, who himself knows and believes in God. Yes, even the devil and his devils believe in God....even if you don't. Like Nimrod.

James 2:18

Thou believest that there is one God; thou doest well: the devils also believe, and tremble.

The AntiChrist will rule on Earth for a short time. In fact, the Bible says that he will rule for 42 months (Rev. 13), which equals 3 ½ years. Ironically, this is the same amount of time that Jesus' ministry lasted. Reader, please understand this clearly: this will happen and the ONLY thing that can save you from this disastrous environment and time is Jesus! There will be some who come to Christ during that time but will face death. The AntiChrist will make war with the saints and win (Rev. 13:7). He will institute 666, the Mark of the Beast, which will govern the global economy. He will be given power to rule the world and everyone will worship him. Like Nimrod.

Revelation 13:8

And all that dwell upon the earth shall worship him, whose names are not written in the book of life of the Lamb slain from the foundation of the world.

When the season of the AntiChrist is done, Christ will return for the final battle. We know it as Armageddon. The more I read about it, the crazier to me someone has to be to actually go to war against God. To do so is recognition of the fact that there is a God after all, which is Satanism' open secret. I digress.

From a rationalized point of view, why would you go to war against a power that's supernatural, books that are thousands of years old tell you the outcome of your rebellion in advance, and the mere fact that all the nations will come together, whose never been unified, will do so to defeat an enemy they know is All-Powerful God himself? Yes, educated, powerful, rich, resourceful, and mighty fools will be destroyed. How can you fight, work, or strive against God, who is a spirit? As crazy as this sounds, millions of people will....

Isaiah 45:9

Woe unto him that striveth with his Maker! Let the potsherd strive with the potsherds of the earth. Shall the clay say to him that fashioneth it, What makest thou? Or thy work, He hath no hands?

Dear AntiChrist...you lose....that's all.

Like Nimrod.

Armageddon and the *AntiChrist*

Before Armageddon happens, the angel that stands inside the sun shall call the birds of the Earth to the field where the AntiChrist will make war with God (Rev. 19:17). They shall be given a feast, the flesh of the wicked that defy God. As a bonus for you, allow us to share a mystery of the faith with you. Where this battle is set to take place, birds have already been migrating to for thousands of years! Yes, they already know the path, they just haven't been called yet to gather for the final feast. They travel to this area to rest and eat off the land. To those who question this, please consider your grade school World Geography class. Remember, your teacher teaching you, or at least I hope you remember, how animals migrate across the planet and have done so for thousands of years. They were designed by God to do so, even if they personally have never taken the trip themselves because they were too young or displaced by human geography. They migrate, regardless of the many cities and highways in their path. They still find a way to do what God called them to do. It's written in their DNA, so is obeying God.

Jeremiah 8:7

Yea, the stork in the heaven knoweth her appointed time; and the turtle and the crane and the swallow observe the time of their coming; but my people know not the judgment of the LORD.

So where will Armageddon take place?

The final battle of humanity will take place in the Megiddo Valley, in Israel, a crossing ground between Europe, Asia, and Africa. Better yet, this is the crossing ground of Noah's 3 sons, Japheth, Shem, and Ham. Shem (Asia), Japheth (Europe) and Ham (Africa). Hundreds of millions of birds fly through this area every year! The path of the Great Rift Valley stretches from Mozambique in Africa to Syria, which is north of Israel, the same area we a discussing. Every year, bird watchers and nature documentary companies fly to this area to catch sight of this event (ex. *Research Hula Valley Bird Festival*). Little do they know, these birds are doing what the LORD said to do. Even though the world will operate in disobedience, the animals will continue to obey God. We all should obey him as the animals do, as nature does.

Hula Valley Festival of Birds in Israel

© The Times of Israel

In the end, the AntiChrist and his followers, the whole world, will be defeated. They will be defeated and a whole world will be defeated. The AntiChrist will fall, just as Nimrod fell, both at the Tower of Babel and when Esau killed him. The AntiChrist will fall along with those that support his cause, no head to rule from and stripped naked of his power and people. This is exactly how Nimrod was destroyed, swiftly, and without remorse. Evil will be defeated and a new Heaven, a new Earth, and a new Jerusalem will be created thereafter. They will be defeated by THE KING OF KINGS, THE LORD OF LORDS. They will be defeated by the LORD God Almighty! They will be defeated by Jesus the Christ! Now that, ladies and gentlemen, is real power!

Romans 8: 37-39

Nay, in all these things we are more than conquerors through him that loved us. 38 For I am persuaded, that neither death nor life, nor angels, nor principalities, nor powers, nor things present, nor things to come, 39 Nor height, nor depth, nor any other creature, shall be able to separate us from the love of God, which is in Christ Jesus our Lord.

Great Rift Valley
© National Geographic

Antichrist Archetypes

Matthew 24: 24-25

For there shall arise false Christs, and false prophets, and shall shew great signs and wonders; insomuch that, if it were possible, they shall deceive the very elect. 25 Behold, I have told you before.

Many have come, many.

Not some, not a few, but many.

When discussing the topic of antichrists, plural, we must understand why Jesus told the apostles and us what was going to happen and what we were going to see so we wouldn't be deceived by those that was going to come. The allowance of the Bible to be put together, even though it has been tampered with, books taken out, books excluded that the Bible references, translations that change understanding, etc., it has been flawless in allowing us to have X-Ray vision on identifying antichrists throughout the ages. God's WORD is sufficient for us and for those who truly seek HIS way. This is why HE warned us of these arch-type antichrists. HIS WORD is a written reminder that helps us see through the nonsense and evaluate what we are looking at. History has shown us so many examples with a clear view that even if the Bible wasn't true or Jesus wasn't accurate, the similarities of so many world rulers that mimic the *World's First AntiChrist* would prove HIM true, accidentally.

In this section, we will go down the timeline of history and highlight many different rulers of different nations, at different times, what they had in common, and how their thought process rivaled God. The prophets told us about such men, from different perspectives. Jesus told us directly. The apostles thereafter, especially the apostle John, gave us specifics that are crystal clear. Our apologies in advance if some of the names and information we provide for you sicken your stomach or demeanor. Some of the information is graphic, but true nonetheless. Again, these are archetypes of Nimrod, the *World's First AntiChrist*. These are men that met a certain criterion. They claim to be king of kings, a world ruler, god in the flesh, god on earth, denier of Jesus is God, mass murderer as a leader, killer of the saints, mass idolator and spiritual manipulator. Like Nimrod.

Archetype = the original pattern or model of which all things of the same type are representations or copies; prototype.

BC = Before Christ **AD** = Anno Domini (means in the year of the Lord)

Sons of the Mindset of Nimrod.

They all started out with good intentions, then evil ruled their hearts.

Nebuchadnezzar II (642-562 BC)

Regarded as the greatest Babylonian king in its history, only Nimrod was regarded as greater amongst the native people of ancient Sumer, Akkad, and Chaldeans. Born the son of king Nabopolassar, Nebuchadnezzar II was named after his grandfather Nebuchadnezzar, a warrior king. He secured his own reputation as a warrior king by rising through the ranks, winning battles and wars along the way to his quest for global domination. He founded the Neo (new) Babylonian Empire by destroying the Assyrian and Egyptian Empires, which are biblically recorded. His victories are historically known, especially the Battle of Carchemish in Syria, avenging the loss of his father. This victory, as the crown prince, allowed Nebuchadnezzar II the opportunity to roll over into kingship riding a tidal wave of confidence and riches. His father would die just a few weeks after the victory.

Nebuchadnezzar II's power grew tremendously. His empire stretched from Mesopotamia to Egypt to Turkey and parts of Thrace. All that is father and earlier Babylonian rulers couldn't do, he did, and he let everyone know about it. Biblically, he was written about as a very arrogant and self-elevating king. He conquered Jerusalem, sacked the city, deported the people back to Babylon to become slaves, and destroyed the kingdom of Judah for good.

As his successors did before him, Nebuchadnezzar was a very skilled builder and restorer. As his military victories wained over the decades, his building projects continued. He rebuilt his capital, Babylon, as well. He built the historical Hanging Gardens of Babylon and restored the world famous yet abominable Ishtar Gate. He built huge monuments of himself, to himself, for others to bow and worship. There are many relics and artifacts that have been found that validate his building projects and vast wealth and power. It was this great power that fed the ego of the man that pushed him to claim himself too to be a god-king with no rival, not even God himself. After the enslavement of the Jews, Nebuchadnezzar II sensed how equal in land mass he was to the great Nimrod. He chose to take on all of Nimrod's titles and began to expand on a project to expand a statute of himself into the heavens, like Nimrod did with the Tower of Babel. He called all the officials of his people to come and worship this image. Only the Jewish princes refused (Shadrach, Meshach, and Abednego, Daniel). In his rage, he had the first three thrown in a furnace, like Nimrod did Abraham, only to get the same result, the followers of God were not burned at all. He had dreams that only Daniel could interpret. One day Nebuchadnezzar II, basking in his own glory, challenged the might of the LORD. While the words were in his mouth, God caused the so-called 'King of the Universe' to become like the "beast" he considered himself to be, which for 12 months, the king wondered in the fields and palaces eating grass like an animal. His body was always wet, his hair was uncut and long like eagle feathers, and his nails like the claws of a bird. After a year was over, God restored Nebuchadnezzar II to his senses and he declared that the God of Daniel was the LORD God of Heaven.

Hanging Gardens of Babylon
© Britannica

Archetype Connection: Nimrod was the first 'king of the Universe.' Nebuchadnezzar II wanted to be Nimrod 2.0.

Key Point: even though Nebuchadnezzar II rivaled the anti-God rhetoric that Nimrod did to provoke God to wrath, he wasn't as bad as Nimrod. Nebuchadnezzar acknowledged God was God....Nimrod never did.

Now I Nebuchadnezzar praise and extol and honour the King of heaven, all whose works are truth, and his ways judgment: and those that walk in pride he is able to abase.

- Nebuchadnezzar II

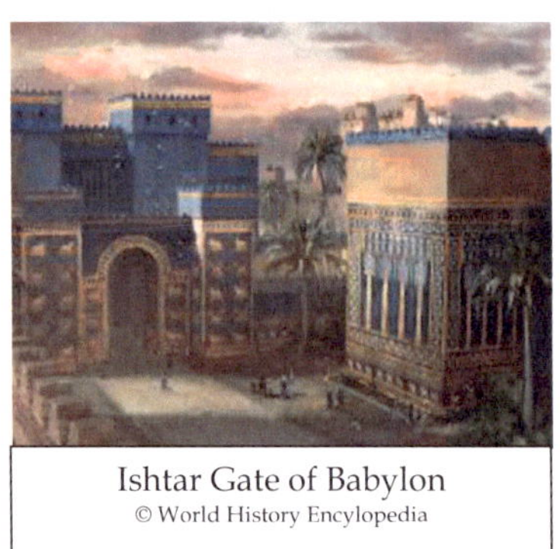

Ishtar Gate of Babylon
© World History Encyclopedia

Alexander the Great (356-323 BC)

The boy who almost conquered the world! This is who Alexander the Great came to be known among the people of his time, even though he wasn't a boy at all. Born Alexander of Macedonia, which is in Greece. Alexander was the son of Philip the One-Eyed, ruler of Macedonia. His father had dreams of ruling all of Greece but knew that defeating the Persians would be the greatest threat to that idea. His vision of a unified Greece was planted into Alexander's head as a child, so his only quest in life was to make this dream a reality for his father.

Alexander the Great
© Britannica

After Philip's assassination, Alexander was made king of Macedonia at the age of 20. From there, he united Greece via war and diplomacy. From there, he conquered his way through the Mediterranean world. He battled Darius III at Gaugamela, dismantled the Persian Empire, and made Babylon his home. Israel, Egypt, the known world at the time was conquered by Alexander. From Babylon, he reached into India, seeking to rule an empire that stretched from Greece to Asia. His dream stretched beyond his father's dream of uniting Greece, he sought to unite the world. He sought to reach the "ends of the world", seeking to reach the Pacific Ocean. He didn't know that there was a world of nations beyond that with China and Japan in front of it. Regardless, at the time, Alexander ruled an empire that was the largest in the history of the planet. After conquering Babylon, he wore the crown of Nimrod and fashioned himself as King of Babylon, the ruler of the world.

Alexander is a huge reason the Bible was put together. He was prophesied about by the prophet Daniel and Zechariah. The quiet time between Malachi and Matthew was the time that Alexander ruled. It was because of Alexander that the known world at the time learned Greek. Jesus spoke Greek as a result of Alexander's conquest. The genius of Alexander was that when he conquered a nation, he taught them his language, Greek, to unite his kingdom. He figured that if the world spoke his language, how could they be divided. This is the same thing Nimrod did until the Tower of Babel. Also, he took on the titles of nations that he ruled, such as Pharaoh, King of Babylon, King of Kings, King of Asia, and most blasphemous, the god-king. The Greeks hated Darius III because he fashioned himself as a god-king, especially Alexander. When he defeated Darius III, and married his daughter, he accepted the title of god-king, and then began to accept worship as a god. When his inner circle confronted him about it, he killed one of his most trusted advisors who knew him since birth. This marked the beginning of the end for Alexander's rule. He was also well known for his love of his famed horse Bucephalus and homosexuality, especially the orgies where young boys were sodomized.

It was in India that Alexander's army mutinied on him. He got sick and finally decided to return home, regroup, raise a new army, then go to Arabia and conquer it. In 323 BC, in his palace in Babylon, Alexander the Great died from alcohol poisoning, at the age of 33. When he died, his kingdom was immediately split among his generals. This great empire he ruled over, established for the record books, feared by those who heard he was coming, was broken apart before his body got cold. That same body was buried in Egypt, not Greece, as he fashioned himself as a living god, pharaoh of Egypt, African. His body and whereabouts have been lost to history as no one knows where his tomb is after Alexandria, the city he built in his own honor, was sunk into the Mediterranean Sea.

Archetype Connection: Rikayon, the first Pharaoh, was a poor man from Nimrod's kingdom. Nimrod was worshipped as a god and the sun, both beliefs Alexander adopted. He ruled Babel, which would later become Babylon, the same place from which Alexander both ruled and died.

Key Point: even though Alexander the Great considered himself a god king with a vast empire, he wanted to be Nimrod. Alexander never reached heaven with his works and projects....Nimrod did.

Sex and sleep alone make me conscious that I am mortal.

- Alexander the Great

Xerxes I (518-465 BC)

The god-king. When addressing Xerses I or coming into his presence, these better be the words you use or face certain death. This is the same king that was made popular in the western world by the movie 300, a tale of the Spartans vs. Persians in a quest for freedom of thought. It was he that the known world feared as historical scholars say Xerses I fielded a moving army of over 1 million soldiers that 'drank rivers dry.'

Xerses I was the son of the Persian king Darius the Great and Atossa (Cyrus the Great daughter). He inherited his father's kingdom over his older brother and immediately began to put down revolts over the empire. In the process, he went from being a prince of great stature to accepting worship as a god. After putting down rebellions in Egypt and Babylon, he puts his eyes and effort into destroying the people who caused his father so many problems, the Greeks. He's responsible for sacking Athens and many other Greek city-states before being defeated and forced back into Asia after the Battle of Salamis. The campaign ended the following year.

Xerxes I

Xerses I is a biblical character. He is one of the main characters in the book of Ester. As you read in the book, Xerses I had access to every woman within his vast empire. He chose Ester because of her natural beauty and commitment to her people. Although historically he is known for having one wife, as scripture tells us who she was, he married Ester and had many other concubines and children outside of his marriage. He was known for building great structures and projects, including those left from his father's plans. He was also known for his belief in Ahura Mazda, the supreme god of Zoroastrianism. He allowed different belief structures of different cultures until someone rebelled. Then, he would not only kill the people, but he would destroy the images of their god in their presence before annihilating them.

Xerses I had vast monuments made of himself and his titles he carried. King of kings, king of Persia, king of Babylon, great king, Pharaoh of Egypt, King of Countries, and the god-king. By accepting worship and claiming Asia and Egypt, Europe was the only place in the known world that he didn't rule. This vast power caused him to have enemies that eventually took his life.

In 465BC, Xerxes the Great was murdered by the commander of his personal bodyguard along with his son Darius, the crown prince. His son Artaxerxes avenged his father and brother's death by killing the commander and his seven sons who were a part of Xerses I royal guard. The man who fashioned himself as the god-king died like a normal man, with his son. The king of kings wasn't killed by a king, but a bodyguard.

Archetype Connection: Nimrod was the first to call himself the king of kings. He was a great builder, such as the Tower of Babel, which is biblically backed. Winning wars, building monuments to yourself, and calling yourself god was Nimrod's original idea of godship, duplicated by Xerxes I with a Persian spin.

Key Point: even though Xerses I called himself the god-king, he worshipped a god other than himself, which wasn't as idolatrous as Nimrod. By default, Xerses I didn't really believe he was god....Nimrod did.

I am Xerses, great king, king of king, the king of all countries which speak all kinds of languages, the king of the entire big far-reaching earth.

\- Xerxes I

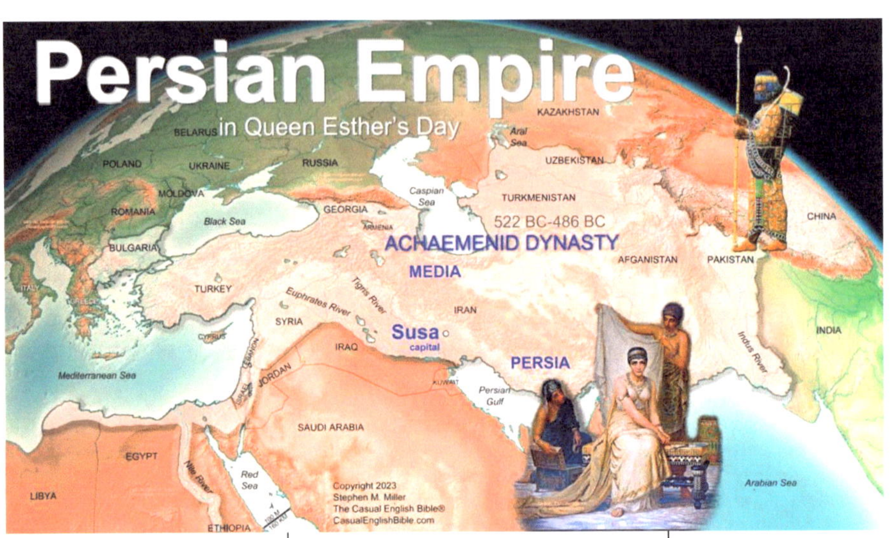

Xerxes I and His Persian Empire
© Casual English Bible

Nero (37-68 AD)

Nero
© British Museum

Historically, Mr. Evil himself. This is the man that even the apostles and first church thought was the AntiChrist that Jesus told us was coming. Imagine that. Imagine how vile and evil this man had to be for the people who walked with Jesus himself to think this was THE AntiChrist. Wow!

Nero was the son of Emperor Augustus' great-granddaughter Agrippina. By the time he was 11 years old, his mother married Emperor Claudius, thus making him the next in line to be Emperor. He was a power-hungry young man from his youth, willing to win at all cause and do as he pleased whenever he wanted. For example, Nero had his mother killed after becoming Emperor even though she was his advisor. He had his wife and stepbrother killed so he could marry his wife. The people of Rome itself thought Nero was demented, self-absorbed, and vile. They knew he was a corrupt man, from the beginning. This man set Rome on fire, which is called the Great Fire of Rome, that nearly destroyed the world capital at the time. While Rome was burning, historians recorded that Nero was in his palace, playing and acting out a play of poetry, while the city burned and people died. He used the fire for two reasons. One, it was an excuse to build what he wanted at the expense of the people. Two, he used it as an opportunity to make the Christians a scapegoat for his actions, giving him a reason to kill a whole group of people, which fed his fetish of seeing people in pain. Nero literally gathered innocent people, namely Christians, burned them alive, publicly, cruelly. He actually burnt their bodies at night time on the roads leading into Rome which served as light posts for those traveling, which is demonic.

To add to that concept, Nero was a sexual and social deviant. He was into all kinds of debauchery, namely homosexuality and different perversions we will not mention here. He is work a separate reading that puts him in a whole different category. Nero built monuments of himself, palaces and building projects to promote himself, all because he was in love with himself, literally. In 67 AD, he married a man because he looked like his ex-wife. He had the boy castrated and still had sex with him, until he died. He was the first openly homosexual emperor of the Roman Empire. Others were homosexual, but none were open about it in this light, none had reached as far as Nero did to have a man castrated to mimic a woman yet penetrate him as a man. It's disgusting any way you look at it. Again, sexual and social deviant.

In the end, Nero was a man that loved himself above all. He almost became the man that Daniel prophesied about, in regards to the AntiChrist. The apostles and first church thought that Nero was him. He is accredited by many historical scholars as the Roman Emperor that had Paul and Peter killed. Regardless, Nero was a man regarded as one of the top most evil men of all time on anyone's list. The more you study his life, it's hard to say it's not true. With that said, Nero, like the others who deemed themselves to be gods among men, committed suicide, on the anniversary of the day he had his first wife murdered.

Archetype Connection: Nimrod was a sexual and social deviant, teaching and indulging in debauchery as its leader. He was man in love with himself and built monuments to himself, Nero followed.

Key Point: even though Nero was a deviant, he was an amateur compared to Nimrod, not even close.

I am at last beginning to be housed like a human being.

- Nero

Nero's Roman Empire

Genghis Khan (1162-1227 AD)

Genghis Khan
© The Sun

The Great Khan, born by the name Temujin, went from prison to power. This man ruled over the largest empire the world has ever seen. He united and ruled over the Mongolian people of north Asia, who was used to being independent people that wouldn't come together to save themselves. By uniting his people and going on a warpath to expand the Mongolian Empire, Genghis Khan is revered in Asia and all around the world for his military prowess, creative mind, and unnecessary cruelty. The name Genghis Khan means 'universal ruler' in his native language.

He fathered so many children that to this day, literally, 1 in every 200 men on this planet are direct Y chromosome descendants of Genghis Khan. That's wild! He only recognized four sons, but overall, no one knows how many children he actually fathered. How did he do this? When Genghis Khan conquered a village, town, city, or nation, he would kill off the men and impregnate the women. When these women would have sons, he would enlist them in the army. When he had daughters, he would marry them off to opposing kings that sought partnership with the Khan. Once married, he would put the king on the front line of war, and after the king died fighting, the kingdom would be ceded over to his daughter, who in turn would cede the kingdom over to him.

The Khan was well known for his brilliant brutality, which is what made him what many military strategists call a war genius. He once killed 1,748,000 people in an hour at the Persian city of Nishapur. He was known for sieging a city then catapulting diseased or dead bodies into the city. His legend speaks of a mini-mountain he had made of dead bodies for passers by, sending a message to all that he was not to be played with. His Golden Horde was known for killing, raping, and pillaging.

Genghis Khan killed so many people in such a short time that he changed the climate on the planet. Reread what I just said, and think about that for a second. It is estimated that he killed close to 40 million people! Many of them were his own people and immediate neighbors, just as scripture said the antichrists would. Scientists have estimated that his killing of so many people in such a short time (decreased heat signature [body heat]) changed the carbon footprint on the planet all while increasing vegetation, removing tons of carbon from the atmosphere. How evil is that? When he died, he had everyone who knew of his burial placed killed, pallbearers and all. Horses, funeral planners, women, children, all. So, to this day no one knows where he was actually buried.

<u>Archetype Connection</u>: Nimrod was known as a mighty hunter of not only animals but humans. He made killing men to subjugate nations a way of life, which was duplicated by Genghis Khan on a climate changing level.

<u>Key Point</u>: even though Genghis Khan ruled over more people, killed more people, fathered more children, he still wasn't as bad as Nimrod. Genghis never ruled the world....Nimrod did.

I am the punishment of God. If you had not committed great sins, God would not have sent a punishment like me upon you.

- Genghis Khan

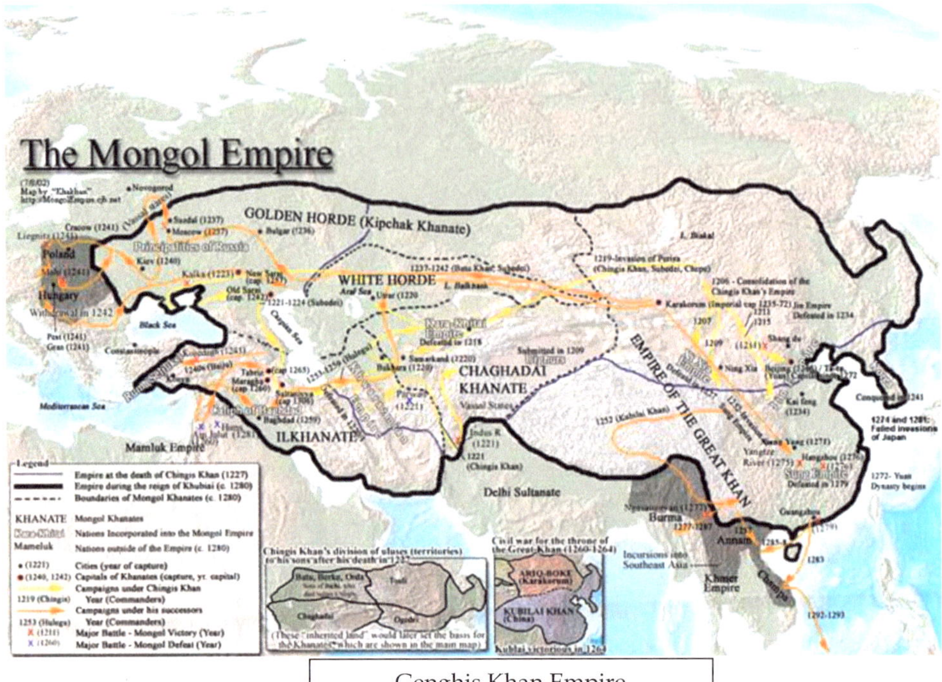

Genghis Khan Empire
© Manchester Historian

Charles V (1500-1558 AD)

Charles V
© The Brussels Times

The Universal Ruler, as he deemed himself, was a Spanish ruler that expanded the European ideology worldwide. Born as the heir to the Spanish throne by his grandfather Maximilian I, the Holy Roman Emperor, after his father died in 1506. He took on the name Charles V after Charlemagne, looking to be as impactful and powerful. From Spain, he established a European world through global conquest. He is known for traveling throughout his empire about 25% of his reign.

Initially a man of peace, Charles became known as a warmonger, expanding the Holy Roman Empire to nations that the Spanish world didn't know existed. He's the ruler that killed off the Aztecs and Incan empires of mid and central America, some of my ancestors. He conquered and became the ruler over Spain, Germany, Italy, Austria, Hungary, Bohemia, Sicily, Sardinia, etc. His titles are so expansive that we would have to make a whole page of them alone (ex. Count of Barcelona, King of the Romans, Duke of Guelders, King of the Indies, etc.). Again, he fashioned himself as the Holy Roman Emperor, which came with a higher title, Universal Ruler.

Charles V had a deformity, an enlarged jaw, due to his family's many years of intermarriages. He was a man that was viewed as physically weak, possible epilepsy. He also was diagnosed with gout because of his consistent diet of eating red meat. This caused him to become a cripple as he aged, which for a traveling king, would have been a painful experience.

In the end, Charles V was known as realizing the term "the empire on which the sun never sets." His expansive empire reached from Europe to the Americas to Africa and parts of Asia. He and the Roman Catholic Church used religion to enslave and destroy civilizations for their own personal gain. Whole nations were wiped out under Charles V that are considered extinct. Not because they warred against Spain, but because Charles V wanted to become ruler of the world. It began with him subjugating his neighbors, his European brothers. He ruled until the age of 56, then gave up his throne. Two years later he died of malaria.

Archetype Connection: Nimrod subjugated his cousins, the Japhetites, then the rest of the known world in Mesopotamia. They were his family, just like Charles V. One of Nimrod's titles was Universal Ruler, which was adopted by Charles V.

Key Point: even though Charles V empire stretched around the world in different areas and called himself the Universal Ruler, he never ruled all nations....Nimrod did.

I came, I saw, God conquered.

- Charles V

Adolf Hitler (1889-1945 AD)

Adolf Hitler
© The HISTORY Channel

Evil. The man responsible for the deaths of over 6 million Jews need no introduction or page of notes to highlight his atrocities. What we will express is how Hitler had a foundational understanding of God and that he was real. Hitler even sang in the choir as a boy and strongly considered becoming a priest.

His Anti-Jewish thought process began when he was younger, learning from Karl Lueger and others how to view the Jews. Those seeds led to what we now Hitler means in the mind of people worldwide. This man went from a Catholic background to denying the divinity of Jesus Christ himself. There are whole documentaries made of Hitler and the Nazis worshipping and summoning demonic entities for technology and power enhancement. The things Hitler, the Nazis, and world governments did and continue to practice are and were blasphemous and abominable before both God and man. The knowledge they received created what we know as NASA. So, with that said, I will close out this section on the man who's name still rings evil almost 100 years after his arrival on the global scene. His name, more so than any other on this list, equates to antichrist. Everything he stood for symbolizes such, especially with his genocide of the Jews. Stomach turning. Sources said he died by suicide in Germany as the Russians and Americans closed in on him in a bunker. Truth is, in declassified documents, Hitler escaped to South America and died in shame, in a hut....which is what the literal name Hitler means in German. The man who sat on top of the world died in a hut.

Archetype Connection: Nimrod consulted with spirits and provoked God to wrath with his idolatrous ways, which was duplicated by Hitler, which almost made him king of the world. It almost happened.

Key Point: even though Hitler is known for his evil and Satanic thought process as he pushed to become ruler of the world, he wasn't as bad as Nimrod. Hitler made a deal with the devil but fell short of delivering rulership over the known world....Nimrod did.

The Christian-Jewish pestilence is surely approaching its end now. It is simply dreadful, that a religion has even been possible, that literally eats its God in Holy Communion.

- Adolf Hitler

Joseph Stalin (1878-1953 AD)

Joseph Stalin
© BBC

Publicly, Joseph Stalin is not as known as Hitler is. Historically, he's Hitler's equal and the man that almost lost Russia in the process of defeating the Nazis. But factually, Joseph Stalin was worse than Hitler, way worse.

Born to a poor family in Georgia, Russia, Stalin rose through the ranks of a Russian Revolution to absolute ruler and dictator. Whereas Hitler killed 6 million Jews, Stalin killed close to 20 million people, most of which were his own. 1 million of those were killed in the early 1930s when he rose to power. After that, through his gulags and secret missions, Stalin had families wiped out for the betterment of the Soviet Union (in his opinion). Famines, forced labor (slavery), deportation, massacres, and inhumane detentions of random citizens marked the rule of Stalin. He was a man that Hitler respected even though Stalin secretly feared the Nazi leader. Stalin was known as a paranoid man that was notorious for having people disappear if they looked at him in a way he didn't like. Generals who did his nastiest biddings were killed at the snap of finger, depending on how he felt that day.

Stalin, unlike the others, was not out for global conquest. Instead, his focus was on a Soviet Union ran world, which is different than running the world from the Soviet Union. His preference was to dominate home, then the state. In order to do so, Stalin used genocide to complete this task. He killed almost 3x as many people as Hitler using this method. He had a dislike of the Jews as well (read the Soviet "Doctor's Plot"). This state of paranoia hunted him to the day he died. Stalin died in his own feces, on the floor, in his office, scared. Doctors say he died of a cerebral hemorrhage, which means he died of a stroke. The man who ruled over the superpower of the world after World War II died alone and scared in 1953.

Archetype Connection: Nimrod narrowed the number of people around him as he was paranoid and afraid that someone was going to kill him and rule in his stead, especially if they got the garments of Adam and Eve. Stalin duplicated this mindset at the expense of millions of lives.

Key Point: even though Stalin didn't seek to rule the world, he became the leader of the world superpower after WWII. Stalin never wanted to rule the world....Nimrod did.

You know they are fooling us, there is no God.

- Joseph Stalin

Mao Zedong (1893-1976)

Another genocidal maniac who killed millions of people, his own. Mao Zedong, former leader of communist China, was a man that had no conscience. It is estimated that he had close to 80 million Chinese people killed. It's disgusting. Mao, although viewed as a madman now, established the People's Republic of China that dominates world markets today. He started the Chinese Cultural Revolution in 1966, which jump started the death of tens of millions of people.

Mao, similar to Genghis Khan, sought to unite his people. But like Stalin, he used genocide to do so. Mao wanted to usher in a new world for the Chinese people and he believed that by using communism under a totalitarianism leadership model, he could do so. Only Genghis Khan killed more people than Mao Zedong. He took China from a small business minded country to the world leading economy and largest standing army. While all this sounds good, millions of people had to disappear in order to do so. In the end, Mao died from a multitude of things: Lou Gehrigs disease, lung complications from heavy smoking, and heart disease. Finally, in 1976, Mao died of several heart attacks over a 7-month period. He died in pain and agony. After he died, China's population exploded from around 500 million people to nearly 900 million.

Mao Zedong
© Biography

Archetype Connection: Nimrod changed the culture on the planet. He taught mankind how to sin against God in ways that no one else has. His teachings continue to send people to Hell, the Anti-God Revolution, just like Mao's Cultural Revolution.

Key Point: even though Mao tried to change the mind of China through his rule, he wasn't as influential as Nimrod. Mao changed how his people changed for a while....Nimrod has changed how the world thinks, even to this day, until the end of time.

Religion is poison. It has two great defects: it undermines the race…(and) retards the progress of the country.

- Mao Zedong

Most of these so-called great and powerful men died horrible, vile, shameful deaths. All charismatic, all empire drivers, all economy creators, all impulsive, all with a god-complex. Only Nebuchadnezzar II died in peace, as an year-old man. Why him? Wasn't he the most like Nimrod? Yes, he was, but unlike the others, he acknowledged t the God of Heaven is God. Not himself nor any deity or man the world claimed was supreme was God, but the LOR of Heaven. The other so-called 'world king' or 'universal ruler' died in their idolatry. No matter how much power these men had, money, resources, influence, worshipped, god-complex thinking, etc., none of them died peaceful, except Nebuchadnezzar II. They all died miserable, isolated, and or alone.

How The "god-kings" Died

Nebuchadnezzar II – acknowledged God, died in peace

Alexander the Great – died of alcohol poisoning

Xerses I – murdered by his bodyguard, along with his son

Genghis Khan – died from an illness after falling from his horse during a siege

Charles V – died ill and crippled, from malaria

Adolf Hitler – died in a hut in South America, poor (allegedly died from suicide in 1945)

Joseph Stalin – died of a stroke in his own feces, alone, for days

Mao Zedong – died of a series of heart attacks

How The "Original god-king" Died

Nimrod – died naked, in the wilderness, with his head chopped off

Ladies and gentlemen, this is not a coincidence. These rulers, and many more of this mindset, died in similar fashion, usually alone and graphically disturbing. For example, Napoleon Bonaparte died of stomach cancer, alone on an island, isolated from the only thing that gave him human connection: power. Why? Because these men chose to follow evil, day after day, until the day they died. They believed the rhetoric, the lies, the worship, the manipulation, the power. They all searched for the crown of Nimrod, with Alexander the Great actually finding it. They all sought to do then outdo Nimrod. Even though they called him different names throughout the ages, they all chased the same platform and power Nimrod attained. Their chasing after Nimrod's impact, for example, is like the US Presidents. Regardless of who you like or who's the next one in line, they are all trying to catch up with the first one, George Washington. He was the only president to be asked to become king. No one else, regardless of what you think or feel. Only Washington was asked to be more than the office of the President. He declined, went home, and died in peace. Sounds like Nebuchadnezzar II's story.

To be clear, evil in the form of Nimrod's is more than just a single man ruling a kingdom, but it's a system, a way of life, a government. Nimrod and his system had unlimited power. Not because of him, per say, but because of the spirit that ruled him that ruled others that only holiness can limit. That's the power of Nimrod's system, the spirit of the AntiChrist. Nimrod gave himself to evil in a way that made it possible to not only rule a people for the time being, but for ages. His way is the base of all evil governments on this planet, regardless of what they call themselves on the surface, they're updated versions of Nimrod's world. He gave evil a human constitution, which is why Satan's organization still prevails in the Earth. Sure, Satan mentally rules this world, but he needs help in order to rule. He is not God, and he knows that. Therefore, he needs help to mask as if he is God, which is a kingdom of the mind. That requires human help.

ne spirit that animates a Satanic mindset is the very spirit of the AntiChrist. This is where Nimrod comes in. His llowance of Satanic influence did something that all the others that followed him couldn't do: his system was the first that God himself had to come down and discipline. None of the others required God to do so so epically as he did at the Tower of Babel. Any system that claims its executive office as a global ruler, "holy" anything, universal anything, god anything, is an expression of the Nimrodic system. This is why we were put on alert by the prophets and Jesus himself about the spirit of the antichrist leading up to THE AntiChrist. This is what makes Nimrod and the spirit of the AntiChrist so unique.

This is also why THE AntiChrist will be so unique....archetype 2.0.

Spirit of the AntiChrist

Matthew 24:24

For there shall arise false Christs, and false prophets, and shall shew great signs and wonders; insomuch that, if it were possible, they shall deceive the very elect.

Ladies and Gentlemen, the spirit of the AntiChrist is real, very real. It's not a new spirit or something that just came around when the Bible was printed in 1455 in Germany on the Gutenberg Press. It's been here for thousands of years. Since Nimrod, this concept, idea, system, plan, government, thought, has been in play. Satan has been looking for THE AntiChrist to come so he can have his fun in the sun. Over the course of human history, Satan has watched closely and influenced many people to rule in his stead. The antichrists that Jesus spoke about, the prophets spoke about, and even the few we mentioned in this work are all pawns that Satan uses to push his agenda. They all believed that they would rise and rule to unforeseen power and prestige. In some shape or form, they all believed they were above humanity, god-like, beyond death. This is also why God sent them all a message, that HE is LORD, above all, HE is the master over death, in which they all died miserable deaths. All, except Nebuchadnezzar II, who ruled in the same city, nation, palace, and place that Nimrod did, was the closest of all the archetypes to Nimrod, but he was humbled by the LORD. He was made to crawl like an animal around his kingdom for all to see. The man that ruled the largest empire on the planet at the time was likened to a beast, an animal, for a year, until the LORD opened his mind for him to see that only the LORD God of Heaven is king of kings, LORD of Lords. This humbling was a message to all, namely Satan, but more specifically, the spirit of the antichrist.

When God made the world, HE made spirits of various types. For example, Satan is a spirit, a fallen angel. Angels are spirits, meant to be messengers of the LORD for the purposes that HE chooses. HE is the Father of spirits, meaning that HE rules over each and every spirit, good and evil. All spirits submit to HIS will, way, and WORD. This includes Satan. This includes the spirit of the AntiChrist. God is the original spirit, creator, LORD. Nothing exists outside of HIM.

With that said, we must take a closer look at the spirit of the antichrist. This spirit is the same that ruled over Nimrod. This spirit has ruled over many people, a spirit that is seducing, unwavering, restless, promising power but delivering slavery and death. In order for us to understand the coming and final AntiChrist, we must understand Nimrod and the spirit of the antichrist that came through him. Since Nimrod, this spirit has been spreading like a virus.

1 John 4:3

And every spirit that confesseth not that Jesus Christ is come in the flesh is not of God: and this is that spirit of antichrist, whereof ye have heard that it should come; and even now already is it in the world.

To Make It Plain, this spirit is not coming, it is already here. It is not just in a world leader, but in your and my world, operating. Yes, ladies and gentlemen, any and every spirit that doesn't confess that Jesus the Christ was not God in the flesh has the spirit of the antichrist. No one is exempt. The spirit itself is the problem, the people who accept it are the byproduct that has given way to the spirit. Our family, friends, neighbors, loved ones, leaders, followers, people we know, and or strangers could carry this spirit. It is a spirit that spreads on the minds and hearts of men, like a virus or bacteria, causing people to accept blasphemy as their truth. Like a virus, it comes in, unassuming. It will attack a cell, communicate with its systems, then seek to shut it down for its own self-gain. Also, like a virus, it can kill you if not treated. This is why we must not believe every spirit, regardless of the person, which could cloud our vision of the LORD, which could lead to not only physical death but spiritual death. We must be clear in our approach to such things so we can stand correct in the eyes of God. This spirit has a few different nicknames but has several attributes that we must pay attention to in order to identify it when we see or experience it.

Spirit of Error

1 John 4:6

We are of God: he that knoweth God heareth us; he that is not of God heareth not us. Hereby know we the spirit of truth, and the spirit of error.

Deceiver (manipulator)

2 John 1:7

For many deceivers are entered into the world, who confess not that Jesus Christ is come in the flesh. This is a deceiver and an antichrist.

Many Before THE One

1 John 2:18

Little children, it is the last time: and as ye have heard that antichrist shall come, even now are there many antichrists; whereby we know that it is the last time.

We all know an antichrist, whether you want to admit it or not. We all know a person who has knowledge of God yet denies the power thereof. They know HE is God Almighty, but they deny that Jesus is God and that HE was in Christ, the anointed one. It's intentional, not an accident.

So how do we identify an antichrist? The Bible is plain. Anyone who doesn't accept Jesus as God in the flesh. It's that simple. The LORD has no respector of person to the point that HE overlooks such an issue. We must understand this concept. It's not the person, per say, but the spirit in the person that influences the mind or heart of a person to not see God clearly. Some people haven't heard the truth of God, which is a different conversation all together. But there are billions of people on the planet that has heard of God, and yet deny that Jesus is God in the flesh. We have people in our everyday life that we have known our whole lives and still don't believe that Jesus is God in the flesh. To be fair, there hasn't been a lot correct and detailed ministry to teach people the truth of the LORD. But that's why books like this are being made accessible for you to alleviate that issue. Ignorance addressed can bring salvation. That's why we must be ready to share the truth of God with everyone for their eternity's sake. The spirit of the antichrist prefers the arrogance of knowledge over the ignorance of wisdom.

As a believer, when we address a person who has such a spirit, being combative and judgmental is not the answer. Instead, treat them as God does you. When they are open and available for the conversation, have it, with grace and truth. Listen first. Humble yourself, be open, seek to understand from their perspective. It doesn't lessen your belief, instead, as I have experienced more times than I can remember, it deepens your faith, if you're rooted in it. Listen, be available. Then, when the time comes, be willing and ready to...

2 Timothy 2: 15

Study to shew thyself approved unto God, a workman that needeth not be ashamed, rightly diving the word of truth.

That's it. It's that simple. We must study the scriptures to learn what and how. The key is studying to understand for self-sake, not for others. That's not what God wants us to do, which for some reason people do. This is why, when asked a question that stretches beyond their quick talking points, they can't answer in a truthful and effective way. Instead, we should study for self, for God to approve, so when we encounter others and they ask questions, you are prepared. Studying for self to the glory of God is honorable. Studying for self for self, is dishonorable. This very concept, when you study for self for self, is antichrist type behavior as well. See how thin of a line it is?

All you can do is what you can do. Take Abraham for an example. When face to face with Nimrod, the World's First AntiChrist, he wasn't combative. All he did was tell the truth of God, personally, then was willing to stand on business. This is why when Nimrod threw him in the furnace, nothing happened to Abraham. We are thrown into the fire as well, just in a different way. The fire we may be thrown into is the flame of scrutiny, ridicule, debate, shame, violence, etc. I've been in all of thee above. It's a challenge, but a fun one if you understand the assignment and that everlasting eternity with God is on the other side of the worst type of reaction you receive. Just as Abraham was unphased by the fire that killed his brother, so should we be unphased by the same fire that may cause our brother to fall when it comes to our belief. Just as God was with Abraham, who prior to this encounter with Nimrod, learned the ways of God himself. Therefore, Abraham was willing to stand on what he learned of God and taught through his life with seasoning words to the world king. Even Nimrod, who had the original spirit of the antichrist, had to accept that not only was Abraham special and anointed, but that the real God of the Universe was in charge and the spirit within him that had deceived the whole world was in error. Again, this is why this work was done, to *Make It Plain*, reach those who had never read the detailed story of Abraham and Nimrod, how to deal with both the antichrists and THE AntiChrist, and above all, save souls to the LORD. Simple.

Reader, do not fear the times that we are living in. The world is what it is and it's going to get worse. My responsibility is not to make you feel better but to tell you the truth to encourage you to do better. The LORD never promised us "feel good." Please show me where HE said that? The world promises you a multitude of ways to feel better. God promised us the actuality of being better. Medicine can make you feel better, but keep you in the hospital or cause an addiction to the feeling you receive from taking a medicine for the ailment you have. Or, you can get the cure, which makes you better, even if it doesn't feel good. The world offers you feelings. God offers you facts. There's a huge difference between the two. The spirit of the antichrist chooses the world. The spirit of God chooses HIM. WE are like HIM!

They Not Like Us!

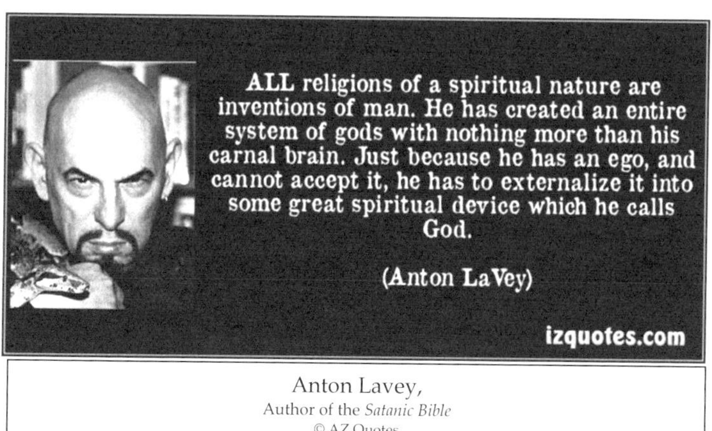

Anton Lavey,
Author of the *Satanic Bible*
© AZ Quotes

AntiChrist Spirits That Rule Over Nations

Ephesians 6:12

For we wrestle not against flesh and blood, but against principalities, against powers, against the rulers of darkness of this world, against spiritual wickedness in high places.

You have no idea, trust me.

People, it's not about waking up anymore. There has been MANY warnings, signs, sirens, and everything else to wake people up to what's going on out here. You can see, hear, feel, touch, taste, imagine, etc., evil. It's everywhere!

NEWS FLASH!!!

Spirits rule over nations!

When people ask why does God allow things to happen the way that they have and how they are currently, in most cases no one takes into consideration what the LORD hasn't allowed to happen. It's really crazy when you think about it. God, the Father of All Spirits, has a system for all spirits to operate in. Order, universal order. HE is God, alone, with none beside him. When it comes to the nations, he has angels that sit over them whose job it is to report to HIM about what's going on, what is to be allowed, protection methods, all kinds of things. Let's be clear, they can only do what they are assigned to do, nothing more. They are angels, which means messenger, so it's not like they have full autonomy to do as they please. Therefore, there is order above our heads, even if there is warring we cannot see. Why did we say this?

The spirit of the antichrist is at war with mankind. There are spirits that rule over certain nations that hinder prayers. Yes, the things that are between you and God go up to the LORD of Heaven. He hears every prayer, especially those that are sincere and truthful unto HIM. Those prayers are like a sound, music in a sense, that the LORD hears. For the great musician HE is, it's like the image of floating notes that go before HIM. God is a spirit, and those that worship HIM must do so in spirit and in truth (John 4:24).

Spirits can see what we can't. They have been assigned to a world that exists outside of ours. They have to get permission to come into ours. Aleister Crowley, the self-proclaimed "Mr. 666" himself, tried to summon a spirit to step through a portal into our 3-D world. The entity was named Lam, which is the very image that every UFO image looked like on TV for the last 100 years. What a coincidence! Regardless, this entity could not step through because he didn't have permission to even though Crowley had a chance to see it. This show the power of evil in this world when empowered by man, which is what God himself warned against at the Tower of Babel (Gen. 10:6). The more mankind discovers the depth of its power given by the LORD himself, the more evil we become. Nimrod was the most dangerous to date to understand this concept. He, like the other world leaders that followed his lead in the spirit of the antichrist, studied the spiritual world in detail and understood what we are teaching here. There are spirits that rule over nations that give certain people power. They have yet to catch on to the fact that this power is only for a time, which is the manipulation of the spirit. Satan doesn't have to do much when the spirit of the antichrist is at work.

When the verse says principalities and powers, it's not just talking about humans, but angels. The titles for angels or spirits that rule over certain areas or regions are considered principalities and powers. Again, we you have no idea. This world that we live in is a multi-layered, multi-dimensional world that God gave mankind dominion over. We know more than we should know but less than what we could know. This is why kingdoms rise and fall. The principalities and powers have influence in ways that occur in the spiritual realm but is manifested in the physical realm. Again, we have no idea.

These are not weak spirits, but spirits that have power beyond the measure that we understand because this hasn't been explained to us. Some spirits have the ability to get in the way of prayers. Yes, you read that correctly! There are spirits that can hinder a prayer or message that comes from us to the LORD. There are people that are devout in their belief, honorable in the eyes of God, whose words move the heart of the LORD. That same person can pray, earnestly, and it seem as though their prayer isn't answered. In most cases, people scramble and look for all kinds of explanations. One that I don't hear at all is that possibly a spirit is blocking it. I've heard that the devil could be blocking it, but that would mean that he is dang near omnipresent, meaning everywhere at one time, which he is not. With all the people praying to God, that would have to be his only job.

I know, this sounds crazy right? Sounds like we're stretching it, huh? There's no way an angel stands guard over certain nations, right? There's no way that spirits can hinder my prayers, especially for the holy ones, right?

Brace yourself....truth is stranger than fiction.

Daniel 10: 12-13

Then said he unto me, Fear not, Daniel: for from the first day that thou didst set thine heart to understand, and to chasten thyself before thy God, thy words were heard, and I am come for thy words. 13 But the prince of the kingdom of Persia withstood me one and twenty days: but lo, Michael, one of the chief princes, came to help me; and I remained there with the kings of Persia.

Let's *Make it Plain*.

Daniel prayed but his prayer was blocked. By an angel. It took the archangel Michael to set him free.

This angel was given an assignment from God based on the prayer Daniel prayed. For 21 days, Daniel waited, humbling himself before God. This messenger was sent on the 1st day to answer Daniel's prayer. However, the prince of Persia hindered the delivery for 21 days. Question: how do we know the prince of Persia is a spirit or angel and not an actual man? Verse 13 tells us that Michael, one of the chief princes, came to help this lesser powerful angel. We know that Michael is the archangel of God. This is the same Michael that cast Satan out of heaven before the creation of the world and rebuked him over the body of Moses.

Revelation 12: 7-9

And there was war in heaven: Michael and his angels fought against the dragon; and the dragon fought and his angels, 8 And prevailed not; neither was their place found any more in heaven. 9 And the great dragon was cast out, that old serpent, called the Devil, and Satan, which deceiveth the whole world: he was cast out with him.

Jude 1:9

Yet Michael the archangel, when contending with the devil he disputed about the body of Moses, durst not bring against him a railing accusation, but said, The Lord rebuke thee.

Needless to say, Michael is a powerful being, an angel of the LORD, who contains substantial power. The LORD saw the dispute and delay then decided to send Michael. This is why the angel that spoke to Daniel said what he said. Without Michael, there is no telling how long Daniel would have had to wait on his response from the LORD.

For this section, let's refocus on Daniel 10:13.

But the prince of the kingdom of Persia withstood me one and twenty days: but lo, Michael, one of the chief princes, came to help me; and I remained there with the kings of Persia.

Now that we know that prince here means angel, we understand that Persia has an angel that not only guarded over it then but still guards it, even though today it has another name. Today, the area that made up the Persian Empire during this time is Iran. The kings of Persia in verse 13 refers to are the 5 kings that Daniel served: Nebuchadnezzar II, Evil-Merodach, Belshazzar, Darius I, and Cyrus the Great. These kings had an angel standing over their kingdom that they didn't know about. Even though they all were influenced by Daniel and served the will of God in some form or fashion, the spirit that was over the kingdom as a whole was in contention with the prayers of Daniel to God, a principality angel. The kings of Persia were idolaters and their nation were a nation of idolaters, meaning idol worshippers.

The Babylonian kingdom, led by Nebuchadnezzar II, were idol worshippers. The next 2 rulers were Babylonian. Darius I was a Mede, and Cyrus was considered a Persian. This spirit, angel, prince, stood over 3 different nations but the same kingdom. The people were a mix of Babylonians, Medes, Persians, and Chaldeans. The nation took on the personality of the spirit that stood over it.

It was a dream of Nebuchadnezzar II, the closet ruler to Nimrod of the antichrist's archetypes, that we learn about the end of the Babylonian kingdom but the birth of 3 future world kingdoms that the world will see before its end. From Nimrod to Nebuchadnezzar, different rulers ruled over the land mass that the Persians eventually took over. Regardless of who ruled, the foundation of evil and idolatry remained the same as the seed of Nimrod had deep roots. It still does. Belshazzar lost the Babylonian kingdom to Darius I the Mede. Cyrus came in a night and took the kingdom from Darius I, making himself the first Persian king. Although only one of them were truly Persian, Cyrus, they all share the same spirit at one point. They all took on this spirit, exhibiting the antichrist spirit that denied the power of God. Nebuchadnezzar II and Cyrus ended their lives as honorable men before God, being used by him in a willing manner, but they all took the throne that Nimrod established. Although both men served God, they did not abolish the ways of Nimrod and destroy the idols of the nation or their kingdom as history has shown us. Therefore, God, in his infinite wisdom, showed us all what was going to be from a global kingdom point of view in the dream of Nebuchadnezzar II, interpreted by the prophet Daniel.

Daniel 2: 31-33

Thou, O king, sawest, and behold a great image. This great image, whose brightness was excellent, stood before thee; and the form
thereof was terrible. 32 This image's head was of fine gold, his breast and his arms of silver, his belly and his thighs of brass, 33 His
legs of iron, his feet part of iron and part of clay. 34 Thou sawest till a stone was cut out without hands, which smote the image
upon his feet that were of iron and clay, and brake them to pieces. 35 Then was the iron, the clay, the brass, the silver, and the gold,
broken to pieces together, and became like the chaff of the summer threshing floors; and the wind carried them away, that no place
was found for them: and the stone that smote the image became a great mountain, and filled the whole earth. 36 This is the dream;
and we will tell the interpretation thereof before the king. 37 Thou, O king, art a king of kings: for the God of heaven hath given
thee a kingdom, power, and strength, and glory. 38 And wheresoever the children of men dwell, the beasts of the field and the
fowls of the heaven hath he given into thine hand, and hath made thee ruler over them all. Thou art this head of gold. 39 And after
thee shall arise another kingdom inferior to thee, and another third kingdom of brass, which shall bear rule over all the earth. 40
And the fourth kingdom shall be strong as iron: forasmuch as iron breaketh in pieces and subdueth all things: and as iron that
breaketh all these, shall it break in pieces and bruise.

Make It Plain

This image that was seen was that of both Nimrod and the AntiChrist, the World's First and the World's Last AntiChrist. Biblical scholars have thought and taught this image to be that of Nebuchadnezzar II. It was not. In verse 38, Daniel told Nebuchadnezzar II to his face that he was the head of gold. He didn't say that the image was him, just the head. Nebuchadnezzar II was the antichrist type that had a mind likened to Nimrod. Just as Nimrod ruled over the world, so did Nebuchadnezzar II. We must keep in mind that the most powerful kingdom on the planet at the time was under Nebuchadnezzar II's rule even though he didn't conquer Egypt when he had the chance after his initial win at the Battle of Carchemish as the crown prince. Still, he was given dominion over all the Earth. But how? Because of the spirit that ruled over the nation. It was on assignment that stood in the gap to maintain the ideology of Nimrod over the ages. This spirit was stronger than other spirits that stood guard over other nations. This is why the angel that spoke to Daniel said that Michael had to help it out of a jam while contending with the prince or spirit of Persia in Daniel 10. Spiritual warfare is real.

The four kingdoms that Daniel told Nebuchadnezzar II about that was in his dream were:

1st kingdom – Gold, Nebuchadnezzar II, Babylonian Empire

2nd kingdom – Silver, Cyrus the Great, Medo-Persian Empire

3rd kingdom – Brass, Alexander the Great, Greek Empire

4th kingdom – Iron and Clay, the Caesars, Roman Empire

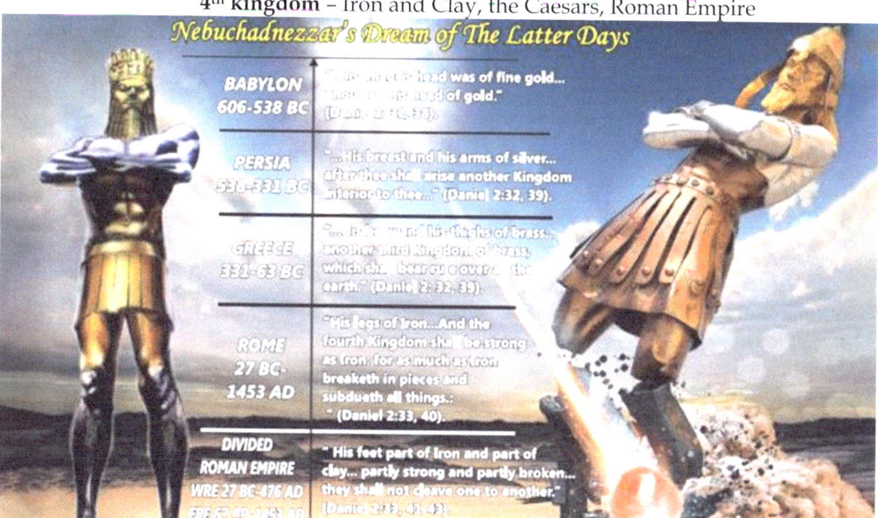

Each one of these kingdoms were expressions of both Nimrod and THE AntiChrist. The kingdom that rose after the Babylonian Empire, the Persians, were amazing and outstanding, but not as powerful as the Babylonian kingdom that Nebuchadnezzar II ruled. The kings of Persia were great, but inferior to the Babylonian kings that stretched from Nimrod to Nebuchadnezzar II. The third kingdom, Alexander the Great and his contributions to the spreading of the Greek language throughout the known world, was and still is a power that connects the planet in a similar way that the world spoke one language pre Tower of Babel. The fourth kingdom has many rulers, beginning with Julius Caesar, that called themselves Caesar. From them we get the world system that still exists to this day. For example, the United States of America is really the United States of Rome. We have the same type of government (republic), military mindset, capitalist structure, glorification of perversion, idol worshiping capital of the world, a rich vs working class, gladiator system that is merged with slaves having the opportunity to win their freedom (sports and politics), celebrity worship, false flag wars, and a mentally sick public whose identity is wrapped in self-elevation at the expense of others while claiming victimization. Rome is even the birthplace of the stock market system (societates publicanonrum). Again, the United States of Rome.

The iron and clay of the feet represent weapons and people as weapons are made of iron and humans made of clay. It has the image of the feet because just as feet travel and hold up the body, the Roman system upholds the evil of the spirit of the antichrist. It also has a worldwide reach, that expands beyond the borders of its 3 predecessor kingdoms. Because of its diversity, it has both the weapons and people to last. Only the stone, you know, the one the builders rejected, can destroy this "image". This stone, which Daniel said was cut out WITHOUT hands, destroyed this image, as verse 34 says. WITHOUT hands was the indicator that this was God, not man. The stone, ladies and gentlemen, was Jesus, the Christ. How do we know that?

Matthew 21: 42-45

Jesus saith unto them, did ye never read in the scriptures, The stone which the builders rejected, the same is become the head of the corner: this is the Lord's doing, and it is marvelous in our eyes? 43 Therefore say I unto you, The kingdom of God shall be taken from you, and given to a nation bringing forth the fruits thereof. 44 And whosoever shall fall on this stone shall be broken: but on whomsoever it shall fall, it will grind him to powder. 45 And when the chief priests and Pharisees had heard his parable, they perceived that he spake of them.

Jesus himself told the Jewish leaders that HE was the stone and they were the builders that rejected him. HE is the stone that Nebuchadnezzar II saw in his dream that Daniel interpreted. As the Christ, HE was the fulfillment of the dream and interpretation. HE didn't come during Nebuchadnezzar II's reign, the 1st kingdom. HE didn't come during the 2nd or 3rd kingdom. How ironic is it that hundreds of years in advance, the king of Babylon saw in a dream the stone crashing into the feet, which is the 4th kingdom, which is the Roman Empire. It just so happens that it was during this time that Jesus came. Daniel didn't see this, the king of Babylon saw it. A man that accepted worship as a god himself, a man that had to be humbled before he died. He saw it, Daniel interpreted it, and it has come to pass. The only part that hasn't happened yet is the complete collapse of the image. This collapse is the end of the world.

Christ told the Jewish leaders in Matthew 21 verse 44 more information to validate who HE was. Not only did HE verify what Daniel said, but HE added that all of those nations will be broken by HIM and that whoever is under HIM after the collapse shall be grinded into powder. Wow! The LORD ain't taking no names! By making this statement, Jesus is letting it be known that all systems, all governments, and everyone that will try to stand in the last day shall be ground to powder. Here, HE is forecasting Armageddon to them and they don't even know it, still don't. This is the wisdom of God, a mystery of the faith. We digress.

The spirit that Christ will crush in the end will be this same spirit that resides in the hearts of men: antichrist. Nebuchadnezzar II saw it but didn't know what he was looking at. The angel that needed the help from the archangel Michael was delayed for 21 days because of it. This same spirit, while in the present, knew that its battle was just for a season. As the angel progressed with the help of Michael, it said something that was fulfilled by history.

Danie 10:20

Then said he, Knowest thou wherefore I come unto thee? And now will I return to fight with the prince of Persia: and when I am gone forth, lo, the prince of Grecia hall come.

Grecia is Greece. This is incredible! As the angel is about to depart from Daniel, he tells the prophet that he must return now that he has delivered his message, but he knows that he must fight with the angel of Persia. This fight would last from Nebuchadnezzar II's reign (605-562 BC) to the year Alexander the Great became the king of Babylon (331 BC). That's almost 280 years! Yes, these being contested with one another for almost 3 centuries until Alexander the Great established new rulership over Greece. This angel that guarded the Persian kingdom had a time in which it could hinder prayers and do other things. When the time was up, it was over. In the physical world, it's the changing of the guard, a new way of life. But in the spiritual world, spirits are in conflict. The angel may be different, but the mindset is the same, which is why Alexander took on the names and idolatrous titles as Nimrod. He even found and wore the crown of Nimrod, made Babylon his capital in the east, rebuilt blasphemous temples, and eventually died in Nebuchadnezzar II's palace. The spirit of the antichrist strikes again.

In conclusion, I hope we now understand what the scripture means when it says that we battle not against flesh and blood but spiritual wickedness in high places. There are not only people in high places of society that are evil that run the world, but there are spirits that exists above that whose job is to guard the nations they are assigned. When we begin to understand this concept, you really begin to understand that nothing you see in this world should throw you off your focus on God. These angels or spirits have a job to do, so do we. If your prayers are hindered, don't worry: 1 God hears your prayer 2 there's a spirit on the way with an answer 3 if you don't get it in time, just look up and give God thanks. Why? Because, if your prayer is being jammed up, know that Michael may be on the way to clear the path for your answer. It's a win-win either way!

Ishtar, My Apologies, **Easter**

Acts 12:4

Now about that time Herod the king stretched forth his hands to vex certain of the church. 2 And he killed James the brother of John with the sword. 3 And ecause he saw it pleased the Jews, he proceeded further to take Peter also. (Then were the days of unleavened bread) 4 And when he had apprehended him, he put him in prison, and delivered him to four quaternions of soldiers to keep him; intending after Easter to bring him forth to the people.

It's right in your face.

We are going to ask you a few simple questions for you to think about in regards to Easter. Basic common-sense questions. Put what you have traditionally learned to the side and take a look. Conclude and judge for yourself. Truth is stranger than fiction.

Question: Is this king Herod of Acts 12 the same Herod that had all the Jewish boys 2 years old and younger killed at the time of Jesus' birth?

Answer: No. The Herod of Jesus' birth is Herod the Great (Matthew 2: 16-18). The Herod of Acts 12 is Herod Agrippa I, the grandson of Herod the Great.

Question: Who was Herod Agrippa I?

Answer: He was the last Jewish king under Roman rule (Herodian dynasty). He was a Jew that ruled Jews on the behalf of the Roman government. He was known as being a good diplomat or middle man between the Romans and Jews. He is responsible for the death of James, the brother of John, and intended to kill Peter after arresting him. He was a good friend of Caligula, arguably the worst and most demonic ruler in Roman history.

Herod Agrippa II
© Bible Archaeology Report

Question: We know Jesus started his ministry at 30 years old (Luke 3:23) and had a 3 ½ year ministry. Herod Agrippa I ruled Judea/Palestine from 41-44 AD, which would have been 6-7 years after the crucifixion of Jesus the Christ. Would he have known about Jesus?

Answer: Yes. He was a friend of both the Jews and Romans. However, he was stark enemy of Jewish believers in Jesus, who would later be classified as Christians.

Question: If Agrippa I was an enemy of the believers in Jesus and a friend of the Jews and Romans, would he celebrate, encourage, or endorse a day dedicated to the resurrection of Jesus?
Answer: No! Agrippa I was an avid enemy of the believers in Jesus. His allegiance was to the Roman government and Jewish officials. Anything and anyone who represented anything against these two were subject to death or imprisonment by Agrippa I. This is why he killed James the son of Zebedee by sword, a disciple of Jesus. This is why he imprisoned Peter with the intent to kill him after Easter, intentionally, to please the Jews (Acts 12:3). He would not have recognized the resurrection of Jesus as it was a slap in the face to both the Roman and Jewish stucture. This same structure made him king over this area. Christ represented the opposite of everything Herod Agrippa I stood for.

Our last question....

Question: Being that Herod Agrippa I was a Jew who doubled as Roman king, would he have celebrated Easter?

Answer: NO! Jews, regardless of where they are in the world, do not celebrate Easter.

Ladies and gentlemen, the Jews do NOT celebrate Easter. They celebrate Passover, which occurs around the same time. Jesus himself didn't recognize Easter, he recognized Passover. It was the reason HE was in Jerusalem the week of his death, as HE was crucified the week of Passover.

John 19:14

And it was the preparation of the Passover, and about the sixth hour: and he saith unto the Jews, Behold your King!

The very next verse tells us everything you need to know about how Herod Agrippa I, the Romans, and the Jews viewed Jesus.

John 19:15

But they cried out, Away with him, away with him, crucify him. Pilate saith unto them, Shall I crucify your King? The chief priests answered, We have no king but Caesar.

There it is. No love, no acceptance, no thumbs up. The Jewish officials and Roman government were anti-Jesus. To this day, Jews don't recognize Jesus as the messiah, savior of the world, God in the flesh. He is viewed as a prophet, but not the LORD, not the Christ. They are still waiting for the messiah to come. This is what separates the Jew from the Christian in basic fundamental beliefs.

With all this being said, reader, there is no way Jesus would have been celebrated and or recognized by the Roman government and Jewish officials 6-7 years after his death and resurrection. No way! His followers, the disciples, couldn't even be seen together in public after his death. They were being hunted and killed or imprisoned for their beliefs. Jesus told them and us that we would be persecuted for HIS name sake (Matt. 5: 11-12). Why then would the same Jesus be celebrated by his enemies shortly after his death? The first people saved were at Pentacost. They were gathered together in secret when the Holy Spirit descended down on them. The multitude of people heard the sound of the believers and 3000 were saved that day (Acts 2), including Mary, the mother of Jesus.

The concept of Easter supposedly marking the resurrection of Jesus the Christ would have been an act of treason against the Roman government. Why then would the early church and apostles, who were Jews culturally, celebrate Easter? They wouldn't. They didn't.
So then, why is it mentioned in the Bible in one place, Act 12:4, which just so happen to be a few years after the resurrection of Jesus?

Because Easter was already being celebrated....before Jesus was born, while he was living, even to this day!

Easter as we know it has nothing to do with Jesus. It has nothing to do with HIS resurrection. It has nothing to do with rabbits. It has nothing to do with colored eggs. Jesus didn't celebrate it. The apostles didn't celebrate it. The early church didn't celebrate it. The believers didn't celebrate it.

So, where does Easter come from?

Nimrod*, the World's First AntiChrist.*

According to Alexander Hislop, a well reknown historian and writer of the book *The Two Babylons*:

From Egypt these sacred eggs can be distinctly traced to the banks of the Euphrates. The classic poets are full of the fable of the mystic egg o the Babylonians; and thus its tale is told by Hyginus, the Egyptian, the learned keeper of the Palatine library of Rome, in the time of Augustus, who was skilled in all the wisdom of his native country: "An egg of wondrous size is said to have fallen from heaven into the river Euphrates. The fishes rolled it to the bank, where the doves having settled upon it, and hatched it, out came Venus, who afterwards was called the Syrian Goddess" – that is, Astarte. Hence the egg became one of the symbols of Astarte or Easter; and accordingly, in Cyprus, one of the chosen seats of the worship of Venus, or Astarte, the egg of wondrous size was represented on a grand scale.

- The Two Babylons, pg. 107

Nimrod's wife, Semiramsis, is responsible for the pagan teachings that became accepted throughout the world. Semiramsis, as we learned before, has different names in different cultures throughout different times. Semiramsis is Ishtar, Astarte, Venus, Diana, etc., same person. That's what make this story so interesting that throws many researchers off the trail. Not us. We understand the assignment and God has given us the discernment to *Make It Plain* for both you and us.

Just as a mother is the first teacher of a child beginning in the womb, Nimrod set Semiramsis up to be the first teacher of his world of anti-God followers. According to ancient Babylonian legend, from Semiramsis comes the origin of Easter and the festivities involved. It began when Semiramsis made herself the moon goddess, recognizing Nimrod her husband as the sun god. She taught the nations that she was dropped from the moon in a large egg, which landed on the Euphrates River. She then hatched out of the shell, appearing as an egg-laying rabbit. The egg and rabbit symbolize fertility, which is why Semiramsis, regardless of her varying names, became the goddess of fertility, love, childbearing, and or sex. She made herself to be the mother of all creation coming from the flood. The egg she emerged from was supposed to be the Ark, which was the biblical Noah, Nimrod her husband's great-grandfather. The timing she taught that she emerged from the egg just so happens to be at the same time of the spring equinox, Easter. See how the legend of Semiramsis, Easter, and eggs begin? Ishtar from the egg.

Following the death of Nimrod, the Sumerian/Babylonian world was in utter chaos, as scripture told us. The family of Nimrod was taken, sold into slavery, split between the nations that had been under the thumb of Nimrod. Whereas this could be seen as a bad thing, his family were the previous teachers of these same nations they became slaves to. For example, Semiramsis, Nimrod's wife, claimed to be pregnant after the death of Nimrod. The child, Tammuz, was taught by Semiramsis to the world that he was the reincarnation of Nimrod. Tammuz, taught by his mother Semiramsis to be the reincarnation of the mighty hunter Nimrod, died, actually killed, by a wild boar at the age of 40 on a hunting trip. Nimrod was killed on a hunting trip by Esau. How ironic, both father and son were killed on hunting trips, as expert hunters?

In response, Semiramsis had the people mourn for 40 days in his honor, a day for each year of his life. This 40-day mourning process became a holiday unto itself within the Babylonian culture. From there, it was adopted and spread throughout the nations. This custom has had different names, but from its beginning it has been called 'Weeping for Tammuz.' Make no mistake, it is 100% demonic in nature as idol worship. Sounds crazy, right? Think this didn't happen? An angel had to take and show the prophet Ezekiel behind closed doors into the Temple and then to the very place where women were actually performing the ritual, in the temple of God.

Ezekiel 8: 14-15

Then he brought me to the door of the gate of the LORD's house which was toward the north; and, behold, there sat women weeping for Tammuz. 15 Then said he unto me, Hast thou seen this, O son of man? Turn thee yet again, and thou shalt see greater abominations than these.

© Shalom Adventure Magazine

This is real ladies and gentlemen. The angel itself called it an abomination. Weeping for Tammuz hasn't stopped. It has continued and is associated with Ishtar, my apologies, Easter. How so? Remember the 40 days of mourning Semiramsis had the people learn and perfom, the ritual. Between Ash Wednesday and Easter, for example, the Roman Catholic Church and other denominations recognize what they call *Lent*. It is the abbreviated form of the word Lenten, which means spring in old English. The root word of Lenten is lang, which means long. Spring represents the lengthening (long) of the days from winter when the days are shorter, in reference to sunlight. During this time, the person observing Lent will fast and remain abstinent from sex for 40 days. This didn't become a holiday or recognized day within the Catholic Church until 360 AD at the Council of Laodicea. That's almost 330 years after the death of Jesus. So, if Jesus, the Jews, the Apostles, and early church didn't recognize this custom, why do we? I get it, the representation of Lent is supposed to be reflective of the 40 days and nights Jesus spent in the wilderness after HE was baptized, but shouldn't Jesus have administered the parameters of this day to the Apostles first? So it could be taught as HE instructed them to do? According to Hislop...

The forty days' abstinence of Lent was directly borrowed from the worshippers of the Babylonian goddess. Such a Lent of forty days, "in the spring of the year," is still observed by the Yezidis or Pagan Devil-worshippers of Koordistan, who have inheritd it from their early masters, the Babylonians. Such a Lent of forty days was held in spring by the Pagan Mexicans, for thus we read in Humboldt, where he gives account of Mexican observances: "Three days after the vernal equinox...began a solemn fast of forty days in honor of the sun." Such a Lent of forty days was observed in Egypt, as may be seen on consulting Wilkinson's Egyptians. This Egyptian Lent of forty days, we are informed by Landseer, in his Sabean Researches, was held expressly in commemoration of Adonis or Osiris, the great mediatorial god.

- Two Babylons

Again, Lent was already being celebrated in different cultures prior to the birth of Jesus. This is why the Roman powers that were at the time blended the pagan beliefs with the believer beliefs and called it a Christian holiday, even though Jesus wasn't either. HIS message was for us to separate from this foolishness, not join it, which is exactly what the Council of Laodicea ignored. This is what makes Satan's kingdom so powerful. It is hidden, disguised, renamed, unseen, but felt, followed, and worshipped. Satan cannot let people see who he really is. He knows that if the world sees him for who he really is, they'll go away from him and make a mockery of him. Don't believe me? Read what God himself said about him...

Ezekiel 28:17

Thine heart was lifted up because of they beauty, thou hast corrupted thy wisdom by reason of thy brightness: I will cast thee to the ground, I will lay thee before kings, that they may behold thee.

2 Corinthians 11:14

And no marvel; for Satan himself is transformed into an angel of light.

This means that he knows he's not what he proports to be, but more powerful than what people think that he is. That's his real power, wisdom. By this corruption of wisdom, God will cast him down so the kings of Earth will see him for who he really is, feeble, like the man behind the curtain of the Wizard of Oz. That's the real story and the reason that people like the story/movie even if they don't know what the story is really telling them. That's what Nimrod, Semiramsis, and Tammuz worked to disguise. It's all a big lie! That's why a day like Easter can be hidden, even from the elect or learned people for so long, because the kingdom of Satan operates as he does, in secret, discreet, unnoticed. By renaming or rebranding anti-God customs, Satan has boosted his power in the minds of man that even some of the most devout and God 1st people fall into the trap of these customs at some point or another. I too have fell victim. Not anymore. While there is nothing wrong with fasting and abstaining from desires, announcing your you-to-God commitment (Ash Wednesday) Jesus himself spoke against. Coincedentally merging the weeping of Tammuz for 40 days with Jesus being in the wilderness after baptism for 40 days is clever, but anti-God. You cannot rebrand evil. It's simply that, regardless of the name or length. What's sad is that Abraham and Isaac stood on the other side of the world while this custom was introduced to the nations as an abomination. The people who still practice this event, including those with a pure heart, claim to be children of Abraham, not realizing their 'father' stood against this. This is how powerful Satan can disguise himself and his agendas throughout the ages.

Therefore, Easter is not a Roman thing. It's not a Christian thing. It's not an American thing. It's not a God thing. It's a Babylonian thing, a Satanic thing, a Nimrod thing. It's a day attached to Semiramsis, Tammuz, and the spring equinox. It's a day specific to Semiramsis and Tammuz, the cursed son of Nimrod. One of Semiramsis' names, nickname or alternate name in a different culture, was Ishtar. Biblically, Asarte, Ashtoreth, Diana. Same woman. Inanna. In different cultures, different names, same woman, same abomination.

Why does the Christian world celebrate Easter? In 325 AD, almost 300 years after the death and resurrection of Jesus the Christ, the Roman Emperor Constantine called together the church leaders at the Council of Nicea. The leaders argued then agreed to make Easter, the ancient Sumerian/Babylonian holiday, the first Sunday after the first full moon following the Spring Equinox. This is why Easter doesn't have a fixed day each year. One year it's in March, the next year it's in April, etc. The bishops believed that Jesus' resurrection took placed on a Sunday, so they attached Easter to the first Sunday after the Spring Equinox.

If you notice, 300 years after the death and resurrection of Jesus, believers were not celebrating Easter. The bishops made this a day that the Roman Church celebrated. From there, the Roman Catholic Church. From there, the Protestant Church when it branched away from the Catholic Church. This is how countless numbers of people for about 1500 years have celebrated a day they have no idea the LORD they love never celebrated but his people were convinced to celebrate. The truth of things are always more interesting than the lies told from them. All it takes is a little common sense and simple history.

For example, the bishops believed that Jesus was resurrected on a Sunday. He was not. I know, that's a huge statement to make. "Everybody" thinks that way, right? The church said it, so it must be true, right? Again, a little common sense and simple history. Check this out...

Jesus was killed on a Friday.
HE stayed in the grave 3 days.
After 3 days, Jesus rose from the grave.
This would make Sunday the resurrection day, as the bishops agreed to.

****Key information**** The Hebrew calendar doesn't begin at sunrise, but sunset, in the evening. When you look at the Creation story, each time God completed his task, it started with Evening. Not morning, but evening. This has been a Jewish cultural truth for thousands of years. We use the Gregorian calendar. The LORD used HIS calendar, the biblical calendar that anyone can see and read about.

Jesus didn't die in the morning, but in the evening. How do we know this?

Luke 23: 44-46

And it was about the sixth hour, and there was a darkness over all the earth until the ninth hour. 45 And the sun was darkened, and the veil of the temple was rent in the midst. 46 And when Jesus had cried with a loud voice, he said, Father, into thy hands I commend my spirit: and having said thus, he gave up the ghost.

Between 6 and 9pm, that's when Jesus died, in the evening. You don't take the morning of Friday and add 3 days from there. Instead, take Jesus at his word, as he told the apostles and us many times, that he was going to raise himself from the dead in 3 days. If you do, guess what day you will get....

Friday Evening to Saturday is one, Saturday to Sunday is two, Sunday to Monday is three. It's that's simple. The beleivers worldwide celebrates Jesus' resurrection on Monday. Only the church in the western world celebrate his resurrection on Sunday, the day of the sun (sun worship), which was a part of the edict from the church as a compromise with the pagan religion. Sun-day was the day to worship the sun in the Roman pagan religion, and a day for the Christian religion to gather and pray to the son, Jesus. None of it has anything to do with the actual LORD, day of worship, etc. As a matter of fact, the day God recognizes, which HE has from the beginning, is the Sabbath. That day is not Sunday, but Saturday (Gen. 2: 1-3). 3 verses for 3 days that Jesus spent in the grave, how ironic. Not voted on, no bishops involved, just God. Again, simple.

Another question, and this will be the final one (please forgive me).

Question: So, if this is true, where did the rabbits and eggs come from in regards to Easter in the western world and customs?

Answer: I thought you would never asked...

In 1572 AD, Germans began to use egg giving to celebrate spring coming forth paralled with the Easter holiday. German immigrants brought the concept of the Easter eggs and bunny rabbits to the US and by the 1800s, candy shops were selling chocolate bunnies for Easter. From there, stories were told to children that alleged that these bunnies delivered baskets of eggs on Easter morning. And just like that, Easter as we know it becomes a celebration with chocolate bunnies and eggs. It LITERALLY had nothing, 0%, to do with Jesus being raised from the death.

All thanks to Nimrod, Semiramsis, and Tammuz.

Ephesians 4: 17-18

This I say therefore, and testify in the Lord, that ye henceforth walk not as other Gentiles walk, in the vanity of their mind, 18
Having the understanding darkened, being alienated from the life of God through the ignorance that is in them, because of the blindness of their heart:

Origins of the *Trinity*

Deuteronomy 6:4

Hear, O Israel: The LORD our God is one LORD:

One God. It's not complicated. One God. It's not a trick or riddle. One God. Not 3 or multiple gods. One God. Not a god with multiple personalities, which is the legal definition of schizophrenia. One God. HE didn't confuse the Hebrews by saying "We" at any point in scripture. One God. Sure, HE used language to explain HIMself in different ways, with many different descriptions of how HE operates, which are called diversities (not personalities).

1 Corinthians 12:6

And there are diversities of operations, but it is the same God which worketh all in all.

Still, One God. Before HIM, there was no God because HE has always been. After HIM will be no God because HE will always be.

Isaiah 43: 10-11

Ye are my witnesses, saith the LORD, and my servant whom I have chosen: that ye may know and believe me, and understand that I am he: before me there was no God formed, neither shall there be after me. 11 I, even I, am the LORD; and beside me there is no saviour.

It's important before moving forward to establish simple scripture coming straight from the LORD God HIMself that HE is One. This is the same doctrine and gospel that the apostles preached. So, that begs the question:

Where does trinity come from that has preached in churches around the world?

Answer: **Nimrod**

Surprised? Don't be, it's Nimrod, the *World's 1st AntiChrist*. After everything you have read in this book, please read the following carefully as this section could be a book all unto itself. The origins of the trinity doctrine is rooted in Nimrod and the Sumerian pantheon of gods then spread throughout the world over the course of time. Buckle up!

Ancient Sumer, then known as Shinar, is universally recognized as the the cradle of civilization.

Not the birthplace of humanity, which is Africa, but the place where mankind began to develop itself into a thriving community of technology and advancement. The Sumerians are acknowledged for creating the wheel, irrigation, domestication of animals, writing (cuneiform), the plow, law codes, beer, and other major advancements in human history. They are regarded as an advanced population that spearheaded human development post-flood. The Sumerians were the offspring and students of Cush, who the oldest global and Sumerian city Kish is named after. In the Sumerian kings list, Kish is named as the first city to be built in the new world. Cush, meaning black or blackface, is the father of Nimrod. Cush, not long after establishing Kish, moved southwest from modern day Iraq to Ethiopia, which for thousands of years was called the land of Cush. He settled near his brothers Mizraim (Egypt), Put (Libya), and Canaan (modern-day Israel), the sons of Ham, the son of Noah.

The Sumerians had their own city-states, meaning they had their own rulers to govern each city as a separate nation unto itself. Each city-state had their own gods and goddesses. They all worshipped elements of nature and different entities they believed deserved their praise and admiration, even if it meant going to war to prove which god or goddess was more powerful to help them succeed. The structure of these city-states would be copied throughout the world into every major culture that branched away from the Sumerians. Again, this is why Sumer, or Shinar, is called the cradle of civilization. They established individual governments, separate and apart, until Nimrod.

When Nimrod became king of Shinar, he built his 4 major cities as scripture says he did (Gen. 10:10): Babel (later Babylon), Erech (later Uruk, Iraq), Accad, and Calneh. These were city states, ruled by Nimrod, as he established more cities to expand his kingdom over the Mesopotamian area. From 4 cities to the whole of the known world, Nimrod ruled them all, as we have described in detail in previous chapters.

In order for Nimrod to rule city-states and keep them in alignment for the 185 years of his reign, he established a universal religion and belief structure that allowed him to group the gods and goddesses in a way that allowed the individual city-states to operate as a collective in an individual way. Different cities called their gods and goddesses different names yet they had the same functions. In other words, he established a New World Order with him as ruler, separate yet collective, vassal kings who acted as governors over their independent cities, unified in their anti-God belief structure while allowing them to use a pantheon of over 1000 different gods to keep them subjected. This seems very complex and exhaustive, so it begs the question: how did Nimrod do this?

Nimrod and his family created a divne trinity

Nimrod figured out that if he established 3 main gods, who would work as 1, he could classify them as the greater gods and the other gods would be considered lesser. All people could worship any god or goddess they wanted, give them any name they so desired in any language, but they would have to unify to worship the main 3. He would accept worship as a god himself, but the greater gods would stand as the supreme gods that were to be worshipped as foundational doctrine while he and his family stood on the forefront to be deified by the people as the "living" gods. This thought process would allow him and his family to become half man/half gods, or demi-gods as the Greeks would later label it. The living gods could change, but the foundational gods would not. The grouping of the gods gave people a choice of worship. The gods you can see and the gods you cannot. Spiritual beings and physical beings. When you align such worship with astrology and folklore stories, the allusion of universal power is accepted by those who don't have the knowledge or information to know better. The only person who would know what was being taught was a lie would have to be the person at the top, the man behind the curtain. An example of such a strong delusion and illusion is exemplified in the global sensational movie *The Wizard of Oz*. Only the man behind the curtain knew better than the lie he was perpetrating, whereas everyone else in the world was fooled. This is what is called a lying wonder (2 Thess. 2:9). This is Satanic in origin.

Nimrod knew better, he knew the real God. He was given power and love from the real God. It wasn't until he realized the power of the clothing or covering he had, which was blessed by God himself, which made him ruler over all mankind due to his ability to be a mighty hunter and warrior. When he achieved the accolades from the people, he became king. He had a choice to give worship to God or receive worship as a god. He chose the latter. From there, his anti-God behaviors increased to unseen before levels of blasphemy. He knew that God was real. He knew that Abraham and his faith in God would end his reign in the Earth because of the dream he had earlier in his life when Abraham was a newborn. His killing of the male children at that time was copied by future tyrannical leaders, such as the Pharaoh of Egypt that killed the male babies in an attempt to stop Moses (Ex. 1:15-22) and king Herod of Palestine attempting to stop the arrival of the messiah Jesus (Matt. 2: 16-18). Nimrod created the blueprint on how to kill to preserve power, even if it's children. Ironically, it was a child, Esau, who would be his killer, the grandson of Abraham. Again, Nimrod knew the truth of God yet he hid it from the people.

Question: What trinity did Nimrod and his family teach? Answer: It's a 2-part answer.

Part 1

The spiritual foundation of the <u>unseen</u>, according to *The Larousse Encyclopedia of Mythology*,

"The universe was divided into three regions each of which became the domain of a god. Anu's share was the sky. The earth was given to Enlil. Ea became the ruler of the waters. Together they constituted the triad of the Great Gods."

- pg 54-55

Anu, Enlil, and Ea

This was their spiritual Trinity

Anu, the sky god. **Enlil**, the air god. **Ea**, the god of the waters.

Anu (also An), god of the sky, was considered the lord of the heavens. Nimrod made Anu's main center of worship to be in Erech, also called Uruk, one of the four cities he built. He was worshipped as the supreme god of the sky. The story taught in the legend of Anu is that from the union with his wife Antu came the Anunnaki, the judges of the dead, the astronaut gods, better known in our times as UFO's. Anu was believed to be the god that empowered the other gods as he roamed through the sky in lightning. He was depicted as a raging bull running above the clouds that creates the thunder sound during storms. As an elder god, only his son Enlil could communicate with him, especially when he is in route across the storming sky. Anu is considered the supreme god of the three.

Enlil (also Ellil), god of the air, was considered the lord of the winds and weather. Nimrod made Enlil's main center of worship to be in Nippur, in the land of Accad of the Akkadians. His temple or 'Mountain House' in Nippur has been discovered by archaeologists for historical research.

Accad is one of the 4 cities that Nimrod built, Accad being in the mountainous region of his kingdom. Depictions of Enlil are written about on the ancient Sumerian tablets. He was worshipped as the 'lord of the air', which ironically is the nickname of Satan (Eph. 2:2) as 'the prince of the power of the air'. He was worshipped as the people prayed for good weather in preparation for a good harvest. More important to note about Enlil is that he is regarded as the king maker, which also ironically aligns itself with Satan again, who God himself calls the god or ruler of this world (2 Cor. 4:4). No one could rule Shinar without his permission, as poems written on the Akkadian history tablets pronounce Enlil as the giver of kingship to whomever he chooses, they will become commander of the world, which is what Nimrod became. Enlil was considered a supreme authoritative figure of finality of the three-person godhead.

Ea (1st named ***Enki***), god of the waters, was considered the lord of the waters. Nimrod made Ea's main center of worship Babel (Eridu), which is where he built the Tower of Babel.

To Ea, also Enki, was the temple Tower of Babel built to wage war against God. Babel is also 1 of the 4 cities that Nimrod built, with Babel (Eridu) being his capital. Ea would evolve into another god, Apsu (also Abzu (alternate for the abyss)), leaving Enki to inherit the title and position of lord of the earth while Ea/Apsu continued as lord of the waters. Ea was the god of ritual purifications, thus the water god power. He was in charge of incantations, sorcery, shapeshifting, and the arts. The very culture of Sumer (Shinar) was attributed to Ea. In history classes across the United States of America, when the cradle of civilization lessons come up about *The Land Between the Two Rivers* or *Mesopotamia*, please know that the very idea of the power of the Tigris and Euphrates Rivers along with its flooding is speaking about Ea, the water god. It is hidden in plain sight as the focus in most lessons are aimed on the Sumerian gods who the people believed caused the floods, but the mere fact that the soil was rich because of the flooding. Notice the deception? Ea was considered an advisor and powerful being in the trinity. **Enki** (also Ea), was the god of the earth. Diffferent name, same being, one coin, two different faces, like a gemini. Nimrod allowed the presence of Enki to come forward as he was the embodiment of Ea in person, wise in his actions and beloved of all the gods. He was regarded as the god of magic, using it to create the Earth. He's also the god of trickery, mischief, exorcisms, healing, fertility, art, and intelligence. Sumerian and Babylonian images show him as a bearded man wearing robes with running waters (Ea) running over his shoulders, symbolizing his ability to give life where he goes. Same god can trick you into thinking this is true. Also, he's always depicted as climbing or ascending the Mountain of the Sunrise or the Heavenly mountains. Sound familiar? Someone else was accused of seeking to climb above the mountain of God to assert themselves above it: Lucifer (Isaiah 14:13-14). He is usually depicted in animals representing fertility such as the fish and the goat. Enki was the most popular and celebrated of the godhead as he was more relatable because of his dual nature.

As you see, these three entities created the first trinity. In association with the so-called christian trinity, these three are represented in similar order. Anu is representative of God the Father, creator of heaven, supreme of the the 3. Enlil is representative of God the Holy Spirit, unseen yet felt like the air, that of which you cannot live without. Ea/Enki is representive of God in Christ Jesus, Enki being an embodiment of the spirit Ea just as Jesus was the embodiment of God in Christ, being wise, majestic, beloved and the supreme giver of human life (ex. The Word, John 1:1). Enki represented both the god of the earth and water, which represents humanity, made of 70% water, 30% dust, 100% of which will return to the earth when we die. All three of these entities were installed as the unseen gods by Nimrod and Semiramis.

Part 2

The physical foundation of what could be <u>seen</u>, according to Alexander Hislop in his book *The Two Babylons*,

> *"The trinity got its start in Ancient Babylon with Nimrod - Tammuz - and Semiramis. Semiramis demanded worship for both her husband and her son as well as herself. She claimed that her son, was both the father and the son. Yes, he was "god the father" and "god the son" - The first divine incomprehensible trinity."*
>
> *- p. 51*

Nimrod, Semiramis, and Tammuz

This was the physical Trinity

Nimrod, the sun god. **Semiramis**, the moon god. **Tammuz**, the reborn sun.

Nimrod, using astronomy, accepted worship as the sun god. The sun, producer of energy, light, measurer of daytime, giver and taker of life, vegetation life source, provider of heat to the earth, was viewed as the power source to sustain life. Crops could not be grown without it, which was paramount in an agrarian based world. Sun worship is associated with kingship, with Nimrod being the king of the world, which made future kings claim to be direct descendants of the sun (ex. Ancient Pharaohs and Ra). The sun is unblinking, all-seeing, enlightening, illuminating, representative of justice, the source of wisdom, unmatched in the earth and heavens. Nimrod was worshipped as the human embodiment of the sun, showing himself to be the ruler of the day, the greatest heavenly being that concentrated its attention on the earth for humanity to have life. Nimrod was considered the supreme of the trinity.

Semiramis, using astronomy and mystery schools, taught the known world worship of the three as the moon goddess. The moon, lesser of the great lights in the sky that shows itself in the night while making celestial cameos in the daytime (to this day), showing its ability to be both leader and follower, as a woman and or queen. The moon represented the rhythm of life, seen as the place to which the dead ascend to, the source of water or wave rhythms, power of rebirth, by which a woman's menstrual cycle can be calculated, its phases representing the growth and decline of all life, harvest was calculated by it as sexual rituals of when or how to produce children. Another key proponent to moon worship was healing, as ancient cultures would lay their food out at nighttime to absorb its rays, believing it gave certain foods the power to cure disease and prolong life. The waves of the sea are determined by the moon. Semiramis, both the mother and wife of Nimrod, was worshipped as the human embodiment of the moon, showing herself to be both benevolent and malevolent, both strong and weak, creator and destroyer, both leader and follower, through and to whom women needed to aspire being that she had dual capabilities and by whom fertility came, both sexually and in nature. Semiramis was considered an authoritative figure of finality and versatility in the literal 3-person godhead.

Tammuz (also Dumuzid), using astronomy, accepted worship as the rebirth of the sun. Tammuz had a split nature, being both celestial and human. The celestial side of him was taught as the son of Nimrod, when Nimrod died, Tammuz was the reborn embodiment of his father, reborn annually in the last month of the year on December 25. Yes, Christmas as we know it is the rebirth of Nimrod or the birthdate of Tammuz, taught by Semiramis to the world. His name Tammuz meant 'son of life'. Tammuz was believed to be the spirit of Nimrod in the flesh. The human deity of Tammuz was that he was the god of the shepherds, representing pastoral needs for the embetterment of the herd and community. Tammuz represented fertile land, grain increase, healthy livestock, abundant milk, safe travels, and even grass to grow in the desert. He also represented marriage, as there were 2 yearly festivals dedicated to him. The 1st festival represented his marriage to Inanna (February/March), the 2nd was the lamenting of his death (March/April), in which the people would wale and cry. According to John Kitto's *A Cyclopaedia of Biblical Literature*,

> *The first day of the month of Tammuz was the day of the new moon of the summer solstice.*
>
> *- pg.825*

This day represented the product of both the sun and moon's union, or in Sumer (Shinar), Tammuz being the offspring of Semiramis and Nimrod, a cause for celebration. However, the next day, according to Geoffrey Bromiley's *International Standard Bible Encyclopedia*,

> *On the second day of the month, there was lamentation over the death of Tammuz, on the 9th, 16th and 17th days torchlit processions, and on the last three days, an image of Tammuz was buried*
>
> *- pg.89*

Tammuz was a beloved figure in ancient Mesopotamia as he represented both the will of heaven and humans. His birth represented new life and love, his death representing lamentation. Tammuz was the most popular of the physical godhead due to his dual nature representing both heaven and human, life and death.

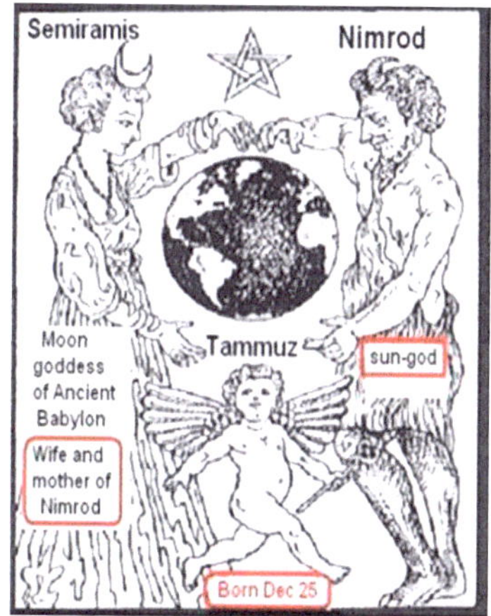

As you see, these three entities created the first real or literal trinity that people could see and believe in. In association with the so-called christian trinity, these three are represented in similar order. Nimrod is representative of God the Father, creator of heaven, supreme of the the 3. Semiramis is representative of God the Holy Spirit, a comforter to all who seek her like the air, that of which you cannot live without. Tammuz is represenive of God in Christ Jesus, Tammuz being an embodiment of the spirit Nimrod just as Jesus was the embodiment of God in Christ, being wise, majestic, beloved and the supreme giver of human life (ex. The Word, John 1:1). Tammuz represented both the sun and moon, which represents the heavenly or divine. All three of these entities were installed as the seen gods introduced by Nimrod, taught in mystery schools by Semiramis, accepted by the world.

This, ladies and gentlemen was the intelligence of Nimrod. This was the original trinity. None of this doctrine has anything to do with God, the LORD God Almighty that Abraham chose to worship. This trinity was the doctrine of the devil, created by the fallen one, given to his greatest human pupil Nimrod, taught by his mother-wife Semiramis. Reborn in his son Tammuz. Blasphemy, 100% Anti-God.

EGYPTIAN TRINITY

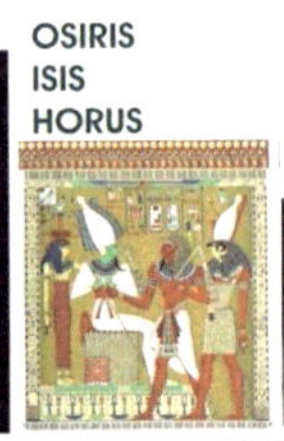

OSIRIS THE FATHER, **ISIS** THE MOTHER, **HORUS** THE CHILD

Question: What other empires did the trinity spread to?

Answer: Every major empire in world history!

Before the dismantling of their family after the death of Nimrod, Semiramis taught this belief structure to their vassal kingdoms. Keep in mind, Nimrod ruled Sumer (Shinar) for 185 years, which means there was plenty of time to teach trinity. This religion became a blueprint for other nations to establish dominance from the top down. Several nations, the major ones listed below, used Nimrod's Trinity to solidify their claim to divine power. The establishing of these temples or schools, later called mystery schools in other cultures and nations throughout history, taught religion from the foundation of Semiramis' doctrine. Observe:

Nation	Nimrod	Semiramis	Tammuz
Babylon	Belus	Ishtar	Tammuz
Egypt	Ra/Osiris	Isis	Horus
Assyria	Ninus	Beltis	Herucles

Canaan	Ba'al	Ashtoreth	Tammuz
Phoencia	El	Astarte	Bacchus
Greece	Zeus	Aphrodite	Dionysus
Rome	Jupiter	Diana	Apollo
Nordic	Odin	Joro	Thor
India	Vishnu	Chandra	Krishna
China	Pan-ku	Hengo	Yi
Mexico	Teotl	Coattlicue	Quetzalcoatl
Scandinavia	Odin	Friig/Freyda	Balder
Israel	Ba'al	Ashtoreth	Tammuz
Catholism	God	Mary	Jesus
Luciferianism	**Lucifer**	**Diana**	**AntiChrist**

After the fall of Nimrod, the next empire to establish themselves was ancient Egypt. Keep in mind, Egypt is named after Mizraim, Nimrod's uncle (Gen.10: 6-8) and at one time during his reign, advisor. The Assyrians, the sons of Asshur, established their kingdom not too long later. Asshur was the son of Shem, a cousin of Nimrod. The Canaanites settled next to the land of Shinar (land of Nimrod). Canaan is the son of Ham (Gen. 10:6), another uncle of Nimrod. The Phoenicians were a different group of Canaanites that were dominant Mediterranean Sea traders. The Greeks stole their information from the Egyptians. The Romans stole their belief structure from the Greeks. Then Nordics from the Romans. The Indians took their information from the Persians, their neighbors to the west who would later rule most of the known world. Persians were the offspring of Abraham through Keturah. The Chinese, biblically the Sinite (Gen. 10:17), were influenced early by the Sumerians (Shinar). Every nation had representatives at the Tower of Babel, which through time and travel, the teachings of Nimrod became global. The speaking of different languages forced people to take what they were taught, change names, add minor differences in characteristics to the characters, yet the core of who the trinity was remains the same. It is not coincidental that all of these nations mentioned above that sit in different pockets of the world throughout the core of human history have these same ideals and beliefs in mind and practice.

Question: Did any of the major kings in Hebrew or Biblical history adopt trinity worship?

Answer: Yes. The wisest of the Hebrew kings, Solomon, adopted this belief.

1 Kings 11: 5-8

For Solomon went after Ashtoreth the goddess of the Zidonians, and after Milcom the abomination of the Ammonites. 6 And
Solomon did evil in the sight of the LORD, and went not fully after the LORD, as did David his father. 7 Then did Solomon
build an high place for Chemosh, the abomination of Moab, in the hill that is before Jerusalem, and for Molech, the
abomination of the children of Ammon. 8 And likewise did he for all his strange wives, which burnt incense and sacrificed
unto their gods.

Ashtoreth is the Zidonian name of Semiramis. Milcom is the Ammonite version of Moloch, the demon that encourages people to sacrifice their children through the fire. Chemosh, the chief god of the Moabites, was the alternate version of the Sumerian/Babylonian Nergal, who just so happens to be the son of Enlil, the god of the air (Satanic), who in the physical form was Semiramis. Chemosh was regarded as the lord of war, disease, and death. Solomon, even in all his wisdom, fell for this belief after falling for the hearts of the women he was in love with. Again, all roads lead back to the Nimrod trinity.

Question: How did God respond to his (Solomon) decision?

Answer: With ANGER!

1 Kings 11: 9-13

And the LORD was angry with Solomon, because his heart was turned from the LORD God of Israel, which had appeared
unto him twice, 10 And had commanded him concerning this thing, that he should not go after other gods: but he kept not
that which the LORD commanded. 11 Wherefore the LORD said unto Solomon, Forasmuch as this is done of thee, and thou
hast not kept my covenant and my statutes, which I have commanded thee, I will surely rend the kingdom from thee, and will
give it to thy servant. 12 Notwithstanding in thy days I will not do it for David thy father's sake: but I will rend it out of the
hand of thy son. 13 Howbeit I will not rend away all the kingdom; but will give one tribe to thy son for David my servant's
sake, and for Jerusalem's sake which I have chosen.

Solomon knew better. Don't misunderstand what you are reading, Solomon knew better. He knew not to follow after other gods. He knew the Mosaic law. He knew the ways of his father David who served the LORD God only. He knew that the LORD God of Israel was One, and One alone. This same Solomon is the same person who being led by the spirit wrote these words earlier in his life, right before he changed his heart and followed after 'strange' women:

1 Kings 8: 59-60

And let these my words, wherewith I have made supplication before the LORD, be nigh unto the LORD our God day and night, that he maintain the cause of his servant, and the cause of his people Israel at all times, as the matter shall require: 60
That all the people of the earth may know that the LORD is God, and that there is none else.

Be mindful, reader, of those who have influence with or over you. If they do not follow the LORD God Almighty, choose wisely the areas of influence that you give them to persuade you. Guard you heart, it's the only one you have.

Question: Considering what we have learned about the nations who were influenced by Nimrod and the original trinity, when these neighboring nations popped up in biblical times, what did God tell the people to do when being offered their belief structure?

Answer: Do not follow them, do not worship them, do not entertain them, have nothing to do with them. It is an abomination unto him.

Please allow for the words of the LORD HIMself to go forth on the topic...

Exodus 20:3

Thou shalt have no other gods before me.

Deuteronomy 5: 8-10

Thou shalt not make thee any graven image, or any likeness of any thing that is in heaven above, or that is in the earth beneath, or that is in the waters beneath the earth: 9 Thou shalt not bow down thyself unto them, nor serve them: for I the LORD thy God am a jealous God, visiting the iniquity of the fathers upon the children unto the third and fourth generation of them that
hate me, 10 And shewing mercy unto thousands of them that love me and keep my commandments.

Deuteronomy 6:14

Ye shall not go after other gods, of the gods of the people which are round about you;

Deuteronomy 12: 2-3

Ye shall utterly destroy all the places, wherein the nations which ye shall possess served their gods, upon the high mountains, and upon the hills, and under every green tree: 3 And ye shall overthrow their altars, and break their pillars, and burn their groves with fire, and ye shall hew down the graven images of their gods, and destroy the names of them out of that place

Joshua 23:16

When ye have transgressed the covenant of the LORD your God, which he commanded you, and have gone and served other gods, and bowed yourselves to them; then shall the anger of the LORD be kindled against you, and ye shall perish quickly from off the good land which he hath given unto you.

Judges 10:6

And the children of Israel did evil again in the sight of the LORD, and served Baalim, and Ashtaroth, and the gods of Syria, and the gods of Zidon, and the gods of Moab, and the gods of the children of Ammon, and the gods of the Philistines, and forsook the LORD, and served not him.

1 Samuel 7: 3-4

And Samuel spake unto all the house of Israel, saying, If ye do return unto the LORD with all your hearts, then put away the strange gods and **Ashtaroth** from among you, and prepare your hearts unto the LORD, and serve him only: and he will deliver you out of the hand of the Philistines. 4 Then the children of Israel did put away **Baalim** and **Ashtaroth**, and served the LORD only.

Jeremiah 2:8

The priests said not, Where is the LORD? and they that handle the law knew me not: the pastors also transgressed against me, and the prophets prophesied by Baal, and walked after things that do not profit.

Jeremiah 7: 8-11

Behold, ye trust in lying words, that cannot profit. 9 Will ye steal, murder, and commit adultery, and swear falsely, and burn incense unto Baal, and walk after other gods whom ye know not; 10 And come and stand before me in this house, which is called by my name, and say, We are delivered to do all these abominations? 11 Is this house, which is called by my name, become a den of robbers in your eyes? Behold, even I have seen it, saith the LORD.

(For the people in the back)

Mark 12: 29-30

And Jesus answered him, The first of all the commandments is, Hear, O Israel; **The Lord our God is one Lord**: 30 And thou shalt love the Lord thy God with all thy heart, and with all thy soul, and with all thy mind, and with all thy strength: this is the first commandment.

If you are struggling with how to deal with breaking this stronghold in your life, family, culture, or area of influence, read the following of how King Josiah decided to counter the idolatry of Nimrod's trinity. Take note of how detailed he was with the names of the gods and goddesses. Examine for yourself, seek prayer and counsel of the LORD as every situation is different and requires discernment on such matters:

2 Kings 23: 4-14

And the king commanded Hilkiah the high priest, and the priests of the second order, and the keepers of the door, to bring
forth out of the temple of the LORD all the vessels that were made for **Baal**, and for the grove, and for all the host of heaven:
and he burned them without Jerusalem in the fields of Kidron, and carried the ashes of them unto Bethel. 5 And he put down
the idolatrous priests, whom the kings of Judah had ordained to burn incense in the high places in the cities of Judah, and in
the places round about Jerusalem; them also that burned incense unto **Baal**, to the sun, and to the moon, and to the planets,
and to all the host of heaven. 6 And he brought out the grove from the house of the LORD, without Jerusalem, unto the brook
Kidron, and burned it at the brook Kidron, and stamped it small to powder, and cast the powder thereof upon the graves of the
children of the people. 7 And he brake down the houses of the **sodomites**, that were by the house of the LORD, where the
women wove hangings for the grove. 8 And he brought all the priests out of the cities of Judah, and defiled the high places
where the priests had burned incense, from Geba to Beersheba, and brake down the high places of the gates that were in the
entering in of the gate of Joshua the governor of the city, which were on a man's left hand at the gate of the city. 9 Nevertheless
the priests of the high places came not up to the altar of the LORD in Jerusalem, but they did eat of the unleavened bread
among their brethren. 10 And he defiled Topheth, which is in the valley of the children of Hinnom, that no man might make
his son or his daughter to pass through the fire to **Molech**. 11 And he took away the horses that the kings of Judah had given to
the sun, at the entering in of the house of the LORD, by the chamber of Nathanmelech the chamberlain, which was in the
suburbs, and burned the chariots of the sun with fire. 12 And the altars that were on the top of the upper chamber of Ahaz,
which the kings of Judah had made, and the altars which Manasseh had made in the two courts of the house of the LORD, did
the king beat down, and brake them down from thence, and cast the dust of them into the brook Kidron. 13 And the high
places that were before Jerusalem, which were on the right hand of the mount of corruption, which Solomon the king of Israel
had builded for **Ashtoreth** the abomination of the Zidonians, and for **Chemosh** the abomination of the Moabites, and for
Milcom the abomination of the children of Ammon, did the king defile. 14 **And he brake in pieces the images, and cut down
the groves, and filled their places with the bones of men**.

If you really want to commit or recommit yourself to the LORD, examine yourself as Josiah did. Check your inventory, and see if the things you have in your possession, the people you have influence over, the gifts of God that's been given to you, the place of worship you attend, your home, your person, your mind, check them. Are they aligned properly? See if they are as polluted as Israel was. My inventory was, so I had to break some things, change my visits to places and people, clean out my house, change my lingo, ask for forgiveness and ask God to cleanse and renew my mind. It was and remains tough! If you are really interested in changing for the LORD so HE will be pleased with you, I encourage you to follow the actions mentioned above by King Josiah. It's not easy, but you must keep in mind Jehovah is watching. What's more important, appeasement now and hell fire later, or hell now and eternity with the LORD God of Heaven forever? I made my choice.

Question: Did or does the Catholic or Protestant Church teach trinity?

Answer: Yes and Yes. They both did, and continue to this day.

Reader, let's be clear: this is not about the Catholic or Protestant Church, at all. The focus should be on the trinity within itself, not the Catholic or Protestant Church dogma. This is not to bow out, deflect, or make excuses, but let's keep the main thing the main thing. Yes, the Catholic Church begin the practice in Europe and when Martin Luther came along with the 95 Thesis, when Protestantism officially separated from Catholicism a little bit later, pieces of the Catholic Church was adopted by the Protestant Movement. This is no different than the Romans stealing from the Greeks, who stole their pantheon of gods and goddesses from the Egyptians, who stole their legends from the Sumerians-Babylonians who predated them. Nimrod, the *World's 1st AntiChrist*, influenced and taught them All.

Here is a brief look into 'Trinity' history within the church:

According to the the *New Bible Dictionary* on the topic of 'trinity',

> *The term trinity is not itself found in the Bible. It was first used by Tertullian at the close of the 2nd century, but received wide currency [common use in intellectual discussion] and formal elucidation [clarification] only in the 4th and 5th centuries.*

There's more...

> *the formal doctrine of the Trinity was the result of several inadequate attempts to explain who and what the Christian God really is ... To deal with these problems the Church Fathers met in [A.D.] 325 at the Council of Nicaea to set out an orthodox biblical definition concerning the divine identity." However, it wasn't until 381, "at the Council of Constantinople, [that] the divinity of the Spirit was affirmed.*

Tertullian was the man who introduced the term 'trinity' into church matters. He called it 'trinitas', in Latin meaning 'threeness'. He admitted in his own written works that he blended pagan (Roman/Babylonian/Egyptian) practices into worship services, knowing that they were not found or backed by scripture. He wrote in his own words in a written doctrinal battle against fellow church father Praxeas,

> *These three are one substance, not one person; and it is said, 'I and my Father are one' in respect not of the singularity of number but the unity of the substance.*

M.I.P.

3 = 1, the substance of God is not the person of God

Jesus saying HE and the Father are One is speaking of their substance, not their person

Reader, Jesus did not teach this. None of the disciples taught this. Paul didn't teach this. Sure, one could summarize and assume that Tertullian meant well, but the scripture alleviates such speculations. God is clear on who HE says that HE is. Who would know better than HIM? Is the appeal to what we were taught by our fathers more important than the words of God himself?

Consider your answer wisely. If you are still in conflict, read the following as Paul simplifies the answer to questions coming from the church in Ephesus about the same issue that Tertullian and several church father theologians eventually disagreed with:

Ephesians 4: 4-6

There is one body, and one Spirit, even as ye are called in one hope of your calling; 5 One Lord, one faith, one baptism, 6 One God and Father of all, who is above all, and through all, and in you all.

How can one conclude that there are multiple with this explanation? Where in scripture, especially here in Ephesians, where Paul doesn't say anything remotely close to there being multiple persons in God? Did Tertullian know better than Paul? Does not the statement of Tertullian mentioned above contradict Ephesians 4: 4-6, at a very simple and basic level? Does or could that not cause confusion?

Did Paul not say...

1 Corinthians 14:33

For God is not the author of confusion, but of peace, as in all churches of the saints.

Martin Luther, nicknamed the great Protestant, who encouraged separation from the Catholic Church, also believed in the trinity. Several of his works are quick google searches where you can read his words and justifications. This shows the power of the doctrine that is rooted and well disguised in church service, even for the man who called the pope the office of the AntiChrist, a branch of Nimrod.

It is no secret that the pagan Roman Empiric ways were adopted into practice by those in the church seeking survival of the Roman system as it decayed and was broken into many different pieces, spreading throughout Europe. It was transformed from the Roman Empire to the Roman Catholic Church. The clever and serpent-like wisdom of the Romans to uphold their legacy and power was to adopt the idea that "*No army can defeat an idea whose time has come*", a quote by Victor Hugo. The idea of Christianity was bigger and stronger than the Roman Empire, and the Romans witnessed this as it emerged through the time of the emperors. The polytheistic Romans admired the undying belief and commitment to Jesus the Christ that they didn't have in their multi-god world. From being banned and killed for their beliefs to Emperor Theodosius declaring Christianity as the official religion of the Empire, the process of blending paganism and monotheism ruled the Roman religious world. It is from this mixing and meshing comes the birth of the Catholic Church. From there, years later in 1054AD, came the Great Schism (the split between the Catholic Church and the Eastern Orthodox Church). Regardless of where you are the perspectives of the splitting of the Catholic church, God has always wanted to be identified as One (Deut. 6:4), not the author of confusion or many doctrines (1 Cor. 14:33, 2 Tim. 6: 3-5). HE did not nor does HE want to be confused with others. This was not the case with Rome, who absorbed so many different customs and traditions that its identity is polytheistic, giving it many heads, many faces, many alliances. It's Satanism at its root. It was the Roman government that had Jesus killed. It was the Roman soldier or centurion that stabbed Jesus in the side on the cross (John 19:34) after HE died. It was the ever-changing Roman system that blended the teaching of Christ with the teachings of the trinity. The whole Roman Empire was created with its famous Triumvirate: Julius Caesar, Pompey, and Crassus. All three of these men were polytheistic. Triumvirate means an association of 3 operating as one. God is not the One to accept this nor share HIS glory with any other person, being, or substance.

Isaiah 42:8

I am the LORD: that is my name: and my glory will I not give to another, neither my praise to graven images.

Any form of worship to any other person or being by definition is considered idolatry. God did not nor does HE accept this behavior. In Catholicism, praying to Mary the mother of the flesh of Jesus the Christ is accepted. This has been a custom of Catholics for centuries. Whereas the idea of paying homage to Mary for accepting the role of bringing the Christ into the world is honorable, there is no part of scripture that praises Mary to such degree that she is to be worshipped and or prayed to. Let's read...

Mary admitted that it was God, NOT her, that allowed the Christ to come through her.

Luke 1: 47-49

And my spirit hath rejoiced in God my Saviour. 48 For he hath regarded the low estate of his handmaiden: for, behold, from
henceforth all generations shall call me blessed. 49 For he that is mighty hath done to me great things; and holy is his name.

Mary was blessed AMONG women, NOT above them.

Luke 1:28

And the angel came in unto her, and said, Hail, thou that art highly favoured, the Lord is with thee: blessed art thou **among** women.

Mary CANNOT save anyone (only Jesus saves).

Acts 4:12

Neither is there salvation in any other: **for there is none other name under heaven given among men, whereby we must be saved**.

Mary told people to do that whatever JESUS said.

John 2: 3-5

And when they wanted wine, the mother of Jesus saith unto him, They have no wine. 4 Jesus saith unto her, Woman, what have I to do with thee? mine hour is not yet come. 5 His mother saith unto the servants, Whatsoever he saith unto you, do it.

Jesus did NOT stop his work for her, valuing the work of God over personal relationships.

Matthew 12: 46-50

While he yet talked to the people, behold, his mother and his brethren stood without, desiring to speak with him. 47 Then one said unto him, Behold, thy mother and thy brethren stand without, desiring to speak with thee. 48 But he answered and said unto him that told him, Who is my mother? and who are my brethren? 49 And he stretched forth his hand toward his disciples, and said, Behold my mother and my brethren! 50 For whosoever shall do the will of my Father which is in heaven, the same is my brother, and sister, and mother.

Mary was NOT saved before everyone else, she was AMONG the 1st to accept the Holy Spirit when it descended at Pentecost, indicating that Mary had to be saved just like everyone else.

Acts 1: 12-14

Then returned they unto Jerusalem from the mount called Olivet, which is from Jerusalem a sabbath
day's journey. 13 And when they were come in, they went up into an upper room, where abode both
Peter, and James, and John, and Andrew, Philip, and Thomas, Bartholomew, and Matthew, James the
son of Alphaeus, and Simon Zelotes, and Judas the brother of James. 14 These all continued with one
accord in prayer and supplication, with the women, and Mary the mother of Jesus, and with his
brethren.

In the end, Paul ended the conversation about prayer to any other person that's not the LORD God himself, especially Mary. Catholics pray to her as the mediator between man and Jesus and God, inferring that God needs help answering prayers or Jesus gets too busy at times and his mother leaves him reminders to do what God is supposed to do. I mean no disrespect, but this is how foolish the ideology of Mary worship appears when weighed verses scripture. It's blasphemous as an insult on the functionality of the spirit of God HIMself!

1 Timothy 2:5

For there is one God, and one mediator between God and men, the man Christ Jesus;

Worship of Mary as a divine being is directly associated with Semiramis worship. In fact, most of the imagery of the Mary and Jesus that has been put in painting and artwork for centuries are copycat images of ancient trinity teachings that directly descend from Semiramis.

BABYLONIAN GODDESS SEMIRAMIS AND GOD-INCARNATE SON

INDIAN GODDESS DEVKA AND INFANT KRISHNA

INDIAN GODDESS ISI AND INFANT ISWARA

Final Question: If what you say is true of Nimrod and the original trinity, will the coming AntiChrist have a trinity as well?

Answer: I thought you would never ask. Yes! He will indeed. Let's read... Revelation

The coming AntiChrist will have an unholy trinity that will run the world. Yes, the trinity, regardless of its origin, has no plans of going anywhere anytime soon. It worked in the ancient world, thrived during the Middle Ages, and will thrive in the last days. Let's be clear about what you just read and breakdown the final trinity.

EGYPTIAN GODDESS ISIS AND SON HORUS

ROMAN CATHOLIC MARY AND GOD-INCARNATE JESUS

GODDESS DIANA OF EPHESUS

Satan, AntiChrist, False Prophet

<u>This is the *FINAL* Trinity</u>

Satan is the dragon. AntiChrist is the beast. False Prophet is just that, the false prophet.

When analyzing the final trinity, let's M.I.P. what you are really looking at before we press forward:

<u>M.I.P.</u>

The Dragon = Anti-God

The Beast = Anti-Christ

The False Prophet = Anti-Spirit

We cannot forget that Satan is the god of the world we live in, contextually meaning that he rules this age (2 Cor. 4:4). God is clearly the master of the universe and allows Satan to rule in this chaos, but it is only for an appointed time and since man chooses sin over righteousness, Satan rules in the hearts of mankind. Satan will seek to use the premise of God as Father, Son, and Spirit to create the narrative of mankind's destruction and his global dominance. The evil one will align his trinity as such:

Satan, as the dragon, Is a spirit that acts as the accuser of mankind. He deceives humanity then accuses them of sin before God. In the beginning, in the Garden of Eden, he is a serpent (Gen. 3:1). In the end, he is a dragon (Rev. 12:9). This shows how much stronger and powerful he has become over the ages. Over the course of time, Satan has sought to get ahead of God by supplanting anti-God beliefs, doctrine, people, schemes, etc. to offset the inevitable power of God and HIS will. From the 1st sin in the Earth to the last one, his entire ambition has been to scourge the image of God (humanity), seeking to take as many lives as he can with him to the bottomless pit when he is cast down and broken forever (Rev. 20:10). The dragon is a vicious creature, split tongued, meaning that he tells part truth, part lie, from the same mouth. His ability to manipulate his appearance and blend in to his surroundings, like a chameleon (also considered a dragon), shows his need to be deceptive in order to survive. It is by his growing power and schemes that he will manifest himself in the coming AntiChrist. By giving his power to the AntiChrist, the full acceptance of trinity will be put on display for the world to be force-fed and accepted against the wishes of God. This was the plan with Nimrod, which by cutting off Abraham, the coming Christ would not have come, but God. Satan is the power behind the trinity.

AntiChrist, as the beast, is a man set to come that will lead the world away from God. This beast, with his many descriptions, will come out of the Sea (Rev.13: 1-3). The "sea" is representative of people, or the Gentile nations. He will be a man who grew up knowing God, just as Nimrod did. He will imitate Christ in many of his mannerisms and speech patterns, all the while denying the power of God as God. In fact, he will blaspheme the LORD, teach others how to do so, and he will become the world leader of a New World Order that will be unrivaled as such in world history! There are many antichrists that has already come in the world as Jesus said (Matt.24:24), from the day to day people we know that deny God and his power all the way to tyrannical rulers of nations (ex. Hitler, Alexander the Great, Mao Zedong, etc.). There have been several leaders over the centuries that became world powers based on deceptive and Satanic backed schemes, all in pursuit for global dominance. They all sought to become or hold the office of Nimrod. In fact, they all take on titles that Nimrod wore in some shape, fashion, or form (ex. King of the World, King, lord, Great Hunter, 1st Crowned King). It's no coincidence. The AntiChrist is the image of the trinity.

Baphomet
Sign of Satan
Originally drawn by French Occultist/Satanist Eliphas Levi in 1856
1st seen in his book
© *Transcendental Magic: Its Doctrine and Ritual*

False Prophet, as the 2nd beast, will be a man that worships the AntiChrist openly, performing wonders and miracles in the eyes of the world. In a social media world, the false prophet will become its greatest influencer, showcasing the power of the AntiChrist on a worldwide scale. This beast will come out of the Earth, symbolic of him coming from the masses. Considering the title of prophet, he will have to be associated with the religious world. He will operate in a similar role as the Holy Spirit of God, directing people back to the AntiChrist. He will also have the power to give life to the image of the AntiChrist. Anyone who won't worship the AntiChrist as he does, he will have killed. It is the false prophet that's going to create the system through which 666 shall be distributed to the world. The False Prophet is the force that will influence and teach the world how to worship the trinity.

Satan, who exists now as a Spirit, will give his power over to the coming AntiChrist. The False Prophet will emerge, doing signs and false wonders to verify the AntiChrist. Satan will still exist as a spirit, but the AntiChrist and False Prophet will be actual people. Let's compare how Satan's trinity will war against the Saints of God (Rev. 13: 7-10):

Jesus went into the world to win it back to God (2 Cor. 5:18) /// the AntiChrist will go into the world to win it over to Satan (2 Thess. 2: 9-12)

God manifested himself in Jesus (2 Cor. 5:19) /// Satan will manifest himself into the AntiChrist (Rev. 13: 2-4)

The mystery of Godliness = God in the flesh (1 Tim. 3:16) /// The mystery of Iniquity = Satan in the flesh (2 Thess. 2: 7-9)

Church of Christ (Col. 1: 15-18) /// Synagogues of Satan (Rev. 2:9)

The Communion Cup (1 Cor. 10:16) /// Cup of Devils (1 Cor. 10:21)

Bride of Christ = Church (Eph. 5:25-27) /// Bride of Satan = Mystic Harlot Church (Rev. 17: 1-6)

Baphomet
(Temple of Satan in Detroit, Michigan)
© BBC.com

In conclusion, the word trinity is no where to be found in the Bible. Do not be fooled. I highly encourage you to look into scripture, get a King James Version or an earlier translated version, the Ethiopic Bible (original), and review the scriptures. The LORD our God is One, not many. HE has many diversities, meaning HE can do many things. HE has many operations, which if HE is God of the universe as HE is, HE has many roles and jobs, thus the meaning of many operations. HE has a nature, which is spirit. He has a personality, which is holy, thus making HIM THE Holy Spirit. HE said in Isaiah 44:6 that beside HIM there is NO God. These are not my words, but HIS. Please keep this in mind. The idea of multi in relation to God is triune, the opposite of HIS words. This shows why and how deceptive Satan and his greatest pupil Nimrod really was. Satan saw the opportunity to create separation from God in the simple, small ways, playing on the psych and verbiage of men to lure them away from the Holy One. He used Nimrod to be the AntiChrist template that influenced the world on several different levels to turn against God to self-elevate himself to god of this world status. By agreeing to do so, even Nimrod and his family grew to considering themselves gods on Earth. Nimrod knew there was a God and beside HIM there was no other, so does Satan. However, Satan's anger towards God and jealousy of humanity has spurred him into this spiritual battle which in the end will finalize in defeat for Satan, the AntiChrist, and the false prophet....so will the belief structure of the trinity.

Isaiah 43: 9-13

Let all the nations be gathered together, and let the people be assembled: who among them can declare this, and shew us
former things? let them bring forth their witnesses, that they may be justified: or let them hear, and say, It is truth. 10 Ye are
my witnesses, saith the LORD, and my servant whom I have chosen: that ye may know and believe me, and understand
that I am he: before me there was no God formed, neither shall there be after me. 11 I, even I, am the LORD; and beside me
there is no saviour. 12 I have declared, and have saved, and I have shewed, when there was no strange god among you:
therefore ye are my witnesses, saith the LORD, that I am God. 13 Yea, before the day was I am he; and there is none that can
deliver out of my hand: I will work, and who shall let it?

The Beast, Nimrod 2.0

Revelation 13: 1-2

And I stood upon the sand of the sea, and saw a beast rise up out of the sea, having seven heads and ten horns, and upon his horns ten crowns, and upon his heads the name of blasphemy. 2 And the beast which I saw was like unto a leopard, and his feet were as the feet of a bear, and his mouth as the mouth of a lion: and the dragon gave him his power, and his seat, and great authority.

Blasphemy. Pure, unadulterated, unapologetic, unwarranted, unwanted, accursed, Blasphemy.

Reader, please understand as we go forward in our explanation of the Beast, he is identified for the name of blasphemy. To be clear, there are 2 types of blasphemy: knowingly and unknowingly. One type of blasphemy you can be forgiven for, the other you cannot. The blasphemy you can be forgiven for is blaspheming out of ignorance, like the Apostle Paul before his conversion:

1 Timothy 1:12-13

And I thank Christ Jesus our Lord, who hath enabled me, for that he counted me faithful, putting me into the ministry; 13 Who was before a blasphemer, and a persecutor, and injurious: but I obtained mercy, because I did it ignorantly in unbelief.

The other type of blasphemy is the one you cannot be forgiven for. Why? Because you know what you are doing and you are intentional about mocking or targeting the HOLY Spirit.

Matthew 12: 31-32

Wherefore I say unto you, All manner of sin and blasphemy shall be forgiven unto men: but the blasphemy against the Holy Ghost shall not be forgiven unto men. 32 And whosever speaketh a word against the Son of man, it shall be forgiven him: but whosoever speaketh against the Holy Ghost, it shall not be forgiven him, neither in this world, neither in the world to come.

The reason why this type of blasphemy against the Holy Ghost or Holy Spirit is unforgiveable is because it is a direct attack against God. How so? Because God is a spirit, and HE is holy. To directly insult the spirit of God is to insult his nature, which is exactly what this type of unforgivable blasphemy is. In verse 32, the nature of the Christ that was Jesus was flesh, which is why that blasphemy could be forgiven, because the flesh that the Christ was in was a different nature and not God. The spirit, however, was God. Therefore, blaspheming the flesh is forgivable. However, blaspheming the spirit is unforgiveable.

The name on the heads of the Beast is Blaphemy....the unforgivable kind, meaning he will know EXACTLY what he is doing.

Revelation 13: 1-2

And I stood upon the sand of the sea, and saw a beast rise up out of the sea, having seven heads and ten horns, and upon his horns ten crowns, and upon his heads the name of blasphemy. 2 And the beast which I saw was like unto a leopard, and his feet were as the feet of a bear, and his mouth as the mouth of a lion: and the dragon gave him his power, and his seat, and great authority.

Now that we understand the word blasphemy relative to the Beast as a foundational truth, we can begin dissecting the scriptures with precision. When we look at the first description of the beast, we see an animal, which is a symbol of his characateristics of the nature of this man, an animal. Not just an animal, but a leopard, which is known for being an apex predator, a stalker, quick, a master hunter, deceptive, able to blend in with its surroundings, stealthy, and strong.

When we look at the feet, it is likened to the feet of the bear, which is strong, tough, able to expand and retract. His mouth, as a lion, means that when he speaks he speaks with authority. Keep in mind, Satan has been identified in the scriptures as a roaring lion, meaning that he is skilled at speaking with authority and will garner the attention of all that can hear (1 Peter 5:8). He will be a leader, charasmatic. All of these animals are carnivores, flesh eaters, unclean animals. This man shall be a man killer.

The dragon, ladies and gentlemen, we know to be Satan (Rev. 12:9). Satan, in verse 2, gives his power to this man, The Beast. Not only would he give him his power, which Satan has never done to anyone, but he also gave the Beast his seat and great authority. This is why the Mark of the Beast will be a global phenomenom, because the man alone won't be able to control the world. There has been archtypes of this man since Nimrod but none has had his power or the power of Satan himself. Satan rules this world, period. Therefore, by giving this man his power, the man will have Satan's power to rule the world, which is the seat scripture is referring to, the seat of Satan as the ruler of this world. Pushing the Mark of the Beast and Satan's agenda can only happen with Satan's authority.

Satan's Seat, Power, and Authority

2 Corinthians 4: 3-4

But if our gospel be hid, it is hid to them that are lost: 4 In whom the god of this world hath blinded the minds of them that believe not, lest the light of the glorious gospel of Christ, who is the image of God, should shine unto them.

The image of God is Christ, the image was not God, but the spirit that was in the Christ, was God. That's what shines on those that believe.

Revelation 13: 3-4

And I saw one of his heads as it were wounded to death; and his deadly wound was healed: and all the world wondered after the beast. 4 And they worshipped the dragon which gave power unto the beast: and they worshipped the beast, saying, Who is like unto the beast? Who is able to make war with him?

Right now, as we speak, the world is running after the beast, who has yet to be revealed. Why? Because the spirit, power, and authority that the Beast will have comes from Satan himself. Therefore, they that worship and run after the dragon, Satan, will also run after and worship the Beast. What we see now in Satanic worship and symbolistic action is nothing compared to what is to come. It's going to get worse. People will try to combat the Beast, but again, he will have the power and authority of the god of this world, which means that he will defeat those that make the attempt to war against him due to his animalistic nature. Remember, this is similar to the mind and nature of Nimrod, the great hunter before the LORD, who hunted and thought as the prey he hunted in the skins of Adam and Eve, made from the hands of God himself. Who by being such a great hunter and carnivore, eventually became ruler of the world by means of killing men, a man killer, like the Beast.

Revelation 13: 5-6

And there was given unto him a mouth speaking great things and blasphemies; and power was given unto him to continue forty and two months. 6 And he opened his mouth in blasphemy against God, to blaspheme his name, and his tabernacle, and them that dwell in heaven.

This same spirit that the Beast will speak such vile and blasphemous things is already in the world. It's happening now, but what's to come will be waaayyyyyy worse! What we see now is an appetizer. What's to come will be the main dish and dessert. For 3 ½ years, the same length of Christ' ministry, the Beast will say what he wants to say, do what he wants to do, and nothing will done about it due to his power, seat, and authority. This is similar to what Nimrod did as ruler of the known world. He did what he wanted and no one could combat him except, Abraham, through the grace and power of God.

The Beast will have power to do miraculous signs and wonders, for the people, who have always sought a sign. He will have the ability to do so because of the power of the devil. He will not only blaspheme God, but he will blaspheme God's name. That name, is not God. God is a title. HIS name, is Jesus. The Beast will not only blaspheme Jesus, but his tabernacle, which is the church. Not only will he blaspheme the church, but he will blaspheme those that are in heaven, meaning he will have a knowledge of the hosts of heaven that are in the presence of God. He will not care nor will he have a fear of heaven. This is similar to Nimrod, who built the Tower of Babel with the idea of replacing God. The idea of the Tower to reach into the heavens was blasphemy. Each brick made and carried for such a purpose was blasphemy.

Revelation 13: 7-8

And it was given unto him to make war with the saints, and to overcome them: and power was given him over all kindreds, and tongues, and nations. 8 And all that dwell upon the earth shall worship him, whose name are not written in the book of life of the Lamb slain from the foundation of the world.

No one will be safe. The saints will not win versus this man. Your old ways, thoughts, family, friends, network, etc. won't matter. He will rule. There will be no in-betweens. This man, this Beast, shall rule with the power of Satan over all of the Earth. Everyone who accepts the Beast will not spend eternity with God. Everyone that goes along to get along, will not spend eternity with God. Those, like Abraham's brother Haran that was thrown into the fire, who was a good man, a good person, shall be reserved for hell fire and burn in that fire for eternity, like Haran who was burned in the fire meant to destroy Abraham. Haran meant well, but didn't fully accept God the same way Abraham did even though he admired his younger brother' belief (Jasher 12: 18-19). Just as Nimrod ruled over the Earth with an iron fist, so shall the Beast.

Revelation 13: 9

If any man have an ear, let him hear. 10 He that leadeth into captivity shall go into captivity: he that killeth with the sword must be killed with the sword. Here is the patience and the faith of the saints.

If you can read this, take heed. It's a signal, a beacon, a siren, a warning, an intentional message to YOU! To me. To the world. The Beast is coming and all of Satan's power will be with him. Those that lead people to getting caught up, will be caught up. Those that kill people will be killed. Reader, please understand: the Beast will leave no stone unturned in his quest for global domination. The one who serves him thinking they will be rewarded for enslaving and killing for him will be get the same measurement in return. There will be no compromise. He will not have patience. He will not have faith. For the believer, the saint, we cannot be God-like with patience and faith. We will not and cannot achieve the term saint unless we accept then process to progress in the struggle of patience and faith. This is and will be a huge differientation between us and them. Satan's nature is not patience, but restless. He doesn't have faith because he knows the real God that the world doesn't. We need faith because we don't know the real God as we should. This is another reason why he will rule. The Beast will know the real God and still blaspheme because he will see the world from the same perspective as Satan himself. This mindset will be similar to Nimrod's, but on a much more devastating scale.

What's interesting about this beast is that it will rise out of the sea (Rev. 13:1). The sea, as stated, is not talking about a mermaid or anything like that. Instead, it's a symbolism to say that the Beast shall rise out of the people. The sea represents people. Therefore, the Beast shall come from amongst the people. When you understand the animal symbolism, this man will be able to relate to so many people because he will be from among them. So, whatever the latest buzz or leading thread or idea or movement, he will know all of it enough to galvanize the people, nations, and governments to follow him.

But wait, there's more....

Revelation 13: 11-12

And I beheld another beast coming up out of the earth; and he had two horns like a lamb, and he spake as a dragon. 12 And he exerciseth all the power of the first beast before him, and causeth the earth and them which dwell therein to worship the first beast, whose deadly wound was healed.

Uh oh! There will be another beast, another man, similar to the first beast. This man, however, has a different appearance and power. He will speak like the dragon, meaning he will speak just like Satan does, which the Beast does. He will have the same power as the Beast, but he will be a messenger for the Beast, the hype man, the one who points you in the direction of the Beast to worship him. A witness. This is why his appearance will be that like a lamb, meaning he will represent innocence, but he will be guilt personified. Both the first Beast and the second beast will have the same spirit. This shows us that there is unity among those that hate God.

Revelation 13: 13-14

And he doeth great wonders, so that he maketh fire come down from heaven on the earth in the sight of men. 14 And deceiveth them that dwell on the earth by the means of those miracles which he had power to do in the sight of the beast; saying to them that dwell on the earth, that they should make an image to the beast, which had the wound by a sword, and did live.

This man will give the people what they want. He will perform signs and wonders, false signs and teachings, that shall be true in the eyes of men. He will not only perform these signs in the eyes of men, but he will do them in the eyes of the Beast. The second man will seek to push the agenda of the first man, performing amazing feats for the world to see. He will go so far to convince the people of Earth to make an image of the man they worship. He will be god to them. The first man shall be a hero to the people because of the wound that should have killed him. Instead, due to his survival, they will view the first Beast as more than a man. The second man will deceive the world, so much so that the people will think that he has the power of God himself. Blasphemy!

Revelation 13:15

And he had power to give life unto the image of the beast, that the image of the beast should both speak, and cause that as many as would not worship the image of the beast should be killed.

This same concept has already happened before. Not with Nimrod, but with the man that is the most like Nimrod in world history, king Nebuchadnezzar II of Babylon.

Daniel 3: 1-7

Nebuchadnezzar the king made an image of gold, whose height was threescore cubits, and the breadth thereof six cubits: he set it up in the plain of Dura, in the province of Babylon. 2 Then Nebuchadnezzar the king sent to gather together the princes, the govenors, and the captains , the judges, the treasurers, the counsellers, the sheriffs, and all the rulers of the provinces, to come to the dedication of the image which Nebuchadnezzar the king had set up. 3 Then the princes, the govenors, and captains, the judges, the treasurers, the counsellers, the sheriffs, and all the rulers of the provinces, were gathered together unto the dedication of the image that Nebuchadnezzar the king had set up; and they stood before the image that Nebuchadnezzar had set up. 4 Then an herald cried aloud, To you it is commanded, O people, nations, and languages, 5 That at ttime ye hear the sound of the cornet, flute, harp, sackbut, psaltery, dulcimer, and all kinds of musick, ye fall down and worship the golden image that Nebuchadnezzar the king hath set up: 6 And whoso falleth not down and worshippeth shall the same hour be cast into the midst of a burning fiery furnace. 7 Therefore at that time, whan all the people heard thesound of the cornet, flute, harp, sackbut, psaltery, and all kinds of musick, all the people, the nations, and the languages, fell down and worshipped the golden image that Nebuchadnezzar the king had set up.

See what we mean? History will repeat itself. If you study the archtypes, you will see that the Beast will mimic the those that came before him in different ways, but none of them will have the total package that he will have. Nebuchadnezzar II already did this, but that's with millions of people on the planet at that time. This will be done with billions of people, with more technology, more power, more outreach, plus the spirit of Satan to be able to enforce punishment. Just like death was promised to anyone who didn't bow down and worship the image of Nebuchadnezzar II, so will death be assured to anyone who decides to wakeup and not bow down to the image of the Beast. Blasphemy!

The second beast will have the ability and power to give life to the image, meaning he will animate and control the thing that he created that will deceive the world. This is wild! This man, the second beast, will have the ability to deceive the so-called seeing people, forcing them into worshipping the Beast, or die. How will he be able to do this? A system.

Revelation 13: 16-17

And he causeth all, both small and great, rich and poor, free and bond, to receive a mark in their right hand, or in their foreheads:
17 And that no man might buy or sell, save he that had that had the mark, or the name of the beast, or the number of his name.

This is the system................the Mark of the Beast.

This system has been running for a long time, testing and prepping for the Beast. For example, the system of indulgences was a prelude to this system. How so? It used the influence of the church under the direct power of the pope to control the economy of everyday citizens who were under the control of the Roman Catholic Church. In today's world, the concept of prosperity preaching is an update to the system. How so? It has programmed people to think money, and that if they give their all, which is ONLY reserved for God, to some man masquerading as a minister, that they will be enhanced and protected in the eyes of God. This is the same con job as the Catholic indulgence fraud. You couldn't find indulgences in the WORD of God then, you can't find prosperity preaching in the WORD of God now. Meanwhile, case after case, exposure after exposure, we see these Anti-God concepts fail. The idea of deceiving the people, get rich in the process, controlling the minds of the everyday person, is system, an anti-God system, but without the mark. Satan has sent his ministers into the Earth to program the people to think a certain way that equates to people serving idols in the pulpit, politics, celebrities, go-getters (financially), etc., this is exactly what the image will be. It is working now on a small scale. Imagine how vast it will be in that day to come. Mass manipulation unlike the world has ever seen!

With that being said, reader, all the money in the world won't protect you from this evil. The richest people on the planet at that time who think their money protects them will find out something that the evil spirits that whisper in their ears won't tell them: Satan doesn't care about wealth. He doesn't care, at all. He has already convinced the world to worship money. An illusion the master illusionist! That's the god of this generation, even down to the infants who learn of money and what it means. Satan has enticed the world into this concept that you should strive to be rich and wealthy with the power to do all of these things, only to use it as leverage to gain power and control over the person and or people who believe this con. He can care less about money, but he doesn't want you to know that. He knows that there is no such thing as money in the afterlife, but the people don't know or understand that. Need proof? Here's an example...

As a black man, there are many black people in the western world who are looking for an identity, walk around claiming Egyptology as their original belief structure. They wear the eye of horus necklaces, bracelets, earrings, etc. Even the women dress like the Egyptian princesses. The pharaohs of Egypt carried their wealth with them into their tombs or pyramids, in full belief that they would need it to pay Anubis, the jackel-headed god of the afterlife. He was charged with protecting their mummified body and the cemetaries of ancient Egypt. What's crazy is that mostly all the treasures of the pharaohs have been robbed, put on display in European and American museums for people to get rich off their riches. No god protected their treasures! Not one metal, stone, or item of clothing went into the afterlife with these mummies. No articles they went into the grave with went into the afterlife. But we have people out here wearing this abomination because they want to belong to something they deem as being more or higher than themselves. Only the people who fell victim to the traps and curses of the builders died from robbing these tombs. Egypt, known for its gold and great structures, doesn't have gold, just structures of past glory that people visit to see that are empty. The gold that Egypt is known for came from their darker skinned brothers from the south in Cush, which was Nubia, modern-day Ethiopia. The pyramids of Meroe predate the pyramids, but I digress. They don't study the Ethiopian way. Why? Because you will find the Queen of Sheba there. You will find Menelik I there, the son of king Solomon and the Queen of Sheba. You will find their belief in the One true God there. Instead, they prefer the Egyptian way. To be clear, this is not to disrespect their work, which is amazing and certainly a place of extraordinary knowledge that should be protected. However, this is to say that the sense of belonging to something is a system that Satan has used to his benefit to deceive the world and Egypt was a breeding ground for the devil himself to launch from.

Many have never even thought about that. He knows better. Therefore, when this time comes, the first Beast will not care whether a person is rich or poor. All he will care about is if a person bows down and worships him. All he will concern himself with is if you get his mark in your right hand or forehead. If you do, you're good with him and his system. If you don't, death.

Question: So, what does the mark of the beast on the hand and head mean?

Answer: Control. The mark on the hand represents control over a man's deeds and doings. The mark on the forehead represents control over a man's mind. Without the mind or hand, no man can buy or sale anything. Commerce, whether fair or unfair, cannot happen with interation (hand) and transaction (head). By taking the mark, you surrender your mind and body to the Beast, which in turns surrenders your soul to eternal hell fire.

Revelation 13:18

Here is wisdom. Let him that hath understanding count the number of the beast: for it is the number of a man; and his number is Six hundred threescore and six.

666.

In order to understand 666, we must go back to the first Beast and look at his heads and understand his system. The number 666 is the number of man, which explains itself being that man was created on the 6th day. The key is not the number, but the system the number represents. It's a money system, which is why no one will be able to buy or sale without it. That's the key, the system.

Revelation 13: 1-2

And I stood upon the sand of the sea, and saw a beast rise up out of the sea, having seven heads and ten horns, and upon his horns ten crowns, and upon his heads the name of blasphemy. 2 And the beast which I saw was like unto a leopard, and his feet were as the feet of a bear, and his mouth as the mouth of a lion: and the dragon gave him his power, and his seat, and great authority.

7 heads, 10 horns, 10 crowns.
7 heads = 7 supreme nations.
10 horns = 10 armies or 10 weapons
10 crowns = 10 rulers

This Beast got his power from a beast, Satan, the god of this world. The world has been conditioned to desire and love money 1st. Therefore, if you are already programmed or preconditioned to desire and respect money 1st over everything (ex. In hip-hop culture it's called MOB), then this system will be easy to accept.

Reader, think for a second. They have already laid out free trial for their study. Take the US Presidency Election as an example or case study. Whenever an election comes up, the powers that be send out celebrities and well-known figures to convince the people to vote a certain way, think a certain way, see things a certain way. People don't think, and the powers that be know that. Instead, the people follow the program. There are people who vote republican just because, democrat just because, black just because, white just because, gay just because, male just because, female just because, liberal just because, conservative just because, etc. If you ask them about the value of their vote, they talk about their voice, thinking it is the same. It is not. They tell people this is a democracy. It is not. It is a republic, which is a starkly different governmental structure than a democracy. The people think that their vote actually counts in a presidential election, their voice. Nevermind that 4x already a person has won more people votes and lost the election. How is that possible? Well, in a democracy, that shouldn't happen. But in a republic, which mean a few represent the many, we have what is called an electoral college. This small group of people are unknown. These are the people who actually vote for the president of the US but again, they are unknown. The word democracy is not even in the constitution, or the declaration of independence. The people who founded this country, the founding fathers as we have been taught, made sure to not give the people the final choice in the matter of choosing their leader because they knew the masses would choose who's the most famous, not who's the most effective. Don't believe me? Go read the Federalist Papers: No. 68, written by Alexander Hamilton, one of the "founding fathers" who is accredited with establishing the financial foundation and mind of America. Need more? God read the 12th Amendment, the one that precedes the 13th Amendment (which set the slaves free), which outlines how the electors vote outside the masses, legally. I digress. The electoral college voters have the right to follow the people's vote, but they don't have to. The presidential debates aren't for the American people per say, it's an open evaluation for the private electors to see the ability of the candidates to convince the unknown voters to choose them depending on their skillset to sway or convince the people to follow them. The private voters and big business are puppet masters, the president is the puppet, the people are the audience thinking they have the remote control of the puppet and the show. That's it.

The system of the Beast will control the masses like so, making people believe they have a choice but in reality, they don't. He will take the next step and do what the 2004 presidential campaign declared as 'Vote or Die'. It's interesting how the person who launched this campaign, Sean 'Puffy' Combs, is now one of the most scrutinized individuals in the world right now for his abuse of the same people he told to vote or die. Again, the system of the Beast at work. I digress.

In the end, reader, understand, the power of the devil and hell itself shall be in one man, the Beast. He shall have a hype man, a forerunner, the False Prophet, which is the 2nd beast. Satan will be the power behind both men. This, ladies and gentlemen, is the trinity, the unholy trinity, orchestrated by Satan himself. Just as he did with Nimrod then, he will do with the Beast to come, who will be greater than Nimrod, making him Nimrod 2.0, unlike any other before him.

The Beast is the AntiChrist.

Repent!!!

Ladies and gentlemen, I pray that you have learned something from this great work. In order to fully hear it, digest it, and understand what we are dealing with, please pray and ask God for the wisdom needed to accept his WORD. We are nothing more than a messenger with a message for those in search of knowledge, understanding, and wisdom of the LORD Jesus Christ. It is he that does the work. We are HIS servants, not servants of ourselves. We bear witness to the fact that there is ONLY One God, and none else. He is God and it is HE that we serve.

If in your reading and searching, you wish to come to the LORD God himself and receive the salvation of the LORD, there is but one way:

Acts 2:38

Then Peter said unto them repent, and be baptized every one of you in the name of Jesus Christ for the remission of sins, and yeshall receive the gift of the Holy Ghost.

Repent, and be baptized, everyone, in the name of Jesus Christ! That's it. For the remission of your sins so you can receive the gift of the Holy Spirit.

The times that we are living in and the ones to come will be unlike any in the history of the planet. However, we have the ability to avoid the calamity of the end if you are in alignment with the LORD God of Heaven if you repent. Why put yourself in danger of hell fire unnecessarily? Why operate in a foolish pride as if you understand more than the LORD himself. Even Atheists agree that the times we are living in are unprecedented. Even the little children can tell you that there is something evil out here. Therefore, we must repent and be baptized in the name of Jesus Christ. Do so and join the body of believers who look to the day and returning of the LORD! This is the path that we take and encourage you to take.

May peace, joy, and the wisdom of the LORD be with you.

We love you!

I love you!

Revelation 22: 16-17

I Jesus have sent mine angel to testify unto you these things in the churches. I am the root and the offspring of David, and the bright and morning star. 17 And the Spirit and the bride say, Come. And let him that is athirst come. And whosoever will, let him take the water of life freely.

Bibliography

Books

The Larousse Encyclopedia of Mythology, 1994, pp. 54-55

Muller, G. (2014). The Ancient Black Hebrews: The Forensic Proof Simply Explained. United Kingdom: CreateSpace Independent Publishing Platform.

Childress, D. H. (2015). Ark of God: The Incredible Power of the Ark of the Covenant. (n.p.): Adventures Unlimited Press.

Oshima, T. (2011). Babylonian Prayers to Marduk. Germany: Mohr Siebeck.

Mark, J. J. (2017, February 08). Nanna. World History Encyclopedia.
Hitchcock, Roswell D. "Entry for 'Jokshan'". "An Interpreting Dictionary of Scripture Proper Names". . New York, N.Y., 1869.
Alexander Hislop, The Two Babylons, pg.51

The Columbia Electronic Encyclopedia, 6th ed. Copyright © 2012, Columbia University Press.

Journal of Biblical Literature Vol. 36, No. 1/2 (1917), pp. 100-111 (12 pages) Published by: The Society of Biblical Literature

John Kitto, ed. (1846), A Cyclopaedia of Biblical Literature: Ibz-Zuz, vol. 2, pg. 825, Mark H. Newman

Bromiley, Geoffrey W. (1995), International Standard Bible Encyclopedia: Q-Z (Reprint, revised ed.), pg. 89, Wm. B. Eerdmans Publishing, ISBN 9780802837844

New Bible Dictionary, 1996

Encyclopedic Dictionary of the Bible, translated and adapted by l. hartman (New York, 1963) 2392–93. s. h. hooke, Babylonian and Assyrian Religion (New York 1953). a. moortgart, Tammuz: Der Unsterblichkeitsglaube in der altorientalischen Bildkunst (Berlin 1949). r. de vaux, "Sur quelques rapports entre Adonis et Osiris," Revue Biblique 42 (1933) 31–56.

Werner, Keller. The Bible as History, pg.331

New Catholic Encyclopedia MUELLER, H.

WARREN LARSON Jesus in Islam and Christianity: Discussing the Similarities and the Differences p. 335

Smith, Jane I.; Haddad, Yvonne Y. (1981). The Islamic Understanding of Death and Resurrection. Albany, N Y: SUNY Press. p. 69.

Qaim, Mahdi Muntazir (2007). Jesus Through the Qur'an and Shi'ite Narrations. Queens, New York. ISBN 978-1879402140.

"Jesus, A Prophet of Allah - Association of Islamic Charitable Projects in USA". www.aicp.org. Retrieved 2021-07-28.

Eph'al, Israel (2003). "Nebuchadnezzar the Warrior: Remarks on his Military Achievements". Israel Exploration Journal. 53 (2): 178–191. JSTOR 27927044.

Olmstead, A. T. (1925). "The Chaldaean Dynasty". Hebrew Union College Annual. 2: 29–55. JSTOR 23502505.

Hislap, Alexander. The Two Babylons, pg. 107

Websites:

https://www.worldhistory.org/sumer/#:~:text=Sumer%20was%20the%20southernmost%20region,land%20of%20the%20civilized%20kings%E2%80%9D

https://www.khanacademy.org/humanities/ancient-art-civilizations/ancient-near-east1/sumerian/a/the-sumerians-and-mesopotamia

https://www.history.com/news/sumerians-inventions-mesopotamia

https://www.abarim-publications.com/index.html

http://www.ugandatravelguide.com/langi-culture.html

https://sitn.hms.harvard.edu/flash/2017/science-genetics-reshaping-race-debate-21st-century/

https://www.icr.org/article/what-happened-days-peleg

http://oracc.museum.upenn.edu/amgg/listofdeities/marduk/

https://www.bbc.com/news/uk-england-lancashire-31623397

http://oracc.museum.upenn.edu/amgg/listofdeities/utu/index.html

http://news.samsungcnt.com/standing-tall-story-behind-skyscraper-foundations/

https://www.guinnessworldrecords.com/world-records/fastest-time-to-climb-burj-khalifa-tower-unassisted-(solo)

http://www.touregypt.net/featurestories/prehistory.htm

https://www.medicalnewstoday.com/articles/319882#understanding-circadian-rhythms

http://historyofkurd.com/english/2020/04/20/%EF%BB%BFhistory-of-the-medes-median-empire/

https://www.worldhistory.biz/ancient-history/59517-text-28-1-the-seventh-campaign-of-ashurnasirpal-ii-an-example-of-an-assyrian-annalistic-account-of-the-ninth-century-bc.html

https://www.degruyter.com/document/doi/10.3138/9781442657052-012/pdf

https://www.health.com/condition/pregnancy/pregnancy-heartburn-and-the-hairy baby

https://www.theosociety.org/pasadena/mysterys/MysterySchoolsGFK.pdf

https://www.tertullian.org/articles/evans_praxeas_eng.htm

https://www.bbc.com/news/magazine-33682878

https://www.brown.edu/Departments/Joukowsky_Institute/courses/materialworlds/files/1308642.pdf

https://medium.com/la-biblioth%C3%A8que/the-fascinating-history-of-the-christmas-tree-1121e051f4b

http://linesandprecepts.com/2016/03/27/the-pagan-origins-of-easter/

https://greekreporter.com/2021/12/14/the-roots-of-christmas-in-ancient-greece/#:~:text=Many%20Christmas%20traditions%20have%20roots,the%20king%20of%20the%20Gods.

https://www.worldhistory.org/article/221/the-mesopotamian-pantheon/

https://www.encyclopedia.com/philosophy-and-religion/ancient-religions/ancient-religion/tammuz

https://www.space.com/15551-nibiru.html

https://oi.uchicago.edu/sites/oi.uchicago.edu/files/uploads/shared/docs/misc_genesis.pdf

http://www.csun.edu/~hcfll004/sumking.html#:~:text=%22After%20kingship%20had%20descended%20from,Alalgar%20reigned%2036%2C000%20years.

http://oracc.museum.upenn.edu/amgg/listofdeities/anunna/index.html

https://www.aicp.org/index.php/islamic-information/text/english/52-isa-jesus-a-prophet-of-allah

https://quran.com/en

https://www.jpost.com/middle-east/iran-news/the-fall-of-soleimnai-and-the-mahdi-doctrine-615654

https://www.iium.edu.my/deed/hadith/abudawood/031_sat.html#:~:text=Narrated%20Abu%20Sa'id%20al,will%20rule%20for%20seven%20years.

https://www.awaytoafrica.com/know-african-roots/#:~:text=Alkebulan%20%7C%20The%20Original%20Name%20For%20Africa

https://scibi.org/?p=18&gclid=CjwKCAiAkp6tBhB5EiwANTCx1Gc3_07pd9HTJDhj-zzj_Mzh6zxFgWdNXBla7_4trE94Q8OMxg07pRoCmgMQAvD_BwE

https://www.jewishencyclopedia.com/articles/1762-arioch

https://science.nasa.gov/universe/stars/

https://cals.cornell.edu/nys-4-h-animal-science-programs/livestock/goats/goat-fact-sheets/goat-herd-behavior

https://www.excelpestservices.com/11-fun-facts-about-pigeons/#:~:text=6.,been%20used%20for%20communication%20purposes.

https://www.ncbi.nlm.nih.gov/pmc/articles/PMC10597482/

https://www.jewishvirtuallibrary.org/tomb-of-the-patriarchs-ma-arat-hamachpelah

Made in the USA
Columbia, SC
02 June 2025

58811851R00209